True Stories from the SAS & Elite Forces

Edited by
Jon E. Lewis

•PARRAGON•

This edition published and distributed by
Parragon Book Service Ltd in 1995
Parragon Book Service Ltd
Unit 13–17 Avonbridge Trading Estate
Atlantic Road
Avonmouth
Bristol BS11 9QD

True Stories of the Elite Forces first published
by Robinson Publishing Ltd 1993

True Stories of the SAS & other Elite Forces first
published by Magpie Books Ltd 1995

Robinson Publishing Ltd
7 Kensington Church Court
London W8 4SP

ISBN 0–7525–1350–8

Typeset by Hewer Text Composition Services, Edinburgh.

Printed in Great Britain

10 9 8 7 6 5 4 3 2 1

CONTENTS

BOOK ONE

True Stories of
THE ELITE FORCES

BOOK TWO

True Stories of the
SAS and other ELITE FORCES

Other books by Jon E. Lewis

True Stories of the Elite Forces
The Mammoth Book of True War Stories
The Mammoth Book of Modern War Stories
The Mammoth Book of Battles
Eye-witness D-Day
Eye-witness 20th Century
The Mammoth Book of the Western
Means to a Kill
Red Handed
Cult TV

True Stories of
THE ELITE FORCES

True Stories of THE ELITE FORCES

Edited by
Jon E. Lewis

•PARRAGON•

Contents

DESERT SCORPION
(Popski's Private Army, Tunisia 1943)
Vladimir ("Popski") Peniakoff 1

SIEGE AT PRINCES GATE
(22 SAS, London 1980)
Jon E. Lewis 32

THE BULL OF SCAPA FLOW
(U-47, North Sea 1939)
Wolfgang Frank 40

OPERATION THUNDERBALL
(Israeli Paras, Entebbe 1976)
Yeshayu Ben-Porat, Eitan Haber and Zeev Schiff 51

WIRELESS RIDGE
(2 Para, The Falklands 1982)
John Frost 68

THE SEA DEVILS
(Italian 10th MAS, Alexandria 1941)
J. Valerio Borghese 87

THE FLYING TIGERS
(American Volunteer Group, China 1941)
Claire L. Chennault 117

SAINT NAZAIRE COMMANDOS
(British Commandos, France 1942)
Adolphe Lepotier 138

ASSAULT INTO HELL
(US Marines, Peleliu 1944)
E. B. Sledge 176

THE TWILIGHT OF THE GODS
(French Foreign Legion, Vietnam 1954)
Jules Roy 190

PROJECT DELTA
(US Special Forces, Vietnam 1964)
Shelby L. Stanton 217

THE LAST RAID ON SIMI
(SBS, Greece 1944)
John Lodwick 225

MIRBAT
(22 SAS, Oman 1972)
Tony Jeapes 234

AIRMOBILITY
(Ist Air Cavalry, Vietnam 1965)
John Pimlott 251

THE MUSSOLINI RESCUE
(SS Special Troops, Italy 1943)
Otto Skorzeny 258

Acknowledgements 276

DESERT SCORPION
Vladimir ("Popski") Peniakoff

Of all the British special forces of the Second World War, none had more romance attached to it than the Army's smallest independent unit – Popski's Private Army. The unit was formed in October 1942 after Major Vladimir Peniakoff ("Popski") of the Long Range Desert Group was persuaded to take an independent command. Stuck for a name for the new force (War Establishment ME WE 866/1), Lieutenant-Colonel Shan Hackett, co-ordinator of special forces in North Africa, jokingly suggested it should be titled "Popski's Private Army". The name stuck, and the War Office even approved it officially. The unit's badge was a silver astrolabe (a type of astronomical measuring instrument), and its brief was to be a highly mobile force gathering intelligence and spreading "alarm and despondency" behind enemy lines in Tunisia and Libya.

Initially, the PPA numbered 23 all ranks, but eventually rose to a total of 195, all volunteers hand-picked by Popski personally. Its raids -- by jeep and three-ton truck- were frequently spectacular successes, and included the discovery of a route to outflank the German-held Mareth Line. Popski's account of that mission, from his autobiography Private Army, *is set out below.*

With the effective end of the war in North Africa in 1943, the PPA was switched to Italy, where the unit operated with the 12th and 27th Lancers until the German surrender. (It was in Italy, in December 1944, that five jeeps of the PPA armed with Browning 0.3 and 0.5 inch machine guns famously engaged two German companies supported by tanks to rescue a group of 27th Lancers trapped in a farmhouse, loosing off 25,000 rounds in the process).

Popski himself was born in Belgium in 1897, the son of intellectual Russian parents. He enrolled at Cambridge University in 1914, but left after several terms to join the French Army as a gunner (the quickest route to the front). With the end of the First World War, he became an engineer and later a sugar manufacturer in Egypt. It was at this time that Peniakoff learned the desert lore – mostly gained in long, solo expeditions in a Model A Ford he called "The Pisspot" – that made him invaluable to the British in North Africa, and he was commissioned in 1939. Nor was Popski the only "foreigner" in his Private Army, which included, as well as Britons, Frenchmen and Arabs. During the Italian campaign, it even incorporated some Italian anti-fascists and escaped Russian POWs.

After the war Popski worked as a liaison officer between the Russian and the British in Vienna. He died in London in May 1951. In the introduction to his autobiography Peniakoff writes: "only to the fools amongst the men of my generation will the realization come as a surprise that we liked war." That liking is evident in what follows, which begins with Popski returning to base after the PPAs' first mission, a somewhat mixed success.

WE SLUNK INTO the wadi at Shweref with our tails between our legs to find a kind of general assembly of L.R.D.G.,* which mercifully took little notice of us. Never had I seen so many patrols together in one place, some going out, some coming home to Hon, where Headquarters had moved from Zella.

Prendergast flew his Waco over on the second day. He listened to our reports and commented: "It was rather unfortunate, wasn't it?" – a very strong rebuke from him. We had no time to cry over spilt milk for the war was moving on. Eighth Army was attacking Rommel at Buerat that very day, expected to be in Tripoli a fortnight later, and wanted urgently information about the Mareth Line. Nick Wilder, now on his way back, had signalled that he had found a pass through the Nefusa range suitable for Montgomery's left hook, some forty miles north of Dehibat, and now the ground leading north from Wilder's Gap to the Mareth Line had to be reconnoitred and a route found, not just for an agile L.R.D.G. patrol, but

* Long Range Desert Group

such as could be negotiated by an armoured division. The defences between Matmata and Jebel Tebaqa had also to be investigated: no time could be lost because in a few weeks, with Rommel's forces established in that desolate area, it would be awkward for us to move around.

Dumps of petrol had been established near the Tunisian border and also at Tozeur, an oasis in southern Tunisia, in the hands of the French troops of North Africa, who were now fighting half-heartedly on our side. Jake Easonsmith had flown over to the Headquarters of First Army in Algeria for this purpose, and had brought back a number of incredible tales. One of these, which never failed to raise incredulous laughter, was that the officers in First Army wore *ties*: "Did they also carry swords and were their men armed with crossbows?"

With these dumps at hand we could now reach Tunisia with supplies to spare for operations: on January 18th, P.P.A., complete and all there was of it, set out in company with Lieutenant Tinker's New Zealand patrol. My orders were to proceed with Tinker to Ksar Rhilane, three hundred miles away, in Tunisia, to reconnoitre with him the going leading up to the Mareth Line; then to get information concerning the defences of the line itself between Matmata and El Hamma. When these reconnaissances had been carried out, my intelligence role would come to an end and I should have a free hand to operate in any area *behind* the Mareth Line and do what harm I could to the enemy according to the information I could collect locally. Thinking of eventual contacts with the officers in ties on the other side, I got these orders written down, stamped and signed (a most unusual procedure with us), and went off to consult my old friend, Bill Shaw, L.R.D.G. intelligence officer. Captain Shaw, a civilian like myself, archaeologist in the Palestinian service before the war, was a veteran desert traveller. He had started with camels, then had joined Bagnold in his early motor trips to Oweinat and the Gilf el Kebir. His name appears in many places on the maps of these areas where dotted lines marked "Shaw 1935" are the result of his running surveys. In the L.R.D.G. from the foundation, he knew more about the desert, its topography, its inhabitants (present and past), and its military possibilities than any man alive, and he could tell what every patrol that had gone out from the first day had done, where it had been and who were the men on it. His memory was prodigious, and though lately he had no opportunities of going out on patrols, he had a gift of describing a route or the clues to a hidden dump as if he had just been there himself. His desert lore was superior even to the Arabs'; it extended to areas where no Arab had ever been.

I went to him to be briefed about southern Tunisia: of the topography he couldn't tell me much more than appeared on the map, for none of us had yet visited this area, but he advised me not to count on being able to penetrate the Grand Erg, the sands of which I would find much less accessible to my trucks than those of the Libyan Sand Sea, and he warned me against the Arabs of Tunisia, whom he believed to be largely disaffected on account of their longstanding hostility to the French. This was bad news to me; I had planned an impregnable and improbable base in the Grand Erg Oriental, and had counted on a network of Arab information similar to the one which had served me in Cyrenaica. I hoped he was mistaken.

A rendezvous was arranged with Nick Wilder on his way back; he would give us fresh information about the southern part of our area which he had just reconnoitred. I was warned that the S.A.S. would probably be operating in the same parts as ourselves, but their movements and indeed also their aims remained obscure, for David Stirling kept his own counsel and preferred not to disclose his plans to possible rivals.

David Stirling, young, tall, good looking and dashing, had become (much against his naturally modest disposition) the romantic figure of the war in the Middle East. He had raised his First S.A.S. Regiment and trained it, at first for parachute operations, then for land fighting in jeeps. With Mayne and a band of friends they had ravaged the German airfields before El Alamein and spread panic amongst the defeated enemy troops after the battle. With a light heart and a cool courage he inspired in his men a passionate devotion and led them to thrilling adventures. Where we plodded, he pranced.

He was captured near Gabes a few weeks later and spent the remainder of the war in captivity.

Yunnie had brought up from Zella the tail of P.P.A., and Hunter had also joined the assembly in Shweref, bringing back with him our Locke and his companions. In this way, by a succession of coincidences, my little band was reunited. I moved forward from Shweref, leaving no one behind.

We had lost Binney, captured in Wadi Zemzem, but we had received a powerful reinforcement which increased our officer strength by fifty per cent: Jean Caneri, our third officer, had turned up in Zella. At the time we left Cairo he was with Chapman, my former companion in the Jebel, engaged in sinking ships in Benghazi harbour. The method they used was to swim at night across the harbour carrying special mines (nicknamed Limpets) strapped to their chests. Having reached a ship, they unstrapped the mine and fixed it to the hull under the water line. The mine was fitted with magnets by means of which it adhered to the steel plates of the ship's hull. They then set the time fuse, swam back to shore, recovered their clothes and walked through the town and on to their hide-out ten miles out in the hills. In due course the mine blew a hole ten feet square out of the hull and the ship went to the bottom.

The liberation of Benghazi had put an end to these exhausting exercises. Caneri, fearing to report back to Cairo in case he should be snatched up once more by the decaying Libyan Arab Force, wandered forward instead and happened to be in El Agheila on January 8th when an L.R.D.G. heavy section convoy came up from Zella for supplies. Caneri had been attached to L.R.D.G. for several months and counted many friends amongst its personnel: he gossiped with these men, heard casually that P.P.A. was stationed in Zella, put his kit on board one of their trucks and reported for duty to Bob Yunnie two days later.

Caneri (we pronounced his name as "Canary") was French. Posted to the French Army in Syria at the declaration of war as a gunner sergeant, he deserted at the time of the fall of France, and came to Cairo where he had spent part of his childhood and had many friends. He promptly enlisted in the British

Army, and was commissioned and posted to the Libyan Arab Force after a period of service in the Abyssinian campaign. He had taken a law degree at the Sorbonne, but having served two years as a conscript he had had no opportunity of being called to the Bar. He was twenty-six years old when he joined us, and at that time spoke in a rather broken English.

I had now two officers according to my heart: experienced and determined men tied closely together by deep friendship, mutual understanding and a common purpose.

Our outlooks differed and were in a way complementary: Yunnie, matter-of-fact as he was, had a romantic side with a touch of flamboyant bravery which gave colour to our undertakings and inspired our men; Caneri, hard and somewhat cynical, had a cold-blooded courage together with a disarming ingenuity: he was both liked and feared – and obeyed. He had a passionate love of tidy details which put order in our affairs where my haphazard negligence produced an incredible confusion. I had imagination, a broad view of our problems and a certain flair for picking out men suitable for our purposes, but without this persevering pair to implement them, most of my plans would have petered out. We had all three of us an obstinate continuity of purpose which urged us on unceasingly and never allowed us to relax.

I could open my heart to them both and yet lose none of my authority: I was thus spared the loneliness which induces a dangerous autocratic pig-headedness in so many commanders incapable of choosing outspoken confidants. With them I was by no means "always right"; I could not take their acquiescence for granted and I had to consider my decisions more carefully than if my orders had invariably been law.

As soon as we set out from Shweref I realized that the minor operations on which some of us had recently been engaged had borne fruit. Our men, no longer merely thrown together by the chance of recruiting, had now some common memories, excitements experienced together, private jokes, a certain pride in their achievements (somewhat magnified no doubt), a desire to do more, and the beginnings of confidence in their fellows and reliance on their commanders. Locke had distinguished himself in trying to drive his jeep down a precipitous face of Jebel Nefusa west of Nalut, where he had gone with Hunter and his patrol. The jeep had turned over and rolled down the slope, a total wreck, Locke and his companion being thrown out unhurt. Amidst Tripolitanian soldiers (in Italian service) who had turned up at this awkward moment, Locke had recovered his guns and all his equipment. To the Tripolitanians he had somehow conveyed that he was a German officer experimenting with a new type of car. Hunter and he had spent the next night in the comfort of an Italian post (January nights are bitterly cold fifteen hundred feet up the mountains) talking gibberish German to one another, and had slipped away quietly before breakfast. Strangely, Locke himself had given me a very sober account – Hunter had been more colourful in describing our pirate's exploits and gave him great praise for his resourcefulness and his presence of mind – but I can't say what stories he told his companions, to whom he was now a bit of a hero, and something of a mascot.

Driver Davies, the Yorkshireman, a storekeeper in civilian life, disgraced himself during the trip from Kufra to Zella by whimpering over a bout of malaria, but after his recovery it appeared that his short illness had brought out a latent forcefulness: he bossed his companions, cheered us all in our days of adversity, and showed so much strength of character and so much fun that he had to be made a corporal, then patrol sergeant and finally quartermaster sergeant.

We had lost one jeep down Jebel Nefusa, leaving us with three only, but Prendergast had arranged that Tinker, on completing his reconnaissance, should hand us over one of his. The two three-tonners were in good order.

We set our course through the Hamada el Homra (the red stony desert), about ten thousand square miles of blank on the map, as yet uncrossed by any of our patrols, which we expected to find very difficult going as it had somehow got a reputation for frightfulness. We were agreeably disappointed: the going was quite good over a rolling plain of firm sand strewn with stones. Coming after the black basalt boulders of the Kharug surrounding Hon, where trucks had to travel snakewise, and, however carefully driven, had their tyres shaved off by the razor-like edges of rock, the Hamada el Homra gave us a holiday drive. The reputation for frightfulness came from the complete absence of vegetation: it is a very empty stretch of desert, without a single bush for a hundred miles, but very lovely, the sand a pearly grey, with red stones about the size of a hand, set in it vertically on edge. When the sun is low on the horizon each slope according to the incidence of light comes out in a different colour, shifting, as the traveller proceeds, from pale coral pink to dark crimson.

One morning I noticed along the top of a slope to my left a multitude of small serrations bobbing up and down. Puzzled, as I thought, by a peculiar form of mirage, I drove idly up the slope: my serrations were the heads, just visible above the skyline, of a herd of gazelle bounding along in the same direction as we were going and keeping pretty well the same speed. There were, we estimated, more than two thousand of them, in one compact mass, bound on some migration of theirs across the inhospitable Hamada. Suddenly the whole herd took a right turn and joined the path of our trucks: in a moment the beasts were amongst us, so close that I had to brake sharply to avoid running one over. On every vehicle rifles came out, but such was the amazement of our men (to whom hitherto a dozen gazelle seen at one time had been a wonder) at the number and the fearlessness of the lovely animals that not a shot was fired. They ran with our moving trucks for a while, then another turn took the herd out of our path over the northern skyline.

Davies mused a long time over the incident. At our next stop he came over to me:

"They must have thought we were another herd of gazelle."

Out of the Hamada we drove into rocky hills looking for the petrol dump. With the "chart and the instructions" we discovered our treasure: cans spread out under rocks and covered with stones. While we were loading, the trucks of T2 Patrol, with Nick Wilder, came lurching down the wadi, like small ships in a choppy sea with the wind astern. They struck their sails and we exchanged the news. Wilder had found the gap in the range which several other patrols had searched for before him, and was now on his way back to Hon to report, refit and set out again. Much of his reconnaissance had been done wearily on foot, but driving, he told us, had been even more exhausting than walking. The going in the corridor thirty-five miles wide between Jebel Nefusa and the Grand Erg sand dunes was the most exasperating he had ever been over, and he sardonically wished us better luck than he had had, for we were bound for the same unattractive parts. We parted the next morning in our opposite directions.

In uncharted country, each patrol endeavoured to break a new route and to cover fresh ground on each voyage: the information brought back was the material from which Shaw and his surveyors built up maps on which layers of colours denoted the nature of the going. These maps were used by Army Headquarters to plan their movements over the desert and were also issued to the units concerned. Thus it happened that the next day we were running along the edge of an unknown escarpment, searching for a gully down which we could drive our trucks into the plain three hundred feet below. The gullies were all found to end in vertical drops; in desperation we chose to build ourselves a ramp at a spot where the cliff face itself had crumbled down somewhat. For five hours we rolled boulders and carried stones, then drove the jeeps down, then the thirty-hundred-weights and finally my heavy, overloaded, three-tonners slithered, lurched and bumped their way down. All the time Italian traffic was running up and down the Sinaun-Nalut track, two miles across the plain. We had a meal and after dark crept across the track and away to the west to rest under cover of very meagre bushes.

The next day we crossed the Tunisian border and immediately encountered the exasperating country Wilder had promised us. Our course lay to the west of his, skirting ochre-coloured dunes, outliers of the Grand Erg Sand Sea, over choppy, closely-packed, sandy hillocks twelve to twenty feet high, overgrown with repulsive bushes. The whole of Tunisia seems to be covered with the decaying carcasses of monstrous, dead animals. In the north, straight, broken-edged mountain ranges sticking out of the plains are sharp backbones from which the flesh has rotted away and flowed down in streams of pus to fill the cesspools of the "shotts" (a shott is a salt marsh); in the south we travelled as on dubious pelts, firm on top but supported underneath only by sagging putrid entrails. In the tracks of our bumping trucks I expected to see oozing viscous purple projections. In my childhood I had one day slithered down a high bank and landed smartly on my bottom on a very dead sheep covered in grass and leaves: the horrible long forgotten memory never left me as long as I stayed in Tunsisia.

We struggled on a few miles a day. The long three tonners alternately bellied on the crests and wedged in the troughs of the sand waves; when we struck easier patches of more undulating ground the brush, thick, dry and brittle, collected under the bellies of the jeeps, jammed the steering and caught fire over the exhaust pipes.

On January 24th we met human beings for the first time, a band of twelve Arabs with two camels, ragged, starved and diseased, sulky and suspicious creatures who accepted our hospitality but kept their shifty eyes averted. I took one of them, Abdel Kerim ben 'Ali el Bendiri, with us, nominally as a guide, in fact as a hostage. I had less difficulty in understanding their speech than I had expected, and our Senussis conversed with them quite easily.

The next morning I decided with Tinker to leave behind all our heavy vehicles and to carry out the reconnaissance northwards with jeeps only. We drove westwards under a hill called Qaret 'Ali, intending to establish our base a few miles inside the sand dunes of the Grand Erg, where it would be safe against surprise by enemy land forces. At our first attempt we realized that the technique which had taken us over the Libyan Sand Sea would not serve us here: the dunes here were made of dirty brown, powdery, silt-like sand, into which our steel channels sank as in water. We gave up the attempt and established our base on a long patch of hard ground, surrounded on three sides by high dunes, a position easy enough to defend as it could only be reached along a narrow neck. Vehicles trying to force an entry would have to negotiate this difficult gap under the fire of our trucks, well covered themselves by low hummocks. To make things more difficult we laid a few mines in the gap, leaving only a passage for our own use. We filled with water from brackish wells under Qaret el Jesseb, three miles to the south. I put Yunnie in charge of the party, handed him our hostage, wished him good luck and left, to be back in four or five days.

Our reconnaissance party was made up of Tinker, his navigator, and two of his New Zealanders in two jeeps, myself, Caneri, Petrie, Yunes and one man in two other jeeps: a nice party to handle, small enough to keep easily under control; as each one of us knew exactly what we were doing I had no worry about a tail that might go astray. Our low vehicles were practically invisible: the only enemy we had to beware of were armoured cars, and as long as we kept off the tracks, which they couldn't leave in this difficult country, we were quite safe. The local Arabs had reluctantly told us that the only German and Italian posts in the neighbourhood were at Duz, Jemma and Kebili. Ksar Rhilane, an old Roman fort twenty miles north of Qaret 'Ali was empty by their account. We first made sure of this, and found the only inhabitant within its crumbling walls an elderly Arab called 'Ali, a former sergeant-major in the French colonial troops, who spoke French, and preserved in his raggedness remains of military swagger. He told us that a number of vehicles similar to ours had been at the fort a few days previously and had driven off northwards (an S.A.S. detachment we concluded), and that two of these men, their jeep broken down and mislaid, had been living at the fort ever since – but they could not be found before we left. Separated in two groups to cover more ground, we made, as nearly in a straight line as we could, for Matmata, two miles short of which we arranged to meet again in the evening. Up, down and round we switchbacked over the hillocks, stopping only to clear the brushwood from under the chassis. In the early afternoon we reached higher ground and better going. Two unknown jeeps came dashing up a slope behind us: I turned to face them and put out a yellow flag, the agreed recognition signal for all our troops operating in Tunisia, but they took no notice, and stopped only when I fired a burst over their heads. They were six hearty paratroopers of the French section of the S.A.S., who had had originally three jeeps (but had smashed one), and now in their eagerness they were rushing off to Kebili for some vague purpose of their own, and wouldn't listen to my warnings of enemy troops, but drove off at an unreasonable speed, waving and shouting excited farewells.

At four o'clock in the afternoon we pulled up in a discreet wadi within sight of Matmata, a small stone-built town perched on one of the last spurs of the Nefusa range. Less than ten minutes later Yunes, posted as a look-out on top of a hill, waved Tinker in. He and I immediately walked towards Matmata over rocks and grassy slopes – this corner of Tunisia was like a real country – and before nightfall we had seen as much as we needed to make a fair sketch of the western approaches to the town. We had even been near enough to look into the sleepy streets, where, apart from a few Arabs, we had only seen two fat German officers, a very different picture from what I had expected of the fortress which guarded the western end of the formidable Mareth Line.

The main defences of the original Mareth Line extended westwards from the coast to Matmata. The gap through which Montgomery intended to launch his left hook extended from this town to the Jebel Tebaqa range: it was the main object of our reconnaissance. We had that day examined the approaches and found a possible route for an armoured division: it remained now to reconnoitre the actual battle ground. We knew that the planners at Eighth Army Headquarters were waiting for the results of our investigations and we made all the haste we could.

During our absence Yunes had been gossiping with some Arab shepherds, to whom he had given out that we were German officers concerned with the building of the new defences, and had given them hopes of employment. He had heard that some of our supposed colleagues were indeed engaged in building strong points along a line extending from Matmata to the eastern tip of Jebel Tebaqa. This was precisely what we had come to investigate; during the next day, roaming gingerly in the twenty mile gap between the two ranges, we saw I believe most of the work being done by the Germans at the time, which was not very much. They were not taking too seriously the possibility of an attack in force west of the Nefusa range. We knew better and felt very powerful in our four little jeeps.

Tinker had a gravity well beyond his years – I believe he was only twenty-two – and a great big, black, bushy beard gave him an elderly appearance. I treated him as a man of my own age, and such was the assurance of his manner that I tended to take his advice in many matters. Several months later I called on the L.R.D.G. in Egypt, where they had gone to refit, and saw most of my friends. Left alone in the mess I went over in my mind the names of those I had wanted to see and found that Tinker had not put in an appearance. An unknown, slim, clean-shaven youth came in, whom I had noticed previously keeping shyly in the background as if he was a new recruit. I asked him:

"Do you know if Lieutenant Tinker is in camp? I particularly want to see him."

Surprised, he laughed.

"I am Tinker. I wondered why you wouldn't speak to me Popski."

At the end of the fourth day of our reconnaissance we considered that we had the answers to the main problems set by Eighth Army: we had found a route – of terribly bad going, but just practicable, from Wilder's Gap up to the western end of the main Mareth Line; behind the line and as far as El Hamma we had found, with the exception of one wadi, the ground free of major obstacles, either topographical or man-made, and we knew the location of the defence works that were built at that time.

Six weeks later the New Zealand Corps, comprising the Second New Zealand Division, the Eighth Armoured Brigade and General Leclerc's force, reinforced later by the First Armoured Division, was to advance along the route we had reconnoitred and to attack Rommel's right wing on the ground over which we had just been wandering. They forced their way as far as El Hamma, outflanked Rommel, compelled him to withdraw his forces to Wadi Akarit and won the Battle of the Mareth Line.

Our share in the coming events was now to pass on our knowledge to Eighth Army, and accordingly we made for our wireless at Qaret 'Ali.

We separated once more: I took an easterly route along the

Nefusa foothills, Tinker went zigzagging towards Kebili, and promised to join us at our base the next day, calling at Ksar Rhilane on the way. With Caneri we struggled on for hours in a maze of hillocks till we emerged on the Kebili Fum Tatahwin road: it was lovely and smooth, the temptation great – we fell, and, ignoring the risk, whizzed along the road. I pulled up to ask a young shepherd how far to the water.

"Quite near," he said, and went on to gossip of other things. As we were leaving he said: "The two cars of your friends are at the well now," and pointed to two Italian scout cars which – unnoticed by us – were drawing water from Bir Soltan a quarter of a mile to the right of the road. I had a hurried conference with Caneri: we were in great spirits, our reconnaissance had been more successful than we had dared to hope, forty miles away only, the comfort of our big trucks would be ours this very night, and we could now afford to enjoy a little fun. I decided to shoot up the Italian cars and investigate the wells. Water supplies, I speciously argued to myself, were a matter of vital importance to a large force moving in the desert: Eighth Army would want to know all about Bir Soltan, and my mission would be incomplete without a report on this water.

We cocked our guns and I led slowly along the road, looking for the turning which led to the wells. The plan was to drive our two jeeps abreast and thirty yards apart, straight at the wells, and open fire at a hundred yards range. Carefully – round a bend – and uphill. My gunner tapped my arm, pointed ahead and said: "Do you see what I see?"

What I saw was the turret of a whacking big tank, hull down by the roadside a hundred yards away. I stuck out my arm for Caneri, turned sharp left off the road, put my foot down and went bouncing along the hillside out of sight. Caneri, who had seen nothing, had the sense to follow me and caught up when I had gone in a wide circle and crossed the road again three miles below the wells. The laugh was on us even more than we knew: I heard later that what I had seen of the turret was all there was – it had no tank underneath! Set up at some time as a machine-gun post to guard the wells, it was not manned.

At another well five miles from Ksar Rhilane where we

stopped for water, an ancient, toothless Arab, nearly unintelligible, made desperate efforts to warn us of some urgent danger. All we could gather was that something had been burnt and that the enemy was about. The poor creature could not know which of us was fighting whom. I thought there might have been a scrap between the French madmen and an Italian patrol from Duz. Anyway, it seemed reasonable not to drive into Ksar Rhilane without first making sure that the enemy wasn't in it: so two miles short of the Roman fort, we concealed our two jeeps in thick bushes, and while we waited quietly for the night to fall I told Caneri of plans I was making. That evening I would write my report to Eighth Army; the next day I would remain at Qaret 'Ali, waiting for Tinker's return. The following day Tinker and his New Zealanders would make for Hon and we would remain to start operations on our own account. I had noticed a telephone line connecting the half-built German strong points off Matmata: we would liberate a field telephone, tap the line, ring up Head-quarters in Gabes and find the times of the supply trains running from the harbour in Gabes to the railhead in Medenine. With this information we would arrange for a train to blow itself up, together with a bridge between Gabes and Katena. If the times turned out suitable, we might simultaneously make a noisy night display in the streets of Gabes as a diversion. I would arrange to give the Germans the impression that our raid had originated from French-held Tozeur, and we would then withdraw in peace for a while to a new hiding place south of Qaret 'Ali. For the next operation I was thinking of breaking past Gabes into central Tunisia. By the time I could be ready for it I thought Eighth Army would be on the Tunisian border, Gabes would be within fighter range of the R.A.F., and our place would be much further back in the enemy rear.

Night came. Caneri and Yunes walked away towards Ksar Rhilane. Busy in my mind with the details of my plans, I lay down on the ground to wait for their return. An hour and a half later the lights of a car showed below the skyline. We brought the guns of the jeeps to bear on the track and waited: I thought Caneri had been captured and that the enemy were now searching for us. Two headlights that might have been those of a jeep appeared over a rise. I made up my mind and flashed R – R – R on my torch. The headlights blinked T – T – T, an agreed reply, and we uncocked the guns. A jeep pulled up, Caneri climbed out, with him was the French lieutenant parachutist. I said:

"I am glad to see you are still alive and free."

He laughed. "I know. But we never got to Kebili. We smashed another jeep, piled the six of us on to the last remaining one and came back to Ksar Rhilane. Now it seems that the enemy has been active. I have heard rumours that three Messerschmidts strafed your camp at Qaret 'Ali yesterday morning and that some of your vehicles have been burnt out."

We drove to the Roman tower. 'Ali, the friendly old sergeant-major, late of the French Army, confirmed the rumour. Two of the Arabs we had met at Qaret 'Ali had ridden to the Italian post at Duz with the information of our leaguer.

I left Caneri and the six Frenchmen concealed outside Ksar Rhilane to intercept Tinker on his return and prevent him from falling into a trap, for if, as I expected, an Italian armoured patrol came down from Duz or Kebili to deal with the survivors of the Luftwaffe raid, the only track they could use ran through Ksar Rhilane. I drove off in the night with 'Ali to guide me to Qaret 'Ali.

The jeep crashed through the malevolent, man-high Tunisian weeds with a continuous crackle. The glare of the headlights gave them repellent, unnatural hues of metallic green and white as they sprang at us out of the night and vanished under the car. 'Ali understood his job; after an hour and a half we turned right into the defile leading to our leaguer; as I drove through my lights suddenly picked out the skeleton of a three-ton truck standing gauntly burnt out amongst flung litter; I drove round the leaguer, counting the wrecks: every one of my trucks and those of the New Zealanders stood burnt to the ribs. There was a deadly hush and no sign of our men.

At the far end of the leaguer we picked up footprints in the sand of many men, a trail leading into the highest dunes. I left the jeep and followed the trail on foot with a torch: up and up I trudged for a quarter of an hour, shouting my name, reached a crest, sank into a hollow, climbed another slope. I was challenged and shone my torch on a figure muffled in a blanket. Bob Yunnie led me to a hollow where his men were sleeping: they were all there, but two New Zealanders had limb wounds and couldn't walk.

He had saved a few pistols and tommy guns, some rations and a few blankets. Thirty cans of petrol which he had buried had been dug up by the Arabs during the night and stolen. All the rest was lost. The Arabs, including our hostage, had vanished.

The extent of my disaster filled me with sombre joy. My mind was swept clean of all the plans and the hopes with which I had been busy day and night during the last three months, and I had not even a flicker of regret for the strenuous preparations and the long efforts now suddenly wasted at the very moment they were about to bear fruit. From my long-cherished plans for defeating the enemy single-handed, my mind switched over in a moment to consider the new and desperate problems which I had now to solve. Exhilarated by the urgency and the difficulty of the task, my brain functioned with a delightful, effortless lucidity, which I had never experienced before, for I am usually a slow and muddled thinker, full of questionings and doubts.

Woefully cheerful, Yunnie told me that early the previous morning three Messerschmidts had dived from just over the high dunes which surrounded the leaguer. The rattle of their machine guns was the first warning he had had. Backwards and forwards they dived and machine-gunned, and flew away after five minutes, leaving his nine trucks ablaze and exploding. He had tried to save our wireless jeep, which had not been hit, but a burning petrol can projected from one of the three-tonners, landed on the truck and put an end to it. Two New Zealanders had bullet wounds and several other men, including Waterson, had suffered superficial burns while they were attempting salvage from the blaze. Expecting an Italian motor patrol, he had withdrawn with his men into the dunes, where they could only be attacked on foot.

We sat talking in low voices, the men asleep around us. A fire had been kindled by our Senussis and they brewed us some tea, for they had salvaged, together with their weapons, their teapots and glasses. While I questioned Yunnie and listened to his replies, a picture of our situation formed itself in my mind with a clarity of detail that owed nothing to any conscious effort of mine. This picture in outline was as follows: the nearest spot at which I could expect to find help was Tozeur, the French oasis on the other side of Shott Jerid. The distance from Qaret 'Ali to Tozeur was roughly one hundred and ninety miles over unknown desert – probably very rough. The enemy, mostly Italian, had known posts along our route at Duz, Kebili and Sabria. They knew of our presence in the area. The nomad Arabs were miserable but actively hostile: they might fight us themselves, and they would certainly attempt to ingratiate themselves with their Italian masters by reporting our movements. Though they were few in numbers we couldn't hope to move through their areas without their knowledge, and we should have to rely on them to show us the wells, and probably for food. We had no wireless.

Our vehicles were five jeeps, with no more than fifty gallons of petrol between them: probably enough to take three jeeps as far as Tozeur.

Counting the Frenchmen and the two S.A.S. men stranded in Ksar Rhilane, our party numbered fifty-one men, two of whom were wounded and unable to walk. The others were ill shod (most of us wore open sandals or gym shoes on our bare feet) and untrained for long marches.

The food available was sufficient for five or six days, on very short rations.

My immediate tasks, in order of urgency, were:

Communicate the results of our reconnaissance to Eighth Army.

Get medical attention for the wounded.

Get our men out of the dunes at Qaret 'Ali, before dawn

if possible, to avoid the risk of their being trapped by an Italian land force, and then march them to Tozeur to safety.

Warn Henry, who was coming up behind us with the Rhodesian patrol, of the danger he was in of being betrayed to the Luftwaffe by the local Arabs.

By the time Yunnie had finished his report I knew how I was going to set about my business. It was fascinating, I thought, to find all the answers without having to rack my brains; I hoped this unexpected power of decision would remain with me for ever, and I looked forward to the next few days with pleasure. I had all the men woken up and sitting around me; with fresh wood on the fire I kindled a bright blaze so as to light their faces for me while I spoke to them; and to give them time to collect their spirits I made the Arabs draw extravagantly on our meagre supplies of tea and prepare a powerful brew of Arab tea for everyone. I myself woke the two wounded New Zealanders and helped them to the fire: they had had a shot of morphia and slumbered heavily.

When I saw that I had everyone's attention I said:

"You may think that something has happened to Tinker that he is not here with me. Tinker is all right. He will be back tomorrow. While you were being strafed here we made, quite a scoop, Tinker and I, and we want to get the news back to Army quick. We have now got no wireless so we shall go over to First Army to find one.

"Our mishap here was brought about by the local Arabs who betrayed us. I know the two who did it. The Arabs here are not like the Senussis; they are paid by the Italians and the Germans.

"The nearest place where we can get in touch with First Army is Tozeur, held by the French. We are going to walk one hundred and ninety miles to get there. We shan't all walk: Tinker and Caneri are going to drive in three jeeps, carrying twelve men, including our two casualties. The rest of us will walk. If possible when the driving party reaches Tozeur they will raise transport and come back to collect the walking party. But we mustn't count on it. I reckon we can walk to Tozeur in eight days and we are going to start in two hours' time so as to get out of this place, which I don't like, before daylight. Also we haven't got much food and we don't want to waste it sitting on our bottoms.

"I shall drive the two casualties to Ksar Rhilane right now and drive back here in the early morning to collect the food and kit which the Arabs haven't looted. Sergeant Waterson will be in charge of the walking party from here to Ksar Rhilane, and Yunes will guide you by the shortest route which does not follow the tracks of my jeep.

"Bob Yunnie, Sergeant Garven and Sergeant Mohammed will remain here for no more than seven days, in case Henry and S Patrol call here on their way to Tozeur. He is to warn them of the danger of betrayal by the Arabs. If Henry does not call they will make their own way to Tozeur.

"With a little luck we shall get out of this jam without any worse trouble than very sore feet. I want you all to keep close together and allow no one to stray. This is not the Jebel. A lonely man will not have a chance amongst hostile Arabs.

"That is all. Thank you very much. Waterson will now call the roll."

My original intention had been to leave Sergeant Mohammed behind alone to convey the warning to Henry, but I had accepted Yunnie's offer to stay with him, and Sergeant Garven, a New Zealander, had also asked to be allowed to remain: he felt, I believe, that L.R.D.G. should be represented on this desperate rear party.

Yunnie, at that time thirty-three years old, was fundamentally a civilian. He held the methods and the discipline of the army in some contempt and preferred – passionately – to go his own way. He claimed now, as a privilege, to be allowed to remain behind on this risky mission: I thought it would compensate him, in a way, for his cruel disappointment at the loss of our equipment, for, he more than anybody else, had had the trouble of getting it together, and now it was all gone while he was still waiting for his first chance to use it.

He thought that, assisted by the craftiness of Mohammed they would be able to survive in spite of the treachery of the local Arabs. Mohammed had been with him on the two hundred mile trek behind the lines, when his Libyan battalion had walked from Ajedabia to Tobruq nearly exactly a year previously: and from that time he had put great faith in his ability.

The two wounded New Zealanders were carried to my jeep, and I drove immediately to Ksar Rhilane, where I left them with Caneri; then back again to Qaret 'Ali to rummage for food by daylight. Waterson and the walking party had left at four guided by 'Ali, on whom Yunes kept an eye.

Bob Yunnie, Mohammed and two men of P.P.A. were collecting tins when I arrived. Fortunately the Arabs had no use for tinned food, and had overlooked it in their very thorough looting, which had even included the theodolite, after it had been salvaged and hidden under a bush.

On my way back for the second time to Ksar Rhilane with our small stock of supplies and my two men, I followed the tracks of the walking party and overtook them about midday as they were resting and waiting for their dinner to be boiled: a large kid which Yunes had bought from some Arabs. They seemed all in good spirits and Waterson particularly ebullient. I believe that, like me, he enjoyed disasters.

At Ksar Rhilane Tinker was very impatient to get our reports sent over to Eighth Army. We decided that he would leave the same evening for Tozeur and First Army, and that my walking party would follow in the tracks of his jeeps. After sending off our messages to Eighth Army, he would try to raise transport and come back along his tracks to meet us and give us a lift. We found that we had enough petrol to send three jeeps to Tozeur, with a few gallons left over for my jeep and the French one which would carry supplies for the walking party and give us the protection of their guns, as long as the petrol lasted.

My walking party consisted of thirty-seven men: seventeen New Zealanders, twelve British, six French and two Arabs. As we were practically unarmed, our chances of avoiding being killed on our two hundred mile march were slender. On our right, and no more than five miles distant from our route, stood the Italian posts in Duz and Sabria. On our left the sands of the Grand Erg prevented us from giving the enemy a wider berth. All along the first hundred miles of our route any Arab who decided to betray us would not have to ride his camel more than a few hours before reaching an Italian post where a reward would be paid for his information. I had no fear of a motorized column, as the Italians possessed no vehicles that could travel over the difficult country we would be crossing, nor could their aircraft hurt us much beyond compelling us to waste time under cover; but they had mounted native troops against which we would be quite powerless once they got on our tracks. And the nomad Arabs themselves with their antique muskets could well snipe us out of existence if ever they discovered how few weapons we carried. In the latter part of our march we ran the risk of encountering patrols of French Goums, who had a reputation for shooting first and asking questions afterwards, and for being rather indiscriminate in their choice of enemies.

My only chance of getting my men through alive lay in bluffing our enemies, Italians and Arabs, and playing them off, one against the other. This I proceeded to attempt without delay. The Italians first; though three days had now elapsed since the air attack, they had shown no signs of sending out a patrol to investigate. I assumed that the reports they must have received of vehicles moving around Ksar Rhilane made them shy of risking a scrap with an unknown number of heavily armed and highly mobile jeeps. I decided to give them a fantastic idea of our numbers. I got 'Ali to invite a few of the neighbouring shepherds to have tea with me at the fort: then, while we were sipping, Caneri drove smartly into the courtyard with two jeeps, came up to me, saluted, pocketed a document I handed to him and departed with a great noisy revving of engines. A moment later Tinker repeated the ceremony with three jeeps, then the French lieutenant with two vehicles, and so on till, in the course of an hour, every one of the fifteen men we had with us at the moment had come up before me and our five jeeps had been displayed nine times over. Hurried alterations were made to the jeep loads between each scene, although I felt sure that to my untrained guests one jeep was as good as another. I knew that in the early hours of next morning an alarmed Italian commander in Duz would be pulled out of bed to listen to reports of fifty jeeps mounting six guns each, all passing through Ksar Rhilane in one afternoon. It would, I hoped, put him on the defensive, clamouring on the telephone for reinforcements from Kebili. A warning no doubt would also reach Sabria, further on our course.

The show over, I went into a huddle with Yunes and 'Abdel Salam to concoct a programme of deception for the use of the Arabs we would meet on our march.

Waterson and his party walked in from Qaret 'Ali later in the afternoon and that evening Tinker and Caneri, with the two casualties and eight men, drove off to Tozeur, taking with them by mistake two of the petrol cans which had been put aside for my use.

The next morning I called my motley party together, gave them my instructions successively in English, French and Arabic, and we walked off in good order for a well, Bir Haj Brahim, twenty-five miles away, where I wanted to spend the first night. Two hours later we were a straggling column stretched over a mile: Waterson and a group of enthusiasts led the pace at a rate that I found hard to keep up. Now and then I got into my jeep and counted the men as they went by, then drove up again, carrying the last stragglers to march with Waterson for a while. In this disorder we were lucky to gather all our men to the well at nightfall. The six Frenchmen insisted on riding in their jeep, and nothing I said could shame them into taking turns at walking and giving lifts to the more footsore of their companions. They were quite unconscious of the precariousness of our position and talked wildly of pushing ahead and clearing away the Arabs for us.

We found some shepherds watering their cattle at the well and tried on them the story we had prepared. Their acceptance gave us hopes that we would also succeed in deceiving warriors less obtuse than these simple-minded lads. The next day we kept better order, stopping every hour and collecting the stragglers each time, but we covered only fifteen miles. We saw no Arabs at all the whole of that day.

On the third day we again did fifteen miles. Some of the men were now going barefooted rather than in open sandals which collect sand between foot and sole and make walking very painful. But their feet were tender and they made slow progress. We camped for the night seven miles from Sabria in sand dunes. The night was so cold that I burnt a hole in my leather jerkin sleeping on the fire; another man burnt his socks off his feet. These comical mishaps considerably helped our morale.

We had seen no Arabs during the whole day, but two men came up to our fire after dark: it seems there was a feud between the tribe which pastured its flocks near Duz and that which kept near Ksar Rhilane and to avoid daily clashes they left an empty no-man's-land to divide their grazings; thus it was our good fortune that gossip seeped through slowly, and rumours of our identity had not reached them.

Like all the tribesmen in southern Tunisia these men were destitute and lived miserably off their thin cattle for which they had no decent grazing. The French, the Italians and also some of their Arab brethren settling on the land further north, had slowly squeezed them out of the rich pastures on which their forefathers had lived in plenty. Hence a surly resentment against all the people in the north, dull grievances which I intended to exploit for our own ends. 'Ali of the Roman castle, who was glib and politically minded as befitted a man who counted himself well travelled and enlightened, had provided me with a knowledge of local politics, sufficient, I hoped, for my dealings with the half-savage tribesmen.

I entertained my visitors as nobly as my means allowed and asked them to inform their sheikh, whose tents were pitched some twenty-five miles to the south-west, of my visit on the following evening. For their pains I gave them a present of money, generous indeed but not so extravagant (I had inquired from 'Ali the Italian rates of pay) as to excite their cupidity. I gave them to understand that I had matters of importance and secrecy to disclose to their sheikh, counting on the Arabs' love of intrigue to keep their mouths shut.

My big bluff had to be made on the next day or never, because after that time I would be out of petrol, and, without the prestige of a car, I couldn't hope to impress the intended victims of my deceptions with my secret importance. My visitors no doubt could not have helped noticing the scarcity of our weapons: so I hinted broadly that with us all was not as it seemed, as our common enemies, the French, would in due course find out to their grief. With this suggestion of secret weapons I sent them home.

On the fourth day we made an early start and walked over twenty miles following the tracks of Tinker's jeeps, to come to rest in the early afternoon two miles from a spring, 'En bu Rdaf. The going over choppy hillocks overgrown with bushes was tiring for the walkers and alarmingly heavy on petrol for the jeeps. We had all suddenly become extremely ragged; every semblance of military smartness discarded, our appearance was that of a band of refugees. The raggedness, however, was not in our hearts: shadowed the whole day by Arab horsemen, we moved in a close group, ready to fight at any moment, the few of us who possessed a weapon disposed at the head and at the tail of our column. My jeep drove a few hundred yards ahead, the Frenchmen in the rear, driving and stopping alternately so as not to outstrip the men on foot. During the afternoon more and more horsemen showed up on both flanks: with old French Chassepot rifles or long Arab muskets slung on their backs, they became bolder as their numbers increased and I thought that it was only out of respect for the twin guns on our jeeps that they refrained from falling on us.

At the evening halt I found that no more than a few pints of muddy petrol were left in the tanks. We drained and strained the last drops from the French jeep and poured it into mine, hoping it would last long enough to enable it to perform its last task. I got ready for a ceremonial call: as I had carried my kit with me in the jeep all the time I had not suffered to the same extent as the others from the disaster at Qaret 'Ali; I managed to dress with some appearance of decency, and strapped on to me a .45 pistol, field glasses compass and empty pouches. Yunes and 'Abdel Salam had salvaged some of their kit together with their rifles, and we made them look spruce enough. They were the only ones in our crowd who wore army boots. I took Locke with me as my gunner and covered his nakedness – for he wore only a pair of khaki shorts – with my sheepskin coat and gave him my spare pair of desert boots, three sizes too big. I armed him with a tommy gun and an automatic – he had also saved his dagger – and briefed him in his new role. Thus arrayed, the four of us drove off to 'En bu Rdaf, the spring of water at which I had arranged to meet my visitors of the previous night. An Arab, impressed from the crowd of onlookers, guided us. At the spring, to my immense relief, I found both my messengers waiting for me: perched on the back of my jeep they escorted us to the tents of their sheikh.

A man of mean appearance with clever shifty eyes, he was sitting under a patched tent with the flaps up. As he rose to greet me I saw that he too had made an effort to smarten himself up: his threadbare burnous was white and fairly clean, but his followers were clad in the usual ragged brown homespun. Assuming my best party manners, I drew out as long as I could the exchange of courtesies, noticing hopefully some preparations for a meal. My host and his followers being unarmed, I unbuckled my belt and threw it in the jeep: my Senussis required no telling and had already placed their rifles under Locke's care. He remained sitting behind his guns and refused mutely invitations to alight.

We sat down under the tent on camel saddles covered with sheep-skins: our host, a poor man, owned neither wooden sofas nor rugs. As we had arranged, Yunes sat next to me to help me in my conversation and interpret when the local dialect became too obscure for my understanding; 'Abdel Salam, a wizened old man of great cunning and sagacity, sat amongst the followers to spread calculated indiscretions.

I wanted to impress my host with the importance of my own person, as well as with the greatness of my condescension in visiting him. My aim was to make him feel flattered and eager to learn the object of my visit; never to suspect that I wanted favours from him. For this reason I dragged out the conversation interminably in polite courtesies and general gossip until the meal was brought in. Yunes, with whom I had rehearsed the proceedings, seconded me admirably, while 'Abdel Salam carried on the good work in the background. We talked and talked, on a multitude of subjects, but never mentioned our purpose. Beyond the fact that I was a high-ranking German officer, and my two friends Tripolitanian sheikhs of high standing, I told him nothing of our intentions and aloofly ignored his pointed questions.

The meal of boiled goat and kuskus was silent as good manners required. When water had been poured over our hands, I asked my host to let down the flaps of his tent and admit inside only his trusted confidants.

I started then on the evening's business. The German command, I said, had become equally distrustful of the Italians and of the town Arabs in the north. As things were going the only consequence of us Germans winning the war in Tunisia would be to replace greedy Frenchmen by even greedier Italians in the possession of the land. What we wanted was a Tunisia controlled by warlike nomads under German supervision, a military base for us in which contented tribesmen would recover the fat pastures which had been filched from them by the French and their scheming town-Arab friends. Truly these town Arabs had now turned against the French and started a Free Tunisia movement but all they wanted was plunder. Our business was not to fight a painful war to the end that fat, deceitful, town dwellers should grow fatter and richer and finally turn us out of the land. Our friends were the faithful nomads, brave soldiers like ourselves; we intended that they should have a share of the rich loot of Gabes, Sfax, Sousse and Tunis, and then pasture their flocks in peace and amity on rich grass lands – no more on God-forsaken parched and barren sand dunes.

In this vein I talked for hours: I never knew I could say the same things in so many different ways. When I tired, Yunes took up the thread and described the fabulous wealth of Tunis (which he had never seen). In the gloom of the far end of the tent 'Abdel Salam murmured to a close circle of enthralled listeners.

What we wanted from the tribesmen, I told my host, was their help to evict all the settlers, French, Italian and Arab alike – when the time came, which was not yet. I had taken the opportunity of my present mission to call on him, a man of influence as I knew, to prepare him for the call. He would understand that the matter must be kept secret from our weak Italian allies. They had still their uses for us at the present time and should not be made suspicious.

Loot, intrigue, treachery, fat pastures, glory – I had exhausted the temptations I could offer my debased Arab host. Under his native composure I felt him excited; cupidity shone in his eyes. I thought he was ripe for further disclosures: I kicked quietly Yunes's leg to draw his attention to the change of subject and said, quite casually:

"I might as well tell you the truth about the occasion which has brought us here. The French in Tozeur have three companies of Tunisian Goum. We hear that the men are much disaffected to their French officers. We have got together the German soldiers I have with me, all picked men, and dressed them up as escaped British prisoners-of-war. In this guise we intend to drift into Tozeur, where the French, unsuspecting, will receive us well and quarter us in the barracks with the Goum. We will get to work amongst the men and one night the three companies will rise, cut their French officers' throats and seize the town. They will be led by my men, every one of whom carries a powerful German automatic pistol concealed under his clothes."

I had done it! I watched Yunes anxiously out of the tail of my eye. He expanded my speech and added a few details. Our host leaned over and in a low voice asked Yunes some questions which I failed to understand. Then Yunes very deliberately lit a cigarette for the host – not from his lighter, but with an ember picked out of the fire. We had arranged this to be a sign that, in Yunes's opinion, the bait had been swallowed.

I went on: "For the sake of likelihood we cannot take our cars into Tozeur. I would like to leave them here if you would care to look after them till I send someone back to collect."

The sheikh agreed and I thanked him casually. Standing up to stretch my legs I heard Yunes whisper to our host:

"These Germans are generous."

We talked of other matters, but I felt that he had something on his mind.

"Will Your Excellency walk with the men? I am very poor but I could provide you with a riding camel, not a good one, but still, one that would go."

I looked at him dreamily, as if I was turning over in my mind vast problems of strategy:

"I leave such matters to be settled by Yunes," I said, and strode out of the tent into the cold night.

When Yunes joined me later it appeared that we were to be provided with two camels, one intended for my personal use, the other to carry our stores. He had also obtained four sheep, one of which was being slaughtered at that very moment to provide supper for our hungry men. The three others would be carried on the camels. It was just as well that he had succeeded in refilling our larder, otherwise the next day would have seen the last of our rations.

Better still than transport and food, he had induced the sheikh to provide a khabir to go with us, a guide who would vouch for us and smooth out unpleasantness which might arise with Arabs of other tribes along our route.

I gave Yunes a gold coin for our deluded host, and I drove back to camp extremely weary and fighting down an unexpected urge to giggle. I said to Yunes:

"We have told many lies tonight. Please God we may be able to tell the truth sometimes after this."

"God be praised," he said piously. "These Arabs are extremely credulous," and he chuckled softly. I shook with uncontrollable laughter.

The next day, fifth out of Ksar Rhilane, we started late. We made camp for the six Frenchmen, who had long ago expressed their determination not to walk and who now asked to remain behind to guard the paralysed jeeps. Failing to convince them of the unwiseness of their choice, I arranged with the sheikh for food and warned them not to forget that they were supposed to be Germans. They laughed: "Anything rather than walk!" They couldn't speak a word of intelligible Arabic so perhaps they couldn't give us away.

The khabir turned up with two camels and three sheep, we

loaded our blankets and few remaining rations, and walked away. We covered twenty miles before nightfall, one hundred and fifteen from Qaret 'Ali. The sixth day I estimated also at twenty miles. Waterson was like a bird, hopping about and cheerful. He had taken special charge of Petrie, who tended to brood but always kept in the van. Most of the New Zealanders walked with these two. They showed no signs of being upset. Some of my English lads dragged behind and required encouragement now and then. Locke, completely unperturbed, walked generally by himself, flapping his feet in my large desert boots. The Arabs were quite at home on the march and somehow their clothes suffered less than ours. The cold, sharp during the night, became unbearable towards morning, and as we couldn't sleep we walked away before dawn.

On the seventh day we saw several horsemen hovering about. The khabir grew nervous and talked of going home. During the afternoon we heard a distant noise of aircraft and we went to ground, dispersed amongst the hillocks. The noise grew and grew and suddenly one of my men stood on top of a hillock waving and cheering, and the next moment we were all doing the same: two hundred feet overhead, fifty R.A.F. bombers in close formation thundered over us on their way to Tripolitania. We still had our noses in the air when I noticed, on the ground this time, coming towards us a school of jeeps wheeling up and down over the hillocks like porpoises in a choppy sea. Tinker, in a hurry as usual, drove up to me. He had four borrowed jeeps with him. Caneri with another four jeeps was searching for us along a shorter route, in case we had lost the original track. I sent Yunes to guide Tinker to the two jeeps we had left with the Frenchmen, and we all sat down and rubbed our feet; we had walked one hundred and fifty miles. In an incredibly short time he was back with our vehicles from the spring from which we had walked in three days. We piled in, six and seven to a jeep, and drove off. That night we slept on the shore of Shott Jerid. The next morning we drove like birds over the mud flats at the western tail of the Shott, fearful of hitting a quagmire and of being engulfed. At eleven o'clock we hit the tarmac road which runs from

Touggourt to Tozeur, and a little after twelve we sat down to lunch in the gaudy dining-room of the Hotel Trans atlantique in Tozeur. We looked very incongruous, sitting in fours at our tables, with white linen, an array of cutlery and three glasses to each of us.

SIEGE AT PRINCES GATE
Jon E. Lewis

The Special Air Service of the British Army burst into the world headlines in May 1980 when it stormed the Iranian Embassy in London to free 26 hostages held by Arab gunmen. It was an unusually public appearance for the SAS, most of whose operations since its foundation in 1941 have been deep behind enemy lines, or in the more shadowy areas of counter-revolutionary warfare.

The man most reponsible for the foundation of the SAS was David Stirling, a young and junior officer of the Scots Guards who tricked his way into the British Army Middle East HQ in Cairo in 1941 in an effort to talk to the Chief of Staff about "a matter of operational importance". He ended up in the office of the deputy Chief, Major-General Neil Ritche, who, impressed with Stirling's audacity, gave him a hearing. The subaltern's idea was to destroy Axis aircraft in the desert while they were on the ground, using a small mobile land unit. Ritche gave the scheme his approval and L Detachment, Special Air Service Brigade was born. (There was in fact no "Brigade"; it was a bluff to fool German intelligence into thinking that the unit was larger than it was, namely a handful of men, three tents and one three-ton truck). The badge of the SAS, the Sword Of Damocles and wings, with the motto "Who Dares Wins", was formally approved in 1942. Most of L Detachment's initial troopers were disbanded commandos who, under Stirling's training and leadership and in close liaison with the Long Range Desert Group, proved to be formidable desert raiders. In January 1943 the 1st Special Air Service Regiment was formally recognised, and three months later the 2nd SAS Regiment was formed. In the same year, Stirling himself was captured by the Germans in Tunisia. After Africa, the regiments fought in Italy and northwest Europe. With the war's end the SAS, along with several other "private armies", was disbanded.

In 1947, however, it was reformed as 21 SAS, with a Malayan Scouts (SAS) unit coming into being in 1950. As its name implied, its chief purpose was to fight in the jungles of Malaya against the communist insurgency. The scouts were officially recognized as the 22nd SAS in 1952. Since that time, 22 SAS has been involved in campaigns in Borneo, Aden, and Oman (see pages 235 ff). Following the massacre of Israeli atheletes at the Munich Olympics in 1972, its counter-revolutionary warfare training and role was stepped up considerably, with the Regiment playing an active, if covert, part in the war against the Provisional IRA in Ireland and mainland Britain. It has also worked alongside the CRW units of other nations, including the West German GSG9 at Mogadishu. It therefore went in to break the siege of the Iranian Embassy at Princes Gate in 1980, the story of which is related below, with a wealth of CRW experience.

AT 11.25 AM ON the morning of Wednesday 30 April 1980, the tranquillity of Princes Gate, in London's leafy Kensington district, was shattered as six gunmen wearing shamags over their faces sprayed the outside of No.16 with machine gun fire and stormed through the entrance. The leading gunman made straight for an astonished police constable standing in the foyer, Trevor Lock of the Diplomatic Protection Group, while the rest, shouting and waving their machine pistols, rounded up the other occupants of the building.

The gunmen – Faisal, Hassan, Shai, Makki, Ali and Salim – were members of Mohieddin al Nasser Martyr Group, an Arab group seeking the liberation of Khuzestan from Ayatollah Khomeini's Iran. No. 16 was the Iranian Embassy in Britain. The siege of Princes Gate had begun.

The police were on the scene almost immediately, alerted by an emergency signal by Trevor Lock, and were soon followed by Scotland Yard specialist units including C13, the anti-terrorist squad, and D11, the elite blue beret marksmen. The building was surrounded, and Scotland Yard hastily began putting in motion its siege negotiation machinery.

While no siege is ever the same as the one before or after it, most follow a definite pattern: in stage one, the authorities try to pacify the gunmen (usually with such provisions as cigarettes and food), and allow the release of ideological statements; in stage two, the hostage-takers drop their original demands, and begin negotiating their own escape; stage three is the resolution.

The Princes Gate siege moved very quickly to stage one, with Salim, the head Arab gunman announcing his demands over the telephone just after 2.35 pm: autonomy and human rights for the people of Khuzestan, and the release of 91 Arab prisoners held in Iranian jails. If his demands were not met he would blow up the Embassy, hostages and all, at noon the following day.

The SAS meanwhile had been alerted about the siege within minutes of its start. Dusty Gray, an ex-SAS sergeant now a Metropolitan Police dog handler, telephoned the Officers' Mess at Bradbury Lines, the SAS's HQ next to the River Wye in Hereford, and said that the SAS would probably be required at the Iranian Embassy, where gunmen had taken over. That night SAS troopers left for London in Range Rovers, arriving at a holding area in Regent's Park Barracks in the early hours of Thursday morning. The official authority from the Ministry of Defence approving the move of the SAS teams to London arrived at Bradbury Lines some hours after they had already left.

Over the next few days the Metropolitan Police continued their "softly, softly" negotiating approach, while trying to determine exactly how many hostages were in the Embassy and where they were located. Scotland Yard's technical squad, C7, installed microphones in the chimney and walls of No. 16, covering the noise by faking Gas Board repairs at neighbouring Enismore Gardens. Gradually it became clear that there were about 25 hostages (as they discovered at the end of the siege, the exact count was 26), most of them Iranian embassy workers. Also hostage were PC Trevor Lock and two BBC sound engineers, Sim Harris and Chris Cramer. The latter, who became seriously ill with a stomach disorder, was released by the gunmen as an act of good faith. It was a bad mistake by the Arab revolutionaries: a debriefing of Cramer gave the SAS vital information about the situation inside the

Embassy as they planned and trained in a new holding area only streets away from Princes Gate itself.

Inside the holding area a scale model of the Embassy had been constructed to familiarize the SAS troopers with the layout of the building they would assault if the police negotiations were to break down. Such training and preparation was nothing new. At the Bradbury Lines HQ, SAS Counter-Revolutionary Warfare teams use a Close-Quarter Battle house for experience of smallarms fire in confined spaces. (One exercise involves troopers sitting amongst dummy "terrorists" while others storm in and riddle the dummies with live rounds).

As the police negotiating team located in a forward base at No. 25 Princes Gate (of all places, the Royal School of Needlework) anticipated, the gunmen very quickly dropped their original demands. By late evening on the second day of the siege, the gunmen were requesting mediation of the siege by Arab ambassadors – and a safe passage out of the country. The British Government, under Margaret Thatcher, refused to countenance the request. To the anger of the gunmen, BBC radio news made no mention of their changed demands, the broadcast of which had been a concession agreed earlier in the day. Finally, the demands were transmitted – but the BBC got the details wrong.

For some tense moments on Saturday, the third day of the siege, it looked as though the furious Salim would start shooting. The crisis was only averted when the police promised that the BBC would put out the demands accurately that evening. The Nine o'clock news duly transmitted them as its first item. The gunmen were jubilant. As they congratulated themselves, however, an SAS reconnaissance team on the roof was discovering a way into No. 16 via an improperly locked skylight. Next door, at No. 18, the Ethiopian Embassy, bricks were being removed from the dividing wall, leaving only plaster for an assault team to break through.

On Sunday 4 May, it began to look as though all the SAS preparation would be for nothing. The tension inside the Embassy had palpably slackened, and the negotiations seemed to be getting somewhere. The gunmen's demands were lessening all the time. Arab ambassadors had agreed to attend a meeting of their COBRA committee in order to decide who would mediate in the siege.

And then, on the morning of Bank Holiday Monday, 5 May, the situation worsened rapidly. Just after dawn the gunmen woke the hostages in a frustrated and nervous state. Bizarrely, Salim, who thought he had heard noises in the night, sent PC Lock to scout the building, to see whether it had been infiltrated. The hostages in Room 9 heard him report to Salim that there was nobody in the Embassy but themselves. Conversations among the gunmen indicated that they increasingly believed they had little chance of escape. At 11.00 am Salim discovered an enormous bulge in the wall separating the Iranian Embassy from the Ethiopian Embassy. Extremely agitated, he moved the male hostages into the telex room at the front of the building on the second floor. Forty minutes later, PC Lock and Sim Harris appeared on the first-floor balcony and informed the police negotiator that their captors would start killing hostages if news of the Arab mediators was not forthcoming immediately. The police played for time, saying that there would be an update on the midday BBC news. The bulletin, however, only served to anger Salim, announcing as it did that the meeting between COBRA and the Arab ambassadors had failed to agree on the question of who would mediate. Incensed, Salim grabbed the telephone link to the police, and announced: "You have run out of time. There will be no more talking. Bring the ambassador to the phone or I will kill a hostage in forty-five minutes."

Outside, in the police forward post, the minutes ticked away with no news from the COBRA meeting, the last negotiating chip of the police. Forty-two minutes, forty-three minutes . . . The telephone rang. It was Trevor Lock to say that the gunmen had taken a hostage, the Iranian Press Attaché, and were tying him to the stairs. They were going to kill him. Salim came on to the phone shouting that the police had deceived him. At precisely 1.45 pm the distinct sound of three shots was heard from inside the embassy.

The news of the shooting was immediately forwarded to

the SAS teams waiting at their holding area. They would be used after all. Operation Nimrod – the relief of the Embassy – was on. The men checked and cleaned their weapons, 9 mm Browning HP automatic pistols and Heckler & Koch ("Hockler") MP5A3 submachine guns. The MP5, a favourite SAS weapon, first came to prominence when a German GSG9 unit used it to storm the hi-jacked airliner at Mogadishu. It can fire up to 650 rpm. The order for the assault teams to move into place was shortly forthcoming.

At 6.50 pm, with tension mounting, the gunmen announced their demands again, with the codicil that a hostage would be shot every forty-five minutes until their demands were met. Another burst of shots was heard. The door of the Embassy opened, and a body was flung down the steps. (The body belonged to the Press Attaché shot earlier in the day. The new burst of shots was a scare tactic.) The police phoned into the Embassy's first floor, where the telephone link with the gunmen was situated. They seemed to cave in to Salim's demands, assuring him that they were not tricking him, and that a bus would be arriving in minutes to take the gunmen to Heathrow Airport, from where they would fly to the Middle East. But by talking on the phone Salim had signalled his wherabouts to the SAS teams who had taken up their start positions on the roof, and in the two buildings either side of No. 16, the Ethiopian Embassy and the Royal College of Physicians. At around this time, formal responsibility – via a handwritten note – passed from the Metropolitan Police to the SAS.

Suddenly, as the world watched Princes Gate on TV, black-clad men wearing respirators appeared on the front balconies and placed "frame-charges" against the armoured-glass window. There was an enormous explosion. The time was exactly 7.23 pm. At the back of the building and on the roof, the assault teams heard the order "Go. Go. Go." Less than 12 minutes had elapsed since the body of the Press Attaché had appeared on the Embassy steps.

The assault on the building came from three sides, with the main assault from the rear, where three pairs of troopers abseiled down from the roof. One of the first party accidentally swung his foot through an upper storey window, thereby alerting Salim to their line of assault. The pair dropped to the ground and prepared to fight their way in, while another pair landed on the balcony, broke the window and threw in stun grenades. A third pair also abseiled down, but one of them became entangled in the ropes, which meant that the rear assault could not use frame charges to blow-in the bullet proof glass. Instead a call sign from a rear troop in the garden sledge-hammered the French windows open, with the troopers swarming into the building on the ground floor. They "negotiated" a gunman in the front hall, cleared the cellars, and then raced upwards to the second floor and the telex room, where the male hostages were held by three gunmen. Meanwhile the pair who had come in through the rear first floor balcony encountered PC Lock grappling with Salim, the head gunman, who had been about to fire at an SAS trooper at the window, and shot the gunman dead.

Almost simultaneous with the rear assault, the frontal assault group stormed over the balcony on the first floor, lobbing in stun grenades through the window broken by their frame charges. Amid gushing smoke they entered and also moved towards the telex room. Another SAS team broke into the building through the plaster division left after the bricks had been removed from wall with the Ethiopian Embassy.

Outside, at the front, the SAS shot CS gas cartridges into an upstairs room where one of the gunmen was believed to be hiding. This room caught fire, the flames spreading quickly to other rooms. (The trooper caught in the abseil rope suffered burns at this point, but was then cut free and rejoined the assault.)

The SAS converged at the telex room, as planned. The gunmen had started shooting the hostages. The Assistant Press Attaché was shot and killed, and the Chargé d'Affaires wounded before the SAS broke in. By then the gunmen were lying on the floor, trying in the smoke and noise to pass themselves off as hostages. What then happened is the subject of some dispute, but the outcome was that the SAS shot two of the gunmen dead. Afterwards, some of the hostages said that the gunmen tried to give themselves up, but were killed anyway. In the event, only one gunman escaped with his life, the one guarding the women in Room 9. The women refused to identify him as a terrorist, and he was handed over to the police. After a brief assembly at No. 14 for emotional congratulations from Home Secretary William Whitelaw, the SAS teams sped away in rented Avis vans. Behind them the Embassy was a blaze of fire and smoke.

The breaking of the siege had taken just 17 minutes. Of the 20 hostages in the building at the time of the SAS assault, 19 were brought out alive. The SAS suffered no casualties. Although mistakes were made in the assault (part of the main assault went in via a room which contained no gunmen and was blocked off from the rest of the Embassy), the speed, daring, and adaptability of the SAS assault proved the regiment an elite amongst the counter-revolutionary forces of the world.

THE BULL OF SCAPA FLOW
Wolfgang Frank

The Second World War was barely six weeks old when, on 13 October 1939, the German submarine Unterseeboot-47 *penetrated the British naval base at Scapa Flow, sinking the battleship* Royal Oak. *It was an audacious blow, one made all the sweeter for the Kriegsmarine in that Scapa Flow had been the site of the scuttling of its High Seas Fleet in 1918. The crew of* U-47 *returned home to Wilhelmshaven national heroes.*

Günther Prien, the commander of U-47, *was a natural U-boat ace and had already claimed the first U-boat victory of the war, a cargo ship on 5 September. An ardent Nazi, Prien had been an unemployed merchant seaman before volunteering for the U-boat arm (all German submarine crew were volunteers) in 1938. He had been appointed commander of* U-47 *just before the outbreak of war.*

After the success of the Scapa Flow raid, U-47 *was sent to the North Atlantic where it wreaked havoc amongst Allied shipping. A type VIIIB submarine,* U-47 *was armed with an 8.8 cm deck gun, a 2 cm anti-aircraft gun and five torpedo tubes (one stern, four in the bows). Its crew was 44 strong. Most of its attacking was done at night, on the surface, with the deck gun, since torpedoes were expensive and the boat could only remain underwater for short periods.*

The following account of the illustrious career of U-47, *including the Scapa Flow raid, is by Wolfgang Frank, the press officer for the U-boat arm during the 1939–45 conflict. He both knew most of the U-boat aces personally and occasionally accompanied them on their voyages.*

It is worth pointing out that the most important consequence of the Scapa Flow raid was that it enabled the head of the U-boat arm, Captain

Karl Dönitz, to persuade the Fuhrer – hitherto uninterested in naval matters – to endorse a massive U-boat building programme. As Dönitz realized, single U-boat raids, though spectacular and morale-sapping for the enemy would not greatly influence the war effort: large numbers of U-boats, organized in flotillas, or "Wolf Packs", to strangle the sea-lanes to Britain could. By the war's end some 600 submarines of the same type as U-47 *had been built.*

IN SEPTEMBER, 1939, one of the "canoes" operating east of the Orkneys found herself off the Pentland Firth, the passage between Scotland and the Orkneys. A strong westerly current caught the boat and swept her through the turbulent narrows. Finding that his engines were not powerful enough to pull him free, the captain, making a virtue out of necessity, carefully surveyed the movement of ships and the defences in the area. On his return he made a detailed report to Dönitz, who at once saw the possibilities of a special operation. After much deliberation he ordered one of his best young officers, Lieut. Günther Prien, to report on board the depot-ship *Weichsel* at Kiel.

As Prien entered the Commodore's cabin he found Dönitz in conference with his own flotilla-commander and Lieut. Wellner, the captain of the "canoe". Charts lay spread on the table before them and Prien's eye was immediately caught by the words "Scapa Flow". The Commodore addressed him.

"Do you think that a determined CO could take his boat into Scapa Flow and attack the ships there? Don't answer now, but let me have your reply by Tuesday. The decision rests entirely with you, and without prejudice to yourself." It was then Sunday. Prien saluted and withdrew, his heart beating fast. He went straight to his quarters and settled down to a thorough study of the problem. He worked away hour after hour, calculating, figuring, checking and re-checking. On the appointed day he stood once again before the Commodore.

"Yes or no?" – "Yes, Sir." A pause. "Have you thought it all out? Have you thought of Emsmann and Henning who tried the same thing in the First World War and never came back?" – "Yes, Sir." – "Then get your boat ready."

The crew could make no sense of the preparations for their next patrol. Why were they disembarking part of their food supplies and taking so little fuel and fresh water with them? Apart from giving essential orders, the captain was uncommunicative, and on the appointed day the U-boat slipped quietly through the Kiel Canal into the North Sea. The nights were dark, the seas running high. While on passage the crew watched their captain closely; although funnel-smoke was sighted several times he never attempted to attack. At last, early in the morning of 13th October, the Orkneys were in sight. Prien gave the order to dive and when the U-boat was resting easily on the sea-bed, he ordered all hands to muster forward. "To-morrow we go into Scapa Flow," he began, and went on talking quietly, making sure that every man knew what he had to do. Then he ordered every available man off watch to turn in; they would need all their strength when the time came.

At four o'clock in the afternoon the boat came to life again and the cook served a specially good meal. Jokes were bandied about and Prien wrote in his log, "the morale of the ship's company is superb." At seven-fifteen all hands went to diving-stations, and the chief engineer began to lift the boat off the bottom; the ballast-pumps sang and the boat began to move as the motors stirred into life. Prien took a first cautious glimpse through the periscope. All clear. He gave the order to surface. The wind had dropped but the sky was covered with light clouds; although there was a new moon, the Northern Lights made the night almost as bright as day.

As they moved into the narrows a powerful rip-tide suddenly caught the boat, just as Prien had expected. He needed every ounce of concentration now and a good deal of luck. The rudder was swung from port to starboard and back again, with full use of diesel engines, to keep the bows steady against the stream. At one moment he had to go full astern to avoid colliding with a blockship. Then he suddenly bent down and shouted through the hatch, "We are inside Scapa Flow!*

At this point his log read, "I could see nothing to the south, so turned away along the coast to the north. There I sighted two battleships and beyond them some destroyers at anchor. No cruisers. I decided to attack the big ships." As the U-boat crept closer still, he could make out the details of the ships. The nearest to him was of the *Royal Oak* class. He went closer, until the bows of the second ship appeared beyond the first. She looked like the *Repulse*. He gave his orders, "Ready all tubes! Stand by to fire a salvo from Nos. 1 to 4!' Endrass, his first lieutenant, was taking aim; the forecastle of the *Repulse*† came into the cross-wires. "Fire!" He pressed the firing key.

The U-boat shuddered as the torpedoes leaped away. There was a moment's agonizing pause. Would they hit? Then a tall column of water reared against *Repulse*'s side. But *Royal Oak* lay motionless as before. A miss? Impossible. Defective torpedo? Unlikely. Minutes went by but the silence of the bay remained unbroken. Had the ships been abandoned? Was the whole of Scapa still asleep? Why no counter-attack from the destroyers? It is almost impossible to believe what happened next. Calmly deciding to make a second attack, the captain took his boat in a wide circle round the anchorage *on the surface*, while the spare torpedoes were being loaded into the tubes. For nearly twenty minutes he cruised round the main base of the British fleet while down below the sweating hands pushed torpedo after torpedo into place. As though the situation were not tense enough already, Prien suddenly noticed one of his junior officers, Sub-Lieutenant von Varendorff, calmly walking round the deck. "Are you crazy?" hissed the captain. "Come up here at once!" Once again Prien moved to the attack – this time at closer range – and once again the torpedoes raced towards their target.

* The entry into Scapa Flow was made through Kirk Sound, which was inadequately blocked.

† Prien mistook the old seaplane-carrier *Pegasus* for *Repulse*, which was not in Scapa Flow. Only *Royal Oak* was hit in both attacks. For the next five months the Home Fleet had to use remote anchorages on the west coast of Scotland, until the defences of Scapa had been put in order.

smoke and water towered into the air while the sky was filled with falling wreckage – whole gun-turrets and strips of armourplating weighing tons apiece. The harbour sprang to life. Morse signals flashed from every corner, searchlights probed and swept, a car on the coast road stopped, turned and flashed its headlights on and off as though signalling, as it dashed back the way it had come.

"Emergency full ahead both!" ordered Prien. "Group up motors. Give me everything you've got!" As the water bubbled and boiled beneath the U-boat's stern, he saw a destroyer coming swiftly towards him, sweeping the water with her searchlight. She began to signal with her Aldis lamp; Prien bit his lip as the bridge beneath him shuddered to the vibration of the screws. His wake showed up all too clearly yet he could not afford to reduce speed. Suddenly the miracle happened; the destroyer dropped astern, turned away and disappeared. A moment later he heard the crash of her depth-charges in the distance. The U-boat scraped past the end of a jetty and then – "We're through! Pass the word, we're through!" A roar of cheers answered him from below. Prien set course for the south-east – and home.

During the long hours of waiting before the attack, the crew had passed round a comic paper; one of the cartoons in it showed a bull with head down and nostrils smoking. "Harry Hotspur," someone had said; that was also their name for their captain. Now, on the way home, Endrass had an idea. Armed with paint-brushes and some white paint a small working party clambered on to the casing and painted on the side of the conning-tower the boat's new crest – the Bull of Scapa Flow.

While crossing the North Sea they listened to the wireless. "According to a British Admiralty report," said the announcer, "the battleship *Royal Oak* has been sunk, apparently by a U-boat. British reports say that the U-boat was also sunk." The men in *U47* smiled. In the afternoon came an official announcement from the German Admiralty: "The U-boat which sank the British battleship *Royal Oak* is now known to have also hit the battleship *Repulse* and to have put her out of action. It can now be announced that this U-boat was commanded by Lieutenant Prien." For the first time the name of Prien was heard by the German people. Prien in Scapa Flow – where twenty years before, the German High Seas Fleet had gone to the bottom!

As the U-boat made fast to the jetty Dönitz could be seen standing next to Grand Admiral Raeder, the cornflower-blue lapels of his uniform clearly visible. The Grand Admiral came on board to congratulate the crew; offering his hand to each man he conferred upon every one of them the Iron Cross, Second Class, while the captain was awarded the First Class of the Order. "Lieutenant Prien," said Admiral Raeder, "you will have an opportunity of making a personal report to the Führer." Turning to Dönitz he then announced before them all that the Commodore had been promoted to Rear-Admiral. Henceforth he would be the Flag Officer Commanding U-boats. That same afternoon Prien and his crew were flown to Berlin. Hitler received them in the Reich Chancellery and conferred upon the captain the Knight's Cross of the Iron Cross.

In June, 1940, *U 47* was patrolling to the west of Scotland, still commanded by Lieut. Prien, the "Bull of Scapa Flow". The weather was calm and mild, the nights so light that one could read a book on the bridge at midnight.

Early one morning the haze lifted to reveal a ship – their first target for days. Just as *U 47* altered course to attack, the target turned too and came straight down at her. Prien lowered his periscope and dived as fast as he could to 180 feet, while the ship rumbled unwittingly overhead. Almost at once he surfaced again, ordering the gun's crew to their stations; but as they were closing up round the gun, an after look-out suddenly reported more smoke astern of the U-boat and Prien realised that a convoy was approaching. He abandoned his original plan and, after sending out a hasty sighting-report to head-quarters, he submerged again.

As soon as *U 47* was running smoothly at periscope-depth, he took a quick look through the lens as it broke surface for a few seconds. He could hardly believe his eyes. Forty-two ships were steaming majestically towards him in open order, seven columns of six ships of all shapes and sizes, escorted by two ancient-looking destroyers and three modern ones. For three hours, still submerged, Prien tried to close on the convoy, but his boat was too slow; steadily he lost bearing on the ships, until they were out of periscope sight. He started to surface but almost immediately a trawler hove in sight and he had to dive; at his next attempt a Sunderland zoomed out of the sun like a fat bumble-bee and forced him below again. Prien now realised that to catch up with that convoy he would have to chase it for at least ten hours, and by then it would be so close to the coast that he would never get near it for aircraft and surface-escorts. As he sat weighing up his chances and scanning the horizon, masts and smoke suddenly appeared to port and a straggler from the convoy came hurrying along, zigzagging violently. So he stayed below the surface, and everyone kept deathly still, as if the U-boat herself were holding her breath like a living thing. "All tubes ready!" Every man was standing tensely at his post. Suddenly the ship turned away; with a curse Prien called for the last ounce of power from his motors as he stood after his prey. "No. 5, stand by . . . fire!" Some seconds later there was a clanging crash. "We've hit her near the funnel!" called Prien triumphantly. "She's the *Balmoral Wood** – look and see how big she is, I'd put her at 5,000 or 6,000 tons." As the water closed over the sinking ship, all that could be seen on the surface were a few large crates, some of which had burst open to reveal aircraft wings and fuselages. "Well, *they* won't be dropping any bombs on Kiel, anyway," commented one of the crew.

All next day Prien carried out a searching sweep on various courses, but sighted nothing. "The Atlantic seems to have been swept clean," he wrote in his log. But his luck changed with the dawn of the following day, for a 5,000-tonner without lights came steaming past, barely 5,000 yards away. Despite the growing daylight, Prien tried to approach on the surface but he was soon forced under by a Sunderland; however, he was determined to get in an attack and once again he surfaced. This time his first hasty look round revealed warships ahead and

* This ship was torpedoed and sunk on 14 June 1940.

merchant ships astern of him; quickly he sent out a sighting signal and dived again, realizing that he had chanced upon the meeting-place of a convoy with its escort. He moved in to attack but soon saw that the twenty ships in convoy were screened by at least four escorts of the *Auckland* and *Bittern* class, while a Sunderland flew above them. His original plan of attack would be of no avail against such a strong escort, so he waited awhile before surfacing and then made a wide sweep round, so as to try his luck from the other side. As night fell he closed in, once more at periscope-depth, and began to look for a likely target. The weather was favourable; white caps of foam on the waves would make it difficult for the enemy look-outs to spot his periscope, and although the sky was cloudy, visibility was good.

Despite all this, it looked as though the U-boat had in fact been sighted, for one of the escorts turned towards *U 47* and came down like a pointer sniffing into the wind for game. The range dropped quickly – 300 yards, 250, 200 . . . Prien was tempted to fire at the escort, but she suddenly turned away and disappeared on a course parallel to the U-boat. With a sigh of relief Prien ordered, "No. 1 ready . . . fire!" His target was a great tanker, deeply laden, which had caught his eye earlier in the day. He did not wait to see the torpedo hit, but turned immediately to his next victim, which was slightly nearer – a ship of about 7,000 tons. "No. 2 . . . fire!" While the U-boat was still heeling, Prien suddenly saw a column of water spouting up alongside a ship he had not aimed at. There had been a slight mishap in the torpedo compartment; the torpedo-artificer had been thrown off his balance by the movement of the boat and had saved himself from falling by catching hold of the firing-grip. As a result No. 3 tube had fired a fraction after No. 2 – but the torpedo had hit a second tanker.

Fifteen minutes later the U-boat surfaced and Prien sprang up to the bridge; it was not yet quite dark and the sea was getting up. Over on the port quarter lay the big tanker with a heavy list, her bows well below the surface, her decks awash. Prien sent for the silhouette-book and soon identified the battered wreck as that of the tanker *Cadillac*,

12,100 tons.* The other ship, of which nothing could now be seen, was presumably one of the *Gracia* class of 5,600 tons. The third had also disappeared. Now for the rest of them!

But it was not to be; a storm blew up and after two days' fruitless search Prien realised that he had lost the convoy. A day later, however, he sighted and sank the Dutch tanker *Leticia*,† 2,800 tons, bound for England from Curaçao with fuel-oil. Late that night, in a freshening sea, yet another tanker was sighted and Prien ordered the gun to be manned, having decided to stop the ship with a couple of well-placed rounds and then sink her at his leisure. "Only five rounds of ammunition left, Sir," warned the coxswain. – "Never mind, we'll use them just the same." Time passed but there was no sign of the captain of the gun. Prien called down the hatchway, "Control room! Where's Meier?" There was the sound of running feet below, then the voice of the control room petty officer. "Meier is lying in his bunk, Sir, and says there's absolutely no point in trying to aim a gun in this weather." Prien could hardly believe his ears; the bridge watch did their best to hide their amusement. "Give him a direct order from the captain to report immediately on the bridge!" When Meier at last appeared he did not trouble to hide his feelings. "In *this* sea, with only a couple of rounds?" – "They *must* hit, Meier!" – "Aye, aye, Sir." Indifferently he moved towards the gun and Prien gave the order to open fire. The tanker turned sharply away as the first shells screamed towards her, but two of them hit her; Meier was excelling himself. "Hit her in the engine-room!" ordered Prien. Another hit – but the target was still moving away. The last of the five rounds went into the breech, and this time the shell-burst was followed by a cloud of grey smoke and a yellow flash. Soaked to the skin, Meier returned to the bridge; the tanker had stopped and the crew were hastily abandoning ship. Throwing a quick word of congratulation to his still impenitent gunner, Prien brought *U 47* into a good firing position and loosed off a torpedo. His log

* Probably the tanker *San Fernando*, torpedoed and sunk on 21 June 1940.
† Sunk on 27 June 1940.

reads: "The torpedo hit and the ship began to sink. Despite the gunfire and the torpedo-hit, her radio operator continued to signal '*Empire Toucan* torpedoed in position 49°20′ North, 13°52′ West' and later 'Sinking rapidly by stern'. Finally he jumped overboard with a flare and was seen swimming away from the ship." Prien immediately steered towards the flare but when he reached the spot, there was nothing to be seen. A brave man had died. . . .

Weeks went by as Prien and his brother captains hunted and sank, watched and waited, shadowed the convoys and "homed" other boats on to them, in fair weather and in foul. When at length the U-boats returned to France for repairs and provisioning, their crews were sent to the new rest-centres at Carnac and Quiberon near Lorient, where they could relax on the beach, bathe, ride and do exactly as they pleased. Here they could let the world go by, as they took the pretty daughters of France by storm and quaffed the local wines; all too soon they would once more be at sea, the perpetual thunder of the diesels around them and the waves foaming and crashing on their decks.

Prien, too, was soon back at sea. One dark and rainy night, he and half a dozen other boats encountered a convoy, which they attacked from all sides at once. This was one of the earliest organized wolf-pack actions of the war, and will go down to history as the "Night of the Long Knives". Torpedo after torpedo raced from its tube to detonate against some ship's side. Ten thousand tons of petrol went up in a fiery ball of white-hot flame a thousand feet high; an ammunition ship exploded with a deafening roar and literally disintegrated; all around was nothing but the bright glow of flames. Some ships stood on end before finally disappearing, some listed heavily and turned turtle, others broke apart, to die a painful death. Everywhere, like a pack of wolves, the U-boats were at the convoy. With all his torpedoes gone, Prien reckoned up the tonnage he had sunk by identifying his victims from the "picture book". Then he took a signal-pad and wrote, "Have sunk eight ships in the convoy totalling 50,500 tons. All torpedoes fired."

The dawn came slowly, marking the end of the "Night of

the Long Knives". The other commanders were also making their reckoning: Kretschmer, Schepke, Frauenheim, Endrass, Bleichrodt, Moehle and Liebe. In two days of operating together they had achieved the staggering figure of 325,000 tons sunk.* Within a few days *U 47* had returned to her base. Prien, as the first U-boat captain to top the 200,000-ton mark, now became the fifth officer in the armed forces to receive what was then the highest decoration – the Oak Leaves to the Knight's Cross.

AFTERWORD

The luck of U-47 ran out on 8 March 1941, when it was sunk by HMS Wolverine, *with the loss of all hands. During its career the boat had sunk 28 ships totalling 160,939 tons.*

* "Night of the Long Knives" – 18/19th October, 1940.

OPERATION THUNDERBALL

Yeshayu Ben-Porat, Eitan Haber and Zeev Schiff

Just after midday on 27 June 1976 Air France Flight 139 was hijacked en route to Paris from Tel Aviv by members of the German Baader-Meinhof gang and the Popular Front for Liberation of Palestine (PFLP). Fifteen hours later, the jet – which had 258, mostly Israeli, passengers and crew aboard – landed at Entebbe, in Uganda. There the four hijackers were joined by other Baader-Meinhof and PFLP members, and personally welcomed by President Idi Amin Dada. On the following day, the 28th, the hijackers, led by Wilfred Böse of Baader-Meinhof, announced their demands to the waiting world: 53 of their comrades, held in prisons in Israel, France, West Germany, Switzerland and Kenya, must be released. Or they would start shooting the hostages.

At first, the Israeli government of Yitzhak Rabin was inclined to negotiate, since non-Jewish hostages were also involved. The Israeli attitude changed, however, when the hijackers released all the hostages who were not Israeli or Jewish, and it became clear that Idi Amin Dada was intransigent in his support for the hijackers. On 3 July, the Israeli cabinet accepted a dramatic rescue plan proposed by Major-General Dan Shomron, general officer comanding paratroopers and infantry.

Shomron's plan called for crack Israeli para teams to land on the runway at Entebbe in Hercules transport planes, from which the paratroopers, led by Lieutenant-Colonel Jonathan "Yoni" Netanyu, would fan out to secure their targets, most importantly the old terminal where the hostages were held. Crucial to the success of Operation Thunderball, as Shomron's plan was now called, was speed and surprise. As a ruse to fool the Ugandan airport guards, the para team detailed to take the old terminal was to drive there from the runway in a black

Mercedes disguised as Amin's personal car. Meanwhile, above the airfield an Israeli Boeing would act as a mobile communications centre.

The account here of Operation Thunderball, is extracted from Entebbe Rescue *by Israeli authors Ben-Porat, Haber and Schiff, and begins with the first Israeli Hercules transports landing on the runway at Entebbe, 23.01 hours, 3 July 1976.*

THE LEAD HERCULES was still taxiing slowly along the runway as a dozen soldiers leaped out and dispersed, several yards apart, on either side. Each of them turned to a nearby runway beacon and placed mobile flashlights alongside them – a precaution in case the control tower shut off the power before the other three planes landed. More soldiers charged out of the belly of the plane as it stopped moving, taking positions around it to combat any possible Ugandan reaction.

Colonel Natan Aloni was standing by the ramp of the first Hercules as it dropped open to allow in a flow of cool night air. At a distance, he could see the control tower – code-named "Aviva." With the stream of air came an army of tiny tropical flies and mosquitoes which beat against the faces of waiting infantrymen. The temperature was 60°.

Aloni, a veteran soldier, had correctly estimated that the hard work would be over as soon as the plane had landed safely. They had already come several hundred yards down the runway, and no one had opened fire. From here on, he was confident that Operation Thunderball could proceed exactly as planned. Shouting "Forward," he ran in the direction of "July" – New Terminal. The force under his command had to seize the control tower to ensure a clear takeoff at the end of the raid.

The mobile beacons placed by paratroops from the first plane were already illuminating the area next to runway "Yuval."

It was cramped and uncomfortable inside the Mercedes. As the pilot swung the nose of the plane around, Tzur Ben-Ami pressed down on his accelerator and the car leaped forward. Old Terminal was over to the right bathed in a pool of light.

The nine men in the Mercedes knew its location, approximately 1,500 yards away, from rehearsals the day before.

Yoni shouted to the other drivers to keep in line, then ordered Tzur to drive slow enough not to arouse suspicion. Ten or fifteen seconds had already elapsed since they had left the plane, and the Mercedes was approaching the old control tower when Yoni and Tzur spotted two figures a couple of hundred yards from them.

"Pay attention now," Yoni ordered as his men gripped their weapons. The Mercedes moved straight ahead, the two Land Rovers close behind. Rain was spattering the windshield.

The two Ugandan guards were now only fifteen yards from them. During rehearsals, Yossi had insisted that Ugandan troops would not stop a Mercedes, and would certainly never fire on it; after all, these were the cars their officers used. Now, therefore, he was no less surprised than his comrades when one of the Ugandans signaled the car to halt. They were only four yards away.

The Mercedes crawled one yard nearer. This soldier could endanger the entire mission, but there was no mistaking his uplifted right arm.

A pistol poked out the right-hand window. The Ugandan fell, but wasn't dead. Nobody had heard the shot that hit him.

"Right, step on it," ordered Yoni.

Tzur Ben-Ami responded immediately.

Michael Golan steered straight into the pool of light that was Entebbe. He glided in to land and taxied straight to his preset offloading point, behind a twenty- or thirty-foot-high hillock next to one of the runways. Flicking on his microphone, Michael confirmed: "I am at 'Katie.'"

Four flight controllers were on duty in the tower. Five minutes earlier, a passenger plane had asked permission to land. Now, something strange was happening to the radar screens – so foreign journalists were told later. The dancing white spots known as "snow" obscured their entire radius of sweep. Having little choice, the controllers sat back to wait patiently till the electronic disturbance abated.

"There's another light plane in the air," one of the controllers remarked, his voice clearly heard over the radios in the Hercules' cockpits. The men were instantly panicked.

Brigadier Dan Shomron had another worry. When the first Hercules braked at its assigned spot, Shomron jumped off the ramp to choose a location for his command team. The sudden silence of the Ugandan airport hit him hard. For one terrible moment, he was sure that the hostages must have been moved from Old Terminal – a fear reinforced by the memory of a crack United States army detachment that reached an American prisoner of war camp in Vietnam only to find it empty. The silence persisted as the second Hercules trundled along the runway to its parking spot.

In the defense minister's office far off in Tel Aviv, the silence seemed almost painful. The ministers sat along the walls and around the desk, some smoking, others leaning toward the intercom as if their attentiveness might coerce it into speech. But the intercom wouldn't cooperate.

Asher Ben-Natan's bottle of Napoleon brandy still stood on the desk. No one touched it. Military secretaries Braun and Poran sat with poised pens, ready to record any word coming from the intercom.

Somebody coughed, and Yitzhak Rabin turned toward him, instantly indignant, in tacit reproach for disturbing the moment.

Shimon Peres closed his eyes and his companions got the impression that he was offering up a silent prayer. He knew that the next ten or twenty seconds were the most critical of all – for the hostages, for the soldiers on the ground in Entebbe, for the army, and for the government of Israel.

Not far from Peres, Mota Gur was listening over his intercom to the command net on the ground in Entebbe. He could hear the first reports coming in to Dan Shomron, but was waiting for a clear picture from his head of Staff Branch, Yekutiel Adam. In the past there had been occasions when Mota had been grateful for his deputy's characteristic lack of loquaciousness, but right now he was dying to know what was happening in Entebbe.

* * *

The Israeli air force Boeing had just landed at Nairobi. The plane appeared to be an El Al jet on a scheduled flight from Johannesburg to Tel Aviv, via Nairobi. Inside the craft, doctors were installing the last items of equipment, ready for what was to come.

Kenyan security men moved in to surround the plane.

The third Hercules was a few feet above the runway when the lights went out. Pilot Ariel Luz was shocked, but only for a fraction of a second. He made a hard landing and let his plane roll forward, hoping to spot the beacons placed by the paratroops from the first plane. Then he applied his brakes, but the heavy craft only rolled to a stop on the grass beside the asphalt runway.

Michael Golan was puzzled. Only a moment ago, the runway lights had been on; now it was pitch dark. He was worried that Ugandan soldiers could creep out from the terminal buildings to attack the three planes already on the ground.

Kuti Adam, circling above in another plane, was desperate for news. He could hear Dan Shomron, could listen to reports from the teams spreading out over the airport, could grasp that the aircraft were landing without difficulties so far – but he knew nothing about the most critical stage of all. Operation Thunderball would stand or fail by what happened to the Mercedes and its companion Land Rovers. If the terrorists or Ugandans realized there were Israelis in the cars, Old Terminal could become a charnel house. Yoni Netaniahu and his men had seconds in which to reach all three entrances to the building – and Kuti Adam still had no word of them.

The fourth Hercules came in to land between the paratroop torches. In the third plane, the pilot was in a cold sweat. Beyond his windows, he saw that his front wheels had stopped three feet from a six-foot-deep trench. Three feet more and Operation Thunderball would have been over for him, his crew, and his passengers.

The Mercedes and its two Land Rover escorts were now speeding into the area between the old control tower and the terminal, close enough to see the covered walkways at the entrances, exactly as described in their preliminary briefing.

Three or four seconds ago, the second Ugandan – the one who hadn't been shot – had vanished from sight. Now he surfaced again, close to the control tower. He hadn't panicked, and he opened fire immediately. A paratroop sergeant in one of the Land Rovers loosed a burst from a Kalashnikov and the Ugandan fell.

"Faster," Yoni shouted.

Tzur Ben-Ami pressed the pedal down as far as it would go. Then the Mercedes jerked to a stop, its four doors already swinging back hard on their hinges, as the occupants shot out from the car. The spot could not have been better chosen – near enough to Old Terminal for a fast entry, but just far enough not to alert the terrorists unnecessarily.

Yoni, Yossi, and their team raced like men possessed toward the three entrances to Old Terminal.

"Those soldiers must be organizing a revolution against Amin," Jaaber commented on hearing two or three shots in the distance outside the building. This was the burst that had cut down the second Ugandan sentry.

Michel Bacos was washing his hands.

Yitzhak David straightened up on his mattress.

Lisette Hadad pulled her blanket over her head and rolled off the mattress onto the floor. Yosef Hadad grabbed a nearby chair and lifted it over his head.

Jean Jacques Maimoni, who was sitting at the far end, lifted his mattress over his body.

Yossi was the first to reach the doorway. The distance from the Mercedes took him at most three seconds. Yoni ran alongside, with the others close on his heels. Behind the rail that ran the length of Old Terminal, Yossi spotted a terrorist who had come out of the building. He fired. The terrorist bent over and ran back in the direction of the doorway.

Wilfried Böse heard the shot and came out to see what was happening. Yossi shot again, but missed. Böse leaped backward and pointed his carbine in the direction of the hostages.

"Retreat!" shouted Böse, turning his head. Yossi shot him.

"Get in," yelled Yoni. "Through the doors!"

Jaaber stood at the far end, gesturing at the terrorist girl in an unmistakable question: "What's going on?"

The girl threw her hand grenade on Jean Jacques' mattress.

Sara Davidson threw herself flat on the floor, then crawled with Uzzi and her two sons toward the corridor to the washrooms. It wasn't far, and it offered the protective sanctuary of a wall. The washrooms were already crowded with terrified hostages who had pressed themselves flat to the floor.

Hana Cohen had lost sight of her son Yaakov. In the chaos, she didn't notice that he wasn't running with her husband and daughter into the corridor. The three of them sprawled on the floor, Pasco Cohen covering his two women with his own body.

Yaakov Cohen tipped over the bench on which he had been sleeping, and covered himself with a mattress.

Ilan Hartuv ran for the corridor.

Yossi raced under the awning and up to the first door. To his horror, he found it was locked. In a fraction of a second, he spun around and hurtled toward the second entrance. He could still hear Yoni egging the others on: "Forward! Forward!" A terrorist suddenly appeared in Yossi's way. He pressed hard on the trigger of his gun – but nothing happened. Empty magazine! Three soldiers hurtled past and into the second doorway. Yossi switched magazines in record time and jumped in after his men. Coming through the doorway, he noticed the terrorist girl standing inside the hall to the left of the door. Another instant and Yossi would have shot her, but the man behind him beat him to it. Hit by a burst, she spun onto the floor near a window. Beyond the group of hostages, who were hugging the floor, a terrorist aimed his Kalashnikov down at the spread-eagled bodies. One of the French crewman screamed: "Don't shoot!"

The terrorist hesitated a second, and it was his last. From ten yards away, Yossi fired a burst that killed him outright.

Across to the right another terrorist managed to fire. He loosed three or four shots that echoed around the hall, then dropped. Amnon Ben-David hit him. He tried to rise and Amnon shot him again.

The paratroopers who had burst through the two open doorways could now take in a sight of utter confusion. A mad mixture of people, beds, mattresses, blankets, overnight bags. The hostages were terrified. After all, it had happened in fifteen seconds – far too quickly for anyone to grasp!

Ron Vardi and his comrades clung to the sides of a command car as it careened across the empty space to the new control tower. Off to one side was a fire station. As Ron watched, it was suddenly pitch black. Somebody had killed the airport lights. At the foot of the tower, the combat team could hear the crackle of shots from elsewhere on the field, but their target was deserted. The four flight controllers were no longer at their stations. An officer scanned the panels, searching for a switch that would restore light to the runways.

Lieutenant Shlomo Lavi raced at the head of his force, riding in two Rabbi field cars, into the Ugandan air force parking area. According to plan, his men were to prevent any attempt by the MIG pilots to get their craft airborne and attack the departing Hercules. Shlomo's mission proceeded smoothly. In minimum time the area was secure, without opposition.

Around the field, men of the Golani and the paratroop detachments were already deployed across main access routes and roads to block any reinforcements from a nearby army camp almost within earshot of Entebbe International.

At the center of the airport, Dan Shomron was losing patience. Still not a word from Yoni Netaniahu, though he could hear the crackle of light-arms fire – rarely a good sign.

Yoni's Land Rover team headed straight for the second floor. Their mission was to secure the building against any attempt to interfere with the transfer of hostages to the aircraft. The first soldier racing up met two Ugandan soldiers on the stairs. They froze. Above them, on the second floor, were more of their comrades. There was some resistance, but it was over in less than a minute and the Israelis were free to mount guard on the roof, where they could survey the entire surrounding area.

The force now inside Old Terminal had a rough idea of the number of terrorists, all of whom had to be taken care of if the evacuation was to proceed safely. While Yossi and his squad went in to the passenger hall, another team ran along the front of the building to the old VIP Room at the far end. As they arrived, the terrorists off duty came tumbling into the corridor.

Two white Europeans came out of a nearby room. For a split second Ilan Gonen held his fire, thinking that these must be passengers off the Aerobus.

"Who are you?" Ilan shouted in English.

No answer. The two men continued their slow walk.

In the defense minister's office, shots could be heard over the intercom. Were it not for the tension and anxiety, Rabin, Peres, and the others might have found time to marvel at the wonders of modern technology that could let them listen to a battle two thousand miles away. Yet, apart from a few crisp orders issued by Dan Shomron, and terse conversations between the plane and the ground below, there was no way of knowing how things were going or whether the hostages were safe. Amos Aron was sending a message to President Ford over the phone to Ambassador Dinitz in Washington: AT THE TIME OF DELIVERY OF THIS MESSAGE, OUR FORCES . . . Dinitz listened in astonishment.

It was only at 11:07 P.M. that Kuti Adam's voice finally came through in the chief of staff's private bureau and the defense minister's room elsewhere in the building.

"Everything's okay. You'll have a precise report immediately."

Everything's okay?

What had happened at Entebbe?

Were the hostages safe?

Were the terrorists dead?

What about casualties?

The prime minister and his defense minister leaned forward, almost unable to bear the tension, praying to hear Dan Shomron's voice.

Mota Gur no longer hesitated. He called Dan directly.

"What's happening there?"

"Everything's all right. I'll report later. I'm busy now."

Again, everything's all right. . . . What's all right?

Yosef Hadad held the chair over his head as protection against terrorist bullets. A bullet hit his chair, and he thought his end had come. Out of the corner of his eye, he could see Böse lying in a pool of blood.

Pasco Cohen lay on top of his wife and daughter, with more hostages on top of him. He lifted himself for a moment to make sure that Zippy wasn't suffocating. A bullet penetrated his thigh, then tore an artery near his bladder.

"I'm wounded," he told Hana quietly, "look after the children."

As Pasco collapsed on the floor of the corridor, Jean Jacques Maimoni panicked at the sight of the hand grenade that had landed on his mattress. The boy jumped to his feet and ran, bent over, toward the washroom corridor. Two bullets hit his back and sent him sprawling on the floor, dead. Yitzhak David, who lifted his body in an attempt to pull Jean Jacques down, took a bullet in his shoulder.

"Who are you?" Ilan Gonen yelled again. But the two Europeans went on walking, as though all the hubbub and chaos had nothing to do with them. The soldier pointed his gun barrel at them. Spotting the flash of a grenade fuse, he let loose a burst, then dropped flat on the floor. The grenade exploded in the corridor, tearing the bodies of the two Europeans but not harming the paratroopers.

Sara Davidson thought she could hear voices speaking Hebrew. They were coming nearer! A loudspeaker boomed through the enclosed space: "This is *Zahal* – the IDF! We've come to take you home! Lie on the floor and wait for instructions! This is *Zahal*!"

Yosef Hadad shouted in a voice clearly heard throughout Old Terminal: "They're ours! They're ours!"

Somebody else lifted a head to call: "Israeli soldiers? Israeli soldiers!"

Baruch Gross peeked into the hall from the washroom

corridor and almost stopped breathing. Before him stood an Israeli soldier. There could be no mistake! But the man's gun was pointing at him. Baruch didn't lose his head: "*Yisrael*!" he shouted the Hebrew word, "*Yisrael*!" The gun barrel turned, and it seemed to Baruch that his life was also turning.

"Lie on the floor," boomed the bullhorn, "we have come to get you and it will be all right!"

Thirteen-year-old Benny Davidson couldn't believe it. Only at noon he had jokingly told his parents and brother that "the army will come to free us tonight at midnight." So he had said it – so what? He didn't mean it, and certainly didn't believe it. And now, one hour before midnight, Israeli soldiers had appeared in Old Terminal. Sara Davidson dropped on top of Ron, while Benny mumbled a prayer.

Hana Cohen didn't lose her head. She was too good a nurse for that. Tearing Pasco's shirt, she bandaged the wound, but the makeshift dressing turned red. The wound was deep. Pasco was losing too much blood.

Yossi ran through Old Terminal checking to see that all the terrorists were dead. Then he called a sixteen-year-old hostage named Michael, and asked him to identify them. Once that was done, Yossi reported to Brigadier Dan Shomron, somewhere on Entebbe's field. Shomron passed the news on to Yekutiel Adam in the Boeing. Adam relayed the message to General Gur. "The transgressors are eliminated," he said quietly. "I repeat, transgressors eliminated."

Four words were all it took to relieve the tension in Shimon Peres' study. A smile flittered across Yitzhak Rabin's face, and Shimon Peres' eyes sparkled. But they still didn't know very much.

The men in the room could now allow themselves a few words of quiet conversation, but their voices were muted. Suddenly the phone rang; General Zeevi from Paris. He was still waiting for new instructions. Who the hell could negotiate this way? Could he please speak to the prime minister?

This time Rabin told Gandhi that there was no more need for French mediation, and he hoped that the general would forgive him for not saying anything sooner. As a military man of many years' standing, Gandhi could understand Rabin's earlier predicament. And he would be delighted to accept the honor of personally informing President Giscard d'Estaing.

On the second floor of Old Terminal, paratroops checked room by room, looking for terrorists or Ugandan troops. Their instructions were to allow the Ugandans to escape, provided of course they didn't offer resistance. Scores of black troops made use of the opportunity to get away, and quickly.

Almost all the Israeli vehicles were now headed toward the old control tower. First place was given to the half-track armored personnel carrier, from which a torrent of lead from bazooka rockets and machine-gun bullets poured onto the tower. Its occupants had been firing on the Israelis for the past few minutes, and the paratroopers could not but admire the courage of the unknown defenders. Finally it seemed that stage two could begin: the hostages could be moved out to the plane that would take them home.

Only now did Yossi realize that he hadn't heard Yoni's voice for at least sixty seconds. He scanned the interior of Old Terminal, but there was no sign of his commanding officer. Running from the building, he found Yoni almost immediately. He lay unconscious on the ground by the building, a doctor and a corpsman in attendance, trying to save his life. He had been shot in the very first minutes after leaving the Mercedes – a bullet in the back, fired from the old control tower, the place that had worried him during yesterday's rehearsal. Yoni had dropped to the ground, mortally wounded, a moment after guiding his men to target.

Yossi, startled to realize that he was now in command of the main force in Operation Thunderball, begged the doctor: "Do everything you can!"

Inside the lead Hercules, Dr. Yosef was getting anxious. He knew that the aircraft now made a huge static target as it sat being filled with fuel. It was vulnerable even without the flashes of firing that the doctor could see through the small portholes. With him were nine more doctors and orderlies, waiting up front for the hostages, praying they weren't wounded – but ready to do their jobs if they had to.

Yitzhak David rubbed his shoulder. Blood was pouring from it. Ilan Hartuv suddenly noticed the sticky red stream, and raised his voice over the din: "Our leader is hurt. Someone come and bandage him." Michael helped Ilan bind the wound and brought him over to the mattress where, until yesterday, his mother had slept. It was empty, but next to it lay Ida Borowitz, her son Boris stooping over her.

Ida's body was covered with blood. Nobody had noticed her die, but the body of a terrorist lay beside her. Had he shot her? Had he decided to die with one of the hostages? Boris hugged the dead body of his mother and wailed: "*Imaleh, Imaleh* – Mother, Mother!" There were tears in the eyes of the people around him, yet the time had not yet come to mourn the dead.

Sergeant Hershko Surin was due to begin demobilization leave the next day, Sunday. His three years of conscript service were almost over. Twelve hours before ending his military career, Hershko dashed into Entebbe Old Terminal. Climbing the stairs to the second floor, he met two Ugandans. One of them was faster than Hershko. Sergeant Surin dropped to the ground, wavering between life and death, his body paralyzed.

By the outer wall of Old Terminal, a doctor labored to save Yoni Netaniahu. It was useless. The brilliant young lieutenant colonel who had come home to serve his people was dying. Yossi Yaar and the others lifted him gently onto a stretcher. For a moment it seemed that Yoni's will to live might overcome. He raised his head as though wanting to say something – then dropped back on the stretcher.

Yossi ordered his men to collect the casualties strewn across the floor. The bodies of Ida Borowitz and Jean Jacques Maimoni were laid on stretchers, as were the ten people injured in the course of the lightning-fast raid. Bullhorns summoned all the hostages back from corridors and side rooms into the main hall. The stunned men, women, and children shuffled in. The paratroopers had to slap a few to bring them out of shock.

The pilot of the first Hercules started his engines and began to move his craft slowly and cautiously toward Old Terminal, stopping 500 yards away. Yossi ordered his men to prepare the evacuation of the wounded and the hostages, although shots were still being exchanged between Israeli soldiers and Ugandans. When it seemed that the gunfire had finally stopped, Yossi picked up a bullhorn and instructed the hostages to check and see that all members of their families were accounted for.

Uzzi Davidson collected together Sara, Benny, and Ron. Yitzhak David, lying on a stretcher, grasped his wife's hand.

Ilan Hartuv was very worried. His mother was still in Mulago Hospital, but what could be done about that?

Outside the terminal, soldiers took position in two lines, forming a funnel straight to the gaping hatch of the Hercules. Yoni's solution for shock and panic would still be used, even if he wasn't there to supervise it. Yet there was another reason: no one wanted a hostage to run into an engine.

Command cars, jeeps, Rabbi field cars, and a Peugeot pickup truck pulled into the area in front of the building as the 104 hostages were started moving toward the waiting plane. There was some panic. Families clung together and rushed for the vehicles. One young girl came out dressed only in bra and panties, as there had been no time to dress. A soldier threw her a blanket, and she wrapped it around herself as she scrambled onto a command car. Shots were still being fired.

Eighteen minutes had passed since the Mercedes began its journey across Entebbe Airport. Now Yekutiel Adam's voice boomed out from a radio in the General Staff "pit," and from the intercoms in Gur's and Peres' rooms: "Mount Carmel. I repeat, Mount Carmel!"

The prime minister and defense minister knew now that the tough part of the mission was almost over. "Mount Carmel" was the code word denoting the start of evacuation from Old Terminal.

Defense Ministry spokesman Naftali Lavi dialed the home of a military correspondent of one of the daily papers. "It's worthwhile to stay awake tonight," he said – but refused to elaborate.

"What's happening?"

Naftali could not explain, so he merely said, "They'll trade terrorists for hostages tonight."

The journalist couldn't swear to it, but there seemed to be a note of mockery in the spokesman's last remark.

The 500 yards now appeared secure, so Yossi gave the signal for the vehicles to move. Across the way, the engines of the Hercules were holding to a steady, muffled roar. Hostages who hadn't found places on the vehicles began to walk toward the plane.

Hana Cohen swept Zippy up in her arms and began to run. Yaakov caught up with her and ran alongside. Pasco, lying on a stretcher, waved weakly to his son as he was lifted inside the Hercules. A team of doctors and orderlies set to work at once to save his life, pushing Hana, who wanted to help, gently aside. Before she even found a seat, she could see a blood-transfusion bag in place as the precious fluid dripped into Pasco's body. The wound was evidently more serious than she had realized.

Dr Yosef leaned over the stretcher that bore the unconscious body of Lieutenant Colonel Jonathan Netaniahu. There was nothing more that could be done. Yoni was dying, and the doctors were powerless to prevent it happening.

Soldiers helped hostages off the vehicles by the ramp of the Hercules, guiding them across the 500-yard walk. Their stunned charges were encouraged to move at a brisk pace, yet there was no need for panic.

Inside the cockpit, the pilot and his crew were already making their pre-takeoff instrument check. Behind them, at the bottom of the ramp, officers and men of the Thunderball force quietly asked each hostage to check that all his family were accounted for. When Captain Bacos approached the ramp, an officer politely asked him to check his family – the crew of Air Force 139. No one was missing. Only Ilan Hartuv remained silent. He was leaving his mother behind in a Ugandan hospital, with no way to save her – but what else could he do? It would be futile to remain in Entebbe. Now, in the doorway of the Hercules, he could only hope that the president of Uganda would extend his protection to Dora Bloch. Still stunned by the events of the last half hour, Ilan pressed forward into the belly of the plane. Like the others, he was still finding it difficult to believe that the week of captivity was nearly over.

Far away across the airport, Lieutenant Shlomo Lavi and his men detailed to guard the Ugandan MIGs were firing at Ugandan soldiers coming from the direction of the terminal. The opposition was heavy enough to force Lavi's team into equally heavy return fire.

Michael Golan, in the cockpit of the second Hercules, was still behind the hillock next to a runway. The MIGs were parked in a lower area of the airport and he couldn't see them, although he did notice flames and a column of smoke ascending into the night sky. It was Shlomo Lavi's men blowing up eleven MIGs – seven 21s and four 17s. Perhaps half the order of battle of the Ugandan air force was now smoke and ashes.

A spirited radio conversation began between Michael and the other three pilots. Minutes ago an attempt had started to refuel the Israeli planes from Entebbe Airport storage tanks. They had brought three pumps and a group of men who had served in Uganda and knew exactly where the airport fuel stocks were kept. One of the planes was already linked up, but the pump was supplying fuel at low pressure. It seemed as if the process was going to take 45 minutes, and the pilots were growing nervous. Finally, the Golani detachment commander radioed a suggestion to Dan Shomron to stop the refueling: "We have succeeded. Why should we take more risks here?"

Kuti and Benny heard the conversation and agreed, ordering immediate takeoff. Never mind reloading the pumps! All of them together are only worth ten thousand dollars! Let Amin have them. Get those planes airborne!

The lead Hercules, with its load of dazed hostages, lumbered onto the long runway, gathered speed, and climbed heavily into the night. In the cockpit, the hands of the clock indicated

11:43; precisely forty minutes after the first plane landed at Entebbe.

"'Hear, O Israel . . .'" One of the passengers recited the ancient prayer, and Baruch Gross picked up the refrain.

WIRELESS RIDGE
John Frost

The British Army's Second Battalion of The Parachute Regiment fought in all the major battles of the 1982 land war between Britain and Argentina for the Falkland Islands (Malvinas). After spearheading the landings at San Carlos on 21 May, the battalion fought its way to Port Stanley against determined Argentinian resistance, via Bluff Cove, Goose Green and Wireless Ridge. The most famous of these battles is undoubtedly Goose Green (where 2 Para commander, Lieutenant-Colonel "H" Jones, won a posthumous Victoria Cross for his charge against an enemy position), but the engagement at Wireless Ridge on 13–14 June was no less dramatic. The Ridge, a spur on the north side of Port Stanley, was heavily defended by troops from the Argentine 7th Infantry Regiment and the Argentine 1st Parachute Regiment. The story of the battle is told here by Major-General John Frost, CB, DSO, MC, who served with 2 Para in WWII, commanding the Battalion from October 1942 until his capture at Arnhem, 1944, where he led the defence of the bridge.

The origins of The Parachute Regiment lie with an initiative of Winston Churchill who, after noting the success of German paratroop operations during Germany's invasion of Holland and Belgium, suggested the formation of a British airborne elite force. The first units began training in June 1940, with volunteers from the units forming The Parachute Regiment in August 1942.

2 PARA'S TASK WAS to capture the Wireless Ridge features, keeping west of the telegraph wires, and Colonel Chaundler's plan called for a two-phase noisy night attack. In Phase 1, A Company would take the northern spur where the ponds were, C Company having secured the start-line. Once this was secure Phase 2 would come into operation, and B and

D Companies would pass through from the north to attack the main Wireless Ridge feature itself. B Company would go to the right (the western end of the ridge), while D Company attacked the rocky ridge-line east of the track.

The mortars would move forward from Mount Kent to a position in the lee of the hillside south of Drunken Rock Pass, and this would also be the site for a static Battalion Headquarters during the attack. H-hour was again to be at about 0030. The importance of digging in on the objectives was emphasised once more, since Wireless Ridge was dominated by both Tumbledown and Sapper Hill, and if enemy troops should still be there at dawn they could make 2 Para's positions untenable.

The orders were straightforward, and the plan simple, involving the maximum use of darkness. As the "O" Group ended the company commanders were told that they would now fly up to Mount Longdon to look at the ground over which they would operate.

The CO went on ahead with the Battery Commander to meet Lieutenant-Colonel Hew Pike, CO of 3 Para, and Major William McCracken, RA, who controlled the artillery "anchor" OP on Mount Longdon. They discussed and arranged for co-ordinated fire support, with 3 Para's mortars, Milan teams and machine-guns all ready to fire from the flank, and Major Martin Osborne's C Company, 3 Para, in reserve.

Back at the gully all was peaceful in the bright sunshine. Suddenly this was shattered as nine Skyhawks appeared further to the north, flying very low in formation and heading due west towards Mount Kent. The effect was electric, for no one expected that the Argentines could still flaunt their air power in this way.

At "A" Echelon, behind Mount Kent, there was no doubt as to who the jets were aiming for. As they came screaming up over the col and rose to attacking height, the formation split: three went for the area where the artillery gun-line had recently been, three went for 3 Commando Brigade HQ, and three attacked "A" Echelon. All the machine-guns opened up, claiming one possible hit as the bombs rained down. Amazingly, there were no casualties from this minor blitzkrieg. But the accuracy of the attack, and its obvious definiteness of purpose, left people wondering if the enemy had left concealed OPs behind, watching Mount Kent, or if satellite photography had shown up the various targets or, possibly, if Argentine electronic-warfare equipment had picked up radio signals from Brigade HQ.

The air raid created delays to all helicopter movement, but eventually the CO was able to fly on to Brigade HQ, while the company commanders were dropped on to Mount Longdon for their own recces. Colonel Chaundler had already been updated on the actual strength of the enemy, which was greater than had been thought, and a new Argentine position had been detected to the east of the pond-covered spur, on a knoll overlooking Hearnden Water and the mouth of the Murrell River.

While the CO was at Brigade HQ, the company commanders were able to study Wireless Ridge in detail from the commanding position on Longdon. It at once became obvious that much of the information so far given to them was inaccurate. What was thought to be C Company of 3 Para proved to be nothing of the sort: Major Dair Farrar-Hockley noticed that it was an *enemy* position of about company strength, situated dangerously on the flank of the 2 Para axis of attack, west of the northern spur. It was also clear that Wireless Ridge proper was heavily defended, with positions which stretched a long way to the east beyond the line of telegraph poles that marked the 2 Para boundary. Strangely, no harassing fire was being brought to bear during the day on any of the Argentine positions, and their soldiers were free to stand about in the open.

The company commanders flew back to Furze Bush Pass, but clearly a major change in plan was necessary. The CO returned from Brigade HQ as evening approached and was told of the situation. "Go away and have your supper. Come back in forty-five minutes and you will have a new set of orders," he said. Meanwhile the move-up of mortars and the adjustment of artillery had been delayed, and as a result the changes to the fireplan had to continue into the night, directed by the OP on Longdon and using illuminating rounds.

Unfortunately for the company commanders, normal battle procedure had already ensured that relevant details of the first plan had permeated to the lowest level. Platoon and section commanders had had time to issue clear and well constructed orders to their subordinates, but now their efforts were all useless, for by the time the company commanders returned with the CO's revised plan, it was too late to go into new details. Such a sudden last-minute change did little for the men's faith in the system, but it was unavoidable and, in any case, the soldiers had by now become stoical, while the cynics among them were not disappointed by this evidence of fallibility at higher levels. Nevertheless, the battalion was able to adapt and change its plans and moved off on time. But Phil Neame had his misgivings about what the SAS to the east of his line of advance was *meant* to be doing, and there was no knowledge of what the SAS was actually *going* to do. Furthermore, no one really knew what was beyond Wireless Ridge to the south, in the Moody Brook area, and everyone would have liked to have known exactly when the 5 Brigade attack on Tumbledown was timed to begin.

The battalion's new plan was for a four-phase noisy night attack. In Phase 1 D Company would capture the newly discovered enemy position west of the northern spur; A and B Companies would then assault the pond-covered hilltop; Phase 3 called for C Company to take the knoll to the east; and finally D Company would roll up the enemy on Wireless Ridge itself, with fire support from A and B Companies, starting in the west and finishing at the telegraph poles.

Fire support was to be lavish in comparison to Goose Green: two batteries of 105-mm guns, HMS *Ambuscade* with her one 4.5-inch gun offshore, and the mortars of both 2 and 3 Para, totalling sixteen tubes. Ammunition was plentiful, and the battalion's mortars had been moved complete from Mount Kent by helicopter, and were thus fresh for action. The Machine-Gun Platoon had also been flown forward. Between the six guns they had enough ammunition to provide a massive weight of fire, and the men were fresh and rather proud of their earlier achievement behind Mount Kent against the Skyhawks. The Milan Platoon was already forward with the battalion – the experience of Goose Green had demonstrated the capability of this precision guided missile against static defences. Finally the light tanks of the Blues and Royals would be there, Scimitars with their 30-mm automatic cannon and Scorpions with 76-mm guns, and both equipped with very high quality night-vision equipment and having superb cross-country performance. All available support was allotted first to D Company, then to A and B in their assault, and finally to D Company again as it traversed the ridge.

As night closed in the tanks, the mortars and the Recce Platoon, which was to secure the start-line, moved up. By now the promise of the day had vanished and snow and sleet were falling, considerably limiting the effectiveness of all the gunsighting equipment, and reducing visibility.

At about 0015 a storm of fire from the supporting artillery and mortars was unleashed upon the Argentine positions. A and B Companies passed by, led by C Company patrols to the new start-line secured by Corporal Bishop's patrol in the relatively safe ground overlooking Lower Pass. At 0045 hours on Monday 14 June, D Company moved over its own start-line further to the west, and headed towards the identified enemy position.

As the company moved forward, the tanks of the Blues and Royals and the machine-guns provided fire support while the artillery increased its rate of fire. Enemy mortar fire in retaliation became heavy. In the rear of the company, Private Godfrey of 12 Platoon had a near miss as a piece of shrapnel cut through his windproof and dug into his boot. He dived for cover – straight into an Argentine latrine!

The weight of supporting artillery and mortar fire was singularly effective, for the enemy on the D Company objective could be seen running away as the company pushed forward, although 155-mm air-burst shelling increased as the Paras began to clear the Argentine trenches, now-abandoned except for a few enemy killed by the barrage. The darkness of the night and the extent of the enemy position caused the company to spread out, creating problems of control. Lieutenant Webster of 10 Platoon counted up to twenty trenches on his right, with more over to the left, where 2nd Lieutenant Waddington's 11 Platoon found the other half of the assault formation.

Occasionally as they moved forward, men would suddenly disappear into the freezing water of an ice-covered pond. Privates Dean and Creasey of 11 Platoon went in up to their necks, and had to tread water to stay afloat until their platoon sergeant, Sergeant Light, dragged them out.

Fire support for the company was immaculate. The tanks used their powerful image-intensifier night-sights to pinpoint targets. Once enemy positions were identified, they fired. As soon as the battalion's machine-gunners saw the strike they, too, opened up. Occasionally the machine-gun fire was too close for comfort, even for D Company, and in the end 10 Platoon Commander called for it to stop.

The opposition had fled, and D Company took its first objective in record time, remaining *in situ* while A and B Companies began their part of the battle. Enemy artillery fire was increasing, however, and Neame therefore decided to push forward for another 300 hundred metres into relative safety, to avoid the worst of the barrage.

Several of those waiting to move on the A and B Company start-lines were reminded of scenes they had seen from films of the First and Second World Wars. As shells landed all around, men lay huddled against the peat, with bayonets fixed. There could be no denying that, for the soldiers, fear of the known was in this case worse than blissful ignorance of the unknown. In the shelter of the peat bogs some smoked, watching the display of illuminants above.

Just as the time came to move, the shelling claimed its first victim, for Colour Sergeant "Doc" Findlay was killed in the rear of A Company, and soldiers from Support and HQ Companies were also wounded. The advance began, the two companies moving southwards parallel to each other, on either side of the track. The men crossed the stream in the valley north of their objective with the tanks firing over their heads. The effect upon the enemy was devastating. In their night-sights the tank crews could see Argentine soldiers running or falling as the accurate fire took effect. The boost to morale that this form of suppressive fire gave was considerable; fundamentally, the battle was being won by supporting arms, the infantry being free to do their own job, which is actually clearing and securing the ground.

On the left, all was going well with A Company. Command and control had been well practised back at Goose Green and now the junior officers and section commanders were quite expert in maintaining direction. Silence was unnecessary and orders were shouted backwards and forwards. The enemy were still shelling as the companies advanced, but now counter-battery fire was being provided by our own artillery. From his own position the CO could see the two companies in extended formation, moving quickly up the hill, the whole battlefield brightly lit by starshell.

Co-ordinating the two assaulting companies' advances was difficult, however. The track provided a boundary of sorts, but controlling upwards of 200 men during a noisy battle over difficult terrain is not easy. Colonel Chaundler had another worry. Earlier, before the battalion had moved up, he had been shown a captured Argentine map which indicated a minefield directly in the path of the assaulting companies. There was only fifteen minutes to go before 2 Para set off – far too late for a change of plan. The CO only had time to brief OC B Company, while John Crosland had none in which to warn his men, and in any case was told to push on regardless, since there would be no time to clear the mines. Only afterwards did Major Crosland tell his men that they had actually moved directly through the minefield without knowing it. Miraculously, no one was blown up on the way.

The ponds on the spur claimed a victim, however, when Private Philpott of 5 Platoon suddenly plunged into over six feet of water. He was dragged out and his section commander, Corporal Curtis, immediately organized a complete change of clothing from the other men in the section, which probably saved Philpott's life.

The two companies consolidated on the objective. There was some firing from the trenches, swiftly silenced as the men of both companies ran in to clear them. Once more the enemy had fled, leaving only twenty or so of their number behind, quickly taken prisoner as they were winkled out of their holes. Radios were still switched on, and several dead lay around the positions. As the men dug in, the enemy shelling increased and it was to continue for the rest of the night at the same level of intensity. Most thought it was worse than Goose Green, but fortunately the abandoned enemy bunkers provided reasonable shelter, although a number of casualties occurred in A Company.

It was now C Company's turn. Already they had had a minor scare on the A and B Company start-line when a Scorpion tank had careered towards Company Headquarters in the darkness. It was hopelessly lost and its commander had to be evacuated after a dose of "hatch rash" – the effect of placing the head in the path of a rapidly closing hatch. The confused vehicle was soon heading in the right direction, but now under the command of Captain Roger Field, who had seized this opportunity to revert to a more honourable role than foot-slogging.

With A and B Companies now firm, C Company was ordered to check out the Argentine position further to the east that had been spotted from Mount Longdon on the previous day. Major Roger Jenner was glad to be moving again, for it seemed that the supporting artillery battery had developed a "rogue gun" and every sixth round meant for the enemy was coming in uncomfortably close to his company. He and his men set off, taking cover occasionally on the way as shells fell close by. There had been no firing from the company objective during the battle, and soon the platoons were pushing round the side of a minefield on to the knoll.

As the Recce Platoon advanced, they could hear noises of weapons being cocked. The bright moonlight left them uncomfortably exposed on the hillside. On the forward edge of the slope were two parallel lines of rock, and on the second line the platoon found a series of shell scrapes, suggesting recent occupation by a body of troops. Once again it seemed that the enemy had left hurriedly, leaving tents and bits of equipment behind in the process. Away over to the east Jenner's men could see the bright lights of Stanley airfield, and could hear a C-130 landing. The company was ordered to dig in, but since an enemy attack on this feature was extremely unlikely the CO changed the orders, and C Company moved up to the pond-covered hill.

If any particular group deserves special praise for what was done that night, then it must be the tanks of the Blues and Royals. Their mere presence had been a remarkable boost to morale during all the attacks that had taken place, and the speed and accuracy of their fire, matched by their ability to keep up with the advancing Paras, had been a severe shock to the enemy. Lance-Corporal Dunkeley's tank, which Captain Field had taken over following the injury to its commander, had alone fired forty rounds from its 76-mm gun.

2 Para was performing superbly, its three first objectives taken with great speed and a minimum of casualties, despite heavy and accurate enemy artillery fire. Whenever the enemy in trenches had sought to return fire they had been met by a withering concentration of fire from the rifle companies' weapons which, coupled with very heavy support, had proved devastating. It is not known whether the Argentines had gathered that they were facing the men from Goose Green, but there can be no question that 2 Para knew.

D Company was now ready to go into the final phase of the attack and began moving forward again to the west end of Wireless Ridge. The tanks and support weapons moved up to join A and B Companies on the hilltop overlooking the D Company objective, and endured the artillery fire as well as anti-tank fire from Wireless Ridge to the south.

12 Platoon was now in the lead. Lieutenant John Page, who had taken over from the tragically killed Jim Barry, looked for the fence, running at right-angles to the ridge, that would guide him to the correct start-line for the assault. Unfortunately there was little left of the fence marked on the maps, and Corporal Barton's section, at the point of the platoon, could only find a few strands of wire to follow. The number of ice-covered ponds added to the difficulty and the intense cold was beginning to affect men's reactions, as they worked their way south to the western end of Wireless Ridge.

Once more, massive fire-power began to soften up the enemy, who apparently still had no intimation that they were about to be rolled up from a flank. The initial idea had been for D Company simply to sweep eastwards along the ridge without stopping, with 11 Platoon on the left, 12 Platoon on the right and 10 Platoon in reserve. There was still uncertainty as to whether Tumbledown to the south had been taken or not, and clearly a battle was still in progress on that mountain as the Scots Guards fought to drive out the Argentines on its summit. But Neame and his D Company had no intention other than to push on regardless, although they knew that if Tumbledown was still in enemy hands by daylight then 2 Para would be extremely vulnerable.

The bombardment of the western end of the Wireless Ridge continued as the platoons advanced. It seemed to have been effective, since no enemy were encountered at all, although, to be certain, 11 Platoon cleared any bunkers they came across on the reverse slope with grenades.

The first part of Wireless Ridge was now clear and across the dip, where the track came up, lay the narrower rocky outcrops of the remainder of the objective. Fire was concentrated on these areas from A and B Companies as tanks, Milans and machine-guns provided an intense concentration on to three enemy machine-gun posts that remained.

Efforts to switch artillery support further forward and on to the area of Moody Brook had unfortunate results. Five rounds of high explosive crashed on to the ridge around and very near the leading D Company platoons. 3 Section of 11 Platoon was caught in the open and, despite screams to stop the firing, it was too late. Private Parr was killed instantly, and Corporal McAuley was somersaulted into some rocks, completely dazed, and had to be picked up by a stretcher party.

There was a considerable delay while a livid Major Neame tried to get the gunners to sort themselves out. It seemed that one gun was off target, as C Company had noted, but at the gun-lines they did not know which, since in the dark it was impossible to note the fall of shot, even if there had been time, and the other battery was not available owing to shortage of ammunition. In the meantime the CO was growing increasingly impatient, urging the D Company commander to press on.

As soon as the gunners could guarantee reasonable support, and with increased efforts from the Blues and Royals, Neame was off again. All through the wait constant harassing fire from the enemy had been landing around the company, so none were sorry to move. Despite the fire pouring on to the ridge-line ahead, enemy machine-gunners continued firing from well sited bunkers, and were still staunchly in action as the platoons advanced.

They moved with 11 Platoon on the left, 12 Platoon ahead on the ridge itself, with the company commander immediately behind and, in the rear, 10 Platoon. 12 Platoon came across an abandoned Argentine recoilless rifle, an anti-tank weapon, as they crossed the start-line, which may well have been the weapon that had earlier been engaging the tanks on the A and B Company positions. The platoon moved down into the gap between the two parts of the ridge line, but as the soldiers passed by some ponds, very heavy machine-gun fire began from their front and illumination was called for as the platoon answered the firing. Corporal Barton came across some orange string, possibly indicating a minefield, but his platoon commander urged him on regardless.

The enemy appeared to be surprised by the direction of the assault, and as the Paras advanced, they could hear an Argentine voice calling out, possibly to give warning of this sudden attack from the west. 10 Platoon came across a lone enemy machine-gunner who lay wounded in both legs, his weapon lying abandoned beside him.

Corporal Harley of 11 Platoon caught his foot in a wire, which may have been part of a minefield, and, fearing that it might be an Argentine jumping mine, unravelled himself with some care. The platoon pushed on, skirmishing by sections until they met a concertina of wire. Fearing mines, Sappers were called for from Company Headquarters, but these could do little in the darkness except tape off the suspect area. In fact channels could be discerned between the concertinas, and these were assumed, correctly, as it turned out, to be safe lanes.

While 11 Platoon was extricating itself from the minefield, Neame pushed 12 Platoon on and brought 10 Platoon out to the left to maintain the momentum. Suddenly an intense burst of firing brought the company to a halt. It was a critical moment. For a short time, *all* commanders had to do everything in their power to get things going again, with platoon commanders and sergeants and section commanders all urging their men on. It was a real test of leadership as several soldiers understandably went to ground.

A brief fire-fight ensued, with 12 Platoon engaging the enemy as they pushed forward on the right overlooking Moody Brook below, where lights could be seen. The moment of doubt had passed, however, and once more the men were clearing bunkers and mopping up with gusto. 10 and 12 Platoons now moved on either side of the company commander. Maximum speed was needed to keep the enemy off balance as they fell back, conducting a fighting withdrawal along the ridge. The tanks continued to fire, directed by the company commander. Unfortunately his signaller had fallen into a shell hole and become separated, thus creating considerable frustration for the CO, who wanted to talk to Neame about the progress of his battle.

During 12 Platoon's brief fight Private Slough had been hit and died later in hospital, and another soldier was wounded.

Enemy artillery fire continued to make life uncomfortable. Fortunately D Company's task was no longer difficult, as most of the enemy bunkers had now been abandoned. 12 Platoon reached the telegraph wires and consolidated there, while the other platoons reorganized further back along the ridge. Shell fire intensified and snipers began to engage from enemy positions further to the east along the ridge.

Neame went up to see the platoon commander, Lieutenant Page. Snipers in the rocks were still firing on the platoon and it seemed that the enemy might be about to counter-attack from the direction of Moody Brook, to the right.

On several occasions the company commander was nearly hit, and his perambulations began to be the cause of some comment. Sergeant Meredith shouted to him, "For God's sake push off, Sir – you're attracting bullets everywhere you go!"

100 metres or so to the east, Argentines could be heard shouting to each other, as though rallying for a counter-attack.

John Page called for fire support, and then ordered his own men to stop firing, for by so doing they were merely identifying their positions. They felt very isolated and vulnerable.

For two very long and uncomfortable hours the company remained under pressure. Small-arms fire mingled with all types of HE fell in and around 12 Platoon's position as the men crouched in the abandoned enemy sangars and in shell holes. John Page continued to move around his platoon, organizing its defences, and suffering a near-miss in the process. He was hit by a bullet, which passed between two grenades hanging on his webbing and landed in a full magazine in his pouch. He was blown off his feet by the shock. "It was like being hit by a sledgehammer and having an electric shock at the same time," he later described the moment. As he lay there a round exploded in the magazine, but fortunately the grenades remained intact, and he was soon on his feet.

Meanwhile the CO was still trying to get in touch with Neame to know the form. Lieutenant Webster, OC 10 Platoon, was momentarily elevated to commanding the company since he was the only officer left near Company Headquarters. As he talked to the CO, voices could be heard below in the direction of Moody Brook. Corporal Elliot's section opened up and automatic fire was returned by perhaps ten to fifteen men. 11 Platoon moved forward to join 10 Platoon in a long extended line along the ridge, the men firing downhill towards the enemy position. Eventually the CO got through to the company commander, who had had a hair-raising time walking along the ridge to discover what was happening. He now informed the CO of his fears of imminent attack.

Sporadic enemy fire from Tumbledown added to D Company's danger, and all the earlier fears of the consequences of delay to the 5 Brigade attack came to the fore. The CO offered to send tanks up but Neame declined, since they would be very exposed on the forward slope fire positions they would be forced to adopt. He would have preferred another company to hold the first part of Wireless Ridge, which as yet remained undefended.

The company reorganized, leaving Corporal Owen's section forward as a standing patrol while 10 and 11 Platoons found dug-outs on the reverse slope. 12 Platoon stayed in its positions near the telegraph poles.

There was little more that the Companies on the northern spur could now do to support D Company. Two of A Company's trained medical orderlies had been wounded by the shelling that still continued, so the platoons had to look after their own casualties – once again the value of the medical training for all ranks was vindicated. Fortunately the helicopters in support that night were fully effective, evacuating casualties with minimum delay, and other casualties were taken back to the RAP on one of the tanks. The enemy artillery fire gave the remainder every incentive to dig, and the possibility of being overlooked by Mount Tumbledown in the morning was an additional spur.

For A and B Companies it was now a matter of lasting the cold night out, which was not without incident. Privates (Jud') Brookes and Gormley of A Company's 1 Platoon had been hit by shrapnel. The rule was to switch on the injured man's easco light, normally used for night parachute descents, to ensure that he would not be missed in the dark. Sergeant Barrett went back to look for Brookes, whose light was smashed.

"All right, Brookes – me and the Boss will be back to pick you up later."

"Ee, Sarge," he replied in a thick Northern accent, "Ah knows tha f– will."

Unknown to them, the men of 3 Platoon were actually sitting next door to thirteen Argentine soldiers, who were taking cover from their own shell-fire. Only later in the morning were they found and taken prisoner.

In B Company, the state of Privates Carroll and Philpott of 5 Platoon was a cause for concern, since both were now suffering from hypothermia after being immersed in one of the ponds. Their section commander, Corporal Steve Curtis, decided to tell the platoon commander. As he ran out into the shelling, a round exploded close by, shredding his clothes almost completely yet, amazingly, leaving him unharmed.

The mortar teams had been busy all night. By now they had moved on to the side of the A and B Company hill to avoid shelling, which had been uncomfortably close at their first position in the bottom of the valley to the north. Improvised bins had helped to reduce the tendency of the mortar tubes to bed into the soft peat, although not completely, and another problem was that tubes would at times actually slip out of their base-plates under recoil. To prevent this, mortarmen took turns to stand on the base-plates as the tubes were fired, and by the end of the night four men had suffered broken ankles for their efforts. The fire they had been able to provide was very effective, however, and all concerned had been determined that, this time, there would be no question of running short of ammunition or of being out of range. The 3 Para mortars on Longdon did sterling work providing illumination.

The Machine-Gun Platoons, too, had been hard at work, their six guns providing intense heavy fire throughout the night. Resupplied by the tanks and by the splendid work of WO2 Grace's Pioneer Platoon, they had had no worries about ammunition. But gradually the guns broke down, and by dawn only two of the six were still in action.

In Battalion Headquarters the second-in-command, the Operations Officer and Captain David Constance had taken turns at duty officer. At one point the second-in-command, Major Keeble, had been able to see the flashes of the enemy 155-mm guns as they fired, but no amount of reporting back produced any countermeasures. Once the drone of a low-flying Argentine Canberra jet was heard, and amidst the din of artillery even larger thuds reverberated as the aircraft dropped its bombs. Private Steele of the Defence Platoon was unlucky: as he lay on the ground a piece of shrapnel caught him in the back. He hardly felt it, thinking that it was only a piece of turf from the explosion – only later did he discover a rather nasty wound where the metal had penetrated.

The CO's party had not escaped either. A stray round hit Private McLoughlin, a member of the Battery Commander's group, and actually penetrated his helmet at the front. The helmet deflected the round, however, and McLoughlin walked away unharmed.

The snipers were in great demand. Their night-sights enabled them to identify the enemy infra-red sights and to use the signature that then appeared in the image itensifier as an aiming-mark. The Commando Sappers had had a relatively minor role to play in the battle, since there were no mines that it was imperative to clear. But, as at Goose Green, they provided a very useful addition when acting as infantry.

On Wireless Ridge at first light, 12 Platoon was still being sniped at from behind and to the right. Further back along the ridge, Corporal Owen had searched a command post. While rummaging in the bunker, he found a map showing all the details of the Argentine positions, as well as some patrol reports. These were quickly dispatched to Company Headquarters and on to Brigade.

Private Ferguson, in Owen's section, suddenly noticed four or five men below them. The corporal was uncertain as to who they could be – possibly 12 Platoon – and told Ferguson to challenge. The latter yelled "Who's there!", and was instantly greeted with a burst of fire that left them in no doubt. Grenades started to explode around Owen and his men as the enemy counter-attacked. The section opened fire, and Corporal Owen shouted for the machine-guns to engage.

10 Platoon meanwhile were firing on either side of the section, and Owen himself blasted away with eight M-79 rounds. The section was soon short of ammunition, and the men began to ferret for abandoned Argentine supplies. Just then the remainder of the platoon moved up to join the section; though uncertain as to exactly where the enemy were, they were determined to prevent the Argentines from regaining the ridge.

Private Lambert heard an Argentine, close in, shouting, "Grenado, grenado!"

"What a good idea," he thought, and lobbed one of his own in the direction of the voice. There were no more shouts.

11 Platoon also saw a group of four men to its front. 2nd Lieutenant Chris Waddington was unable to make out who they were and, thinking they might be 10 Platoon, shouted to them to stop. The four men took no notice, so he ordered a flare to be put up – the figures ran off as the platoon engaged with small arms and grenades. The orders not to exploit beyond the ridge-line meant that not all the enemy positions had been cleared during the night, and it seemed that some stay-behind

snipers had been left there, and it was probably these that had given 12 Platoon so much trouble. But the counter-attack, such as it was, had fizzled out. Artillery fire was called down on Moody Brook to break up any further efforts at dislodging D Company. Down below the ridge a Landrover could be seen trying to get away. Lance-Corporal Walker fired at it and it crashed.

11 Platoon now came under extremely accurate enemy artillery fire, possibly registered on the flashes of their weapons. Major Neame therefore ordered them to cease firing with small arms, intending to continue the battle with artillery alone. Moody Brook was deserted, however. In the distance the men of D Company noticed two Argentine soldiers walking off down the track as if at the end of an exercise.

In the light of dawn it appeared to the Paras on the ridge that a large number of enemy troops were moving up to reinforce Sapper Hill to the south-east. Neame called for artillery with great urgency, but no guns were available. After a further twenty minutes or so, by which time the enemy had reached the top, the target was engaged. Meanwhile other Argentines could be seen streaming off Tumbledown and Harriet – 5 Brigade had won its battles.

As D Company began to engage this new target the CO arrived. He confirmed Neame's orders to fire on the enemy retiring towards Stanley, and the company now joined in with machine-guns in a "turkey shoot". John Greenhalgh's helicopters swept in and fired SS-11 rockets and, together with two other Scouts, attacked an Argentine battery. The enemy AA was still active, however, and all the helicopters withdrew.

The retiring Argentines on Tumbledown had made no reply to the helicopters, and their artillery had stopped. It was obvious that a major change had occurred. The news was relayed to the Brigadier, who found it difficult to believe what was happening. But the CO realised how vital it was to get the battalion moving into Stanley before the enemy could rally, and A and B Companies, together with the Blues and Royals, were ordered to move as fast as possible up on to Wireless Ridge. The Brigadier arrived, still disbelieving until

Colonel Chaundler said, "It's OK, Brigadier, it's all over." Together they conferred as to what to do next. D Company ceased firing on the fleeing enemy on the far hillside, and the order was given that men were only to fire if fired upon first. Permission was then given for the battalion to move on.

B Company, by now on the ridge, was ordered down into Moody Brook. Corporal Connors's section of 5 Platoon led the way, still expecting to come under fire from the "Triple As" on the race-course. The other two sections covered him forward. He cleared the flattened buildings of the old barracks and Curtis's section took over, clearing the bridge over the Murrell River and the building on the other side, while all the time their platoon commander was exhorted, "Push on, push on!" They remained cautious, fearing booby traps or a sudden burst of fire.

A Company now took the lead as B Company, covering A's advance, moved south on to the high ground on the far side of the valley, above the road, passing through three abandoned gun positions on the way. The tanks of the Blues and Royals moved east along Wireless Ridge to give support if it should be necessary. A Company was well on the way down the road into Stanley, with C and D Companies following, when Brigade announced a cease-fire. Cheers went up, and red berets quickly replaced steel helmets. Bottles of alcohol miraculously appeared to celebrate with. Relief, elation, disbelief – all in turn had their effect.

Major Dair Farrar-Hockley led his men towards the race-course, past the abandoned guns that had been spotted so many hours earlier yet had remained operational in spite of requests for artillery fire. According to civilians afterwards, the Argentines still on the outskirts of Stanley simply broke and ran when they heard that "the Paras" were coming. The leading elements of the battalion arrived in Stanley at 1330 hours, on Monday, 14 June some five hours before the official cease-fire, with 2nd Lieutenant Mark Coe's 2 Platoon the first into the town. They were the first British troops into the capital.

Eventually all the companies were brought into the western outskirts, finding shelter amongst the deserted houses, a few of which had suffered from stray shells. One or two dead Argentine soldiers still lay in the street where they had been caught by shell-fire. On the race-course the Argentine flag was pulled down and Sergeant-Major Fenwick's Union Jack once more served its purpose.

THE SEA DEVILS
J. Valerio Borghese

Without doubt the most effective Italian special unit of WWII was the Underwater Division of the 10th MAS (motor torpedo boat) Flotilla, the pioneers of the manned or "human" torpedo. First developed by Sub-Lieutenants Tesei and Toschi of the Italian Navy in 1936, the human torpedo was an electric underwater chariot – ridden by a crew of two frogmen – with an explosive warhead, which was detached and clamped to the hulls of enemy ships by means of magnets.

Initially, 10th MAS operations with the human torpedo were dogged by ill-luck and equipment malfunction, but in September 1941 the unit succeeded in spectacularly sinking two British naval tankers and a cargo ship carrying high-explosives at Gibraltar.

Yet the Gibraltar raid, though a tonic for the Italian Navy after the defeats at Taranto and Cape Matapan, was but a prelude to the 10th MAS's next exploit, the attack on the British Mediterranean fleet at Alexandria Harbour, 18–19 December 1941. The event is described below in an extract from Sea Devils, *the autobiography of Count Julio Valerio Borghese, the onetime head of the Underwater Division of the 10th MAS. In the attack itself Borghese commanded the submarine which transported the human torpedoes to the target area.*

THE OPERATION AGAINST Alexandria was most carefully thought out. The most important requirement was the maintenance of absolute secrecy, that indispensable coefficient of success in any action, and particularly in those where the vulnerability of a handful of half-naked men, plunged underwater in the dark depths of an enemy harbour, had to overcome armour-plates, barriers and a hundred methods of watching for and spotting them, and also thousands of people on dry land, operating from cover and behind defences on mole and ships, whose business it was to discover and destroy the assailant.

Wide use was made of air reconnaissance for the obtaining of information and photographs with a view to keeping us informed about the usual moorings of vessels and the nature of the protective measures employed (net obstructions, etc.). Great care was also taken in preparing materials: the human torpedoes, which were now in good shape, as had been verified during the last mission to Gibraltar, were brought to the highest level of efficiency.

The *Scirè* was again appointed to carry out the approach. Her gallant crew, now thoroughly accustomed to such experiences, remained unchanged. All its members, after their usual period of rest in the Alto Adige, were in excellent physical trim.

The senior group of pilots had been given a long training by myself in carrying out exercises similar to the performances they would have to accomplish at Alexandria (they were, however, not told the final object of the courses and defence negotiating they were ordered to do). In other words, practice took place at night in the actual conditions prevalent in the enemy harbour, their difficulties being, wherever possible, increased. Thus, while the operators were being trained to economize their strength in view of the prolonged and difficult nature of the assigned task, we ourselves were obtaining the data necessary for the study of the plan of operations and had the opportunity of verifying, as if we had made a survey on the spot, the methods to be adopted for the job, the periods required to complete the various stages and the precautions needed to circumvent difficulties and elude enemy detection, as well as, lastly, to check the degrees of skill acquired by individual operators.

One day we called them all together; Forza made the following very brief speech to them: "Now, boys, we want three crews for an operation in the very near future; all I can tell you about it is that it differs from the Gibraltar operations in the fact that return from it is extremely problematical. Is there anyone who would like to take part in it?" Without an instant's hesitation they all volunteered. Accordingly, we of the Command had the delicate task of making a selection. Finally, the crews were as follows: Lieutenant Luigi Durand de la Penne and P.O./diver Emilio Vianchi; Engineer Captain Antonio Marceglia and P.O./diver Spartaco Schergat; Gunner Captain Vincenzo Martellotta and P.O./diver Mario Marino.

These men were chosen because they were the pick of the bunch. De la Penne, leader of the group, was a veteran of the previous missions to Gibraltar and the rest were all equally vigorous, steady and resolute fellows, in mind as in body. It was pure chance that the three officers represented three different services of the Navy: deck, engines and guns.

The reserve crew consisted of Surgeon Sub-Lieutenant Spaccarelli and Engineer Lieutenant Feltrinelli, both belonging to a lower age group than the others but equally keen.

The usual instructions were given: absolute secrecy was to be maintained without exception for anyone, whether comrades, superior officers or, naturally, relatives; training, now openly designed for this particular operation, was to be intensified; each man's private affairs were to be settled in view of his imminent departure for a length of time which could not be foreseen; at worst, it might be for ever, at best there would be some years of imprisonment.

Meanwhile, all the wheels of the machine began to go round. This kind of operation, if it were to have any decent chance of success, had to be thought out to the last detail; the whole of an extensive organization had to be got ready; there were a thousand details to be studied and put into practice: from the collection of hydrographic and meteorological data to intelligence as to enemy vigilance; from the taking of aerial photographs of the harbour to the arrangement of safe and extremely rapid channels of radio liaison with the submarine, so that the latter could be informed, immediately before the operators were dropped, as to the number and disposition of units on the night of the operation; from the determination of suitable ciphers to getting materials ready for action; from composition of the series of operational orders to the training of operators so as to bring them to the maximum of physical efficiency by the pre-arranged day; from the study of navigation and the best routes of approach for the submarine and those for the forcing of the harbour by the pilots, to research on new devices for causing the enemy maximum damage should the occasion arise; in a word, the proceedings were exactly the opposite of what the phrase "assault craft" might be supposed to mean; there was to be nothing in the nature of making a dash, nothing was to be left to chance, all impulsiveness was to be held in check; on the contrary, everything was to be coolly calculated and every technical and ingenious resource was to be exploited to the fullest extent possible.

During this preparatory phase, we were afflicted by the grievous loss of a valued collaborator; this was Lieutenant Sogos, belonging to the Command of the Tenth. While he was in transit to Athens for consultation with the military authorities there, his young and promising life was cut short by a wretched traffic accident.

At last the time came to start. On the 3rd of December the *Scirè* left La Spezia, ostensibly on an ordinary cruise, so as not to arouse curiosity among the crews of the other submarines at the base.

My gallant, steady and reliable crew neither knew nor wished to know where we were going, so as not to be burdened with a secret which, like all secrets, would be difficult to keep; they only knew that we were on another dangerous operation, perhaps as dangerous as the former ones, perhaps more so; they had confidence in their commander and in their vessel, to which each of them had devoted every care during the period of preparation, knowing well that it was on the proper functioning of the elements of which it was composed that the outcome of the venture, its success and the very lives of all aboard depended.

We had scarcely left harbour, at twilight, so as to elude any indiscreet watchers, when a lighter approached us; it was carrying the human torpedoes 221, 222 and 223, which had just left the works at San Bartolomeo in the pink of condition, as well as the operators' clothing and breathing sets; such was the slight equipment necessary to transform three pairs of men into three engines of destruction.

The operators checked over their craft with a sort of tender solicitude. Each possessed his own; he had done his training with it and knew its good points, its shortcomings and its caprices; he placed it in the appropriate cylinder (de la Penne's was forward, those of Marceglia and Martellotta astern), settling it in such a way as to avoid risking shocks and injury to it. Finally, late at night, everything was fixed to rights; we took leave of the lads, who would rejoin us at the last moment by 'plane, and set out, hugging Tino Island, along the safety route through the minefields. It was 2300 hours on the 3rd of December, 1941. "Operation EA 3", the third attempt of the Tenth Light Flotilla against Alexandria and the ships of the British Eastern Mediterranean Fleet, had begun.

We proceeded normally along the courses set until we made the Sicilian coast; here a curious episode occurred which is worth relating. The Cape Pelorias signal station sent out a Donath (nocturnal signalling lamp) message in clear: "Submarine *Scirè*." A piece of madness! Did they want everyone to know that the *Scirè*, the only submarine in the Italian Navy equipped to carry assault craft, was at sea? Not much of a secret, apparently, though such trouble had been taken to keep it! Off the San Ranieri (Messina) lighthouse a launch belonging to the Naval Command approached us. I was handed an envelope; we immediately resumed navigation. The note was from the Supreme Naval Command informing me of the position of the allied vessels then at sea in case I met them. And the Messina Naval Command told me that an enemy submarine had been seen a few hours before close to Cape dell'Armi, firing torpedoes at one of our convoys.

I had, in fact, to pass near Cape dell'Armi; I decided to give it a wide berth and cruised along the coast of Sicily as far as Taormina. There I sighted a submarine which appeared to be motionless. I kept my bows turned towards it (one can never take too many precautions) and signalled it. I couldn't make head or tail of the answer: the vessel was clearly one of the enemy's. The situation being what it was, both of us being surfaced and visible to each other (it was a bright moonlight night), and considering my orders and my special task, as well, finally, as the fact that my adversary had two guns and I had none, I sent a signal to the Messina Naval Command that I had seen an enemy vessel and continued straight on my course towards the Eastern Mediterranean. And the enemy submarine? Well, she started off on a course parallel to my own! We proceeded in this way, side by side, with about 3000 metres between us, like the best of friends, for about an hour; after this, the other submarine, as unexpectedly as it had joined me, left me to myself and turned back towards Taormina. Strange things happen at sea in time of war! The next day we encountered a melancholy spectacle. We were passing through waters strewn with wreckage and flotsam of every description, including many life-belts; one of our convoys had been surprised during the past few days. On the 9th we reached Leros and entered Port Lago, which I knew well, having made a long stay there, years before, while in charge of the *Iride*. It is a magnificent natural inlet, protected on three sides by high, rocky mountains, while on the other lies a pleasant little village, built entirely during the last few years, with its inn, church and town hall; it looked like a corner of Italy transferred to this Aegean island. I moored at the pier outside the submarine barracks; and was at once visited by Spigai, a career colleague of mine, in command of the 5th Submarine Flotilla at Leros. He put himself at my disposal with the affection of a good comrade. The first thing I did was to cover the *Scirè*'s cylinders with enormous tarpaulins; we were ostensibly a submarine belonging to another base which had put in here on account of serious damage sustained while fighting and was in need of prolonged repairs. Leros was full of Greeks and no precaution could be excessive. Six technicians flown from Italy for the purpose proceeded, meanwhile, to give the "pigs" a final check-over.

On the 12th, the 10 operators arrived, also by air. To keep them out of sight, they were given quarters in the transport *Asmara*, which was moored in the deserted bay of Parteni, at the opposite end of the island; the same anchorage had been used by Faggioni's detachment and the Suda *E*-boats. The lads spent the last few hours before their operation in the peace and quiet of that isolated roadstead, with nothing to distract them and no dangers to be encountered; on the 13th, I paid them a visit and we studied the operational plan in detail, also examining the latest aerial photographs of the harbour and the data I had been receiving (only very few messages up to now); we also gossiped a little, possibly to distract our minds for a while from the subject on which we had been concentrating our whole attention for the last month.

Admiral Biancheri, Commander-in-Chief of the Aegean naval sector, arrived at Leros from Rhodes. He wanted us to carry out exercises and tests in his presence, there and then, at Port Lago! I took advantage of my orders giving me full authority during the operation to decline the invitation. The admiral expressed his disappointment and his convinced opinion that "we shan't do any good if we cut training short".

I could not lose time. The favourable lunar phase had begun, the nights being absolutely dark; weather reports were good. I resolved to start on the 14th of December. I kept in continuous touch with Forza, who had gone to Athens on the 9th to take charge of and co-ordinate air reconnaissance services, intelligence reports, the issue of weather bulletins and radio liaison with the *Scirè*.

The plan of operations provided for the arrival of the *Scirè* on a certain evening, a few thousand metres from the entrance to Alexandria harbour; as it was assumed that everything would be in darkness (owing to the black-out), it had been arranged that, in order to facilitate the submarine's landfall, the coast being low-lying and without conspicuous features, and to allow her to identify the harbour (for the success of the operators' raid would depend largely on the precision with which the point of their release was determined), on the evening before, and also on the one of the action, our aircraft would bomb the harbour. The submarine would then release the operators. The latter, proceeding on courses laid down beforehand, as soon as they arrived in front of the harbour, would have to overcome the obstructions and attack the targets previously assigned to them by the commander of the *Scirè*, who would base his orders on the latest data transmitted to him by radio. After attaching the charges to the hulls of the targets, the operators were to lay a certain number of floating incendiary bombs with which they had been supplied. These bombs would go off about an hour after the warheads had exploded and were intended to set alight the oil which would by then have spread from the ships which had been attacked; it was expected that this would cause fire to break out in the harbour, affecting all the vessels therein, together with the floating docks, the harbour installations and the warehouses . . .; thus putting the chief enemy naval base in the Eastern Mediterranean utterly out of action.

The *Scirè*, directly the operators had been dropped, was to start back. The pilots had been told which zones of the interior of the harbour were considered the least vigilantly watched, where they were to land on conclusion of the operation and what routes they were to take to get clear of the harbour area in the shortest possible time. Plans had also been laid for their rescue: on the days following the action the submarine *Zaffiro* (commanded by Giovanni Lombardi) would shuttle for two consecutive nights 10 miles off Rosetta in the Nile delta; such operators as eluded immediate capture would be able to reach her by any boat they could find on the coast.

The *Scirè*, with the pilots aboard, left Leros on the morning of the 14th. She proceeded without incident and, so to speak, in secret; by day we submerged, surfacing only at night, to charge the batteries and freshen up the atmosphere aboard. The task of the *Scirè* was, as usual, to find a method of getting as close as possible to the enemy harbour, without arousing prohibitive alarm or allowing her presence to be suspected. Discovery would mean arousing anti-submarine measures; a remorseless pursuit would begin, which would prevent us from carrying out the operation. We therefore took the strictest precautions. And as we might be detected by hydrophones as a result of normal sounds aboard the submarine, we had to proceed noiselessly, muffling the machinery. The intelligence we had received on setting out was to the effect that Alexandria harbour was surrounded, like all other harbours in time of war, by minefields. To quote the report: "*Fixed and mobile defences ascertained*: (a) minefield 20 miles NW of harbour; (b) line of 'lobster-pots' arranged at a depth of 30 fathoms in a circle with a radius of about six miles; (c) line of detector cables closer in; (d) groups of 'lobster-pots' in known positions; (e) net barriers relatively easy to force; (f) advanced observation line beyond minefield."

How could all these dangers be circumvented? How could the minefields be evaded if we did not know the security routes? Or the "lobster-pots"? Or the detector cables?

In order to reach the target we were obliged, after a certain stage, to trust to luck; there was nothing else to do. But luck can be "assisted", especially when the matter in hand is a complex one. I had therefore decided that, as soon as we reached a depth of 400 metres (which would probably be where the minefields started), we would proceed at a depth of not less than 60 metres, since I assumed that the mines, even if they were anti-submarine, would be located at a higher level; if the submarine should then collide with one of the mooring cables, I felt sure that the latter would slide along her sides, which were accurately streamlined and carefully cleared of all adherent matter, without getting caught up anywhere, till it fell harmlessly astern. There was nothing else I could do to elude the peril of the mines, except, naturally, to trust to luck.

The other difficulty was that of taking the submarine to the *precise* point prearranged; in other words, to navigate with the exactitude of a draughtsman working with compass and ruler, despite the drifting caused by underwater currents, which are always difficult to deal with, and despite, above all, the impossibility of ascertaining one's position from the moment when, at dawn of the day appointed for the operation, the submarine would be obliged to submerge (so as not to be detected from the enemy base) and proceed at a great depth (to avoid mines), until the time came to release the operators.

The solution of this problem of underwater navigation cannot be reached without perfect control of the speed of the vessel; the course has to be laid and kept to with great precision (so as to eliminate errors due to faulty steering) and finally position has to be determined from variations in depth quota, the only hydrographic factor which can be ascertained in a submerged submarine; here we are in a sphere closer to that of art than to the science of navigation.

Everyone aboard gave me effective help, officers, petty officers and seamen. Each man, in his own special department, took care that his services should be regularly maintained and that his machinery should function in such a way as to prevent any unforeseen accident which might compromise the success of the operation.

Ursano, my second-in-command, had the general supervision of routine aboard; Benini and Olcese, the two efficient navigation officers, helped me in following the course and with the tricky business of dealing with codes and communication; while Tajer, the chief engineer, regulated the performance of the machinery (engines, electric batteries, air supply, etc.) and kept the respective services in order. The petty officers were first-rate: Ravera was chief mechanic, Farina chief torpedo-gunner, and Rapetti chief electrician; the wireless operators kept us in continuous touch with Rome and Athens; all were praise worthy in the discharge of their various duties. Last but not least there was the cook (a seaman to whom this task had been allotted; he was a mason in civil life) who became the martyr aboard; he was on his feet 24 hours out of 24 at the tiny, red-hot electric stoves, whatever the sea was like, concocting from dry rations dishes to satisfy the tastes and digestions of 60 people, as well as hot drinks for those on night watch and solid meals to keep up the spirits of the operators.

The latter, meanwhile, in perfect serenity (for the die was now cast) stored up their energy by resting. De la Penne, with his big fair head of rumpled hair, was generally to be found lying in his bunk asleep. Even as he slumbered he would every now and then stretch out an arm, put his hand into a drawer and extract a large fruit cake, which he ate up at a great rate. Then he would blissfully turn over and go back to his dreams.

Martellotta, permanently in good spirits, occupied another bunk. "Peace and good will!" was his invariable greeting; a heartening phrase. Marceglia, a giant of a man, with a tranquil temperament and something stately about him, was absorbed in study: his *basso profondo* tones were rarely heard and, when they were, it was to make some technical request or utter some comment on the operation. Feltrinelli, Bianchi, Marino, Schergat, Favale and Memoli all managed to find acceptable accommodation among the ship's equipment and spent their days in unbroken repose, only interrupted for the necessary more than substantial meals.

Public health was in the hands of Spaccarelli, surgeon, diver and reserve crew leader; every day he put the pilots through a thorough medical examination; it was essential to have them in the pink of condition on the day of the operation, which was now at hand.

The pilots remained very calm: the difficulties and dangers of which they were naturally well aware did not make them uneasy but merely increased their determination; anxiety and strain were inevitable, but did not find expression; talk went on at the ordinary level of cheerful tranquillity characteristic of life aboard; there were periods of gay hilarity, when facetious repartees were exchanged.

They were really extraordinary fellows, those lads; they were about to undertake action which would require the exploitation of their whole physical and moral energy and put their lives in peril at every moment, hour after hour; it would be a mission from which, *at best*, they could only hope to emerge as prisoners of war, and yet they preserved the attitude of a team of sportsmen off to play their customary Sunday game.

Meanwhile the *Scirè* encountered, on the 16th of December, a heavy storm.

In order to avoid exposing materials, and above all our operators, to excessive strain, I remained submerged even at night, the moment our supplies of air and electricity had been taken in.

The same day I wrote:

> In consequence of the bad weather and the lack of exact information as to the number and size of the enemy units in harbour, I decided to postpone the operation for 24 hours from the night of the 17th/18th to that of the 18th/19th. (From my official report.)

On the 17th of December I added:

> In view of the ship's position and the favourable weather conditions I decided that the operation should take place on the evening of the 18th, hoping that I should meanwhile receive precise intelligence regarding the presence of vessels in harbour.

This was a hope that was soon realized. The same evening we obtained at last, to our great delight, confirmation from Athens that both the two battleships were at Alexandria.

The word was now: forward! Throughout the day, on the 18th, the *Scirè* proceeded through a zone which we presumed to be mined, at a depth of 60 metres, over bottoms which rose rapidly as we approached the coast, till we slipped over them like a silent and invisible tank, "continually regulating our movements in accordance with the rise of the sea-bed, till at 1840 hours we found ourselves at the prearranged point, 1.3 miles by 356° from the lighthouse at the west mole of the commercial harbour of Alexandria, at a depth of 15 metres".

Preparations were made for release of the operators. As soon as I had discovered, by a survey taken through the periscope, that the darkness was complete, I surfaced just sufficiently to enable the trapdoor to be opened ("outcrop level", as it is technically known) and came out on the conning tower. The weather was perfect: it was pitch-dark; the sea very smooth and the sky unclouded. Alexandria was right ahead of me, very close. I identified some of its characteristic buildings and determined my position; to my great satisfaction I found that we were within a metre of the pre-arranged point. This was an exceptional result after 16 hours of blind navigation! Immediately afterwards, with the pilots wrapped in their rubber suits and wearing their breathing sets, the ceremony of leave-taking began; we neither spoke nor embraced one another: "Commander," was all they said, "give us the good-luck kick, will you?" And with this strange rite, into which I put all I knew, so that my good wishes might be evident, the farewell ceremony terminated.

The first to go up were the two leaders of the reserve crews,

Feltrinelli and Spaccarelli. Their job was to open the cylinder doors, to save the operators the fatigue of doing so.

One by one, de la Penne and Bianchi, Marceglia and Schergat, Martellotta and Marino, covered from head to foot in their black suits, their movements encumbered by their breathing gear, went up the ladder and disappeared into the darkness of the night and the sea. I submerged to the bottom.

A few minutes later the hydrophones told us that the three crews were on their way. "God be with them," I prayed, "and speed them well!"

Inside the submarine we waited for the sounds of blows struck against the deck, the agreed signal to be made when the doors of the cylinders, now empty, had been closed and the reserves were ready to be taken aboard again. When at last we heard them, I surfaced. Feltrinelli told me, in a voice broken by emotion, that as he could see no sign of Spaccarelli, he had gone astern to look for him: by pure chance he had stumbled against something soft on deck; he had discovered by groping (for we must not forget that the scene took place underwater at night) that it was the missing Spaccarelli, who seemed lifeless. I instantly sent up two other divers, who had been kept ready for any emergency; Spaccarelli was lifted up and lowered down the ladder into the interior of the submarine. I descended to the bottom again and began to head for home, following precisely the same course which had proved to be safe during my approach.

The unfortunate Spaccarelli was forthwith relieved of his mask, breathing set and diver's suit and put to bed; he was quite blue in the face, his pulse was imperceptible and he was not breathing; he showed every normal symptom of having been drowned.

What was to be done? The mission's surgeon was not much use to us in this extremity, for he himself was the victim. I arranged for two men to give him continuous artificial respiration; I rummaged in the medicine chest and had him injected with the contents of all the phials that, judging from the description of the ingredients, seemed capable of exercising a stimulating action on the heart and circulation; others gave him oxygen (the air aboard was emphatically unsuitable in this case); all the resources of our extremely slender store of medicaments and of our still slenderer knowledge of medicine were brought into play in the attempt to achieve what appeared to be an utter impossibility, the resuscitation of a dead man.

Meanwhile the *Scirè*, with this dramatic episode taking place aboard her, slipped along the sea-bed, further and further away from Alexandria. We took care not to reveal our presence in any way; discovery would have been fatal to the six adventurous lads who were at that very moment engaged in the crucial phase of the operation. But the submarine was not responding very well to my directions: the cylinder doors astern had been left open, a circumstance which made it difficult for me to keep my depth and maintain trim. As soon as we were some miles from the coast I surfaced to close them. I noticed that the Ras el Tin Lighthouse was functioning; a number of lights which I had not seen before showed at the entrance to the harbour; units were evidently going in or out; I hoped the operators would be able to take advantage of the fact. As for the cylinders, I found that they could not be closed on account of damage to one of the doors.

I continued on my course of withdrawal, remaining submerged, for the zone we were now crossing had been notified as constituting the minefield. After three and a half hours' continuous artificial respiration, a number of injections and some applications of oxygen, our surgeon, who had till then shown not the smallest sign of life, drew his first wheezing breath; it was a deep, hoarse sound, resembling a death-rattle. But it meant he was alive and we could save him! A few hours later, in fact, though his condition was still serious, he got back the use of his voice and was able to tell us that while he was making a terrific effort to close the starboard cylinder door, which stubbornly resisted every attempt he made, the effects of the oxygen he was breathing and those of water pressure at the depth involved had caused him to faint; luckily he fell on deck and did not slip overboard, as might very easily have happened, for there were no rails or bulwarks to the vessel (they had been removed to prevent the mine-cables from catching on them).

At last, on the evening of the 19th, since we were now presumably clear of the minefields, the *Scirè* surfaced, after 39 hours of submersion, and set course for Leros. On the evening of the 20th we received the following wireless communication from the Naval Supreme Command: "Photographic reconnaissance indicates two battleships hit." There was great enthusiasm aboard; no one had doubted it would be a success, but to have our expectations confirmed so soon gave us great satisfaction.

On the evening of the 21st, as soon as we had docked at Port Lago, we took Spaccarelli ashore to the local naval hospital. He was now out of danger but still required a good deal of attention in consequence of the severe shock he had experienced.

The return of the *Scirè* from Leros to La Spezia proceeded without any notable incidents, except that on Christmas Day, while the submarine was off Bengazi and the crew were listening to the Pope's speech on the loudspeaker, an aircraft of unidentified nationality came a little too close to the vessel and got within range of our four 13.2 machine-guns; the natural retaliation was the dropping of five bombs about 80 metres astern of us, which did no damage. Our Christmas pies!

On the 29th of December the *Scirè* arrived at La Spezia. Admiral Bacci, now chief of the North Tyrrhenean Sector, was waiting for us, on the pier; he brought us greetings and congratulations from Admiral Riccardi, Under Secretary of State for the Navy.

I was glad of this tribute to my gallant crew, who had worked so hard, with such efficiency and courage, in bringing our submarine back to harbour after 27 days of operational service, 22 of them at sea, and had covered without mishap 3500 miles, thus contributing to a great victory for Italy.

How had it fared with the operators, whom we had left in the open sea, outside Alexandria harbour, astride their fragile torpedoes, plunged beneath the waves in the darkness of night, surrounded by enemies in ambush? The three crews had left the submarine in company and commenced approach along the pre-arranged routes.

The sea was very calm, the night dark. Lights in the harbour permitted the pilots to determine their position, which they found to be precisely as planned. They went ahead so coolly that at one point, as de la Penne relates in his report, "as we were ahead of schedule, we opened our ration tins and had a meal. We were then 500 metres from the Ras el Tin Lighthouse."

At last they reached the net defences at the harbour's entrance.

> We saw some people at the end of the pier and heard them talking; one of them was walking about with a lighted oil-lamp.
>
> We also saw a large motorboat cruising in silence off the pier and dropping depth-charges. These charges were rather a nuisance to us.

While the six heads, only just above water, were looking, with all the concentrated attention of which they were capable, for a gap in the net, three British destroyers suddenly appeared at the entrance to the harbour, waiting to go in: guide lights were switched on to show them the way and the net gates were thrown wide open. Without a second's hesitation our three assault craft slipped into the harbour with the British destroyers: they were in! They had lost sight of one another during this manœuvre, but they were now close to their targets. The latter had been distributed as follows: de la Penne was to take the battleship *Valiant*, Marceglia the battleship *Queen Elizabeth* and Martellotta was to look for the aircraft-carrier; if she were not in harbour, he was to attack a loaded tanker in the hope that the oil or petrol which would issue from it would spread over the water and thus furnish excellent fuel for the floating incendiary bombs the operators were to scatter before abandoning their "pigs".

We will now take up the stories of the individual crews.

De La Penne – Bianchi. Inside the harbour, after passing the interned French warships, the presence of which was well known, de la Penne sighted, at the presumed anchorage, the huge dark mass of the target assigned to him, the 32,000 ton battleship *Valiant*. As he approached her, he encountered the anti-torpedo net barrier: he got through it *surfaced* "in order to lose as little time as possible, for I found that my physical condition, owing to the cold, would be unlikely to let me hold out much longer". (His diver's suit had been leaking ever since he had left the submarine.) He had no difficulty with negotiation of the net: he was now 30 metres from the *Valiant*; it was 19 minutes past two. He touched the hull, giving it a slight bump; in performing the evolution necessary to get beneath the hull, his "pig" seemed to take on extra weight and went to the bottom in 17 metres of water; de la Penne dived after it and discovered to his amazement that there was no sign of his second pilot. He rose to the surface to look for him, but could not see him; everything was quiet aboard the battleship; no alarm had been given. De la Penne left Bianchi to his fate, returned to the bottom and tried to start the engine of his craft to get it underneath the hull, as it had meanwhile moved some distance away. But the engine would not start; a rapid check-over soon showed what the trouble was: a steel wire had got entangled in the propeller.

What was to be done? All alone, with his craft immobilized on the sea-bed a few metres from the target, de la Penne resolved to try the only possible expedient: this was to drag the "pig" by main force, finding his direction from the compass, beneath the battleship. Speed was essential, for he feared that at any moment the British might pick up his second pilot, who had probably fainted and would be floating about close by . . .; the alarm would be given, depth-charges would be dropped, his operation and those of his companions would be doomed to certain failure, for they would be at work only a few hundred metres away. With all his strength, panting and sweating, he dragged at the craft; his goggles became obscured and the mud he was stirring up prevented his reading the compass, his breath began to come in great gasps and it became difficult to breathe at all through the mask, but he stuck to it and made progress; he could hear, close above him, the noises made aboard the ship, especially the sound of an alternating pump, which he used to find his direction. After 40 minutes of superhuman effort, making a few inches at every pull, he at last bumped his head against the hull. He made a cursory survey of the position: he seemed to be at about the middle of the ship, an excellent spot for causing maximum damage. He was now almost exhausted; but he used the last vestiges of his strength to set the time fuses; in accordance with the orders he had received he regulated them so as to cause the explosion at five o'clock precisely (Italian time, corresponding with six o'clock local time). He did not release his incendiary bombs, for when they rose to the surface they would reveal the presence and the position of the threat now established under the hull with the fuses in action. He left his craft on the sea-bed under the vessel and swam to the surface. The moment he got his head above water he removed his mask and sank it; the fresh, pure air revived him; he began to swim slowly away from the ship. But someone called out to him, a searchlight picked him out, a burst of machine-gun fire brought him to a halt. He swam back towards the vessel and climbed out of the water on to the mooring-buoy at the bows of the *Valiant*. He found there his second pilot Bianchi, who, after fainting, had risen to the surface like a balloon and on regaining consciousness had hidden himself on the buoy so as not risk causing an alarm which would have disturbed the work of his leader. "Aboard they were making facetious remarks, believing that our operation had failed; they were talking contemptuously about Italians. I called Bianchi's attention to the probability that in a few hours they would have changed their minds about the Italians." It was then about 3.30. At last a motorboat turned up and the two "shipwrecked" men were picked up by it and taken aboard the battleship. A British officer asked who they were, where they had come from and expressed ironical sympathy with their lack of success. The two operators, who were now prisoners of war, made clear who they were, by handing over their military identity cards. They refused to answer any other questions. They were taken in the motorboat, separated from each other, to a hut ashore, near the Ras el Tin Lighthouse. Bianchi was the first to be cross-examined: on leaving the hut he made a sign to de la Penne indicating that he had said nothing. It was then the latter's turn: naturally, he held his tongue; the Britisher, who had a revolver in his hand, seemed to be an excitable sort of fellow, "I'll soon find a way to make you talk," he said, in excellent Italian. The men were taken back aboard the *Valiant*: it was then four o'clock.

They were received by the commanding officer, Captain Morgan, who asked them where the charge was located. On their refusing to answer, the two men, accompanied by the officer of the watch and escorted by an armed picket, were placed in one of the holds forward, between the two gun-turrets, not very far from the point at which the charge would explode.

We will now let de la Penne take up the tale.

Our escort were rather white about the gills and behaved very nicely to us; they gave me rum to drink and offered me cigarettes; they also tried to make us talk. Bianchi sat down and went to sleep. I perceived from the ribbons on the sailors' caps that we were aboard the battleship *Valiant*. When there were about 10 minutes left before the explosion, I asked if I could speak to the commanding officer. I was taken aft, into his presence. I told him that in a few minutes his ship would blow up, that there was nothing he could do about it and that, if he wished, he could still get his crew into a place of safety. He again asked me where I had placed the charge and as I did not reply had me escorted back to the hold. As we went along I heard the loudspeakers giving orders to abandon ship, as the vessel had been attacked by Italians, and saw people running aft. When I was again in the hold I said to Bianchi, as I came down the ladder, that things had turned out badly and that it was all up with us, but that we could be content, since we had succeeded, in spite of everything, in bringing the operation to a successful conclusion. Bianchi, however, did not answer me. I looked for him and could not find him. I supposed that the British, believing that I had confessed, had removed him. A few minutes passed (they were infernal ones for me: would the explosion take place?) and then it came. The vessel reared, with extreme violence. All the lights went out and the hold became filled with smoke. I was surrounded by shackles which had been hanging from the ceiling and had now fallen. I was unhurt, except for pain in a knee, which had been grazed by one of the shackles in its fall. The vessel was listing to port. I opened one of the port-holes very near sea level, hoping to be able to get through it and escape. This proved to be impossible, as the port-hole was too small, and I gave up the idea: but I left the port open, hoping that through it more water would enter. I waited for a few moments. The hold was now illuminated by the light which entered through the port. I concluded that it would be rash to stay there any longer, noticing that the vessel was now lying on the bottom and continuing slowly to list to port. I climbed up the ladder and, finding the hatchway open, began to walk aft; there was no one about. But there were still many of the crew at the stern. They got up as I passed them; I went on till I reached the Captain. At that moment he was engaged in giving orders for salvaging his ship. I asked him what he had done with my diver. He did not reply and the officer of the watch told me to be silent. The ship had now listed through 4–5 degrees and come to a standstill. I saw from a clock that it was a quarter past six. I went further aft, where a number of officers were standing, and began to watch the battleship *Queen Elizabeth*, which lay about 500 metres astern of us.

The crew of that battleship were standing in her bows. A few seconds passed and then the *Queen Elizabeth*, too, blew up. She rose a few inches out of the water and fragments of iron and other objects flew out of her funnel, mixed with oil which even reached the deck of the *Valiant*, splashing everyone of us standing on her stern. An officer came up and asked me to tell him on my word of honour if there were any other charges under the ship. I made no reply and was then again taken back to the hold. After about a quarter of an hour I was escorted up to the officers' mess, where at last I could sit down, and where I found Bianchi. Shortly afterwards I was put aboard a motor-boat, which took me back to Ras el Tin. I noticed that the anchor, which had been hanging at the bows, was now underwater. During transit an officer asked me whether we had got in through the gaps in the mole. At Ras el Tin we were locked in two cells and kept there until towards evening. I asked whether I could be given a little sunlight, as I was again very cold. A soldier came, felt my pulse and told me that I was perfectly all right.

Towards evening we were put into a small lorry and transported therein to a prisoner-of-war camp in Alexandria. I found some Italians in the camp who had heard the explosions that morning. We lay down on the ground, without having had any food, and, though we were soaked through, we slept till the following morning. I was taken to the infirmary for treatment of my knee injury and some Italian orderlies gave me an excellent dish of macaroni. The next morning I was removed to Cairo. (From the report handed in by Lieutenant Luigi de la Penne on his return from prison.)

In 1944, after de la Penne and Bianchi had come back to Italy from prison, they were awarded the gold medal for gallantry in war. And he who pinned the medal on the chest of de la Penne was none other than Admiral Morgan, formerly commanding officer of the *Valiant* and at that time chief of the allied naval mission in Italy.

Marceglia – Schergat. Approach commenced in company with de la Penne on the pre-arranged course. About midnight they saw the guide lights at the entrance to the harbour switched on; it was clear that units were either going in or coming out. Violent shocks were felt against the casing of the "pig", as though it had crashed against some metallic obstacle, accompanied by strong contraction of the leg muscles of the pilots: these were the effects of depth-charges dropped by the enemy at the entrance to the harbour to prevent "unwelcome visits". As they slipped into the entrance channel they noticed, much to their surprise and satisfaction, that the net gates had been opened. Shortly afterwards, towards one o'clock, they had to take rapid evasive action to avoid being run down by three destroyers which were just coming in. Marceglia resumed the pre-arranged course: "in no time at all found myself face to face with the whole massive bulk of my target." He came upon the anti-torpedo net, got through it and, now that the way was clear, submerged beneath the hull, in line with the funnel. With the aid of his second pilot, Marceglia precisely carried out manoeuvre: he clamped a loop-line connecting the two bilge keels and attached the warhead of his torpedo to the central point of the line, so that it hung about a metre and a half below the hull; then he set the fuse in motion. It was then

3.15 a.m. (Italian time).

> I tried to analyse my sensations at that moment. I found that I did not feel particularly thrilled, but only rather tired and just starting to get cold. We got astride our craft again: my diver made me urgent signs to surface, as he was just about all in. I pumped in air to surface; the craft only detached itself from the bottom with difficulty, then at last it started to rise, at first slowly, later more rapidly. So as not to burst out of the water too suddenly, I had to exhaust; the air bubbles attracted the attention of the watch aft. He switched on a searchlight and we surfaced right into its rays. We ducked down on the craft to make the target as small as possible and prevent our goggles from reflecting the light. Shortly afterwards the searchlight was switched off; we started on our return, which took us past the bows of the ship; a man was walking up and down the fo'c'sle deck, I could see his cigarette glowing; everything was quiet aboard. We got out of the obstructed zone and, at last, took off our masks; it was very cold; I couldn't prevent my teeth chattering. We stopped again and began distributing our incendiaries after setting the fuses. (From a report by Engineer Captain Antonio Marceglia.)

They then set off for the spot on which they were to land: it was the area which, according to our maps and intelligence reports, was the least strictly guarded and furnished the most convenient access to the city.

While still some distance from land they set going the fuse of the craft's self-destructor and sank her; they swam ashore, removed their breathing sets and rubber suits, cut everything to pieces and buried the strips under the rocks. Then they waded ashore: it was 4.30 a.m.; they had been in the water exactly eight hours.

Marceglia and Schergat succeeded in leaving the harbour area unobserved. Posing as French sailors, they entered the city of Alexandria; after wandering about for some time, they made their way to the station to take the train for Rosetta and try to rejoin the submarine which would be lying about 10 miles out to sea at certain pre-arranged times, a night or two later. But at this point their troubles began: the sterling with which they were supplied did not circulate in Egypt; they wasted a lot of time trying to get it changed and were not able to leave until the evening. At Rosetta they spent the night in a squalid little inn, hiding from frequent visits by the police; next day, in the evening, they made for the seashore, but were stopped by the Egyptian police, recognized as Italians and turned over to the British naval authorities.

Their attempt to evade capture was thus frustrated.

Marceglia's operation may be characterized as a "perfect" one, meaning by this phrase that it was performed without a hitch at every stage and nothing unforeseen happened. In a letter he wrote me some years later he observed: "As you can see, Sir, our performance had nothing heroic about it; its success was due solely to the preparations made, the specially favourable conditions under which it took place and above all the determination to succeed at all costs."

Preparations, determination and luck were rewarded with the gold medal for gallantry in war, which both Marceglia and Schergat obtained on their release from prison.

Martellotta – Marino. Martellotta writes in his report:

Aboard the submarine *Scirè* at 1630 on the 18th December 1941, I received from Lieutenant-Commander Borghese the following operational orders: "Attack to be made on a large loaded tanker and six incendiaries to be distributed in its immediate neighbourhood."

The presence which had been notified of 12 loaded tankers in harbour at Alexandria, with a total tonnage of 120,000, was sufficient indication of the importance of the order received: the fire which might be started would be capable of reaching such proportions as to bring about the entire destruction of the harbour itself, with all the units present and all the shore installations.

Nevertheless, I felt obliged to reply: "Sir, I shall obey your orders; but I should like you to know that my diver and I would rather have attacked a warship."

The Captain smiled at this remark of mine and, to please me, since he was aware that there was a possibility of an aircraft-carrier having returned to the harbour, he modified the original operational orders to read: "Search to be made for the aircraft-carrier at its two normal anchorages and attack to be made on it if found; otherwise, all other targets consisting of active war units to be ignored and a large loaded tanker to be attacked with distribution of the six incendiaries in its immediate neighbourhood."

Martellotta had a certain amount of trouble in opening the door of the cylinder and asked Spaccarelli to help him (this was the difficulty which involved Spaccarelli in the adventure related above); he finally joined the other two crews and continued approach in their company as far as the entrance net gate.

I felt shocks from depth-charges and violent pressure against my legs, as though they were being crushed against the craft by some heavy object. I put on my mask and, so as to avoid injury from the frequent shocks being inflicted at vulnerable parts of my body, I ducked in such a way as to lie low in the water, but with heart, lungs and head above the surface. I told Marino, my diver, to put on his mask also and to take up a similar position, but facing aft, since I was unable myself to keep an eye open in that direction, engaged as I was in looking ahead and having only the limited area of visibility which the mask allowed.

We arrived in these positions at the entrance to the harbour . . . We did not find obstructions, as we had expected, at the pier-heads: the channel was clear.

We went ahead very slowly. Suddenly, my diver, Marino, thumped me on the shoulder and said: "Hard a-starboard." I instantly swerved in the direction indicated, putting on speed, but the craft struck the buoys of the fixed interior barrier, being driven against them by the waves from the bow of a ship which had caught me up as it entered the harbour. It was a destroyer, showing no lights and going at about 10 knots; I distinctly heard chains clashing at her bows and saw members of the crew on deck getting ready to moor. It was then 0030 hours on the 19th December. I got going again and, taking advantage of the waves made by a second destroyer as it entered the harbour, I slipped in with it, still surfaced and passing within about 20 metres of the guardship.

Martellotta, therefore, was now inside the harbour; he

started looking for the aircraft-carrier at its two habitual anchorages; he could not find her (as a matter of fact she was not in harbour that night).

But he did sight a large warship; believing her to be a battleship, he initiated attack; he had already got under her hull when he discovered that she was, on the contrary, a cruiser and with great reluctance, in obedience to orders received, abandoned the attack; just as he was clearing her after-davits he was caught in the rays of a pocket-torch aboard her: some seconds of utter immobility ensued, during which he felt as if even his heart had stopped beating; then the torch went out. He made for the zone of the tankers. Martellotta was now beginning to notice signs of strain: his head ached and he had to vomit; he could no longer keep the mouthpiece of the mask between his lips; he took it off and went ahead surfaced. There were the tankers. "I sighted a large one, heavily loaded, which I guessed to be about 16,000 tons." Not being able to submerge, he decided to carry out the attack from the surface: while Martellotta kept the "pig" under the stern of the tanker, the second pilot, Marino, fastened the charge beneath the hull. By 2.55 the fuse had been set going. While this operation was proceeding, a smaller tanker had come alongside the one under attack.

> When Marino rose to the surface and saw her, he said: "Let's hope she stays here another three hours and then she'll have her hash settled too." Next, we started off again, for distribution of the incendiaries: we moored them, after setting their fuses, about 100 metres from the tanker and 20 metres apart.

The operation having been carried out in detail so far, the final stage began: this would be the attempt to escape so as not to fall into the hands of the enemy. They got ashore at the agreed place without incident, destroyed, by way of preventive action, their breathing sets and divers' suits and sank the "pig" after setting the self-destructor fuse. Then they went ashore.

> I set off with Marino to get clear of the harbour zone and enter the city: we were stopped at a control point and arrested by some Egyptian customs officials and police, who summoned a second

lieutenant and six privates of the British Marines. We were taken to an office occupied by two lieutenants of the Egyptian police, who started cross-examining us; while I was answering the questions put to me in as evasive and vague a manner as I could, a British naval commander arrived and requested the senior of the two Egyptian officers to hand us over to the British. The Egyptian refused to do so in the absence of any authority from his Government, pointing out that, as he had found us to be Italians from the documents we carried and Egypt was not at war with Italy, he would have to get special instructions.

The British Commander, after obtaining the necessary authorization from his Admiral, made a personal application to the Egyptian Government for the instructions required and succeeded in getting us handed over.

My waterproof watch was on the table with the other articles taken possession of and I never took my eyes off it. Shortly after 5.54 a.m. a violent explosion was heard, which shook the whole building. A few minutes later, as we were getting into a car to follow the British officer, a second explosion was heard, further away, and after the car had started a third. At the Ras el Tin naval headquarters we were briefly interrogated, courteously enough, and then despatched to the concentration camp for prisoners of war at Cairo. (From the report of Gunner Captain Vincenzo Martellotta.)

Martellotta and Marino, on their release from captivity, were also awarded the gold medal for gallantry in war.

The Italian War Bulletin N. 585 of the 8th of January, 1942, gives the following account of the success of the operation:

On the night of the 18th December assault craft of the Italian Royal Navy entered the harbour of Alexandria and attacked two British battleships anchored there. It has only just been confirmed that a battleship of the *Valiant* class was seriously damaged and put into dock for repairs, and is still there.

The following Bulletin, N. 586 of the 9th of January, rounds off the information as follows:

In the operation conducted by assault craft of the Italian Royal

Navy in the harbour of Alexandria and reported in yesterday's Bulletin we now have definite further intelligence that, in addition to the *Valiant*, a second battleship of the *Barham* class was also damaged.

Such was the modest announcement of a naval victory unparalleled throughout the war for precision of execution and importance of strategic results. At the cost of six men captured, there had been sunk, in addition to a large tanker, two 32,000 ton battleships, the last of those at the disposal of the British in the Mediterranean. Crippled by the charges applied to their hulls by the daring members of the Tenth Light Flotilla, the vessels were at a later date, after much expenditure of energy and materials, refloated, patched up for the time being and then transferred to quiet and distant yards for refit: but they made no further contribution to the war and immediately after the cessation of hostilities they were removed for demolition.

The losses of the *Valiant* and the *Queen Elizabeth*, following those of the *Ark Royal* and the *Barham* in the Mediterranean and almost contemporaneous with the destruction of the *Repulse* and the extremely recent *Prince of Wales* in Indonesia at the hands of Japanese aviators, brought about a most critical situation for the British Navy, which was only retrieved after a long lapse of time and then only by means of American assistance.

The strategic position in the Mediterranean was now reversed: for the first (and last) time in the course of the war the Italian Navy achieved crushing superiority and dominated the Mediterranean; it could therefore resume, with practical immunity, supplies to the armies overseas and carry out transport of the German *Afrika Corps* to Libya, thus causing the defeat, a few months later, of the British Army, which was driven out of Cyrenaica.

Even more could have been done: Italy's naval superiority at that time was such as to permit her armed forces to undertake a direct attack against the pivot of the war in the Mediterranean (and perhaps not only in that theatre of war), namely, Malta. An invasion force transported by a convoy protected by the entire Italian Fleet, when our battleships would be opposed by *no* such British vessels, would have eliminated that obstacle in the heart of the Mediterranean, which had done us so much harm already and was to do us even more later on. Such an operation would have disposed of the difficulties which the Italian Navy had to encounter, for months afterwards, in supplying our African army.

In view of the disproportion between naval forces, the operation would certainly have succeeded, though it might have been accompanied by serious losses. When the thorn in the flank of Italy's line of communication across the Mediterranean had thus been eliminated, the occupation of Egypt would only have been a question of time, bringing with it incalculable consequences for the outcome of the war.

The responsibility for losing this opportunity rests, in my opinion, on the Italian General Staff and, still more, upon the German High Command which, by refusing to supply the necessary fuel for our warships and aircraft, "again displayed its underestimation of sea power in the general conduct of the war and in particular of the importance of the Mediterranean in the general picture of the entire conflict". (From the report of Admiral Weichold, a German liaison officer attached to the Italian Supreme Naval Command, submitted to the Anglo-Americans after the war.)

The great victory at Alexandria was therefore only partially exploited: the British were given time to draw naval and air reinforcements to the Mediterranean to such an extent that a few months later the situation was again reversed, to our disadvantage; it continued to deteriorate until the final collapse, of which the withdrawal from North Africa in May 1943 was the obvious proof.

But how great the danger which threatened the enemy was, and how near we were, after the blow delivered at Alexandria, to achieving decisive victory, was indicated, more clearly than by anyone else, by the man who, being in charge of the conduct of the war on the other side, realized it most fully: Winston Churchill. In a speech before a secret session of the House of Commons on the 23rd of April, 1942, after announcing the loss of the *Ark Royal*, the *Barham*, the *Repulse* and the *Prince of Wales*, he continued as follows:

A further sinister stroke was to come. On the early morning of December 19 half a dozen Italians in unusual diving suits were captured floundering about in the harbour of Alexandria. Extreme precautions have been taken for some time past against the varieties of human torpedo or one-man submarine entering our harbours. Not only are nets and other obstructions used but underwater charges are exploded at frequent irregular intervals in the fairway. None the less these men had penetrated the harbour. Four hours later explosions occurred in the bottoms of the *Valiant* and the *Queen Elizabeth*, produced by limpet bombs fixed with extraordinary courage and ingenuity, the effect of which was to blow large holes in the bottoms of both ships and to flood several compartments, thus putting them both out of action for many months. One ship will soon be ready again, the other is still in the floating dock at Alexandria, a constant target for enemy air attack. Thus we no longer had any battle squadron in the Mediterranean. *Barham* had gone and now *Valiant* and *Queen Elizabeth* were completely out of action. Both these ships floated on an even keel, they looked all right from the air. The enemy were for some time unaware of the success of their attack,* and it is only now that I feel it possible to make this disclosure to the House even in the strictness of a Secret Session. The Italian fleet still contains four or five battleships, several times repaired, of the new *Littorio* or of the modernized class. The sea defence of the Nile valley had to be confided to our submarine and destroyer flotillas, with a few cruisers, and of course to shore based Air forces. For this reason it was necessary to transfer a part of our shore based torpedo-carrying aircraft from the south and east coasts of England, where they were soon to be needed, to the north African shore . . .

The decoration, that of the Military Order of Savoy, which was conferred upon me, on the King's own initiative, after the Alexandria operations, was accompanied by the following citation:

Commanding officer of a submarine detailed to the Tenth Light

* This assertion is disproved by the Italian war Bulletins quoted above. (Author's note.)

Flotilla for special assault craft operations, he had already successfully carried out three daring and difficult undertakings; he studied and prepared, with great technical competence and shrewdness, the plan of a fourth operation, for forcing a further enemy base. He took his submarine close in to the heavily fortified harbour, facing with cool determination the risks incurred from the defence measures and vigilance of the enemy, in order to put the assault craft in the best possible position for forcing the enemy base. He then launched the assault craft in an action which achieved a brilliant success, leading as it did to the infliction of serious damage upon two enemy battleships.

THE FLYING TIGERS
Claire L. Chennault

The legendary Flying Tigers squadron – more properly the American Volunteer Group of the Chinese Nationalist Airforce – were the brainchild of Claire Chennault, a former USAAF pilot who had become the air adviser to the Chinese government of Chiang Kai Chek. Chennault's appointment in 1937 had virtually coincided with the Japanese invasion of China, to which the CNAF had only been able to put up a token resistance. Eventually, though, Chennault persuaded the Chinese government to bolster its airforce by buying 100 Curtiss Tomahawk fighters (P-40s) from the US, while he himself – with President Roosevelt's permission – recruited volunteer pilots for it from the US airforces. By spring 1941, 109 pilots from the US Marine Corps, the US Navy, the USAAF and civilian flying clubs had joined the American Volunteer Group (AWG).

Training lasted until December 1941, in which month the AWG flew its first missions against the Japanese. By now the USA itself was at war with Japan, but the Tigers retained their volunteer status until the summer of 1942, when they were reorganized as the 23rd Fighter Group of the USAAF. In seven months of fighting, the pilots of the AWG, in their shark-mouthed P-40s, had shot down 297 Japanese aircraft for the loss of 80 planes over the skies of China and Burma.

Below is Colonel Claire L. Chennault's personal account of the first AWG sorties against the Japanese, December 1941.

MY WORST FEARS in thirty years of flying and nearly a decade of combat came during the first weeks after the attack on Pearl Harbor over the possibility of getting caught on the ground by a Japanese air assault on the A.V.G. at Toungoo. This fear had been gnawing at me ever since mid-October when the volunteer group began to take shape as a combat unit and I ordered the first aerial reconnaissance over the Japanese-built airfields in Thailand. I knew the Japanese were well informed on the condition of my group. I also knew they would have scant regard for the neutrality of Burma if they considered the A.V.G. a real menace to their activities in China. After Pearl Harbor I considered a Japanese attack on Toungoo a certainty. My only thought was to meet it with my planes in the air. During my long fight against the Japanese I constantly strove to put myself in the place of the enemy air commanders and diagnose their probable tactics. Generally my experience proved I allotted them too much credit.

Nearly half the A.V.G. men at Toungoo were Navy men and many of them had served at Pearl Harbor. I too had my own memories of Hawaii in the days when the 19th Fighter Squadron, which I commanded, was based on Ford Island as part of the air defenses of Pearl Harbor. In 1925 we experienced one of the Japanese attack scares that periodically swept the islands. It proved to be a baseless rumor. However, for three weeks I had the 19th Fighter Squadron warming up their planes in the dark of early morning. We took off before the first streaks of dawn to rendezvous over Oahu at 10,000 feet where it was already day. We patrolled the approaches to Pearl Harbor until long after sunrise hit the ground. There were no orders from my superiors to stand this alert, and our squadron took a lot of ribbing for the performance. I knew, as does every Regular Army officer, that the first responsibility of a unit commander – whether he heads an infantry platoon or an air force – is to take measures to ensure his own unit against tactical surprise by the enemy. The transition from peace to war comes hard for civilians, but for professional soldiers there is no excuse. If I had been caught with my planes on the ground, as were the Air Corps commanders in the Philippines and in Hawaii, I could never again have looked my fellow officers squarely in the eye.

The lightness with which this cardinal military sin was excused by the American high command when committed by Regular Army officers has always seemed to me one of the more shocking aspects of the war. Americans have been prone to excuse the failings of their military leaders partly because of the glow of final victory and partly because they still lack all the facts from which to form an honest and accurate appraisal – facts that have been carefully withheld from the public under the guise of censorship allegedly necessary to military security. It is high time the American people made it their business to find out more about why the men they paid for twenty years to provide for the national defense were so pitifully unprepared for the catastrophe that nearly engulfed us all. The penalty for the failure to do so will be a new and even more disastrous Pearl Harbor.

The Japanese attack on Hawaii confronted me with an abrupt change in plans. Although my fighter squadrons at Toungoo were ready for action, other phases of the project were in a more precarious state. Except for the P-40 tires sent by General MacArthur and Admiral Hart from the Philippines, we had no spares so vitally needed to keep the planes repaired after combat. Hudson bombers for the Second American Volunteer Group were parked on Lockheed's airport at Burbank, California. They were immediately taken over by the Air Corps, and we heard no more of them until they arrived in China for the Chinese Air Force in the late summer of 1942. A sizeable group of bomber crews already at sea on their way to Burma were diverted to Australia and inducted into the U.S. Army. First shipment of replacement fighter pilots met the same fate.

Events of December 7 and 8 made it clear that the fighter group was the only salvage from all the elaborate plans that had been so painstakingly woven in Washington. Had I known then that for over a year this fighter group would be the only effective Allied air force to oppose the Japanese on the Asiatic mainland I probably would not have entered the combat with such high hopes.

It was immediately evident that both ends of the Burma Road would have to be defended from heavy air assaults since the wrecking of Rangoon, the port of entry, and Kunming, the main division point in China, by air attack would offer a relatively cheap and effective means of tightening the Japanese fingers on China's throat without draining the far-flung enemy offensives in the southern Pacific. Rangoon was the only funnel through which supplies could still come to China. Kunming was the vital valve in China that controlled distribution of supplies to the Chinese armies in the field.

From the beginning there was dissension among the new Allies. The Generalissimo offered the British six divisions of his best troops and all of his heavy motorized artillery for the defense of Burma. The British spurned the offer, and Chiang's troops sat idle in Yunnan until March 1942 when the fall of Rangoon finally convinced the British they needed help. The British however showed no such reluctance over the American Volunteer Group of the Chinese Air Force. They pressed hard for transfer of the entire group to Rangoon to operate under R.A.F. command.

I opposed this transfer just as stubbornly as the British refused the help of Chinese ground troops. Early in the fall I conferred with Group Captain Manning over the aerial defense of Rangoon. He then had no warning net and only a single runway at Mingaladon, ten miles from Rangoon, on which to base his fighters. I suggested he build some dispersal fields to the west of Rangoon and fill in the gap between the new fields and the Thailand border with a network of air spotters' posts linked by special telephone and radio. With those facilities our fighters would have been able to meet the enemy over Rangoon with plenty of warning and altitude and be securely protected on the ground at fields beyond the Japs' range. I had learned early in this long game against the Japanese that it is suicide to fight air battles without adequate warning of the enemy's attacks and a main base out of his range. Manning, however, regarded his single runway within Japanese range as adequate and placed a reliance on his combination of radar and long-distance phone that was never borne out by experience. Manning had also committed the R.A.F. under his command to combat tactics that I regarded as suicidal. By serving under his command, I would have lost my own authority over the group and forced my pilots to accept his stupid orders. All during the period we were negotiating for transfer of all or a part of the A.V.G. to Rangoon, Manning refused to allow me to enter his fighter-control room or become familiar with any of the facilities that we were supposed to use jointly in the air defense of Rangoon.

We finally worked out an agreement, satisfactory to both the Generalissimo and the British, whereby one squadron of the A.V.G. would assist the R.A.F. in the defense of Rangoon with the other two squadrons to be stationed at Kunming, the China end of the Burma Road, where we had adequate warning net and dispersal fields. The Rangoon squadron remained under my direct command subject only to operational control by the senior R.A.F. officer in Burma. In this way the American pilots remained free to use their own tactics while coming under strategic direction of the R.A.F. Manning agreed to provide housing, transportation, food, and communications for the American squadron at Rangoon. This he failed to do.

The day after Pearl Harbor (December 9 by our calendar) we had half a dozen false alerts. With each new clang of the brass warning bell, Tom Trumble, my secretary, grabbed his rifle and tin hat and dashed for the slit trenches while I slung on my binoculars and trotted to the control tower. On December 10 Thailand "surrendered" to the Japanese, and enemy troops, ships, and planes poured into Bangkok to establish a base for the assault on Burma and Malaya. I sent Erik Shilling on a photo-reconnaissance mission over Bangkok in a special stripped-down P-40 equipped with an R.A.F. aerial camera. This improvised photo plane was about 18 miles per hour faster and could climb 3,000 feet higher than the average P-40, but it was completely outclassed by the speedy Japanese high-altitude photo planes that continued to do their work unmolested over Asia until the first Lockheed Lightnings (P-38) arrived in China in the summer of 1943. Escorted by Ed Rector of Marshal, North Carolina, and Bert Christman of Fort Collins, Colorado, in regular P-40s, Shilling photographed the docks and airfields of Bangkok from 26,000 feet.

When I saw his pictures, I exploded. Docks along the Menam River were jammed with enemy transports disgorging troops and supplies. Don Maung airdrome outside the city was packed with Japanese aircraft, parked wing tip to wing tip and awaiting dispersal to the chain of advanced bases closer to the Burma border. A dozen bombers could have wrecked the Japanese air offensive in twenty minutes.

This was but one of the many times during the war when a kingdom was lost for want of a few planes.

The Third A.V.G. Squadron commanded by Arvid Olson, of Hollywood, California, moved to Mingaladon airdrome on December 12 to join the R.A.F. in the defense of Rangoon. At Toungoo we encouraged every possible movement rumor about the rest of the group to confuse the Burmese spies while we tied up our loose ends preparatory to establishing a new base at Kunming. There were still twenty-five pilots not sufficiently trained to be turned loose in combat and a dozen P-40s under repair at Toungoo, but when the radio crackled from Kunming that the Japanese were bombing the city on December 18, it was apparent that the time to move had come.

The group was so organized that everything essential to immediate combat operations could be airborne. Permanent base personnel and supplies left Toungoo by truck convoy up the Burma Road. Three C.N.A.C. transports swooped down on Toungoo on the afternoon of the eighteenth and whisked me, my combat staff, and the oxygen, ammunition, and spare parts we needed for fighting to Kunming before dawn the next day.

The First and Second Squadrons flew from Toungoo to Kunming on the afternoon of the eighteenth with a refueling stop at Lashio. At Toungoo the First Squadron circled on patrol covering the Second Squadron's take-off, and at Kunming the roles were reversed as the Second stayed in the air until the First Squadron had landed, refueled, and was ready for combat again at Kunming.

By dawn on the nineteenth we had thirty-four P-40s ready to fight at Kunming with a fighter-control headquarters hooked into the Yunnan warning net and the Chinese code rooms that were monitoring Japanese operational radio frequencies and decoding enemy messages. For the first time since mid-October I breathed easier.

It was this kind of lightning mobility that was necessary to realize the full potential of airpower. To achieve it meant that I would always have to operate on a skeletonized basis with airmen doubling in ground duties and a few key men doing the work of an entire staff. It meant that I could never afford the excess staff personnel required by more orthodox military organizations.

It was this ability to shift my combat operations six hundred and fifty miles in an afternoon and a thousand miles in twenty-four hours that kept the Japanese off balance for four bloody years and prevented them from landing a counterpunch with their numerically superior strength that might easily have put my always meager forces out of business.

We had little strain on our patience for the first pay-off on these tactics. December 19 passed quietly with three P-40 reconnaissance patrols over southern Yunnan but no sign of life from the enemy. At 9:45 A.M. on the twentieth my special phone from the Chinese code room rang. It was Colonel Wong Shu Ming, commander of the Chinese Fifth Air Force and Chinese chief of staff for the A.V.G. His message said, "Ten Japanese bombers crossed the Yunnan border at Laokay heading northwest."

From then on the battle unfolded over Yunnan as it had done a hundred times before in my head. Reports filtered in from the Yunnan net as the enemy bombers penetrated deeper into China.

"Heavy engine noise at station X-10."

"Unknowns overhead at station P-8."

"Noise of many above clouds at station C-23."

Position reports recorded on our fighter-control board added up to a course designed to bring the enemy bombers to about fifty miles east of Kunming, from which point they would probably begin the circling and feinting tactics designed to confuse the warning net before their final dash to the target.

I ordered the Second Squadron to make the interception. Jack Newkirk, of Scarsdale, New York, led one four-plane element in search of the bombers while Jim Howard, of St. Louis, son of former medical missionaries in China, led another four-plane formation on defensive patrol above Kunming. Sixteen planes of the First Squadron commanded by Robert Sandell, of San Antonio, Texas, were held in reserve in the stand-by area west of Kunming, ready to join the fray at the decisive moment.

I fired a red flare sending the Second and First Squadrons into the air and drove with my executive officer, Harvey Greenlaw, and interpreter, Colonel Hsu, to the great timbered clay pyramid looming above the grassy mounds of a Chinese graveyard on a gentle slope overlooking the field. This was our combat-operations shelter with a duplicate set of radio and phone communications. Inside the dark, dank interior we studied the plotting board by the light of matches held by Greenlaw while Hsu took phone reports from the Chinese net. Outside, the winter air of the Kunming plateau was crisp and clear. Scattered puffball clouds floated lazily above the city at 10,000 feet. Weather reports to the south indicated a solid overcast brushing the mountain peaks.

This was the decisive moment I had been awaiting for more than four years – American pilots in American fighter planes aided by a Chinese ground warning net about to tackle a formation of the Imperial Japanese Air Force, which was then sweeping the Pacific skies victorious everywhere. I felt that the fate of China was riding in the P-40 cockpits through the wintery sky over Yunnan. I yearned heartily to be ten years younger and crouched in a cockpit instead of a dugout, tasting the stale rubber of an oxygen mask and peering ahead into limitless space through the cherry-red rings of a gunsight.

Suddenly voices broke through the crackling radio static.

"There they are."

"No, no, they can't be Japs."

"Look at those red balls."

"Let's get 'em."

Then maddening silence. I ordered Sandell's reserve squadron to dive to Iliang about thirty miles southeast of Kunming along the Japs' line of probable approach. There was nothing more on the radio. The Chinese net reported the bombers had reversed course and were heading back toward Indo-China. Sounds of gunfire were heard, and the heavy fall of Japanese bombs in the mountains near Iliang was reported. There was nothing to do but return to the field and wait.

Chinese were already streaming back to the city from their refuge among the grave mounds, incredulous that no bombs had fallen. Howard's patrol over Kunming came down. They had seen nothing. Newkirk's flight returned, sheepish and chagrined over a bad case of buck fever on their first contact with the enemy. They had sighted the Jap formation of ten gray twin-engined bombers about thirty miles southeast of Kunming, but for a few incredulous seconds could hardly believe the bombers were really Japs. The bombers jettisoned their bombs, put their noses down for speed, and wheeled back toward Indo-China. By the time Newkirk's flight recovered and opened fire, the bombers had too big a lead – too big that is for everybody except Ed Rector. The last the other pilots saw of Rector he was still chasing the Japs at full throttle.

Finally Sandell's squadron came straggling in. From the whistling of the wind in their open gun barrels and the slow rolls as they buzzed the field, we knew they had been in a fight. They had sighted the Jap formation in full retreat over Iliang about thirty miles southeast of Kunming, scuttling along on top of a solid overcast with Rector still in pursuit.

As the P-40s dived to attack, everybody went a little crazy with excitement. All the lessons of Toungoo were forgotten. There was no teamwork – only a wild melee in which all pilots agreed that only sheer luck kept P-40s from shooting each other. Pilots tried wild 90-degree deflection shots and other crazy tactics in the 130-mile running fight that followed. Fritz Wolf of Shawano, Wisconsin, shot down two bombers and then cursed his armorer because his guns jammed.

When he landed and inspected the guns, he found they were merely empty. When the P-40s broke off three Jap bombers had gone down in flames and the remainder were smoking in varying degrees. Ed Rector was the only A.V.G. casualty. His long chase left him short of gas, forcing him to crash-land his P-40 in a rice paddy east of Kumming with minor injuries.

Back at the field most of the pilots were too excited to speak coherently.

"Well, boys," I told the excited pilots, "it was a good job but not good enough. Next time get them all."

I herded them into the operations shack for an hour before

I let them eat lunch. We went over the fight in minute detail pointing out their mistakes and advising them on how to get all the bombers next time. Not until the spring of 1945 did I learn how close Sandell's flight had come to getting all the Japs in that first fight of the A.V.G.

Lewis Bishop of De Kalb Junction, New York, an A.V.G. pilot shot down five months after the Iliang battle and taken prisoner in Indo-China, met the Japanese pilot who led the raid. The Jap said his crew had been the sole survivors of the mission. Nine of the ten bombers had failed to return.

Bishop was a prisoner of the enemy for three years. He finally escaped by jumping from a moving train in North China while being transferred from Shanghai to Manchuria. He reached me in Kunming early in 1945 to write the final footnote to the A.V.G.'s first fight.

Japanese airmen never again tried to bomb Kunming while the A.V.G. defended it. For many months afterward they sniffed about the edges of the Yunnan warning net and dropped a few bombs near the border but never ventured near Kunming. Our border patrols shot down a half dozen of these half-hearted raiders, and by the spring of 1942 we were on the offensive carrying the war deep into Indo-China with dive-bombing and strafing missions. The Japs waited until sixteen months after their first defeat to launch another mission against Kunming in the spring of 1943, when they knew I was in Washington attending the Trident Conferences of the British-American Combined Chiefs of Staff. Then they brought thirty fighters to protect their bombers.

Although the A.V.G. was blooded over China, it was the air battles over Rangoon that stamped the hallmark on its fame as the Flying Tigers. The cold statistics for the ten weeks the A.V.G. served at Rangoon show its strength varied between twenty and five serviceable P-40s. This tiny force met a total of a thousand-odd Japanese aircraft over southern Burma and Thailand. In 31 encounters they destroyed 217 enemy planes and probably destroyed 43. Our losses in combat were four pilots killed in the air, one killed while strafing, and one taken prisoner. Sixteen P-40s were destroyed. During the same period the R.A.F., fighting side by side with the A.V.G., destroyed 74 enemy planes, probably destroyed 33, with a loss of 22 Buffaloes and Hurricanes.

Winston Churchill, then prime minister of the United Kingdom, added his eloquence to these statistics, cabling the Governor of Burma, "The victories of these Americans over the rice paddies of Burma are comparable in character if not in scope with those won by the R.A.F. over the hop fields of Kent in the Battle of Britain."

Air Vice Marshal D. F. Stevenson, who replaced Manning in January 1942, noted that while the ratio of British to German planes in the Battle of Britain had been 1 to 4, the ratio of Anglo-American fighters to Japanese planes over Rangoon was 1 to from 4 to 14.

The Japanese began their aerial assault on Rangoon with a strength of 150 fighters and bombers based on a few fields in southern Thailand. In Burma, the Allies could muster only 16 P-40s of the A.V.G., 20 Buffaloes of the R.A.F., some ancient British Lysanders of the India Air Force, and a few Tiger Moth training planes. As I anticipated, the radar-phone combination of the R.A.F. warning system failed to provide adequate warning. Many times the only warning my pilots received was a hurried phone call, "Bombers overhead," or the noise and dust of the R.A.F. Buffaloes scrambling for an alert. Numerous A.V.G. interceptions were made only after the enemy finished bombing and was leaving the target due to the inadequate warning. When the R.A.F. indicated that its only attempts to bolster the warning system consisted of providing advanced ground troops with heliographs to flash warning messages, I fought vigorously to withdraw the A.V.G. from what I considered an unnecessarily exposed position. Only the heavy pressure of the Anglo-American Combined Chiefs of Staff and the Generalissimo prevented me from doing so.

Shortly before the Rangoon battles began, the A.V.G. suffered its final blow from William D. Pawley. The contract between Pawley and the Chinese government provided that I could call on Pawley's Central Aircraft Manufacturing Company for technical personnel, tools, and materials for repairing damaged P-40s of the A.V.G. At a conference with

General Chow, chief of the Chinese Aeronautical Commission, in September it was agreed that all A.V.G. repair work west of the Salween River would be handled by CAMCO's Loi-Wing plant, located in Yunnan just across the Burma border, while the Chinese Air Force repair shop in Kunming would do all servicing east of the Salween.

As damaged planes began to pile up during training at Toungoo, I made repeated requests to Pawley for men and materials from his Loi-Wing plant to repair them. A few CAMCO men were sent to Toungoo but it was decided to do only emergency work there and to ship badly damaged planes over the Burma railroad to Lashio and thence by truck to the Loi-Wing factory. A number of P-40s were shipped to Loi-Wing, but after they arrived, little work was done on them.

CAMCO was engaged in the assembly of Curtiss-Wright Model 21 fighters and some trainers, which Pawley had already sold to the Chinese government. Pawley claimed that repairing A.V.G. planes interfered with his assembly program. I argued that repair of proven combat planes for experienced pilots rated higher priority than the assembly of trainers and experimental fighters. We also disagreed over the need for an A.V.G. squadron to be stationed at Loi-Wing for the protection of his factory. At that time the possibility of enemy air action against Loi-Wing was too remote to be considered seriously.

In mid-December Pawley issued an order to his American employees at Loi-Wing, forbidding them to touch an A.V.G. plane, and followed this with a radio to me that, as of January 1, CAMCO would do no more repair work on A.V.G. P-40s. I replied that Pawley's inability to do this work was regretted, but we would manage without him.

Loss of the CAMCO repair base was a serious blow to the group since we were already fighting over Rangoon. I took the matter to the Generalissimo in Chungking. He ordered the Chinese manager of CAMCO, Colonel Chen, to continue repairing A.V.G. planes. Chen did an excellent job for us until the plant was burned and abandoned in the face of the Japanese advance into Yunnan. The Chinese government acquired Pawley's interest in CAMCO, and he flew off to India where he had already begun construction of another aircraft plant.

I have always suspected that Pawley, like the Japanese, thoroughly believed the British and American intelligence reports that the A.V.G. would not last three weeks in combat. At any rate on the occasions when he had a chance to provide the A.V.G. with badly needed assistance, Pawley exhibited what I considered a remarkable lack of co-operation. It was only after the A.V.G.'s combat record had made the organization world famous that Pawley made strenuous efforts to have himself identified with it, even to the extent of attempting to secure an honorary membership of the Flying Tigers Incorporated, the only authentic postwar organization of former A.V.G. men, by offering a ten-thousand-dollar contribution to the corporation's funds. His offer was flatly rejected by the membership, who apparently felt that a few repaired P-40s during the dark days of 1941–42 would have been more valuable to them than a postwar check. After a succession of wartime manufacturing ventures, Pawley embarked on a diplomatic career as ambassador to Peru and Brazil. No doubt he found the Medal for Merit awarded him for "organizing the Flying Tigers" useful in his new work.

Two days before Christmas the Japanese shot their first aerial bolt against Rangoon with 54 bombers escorted by 20 fighters. The low fighter-bomber ratio indicated that the Japanese were confident and expected little trouble from the Allied air defense. There was no warning at Mingaladon. The Third Squadron was casually ordered to clear the field. While still climbing they were informed by R.A.F. fighter control, "Enemy approaching from the east."

The Japanese had finished bombing and were on their way home before the A.V.G. sighted the formation. Jap fighters were diving on the city, strafing the crowds of civilians who jammed the streets to watch the raid. One bomber formation hit Mingaladon Field, and the other laid their eggs along the docks. In the brief fight that followed, the Americans shot down six Japanese planes and lost two of their own pilots – Neil Martin of Texarkana, Arkansas, riddled by a quartet of

Jap fighters, and Henry Gilbert of Bremerton, Washington, blown up by the top-turret fire of the bomber formations. The R.A.F. failed to make contact.

This raid put the torch of panic to Rangoon. Those who were rich enough to do so fled for their lives to India. Native Burmese rioted, looted, and began potting stray Britons. All the native cooks and servants fled from Mingaladon, leaving the A.V.G. without a mess. For two days they lived mainly on stale bread and canned beer, of which there seemed to be an ample stock.

On a cloudless Christmas day with the temperature at 115 degrees in the sun the Japanese came back to finish off Rangoon. They figured 60 bombers and 30 fighters would be ample for the job. This time 12 P-40s were waiting at altitude and sailed into the Japanese formations as they droned toward the city. "Like rowboats attacking the Spanish Armada," one observer on the ground described the attack. The R.A.F. put 16 Buffaloes into the fray later.

"It was like shooting ducks," Squadron Leader Olson radioed me at Kunming. "We got 15 bombers and 9 fighters. Could put entire Jap force out of commission with whole group here."

A.V.G. losses were 2 planes. Both pilots bailed out safely. The R.A.F. got 7 Jap planes and lost 9 Buffaloes and 6 pilots.

William Pawley happened to be in Rangoon that memorable Christmas and apparently suffered a slight change of heart in his attitude toward the A.V.G. He loaded a truck full of food and drink in Rangoon and drove it to Mingaladon to present the Third Squadron with Christmas dinner. Under the shade of banyan trees around the airport rim, with the smoke of burning Japanese wrecks still rising from the jungles beyond, the Third Squadron squatted to a dinner of ham and chicken liberally lubricated by beer and Scotch. The rest of the group, eight hundred miles to the north on the frosty Kunming plateau, dined on Yunnan duck and rice wine.

After the Christmas battle, the Third Squadron had only 11 serviceable P-40s left. Olson radioed for help, and I sent the Second Squadron, led by Newkirk, to relieve him. By the first week in January the transfer was completed, and the pattern of the Japanese effort against Rangoon became apparent.

While they gathered strength for another mass daylight assault, the Japanese sent night bombers to harass Rangoon, slipping in singly all night long to gain maximum nuisance value. A.V.G. efforts to halt them were unsuccessful, but the R.A.F. bagged several. Meanwhile the A.V.G. took the offensive, prowling the enemy fields in Thailand to smash their planes on the ground. Newkirk and "Tex" Hill led many of these early strafing attacks on the Jap airfields.

While the A.V.G. P-40s fought to keep the port of Rangoon open, our ground crews were working like beavers on the docks loading truck convoys with lend-lease equipment for shipment up the Burma Road to China. It was during this period, with the hot breath of the Japanese blowing on our necks, that the Burma Road first delivered twenty thousand tons a month to China. These supplies, trucked out of Burma before the fall of Rangoon, enabled the A.V.G. to continue operations in China long after every land line of communication with that unhappy land had been severed by the enemy. Every type of A.V.G. nonflying personnel, including our chaplain, Paul Frillman, of Maywood, Illinois, sweated like coolies on the Rangoon docks during those hectic weeks.

By the last week in January the Japanese were ready for another knockout attempt on Rangoon. From January 23 to 28 six major attacks of up to one hundred planes each rolled over the Burmese port. It was a tribute to the Anglo-American fighter pilots that the Japanese formations had switched to a three-to-one ratio of fighters protecting small bomber formations.

On January 23 and 24 the Japanese tried to floor the A.V.G. with a series of one-two punches. They led with a fighter sweep designed to get the Allied fighters into the air and use up their fuel. Then a second wave was scheduled to deliver the knockout punch while the A.V.G. and R.A.F. were on the ground refueling. It was a good plan but it didn't work. A.V.G. ground crews were too fast on refueling and rearming the P-40s and had them ready to fight again before the second wave of Japs appeared. By January 28 the Japs were sending over only large fighter formations, and the score for this offensive stood at 50 Jap planes destroyed against a loss of 2 A.V.G. pilots and 10 R.A.F. pilots killed.

Newkirk radioed Kunming, "The more hardships, work, and fighting the men have to do the higher our morale goes. Squadron spirit really strong now."

However strong the Second Squadron's spirit, they were down to ten P-40s, so I sent Bob Sandell and his First Squadron to take up the burden at Rangoon. The Japanese ground offensive into Burma had begun to roll during the last weeks in January, and it was evident that the British had neither the men, equipment, nor leadership to stop it.

Before I left the United States in the summer of 1941 I asked a few friends in Louisiana to watch the newspapers and send me any clippings about the A.V.G. Now I was being swamped with clippings from stateside newspapers, and my men were astonished to find themselves world famous as the Flying Tigers. The insignia we made famous was by no means original with the A.V.G. Our pilots copied the shark-tooth design on their P-40s' noses from a colored illustration in the *India Illustrated* Weekly depicting an R.A.F. squadron in the Libyan desert with shark-nosed P-40s. Even before that the German Air Force painted shark's teeth on some of its Messerschmitt 210 fighters. With the pointed nose of a liquid-cooled engine it was an apt and fearsome design. How the term Flying Tigers was derived from the shark-nosed P-40s I never will know. At any rate we were somewhat surprised to find ourselves billed under that name. It was not until just before the A.V.G. was disbanded that we had any kind of group insignia. At the request of China Defense Supplies in Washington, Roy Williams of the Walt Disney organization in Hollywood designed our insignia consisting of a winged tiger flying through a large V for victory.

Although the Flying Tiger victories made ready front-page copy for an Allied world rocked by a series of shattering defeats, I noticed too much tendency to attribute our success to sheer derring-do or some mystical quality and not enough on the solid facts on which our triumphs were really based.

Whatever its later shortcomings, the Curtiss-Wright P-40

was an excellent fighter for the battles over Rangoon, all of which were fought below 20,000 feet. At those altitudes the P-40 was better than a Hurricane and at its best against the Japanese Army Nates and Navy Model Zeros. The two .50-caliber machine guns gave the P-40 a heavy, fast-firing gun that neither the British nor Japs could match. Pilot armor saved many a P-40 pilot's life, and the heavy rugged construction, though a disadvantage in maneuverability, was certainly an advantage in field maintenance and putting damaged planes back into battle. P-40s could be repaired after damage that would have made a Japanese plane a total loss.

The ground crews were a vital factor that most newspaper correspondents on the spot overlooked. It was the speed with which the ground crews repaired, refueled, and rearmed the P-40s that kept the A.V.G. from being floored by the Japanese one-two punches. The ground crews displayed ingenuity and energy in repairing battle-damaged P-40s that I have seldom seen equaled and never excelled. Their performance at Rangoon was in many ways symbolic, for in all the long years of the war to come, it was American maintenance that was one of the keystones in our eventual arch of triumph. Until the very end of the Rangoon holocaust our ground crews managed to keep a minimum of 10 P-40s ready to fight every day. In contrast the R.A.F. commander, Air Vice Marshal Stevenson, complained of his maintenance men who allowed a squadron of 30 Hurricanes arriving in January to slump to 11 planes fit for combat by mid-February and only 6 by March. I had never favored liquid-cooled engines for combat planes but the Allison engines in our P-40s certainly did more than the manufacturer claimed for them.

Our leadership at Rangoon was also superior. All of the squadron leaders who saw action there – Olson; Sandell and Newkirk before they were killed; "Tex" Hill of Hunt, Texas; and Bob Neale, of Seattle, Washington, were leaders of the highest quality. It was no accident that Hill and Olson became full colonels and commanded Army Air Forces fighter groups in combat or that the A.A.F. offered a lieutenant colonelcy to Bob Neale, who entered the A.V.G. as a Navy ensign.

Above all it was the kind of teamwork that is so typically American, wherein there is plenty of scope for individual brilliance but everybody contributes toward a common goal. You can see it on an autumn Saturday afternoon in a top-notch football team. It will take the same kind of well-co-ordinated teamwork to operate a guided-missile or push-button group in the next war or to pull us through the perils of peace.

In January my annual attack of chronic bronchitis laid me low in Kunming, and a projected trip to Rangoon had to be canceled. I alternated between brief spells in my airfield office and longer sieges in my sickbed at the University of Kunming where the A.V.G. was quartered. A radio was installed near my bed, so I could listen to the radio chatter of my pilots during their fights over Rangoon. It was over this radio that I heard of the Japanese attack on Toungoo, February 4. They struck at 6 A.M. There was no warning. All personnel were asleep. The operations building and a hangar were destroyed by direct hits; three P-40s still under repair were wrecked; and half a dozen R.A.F. Blenheims burned. That might all too easily have been the fate of the entire A.V.G. eight weeks earlier.

After the fall of Singapore in mid-February, the Japanese transferred the crack air units that blasted the R.A.F. out of the Malayan air to Thailand to join the assault on Rangoon. These reinforcements boosted enemy plane strength available to attack Rangoon to four hundred planes. Before the month's end, they were hammering at the city with two hundred planes a day.

It was during this period that a handful of battered P-40s flown by Bob Neale's First Squadron pilots wrote the final lurid chapter in the A.V.G. history of Rangoon. Neale had become First Squadron leader after the death of Bob Sandell, who died flight-testing a repaired P-40 over Mingaladon. Since the fall of Rangoon was already looming, Neale no longer retained damaged planes at Mingaladon but had them flown or shipped north by rail. About this time I also ordered Neale to cease all strafing and bomber-escort missions due to the worn condition of the P-40 engines, which were long overdue for overhaul. The fact that shark-nosed planes were observed flying north and were no longer seen over Thailand airdromes or accompanying R.A.F. bombers gave rise to rumors that the A.V.G. had left Rangoon. Neale radioed me for orders regarding the actual evacuation. I replied, "Expend equipment. Conserve personnel utmost. Retire with last bottle oxygen."

Neale took me literally. With 9 P-40s he waited for the final Japanese daylight assaults with their crack units from Singapore. R.A.F. strength had dwindled too. All the Buffaloes had been lost in combat or accidents. Thirty Hurricane reinforcements had shrunk to a dozen serviceable planes. New reinforcements of 18 Hurricanes and Spitfires being ferried from Calcutta to Rangoon cracked up in the Chin Hills with a loss of 11 pilots. When the Japanese began their final aerial assault on February 26, there were only 15 Allied fighters to meet the attack by 166 enemy planes. They fought off three raids on the twenty-fifth with the A.V.G. bagging 24 Jap planes. The next day was even worse, with 200 enemy planes over Rangoon. The A.V.G., now reduced to 6 P40s, bagged 18 Jap fighters to bring their two-day total to 43 enemy aircraft without loss to themselves.

In those two days of almost constant air fighting Neale's detachment turned in one of the epic fighter performances of all time. With the best of equipment it would have been a brilliant victory, but under the conditions Neale and his eight pilots fought, it was an incredible feat. The report of Fritz Wolf, who left Rangoon just before the final battles began, describes those conditions well.

> Planes at Rangoon are almost unflyable. Tires are chewed up and baked hard. They blow out continually. We are short on them, and battery plates are thin. When we recharge them, they wear out within a day. There is no Prestone oil coolant in Rangoon. British destroyed the battery-charging and oxygen-storage depots without any advance warning to us so we could stock up. We are completely out of auxiliary gear shifts and they are wearing out in the planes every day.

Fresh food of any kind is completely lacking. We are living out of cans. Water is hard to get. Most of the city water supply has been cut off.

Dust on the field fouls up the P-40 engines considerably. It clogs carburetion so much that it is dangerous to increase manifold pressure when the engine quits cold. Entire carburetion systems are cleaned on the ground, but they are as bad as ever after a single day's operations. This tendency of engines to quit makes it hard to dogfight or strafe. Of the eight planes that took off for an air raid two days ago, only five got off the ground.

Conditions in Rangoon are getting dangerous. Authorities have released criminals, lunatics, and lepers to fend for themselves. Natives have broken into unguarded liquor stocks and are in a dangerous state. There are continual knifings and killings. Three British were killed near the docks a few nights ago. Stores are all closed. At least twenty-five blocks of the city are burning furiously. All fire trucks were sent up the Prome Road to Mandalay several weeks ago.

Our only contact with British intelligence was a visit from one officer about ten days ago. There seems to be little co-operation between the R.A.F. and British Army and less between the R.A.F. and us. It seems certain that the Japanese have crossed the Sittang River (only eighty miles from Rangoon), but we have had no word on it.

On the night of February 27 the R.A.F. removed the radar set from Rangoon without previous notice to the A.V.G. For Neale that was the last straw. The next morning he sent four of his remaining six P-40s to cover the route of the last A.V.G. truck convoy to leave Rangoon. He and his wingman, R. T. Smith, later an A.A.F. fighter group commander, stayed to make a final search for an A.V.G. pilot who had bailed out over the jungle some days before. Neale ripped out his own radio and enlarged the baggage compartment to hold a stretcher case if the pilot turned up injured. Neale and Smith sweated out February 28 waiting for news of the lost pilot, Edward Liebolt. The next day the Japanese cut the Prome Road, last land line of retreat from Rangoon. Neale and Smith jammed two cases of whisky into Neale's baggage compartment and took off for Magwe, two hundred miles to the north. Two days later the Japanese Army entered Rangoon.

The battle of southern Burma was over.

SAINT NAZAIRE COMMANDOS
Adolphe Lepotier

The assault by British Army Commandos on the port of Saint Nazaire, on the occupied Atlantic coast of France, is widely considered to be the greatest seaborne raid of World War II. The port, which lies at the mouth of the Loire, had been a major target for the British from the time of the German occupation. Not only did it contain the largest dry-dock in the world – thus the only one which could facilitate the gigantic German battleships Tirpitz, Scharnhorst *and* Gneisenau *– it was also an important U-boat base in the Battle of the Atlantic.*

A major target, but not an easy one. Saint Nazaire was outside the range of most RAF bombers, and was heavily defended by the 28 heavy guns of the German 280 Naval Atlantic Battalion, plus a battery of railway-mounted 240 mm guns at La Baule, seven miles inland. The port also bristled with anti-aircraft artillery, and was serviced by 6000 German personnel. Moreover, the dry-dock itself – which had to be destroyed for any raid to be considered successful – had an outer caisson (wall) of steel some 35 feet thick.

In the Commandos' raid on Saint Nazaire they were accompanied by the Royal Navy escort destroyers Athelstone *and* Tynedale, *16 motor launches, a motor torpedo boat (*MTB74*) and a motor gun boat (*MGB314*). To break the caisson of the* Normandie *dock, an old destoyer, HMS* Campbeltown, *was packed with four and a quarter tons of high explosive on a time-delay pencil fuse, to be delivered by head-on ramming. This account of Operation Chariot is by the French admiral and military historian, Adolphe Lapotier. It begins with the British flotilla approaching the French coast on the night of 27 March 1942.*

THE HOURS PASSED and night drew nearer. The occupied coast was no longer far away, and the enemy had not yet given any sign of life. For the men whose nerves were keyed up this seemed incredible, and their morale rose proportionately. The *Tynedale* had obviously been quite right about her submarine.*

As a last precaution, the course of the formation was maintained in the direction of La Pallice until nightfall, so that should an enemy plane appear it could still be mistaken about the destination of this unusual task force.

"Nevertheless," said Ryder, "when night fell we all felt immensely relieved."

At 20.00 hours, seventy miles south-west of St. Nazaire, *Atherstone* slipped M.G.B. 314. Ryder, Newman and their small staff got into the small boat, which got under way to accompanying cheers from the crew.

"Don't forget I've been a good father to you," signalled *Atherstone*.

The *Campbeltown* also slipped the M.T.B. 74 which, after a few cavortings, took her place in the queue.

During this time the remaining M.L.s took up their position in the assault formation, with M.G.B. 314 ahead. Behind her came the *Campbeltown*, and astern and on the flanks the leading motor-boats of the two columns.

The *Tynedale* and *Atherstone* took up their positions provisionally about a mile apart to increase their chances of finding the submarine H.M.S. *Sturgeon*, which had taken up a position by day forty miles south-west of St. Nazaire to act as marker. It had to show a discreet light, directed south-west.

"M.L. 341 signals damage to her engine," reported Pike, the skilful signalman of M.G.B. 314.

"Tell her to transfer her Commandos to one of the M.L.s astern."

The M.L. 446 took them off and struggled to rejoin the column, leaving M.L. 341 to her own devices.

* It was learned later that this submarine was not sunk and signalled effectively that it had been attacked by two destroyers sailing on a south-westerly course.

"Light ahead."

This small light on the water could only be the discreet lamp of the *Sturgeon*. A few minutes later the M.G.B. sighted the submarine. They were close enough to thank him by megaphone. They had reached point Z of the plan. Here the escorting destroyers had to patrol, while waiting for the return of the survivors from the raid. They vanished in the darkness, while the small wooden boats and the doomed destroyer advanced alone into the semi-circle of enemy guns of all calibres.

The lights of various fishing-boats appeared on both bows. Ryder thought this was proof that the enemy had not got wind of the attack. This encounter also seemed to him a piece of luck, for the enemy radar would find it difficult to distinguish the suspicious echoes among all the normal ones given by the fishing-boats of a type and volume similar to those of the M.T.B.s.

Towards midnight they saw gun flashes in the distance, in the direction of St. Nazaire. As they approached nearer, they could make out the classic pattern of flak; searchlight beams, the firework display of shells and luminous tracers crossing each other in the sky. This evidence of the presence of friendly aircraft at the promised hour was very comforting.

As they approached the Châtelier Buoy they began to make out the coast to port. The *Campbeltown* received the order to set course at 50° and to guide the formation, for in order to use her rudimentary radar, whose transmitting and reception beam was set fore and aft, the M.G.B. would be obliged to manœuvre constantly while taking the bearings. At the same time, however, she zigzagged to take soundings in front of the columns.

On the fluorescent radar screen the luminous teeth of the "pipes" appeared and disappeared, according to the evolution of the boat, each time it set its course on some protruding object. A very much larger "pipe" appeared when it headed to port. Their course allowed them to pinpoint this obstacle, and at 01.25 hours they could distinguish the big Morées Tower, 400 yards away to the north.

After thirty-three hours of navigation, out of sight of land, the British ships had arrived exactly at their fixed point, despite changes of course and the variable currents met with on the way. Their meeting with *Sturgeon* was another example of the precision of this navigation.

This was the moment when the excitement reached its climax. They were nearing the target. It seemed more and more improbable that the Germans realized eighteen enemy ships were entering a roadstead where they had concentrated every conceivable weapon of lookout, detection and defence.

They wondered if this indifference were merely a ruse and whether they intended to let them come close in before crushing them at one blow.

For the *Campbeltown* there was an additional worry. Was there enough water for her to pass over the Mindin sand bank?

Suddenly all the men on the bridge looked at each other anxiously. By a vibration of the hull beneath their feet, which could deceive no sailor, they realised that the destroyer had touched bottom.

Would she get across?

They bent anxiously over the side to gauge the slowing down of the wake. Their speed seemed constant.

Another jolt. Another anxious moment. They had made it!

Their mates in the M.L.s did not know that a few inches less water and the *Campbeltown* would have been stopped for good a few hundred yards from the goal, even before the enemy had intervened.

But could the Germans wait much longer?

Nerves were keyed up to breaking-point, waiting for what would happen from one minute to the next.

What form would it take?

At that moment the sky was entirely covered by low cloud, through which the moonlight hardly trickled. White wisps of mist floated past from time to time.

On board the M.G.B. they could already make out the dark lines of the outer harbour, just as twenty-four years before the men on the *Vindictive* had seen the Zeebrugge mole a few seconds before the battle began.

Suddenly the narrow beam of a searchlight from the bank lit up the roadstead. The strip of light fell astern of the flotilla.

For a few seconds, while several hundred men held breath, it moved slowly and drew near to the rear motor-boats. A moment before it reached them it went out.

Was it possible that once more the enemy had let slip the opportunity of discovering the attackers?

They did not have to wait long for the answer. Less than a minute later all the searchlights of the two banks went on simultaneously, focused on the roadstead, which was suddenly lit up as bright as day.

Despite the dark, dull paint of the hulls, all the boats were visible at once by the silver foam of their wakes. It reminded one of the appearance of the Moors in the Quadalquivir at Seville, described by Corneille:

La flotte qu'on craignait, dans le grand fleuve entrée,
Croît surprendre la ville et piller la contrée.
Les Maures vont descendre et le flux et la nuit
Dans une heure à nos murs les amènent sans bruit.
. . .
L'onde s'enfle dessous et d'un commun effort
Les Maures et la mer montent jusques au port . . .

But it was no more a question of one hour, as in the poem. In ten minutes the *Campbeltown* would have reached the target unless she suffered some major damage.

Each of the commanding officers ordered: "Full speed ahead!"

They had to start at once now, trying to delay the enemy from opening fire.

Since there was no longer any question of concealing the approach of the ships, they must try and fox the defences by trying to deceive them about their nationality. It was with this in view that the *Campbeltown* had been given the shape of a German destroyer of the identical class of those signalled that very day at sea off St. Nazaire. International law forbids hiding under an enemy flag at the moment of opening fire, but the British hoisted White Ensigns, tattered and blackened by smoke and spray – flags which a yeoman of signals would have considered unserviceable, even for stormy weather.

The little signal searchlight of a coastal battery spelt out its recognition letters in morse. The British ignored them. Leading Yeoman Pike, of the M.G.B., replied at first by illegible flashes; and to another searchlight at the entrance to the harbour, which questioned in turn, he transmitted the letters which the battery had given. A few shots were fired sporadically over their bows.

This was the moment to play the last card.

"Go ahead, Pike."

Pike, who knew how to transmit in German, signalled to his unknown interrogator: "Wait." Then he gave the indication, known to the English, of a German destroyer, followed by a long message in German, preceded by the word "Urgent": "Two vessels damaged in the course of an engagement with the enemy, request entrance to the port immediately." He finished by the signal which meant: "I still have something else to transmit."

He was about to send a message to his other interrogator, when the light batteries of the port opened fire more strongly, although still hesitatingly. Taking his most powerful Aldis lamp, Pike slowly flashed the letters of the international signal code, which meant: "I am a friend – you are mistaken."

The firing ceased again.

In another six minutes the *Campbeltown* would have reached the lock-gate. Her chances improved considerably with each second gained. The British knew that on the quays there were light cannon and machine-guns, and 40-mm. guns on Mindin Point. The heavy coastal batteries could not fire so near the port. It would therefore need a really unlucky shot to stop the destroyer now.

At last the Germans understood what was up. The storm broke loose. The only thing to do was to reply as best they could, and the leaping curves of the multi-coloured tracers crossed each other between the banks and the ships with their powerful wakes.

At that moment the M.G.B. passed a German armed trawler anchored just opposite the southern entrance. She gave it a few bursts from her pompom, and all the British ships astern followed suit as they passed the unfortunate vessel. As she dominated the M.L.s by her height, the German batteries in turn, taking her for a target, finished by sinking her.

The battle was an unequal one between the British crews, in the open, lit up by searchlights on the deck of their wooden M.L.s loaded with petrol, and the German artillery comfortably installed behind the concrete walls of their pill-boxes, hidden in the shadow of the quays and the buildings. However, the accurate fire from the sea slowed down the fire on land. It must also be mentioned that as they approached the Vieille Entrée the ships could concentrate their fire on the batteries surrounding it, while the other German coastal defences could no longer intervene.

On the bridge of the *Campbeltown* Beattie knew that on the promptness of his judgment and of his reflexes in these last moments depended the success of the main operation. Spitting clouds of smoke, the destroyer was now making nineteen knots. Each change of course had to be given in a split second. He could only make out indistinctly the details of the port in the blinding glare of the searchlights, hampered by the tracers, some of which burst on board and ricochetted in stars on the armour plating of the bridge. He suddenly noticed that his ship was heading for the end of the Vieux Môle.

"Starboard 10. Midships."

"Port 20."

Then he had to swing almost 60° to approach the gate, bows on.

The destroyer drew near. Thank God – it was in perfect alignment.

Instinctively everyone crouched. With an appalling ripping of metal, a huge spray of sparks and flames spurted from the bows. The shock was less violent than had been expected. In the engine-room they wondered whether they had really hit.

The plan had reckoned on the ramming taking place at

01.30 hours. It was 01.34 hours. The ship had penetrated almost to the opposite face of the lock-gate; in other words, to a depth of about thirty-three feet. All the forward bulkheads, torn to pieces, were firmly attached by their debris to those of the aperture. The upper part of the stern rose about six feet above the gate.

Immediately the eighty Commandos unrolled their rope ladders and climbed down from both sides onto the improvised quay. They ran off to their targets, covered by the destroyer's 20-mm., while, by the light of their torches, the special squad ran down into the holds to set the scuttling fuses.

On a level with the Vieux Môle, the M.G.B. had veered seawards to leave the *Campbeltown* a free run. She continued to reply to the fire from the light guns posted on both sides of the Vieille Entrée.

Ryder had been relieved to hear the destroyer's crash, punctuated by the spray of sparks, and to see the Commandos climbing down onto the improvised quayside.

The M.L.s of the starboard column had to land their assault troops at the stone stairs to the right of the Vieille Entrée and the jetty of the Mindin Ferry to the left of this same entrance, from the river side.

Unfortunately M.L. 192, which was leading this column, was the first to be hit by a shell, which set her on fire. Lieutenant-Commander Stevens, R.N.V.R., Flotilla Leader in Command, veered to port through the neighbouring column and managed to beach on the shallows south of the Vieux Môle.

Blinded and disturbed by this accident, the captains of M.L. 262 and 267, who were behind, missed the Vieille Entrée and had to make a complete circle in the roadstead before spotting their position again.

The next, M.L. 268, turned at the right moment to her landing point, but before reaching it was set on fire by a shell.

M.L. 156, the fifth in this column, was badly hit at the beginning of the action. More than half her crew and Commandos were out of the battle. The wheel was out of action.

It had to turn off and try to get astern of the last boat still under way.

The last boat in this column, M.L. 177 refused to be discouraged by the lot of those in front and managed to disembark her Commandos at the ferry jetty. At the same moment the M.G.B. put Colonel Newman and his staff ashore at the stairs opposite. When the M.L. 177 drew astern to leave her landing point Ryder gave it orders by megaphone to go alongside the *Campbeltown* and take off the survivors of the crew. In the meanwhile the M.G.B. made off and came alongside the stairs once more, near the lock-gate, its bows towards the Loire.

The M.T.B. 74, which approached, was hailed and stayed with the M.G.B. to await instructions. After their detour the M.L.s 262 and 267 managed to disembark their troops on the south bank of the Vieille Entrée, but they were so violently repulsed that they had to re-embark and retire beneath heavy fire.

The troops in the boats of the port column had to be disembarked at the stone stairs on the north side of the Vieux Môle.

Their main task was to take possession of the old port, which consisted of a small islet, bounded by the Loire, the St. Nazaire basin and the Vieille and Nouvelle Entrées. In order to do this they had to blow up the locks and the swing bridges connecting the islet and the mainland. The crews landed from the *Campbeltown* and the M.G.B. on the Penhoët islet, bounded by the lock and the St. Nazaire basin, had to join up with the others across the Vieille Entrée swivel bridge, which would be later destroyed, so that the general re-embarkation on the Vieux Môle would not be disturbed.

The M.L. 447, the leading ship of this column, approached the Vieux Môle to port, but was set on fire before she arrived.

The M.L. 457 which followed did not hesitate to attempt the same manœuvre and managed to land her troops. Manœuvring to return to the stairs, the enemy concentrated their fire on it and set it on fire.

Passing between the two flaming boats, the M.L. 307 made her way along the mole. She was machine-gunned at point-blank range in enfilade and grenades were hurled at her from the wall. Her fire killed several Germans on the jetty, but she had suffered several casualties, and after beaching had to set off again to attack the batteries and searchlights at Mindin.

Blinded by the searchlights, the flames and the smoke from the burning ships, Lieutenant Horlock overshot the mole. He brought his ship back to the boarding point, but came up against even stronger opposition, which forced him to turn back. Henderson, the last in the line, found himself in the same difficulties.

We have seen that M.L. 446 took on board the passengers from M.L. 341, which broke down before entering the Loire. Arriving in turn near the Vieux Môle, Lieutenant Falconer saw that the majority of his Commandos were already out of the battle. After a consultation with their N.C.O.s, he gave up the attempt at landing.

To sum up. Of all the M.L.s of the port column only M.L. 457 managed to land her troops. By an additional piece of bad luck, she was carrying a demolition group, badly equipped to fight an advance-guard action at a particularly well-defended point.

There remained the M.L.s armed with torpedoes. The M.L. 270 was hit in the stern as she was trying to silence the guns at the Vieille Entrée. She had to pull away. The M.L. 160 brought the valuable support of her fire to this zone and then returned to the Vieille Entrée, where she fired her torpedoes at a ship anchored in the outer harbour, without being able to observe the results of her fire. Lieutenant Boyd then went to the rescue of the burning boats near the Vieux Môle. He fished out three men and made a stern manœuvre to come alongside the only part of the M.L. 447 which was not yet ablaze. Surrounded by flames and smoke, he managed to embark eight soldiers, six of whom were wounded, four sailors, and, finally, in accordance with the rules of the sea, Lieutenant Platt, who completed the first day of his first command in this unforgettable manner.

The M.L. 298 fired on the batteries to the east of the lock and then on those on the Vieux Mole. Crossing a sheet of burning petrol, she caught fire. Becoming a concentrated target for the enemy, she blew up with all aboard.

On board the M.G.B., stuck against the north quay of the Vieille Entrée, Ryder did not know what had happened. The blinding searchlights pin-pointed target after target. Bursts of tracers, sparkling with gold, flame colour or silver, made the water spout on the glassy surface of the river. Tall flames and heavy black smoke rising from the boats transformed them into living torches, and a sheet of blazing petrol spread all around them. How could anyone follow the action of the various boats in these conditions? Moreover, his aerial had been shot away at the beginning of the battle. When the M.G.B. drew alongside the stairs for the second time he saw a large part of the *Campbeltown* crew arrive, carrying their wounded, but among them there was no officer capable of telling him the exact situation of the ship. He decided to go and see for himself. Pike followed at his heels to serve as a bodyguard, brandishing a broken bayonet he had found in a corner.

Hardly had the two men taken a few steps than a sentry barred their passage with a very determined air. The naval chief of the raid hastily reassured him and gave the naval password, which in actual fact was his own name – "Ryder".

The destroyer was in the exact position desired. She seemed abandoned. While the two men took shelter from bullets behind the wall of a small building, the stern was shaken by the explosion of the scuttling charges and slowly sank. There was nothing to be done except to return to his M.G.B.

At that moment they heard dull explosions coming from the pump-house and the manæuvring cabin of the lock-gate. The Commandos had carried out their missions.

For Ryder, the immediate problem was the re-embarkation at the Vieux Môle. He made his way there with his boat.

Also, it remained to utilize the torpedo mines of M.T.B. 74, since the *Campbeltown* had fulfilled her mission. They were fired against the outer gate of the Vieille Entrée lock. They hit it full in the middle and sank silently against it, as had been foreseen. After this manœuvre, the M.T.B. came alongside the M.G.B. and took aboard nine survivors from the destroyer.

"Return to England at full speed," ordered Ryder.

With her forty knots, this M.T.B. was the one with the greatest chances of coming undamaged out of this inferno.

As soon as the M.G.B. came out of the Vieille Entrée Ryder was unpleasantly surprised to find that the Vieux Môle was still stoutly defended by the enemy. The hulks of the burning M.L.s bore witness to the bitterness of the struggle. At that moment an M.L., making a new attempt, was caught in the violent fire from a concrete blockhouse on the extremity of the mole. The roofs of the neighbouring sheds were bristling with machine-guns, which added their deadly fire to that coming from the pill-box. Beneath this hail the M.L. was pierced by incendiary bullets and retired in turn, burning fiercely.

Before the M.G.B. could bring any support, another M.L. entered the slaughter. It was immediately hit and its burning petrol spread out over the black waters of the river.

Savage, the gun-layer of the M.G.B.'s pompom, directed his fire at the embrasure of the blockhouse, which momentarily ceased fire.

"Try and knock out the machine-guns on the roofs," said Curtiss.

This was very difficult, because they were situated slightly to the rear. The shots went too high and were lost, without leaving any traces, and those which were too short crashed against the walls, without effect. The M.G.B., on the contrary, lit up by the searchlights, was a magnificent target. So much so, in fact, that the 40-mm. guns from Mindin were able to fire on her across the estuary and threw up sprays of water nearer and nearer round the boat.

The blockhouse on the mole woke up again and was once more silenced by Savage's accurate firing, but unfortunately the gunner was hit by a shell and killed at his gun. It was an irreparable loss at a crucial moment.

Ryder ordered Curtiss to return to the Vieille Entrée.

There the battle was raging furiously. The quays and roofs were lit up for a moment with flashes from new guns.

Some Germans climbing aboard the *Campbeltown* succeeded in getting one of the oerlikons in action and began to enfilade the entrance.

One could no longer recognize friends and foes.

The battle became more and more unequal. The Germans could multiply indefinitely the guns firing on the estuary which could not be reached from the river, while the boats, which formed ideal targets, were nearly all out of action. Both points of possible re-embarkation seemed to be in the hands of the enemy. As far as his eyes could see along the estuary, Ryder was met with the spectacle of blazing or sinking M.L.s. Among the fifty men crowding on the M.G.B., the number of wounded grew from minute to minute.

A quick decision had to be made. A smoke-float was thrown into the water. After a brief consultation it seemed obvious that the moment had come when the only hope of saving the survivors of the M.G.B. was to put out to sea at full speed. The rudder and the engines still seemed intact. At any moment one of these vital parts might be hit.

With death in his heart when he thought of his abandoned comrades ashore, Ryder ordered: "Full speed ahead, course south-west."

At twenty-four knots, the M.G.B. leapt forward among the hulks, which were now sinking, and the sheets of flaming petrol. The wake which she threw upon each side of her keel attracted the cross-beams of the searchlights and the dangerous tracers which thrashed the water around her.

What had happened ashore?

The motto of the Commandos – "Quick in and quick out" – was particularly applicable at St. Nazaire, since it was estimated that the garrison numbered about ten thousand men – sailors, infantry, gunners, flak, Todt workers, etc.

In actual fact Me Grimaud, who at the time was attached to the Mayor of St. Nazaire, told me that more than a hundred thousand Germans were in the region around the Loire estuary from Pornichet Point to St. Gildas.

Newman had split his forces into small groups, with orders to carry out in the minimum of time the exact tasks for which the men had been so carefully trained. The disadvantage of this procedure was that for each group which failed to land some mission would not be carried out. In actual fact it was precisely the groups entrusted with the task of capturing and holding the re-embarkation point which could not carry out their mission.

But could one operate any differently in the short time available?

Furthermore, on such a long crossing, each M.L. could only carry fifteen men in addition to its own crew. This meant splitting up the Commando; and the troop which was the main formation of these special forces, comprising sixty-five men, was broken.

Each team had studied, down to the smallest detail, the model of St. Nazaire harbour, reconstructed from the R.A.F. reconnaissance photos. On this model all the quays, sheds goods yards, sluices, bridges, cranes, railway lines, trenches and pill-boxes were built to scale and in their actual aspects.

The Commandos in the *Campbeltown* were split into five groups of between ten to twenty men each.

Assault groups were ordered to capture the flak emplacements on either side of the lock-gate. The first group was then to destroy the oil reservoirs and to prevent the arrival of enemy reinforcements from this direction. The second had to make a bridgehead on the north side of the Vieille Entrée to collect all the *Campbeltown* groups once they had carried out their tasks.

Two demolition groups had to blow up the pumping station and the machinery of the north and south caisson gates. The fifth group, composed of Major Copland, second in command to Newman, and eight other men, was to supervise the assault from *Campbeltown* and the re-embarkation at Vieux Môle.

After the ramming, Lieutenant Roderick, at the head of the east assault group, captured the light batteries between the lock-gate and the Loire. He then went on to the mounds which covered the oil reservoirs. A hundred yards farther on he ran up against stiff opposition from German reinforcements, which greatly outnumbered his own group. As there was no possibility of pushing on farther, he held the enemy until the moment he took a spray of tracers for the signal to retire, and fought his way back towards the Vieille Entrée.

Captain Roy and his men landed at the same time on the Penhoët islet, quickly took the positions adjoining the quay. It now remained for him to put out of action the machine-guns on the terraced roof of the pumping station. The big cube-shaped building stood close beside the lockgate.

"Follow me," ordered Roy; and like Indians on the warpath, his men went forward in silence, skirting the west wall.

The attention of the German gunners was obviously concentrated on the southern side, towards the roadstead. At the foot of the north wall everything was quiet. "Attach the ladders to the edge of the roof."

Light ribbons of rope ladder were unrolled like serpents and, after a few attempts, hung down from the wall.

"All together, up you go!"

In the excitement, and deafened by the noise of their own firing, the German gunners did not see the smeared faces with their flat steel helmets suddenly emerge over the parapet of the roof. In an instant they were put out of action by a few unexpected tommy-gun bursts. Climbing down from their terrace, Roy and his men proceeded to hold the bridgehead, as arranged, in front of the bridge crossing the Vieille Entrée.

While they were attacking the roof, the sabotage squad had forced an entrance into the building.

The huge iron door was locked.

"Give me the gun cotton," called Lieutenant Chant.

In a flash the explosive was in place; retreat, crash, lock broken.

"Come on! Look out – it's a vertical descent."

He rushed down the iron ladder which led to the turbines, forty feet below.

"You know your jobs. You take the switchboards, you the valves down there at the bottom to the left. You get on with the electric motors and we'll look after the transformers."

"Everything O.K.? Have you checked everything? Well, get out quick."

Almost simultaneously the explosions shook the ground.

Chant immediately went back to inspect the damage.

"Not a bad job," he said to his men. "I hope they'll enjoy it when they return. Set the transformer oil on fire. It won't do any harm."

At the same moment the team at the control post of the southern lock-gate blew up the machinery.

For their part, Lieutenant Etches and seventeen men ran off towards the north of the lock. They placed their charges along the gate in such a way as to scuttle it and to prevent it being manœuvred. The northern control post was completely destroyed and set on fire.

In this way all the teams from the *Campbeltown* carried out their missions with conscientious rapidity.

On landing from the M.G.B., Colonel Newman, his adjutant Captain Day and the six other men of his staff made their way towards the building situated south of the Vieille Entrée bridge, where it had been planned to make a temporary headquarters.

They ran into a German sentry, who, under the threat of a tommy-gun, declared that the building in question was occupied by a German headquarters.

"Go and tell them to come out with their hands up," Newman told him.

The man disappeared. No one came out, but a boat in the basin opened fire on them. Very opportunely, they were reinforced by Haynes' group – the only one which was able to land from M.L. 177 on the Mindin Ferry pontoon near the Vieille Entrée. The rest of the troops which were to have brought the material, and in particular the special flares with thirty-five red and green stars intended for the re-embarkation signal, could not get ashore from M.L. 267.

They had to act quickly. The German destroyers anchored in the basin now added their fire to that of the machine-guns mounted on the roof of the submarine pen. While Haynes replied with his 2-in. mortar, the German headquarters was cleared with grenades and taken over by the Commandos.

The M.L. 192, leader of the starboard column, hit at

the start, was steered by the Flotilla Leader, Lieutenant-Commander Stevens, towards the shallows south of the Vieux Môle. On board were Captain Burn and fourteen men charged to capture the two flak nests on the extreme north of the Penhoët islet, near the swivel bridge separating the two basins.

After being landed between the outer harbour and the Vieux Môle, Burn and the survivors of his group managed to cross the St. Nazaire islet as far as the Vieille Entrée. After this they followed the west quay of the Penhoët islet to their objective, which they found unoccupied. The installations were burnt.

Swiftly, after operating on the Penhoët islet, all the groups retired to headquarters and reported to Newman that their tasks had been carried out. Major Copland came back with his group and discussed with his chief the possibilities of re-embarkation.

The moment had come to retire to the Roy bridgehead, south of the Vieille Entrée. In default of the flares which had been arranged a runner was sent. Corporal Harrington rushed over the bridge, which was swept by fire from the destroyers and from the submarine base, and returned with Roy's group.

So far everything had gone well ashore, but what would be the reaction of these men when they learnt that all hope of re-embarkation had to be abandoned?

The only group landed on the Vieux Môle was Captain Pritchard's demolition squad, which had to blow up the swing-bridge and the southern lock-gate of the Nouvelle Entrée.

As soon as they were ashore these men came under violent simultaneous fire from the mole pill-box, the roof of a nearby shed and the very tall building near the submarine pen, from where the Germans were able to enfilade the street that crossed the old port on a level with the mole. While they were seeking shelter in vain behind some railway trucks several of them fell, including Captain Pritchard. They were joined by the covering group of five men under Lieutenant Watson, who had landed from the same M.L.

They decided to make their way to the swing-bridge by skirting a shed to reach the basin quay, but as soon as they tried to round the corner of this building they were caught once more in a converging fire from the destroyers and the machine-guns of the submarine pen. Time was slipping by. They had to get it over. Watson decided to make an attempt at all costs to reach the Nouvelle Entrée in a succession of rushes.

"Everyone set?"

At that moment a man rushed towards them, shouting an order. It was a runner from headquarters, giving the order for a general assembly at the Vieux Môle.

Very disappointed at the thought of not having carried out their mission, they assembled near an old building fifty yards west of the mole.

It was here that the real tragedy awaited these men.

Not a single M.L. lay alongside, and as far as the eye could see over the roadstead, hulks were still burning, surrounded by sheets of burning petrol.

All hope of being re-embarked had to be abandoned. Newman immediately called Copland and Day for a discussion behind a railway truck and told them of his intention to force a passage through the town. He would let the men split up in the country, so that they could try and make their way back to England through Spain, or any other way they chose.

These men, armed against all physical and moral ordeals, were by no means downcast at the tragedy of their situation. They had long been prepared for the worst eventualities. This was one of those which always have to be envisaged in such forays.

"We knew," said one of them, "that unless there was a surprise at the last moment we had little chance of ever being re-embarked."

Newman was perfectly cool and even made a few jokes.

"What a magnificent moonlight night. A night for lovers, eh?"

After telling them that they could now fend for themselves and try and get back to England, he added, with almost cockney humour, "Perhaps the smartest of you boys will be able to paddle home in your rubber boots. What do you think?"

Major Copland organised a defence round a line of railway trucks, which served as a temporary shelter. The machine-guns from the rooftops began to concentrate their fire in this direction.

An enemy group advanced, shouting, "*Heil Hitler.*" Newman held his fire until the Jerries were twelve yards away. They were all mown down by bursts of tommy-gun fire, but gradually the enemy pressed home his advantage. The firing increased in intensity. Hand grenades were thrown over the trucks.

There was not a moment to be lost.

Swiftly Newman and Copland split the men up into groups of twenty, which were to try, independently, to make their way through the town. To get out of the "islands" some had to cross the iron turn-table of the railway track at the Nouvelle Entrée. The others would take the swivel-bridge between the Penhoët and the St. Nazaire basins.

The groups led by Newman, Copland and Day dashed towards the turn-table, lit up brightly by the moon and sprayed by wicked fire from the destroyers and the rooftops. Advancing in short rushes, the men crossed the bridge, while the bullets spattered or burst against the metal plates, and entered the main street facing them. Some German motor-cyclists riding towards them were wiped out immediately.

A little farther on they noticed a stationary car with all its lights on. They sensed a trap.

"So much the worse," said Major Copland. "I'll have a try. It's really too good an opportunity."

He tried in vain to start the car.

"Pity," he said. "It would have been an elegant way of going for a ride in the country. I don't think we'd better look and see what's wrong with the engine." Newman's idea was to get out of the main streets as soon as possible and go through the gardens of the houses in an attempt to reach the country. The best way of doing this was to split up into small groups of two or three men.

A Canadian who managed to get back to England a few

months later hid with a comrade in a courtyard. He knocked on the door, and as soon as it was opened he said: "Where's the back door?" Without further explanation, the two men forced their way through the house and found themselves in a garden, at the back of which was a pile of logs, which allowed them to leap the wall into a second garden. Dawn would soon replace the sinking moon. It was impossible to reach the country in broad daylight. They had to find some place to hide. After crossing some more gardens, they noticed a cellar window at the foot of a wall, at ground level. They slipped inside and spent the whole day in this cramped hiding-place between the floorboards and the soil.

They were too uncomfortable to be able to sleep, and they could hear all the comings and goings of the occupants just over their heads. They heard gunshots, tommy-gun bursts, and thought that some of their comrades must be waging their last battle. Between eleven o'clock and midday a tremendous explosion shook the earth. They looked at each other and said, with one accord: "That's the good old *Campbeltown.*"

Towards midnight the two men climbed out of their hole and were at last able to stretch their aching limbs. They leapt over the garden wall and found themselves in a deserted street.

Still that bloody full moon. They made for the country by the stars and skirted close to the walls. They passed in front of a house, from which they heard the sound of German songs. The temptation of bursting in the door and emptying their tommy-gun magazines was very great, but common sense took the upper hand, and they went on their way. Eventually the town lay behind them.

Another group entered a cul-de-sac, and just as they turned back found their passage barred by some Germans. The British forced a passage and then, as dawn was near, they took refuge under the floor of a bomb-damaged house. The seriously wounded men were left lying not far from an enemy post, and those who were still fit decided to leave their hiding-place in twos at half-hour intervals during the following night.

Shortly before midday they, too, heard the violent explosion and interpreted it, without hesitation, as their comrades had done. During the evening a German patrol entered the ruins. One of the men bent over the yawning hole.

In the darkness the Commandos were watching his movements with their fingers on the triggers of their tommy-guns.

The German stood up and uttered a few words which the British, to their great relief, interpreted as meaning: "There's no one there." He walked away with the rest of the patrol.

From 21.00 hours onwards the Commandos came out in pairs at half-hour intervals, to take their chance. One of them who was too seriously wounded shook his mates by the hand and said that he would give himself up as a prisoner.

Many more men remained with Colonel Newman. They went from street to street, diving into alleys to avoid enemy trucks, which were firing in all directions. They, too, realized that they could not reach the open country before daylight. Their ammunition was practically exhausted. Many of the men were urgently in need of attention. Among them was Lieutenant Etches, who had led the demolition squad at the northern lock-gate. He was wounded at the beginning of the action on board the *Campbeltown* and, after carrying out his mission at the other end of the lock, had fought until this moment to remain with his chief.

Newman led them to a cellar which he had discovered by chance. The wounded men were bandaged. The remaining rations and ammunition were checked and redistributed to give the unwounded men a chance of getting away the following night. Suddenly they heard the sound of hurrying footsteps and orders shouted in German. In a flash the house was surrounded by a substantial force.

"Come out with your hands up or else we'll bomb you out!"

The situation was hopeless. They had to carry out the order.

Of the men we saw leave the harbour only five escaped capture and returned to England.

Newman wondered if the speed of the German reaction had not been due to a previous warning.

The delay in opening fire on the flotilla showed without a doubt that its arrival had been a surprise, but all the military and auxiliary German organizations had been on the alert for an hour since the air raid.

The German anti-aircraft measures included the alert of all detection apparatus, of all searchlights, quick-firing guns, patrols for the maintenance of order, first-aid teams and fire fighters, both on land and on board the warships anchored in the basins.

As soon as the approach of the amphibian task force was discovered, all these measures were immediately directed against it. Even more so, since the British planes, numbering about a hundred, which had flown over the town had not dropped their bombs because they did not consider visibility good enough to find their target accurately.

In actual fact this air raid did more harm than good. Instead of diverting the defence, it merely put it on the alert.

The M.G.B. sped away like a thoroughbred when given its head. The water, more crushed than torn beneath the bows well out of the water, and threshed by the screws, burst behind them in a broad, long, silver wake, which bubbled furiously.

"That's fine and dandy – they're still firing at the smoke-screen."

In their haste to finish off this last surviving boat the German gunners had not seen it leave the cloud of smoke thrown off by the smoke-float, and continued to aim on the latter.

The estuary was too well lit by the moon and the searchlights for the broad, increasing wake not to draw the attention of the other batteries. One after the other they went into action, but, misjudging the wake and the speed of the craft, they fired at its stern.

"M.L. on the port bow."

It was a survivor which the M.G.B. would quickly outstrip. It would have been useless to wait, as they could have afforded it no protection.

"Give her a smoke-screen when we draw level," said Ryder; "that's all we can do to help her get out of the jam."

At this speed the M.G.B. would soon be out of range of the quick-firing flak guns. Gordon Holman, the only war correspondent with the party, looked after the wounded. The few other unwounded men helped in this task, and Curtiss took the wheel himself to allow the topman to give a hand to his comrades.

"That's a big fellow."

A red flash burst on the dark coast, followed by a growl of thunder. A few seconds and tall "poplar trees" rose from the water some way ahead.

"Straddled by the first salvo, eh? Those fellows must have some good layers who can gauge the speed of their target."

"What an honour for our cockleshell!"

The sprays of water raised by the salvos were still in the air when the M.G.B. reached them, and Curtiss was obliged to manœuvre between them so as not to wreck his boat. These zigzags might confuse the layers.

The seconds passed. Already the extremities of the searchlight beams merged with the unreal lunar light, and yet the big shells, with the same regularity, kept planting an avenue of poplar trees on either side of the small craft. It was obvious that the Germans were following all the movements of their little quarry with radar.

At last the rhythm of the flashes, punctuated by the sound of the bursts, died down and ceased, without the batteries having been able to sink this small fugitive.

Their respite was short-lived.

"Motor launch on the starboard bow. Another one we've probably caught up with."

A sudden familiar dry crackle in the petrol tank punctuated the shots which came from the unknown craft. It was a German E-boat.

"Are we going up in flames?"

The seconds seemed like centuries, while Curtiss took avoiding action to give the enemy the slip. With this movement, the forward gun, the only one still able to fire, was masked by the superstructure. As soon as it became clear, the skipper bore down on the German to return his fire.

To the great relief of the British, luck was on their side once more. Their petrol did not catch fire and, on the contrary, after the first bursts from the oerlikon, bright flames spurted on board the enemy vessel, which was left to its fate.

"Another M.L. ahead."

This time they were not going to mistake her nationality. She gave her recognition signals. It was M.L. 270, still steering with the handwheel. As they were now out of range of the shore batteries, Ryder reduced speed to twelve knots to sail in company with her. He set course for point Y, thirty miles south-west of St. Nazaire, the first rendezvous planned for the homeward journey.

The sea was still calm and extraordinarily phosphorescent. Hosts of silver spangles glittered in the wakes. Towards 04.25 hours a bright gleam, which they wrongly interpreted as the explosion on the *Campbeltown*, appeared in the direction of St. Nazaire, and a few minutes later the two craft arrived at point Y.

"Nothing in sight."

The spot was too unhealthy for the two little vessels to hang about at that moment.

"Let's be on our way," said Ryder.

An hour later they noticed to the north the usual exchanges of tracer shells. They would only know later what was going on in that direction.

An hour passed and then another exchange of gunfire, this time much nearer. Shots of greater calibre and no tracers, but the flashes to be seen in the east. Ships with that type of gun must be at least destroyer class.

"Perhaps they're the five famous Jerries we were warned of."

There was nothing to be done but to carry on out to sea, for it would soon be dawn. The officers scanned the horizon around them with their binoculars as its circle grew larger.

Something to stern. It was an M.L. Another to port about a mile away. They gave their recognition signals. The former was the M.L. 156 and the latter the M.L. 446, both of which, as we have already seen, had to give up landing their troops on account of the heavy losses suffered during the approach. The M.G.B. turned about to pick up the M.L. 156.

"Destroyers in sight."

"Are they Jerry's or ours?"

There were two of them searching on the exact itinerary of their homeward course. No mistake this time – they were the *Atherstone* and the *Tynedale*.

The former arrived swiftly alongside the M.L. 156. It was high time, for she was shipping water fast and the survivors were in a state of extreme exhaustion. Fortunately the state of the sea allowed them to be taken aboard the destroyer. Letting the M.L. sink, the latter came alongside the M.G.B.

On board Ryder's craft the dawn revealed a heartbreaking sight. The bridge was covered with wounded men, huddled in all the corners, and blood was running all over the deck. The hull and superstructures – particularly in the bows – had been pierced by small shells, including the last salvo from the E-boat, which had hit a petrol tank.

Despite the calm sea, it was not easy to hoist the wounded men aboard the *Atherstone*. They managed it somehow. In the meanwhile the *Tynedale* had taken aboard the survivors of the M.L.s 270 and 446.

This operation took about half an hour, during which time there was every fear of an irruption by the five German destroyers, for Ryder, as he boarded the *Atherstone*, learned that the battle he had seen to the east was an exchange of shots between the two British destroyers and the Germans in question.

Lieutenant-Commander Jenks told him what had happened.

"We had to patrol parallel to the shore on either side of point Y to await your return. We had to avoid at all costs revealing our presence before the start of your action, for fear of arousing the suspicion of the enemy as to the true reason for this unusual incursion off St. Nazaire.

"We knew that your chances of getting back to England depended to a large extent on our skill in being there in a place to help you at the time of the rendezvous. The signal from Pompey made us fear that we might meet the five German destroyers, a force at least double our own.

"Moreover, we knew how things had gone at St. Nazaire. We spent a very anxious night. After half-past two we received departure signals in succession from M.L.s 177, 160, 307 and 443. That was all.

"Towards half-past four, when we were in the neighbourhood of point Y, I noticed three groups of M.L.s heading for the open sea.

"Those at least have got through, I thought. An hour later, as dawn was about to break, we put five miles between us to scour the return route and come to the assistance of strugglers.

"Dawn broke and the horizon grew larger from minute to minute.

"And then we saw them. Not our M.L.s, but the enemy destroyers.

"All five of them in line ahead to port, with the characteristic silhouette of the *Moewe* class, which we copied so well on the *Campbeltown*.

"We had to lure them away from the M.L.s somehow, so sailed southwards and the *Tynedale* tried to join me at top speed. The enemy followed our movements and opened.

"For ten minutes it concentrated its fire on the *Tynedale*, which replied energetically. She was hit twice, but registered a hit on the third German destroyer of the line. We broke off action and put out a smoke-screen. Despite his evident superiority in numbers, the enemy did not give chase."

In his report the officer in command of the German flotilla tried to explain this lack of fighting spirit by damages to his engines, which, he said, reduced the speed of his flotilla to eighteen knots.

What happened to the other M.L.s?

In addition to the group found by the destroyers at dawn, the M.L.s 443, 307, 160 and 306 also managed to reach the open sea.

After the setback at the attempted approach to the Mindin ferry pontoon the M.L. 267 made off on fire and had to be abandoned by the survivors. The M.L. 177, which managed to disembark Haynes' troop at this point, approached the stern of the *Campbeltown*. She embarked the part of her crew which did not join the M.G.B. at the north stairs on land, including Lieut.-Commander Beattie and his officers. As soon as this operation was completed she set a course for the open sea at fifteen knots. Would she manage to come undamaged through this infernal circle with her precious crew? Somehow she did. She weaved among the vicious little sprays from the flak and sped farther out to sea, minute by minute. Another few seconds and she would be out of range.

A ripping of wood and spurts of flames dashed this last hope to the ground. The fire spread rapidly. They had to abandon ship. The wounded men were put in carley floats, to which the more or less unwounded clung. For four hours these men were buffeted in the cold water, lit up by the sinister gleams of the burning hull. In the early morning a German trawler spotted them and picked them up. Several of them died from exhaustion.

Beattie was among the survivors. A few months later the German military commandant of his oflag ordered a ceremonial parade and solemnly read out the citation of the V.C. which had been awarded to him as a tribute to the crew of the *Campbeltown*.

The M.L. 298 suffered a similar fate after completing at least a mile of the return journey. As for the famous M.T.B. 74, which with her thirty knots seemed to have the best chance of not being hit, once out at sea her skipper exposed her courageously to danger, by trying to rescue the crew of one of the burning M.L.s. By stopping, she made an easy target for the enemy and was set on fire in turn, a victim of his chivalrous comradeship.

Let us return to the last M.L. of the port column. Her skipper, Lieutenant Henderson, tried in vain to land his passengers at the Vieux Môle. At two o'clock, with only one oerlikon in action and many of his men wounded, he had to give up his attempt unless he wished to share the fate of all the craft which came under the reinforced fire from the pill-boxes and the neighbouring roofs. He had to retire.

"Full speed ahead. Drop a smoke-float."

Pursued by sprays of flak, the M.L. 306, making eighteen knots, miraculously escaped any fatal hits. The big batteries, busy no doubt with the M.G.B., neglected her and she was soon out of range.

The worst seemed to be over. They were already forty-five miles away from the rat-trap. It was half-past five. It would soon be dawn, and in daylight there would be more chance of joining up with their friends.

"Hell! What are those shapes I can make out on the port bow? They're too tall for M.L.s. They must be at least destroyers, and there are too many of them to be ours."

"Stop!"

They had to endeavour not to be seen until they could identify the suspicious craft. For a small M.L. at night, the first thing to do was to eliminate the revealing wake. Perhaps in these conditions they could escape the enemy spotters and pass for one of those many fishing-boats they had passed the night before in these waters. It was dark enough to hope they would not be noticed.

The unknown ships passed a hundred yards away from the M.L. At that distance they could make out the silhouettes of the German *Moewes*.

Moments of great anxiety. They passed. They were already far away. There was no sign to show that they had spotted the M.L.

"On our way."

The engines started. The screws sent a cloud of phosphorescent bubbles to the surface. Did this betray them or had the enemy already spotted them? At that moment the rear destroyer's searchlight lit them up and the flotilla turned about with the obvious intention of attacking them.

To these five heavily armed hunters the harmless laggard only seemed worthy of a little buckshot. The macabre dance of the tracers which they thought they had left behind began again.

Henderson replied with the only gun in action and the enemy was so close that the Commandos fired bursts of their Bren-guns.

Continuing his manœuvre, the leading destroyer got into position to ram its fragile adversary.

"Full speed ahead! Hard to starboard! Hard to port!"

With these movements, the M.L. 306 avoided the bows of the German and followed him round.

This game of cat-and-mouse could not go on. The hunters grew impatient. As buckshot was not enough, let's try a dose of shells.

Profiting by a moment when the M.L. was fifty yards away, the destroyer trained her guns on her. A 4-in. shell carried away the bridge, with the skipper. The surviving officers were seriously wounded.

The enemy drew alongside the immobilized M.L. and in bad English ordered the survivors to surrender. As they had no more means of continuing this unequal struggle, the survivors climbed aboard the enemy ship.

"Aircraft due east."

The rescue over, the British destroyers and the three M.L.s still afloat got under way.

The suspicious plane grew larger and the noise of its engines louder. It was a Heinkel III. The gun crews were at action stations, but after a reconnaissance at a respectful distance the plane took as its target the M.L. 156, which had been abandoned to stern. After an abortive attempt it registered a direct hit, thus completing the task the *Tynedale* had intended to carry out later – to prevent her falling into the hands of the enemy.

The Heinkel would obviously report the British squadron and they would now be subjected to constant air attack throughout the day.

"Aircraft to the north." The game went on.

But they had a surprise. The first Beaufighter from Coastal Command came to their rescue.

It arrived at the right time. The other plane from the east would find his answer in his own element. It was a Junkers

88. All the spectators below followed the opening moves of this strange combat with the keenest interest.

What was happening? The Beaufighter was behaving in the strangest manner. It looked as though it were going to ram the Ju.

That was it. The two machines collided and their entangled debris crashed into the sea. The *Tynedale* searched in vain for survivors.

"Bearing 315 degrees. Two unidentified ships."

"Identify them."

Reply: "H.M.S. *Cleveland* and *Brocklesby*." The two reinforcing destroyers announced the day before by Plymouth. Better late than never.

Signal from the *Cleveland*: "I am taking over. Stop. Have just met three M.L.s on their way to England."

Commander Sayer, the senior officer of the ships present, took over command, to Ryder's great relief. Exhausted by the responsibilities of that terrible night, he could now relax.

The M.L.s were the 160, 307 and 443, which, as we saw, got away from St. Nazaire.

The new commander immediately had grave decisions to take. The fine weather from the east, which had held so far, was rapidly changing. The normal west wind had sprung up and was increasing in strength. The sea, which had been calm a few moments before, began to rock the M.L.s and to slow them down more and more. They began to ship water through all the holes received in the battle. Many of the seriously wounded would not survive unless they received quick attention in hospital.

The slowing down was even more disturbing, since they were still only sixty miles from the enemy coast and without air cover, after the Beaufighter crashed. Low clouds scudding from north-west to south-east offered magnificent cover for attacking aircraft. The latter had no intention of relinquishing their prey and attacks continued throughout the morning, but so far without damage to the ships. During one of these attacks, the *Brocklesby* shot down a Ju. 88, but the luck could easily change.

All this time the Aldis lamps were repeatedly in action. Sayer kept asking the M.L. skippers: "What is the state of your craft?"

"We're shipping a lot of water – we shall be obliged to reduce speed even more. If the sea increases we shall have to heave to."

To heave to, of course, meant to abandon the convoy and to lay head on to the waves on the spot. There was no question of going to these extremes, particularly in view of the dilapidated state in which the M.L.s were at the moment. The captain had to take his decision. Before the operation became impossible he must get the crews on board the destroyers and scuttle the M.L.s.

Very intelligently Commander Sayer sent the signal: "Prepare to abandon ship and scuttle."

The operation was carried out early in the afternoon. It was high time. Fortunately there were only fit men on board, for they had profited by the calm before dawn to evacuate the wounded. It was with sinking hearts, as every sailor can understand, that the skippers saw the small craft, to which their destinies had been bound during the battle, disappear beneath the waves.

After this painful but necessary surgical operation the four destroyers could increase their speed to twenty-five knots and deploy in an effort to find the three other M.L.s they had met that morning.

That evening the *Cleveland* picked up a message from them. Commander Sayer ordered the *Atherstone* and the *Tynedale* to make for Plymouth at full speed and to disembark the wounded as quickly as possible. The *Cleveland* and the *Brocklesby* tried in vain to get into contact again with the three M.L.s.

The latter, under the command of Lieutenant Platt, a survivor of M.L. 447, and the senior officer of the party, continued with their crossing unescorted. They beat off enemy aircraft with their oerlikons.

The first attacker, a Heinkel III, was shot down and crashed into the sea. A big Blohm and Voss, despising these frail adversaries, ventured too near, was greeted by a firework display, and after being hit broke off the engagement.

One of the most serious difficulties was their fuel consumption. If the sea delayed them any more they would be out of juice before arriving at the English coast.

At last they came in sight of land.

"Direct course for Falmouth."

To leeward of the Lizard the sea grew calmer. They arrived just in time, with barely a few gallons of petrol left in their tanks.

We remember that the M.L. 341, which had engine trouble at the entrance to the Loire, transferred her Commandos on board the M.L. 446. Having tried in vain to rejoin the expedition, she was obliged to turn for home. This was the fourth M.L. which managed to get home out of the eighteen which had embarked forty-eight hours earlier, full of faith and keenness, upon this memorable adventure.

And what of the people of St. Nazaire?

Woken up by the wail of the air-raid siren, some went down into their shelters; others, without leaving their rooms, tried to see the firework display in the sky through closed shutters during a strictly enforced blackout.

They heard the drone of a great number of planes grow louder and then fade away without it being accompanied by the terrible explosion of the bombs which such a noise usually heralded.

The searchlight beams broke on the low clouds, which the flak tracers pierced in their fury.

Silence followed, but the all-clear signal was not given.

Suddenly the crackle of small-arms fire started, hesitant at first and then suddenly unleashed and increasing in volume. An extraordinary thing, this time the trajectories did not rise to the sky. The searchlights and the fire of the German guns were trained on the roadstead.

The more inquisitive townsmen, whose windows looked out onto the sea-front, could see in the beams of the searchlights a group of ships, one of which, larger than the others, was a destroyer type. They were making at full speed towards the port.

"I had a close view of a fast ship making for the Place du

Basin," said M. Gordé, who had been smoking a cigarette on his balcony in the rue Thiers.

"The British fire rained on the town, skimming the roofs or bursting against the façades. Me Grimaud, the Deputy Mayor, told me that, not knowing what was happening in the roadstead, he thought at once: 'The Boche are losing their heads. Now they're machine-gunning the streets and the houses'."

"They're firing low."

This was the news which spread from cellar to cellar and naturally to the A.R.P. headquarters – rue de l'Hôtel de Ville.

M. Compradon, the head of the A.R.P., took the receiver off the telephone, which had just rung.

"Doctor Bizard here, Chief Warden of the Naval Prison. British destroyers are making for the south entrance. We are being heavily shelled."

"Don't talk rubbish."

The communication was interrupted. Runners arrived in quick succession.

"They're fighting in the streets of Old St. Nazaire."

"The British troops are infiltrating the yards."

"The Boche can't get over it – they don't know where to strike."

M[e] Grimaud told me that, intrigued by this continued sound of machine-gun fire and knowing nothing at his post in the fire station, he telephoned to the Town Hall headquarters.

"What's going on?"

"There's a landing."

"Are you pulling my leg?"

Monsieur Lecornu, the Sub-Prefect, took out the A.R.P. ambulances and tried to get them through the German cordons. The soldiers cried, "*Zivilisten heraus.*" When he got to headquarters he phoned M. Deniaud, the Departmental A.R.P. Chief, and tried to convey indirectly the sensational news.

At the moment of the air-raid alert the Germans who had no action stations took shelter with their weapons. When their officers realised the new form of attack which had been launched against them they had great difficulty in arming and regrouping their men into counter-attack detachments.

"A landing, a landing!" repeated the bewildered soldiers, without really knowing what was happening.

On the Boulevard Albert Ier, the Town Major von Trotha, who confirmed the news to M. Lecornu and gave him instructions what route to take with the ambulances, assembled his men, revolver in hand, and led them to the old town. Trucks loaded with German soldiers roared noisily through the streets in the direction of the harbour. Sentries were posted at every street corner.

Many of the French began to think that an attack from the sea, accompanied by an air raid, so far from the nearest Allied bases, could only be a major operation, designed perhaps to open the famous Second Front which had been so long discussed.

They were about to witness one of those historic moments – dangerous moments for unarmed witnesses, looked upon with suspicion by the occupying forces! Some of them who had managed to conceal a weapon decided to go down into the streets when the time came to lend a hand to the liberators.

Before dawn the noise of firing spread from the old harbour to the town and then ceased at daybreak. The German patrols continued to search the cellars and the houses, crying, "Tommies, Tommies." They evacuated the civilians and proceeded to carry out their usual perquisitions, firing at the least provocation. Me Grimaud was nearly hit by a burst of machine-gun fire. A young A.R.P. worker was wounded outside the Town Hall. In all, three of the town folk were killed during the night.

It is impossible to portray the amazement of my compatriots when they saw the British in battle dress or Scots in their kilts appear in their houses or cellars. Seventeen of them descended into the shelter of the Caisse d'Epargne, asking for a plan of the town and for civilian clothes. Then they went to the Town Hall police station, where they were surrounded by overwhelming German forces. A police official intervened to avoid a general massacre and negotiated their surrender.

The cellar where Newman and about thirty of his men took refuge was just opposite the Kommandantur. This accounts for the swift descent of the Germans, who captured them in their shelter.

As day broke, from the Boulevard de L'Ocean could be seen the horrible sight of the estuary in flames, with the M.L.s burning like torches in the water. About 05.25 hours (4.25 British time) one of them exploded with a tremendous fracas, making the window-panes rattle. This was the explosion that the M.G.B. saw from out at sea and wrongly interpreted as being the *Campbeltown*.

In the town order was not restored until half-past eight. The event was eagerly commented. The first B.B.C. broadcast at 6.30 was laconic. "A raid has been carried out on St. Nazaire. All the objectives were reached. Further details will be given on the return of the expedition."

This left the stage clear for enemy propaganda. The first German communiqué read: "British forces tried to land in the bay of St. Nazaire. Caught by the fire of the shore batteries and the flak, they suffered considerable losses. The few elements who landed were immediately surrounded and wiped out. The majority of the naval units were sunk."

The second communiqué gave more details:

"An old American destroyer loaded with explosives, which was to have rammed the lock-gate, blew up without having reached the target. A destroyer, nine fast motor-boats and four motor torpedo launches were destroyed. In addition to his severe losses, the enemy left more than a hundred prisoners in our hands. No German war unit has been lost and no damage has been caused to the submarine base."

According to what the townspeople of St. Nazaire could see and hear, the German version appeared, alas, to be true. During Saturday morning, 28th March, with aching hearts, they saw trucks loaded with British prisoners, most of them wounded, on their way to the camps at La Baule. Access to the harbour yards was forbidden. Until ten o'clock sporadic firing could be heard in the town.

Shortly before midday a formidable explosion rocked the houses and broke all the windows in a large radius round the port. A heavy silence followed. The occupying forces were obviously flabbergasted. A few isolated shots rang out during the course of the following night.

In the morning of the 29th the workers and dockers who tried once more to reach their work in the port found that the Germans were completely disorganized. Having heard the B.B.C. story of the *Campbeltown*'s mission and the German-controlled radio proclaim that she blew up before reaching the target, the most inquisitive did their best to approach the lock from where the terrible explosion the night before seemed to have come. The disorganization of the German services allowed them to get there.

A hideous spectacle met their eyes. The quays near the outer lock-gate were literally piled with corpses. Others were floating in the lock, whose south gate seemed to have disappeared. Shreds of uniform allowed them to recognise the macabre remains of German soldiers of all ranks. Fatigue parties were fishing the bodies out of the water and piling them up. They spread sand on the more bloodstained spots.

Contrary to the normal military behaviour of the Germans, there seemed to be a lack of organization and efficiency. Judging it more prudent not to linger in the vicinity, the French dockers returned to their workshops or yards and questioned the German workers as to what had happened.

They learnt that the *Campbeltown* had approached the caisson-gate, right in the middle, and had rammed it, without making a total breach, which would have allowed the sea to invade the lock.

The German admiral Kellermann, the commandant of the base, went on board, accompanied by several officers and engineers, to study the wreck. He worked out the best means of rapidly disengaging it from the door and repairing the breach. Behind the cordons of troops some Germans tried to approach and take a look at the enemy destroyer. After sizing up the position, the German admiral left, but several officers remained on board to make further investigations.

We shall probably never know if those experts discovered the famous bomb bay. One thing is certain: the fuses do not appear to have functioned, since it was shortly before midday, after a delay corresponding to that of the explosive pencils introduced into every third depth charge on entering the roadstead, which produced the explosion.

The effect of igniting about four tons of powerful explosive in such conditions is difficult to imagine in all its sinister horror. From information obtained later by the British it was discovered that sixty officers and three hundred and twenty private soldiers were killed by this explosion. The caisson-gate was subjected to such pressure that it literally crumpled at the point of ramming. Its ends protruded from their hinges in the quayside and the swift entrance of the sea forced it inside and thrust it up against the west wall.

Under the effect of this cataclysm, which forecasts what the explosion of an atomic bomb would be like in an outer port, the lock was suddenly invaded by the sea. Two huge cargo ships which were in dry dock were instantaneously lifted up like straws and flung against the northern door, causing great damage to it. But strange as it may seem, they themselves remained afloat without sustaining any major damage. The scuttled stern of the *Campbeltown* was flung to the end of the lock. The pumping station, already sabotaged by the Commandos, was destroyed. In this way the main goal of the raid – putting the great lock of St. Nazaire out of service for a long time – was a complete success, but the British only learned of this later.

AFTERWORD

Of the 619 officers and men of the Royal Navy and British Army Commandos (mostly drawn from No. 2 Commando) who went up the Loire on that fateful day in March 1942, 159 were killed, 200 wounded and captured. It was an action marked by extraordinary bravery: no less than five Victoria Crosses were awarded to the St. Nazaire raiders. The citations were careful to express gratitude not only to the individuals concerned, but to the services they were from. Those awarded the VC were Lieutenant Commander S. H. Beattie, the captain of the Campbeltown, *Lieutenant-Colonel C. Newman, Commander R.E.D. Ryder, Able Seaman W. Savage and Sergeant*

T. F. Durrant. The latter was awarded the VC posthumously for attempting to defend his Motor Launch against the German destroyer Jaguar *whilst severely wounded. The award was recommended by a German officer who witnessed Durrant's bravery.*

ASSAULT INTO HELL
E. B. Sledge

Eugene Sledge served as a mortarman with the 1st Marine Division of the United States Marine Corps in the Pacific during WWII. He took part in the invasion of the Japanese-held island of Peleliu – a little known but uncommonly bloody battle – in September 1944, and later in the invasion of Okinawa. His memoir of that time, With the Old Breed, *is one of the finest to emerge from the Second World War. In the following pages from the book, he describes the 1st Marine Division's assault on Ngesebus, a small island off Peleliu.*

The 1st Marine Division occupies a place of special honour in the history of the United States Marine Corp, being the sole Marine Division to have had units fight in all America's major wars in the twentieth century: its Fifth Regiment fought at Belleau Wood in 1918 (so ferociously that the Germans nicknamed its members Teufelhunden, *or "devil dogs"); during WWII, the 1st Marine Division fought at Guadalcanal and Cape Gloucester, as well as Peleliu and Okinawa; it was the only Marine division to fight in Korea and, along with the 3rd and 5th Marine Divisions, it fought in Vietnam.*

EARLY THE NEXT morning our battalion made a successful assault on a small hill on the narrow neck of northern Peleliu. Because of its isolated position, it lacked the mutual support from surrounding caves that made most of the ridges on the island impregnable.

At this time the rest of the regiment was getting a lot of enemy fire from Ngesebus Island. The word was that several days earlier the Japanese had slipped reinforcements by barge down to Peleliu from the larger islands to the north; some of the barges had been shot up and sunk by the navy, but several hundred enemy troops got ashore. It was a real blow to our morale to hear this.

"Sounds just like Guadalcanal," said a veteran. "About the time we think we got the bastards boxed in, the damn Nips bring in reinforcements, and it'll go on and on."

"Yeah," said another, "and once them slant-eyed bastards get in these caves around here, it'll be hell to pay."

On 27 September army troops took over our positions. We moved northward.

"Our battalion is ordered to hit the beach on Ngesebus Island tomorrow," an officer told us.

I shuddered as I recalled the beachhead we had made on 15 September. The battalion moved into an area near the northern peninsula and dug in for the night in a quiet area. It was sandy, open, and had some shattered, drooping palms. We didn't know what to expect on Ngesebus. I prayed the landing wouldn't be a repeat of the holocaust of D day.

Early in the morning of 28 September (D + 3) we squared away our gear and stood by to board the amtracs that would take us across the 500–700 yards of shallow reef to Ngesebus.

"We'll probably get another battle star for this beachhead," said a man enthusiastically.

"No we won't," answered another. "It's still just part of the Peleliu operation."

"The hell you say; it's still another beachhead," the first man responded.

"I don't make the regulations, ole buddy, but you check with the gunny, and I'll betcha I'm right." Several mumbled comments came out about how stingy the high command was in authorizing battle stars, which were little enough compensation for combat duty.

We boarded the tractors and tried to suppress our fear. Ships were firing on Ngesebus, and we saw Marine F4U Corsair fighter planes approaching from the Peleliu airfield to the south. "We gonna have lots of support for this one," an NCO said.

Our amtracs moved to the water's edge and waited for H hour as the thunderous prelanding naval gunfire bombardment covered the little island in smoke, flame, and dust. The

Corsairs from Marine Fighter Squadron (VMF) 114 peeled off and began bombing and strafing the beach. The engines of the beautiful blue gull-winged planes roared, whined, and strained as they dove and pulled out. They plastered the beach with machine guns, bombs, and rockets. The effect was awesome as dirt, sand, and debris spewed into the air.

Our Marine pilots outdid themselves, and we cheered, yelled, waved, and raised our clenched fists to indicate our approval. Never during the war did I see fighter pilots take such risks by not pulling out of their dives until the very last instant. We were certain, more than once, that a pilot was pulling out too late and would crash. But, expert flyers that they were, they gave that beach a brutal pounding without mishap to plane or pilot. We talked about their spectacular flying even after the war ended.

Out to sea on our left, with a cruiser, destroyers, and other ships firing support, was a huge battleship. Someone said it was the USS *Mississippi*, but I never knew for sure. She ranked with the Corsairs in the mass of destruction she hurled at Ngesebus. The huge shells rumbled like freight cars – as the men always used to describe the sound of projectiles from full-sized battleships' 16-inch guns.

At H hour our tractor driver revved up his engine. We moved into the water and started the assault. My heart pounded in my throat. Would my luck hold out? "The Lord is my shepherd," I prayed quietly and squeezed my carbine stock.

To our relief we received no fire as we approached the island. When my amtrac lurched to a stop well up on the beach, the tailgate went down with a bump, and we scrambled out. With its usual din and thunder the bombardment moved inland ahead of us. Some Company K Marines on the beach were already firing into pillboxes and bunkers and dropping in grenades. With several other men, I headed inland a short distance. But as we got to the edge of the airstrip, we had to dive for cover. A Nambu (Japanese light machine gun) had cut loose on us.

A buddy and I huddled behind a coral rock as the machine-gun slugs zipped viciously overhead. He was on my right.

Because the rock was small, we pressed shoulder to shoulder, hugging it for protection. Suddenly there was a sickening crack like someone snapping a large stick.

My friend screamed, "Oh God, I'm hit!" and lurched over onto his right side. He grabbed his left elbow with his right hand, groaning and grimacing with pain as he trashed around kicking up dust.

A bypassed sniper had seen us behind the rock and shot him. The bullet hit him in the left arm, which was pressed tightly against my right arm as we sought cover from the machine gun out front. The Nambu was firing a bit high, but there was no doubt the sniper had his sights right on us. We were between a rock and a hard place. I dragged him around the rock out of sight of the sniper as the Nambu bullets whizzed overhead.

I yelled, "Corpsman!" and Ken (Doc) Caswell, the mortar section corpsman, crawled over, opening his pouch to get at his first aid supplies as he came. Another man also came over to see if he could help. While I cut away the bloody dungaree sleeve from the injured arm with my kabar, Doc began to tend the wound. As he knelt over his patient, the other Marine placed his kabar under the injured man's pack strap and gave a violent upward jerk to cut away the shoulder pack. The razor-sharp blade sliced through the thick web pack strap as though it were a piece of string. But before the Marine could arrest its upward motion, the knife cut Doc in the face to the bone.

Doc recoiled in pain from the impact of the knife thrust. Blood flowed down his face from the nasty gash to the left of his nose. He regained his balance immediately and returned to his work on the smashed arm as though nothing had happened. The clumsy Marine cursed himself for his blunder as I asked Doc what I could do to help him. Despite considerable pain, Doc kept at his work. In a quiet, calm voice he told me to get a battle dressing out of his pouch and press it firmly against his face to stop the bleeding while he finished work on the wounded arm. Such was the selfless dedication of the navy hospital corpsmen who served in Marine infantry units. It was little wonder that we held them in such high esteem. (Doc later got his face tended and was back with the mortar section in a matter of a few hours.)

While I did as Doc directed, I yelled at two Marines coming our way and pointed toward the sniper. They took off quickly toward the beach and hailed a tank. By the time a stretcher team came up and took my wounded friend, the two men trotted by, waved, and one said, "We got the bastard; he ain't gonna shoot nobody else."

The Nambu had ceased firing, and an NCO signaled us forward. Before moving out, I looked toward the beach and saw the walking wounded wading back toward Peleliu.

After we moved farther inland, we received orders to set up the mortars on the inland side of a Japanese pillbox and prepare to fire on the enemy to our company's front. We asked Company K's gunnery sergeant, Gy. Sgt. W. R. Saunders, if he knew of any enemy troops in the bunker. It appeared undamaged. He said some of the men had thrown grenades through the ventilators, and he was sure there were no live enemy inside.

Snafu and I began to set up our mortar about five feet from the bunker. Number One mortar was about five yards to our left. Cpl. R. V. Burgin was getting the sound-powered phone hooked up to receive fire orders from Sgt. Johnny Marmet, who was observing.

I heard something behind me in the pillbox. Japanese were talking in low, excited voices. Metal rattled against an iron grating. I grabbed my carbine and yelled, "Burgin, there're Nips in that pillbox."

All the men readied their weapons as Burgin came over to have a look, kidding me with, "Shucks, Sledgehammer, you're crackin' up." He looked into the ventilator port directly behind me. It was rather small, approximately six inches by eight inches, and covered with iron bars about a half inch apart. What he saw brought forth a stream of curses in his best Texas style against all Nippon. He stuck his carbine muzzle through the bars, fired two quick shots, and yelled, "I got 'em right in the face."

The Japanese inside the pillbox began jabbering loudly.

Burgin was gritting his teeth and calling the enemy SOBs while he fired more shots through the opening.

Every man in the mortar section was ready for trouble as soon as Burgin fired the first shot. It came in the form of a grenade tossed out of the end entrance to my left. It looked as big as a football to me. I yelled "Grenade!" and dove behind the sand breastwork protecting the entrance at the end of the pillbox. The sand bank was about four feet high and L-shaped to protect the entrance from fire from the front and flanks. The grenade exploded, but no one was hit.

The Japanese tossed out several more grenades without causing us injury, because we were hugging the deck. Most of the men crawled around to the front of the pillbox and crouched close to it between the firing ports, so the enemy inside couldn't fire at them. John Redifer and Vincent Santos jumped on top. Things got quiet.

I was nearest the door, and Burgin yelled to me, "Look in and see what's in there, Sledgehammer."

Being trained to take orders without question, I raised my head above the sand bank and peered into the door of the bunker. It nearly cost me my life. Not more than six feet from me crouched a Japanese machine gunner. His eyes were black dots in a tan, impassive face topped with the familiar mushroom helmet. The muzzle of his light machine gun stared at me like a gigantic third eye.

Fortunately for me, I reacted first. Not having time to get my carbine into firing position, I jerked my head down so fast my helmet almost flew off. A split second later he fired a burst of six or eight rounds. The bullets tore a furrow through the bank just above my head and showered sand on me. My ears rang from the muzzle blast and my heart seemed to be in my throat choking me. I knew damned well I had to be dead! He just couldn't have missed me at that range.

A million thoughts raced through my terrified mind: of how my folks had nearly lost their youngest, of what a stupid thing I had done to look directly into a pillbox full of Japanese without even having my carbine at the ready, and of just how much I hated the enemy anyway. Many a Marine veteran had already lost his life on Peleliu for making less of a mistake than I had just made.

Burgin yelled and asked if I were all right. A hoarse squawk was all the answer I could muster, but his voice brought me to my senses. I crawled around to the front, then up on top of the bunker before the enemy machine gunner could have another try at me.

Redifer yelled, "They've got an automatic weapon in there." Snafu disagreed, and a spirited argument ensued. Redifer pointed out that there surely was an automatic weapon in there and that I should know, because it came close to blowing off my head. But Snafu was adamant. Like much of what I experienced in combat, this exchange was unreal. Here we were: twelve Marines with a bull by the tail in the form of a well-built concrete pillbox containing an unknown number of Japanese with no friendly troops near us and Snafu and Redifer – veterans – in a violent argument.

Burgin shouted, "Knock it off," and they shut up.

Redifer and I lay prone on top of the bunker, just above the door. We knew we had to get the Japanese while they were bottled up, or they would come out at us with knives and bayonets, a thought none of us relished. Redifer and I were close enough to the door to place grenades down the opening and move back before they exploded. But the Japanese invariably tossed them back at us before the explosion. I had an irrepressible urge to do just that. Brief as our face-to-face meeting had been, I had quickly developed a feeling of strong personal hate for that machine gunner who had nearly blasted my head off my shoulders. My terror subsided into a cold, homicidal rage and a vengeful desire to get even.

Redifer and I gingerly peeped down over the door. The machine gunner wasn't visible, but we looked at three long Arisaka rifle barrels with bayonets fixed. Those bayonets seemed ten feet long to me. Their owners were jabbering excitedly, apparently planning to rush out. Redifer acted quickly. He held his carbine by the barrel and used the butt to knock down the rifles. The Japanese jerked their weapons back into the bunker with much chattering.

Behind us, Santos yelled that he had located a ventilator

pipe without a cover. He began dropping grenades into it. Each one exploded in the pillbox beneath us with a muffled *bam*. When he had used all of his, Redifer and I handed him our grenades while we kept watch at the door.

After Santos had dropped in several, we stood up and began to discuss with Burgin and the others the possibility that anyone could still be alive inside. (We didn't know at the time that the inside was subdivided by concrete baffles for extra protection.) We got our answer when two grenades were tossed out. Luckily for the men with Burgin, the grenades were thrown out the back. Santos and I shouted a warning and hit the deck on the sand on top of the pillbox, but Redifer merely raised his arm over his face. He took several fragments in the forearm but wasn't wounded seriously.

Burgin yelled, "Let's get the hell outa here and get a tank to help us knock this damn thing out." He ordered us to pull back to some craters about forty yards from the pillbox. We sent a runner to the beach to bring up a flamethrower and an amtrac armed with a 75mm gun.

As we jumped into the crater, three Japanese soldiers ran out of the pillbox door past the sand bank and headed for a thicket. Each carried his bayoneted rifle in his right hand and held up his pants with his left hand. This action so amazed me that I stared in disbelief and didn't fire my carbine. I wasn't afraid, as I had been under shell fire, just filled with wild excitement. My buddies were more effective than I and cut down the enemy with a hail of bullets. They congratulated each other while I chided myself for being more curious about strange Japanese customs than with being combat effective.

The amtrac rattling toward us by this time was certainly a welcome sight. As it pulled into position, several more Japanese raced from the pillbox in a tight group. Some held their bayoneted rifles in both hands, but some of them carried their rifles in one hand and held up their pants with the other. I had overcome my initial surprise and joined the others and the amtrac machine gun in firing away at them. They tumbled onto the hot coral in a forlorn tangle of bare legs, falling rifles, and rolling helmets. We felt no pity for them but exulted over their fate. We had been shot at and shelled too much and had lost too many friends to have compassion for the enemy when we had him cornered.

The amtrac took up a position on a line even with us. Its commander, a sergeant, consulted Burgin. Then the turret gunner fired three armor-piercing 75mm shells at the side of the pillbox. Each time our ears rang with the familiar *wham – bam* as the report of the gun was followed quickly by the explosion of the shell on a target at close range. The third shell tore a hole entirely through the pillbox. Fragments kicked up dust around our abandoned packs and mortars on the other side. On the side nearest us, the hole was about four feet in diameter. Burgin yelled to the tankers to cease firing lest our equipment be damaged.

Someone remarked that if fragments hadn't killed those inside, the concussion surely had. But even before the dust settled, I saw a Japanese soldier appear at the blasted opening. He was grim determination personified as he drew back his arm to throw a grenade at us.

My carbine was already up. When he appeared, I lined up my sights on his chest and began squeezing off shots. As the first bullet hit him, his face contorted in agony. His knees buckled. The grenade slipped from his grasp. All the men near me, including the amtrac machine gunner, had seen him and began firing. The soldier collapsed in the fusilade, and the grenade went off at his feet.

Even in the midst of these fast-moving events, I looked down at my carbine with sober reflection. I had just killed a man at close range. That I had seen clearly the pain on his face when my bullets hit him came as a jolt. It suddenly made the war a very personal affair. The expression on that man's face filled me with shame and then disgust for the war and all the misery it was causing.

My combat experience thus far made me realize that such sentiments for an enemy soldier were the maudlin meditations of a fool. Look at me, a member of the 5th Marine Regiment – one of the oldest, finest, and toughest regiments in the Marine Corps – feeling ashamed because I had shot a damned foe before he could throw a grenade at me! I felt like a fool and was thankful my buddies couldn't read my thoughts.

Burgin's order to us to continue firing into the opening interrupted my musings. We kept up a steady fire into the pillbox to keep the Japanese pinned down while the flamethrower came up, carried by Corporal Womack from Mississippi. He was a brave, good-natured guy and popular with the troops, but he was one of the fiercest looking Marines I ever saw. He was big and husky with a fiery red beard well powdered with white coral dust. He reminded me of some wild Viking. I was glad we were on the same side.

Stooped under the heavy tanks on his back, Womack approached the pillbox with his assistant just out of the line of our fire. When they got about fifteen yards from the target, we ceased firing. The assistant reached up and turned a valve on the flamethrower. Womack then aimed the nozzle at the opening made by the 75mm gun. He pressed the trigger. With a *whoooooooosh* the flame leaped at the opening. Some muffled screams, then all quiet.

Even the stoic Japanese couldn't suppress the agony of death by fire and suffocation. But they were no more likely to surrender to us than we would have been to them had we ever been confronted with the possibility of surrender. In fighting the Japanese, surrender was not one of our options.

Amid our shouts of appreciation, Womack and his buddy started back to battalion headquarters to await the summons to break another deadlock somewhere on the battlefield – or lose their lives trying. The job of flamethrower gunner was probably the least desirable of any open to a Marine infantryman. Carrying tanks with about seventy pounds of flammable jellied gasoline through enemy fire over rugged terrain in hot weather to squirt flames into the mouth of a cave or pillbox was an assignment that few survived but all carried out with magnificent courage.

We left the craters and approached the pillbox cautiously. Burgin ordered some of the men to cover it while the rest of us looked over the fallen Japanese to be sure none was still alive; wounded Japanese invariably exploded grenades when approached, if possible, killing their enemies along with themselves. All of them were dead. The pillbox was out of action thanks to the flamethrower and the amtrac. There were seven enemy dead inside and ten outside. Our packs and mortars were only slightly damaged by the fire from the amtrac's 75mm gun.

Of the twelve Marine mortarmen, our only casualties were Redifer and Leslie Porter, who had taken some grenade fragments. They weren't hurt seriously. Our luck in the whole affair had been incredible. If the enemy had surprised us and rushed us, we might have been in a bad fix.

During this lull the men stripped the packs and pockets of the enemy dead for souvenirs. This was a gruesome business, but Marines executed it in a most methodical manner. Helmet headbands were checked for flags, packs and pockets were emptied, and gold teeth were extracted. Sabers, pistols, and *hari-kari* knives were highly prized and carefully cared for until they could be sent to the folks back home or sold to some pilot or sailor for a fat price. Rifles and other larger weapons usually were rendered useless and thrown aside. They were too heavy to carry in addition to our own equipment. They would be picked up later as fine souvenirs by the rear-echelon troops. The men in the rifle companies had a lot of fun joking about the hair-raising stories these people, who had never seen a live Japanese or been shot at, would probably tell after the war.

The men gloated over, compared, and often swapped their prizes. It was a brutal, ghastly ritual the likes of which have occurred since ancient times on battlefields where the antagonists have possessed a profound mutual hatred. It was uncivilized, as is all war, and was carried out with that particular savagery that characterized the struggle between the Marines and the Japanese. It wasn't simply souvenir hunting or looting the enemy dead; it was more like Indian warriors taking scalps.

While I was removing a bayonet and scabbard from a dead Japanese, I noticed a Marine near me. He wasn't in our mortar section but had happened by and wanted to get in on the spoils. He came up to me dragging what I assumed to be a corpse. But the Japanese wasn't dead. He had been wounded severely in the back and couldn't move his arms; otherwise he would have resisted to his last breath.

The Japanese's mouth glowed with huge gold-crowned

teeth, and his captor wanted them. He put the point of his kabar on the base of a tooth and hit the handle with the palm of his hand. Because the Japanese was kicking his feet and thrashing about, the knife point glanced off the tooth and sank deeply into the victim's mouth. The Marine cursed him and with a slash cut his cheeks open to each ear. He put his foot on the sufferer's lower jaw and tried again. Blood poured out of the soldier's mouth. He made a gurgling noise and thrashed wildly. I shouted, "Put the man out of his misery." All I got for an answer was a cussing out. Another Marine ran up, put a bullet in the enemy soldier's brain, and ended his agony. The scavenger grumbled and continued extracting his prizes undisturbed.

Such was the incredible cruelty that decent men could commit when reduced to a brutish existence in their fight for survival amid the violent death, terror, tension, fatigue, and filth that was the infantryman's war. Our code of conduct toward the enemy differed drastically from that prevailing back at the division CP.

The struggle for survival went on day after weary day, night after terrifying night. One remembers vividly the landings and the beachheads and the details of the first two or three days and nights of a campaign; after that, time lost all meaning. A lull of hours or days seemed but a fleeting instant of heaven-sent tranquility. Lying in a foxhole sweating out an enemy artillery or mortar barrage or waiting to dash across open ground under machine-gun or artillery fire defied any concept of time.

To the noncombatants and those on the periphery of action, the war meant only boredom or occasional excitement; but to those who entered the meat grinder itself, the war was a nether world of horror from which escape seemed less and less likely as casualties mounted and the fighting dragged on and on. Time had no meaning; life had no meaning. The fierce struggle for survival in the abyss of Peleliu eroded the veneer of civilization and made savages of us all. We existed in an environment totally incomprehensible to men behind the lines – service troops and civilians.

* * *

A trip inside the pillbox by Redifer and Burgin solved the mystery of how some of the occupants had survived the grenades and shell bursts. (Burgin shot a soldier inside who was feigning death.) Concrete walls partitioned the bunker into compartments connected by small openings. Three or four enemy soldiers occupied each compartment which had its own firing ports to the outside. Each would have had to be put out of action individually had we not had the help of Womack and his flamethrower.

When our gunny came by and saw the results of our encounter with the pillbox he had thought was empty, he looked sheepish. He gazed in amazement at the enemy dead scattered around. We really razzed him about it – or rather, we gave him the nearest thing approaching the razz that we Marine privates dared hand out to the austere personage of Gy. Sergeant Saunders. I have thought often that Burgin should have been decorated for the fine leadership he exhibited in coordinating and directing the knockout of the pillbox. I'm sure men have been decorated for less.

We set up our two mortars in a large crater near the now knocked-out pillbox and registered in the guns for the night. The ammo carriers dug into the softer coral around the edge of the crater. An amtrac brought up rations and a unit of fire for the company. The wind began to blow briskly, and it got cloudy and heavily overcast. As darkness settled, heavy clouds scudded across the sky. The scene reminded me of hurricane weather on the Gulf Coast back home.

Not far behind us, the heat of the fire burning in the pillbox exploded Japanese grenades and small-arms ammunition. All night occasional shifts of wind blew the nauseating smell of burning flesh our way. The rain fell in torrents, and the wind blew hard. Ships fired star shells to illuminate the battlefield for our battalion. But as soon as the parachute of a star shell opened, the wind swept it swiftly along like some invisible hand snatching away a candle. In the few hundred yards they still held at the northern end of the island, the enemy was fairly quiet.

The next morning, again with the help of tanks and amtracs, our battalion took most of the remainder of Ngesebus. Our casualties were remarkably low for the number of Japanese we killed.* In midafternoon we learned that an army unit would relieve us shortly and complete the job on the northern end of Ngesebus.

* Official accounts vary somewhat as to the actual casualty figures for Ngesebus. However the Marines suffered about 15 killed and 33 wounded, while the Japanese lost 470 killed and captured. Company K suffered the largest portion of the casualties in 3/5 by losing 8 killed and 24 wounded. This undoubtedly resulted from the presence of a ridge and caves on Ngesebus in our sector.

THE TWILIGHT OF THE GODS
Jules Roy

The Vietnamese hamlet of Dien Bien Phu was the graveyard of the French Foreign Legion, but also the site of its most heroic stand in modern times. In 1953 the French Army High Command in Vietnam (then a French colony) decided to garrison the hamlet in order to prevent Viet Ming excursions into neighbouring Laos. The problem with Dien Bien Phu, unseen by the High Command, was that it lay in the middle of a natural geographical bowl, surrounded by a ring of small hills. On these hills were placed eight French strongpoints (allegedly named after the mistresses of the garrison commander, Colonel de Castries). But if ever the French were to lose control of the strongpoints, they would lose strategic control of the valley.

At 1700 on 13 March 1954, 37,500 men from the cream of the nationalist-Communist Viet Minh attacked the outlying strongpoints at Dien Bien Phu. The onslaught was stunning, not least because the Viet Minh, under Vo Nguyen Giap's generalship, had managed to bring heavy guns into the area undetected. The first French outpost, Beatrice, fell on 14 March, Gabrielle on the following day. Thereafter Giap could pound the garrison in the valley with impunity.

Against all the odds the garrison held out until the 7th May. The remaining outposts were only surrendered after days of bloody, often hand to hand, combat. The brunt of the fighting was borne by just 3000 Legionaires – out of a total French force of 10,500 – from the 13th Legion Half-Brigade, the 1st Foreign Legion Parachute Battalion, and the 2nd and 3rd Foreign Legion Infantry Regiments. Alongside them was another elite French force, the 6th Colonial Parachute Battalion, led by the legendary Major Marcel Bigeard.

The account of the last day of the French stand below is from Jules Roy's The Battle of Dien Bien Phu, *one of the greatest pieces of twentieth century war reportage. The battle cost the lives of 1500 Legionaires. It was also the de facto end of French rule in Vietnam.*

THE NIGHT OF MAY 6–7, 1954

AT ISABELLE, ALL the 105-mm. guns but one had been destroyed. On Éliane, where a terrible storm of shells had just broken, Major Botella heard Langlais calling Bréchignac on the radio.

"Young Pierre calling Brèche, Young Pierre calling Brèche, who is that deluge meant for?"

"Brèche calling Young Pierre; it's for Éliane 2."

The shelling moved to Éliane 3, then to Éliane 4, while the guns on former Éliane 1 and Mont Fictif opened fire. Langlais sent three tanks still capable of movement over to the left bank, at the foot of the peaks.

At 1815, hard on the heels of their last salvo, the Viets, wearing gauze masks, hurled themselves against Éliane 2. Using radio communication between its companies and battalion command posts for the first time, the 98th Regiment was in position in front of the peaks of Éliane 4.

Botella replied with his mortars and his recoilless guns. The Viets got as far as his command post but were driven back by Vietnamese troops, who, when they had good officers and NCOs, fought as fiercely as their brothers on the other side, just as North Koreans and South Koreans had fought one another. One of their officers, Captain Phan van Phu, saw his company reduced to thirty men.

At 2100 hours, signals orderly Tran ngoc Duoï of the People's Army went into action with his unit. In the white light of the flares which had taken the place of the moon in its first quarter, he could make out the movements of the counterattacks. In spite of shell splinters in his head and right leg, he refused to allow himself to be evacuated, sheltered a wounded platoon commander and went on carrying out his orders with a limp. When a dynamiter was killed, he took his charge, placed it, lighted it and went back to his mission. The Viet troops were cut to pieces by the mortars, but the following waves covered them and went on.

On Éliane 2, which was held by two companies of the 1st Battalion, Parachute Chasseurs, under Captain Pouget, a Viet jumped in front of Sergeant Chabrier, pointed an automatic pistol at him and shouted, "Give yourself up. You're done for – " then fell back dead. At 2300 hours a great silence suddenly descended on the position, and Pouget said to himself, "Perhaps they're going to let us have a bit of peace?" But then, like the spray of a huge black wave breaking almost noiselessly against a jetty, the earth was hurled high into the air by the thousands of pounds of explosive in the Viet mine, and fell with a thunderous din on the roofs of the shelters and into the trenches. The crater which opened under the defenders' feet and buried them still exists. The vegetation has not returned to it, but the rains fill it in a little every season.

The shock troops, who had been waiting for the signal of the explosion to go into action, felt the earth rumble and hurled themselves screaming at the shattered position. Section Leader Dang phi Thuong, under the orders of the commander of No. 7 Platoon of the 3rd Company of the 98th Regiment, advanced rapidly through the hail of bullets from automatic weapons toward the smashed blockhouses, but found his way barred by the fire from Sergeant Chabrier's platoon, which mowed the attackers down and toppled them into the muddy crater which the mine had opened. "What a sight for sore eyes!" cried one of the machine gunners. But the weapons ended up by jamming, the stocks of ammunition by running out, and the swarm of Viets overran the position. The 12.7-mm. machine gun on the tank "Bazeilles" was the last to fall silent.

At midnight, the five Dakotas which were to drop the last company of reinforcements asked, in the interests of their safety, that no more flares be sent up. Langlais and Bigeard hesitated. Even if it was dark, how could the pilots make out the tiny dropping zone in the midst of all the fires of the battle? Wouldn't the Viets take advantage of the darkness to resume the attack? Near the door of the Dakota, the pockets of his battle dress stuffed with whisky for General de Castries and brandy for Langlais, and worried in case he should break his bottles when he landed, Captain Faussurier waited for the green lamp to light up. Finally Bigeard queried Lieutenant Le Page on the radio.

"The flares must come first," Le Page replied unhesitatingly.

Langlais ordered the planes to turn back, and the men of the 1st Battalion, Parachute Chasseurs, returned to Hanoï, sick at heart. In the shelter of the camp headquarters where Geneviève de Galard was sleeping, sheltered under a table, on a mattress of parachutes, Bigeard felt a certain comfort at the thought that the sacrifice of that company had been avoided; a hundred men could no longer alter the course of events. Calls for help were jamming the lines to the artillery and the radio links with the strong points. As for the enemy radio receivers, they resounded with shouts of victory.

With one of his radio operators killed and the other hit by a bullet in the stomach, Pouget had stopped answering calls from the main position. He had been given up for dead and no more calls had been sent out to him. At four in the morning, he operated his transmitter himself and got through to Major Vadot.

"I've reoccupied all of Éliane 2, but I've only thirty-five men left. If we're to hold out, you've got to send me the reinforcements you promised. Otherwise it'll all be over."

"Where do you expect me to find them?" Vadot answered calmly. "Be reasonable. You know the situation as well as I do. Not another man, not another shell, my friend. You're a para. You're there to get yourself killed."

On the wavelength of the Éliane command network the Viets played the record of the "Song of the Partisans," and now and then their waiting voices took up the refrain:

Friend, can you hear the black flight of the crows
In the plain? . . .

"The swine," muttered Pouget, "the swine."

At Éliane, Botella had fifty mortar shells left and a few cases of grenades. The loudspeakers of Bigeard's radio receivers vibrated: "Dédé calling Bruno, the ammunition's running out."

"Brèche calling Bruno, we're nearly finished."

On all the hills, the strong points changed hands several times within a few hours: The enemy hurled himself at any breach he made, then fell back in disorder. Dead and wounded dropped to the ground. On the west face, Claudine 5 was overrun, near a tank which could not fire any more.

Sitting out in the open near his radio set, Pouget watched the 120-mm. mortar shells pounding Éliane 4 where Botella was holding out. The ground was cracking open. Pouget saw some Viets running along the crest of Éliane 4, lit up by the flares dropped by the planes. Down below, Dienbienphu was burning and fireworks were spurting from the shell stores. Now and then a few stars appeared through the clouds which filled the darkness.

At 0410, before his eyes, along the whole front of Éliane 2, the Viets stood up without firing. Pouget heard them shouting: "Di di, di di! Forward, forward!"

The survivors of Éliane 2 had one machine-gun charger and one grenade left. Pouget ordered the sole remaining lieutenant and those men who could still walk to return to the main position, and, falling back from one hole to the next, found himself reunited with them at the foot of the peak, in a trench full of corpses which they piled up to protect themselves.

Another shrieking tidal wave surged from the ground and broke over the 5th Battalion, Vietnamese Paratroops, covering Captain Phu; but a handful of Legionnaires and paratroops counterattacked again, recaptured some lost trenches, pushed aside the dead and dying to place their machine guns in position, and brought their fire to bear on the shadows in the flat helmets. Officers who were not yet twenty became company commanders or died when, like Second Lieutenant Phung, they called for mortar fire to be directed on them. Of the 6th Battalion, Colonial Paratroops, twenty men remained alive around Major Thomas. Sergeants gathered survivors together and rushed into the attack. Who would be victor or vanquished when this night came to an end? To help the men hanging onto the last peaks, Langlais withdrew some platoons from battalions in the center and threw them into the action among the burning eastern peaks. Everywhere men stumbled over shattered bodies. In the light of the flares which the wind carried toward the mountains, faces ran with sweat and with thick black ink. On Éliane 2, where since four in the morning nobody had answered Bréchignac's calls, the groaning of the wounded filled the dawn. Behind the eastern crests, the sky was turning golden.

MAY 7, 1954

On Éliane 10, at the foot of the peaks, day was breaking. The enemy was advancing everywhere, searching the shelters. Besieged in a block-house, Lieutenant Le Page managed to escape with a couple of men. The miracle was that Éliane 4 was still alive, that Bréchignac and Botella were still in command, calling for help. But what help could they be given? Lemeunier went into Langlais's shelter; he had gathered together a few Legionnaires and was ready to fight his way to the west.

"Not to the west," said Langlais. "To Éliane 4 where they're still holding out."

Langlais emerged from his shelter into the brutal light of summer. In the sky, Dakotas were dropping supplies. In all the trenches leading to the hospital, pitiful files of men trampled on corpses gradually being buried by the mud. Wounded men nobody could attend to any more were left where they lay. Turned loose by the Viets, who had told them, "Go back to your people and tell them we are coming," some battalion medical officers got through to Grauwin with the half-naked cripples who had returned to the fight a few days before.

On the other side of the river and the shattered ammunition dump swarmed the hundreds of men who had taken refuge weeks before in holes in the river banks in order to avoid the fighting, and whom Langlais compared to the crabs on tropical coasts. Dregs of humanity, deserters – Langlais could not find words sufficiently contemptuous for them. He could have mown them down with machine-gun fire or crushed them with a few 105-mm. salvos, but he turned away in disgust. Like Bigeard now, he was beyond all that. Like Béatrice, Gabrielle, Anne-Marie, Huguette and Dominique, Éliane had a new lover . . .

Under the bursts of automatic-pistol fire, Pouget had felt the corpses he was sheltering behind tremble. A grenade exploded near his helmet, stunning him. As in a nightmare, he heard a little nasal voice saying, "You are a prisoner of the Democratic People's Army of Vietnam. You are wounded. We shall take care of you. Can you walk?"

He looked up at his victor in the gauze mask.

"And my comrades?"

"We shall attend to them. Their wounds will be dressed. The medical orderlies are coming."

Pouget got laboriously to his feet. It was all over for him. He was stripped to the waist, with no weapons or marks of rank, hairy and haggard. Somebody helped him to walk. His radio operator leaned on his shoulder.

> Friend, can you hear the muffled cry of the country
> Being loaded with chains?

He was no longer strong enough even to hum the tune the Viets had been broadcasting all night. Defeated, he refused to resign himself. At the end of the suffering and humiliation that awaited him and were already escorting him, he knew that he was going to find the great explanation and salvation.

Suddenly the artillery in the east opened fire again and the shells started falling once more. Long, deep, whistling notes pierced the general din. Hope suddenly mingled with amazement. Captain Capeyron, Sergeant Sammarco, Corporal Hoinant and a great many others, surprised to see the first salvos fall between the positions, turned toward the west. Voices cried, "It's Crèvecoeur!" Faces revealed a joy which did not yet dare express itself freely, but which would burst forth a torrent ready to turn against the course of fate and carry everything with it. Yes, it must be the Crèvecoeur column, which the radiotelegraphers had been claiming to be in touch with for days and which they had said was approaching, which was swooping down from the mountains into the valley with an apocalyptic din. Men did not know whether to shriek or weep for joy. They were already hoisting themselves out of their holes when the range lengthened, reached the command posts and crushed the innocents getting ready to meet their saviors. They were expecting Crèvecoeur, but what they heard was the thunder of Stalin's organs.

Three men dressed in mud, haggard, their faces black with stubble and smoke, staggered up and collapsed on the ground. Bigeard bent over one of them and took his hand. Was he crying? It no longer mattered at this moment when everything had been surpassed, when the grandeur of the ordeal made them giddy, when words were no use except to those witnessing from afar the death agony of Dienbienphu. Bigeard, who had never been known to utter a cry of commiseration, simply said over and over again, "Poor Le Page . . ."

He was weeping for a whole body of knights massacred in vain because a general had flung his army into the enemy's trap, giving in to the bluster of those who had urged him to throw himself into the wolf's jaws. Among those who would be cited among the dead and the prisoners, how many names represented the flower of that army, sacrificed turn and turn about, for centuries past, for great causes and solemn idiocies! Bigeard had a vague suspicion that the disaster taking place had achieved nothing but a crucifixion, of which countless former high commissioners, secretaries of state or prime ministers were already washing their hands with affected delicacy. Obsessed by the idea of the coolie's pole on his shoulder, he could not yet imagine what was waiting for him. Who could tell? The diplomats were gathered together at Geneva; everything might be arranged at the last moment. He did not know that the men by whose fault battles are lost are not those whom they kill. Without suspecting it, it was himself that Bigeard discovered beneath the masks of clay and blood drying on his lieutenants' faces.

"Stop shelling . . ." Bréchignac had just asked Bigeard to spare Éliane 4 a bombardment that would kill off the wounded when he received a report from Botella that any further resistance was impossible. Botella then called Bigeard.

"Dédé calling Bruno, Dédé calling Bruno . . ."

It was the same metallic voice which used to announce, "Objective reached." Bigeard pressed the transmitter switch.

"Bruno here."

"Dédé calling Bruno. It's all over. They're at the command post. Goodbye. Tell Young Pierre that we liked him."

A click. A curter voice: "I'm blowing up the radio. Hip hip hooray . . ."

It was nine o'clock. On the heights surrounding Éliane 4, in the rice fields in the ravines, swarmed a host of little armed men, dressed in coarse green cloth, with sandals cut out of tires on their feet, helmets of interlaced bamboo decorated with the ruby of a red star on their heads, and gauze masks over their faces, who came running out of their hiding places in the forests and mountains. They reached the crests of Éliane in a huge roar which was carried along in waves by gusts of wind as they arrived on the summits. Spreading out over the sides and ridges of the Élianes, they uttered shouts of triumph and raised their weapons in a victorious gesture at sight of the yellow curves of the river and the plowed fields of the entrenched camp. On the double crest of Éliane 4, they could be seen jumping over the ruined trenches, crossing the tangled barbed-wire defenses, and stepping over piles of corpses lying on top of one another in the macabre reconciliation of death, or stretched out on their backs, their arms open, their faces eaten by flies, their mouths still full of a last groan, men fallen from their crosses, nailed to the pulverized ground among the wretched wooden supports of the shelters, or swimming in the slimy mud.

In the face of this swarm of human insects sprung up from all sides, the artillery of the entrenched camp, nearly out of ammunition and gun crews, remained silent. It had three hundred 105-mm. shells left and ten 120-mm. Fighters dived out of the sky, dropped bombs, fired their machine guns and spread disorder for a moment, but the swarm gradually resumed its advance when the planes disappeared after the ten minutes at their disposal. Botella decided to stay at his command post, but ordered Second Lieutenant Makowiak to rejoin the main position with a few uninjured men and a few wounded who could still walk. Soon afterward, the Viets surrounded him and took him into their lines. Section Commander Dang phi Thuong, second-in-command of Platoon No. 7 of the 98th Regiment, returning the action to give Élaine the *coup de grâce*, saw him go by, surrounded by guards, bare-headed and balding, on his way to the first regrouping center where he would find Bréchignac and Pouget, mute with misery. At Opéra, Bizard was holding out and getting ready to launch a counterattack against the Élianes, but Langlais incorporated him into the defense system of the main position.

Capeyron, who was searching near Éliane 2 for some men from his company who had gone up there during the night, was hit by some grenade splinters which slashed his left wrist and groin like a razor.

At ten o'clock, from his office in the citadel at Hanoï, Cogny called Castries. The storms moving over the whole region crackled in the receivers. The conversation, which might be the last contact with the entrenched camp, was recorded in the radio room.

"Good morning, my friend," said Cogny. "What resources have you got left?"

Castries's voice was clear, slow, deliberate; a little shrill, as it always was on the telephone. Now and then, he searched for a word, corrected himself, repeated himself. Cogny punctuated his remarks with muffled words of acquiescence.

"The 6th Battalion, Colonial Paratroops, the 2nd Battalion, 1st Parachute Chasseurs, and what was left of the Algerian Rifles."

"Yes."

"In any case, there's nothing to be done but write the whole bunch off."

"Yes."

"Right . . . At the moment, that's what's left, but greatly reduced of course, because we took, we drew on everything there was on the western perimeter in an attempt to hold out in the east . . ."

"Yes."

"What's left is about two companies from the two BEPs put together . . ."

"Yes."

". . . three companies of Moroccan Rifles, but which are no use at all, you realize, no use at all, which are completely demoralized . . ."

"Yes."

". . . two companies of the 8th Assault . . .

"Yes."

". . . three companies of BT2s, but that's only to be expected because it's always that way, it's the Moroccan Rifles and the BT2s that have the most men left because they don't fight."

"Of course."

"Right, and out of the 1st Battalion, out of the 1st Battalion, Foreign Infantry, there're about two companies left, and about two companies of the 1st Battalion, 13th Demibrigade. It's . . . they are companies of seventy or eighty men."

"Yes. I see."

"Well, there you are . . . We're defending every foot of ground."

"Yes."

"We're defending every foot of ground, and I consider that the most we can do . . ."

Static suddenly interrupted the transmission.

"Hello, hello," Cogny repeated.

"Hello, can you hear me, General?"

". . . that the most you can do?"

". . . is to halt the enemy on the Nam Youm. Right?"

"Yes."

"And even then we would have to hold the bank, because otherwise we wouldn't have any water."

"Yes, of course."

"Right, So, well, that's what I suggest we try, I'll try to bring that off, ah, I've just taken, I've just seen Langlais, we're in agreement about that. And then, damn it all, I'll try, I'll try, conditions permitting, to get as many men as possible out toward the south."

"Good. That'll be by night, I suppose?"

"What's that?"

"By night?"

"Yes, General, by night of course."

"Of course. Yes."

"And I . . . I need your permission to do that."

"All right, fellow."

"You give me permission?"

"I give you permission."

"Anyway, I'll hold out, I'll try to hold out here as long as possible, with what is left."

Castries paused for a while, then intimated that he had nothing more to say.

"General?"

"Yes, all right."

"That's it . . ."

"From the ammunition point of view, have you . . . is there anything to be recovered?" Cogny asked very quickly.

"Ammunition. That's more serious, we haven't any."

"There isn't anything that . . ."

"We don't have any, you see. There are still a few 105-mm. shells, but . . ."

A sentence in the transcript is undecipherable. Castries may have referred to 155-mm. shells, for all those guns were unserviceable.

". . . they aren't any use here."

". . . for the moment. And as for the 120-mm., the 120-mm. shells . . ."

"Yes."

"I still have, I must still have, between 100 and 150."

"Yes."

"Which are all over the place, you see."

"Yes, of course." Cogny repeated.

"Which are all over the place. We can't . . . it's practically impossible to collect them. Obviously the more you send, the better, eh?"

"Yes."

"So we'll hold out, we'll hold out as long as possible."

"I think the best thing," said Cogny, talking fast, "would be for the Air Force to put in a big effort today to bring the Viets to a halt."

"Yes, General. The Air Force must keep up its support, eh? Nonstop, nonstop. Yes, and about the Viets, I'll put you in the picture as to how they stand."

"Yes."

"In the east the Viets have thrown in everything they've still got."

"Yes."

"Including two regiments of the 308th Division."

"Really? Yes."

"You see? On the western perimeter at the moment there isn't anything, there can't be anything but the 36th Regiment."

"The 36th, yes, I think so too."

"Just the 36th Regiment, eh? The 102nd Regiment . . ."

Suddenly he was cut off.

"Hello, hello," Cogny repeated in a panting voice while the technicians tried to re-establish contact.

"Can you hear me?" Castries continued.

"The 102nd Regiment, you were saying?"

"Yes, General."

"The 102nd Regiment?"

"Just that they've been thrown in on the eastern perimeter . . ."

"Yes."

". . . the 102nd Regiment and the 88th Regiment."

"That's it."

"You see? Plus what . . . plus what remained of the 312th . . ."

"That's it. Yes."

". . . and now the 316th."

"Yes."

"You see?"

"They've thrown everything in on the eastern perimeter," said Cogny.

"But you see, as I foresaw, the 308th, as I think I've already mentioned, escapes me, you see, as usual."

"Yes, that's it . . . Good, well, what about the withdrawal to the south?" asked Cogny. "How do you envisage it? Toward Isabelle or a scattered movement?"

"Well, General, in any case, in any case they'll have to pass south of Isabelle, won't they?"

"Yes, that's right."

"But I'll give orders, I'll give orders to Isabelle, too, to try, to try to pull out, if they can."

"Yes. Right. Well, keep me in the picture so that we can give you the maximum air support for that operation."

"Why, of course, General."

"There you are, my friend."

"And then, why, damn it all, I'll keep here, well, the units that don't want to go on it . . ."

"That's it, yes."

". . . the, how shall I put it, the wounded of course, but a lot of them are already in the enemy's hands, because there were some in the strong points, Éliane 4 and because . . . and Éliane 10."

"Yes, of course."

"You see? And I'll keep all that under my command."

"Yes, fellow."

"There you are."

"Good-bye, fellow."

"I may telephone you again before . . . before the end."

"There now, good-bye, Castries, old fellow."

"Good-bye, General."

"Good-bye, fellow."

Castries put down the receiver. Two hundred miles away, Cogny did not look at the officers standing silently around him. Sweat was running down his forehead. Hanoï lay crushed under the heat of the storm which refused to break.

At midday, Bigeard went to see General de Castries.

"It's all over," he told him. "If you agree, I'll get out of here at nightfall with my men. But we've got to make the Viets think that we're still holding out, and to do that the artillery, mortars and automatic weapons have got to keep on firing. Leave a good man here – Trancart, for instance."

"No," replied Castries. "I won't give that job to anybody.

I'll stay, Bruno, old fellow. Don't worry; we'll keep on firing all night. At daybreak we'll cut our losses."

At 1300 hours, Captain Capeyron took up position on Junon with fifty-four Legionnaires. Sergeant Sammarco, at whose feet a 75-mm. shell had landed without exploding, said to a pal, "If we get out of this alive, we'll get blind drunk for a fortnight." In readiness for the sortie, Sergeant Kubiak emptied the flasks of rum in the "Pacific" ration crates into his water bottle. Langlais, Bigeard and their staff officers had some hot soup. Together they studied the situation and summoned the battalion commanders who were going to take part in "Operation Bloodletting." Tourret, Guiraud and Clémençon were unanimous in the opinion that it was impossible. However slim the chances of success, for they were completely cut off, they would have to make the attempt, but the Viets occupied the whole of the left bank, except for the bridge which they were trying to capture, and, like broken-down horses on the point of collapse, paratroopers and Legionnaires were at the end of their tether. One of the two boxers had been knocked out.

At 1530, accompanied by Bigeard, Lemeunier and Vadot, Langlais went to see General de Castries. He did not know that a telegram sent from Dienbienphu at 1400 hours had fixed the cessation of hostilities for seven the next morning. At Isabelle, where there were still two thousand shells left for a solitary 105-mm. gun, Colonel Lalande had permission to attempt a sortie. Castries was free to decide Langlais's fate and that of the remaining officers and men. He said to Bigeard, "You're going to pay dearly for all this, Bruno. You ought to try to make a break for it with a few men."

Who could possibly pull off that sortie? Perfectly calm and self-assured, Castries agreed that within five miles all of them would be overcome by exhaustion. Castries dismissed the officers and remained alone with Langlais. Exactly what they said to each other has been forgotten. Between the remarks exchanged with Bigeard, or by radio with Cogny, everything has become confused. Besides, what can they add to what was? Even monks end up, under the influence of communal life, hating one another.

These two men so different in character and methods no longer had any grounds for dispute. Who bore the responsibility for the fall of Dienbienphu? Neither of the two. Outstripped by events, Castries had failed to react at the right moment, but he had not wanted this post for which he was completely unsuited. He had not deceived anybody; others had been mistaken about him. He had been honest enough to warn Navarre, "If it's a second Na San that you want, pick somebody else. I don't feel cut out for that." And he had lacked the necessary humility to see that he ought to be replaced. Cynical and frivolous as he was, was it his fault also that he didn't like Langlais and Langlais didn't like him? Was Langlais also to blame if, preoccupied with the patrols he had been ordered to organize every day, he had been unable to rehearse the counterattacks intended to recapture outposts which nobody expected to fall? To imagine that he should have demanded the necessary time and resources from Castries and Gaucher is to be wise after the event. It is necessary to go back in time, to breathe the atmosphere of optimism which reigned among the garrison, to hear the roar of Piroth's artillery when it fired its salvos into the mountains at the slightest alert. Who had had any premonition, at the time, of the disaster which had just occurred? As for his animosity toward Castries, that was only skin-deep. Langlais had made offensive remarks on several occasions about Castries's reluctance to leave his shelter, but if everybody paid homage to Langlais's spirit, who hadn't quarreled with him and suffered from his anger and bad temper?

"It's all over," said Castries. "We mustn't leave anything intact."

A brief access of emotion suddenly misted over Castries's eyes and froze Langlais's icy features. When Langlais saluted, Castries stepped forward with his hand outstretched, and Langlais, without saying a word, threw himself into his arms.

About 1600 hours, in the course of a radiotelephone conversation, Lieutenant Colonel de Séguins-Pazzis offered Colonel Lalande the choice between a pitched battle and an attempted sortie toward the south. Lalande was given no indication that the main position would not hold out until the following morning. He chose a sortie at nightfall, issued the orders prepared for that purpose, and sent out reconnaissance patrols toward the south, along both banks of the Nam Youm, to gauge the resistance the enemy was likely to offer. Since the direction of the sortie had been altered from the southwest to due south, there were no maps or guides available. Moreover, only one track seemed to be practicable, by way of Muong Nha, Ban Ta Mot and Ban Pha Nang, and Lalande had to change his plan.

On returning to his command post, Langlais gave orders for the destruction of all weapons, optical and signals equipment. Bigeard remained aloof from all this. The news spread at once that surrender was imminent. Sergeant Sammarco had the barrels of rifles and machine guns thrust into the ground for the last cartridges to be fired. With incendiary grenades they soldered the breeches of the 105-mm. guns or melted the mortars and the bazookas. The ammunition was thrown into the river. The engines of the tanks which were still in working order were raced without any oil. The chaplains gathered together their chalices and holy oils. Grauwin buried a few bottles of penicillin with markers to indicate their position.

The fighting began again and the Viet battalions gradually advanced toward the center, surrounding paratroop units which fell immediately. There was no longer any question of fighting. Already, on the left bank, white rags were being waved among the Moroccans and the river-bank population. Dressed in green, with motley scraps of parachute material in their helmets and their duck trousers rolled up to the knees, the Viets appeared from all sides, in a silent, overwhelming flood. The river was crossed at 1700 hours. Hearing his battalion commander utter an oath, Sergeant Kubiak turned toward Castries's command post over which a huge white flag was waving. It suddenly occurred to Captain Capeyron that he ought to burn the 3rd Company's flag. Bending over the fire which his Legionnaires had hurriedly lit, he had just seen the last letters of the word "Loyalty" embroidered on the silk eaten up by the flames when the Viets arrived. A Viet officer gave the order: "Hands up!"

Capeyron did not obey. Some Viets came up and kicked him

in the buttocks. Some Legionnaires broke ranks to intervene. Pale with humiliation, Capeyron restrained them.

"Don't move. It's too late."

In all the trenches on Éliane, the Viets began piling up the corpses from both sides and covering them with earth. On the summit of Éliane 2, they erected a sort of bamboo cenotaph, thirty feet high, which they decorated with white silk parachutes.

Algerians and Moroccans who had remained in hiding for days and nights on end came out into the open, waving rags and, naturally choosing the word which in all the armies of the world has always meant the end of fighting and the fraternization of former enemies, shouted, "Comrades!"

Company Commander Tho, entrusted with the task of establishing a clearing station, found the prisoners unusually docile; most of them stretched themselves as if they had been lying down for a long time and did breathing exercises. They were sent to the rear in groups of ten or so, without guards, simply being shown the way to the first collecting center. The head of the surgical block at Him Lam, Dr. Nguyen duong Quang, a pupil of Professor Tung, had tents made of parachute material put up to shelter the wounded, and started for the hospital.

"Here they come." These were the words you heard everywhere. In his shelter, Langlais hurriedly burnt his letters, his private notebook, the photographs of the woman he loved and even his red beret. He kissed Geneviève de Galard and gave her a message for his mother while his staff officers destroyed the command archives and the typewriters. He put on his old bush hat, which made him look like a melancholy sailor in a sou'wester. Why had he burnt his red beret when Bigeard had kept his? It was because he was afraid the Viets would use it as a trophy; unconsciously, he also wanted to spare what he held dearest in the way of military uniform the humiliation of defeat. Born for action, he suddenly found himself deprived of everything and at a loss as to what to do, whereas Bigeard, without decorations or marks of rank, but with his red beret pulled down over his head, was already preparing his escape; he rolled a nylon map of the highlands round his ankle and thought of hiding in a hole, under a pile of parachutes. Why shouldn't he succeed in escaping?

Little by little, the camp started swarming with activity, while clouds of smoke rose into the air and the ground shook with the explosions of material being blown up. Demoralized by the savagery of the fighting and by the bombardment which had gone on without stopping since the evening of May 1, thousands of haggard men, who had been drinking the yellow river water out of buckets since the purification plant had been destroyed, regained hope of surviving. Spontaneously, as if they had been slaves all their lives, they formed up in columns, knotted little squares of white material to the ends of sticks, and allowed themselves to be driven toward the northeast along the sides of Route 41 beneath the contemptuous gaze of the Legionnaires and the paratroopers. These were not the pictures of the disaster which would be taken a few days later by cameramen rushed to the spot to reconstruct, with docile North Africans disguised as paratroopers, the scenes the Vietminh had dreamed of. How many were there, at that moment, who preferred captivity to insolence? Ten thousand? And are we entitled to think that Dienbienphu would never have fallen if they had fought like the other two thousand who were preparing to force a way out?

The guns destroyed, the sandbags ripped open, the shelters in ruins, the burned-out trucks lying in puddles of yellow water – everything showed that the defeat was complete. Dirty parachutes covered the hills and the valley, hung on the river banks, clung to the parapets of the bridge and the barbed-wire entanglements like torn spiders' webs. There could no longer be any doubt about it: all was lost. Some, like Sergeant Sammarco, said to themselves, "It wasn't worth the trouble of killing so many people." Most remained silent. Corporal Hoinant, who had never seen anybody but his chief, Major Guiraud, could not understand anything any more. He had been told that it was essential to hold out until the Geneva Conference was over, and now they had just given in. As for hoping, he had abandoned all hope since he had been deceived with the assurance, repeated every day, that Crèvecoeur was on the way.

"Come out with your hands up . . ."

If the fortunes of war had gone the other way, Hoinant and Sammarco considered that the victory of the paratroops and the Legion would have been more harshly imposed on the defeated side. Neither of them had witnessed the humiliation inflicted on Captain Capeyron and, through him, on all the vanquished. They noted the correct behavior and lack of hatred of the Viets, who said to them, "The war is over." Perhaps. Commandos jumped down into the trenches, holding their noses because the smell was so atrocious, and ransacked the command posts in search of documents. Others, in token of their joy, threw grenades into the river, where they exploded with a muffled noise. Grauwin inspected the uniforms of his medical orderlies and distributed armlets on which red crosses had been painted with Mercurochrome.

"Whatever you do," Grauwin told his team, "don't leave my side."

In Hanoï, where he had heard Castries outline the situation to him once again, Cogny had the signal switched to the floor below, to General Bodet, whom Navarre had left on the spot to represent him and who wanted to bid Castries the official farewell, worthy of the Commander in Chief and his brilliant deputy.

Bastiani, Cogny's chief of staff, intervened.

"Wait a minute," he said to Cogny. "You didn't mention the question of the white flag."

Catapulted out of his seat by a terrible premonition, Cogny rushed downstairs and burst into Bodet's office just as Navarre's deputy, in his shrill little voice, was saying to Castries, "Good-bye, my friend. And all the very best. You've put up a good fight."

Cogny pushed him to one side and snatched the receiver from his hand. Navarre had never conceived the possibility that the white flag might be hoisted. In his directive of April 1, he had declared that under no circumstances was the idea of capitulation to be considered.

"Hello, hello, Castries? . . . Hello, Castries?"

"General?"

"Look, man, naturally you've got to call it quits. But one thing certain is that everything you've done so far is superb. You mustn't spoil it all now by hoisting the white flag. You're overwhelmed, but there must be no surrender, no white flag."

Did Castries suddenly realize the extent of his blunder? Probably nobody will ever know, and General de Castries and Séguins-Pazzis will take their secret to the grave. What is striking about the recording of this conversation – and the copies I have heard have been cut at precisely this point – is Castries's embarrassment after Cogny's injunction and the argument he uses to justify himself. To justify himself for what if not for having hoisted the white flag?

"Ah! Very good, General," Castries replied after a pause, in a heart-broken voice. "It was just that I wanted to protect the wounded."

"Yes, I know. Then protect them as best you can, letting your [. . .] act on their own [. . .] What you've done is too fine to be spoilt like that. You understand, don't you?"

"Very good, General."

"Well, good-bye, fellow, see you soon."

There was no "*Vive la France*!" as the commander of the entrenched camp was reported saying. Radio operator Mélien, who was putting the signal through from an office near Castries's, concluded for the benefit of his opposite number in Hanoï, "The Viets are a few yards away. We're going to blow up the transmitter. So long, fellow."

The white flag which Sergeant Kubiak had seen flying over Castries's command post while Bigeard and Langlais were getting ready in their shelters to receive the Viets was hurriedly taken down.

Cogny informed Madame de Castries of the fall of Dienbienphu and asked her to keep the news secret. In Cogny's anteroom Mr. Hedberg, a journalist on the *Expressen*, was waiting.

There was the sound of feet running over the roof of the shelter. When Platoon Commander Chu ta Thé's squad reached the superstructure of Castries's command post at a gallop, did it unfold and wave the red flag with the gold star that day, or was the scene reconstructed later? On the French side, nobody knows. The only flag that Sergeant Kubiak saw flying over Castries's command post was the white one. He stated this in writing, and the official periodical of the Foreign Legion published his story in its issue of April, 1963, without anyone protesting.

When the Viets entered the command post and pushed aside the door curtain, Castries was waiting for them standing, unarmed, his sleeves rolled up. He had changed his shirt and trousers and, as usual, was wearing his medal ribbons. The parachutist Sergeant Passerat de Silans, who belonged to Langlais's signals section, maintains that at the sight of the submachine guns aimed at him Castries cried, "Don't shoot me." This doesn't sound like Castries, who may have said, in an attempt to change the squad's threatening attitude, "You damn fools, you aren't going to shoot, are you?"

Grauwin glanced toward the sap and caught sight of Castries, pale under his red forage cap, a cigarette between his lips, dazzled by the sunlight. He was promptly driven away in a jeep to be questioned by the Viet Military Intelligence. Did Grauwin also see, as he would subsequently write, Langlais, with his frozen, unseeing face, and Bigeard, his head bent under his beret, swept away in a crowd of prisoners? Langlais and Bigeard had come out together, without putting their hands up, but at a different time from Castries, whom they would not see again for ten days. Grauwin, his heart pounding, went down to the hospital. A Viet soldier, his legs covered with mud, his belt hung with grenades, appeared and gestured toward the sap.

"Outside!"

In the operating theater, where Lieutenant Gindrey of the medical service was bending over a torn body, men lay groaning on stretchers, waiting their turn. Followed by Geneviève de Galard and his medical orderlies, Grauwin came out onto the terreplein, where some wounded men, who had just been put down near some rotting corpses, watched him go by like salvation disappearing from sight.

In the vicinity of the command post, the Viets called for Langlais, who went toward them.

"That's me."

He was surrounded and Bigeard followed him, walking among his staff. The Viets also shouted, "Bigeard! . . . Where is Bigeard?"

His hands thrust deep into his pockets, Bigeard went on walking in the long column, anonymous and walled up in a silence from which he would not emerge for days, ready to seize the slightest opportunity to escape. They could look for the wolf Bigeard themselves. He carried nothing on him, not a single packet of cigarettes or tin of rations, while some prisoners were bent under suitcases stuffed with food. His faithful orderly, knowing what he was like, had taken a carton of Lucky Strikes for him from Castries's command post. No doubt Bigeard knew that he was down on the canvas, but he was already getting to his feet. The fight wasn't over. Nothing was over as long as life went on flowing through his veins. This business was not simply an affair between the West and the rebels, the Expeditionary Corps and the People's Army; it was a scrap between the Viets and himself. How had these little men, the youngest of whom looked like boys of fifteen and who had always avoided battle for fear of meeting their match, managed to win? How were fresh humiliations to be avoided in the future? What lessons were to be learned from this affair and from this army of ants which had fought on empty bellies but with their heads full of the ideas and the hope with which they had been crammed? These were the questions which haunted him. He, too, had heard the "Song of the Partisans" all night on the Viet wavelength. He felt sick at heart.

For the moment, shutting out everything around him, his shoulders hunched so as not to irritate anybody, he watched through half-closed eyes for any relaxation of the guards' supervision so he could escape into the mountains with a few companions, as Second Lieutenant Makowiak would do, reaching an outpost in Laos. From the generosity of the People's Army, Bigeard expected nothing. Defeated, he would suffer the lot of the defeated, without ever accepting it. "Poor bastards." He kept repeating this insult to punish himself and the simpletons who had thought they were bound to win because their camp was stuffed with artillery and heavy machine guns and received supplies every day by air from Hanoï. Perhaps he remembered that at Agincourt, too, the French had despised the enemy and had prepared for battle with the same arrogant self-assurance. But above all else, there must be no tears such as he had seen on the faces of some of his comrades. Victory over the ants of the totalitarian regimes was won in other ways; as for the victory parade, led by a band through the streets of a capital, which some officers had vaguely dreamed of, once the Viets had been laid out in the barbed-wire entanglements, Bigeard laughed at the idea. Here it was, the victory planned by the staffs of the Expeditionary Corps and approved by the government. He did not know that in a few weeks the prisoners would be gathered together and made to march all day long, with bowed heads, in columns of eight, a procession of shame escorted by little men armed with automatic pistols, in front of the cameras of the Communist world; but when he was asked to take part in the reconstruction of the capture of the command post, he would reply, "I'd rather die." And the Viets would not insist.

If the Viets were calling for Bigeard everywhere, it was because they wanted to see at close quarters the wolf finally in captivity with the sheep. How could they recognize him with nothing to distinguish him from the men plodding like a procession of caterpillars toward the northeastern heights?

Under a sky suddenly empty of planes, the little group of doctors crossed the bridge. The last packages of the seventy tons which twenty-eight Dakotas had dropped during the morning were spread out; 105-mm. shells, food supplies, small arms, pharmaceutical products, canned milk, everything henceforth belonged to the victor. On the other bank the medical team was stopped and Grauwin was ordered to return to care for the wounded. Dr. Nguyen duong Quang had just inspected the hospital, which he had found far better equipped than his own; he had noted that the Vietminh soldiers were treated on an equal footing with the French. Touched by Grauwin's sadness, he had some coffee brought to him.

At 1755 a dispatch from Cogny asked Colonel Lalande at

Isabelle to tell him his plans for the coming night. Lalande was still unaware that the main position had fallen. He learned it only at 1830 from the decoding of a message and the sudden opening of a bombardment which blew up his ammunition dumps, cut his telephone wires and set fire to his dressing station. After which the Vietminh radio told him on his own wavelength, "It is useless to go on fighting. The rest of the garrison are prisoners. Give yourselves up."

About 2000 hours, guided by the Thais who had not yet dared to desert and wanted to disappear into the country, the 12th Company of the 3rd Foreign tried to escape along the right bank, following the curves of the river. Radio contact was poor and it was difficult to follow its progress. From the firing which broke out, it was possible to locate more or less accurately the points where it had met Viet resistance. A little later, the 11th Company set off between the track and the left bank. About 2100 hours, silence seemed to indicate that it had succeeded. One by one, in the total darkness, all the units followed, laboriously extricating themselves from the barbed-wire entanglements and the muddy trenches. The noise of fighting came from the south, where the 57th Regiment was barring the way with one battalion on each side of the Nam Youm. At 2300 hours, Captain Hien, who with a third battalion was blocking the junction of the Nam Youm and the Nam Noua, where Route 41 met the track from Laos, was ordered to return. An attack created disorder among the bulk of the units, cut them off, split them up and overwhelmed them. Soldiers of the People's Army and the Expeditionary Corps mingled with one another. Voices shouted, "Don't shoot. You will be well treated." Colonel Lalande then decided to try to hold out on the spot and ordered his units to return to Isabelle, where utter confusion reigned.

In Paris, it was nearly five o'clock. M. Joseph Laniel, the Prime Minister, mounted the tribune of the National Assembly to announce, in a voice which he tried to keep steady, the fall of Dienbienphu. All the deputies, except those on the Communist benches, rose to their feet. The stupor of defeat suddenly weighed upon the city, where the papers were publishing dispatches which had arrived out of order, mutilated by the Saigon censorship. A special edition of *France-Soir* carried a banner headline spread over eight columns: "DIENBIENPHU HAS FALLEN." *Le Monde* announced that the plane of Bao Dai, who had been accused for some days of delaying the evacuation of the wounded by his stay on the Côte d'Azur, had narrowly escaped an accident. The weather was fine that Friday afternoon, and the chestnut trees in the Bois de Boulogne and along the quays were in flower. The theaters and movie houses would be open that evening as usual.

About one o'clock in the morning of May 8, a small group of French-speaking Viets waving a white flag advanced toward the command post of Isabelle. "Let us pass," they told the soldiers who stopped them. "We want to see your commander, Colonel Lalande." Colonel Lalande agreed to see these envoys, who told him, "All further resistance is useless. Don't be stubborn." Lalande then gave orders for a cease-fire.

For Bigeard and Langlais the darkness was falling, whereas it seemed to Captain Hien as if a long night had come to an end. Everywhere the news of the victory spread like wildfire from village to village. Professor Tung, on his way toward the hospitals in the rear, had learned it at 2000 hours. Already people were shouting, "It's all right. We know." The entrenched camp looked like a huge flea market where the victors were dividing their booty of bars of soap, flashlights and canned foods. Lights were shining in the basin, where there was no longer any fear of air raids which would kill as many French as Viets. Yet planes continued to fly over the region, ready to drop flares or bombs on the poor stars in the valley.

General Navarre's former aide-de-camp was marching with ten thousand prisoners toward the Tonkin camps. The Viets had tied his hands behind his back because he had refused to answer their questions. Throughout the world, where Waterloo had created less of a sensation, the fall of Dienbienphu had caused utter amazement. It was one of the greatest defeats ever suffered by the West, heralding the collapse of the colonial empires and the end of a republic. The thunder of the event rumbles on.

PROJECT DELTA
Shelby L. Stanton

The US Army Special Forces – the Green Berets – was formed in 1952 to fight unconventional warfare in unconventional wars. Initially regarded with suspicion, if not hostility, by the US military hierarchy and government, the Green Berets were expanded in 1961 by President Kennedy, who believed that their counter-insurgency skills could play a vital part in defending US interests – in particular, in South East Asia, where the country was becoming embroiled in the Vietnamese War.

By 1963 some 1500 Green Berets from 5th Special Forces Group were in place in Vietnam. Highly trained in the arts of jungle combat, and equipped with specialist equipment (including the STABO rig, which allowed personnel to be lifted into a helicopter while still firing their weapons), the Special Forces were assigned to reconnaissance and sabotage work deep in communist-held territory.

As a refinement to their operations, the Special Forces in Vietnam set up Project Delta in 1964, a self-contained group designed to carry out the most dangerous missions against the Viet Cong and NVA. Run jointly by the US and South Vietnamese Special Forces, Delta was organized into 16 recon teams, each composed of two US Special Forces and four native peoples ("indigs"), mostly from the Nung tribe. Other Delta personnel were operated as "Roadrunners", indigs disguised as Viet Cong who infiltrated enemy routes and bases. The assault element of the project, used to "neutralize" enemy targets identified by the recon and Roadrunner teams, was a South Vietnamese Ranger Battalion, the 91st Airborne.

This account of the work of Special Forces Delta Project is from Green Berets at War *by Shelby L. Stanton, a former captain in US Army Special Forces.*

* * *

THE FIRST INTELLIGENCE-GATHERING missions were costly, since these tasks placed a premium on mastering difficult techniques, with little chance for error deep in Viet Cong territory. During Operation MASHER in the first month of 1966, the 1st Cavalry Division requested Project DELTA reconnaissance assistance in the jungled An Lao Valley of Binh Dinh Province. Major Charlie Beckwith's Detachment B-52 left Nha Trang in C-123 aircraft and landed at Bong Son on 26 January 1966. The schedule provided insufficient preparation prior to the commitment of the recondo teams. They were inserted into the operational area the very next evening, despite marginal weather. Operation 2-66 in the An Lao Valley was one of the worst disasters to befall Project DELTA in the Vietnam War.

Sfc. Henry A. Keating's Team Eskimo was composed of five Special Forces sergeants. In a skirmish with Viet Cong on the morning of 28 January. Staff Sergeant Dupuis suffered a head wound from grenade shrapnel. The team climbed a ridgeline overlooking the valley and radioed for extraction. The helicopter spent two hours unsuccessfully searching for the team in the drizzling rain. The aircraft returned after refueling, spotted Keating's panel, and dropped rope ladders to them in the high elephant grass.

Team Capitol, a six-man American team under Sfc. Frank R. Webber, Jr., scouted several trails on 28 January but was spotted by woodcutters. Webber led his men to higher ground where they spent the night. Heavy fog and rain hampered their difficult trek through the tropical underbrush, which became so thick at the base of a rock cliff that they were forced to crawl on their hands and knees. At noon on 29 January, the team reached a small clearing, assumed defensive positions, and prepared to discuss its next move. Suddenly, Viet Cong automatic rifle fire ripped through the foliage. Sfc. Jesse L. Hancock was killed instantly and S. Sgt. George A. Hoagland III collapsed on his back, mortally wounded. Both Webber and Sfc. Marlin C. Cook were also wounded in this initial volley of fire.

The surrounding jungle was so dense that no one knew where the firing was coming from. Cook had been hit in the stomach and back. Although paralyzed from the waist down, he returned fire into the shrubbery. Webber's lower arm was shattered, but he also fired into the foliage as S. Sgt. Charles F. Hiner ran over to Cook's position, took the radio from his backpack, and frantically called for assistance. S. Sgt. Donald L. Dotson was shot through the chest and killed while trying to move across the clearing.

Hiner managed to contact an aircraft, and the team emergency was relayed to the forward air controller. After spotting Hiner's red smoke grenade, the control aircraft departed to guide two helicopter gunships to the team position. After some initial confusion in relocating the shattered team, the helicopters were overhead and responded to Hiner's desperate pleas to make gun-runs on his own perimeter. Hiner was wounded, but the VC fire became sporadic. Webber crawled back from the edge of the clearing and dragged Cook with him to the rock where Hiner was. Minutes later Cook was killed by helicopters strafing through the middle of the clearing.

Hiner and Webber were the only team members still alive, and they were both faint from loss of blood. Hiner kept passing out over the radio, but he regained consciousness in time to hear that Lieutenant Holland's reaction team was working its way to them and needed signal smoke. Ten minutes later the rescue group reached them. Rope ladders were used to lift the two wounded sergeants and four bodies out of the jungle.

The third team, Roadrunner, was led by Sfc. Marcus Huston. They exchanged gunfire with Viet Cong near a stream and were evading uphill on 28 January, when they came under fire for the second time. Staff Sgt. Frank N. Badolati was hit in the upper left arm with such force that the arm was nearly severed. Sfc. Cecil J. Hodgson's rifle was blasted out of his hands. The other sergeants opened fire and provided covering fire as the team ran from the area. Badolati begged the team to leave him and save themselves. A tourniquet was applied to his arm and morphine was administered four times during the retreat. The team paused to radio a distress call near a rock ledge and was inadvertently split up by renewed fighting.

Huston and Staff Sergeant McKeith took Badolati with them, although he protested, encouraging them to continue without him. Badolati realized that his comrades would stop if he did, so he kept moving through sheer willpower. Finally, his wounds forced him to halt, and he told Huston, "Save yourselves." Huston and McKeith placed Badolati among the boulders near a mountain stream, where they prepared for a final stand. Badolati died during the next two hours. They put his body at a fork in the stream and continued moving until dark. The next morning, Huston and McKeith's panel was sighted by an L-19 aircraft, and the forward air controller diverted an extraction helicopter to them.

The other element under M. Sgt. Wiley W. Gray was involved in another firefight before they could reach the emergency pickup point. Gray heard S. Sgt. Ronald T. Terry yell that he had been hit and turned around to see him holding his side with both hands. Within seconds Terry was shot again and killed. Gray could not find Hodgson (later declared missing in action). Suddenly helicopter gunships appeared overhead, strafing the area as part of the Huston-McKeith extraction. The confusion enabled Gray to escape, and later that afternoon he was able to signal rescue helicopters with his flare pistol.

Major Beckwith was wounded in his helicopter during the extractions and replaced. After Operation 2–66, Project DELTA was overhauled and conducted multiple reconnaissance missions across the Central Highlands throughout I and II CTZ. The next combat fatality did not occur until Operation 10–66 (9 August to 5 September 1966) while DELTA was under the operational control of the 196th Infantry Brigade in War Zone C. In that operation DELTA teams that had infiltrated from Song Be and Tay Ninh reconnoitered extensive trail networks entering the area from Cambodia. The Viet Cong were reluctant to engage the Special Forces, possibly from fear of airstrikes, but on the afternoon of 27 August, contact was lost with Team #2.

Maj. Robert E. Luttrell, commanding Detachment B-52, was aloft with the air relay pilot and spotted a red panel, smoke, and a signal mirror being flashed at them. Helicopters were dispatched to the scene, and medical Sgt. Timothy O'Connor dashed out under heavy fire to place seriously wounded patrol advisor Sgt. Johnny Varner in the pickup aircraft. O'Connor was wounded in the leg trying to reach Sgt. Eugene Moreau, who already appeared dead. An LLDB team member crawled into the helicopter from the other side, and they lifted off as automatic weapons fire cut across the landing zone. Shortly thereafter, another LLDB team member was spotted in the forest and taken out by McGuire rig. The 4th Company, 91st Airborne Ranger Battalion, arrived on the battlefield after dark and retrieved the bodies of Moreau and LLDB Corporal Mo. Although Operation 10–66 resulted in one Special Forces soldier killed and another four wounded, extensive DELTA-directed airstrike damage was inflicted on Viet Cong installations.

Project DELTA returned to War Zone C in Operation 12–66 during late September, after vainly searching for a downed F4 Phantom crew near Cam Ranh Bay. Airstrikes were used to silence several VC base facilities. On 15 October the unit was dispatched to Khe Sanh in Operation 13–66 and found an extensive storage area just south of the DMZ near the Laotian border. Aerial bombing caused large secondary explosions and intense munitions fires. During the second phase of the operation, a patrol was destroyed by the North Vietnamese on 2 December 1966. Sgt. Irby Dyer III was killed, and the LLDB survivors last saw S. Sgt. Russell P. Bott attending to the wounded patrol leader, Sfc. Willie E. Stark, whom he refused to abandon even though they were surrounded and outnumbered.

The next three operations (1–67 through 3–67) were cancelled by intensive training in Nha Trang. Project DELTA reentered the An Lao Valley under the 1st Cavalry Division in Operation 4–67. Commencing 4 March 1967, fifty-two reconnaissance missions verified slight Viet Cong presence, since bivouac and way stations had fallen into disuse and trail activity was light.

Project DELTA entered the A Shau Valley west of Hue on 10 April 1967 during Operation 5–67. Forty-eight patrols gained vast intelligence value at the cost of five wounded Special Forces members. The sweeps proved that the NVA were using the valley as a major infiltration corridor, had linked Route 922 from Laos to other roads, and were using vehicular convoys at night. DELTA elements directed hundreds of airstrikes into the area and substantially reduced the North Vietnamese traffic.

The A Shau intrusion was also harrowing. On the afternoon of 14 May, Staff Sergeant Gleason's Reconnaissance Team #1 was being landed when the helicopter was blasted by automatic weapons fire, causing it to lose all oil pressure. The pilot crash-landed, and everyone formed a defensive circle around the downed aircraft. One NVA machine gun was silenced, and after dark another helicopter lifted out the crewmen and three LLDB soldiers. Staff Sergeants Gleason and Brierley remained with an LLDB soldier and were joined by a DELTA sergeant who had voluntarily left the recovery aircraft to make room for those taken out. A second helicopter trying to reach them struck the trees with its rotor and crashed only twenty yards away. The crew and another Special Forces sergeant joined the first group. All personnel were extracted under flarelight at 9:30 P.M., without further incident.

Operations SAMURAI I to III extended Maj. Charles "Chuck" A. Allen's DELTA searches from the northern stretches to the A Shau Valley into Happy Valley, west of Da Nang, where further infiltration was discovered from 10 July through the end of October 1967. Elements overran an NVA aid station, capturing numerous documents and prisoners. In the Happy Valley area DELTA ranger, roadrunner, and recon forces fought a series of firefights with the *368B NVA Rocket Regiment*, which had been bombarding the Da Nang area.

From 27 November 1967 to 28 January 1968, Major Allen moved his unit into the Plei Trap Valley along the Laotian border of II CTZ for Operations SULTAN I and II. His teams confirmed that the *32d NVA Regiment* had moved into the area following the battle of Dak To. Project DELTA moved north again into the A Shau Valley for Operations SAMURAI IV and V, which lasted from 3 March until 20 May 1968. General Westmoreland ordered the unit to help interdict infiltration routes leading into Hue. Despite unfavorable weather and the first real jump in casualties, the Special Forces and LLDB rangers engaged the North Vietnamese in a series of deliberate confrontations.

Operation ALAMO was conducted next in the III CTZ Song Be River area near Cambodia. Project DELTA was under control of the 5th ARVN Division. The lack of helicopters necessitated reducing the usual twelve reconnaissance teams operating at any one time to only six. Twenty-seven missions were conducted during a month of September patrolling that uncovered a large number of base sites, hospitals, ammunition stocks, and food caches. Project DELTA was responsible for the discovery of a number of high speed, bamboo-matted infiltration trails.

Project DELTA was displaced north on Operation WAR BONNET in the An Hoa vicinity but returned south to Binh Long Province in III CTZ during Operation ARES on 16 November 1968. Eighty-five missions identified a major rear service and supply area there. On 29 March 1969 the unit was flown back into I CTZ and placed under the control of the 101st Airborne Division (Airmobile). During Operations CASS PARK I and II, followed by TROJAN HORSE I and II, reconnaissance teams scoured the Vuong River Valley, An Hoa basin, and northwestern fringes of the country. Captured documents enabled the 3d Marine Division to gain additional appraisals of several regiments and battalions operating in its area.

During Operation CASS PARK II, Roadrunner Team #103 was infiltrated southwest of An Hoa on 17 June 1969. Two days later they spotted thirty NVA walking along a trail, followed by one 37mm antiaircraft gun that was being pulled by two water buffaloes. Reconnaissance Team #1A had spotted something much prettier the day before. Their final report stated:

> 181515H Vic[inity] coord[inates] Z0085002, tm [team] obsrd [observed] a group of 12 VC moving NE, all were walking and dressed the same as en[emy] mentioned before, all had wpns [weapons] but no packs nor web gear. Approx[imately] in the center of this group tm obsrd a Caucasian female. The Caucasian female was dressed in white shirt, dark pants, with

> her shirt tucked in her pants. She was without head gear. Her clothes were clean and neat. Hair was strawberry blond, roughly shoulder length. Smooth light skin. Weight approx 140 to 145 lbs, height 5′6″, large bust, female was not carrying anything. She was not under duress. She seemed well fed and in good health.

Project DELTA stayed in the north until 9 November 1969. During the last three weeks of December, Operation YELLOW RIBBON verified lack of major NVA activity west of Pleiku within the previous six months. Project DELTA undertook Operation SABER AND SPURS on 11 February 1970 and was attached to another Special Forces unit for the first time in detachment history. Working under Company A at Bien Hoa, sixty-three missions confirmed that certain NVA rear service units were still using northern portions of III CTZ but fled at the sight of patrols. The same task was continued in Operation CAVALRY GLORY.

On 10 May 1970 Project DELTA commenced its last two operations in Vietnam, DELTA DAGGER I and II. Operationally controlled by the 101st Airborne Division (Airmobile), the unit swept through southwestern Quang Tri Province and adjacent Laotian border regions. There were no significant contacts or sightings after the end of May, and on 31 June Maj. George F. Aiken's Project DELTA ceased all tactical operations and returned to the rear base at Nha Trang. The personnel were reassigned and Detachment B-52 was deactivated on 31 July 1970.

Project DELTA was a very successful Special Forces long-range reconnaissance operation. The intelligence provided the identities of more than seventy NVA/VC units and enabled the capture of numerous supply caches, documents, and prisoners. It rendered vital information on enemy troop concentrations, infiltration networks, extent of fortifications, and lack of activity in areas planned for extensive allied search operations. The data were often gained in remote and largely inaccessible areas of the country, and were produced with minimal casualties.

THE LAST RAID ON SIMI
John Lodwick

The Greek island of Simi, occupied by the Germans in 1941, was a favourite stomping ground of the British Special Boat Squadron during WWII. The SBS raided Simi – even controlled it temporarily – on numerous occasions. As a result, the Wehrmacht was forced to strengthen the island's garrison with troops diverted from other fronts. It is estimated that as many as 18,000 German troops were tied down by the actions of the 250-strong SBS against Simi and the other Aegean islands.

Formed in 1942 from a marriage of SAS's D Squadron and the Commando Special Boat Sections, the SBS's main area of activity was the Aegean, but it also fought in the Mediterranean and Adriatic Seas. It was led by Major the Earl Jellicoe, an early member of David Stirling's 1 SAS.

The SBS was unorthodox in its dress (which consisted of any Allied uniform to hand), armament (the German MP38/40 was a favourite weapon) and parade-ground discipline. It was also pervaded by a very British sense of "dashingness", perfectly encapsulated in an incident where a junior officer, David Clark, landed on a German occupied island, walked in to the officers mess, and said: "It would be all so much easier *if you would just raise your hands."*

Yet the appearance of casualness in the SBS was deceptive and training for the unit at its specialist camp at Athlit in the Palestine was gruelling, including many hours instruction in the use of folboats and Greek caiques.

The SBS – the inspiration for Alistair Maclean's novel, The Guns of Navarone *– was disbanded in 1945, although much of its ethos lives on in the elite unit which bears the same name today, the Special Boat Squadron of the Royal Marines.*

The account here is of the SBS's last action against Simi, that of July 1944. It comes from John Lodwick's classic and evocative memoir of life and war in the Squadron, The Filibusters.

THE SIMI OPERATION had been considered for some time, but as long as the enemy possessed destroyers in the Aegean, it had never looked practicable. Destroyers can interfere with landing operations, even at long range and at short notice. At the beginning of the year, there had been four destroyers in the Eastern Mediterranean. Only very gradually were they eliminated.

The German navy in those waters seldom put to sea.

In March, one of these ships was damaged by a British submarine. Later, a second received a bomb amidships from a Beaufighter. Two remained lurking in Leros. In this emergency, Brigadier Turnbull requested London to send him out a small party of Royal Marine Boom Commando troops. A wise move, for though there were still many men in the SBS to whom folboating was second nature, the art of infiltration by canoe had undoubtedly declined since the days of 'Tug' Wilson. Folboats, when used at all, were now used to land personnel, their role being no more aggressive than that of a gondola.

When Turnbull's marines first arrived in the Middle East the experts were inclined to scoff. Their attitude of condescension was abandoned when it was seen with what precision the newcomers handled their craft. In mid-June they went into Portolago Harbour, Leros, crossed two booms, sank the surviving destroyers with limpet charges and emerged without loss.

The way was now clear for Simi.

On 6th July Stewart Macbeth returned to base. He had made a personal reconnaissance of the island and pin-pointed the enemy dispositions. Two days later the striking force, under Brigadier Turnbull himself, comprising ten motor launches, two schooners, eighty-one members of the SBS and one hundred and thirty-nine from the Greek Sacred Squadron were concentrated in Penzik Bay, Turkey, under camouflage. Three parties were constituted: Main Force, under the Brigadier with Lapraik deputizing; West Force, under Captain Charles Clynes; and South Force, under Macbeth. On the night of July 13th the landings were made, and despite great enemy vigilance, passed everywhere unobserved. The only casualities suffered consisted of two Greek officers who fell into the water with heavy packs. They were drowned.

The approach marches were difficult but all three forces were lying up and overlooking their targets before dawn. At first light a barrage was opened upon Simi Castle – the main enemy stronghold – by mortars and multiple machine-guns. Two German "Ems" barges which had left harbour a few minutes before zero hour now came scuttling back. They had sighted the force of five British launches which was coming in to bombard the castle. Both motor launches and the SBS opened fire on these ships. Presently, large white flags could be seen waving from their bridges before they ran ashore and were captured in good working order.

"Stud" Stellin was clearing Molo Point. He had taken his first objective without opposition. Ahead of him, Germans were running up the hill to man their machine-gun posts.

"I took a shot with my carbine," said "Stud", "but misfired. I therefore called upon Private Whalen to give them the works. We strolled in with grenades, and I think that everybody went a little mad. Soon, all the enemy were either down and dead, or up and waving their hands."

Stellin locked these prisoners in a church, left a sentry outside it and moved on to his next objective.

Clynes, scheduled to attack gun positions, gave them three minutes softening from his Brens and then ordered his Greeks to charge. "All I can remember, then," he said, "is a general surge up the slope and two small and pathetic white handkerchiefs waving at the top of it. I ordered a 'Cease fire' all round, and began to count my prisoners."

By 0900 hours, Main Force Headquarters and the Vickers machine-gun and mortar troops had advanced to within 800 yards of the castle. Fire was intensified upon this target from all sides, mortar projectiles crashing on the battlements and nine-millimetre tracers searching every embrasure. The enemy reaction was spirited and indicated that they had by no means abandoned hope. Stellin, moving his patrol to clear some caïque yards, received most of the attention.

"The stuff started to whizz about. We had to cross a bridge. Somebody in the castle had a very accurate bead on that bridge. We doubled, but Lance-Corporal Roberts, Private Majury, and Marine Kinghorn became pinned down under a low parapet, the slightest movement causing fire to be brought upon them. I told them to stay there . . ."

They did. They were not able to get up until the castle surrendered three hours later. Roberts, who attempted to while away the time by lighting a cigarette, raised his head an inch or two. He received a bullet graze from the temple to the neck.

Clynes had also been sent down to the caïque yard with orders to clear it. On the way he met Lieutenant Betts-Gray, who throughout the action did excellent liaison work. Betts-Gray was hugging the rocks, pursued by a hail of fire. Clynes and his patrol were presently pinned down in their turn. Private Bromley was hit in the arm, and Betts-Gray, who had had miraculous escapes all day, in the buttocks once, and in the back twice, was assisted into a house and put to bed.

To the south, Macbeth and Bury, with their forces, had assaulted a monastery position after considerable mortar preparation. The surviving enemy were driven down a promontory towards the extremity of the island, where Macbeth called upon them to surrender. The first demand written by Bob Bury, was rejected haughtily by the defenders as illegible. It was rewritten with the aid of a young Greek girl, who volunteered to carry it through the lines. This civilian armistice commission was successful and thirty-three more of the enemy laid down their arms.

Around the castle, the situation had developed into a stalemate, with mortar fire causing the garrison casualties and discomfort, but not sufficient in itself to bring about their surrender. Neither Brigadier Turnbull nor Lapraik considered that the position could be taken by direct assault. They decided to consolidate, make the maximum display of force at their disposal and institute surrender parleys.

Accordingly, Brigadier Turnbull sent a German petty-officer, commanding one of the "Ems" barges, up under escort, with instructions to inform the enemy that they were completely surrounded, that the rest of the island was in British hands, and that further resistance on their part was as senseless as it was likely to prove costly.

The petty-officer returned an hour later. It appeared that the enemy were prepared to talk business. Lieutenant Kenneth Fox, a German speaker, now returned to the castle with the same man. A further hour elapsed during which the only incident was the emergence of a party of Italian *carabinieri* from the stronghold, weeping, and waving a Red Cross flag.

"I thought I recognized one of these fellows," said Lapraik, "and sure enough it was the old rascal who had given us so much trouble during our previous occupation of Simi. He grew very pale when he saw me . . ."

Lieutenant-Commander Ramseyer, the naval liaison officer, was then sent up to expedite matters. He found Fox and the German Commander in agitated conference and himself in imminent danger from our mortar fire. At last, the capitulation was arranged and the garrison marched out. They had barely been collected and counted when three Messerschmitts flew over the port and dropped antipersonnel bombs.

"Too bad," the German Commander is reported to have said, shaking his head. "You see, that's what comes of being late. I thought they had forgotten about us. I radioed for them five hours ago."

Prisoners taken in this action totalled 151, of whom seventeen were wounded. Twenty-one Germans and Italians had been killed. The SBS and Sacred Squadron losses were as usual microscopic, and, apart from the two Greek officers drowned, not a single man was killed. Six were wounded.

As soon as the Messerchmitts had disappeared, tea was taken by both armies in the caïque yards. Sausages were fried and an ox, provided by the delighted population, roasted on a bowsprit. As for the prisoners, they were so delighted to find themselves treated deferentially instead of being shot out of hand, that they revealed the existence of many a cache of wine in their living-quarters. Bottles were transferred to the SBS packs, to be drunk at base.

Meanwhile, Lapraik, Macbeth, and Stellin, well known on the island, were borne to the town hall, where many speeches were made. The town jail was thrown open to the accompaniment of a furore which would have done credit to the storming of the Bastille. Unfortunately, only one prisoner was found inside and he, a Fascist, refused to be liberated.

"I admired these islanders," said Lapraik, "intensely; for they well knew that we could not remain and were rightly apprehensive of reprisals. But this did not diminish in any way their enthusiasm, though they were aware that hostile eyes were watching them, recording every incident. In the end, we caused them immense relief by taking the fifteen foremost quislings away with us."

General demolitions were begun by Bill Cumper and installations as varied as 75-mm. gun emplacements, diesel fuel pumps and cable-heads, received generous charges. Ammunition and explosive dumps provided fireworks to suit the occasion. In the harbour, nineteen German caïques, some displacing as much as 150 tons, were sunk. At midnight the whole force sailed, the prisoners being crowded into the two "Ems" barges. Stellin, with his patrol and Captain Pyke, Civil Affairs Officer, remained behind as rear party, with instructions to report subsequent events on Simi, and to distribute nearly thirty tons of food which had been brought in for the relief of the civilian population.

The German reaction was as expected, and followed the traditional pattern of attempted intimidation preceding assault. On the following morning the town was heavily bombed. Stellin and his men sat tight in their slit trenches. When it was all over they emerged to find, as they had hoped, that two enemy motor launches were attempting to enter the harbour. Such accurate fire was opened on these ships that they withdrew, blazing. So did Stellin, whose keen ear had detected the approach of more bombers, and who knew that this was the prelude to reoccupation of the island.

At three o'clock, from one of the more remote mountains, he watched the German flag hoisted over the citadel. But

Stellin's adventures were not yet over; that night the launch re-embarking his party, encountered an "E" boat on the return journey. So many and so various were Stellin's store of captured weapons that every man in his patrol was able to take a personal hand in the battle with a machine-gun. The "E" boat was left in a sinking condition.

The great raid on Simi marked the end of SBS intervention in the Aegean. It had always been intended that the Sacred Squadron should take over this, their natural theatre of operations, as soon as they were fully trained and in a position to assume the heavy commitments involved. That happy state of affairs had now been achieved and Lapraik, instructed by Brigadier Turnbull, was able to write to the Greek Commander: "Your group will operate in the Aegean until further notice. For the present, you will confine yourself to reconnaissance, but in September, raiding activities will be resumed upon a much larger scale. Sergeant Dale, SBS, will remain attached to you for Intelligence purposes."

Lapraik, with his men, his prisoners, and his booty, withdrew to Castelrosso, and from Castelrosso to Beirut for a well-deserved holiday. Here they were met by the news that the SBS had been asked for in Italy for the purpose of attacking targets in Jugoslavia and Albania. Turkish waters would see them no more.

But it is not possible to leave those waters without some description of the extraordinary life led by all ranks there when not on operations.

Picture the deep, indented Gulf of Cos, with uninhabited shores and sullen, fir-covered mountains rising abruptly from the water's edge. In this two hundred miles of coastline it would not be easy for you to find the SBS, but if you were wise, you would look for some bay screened by small islands suitable for training purposes. Again, if you were wise, you would consult your map in search of one of the few streams from which drinkable water might be drawn.

Entering this bay, you would at first judge it to be empty. Closer inspection would show you a large, squat, ugly schooner lying close to one shore, with her gang-plank down and a horde of dories, folboats, rubber dinghies, and rafts nuzzling one flank like kittens about the teats of their mother. Farther off, a full mile away, lie five or six motor launches and an MTB under camouflage, and within gin-and-lime distance of them a sleeker, trimmer, cleaner caïque, which is obviously naval property. In this area, too, are other subsidiary caïques. The intervening water is dotted with small boats from which men are fishing . . . mostly with grenades.

Let us approach the large and ugly schooner. She is the *Tewfik* of Port Said, the SBS depot ship. In her vast stern a naked figure is crouching, and whittling at something with a knife. It is Lassen, and he is making a bow with which to shoot pigs. Down below, in the murky cabin at the foot of the steep companion-way, David Sutherland, pipe in mouth, is writing an operational order. Beside him are rum bottles, magnums of champagne from Nisiros reserved for special occasions, and a neat list showing the casualties inflicted on the enemy during the current month . . . and our own.

"Blyth, Captain H. W., plus 4 – OUT – 4.4.44. Due in 12.4.44. Overdue. Target, CALCHI."

Presently, Sutherland reaches a difficult point in his work. He takes the pipe from his mouth and shouts:

"Corporal Morris."

A tall, angular, serious, and bespectacled figure comes bowling down the companion-way with a file in his hand. Curiously enough, it is the file which Sutherland wants, for Morris possesses second sight. Morris retires. His typewriter, seldom silent, begins clicking again in the distance.

Just forrard of the poop, Sergeant Jenkins, known colloquially as "The Soldier's Friend" by reason of his claims to satisfy everyone, is trying to do three things at once. Sergeant Jenkins is accusing one SBS man of pinching a tin of sausage meat, endeavouring to prevent another from doing the same thing under his very nose, and issuing orders to the Greek cooks concerning dinner.

"Not octopus again," he begs them. "Not octopus, *please*."

On the hatch beside him, Nobby Clarke, his magnificent moustache stained by indelible pencil marks, is endeavouring to write an operational report under difficult conditions. Two American war correspondents recline on the same hatch in deck-chairs. They are polishing recently acquired Lügers.

Farther forward, Guardsmen O'Reilly, Conby, and D'Arcy, mugs of rum and tea in their hands, are discussing the good old days in Libya. In the black hole behind them which is the main men's quarters, the severe and well-cropped head of Staff-Sergeant-Major John Riley can be seen. Riley, oblivious of the noisy and vulgar game of pontoon going on in his immediate neighbourhood, is playing bridge.

In the forepeak, German prisoners, poking their heads up inquisitively, are being given cigarettes by almsgivers.

Towards dusk, the scene becomes more animated, and the immense capacity of the British soldier for slumber less noticeable. The headquarter signallers are pursued, for they alone have news of what is going on in the latest raids. Perhaps a motor launch returns with the personnel from one of these raids . . . another is almost certainly setting out to continue them. Men who have been bathing, fishing, bartering with the local Turks, return, demanding supper loudly. Aft, Paddy Errett, Cumper's deputy, is cursing and producing perfectly packed explosive charges at two minutes' notice.

A motor boat chugs alongside, and Sutherland is whisked away to Levant Schooner 9, where Lieutenant-Commander Campbell, sherry glass in hand, is entertaining a couple of MTB skippers with the details of their coming patrol, which, to-night, will be north of Cos. "E" boats are expected.

Sutherland and Campbell confer, confide, plot, send signals . . .

Keith Balsillic is zero-ing a German sniper's rifle found in Piscopi.

Marine Hughes is eating a tin of peaches . . .

"Brown Body" Henderson is unable to find any volunteers for P.T.

South of Samos, Harold Chevalier, two days out from base, has just ordered a German caïque to heave-to.

MIRBAT
Tony Jeapes

Just after dawn on 19 July 1972 an eight-man SAS detachment known as a "BATT" (British Army Training Team) stationed in Mirbat, Oman, was attacked by 250 communist guerrillas or Adoo. *The events of that remarkable day are described below by Colonel Tony Jeapes, a former SAS regimental commander in Oman.*

The Sultanate of Oman – a British ally, and strategically important Gulf nation – had been in a state of civil war in its southern province of Dhofar since the 1960s. Originally Arab nationalists, the insurgent Adoo *had passed to Stalin-type Communism, aided and sponsored by South Yemen. The* Adoo *were a formidable enemy, brave, well-trained and equipped with Soviet arms. (In the attack on the SAS BATT they also had a Carl Gustav rocket launcher.) However, their appeal had been weakened latterly by a new Sultan, Qaboos, who had wooed over elements of the insurgents with promises of material progress. What the* Adoo *needed to reassert their influence was a magnificent victory in Dhofar against the Sultan's Armed Forces, the* firqat *(guerrillas who had changed sides), and the Sultan's British helpers, the SAS. Hence the attack on Mirbat.*

19 JULY 1972

THE LAST FEW moments before a dawn attack are always ones of tension. So they were now. Two hundred and fifty men lay or knelt, silent except for the occasional chink of weapon on stone, a low cough or quiet whisper, staring into the darkness. Behind rose the great blackness of the jebel massif hidden in the monsoon drizzle. Before, twelve hundred yards away, lay Mirbat.

As the seconds slipped away, commanders, like commanders anywhere, would be going over the plan in their minds yet again to make certain that nothing had been missed out. Did every man know what he had to do? The weapons had all been checked and they worked. The radios were netted in all right. The artillery sights had been checked for range and elevation. The correct ammunition had been dumped by the correct guns. Everything seemed "go", but what if . . .? What if the enemy knew, and even now were standing to their weapons, waiting. It was unlikely. Security had been good. The fighters, all young, all well indoctrinated in the cause, all heavily motivated, had moved over the jebel in parties of forty with a security screen in front to clear out the villages they would have to pass through. In any case, they did not even know themselves where they were going until they had been briefed up on the jebel the previous night.

Ironically, the enemy had helped, too. It was a year since they had identified the party cell in town and rounded it up, and their grip was now too tight on the town to establish another. So there could be no leak from there.

With luck, few enemy should be left in the town to defend it anyway. They had fallen nicely for the decoy patrol sent down on the plain two days before and most of them were now chasing a will-o'-the-wisp, near the jebel. But that 'what if' always remains at the back of a commander's mind.

The fighters would be concerned with more immediate matters, like keeping warm in the pre-dawn monsoon chill. All along the line men would pull their shamags tighter around their heads or flap their arms against their sides, half wanting to get up and get moving, half frightened at what the next hour would bring. Riflemen would seek nervous relief by checking their weapons and equipment for the tenth time. Were safety catches on safe, bayonets properly fixed, pouches buttoned up? Gunners leant forward to check their dial sights yet again by the little lamps that glowed faintly above them, and the gun numbers felt to see that the shells were properly fused and easily to hand.

To the left, the drab sky was slowly lightening. To the right sounded a faint crackle of small arms, a burst or two of machine gun fire and the dull thud of exploding grenades.

That was the enemy picket forward of the town on Jebel Ali being taken out. It was time.

All along the line arms swept downwards and men turned away from the blast with their hands over their ears as the barrage began. Shells and mortar bombs began to rain down upon the town. At the same time two hundred determined young men clambered to their feet and began to move steadily forward in line abreast. The battle of Mirbat had begun.

The commander of the eight-man BATT in the town was Captain Mike Kealy, who was to win the DSO for his exploits that day. To say that Kealy was worried about how he would behave when he heard his first shot fired in anger would be an over-statement. Nonetheless, commanding a platoon of nineteen-year-old fusiliers in Germany was very different from finding yourself in command of a troop of 28-year-old hardened SAS veterans, experienced in battles fought across half the world during the British Empire's death throes. It was a neurosis at the back of the mind of most newly joined SAS troop commanders. So his feelings when he woke with a start as the first shell exploded, he told me, can not have been unlike those of the young men already advancing, unknown to him, towards the town – half apprehension, half relief.

As he fumbled for his torch, a second explosion shook BATT house and pieces of dried mud fell on top of him. Dust filled the room. Coughing, he grabbed his rifle and belt, slipped on his flipflops and stumbled out into the fresh air. A makeshift bamboo ladder led up to the roof where most of his team were already waiting. It was just beginning to get light. He glanced at his watch – 0530.

The lean hard figure of Corporal Bob Bradshaw paced over to him. Instinctively, although the enemy were far away, he talked in a low voice, pointing out the flashes of the enemy guns on the Jebel Ali and explaining the layout on the roof. Two machine-guns, a GPMG and a heavy Browning .5, had been mounted in sand-bagged sangars.

Kealy looked over to the two dark figures of Lance Corporal Pete Wignall and Corporal Roger Chapman and the long barrels of their machine-guns silhouetted above the sand-bagged walls against the lightening sky. It was just light enough now to see the fort also, a large square Beau Geste affair seven hundred yards to the north-east. A motley group of Dhofar Gendarmerie and askars manned it, tribesmen brought down from the north under the reign of the old sultan and armed with old bolt action .303 rifles.

Nearer, to the north-west and almost within hailing distance stood the wali's house. Its roof stood at the same height as BATT house and Kealy could just make out some figures moving about it. To the south two hundred yards away lay the houses of the town, now covered by a pall of mud dust from the incoming shells. He could hear screams and some men were shouting.

A shell screeched overhead and they all ducked as it exploded behind the house. Then came a succession of explosions a few seconds apart from the base of the house. They shook Kealy for a moment until he realised it was the BATT mortar returning fire. Behind Bradshaw the bulky reassuring figure of Trooper Savesaki was talking in Arabic on the radio. He reported that the firqat leader had just told him he had forty men out towards the jebel somewhere. Only greybeards and children remained.

"Where's Labalaba?" Kealy asked, knowing that where one Fijian was the other would not be far away. Bradshaw looked up from his mortar plotting board and jerked his head towards the fort. Trooper Labalaba was manning the 25-pounder with the Omani gunner, he said.

A burst of heavy machine gun bullets crack-crack-cracked close by followed by a long burst from the BATT .5 Browning. Empty brass cases tinkled brashly on to the roof. The air was rent by unending continuous noise now, the mind-bending explosions of incoming shells, the crashing thuds of the BATT mortar returning fire, the spitting crackle of enemy machine-gun fire and the steady booming of the BATT heavy machine-gun in reply. Kealy forced himself to think above the racket. He knew the firqat leader had sent a strong patrol out after the small enemy group reported at the base of the jebel, but he had not realised that so few firqat remained. There was nothing anyone could do but if the patrol fell foul of the sort of firepower now being directed at Mirbat . . .

Then, what was this? The adoo had never attacked with this intensity before. Was it just a stand-off attack or would they combine it with an infantry assault? He told me that he felt his first real pang of apprehension as he counted up his defences: say, thirty men in the fort – they would fight back but they would be no use for anything except a threat to the fort itself, the few firqat left behind in the town, the eight SAS men including himself, and the Omani gunner with the 25-pounder artillery piece dug into its pit beside the fort. He ducked as an explosion sent pieces of shrapnel thudding into the sandbags by his head.

Savesaki was listening intently to the radio. He turned to Kealy, his face as impassive as ever but his eyes betrayed him. Labalaba had been hit in the chin he said. Kealy nodded to his suggestion that he should go and help his countryman at the big gun.

"Take some extra medical kit and keep low."

For all his muscular bulk, Savesaki was one of the finest rugby forwards in the West Country. If anyone could make it, he would. Nonetheless all those at the BATT house stared with nerves tingling as the big Fijian raced towards the fort swerving and dodging between the explosions while bullets kicked up spurts of sand at his feet. A cloud of dust obliterated him – but as it cleared he was still seen running, until at last he disappeared from view behind the gun's sangar wall. At BATT house men breathed again.

Chapman was the first to see them and pointed out to Kealy a group of twenty men walking confidently towards the perimeter wire fence that surrounded the three sides of the town not bordered by the sea. The fort lay inside the north-eastern corner of the wire and within forty yards of it. Kealy studied the group through his binoculars. It was now light enough to see them clearly, but still he was uncertain. They could be some of the firqat returning, or a patrol the Gendarmerie might have sent out without telling him. They appeared too cool and confident to be adoo.

Suddenly all doubts were removed. At a signal, the men

started to run into an extended line, raising their weapons to their shoulders. The crackle of small arms fire sounded paltry against the ear-splitting noise of the bursting shells. Chapman did not wait for orders. Short sharp bursts of fire ripped through the haze like a succession of tiny comets into the groups of running men, the ricochets bouncing and arching gracefully into the air until they burnt out. As if it was a signal to begin, the whole corner near the fort erupted with the sound of machine guns and rifles mixed with the explosion of shells. All the enemy's fire seemed to be directed at the fort and the SAS men looked on with disbelief as it disappeared from sight. A cloud of brown smoke and dust, lit up in spasms by the bright flashes of shell bursts against the walls, hid the fort entirely. Above it all sounded the vicious cracking explosions of the big gun by the fort as it fired its 25-pound shells point blank at the wire forty yards in front of it.

The radio crackled but Kealy could not hear what it said above the racket. He thought it was the gun pit but could not be sure. In any case, Wignall and Chapman, their over-heated gun barrels sizzling in the wet, were shouting for more ammunition. Together with the two uncommitted men, Corporal Reynolds and Trooper Tobin, Kealy hauled up the heavy steel boxes from below until their shirts were as smoked from sweat as from the steady monsoon drizzle.

The plain was now full of groups of ten to twelve men, sometimes in full view, sometimes hidden as they crossed a dip, all moving steadily towards the town. The battle still raged around the fort, and keeping the GPMG firing in that direction, every other BATT weapon was brought to bear on the approaching infantry. But the enemy now realized where most of the return fire came from and had ranged in on BATT house with machine-guns, the bullets thudding into the mud walls and sandbags or cracking viciously about the soldiers' heads. But nobody had yet been hit and still the BATT machine-guns hammered back.

The enemy reached the wire and began to breach it. Men tore at it with their hands. Others threw a blanket over it and scrambled across; it was little more than a cattle fence and could not hold them for long. Bradshaw told me that his attention was taken by the leader, standing in full view astride the wire, shouting and waving his men on, his rifle held out full stretch above his head. In his khaki uniform, his peaked cap and his bandoliers across his chest it struck Bradshaw that he looked like a hero from some Red Chinese poster. For a moment he watched in admiration then reluctantly lined up his rifle sights on the man and fired. Missed! Again he fired, and missed. Damn! He paused a second to steady himself, forcing his body to obey. Breathe in . . . breathe out . . . hold it . . . a nice steady pressure . . . the rifle kicked, and the man crumpled.

Several men were across the wire and running towards the fort. Others were caught. Kealy recalled that a figure lay doubled up over it like a rag doll. Bradshaw remembered that another hung head down, his arms and legs spread wide in grotesque crucifixion. Two others crossed the wire and fell immediately, one his leg jerking frantically. Another staggered about, both hands pressed to his face.

Kealy fought to think, think, think, his head a great drum of noise. Suddenly he realised that apart from a terse contact report at the beginning he had not told BATT Headquarters thirty miles away what was going on. He scrambled hastily down the rickety ladder into the courtyard and to the long range radio, forcing his voice to sound calm as he described the situation as clearly as he could. The mist was still down to about a hundred and fifty feet, he said, but nonetheless he wanted a helicopter to evacuate Labalaba and no doubt there were more casualties, and the jets were to be stood by to fly as soon as the weather allowed.

Back up on the roof a minute later, the fighting had died down. Although the cracks and thuds of battle still sounded spasmodically, it seemed very quiet, as if the whole battlefield were waiting for something. Bradshaw told him that he could still get no reply from the gun pit.

Kealy picked up the radio and called the gun pit yet again. Now very worried, he told Bradshaw to take over command at the house while he went over to the gun pit to find out what had happened to the others. A violent argument followed for a minute as all three men began to buckle on their belt equipment. Bradshaw and Wignall were needed at the house, Kealy insisted, but very well, he would take Tobin. He was a medic and would be useful.

"You won't get far in those," grinned Bradshaw and Kealy flushed as he realized that he was still wearing the flip flops he put on when he got out of bed. He dropped down into the courtyard and made his way quickly back to his room.

When he came out, Tobin was waiting, his medical pack slung over his shoulder, his drab green shorts and shirt grimy with burnt oil and dust. Like all of them he was bareheaded. He carried his rifle easily in one hand and his belt order, containing all an SAS soldier needs to fight and live with, was clipped about his waist. They opened the wooden gates and stepped out past the sand-bagged pit where Trooper Harris fussed over the mortar sight.

A shallow wadi, perhaps two feet deep, ran parallel to the direct route to the fort but seventy-five yards to the right. The occasional bullet still came near but it was quiet enough to set off up the wadi, trusting to its low rim if they should have to take cover. A brick laundry house stood a hundred yards up and the two men stopped briefly to shake hands with the ancient in charge.

They had not gone more than another hundred yards when a burst of machine-gun fire crackled viciously between them, the breeze of the passing bullets plainly felt by Kealy. Both men flung themselves flat for a few seconds and then, one man firing, one man running, with bullets cracking and humming about their ears they dashed in short sprints for the protection of the gunpit. Tobin reached it first, vaulted the wall and disappeared. One glance told Kealy that there was no room in the gun pit itself, but a few feet to the side and dug into the ground was a sand-bagged ammunition bay. He leapt the body of a dead gendarme and threw himself into the bay where he lay gasping from the final sprint. Suddenly he realized that he was not alone. He spun round. Crouching under the lip of the sandbag-covered lid was another gendarme, his lips pulled back over his teeth, his face a mask of terror.

Glancing over to the gun pit again, Kealy saw that Tobin was applying a drip to the seriously wounded Omani gunner at the side of the bay, whilst Trooper Labalaba was crawling across towards him, his face grey and bloodstained under the khaki shell dressing that covered his chin. The Fijian tried to smile with his eyes and his mumbled words were barely distinguishable, but he explained that Savesaki was badly hit in the back and had lost a lot of blood. He was still conscious, however, and was covering the left side of the fort.

A huge explosion hit the edge of the bunker. Both men were thrown against the edge of the pit and stinging sand cut their faces and hands. The crackle of incoming bullets rose to a crescendo and put an end to any more talk as the two men thrust their rifles over the crest of the pit. A series of double cracks, the hallmark of an SAS rifleman, rang out from the other side of the gun pit.

"Boss, they're through the wire." Savesaki's voice sounded faintly above the din. The enemy had pierced the wire and were now crawling and running up to the fort itself. Labalaba dashed to the gun, traversed it as far right as he could and fired. Its deafening crash, smoke and recoil filled the pit. He slapped the breech handle back and the empty brass case dropped smoking on to the sandy floor. Turning, the big Fijian reached for another shell, slammed it home with one hand and, as the breech clanged shut, pitched forward without a sound.

Kealy lifted his head above the pit and in half of one second registered two things: first, several enemy had crept around his side of the fort, and second, a small green grenade was fizzing two feet from his head. He ducked and a split second after the explosion raised his head again. A man was leaning around the wall aiming a Kalashnikov at him. He took a snap shot and the man spun and fell. Another replaced him. Kealy fired at him, too: a double tap, crack-crack. A chip of stone fell off the wall and the man ducked.

"Sav, take the left, I'll take the right," he shouted. Another crash and more smoke as the 25-pounder fired again. He looked around to see Tobin reloading. Within seconds Tobin fell too, mortally hit. Urgently, Kealy spoke into the radio and told Bradshaw to get both machine-guns to spray either side of the fort and to fire the mortar as close in as he could get it.

Bradshaw's cool voice acted as a tonic. The jets were on their way he told him, but already Harris was hugging the mortar clear of its bipod against his chest to shorten the range while someone else dropped the bombs down the barrel. He could not get closer.

The SAS machine-gun fire crackled and spat about the fort and Kealy stopped firing for a moment to let his rifle cool down. He realized he was running short of full magazines and then he remembered the frightened man. He turned to look at him. For a second, he later told me, he thought of telling the man to fight, but their eyes met and he suddenly knew the man would kill him if he tried. Instead, he thrust his empty magazines at him. "Fill those," he snapped. The gendarme set to work feverishly.

Another flight of grenades came bouncing and hissing towards the gun pit. In horror he watched one roll to the lip of the pit and then drop in, to lie smoking out of reach. He pressed his body against the side of the pit and screwed up his face at the pain he knew must come . . . until with a tame little "phut" it went out. A dud. Desperately, he put his rifle over the top again and searched for a target. The air was full of the stench and noise of battle. Something passed through his hair. Another fanned his neck. Suddenly the thumping of cannon fire sounded alongside and shells hissed overhead as the first Strikemaster jet made its run.

His fingers clumsy in his haste, he dragged out a fluorescent marker panel and placed it over the body of the dead gendarme, but the cannon fire was striking well the other side of the fort. As a second jet came in to strafe, adoo began running back into the wadi behind the fort for shelter. A black bomb detached itself from the aircraft and plummeted into the wadi where they were hiding, to explode in earth-quaking thunder and a cloud of black smoke.

The jet strike did its work and gradually a second lull crept over the battlefield as the noise of men trying to kill each other died down. Kealy scrambled over to where Savesaki was leaning wearily against the far wall of the gun pit and from where he could best see the left side of the fort. The side of his head was matted with blood and his shirt was caked a dull brown but his face was as impassive as ever. It struck Kealy how his steady brown eyes contrasted with the whites of the gendarme in the ammunition bay.

The two men looked up at the walls of the fort. The question was who held it? They could only see one wall properly. One of the others could have been breached. Kealy recalled that a dead gendarme, dressed in a black shirt, lay slouched over an embrasure, his rifle pointing to the sky. There was no sign of life.

Savesaki was both a medic and an Arabic speaker. He eased himself up.

"Oh soldiers!" he shouted. "How are you? Are you alive? Is all well? My captain wishes to speak to your officer."

Silence.

He tried again, this time with more success: at least he was answered.

"*Abadan*! Never!"

Kealy decided it was not worth pressing the matter for the moment and clambered across to comfort the wounded men and re-dress their wounds according to Savesaki's instructions. He gave them a sip of water and made them as comfortable as he could but there was little enough he could do. Then he pulled the dead men to the side of the pit out of the way and covered them with a groundsheet.

The jets made one more strike, this time on to Jebel Ali on Bradshaw's directions and disappeared into the mist back to Salalah to re-fuel and re-arm. Then Bradshaw radioed Kealy to say that he was sending Harris, another medic, over to him. And that reinforcements were on their way.

Von Clausewitz wrote "War is the province of chance", and the chance that a second SAS squadron would be in Dhofar on that day stood at three per cent. The chance that the main body would have arrived from England only the previous day and were not therefore already in the hills stood at less than one per cent. Most of the officers and senior NCOs had been in the advance party and were already taking over positions on the jebel from the outgoing squadron so only the younger soldiers were left in Salalah. And at 0800 hours that morning, the squadron commander, his sergeant major and twenty-one soldiers paraded all set to go to a nearby range to test fire their weapons as part of the normal routine of taking over. They were heavily armed for such a small group – nine GPMGs and four M79 grenade launchers between them, and every other man carried a semi-automatic rifle.

By this time the action at Mirbat had been going on for two and a half hours and that the attack was a major one could not be in doubt. The outgoing squadron commander, Major Richard Pirie, appreciated that the only way he could get any help to Mirbat in time was by air, despite the monsoon, and had already moved to the SOAF headquarters at Salalah airfield to set up a joint operations centre. There he could himself brief the pilots on the exact state of affairs they would meet on arrival, control the movements of reinforcements and re-supplies and arrange the evacuation of casualties.

So it was to the airfield that the twenty-three now went and after a careful briefing climbed aboard three SOAF helicopters bound for Mirbat. The mist was well down and the three aircraft felt their way cautiously along the coast only a few feet above the waves before landing to the south-east of the town according to plan.

Quickly the force deployed into two ten-man "hit" groups and a command group, and in minutes came under fire. The adoo must have estimated that in a little force like this, two thirds the size of an infantry platoon, a maximum of three machine guns would be carried. But this had nine, the fire power of an infantry company. They quickly disposed of the adoo facing them and, moving in bounds, group by group, and even within groups, two or three men dashing forward covered by the fire of the remainder, the squadron moved towards the town killing as they went.

The firqat also, at least those who were not out beyond Jebel Ali with the fighting patrol, were fighting hard. Not content to remain in the town, they lay scattered in twos and threes behind every rock and in every fold of the ground between the enemy and the town. The enemy were in effect in a trap, caught between the anvil of the firqat and the hammer of the advancing SAS.

It was this that worried Kealy. He had just returned from a one-man foray into the wadi where the bomb had landed to check that it was clear of enemy. He could hear the crackle of fire to the south-east and he knew that the relief was approaching the town from that direction. Unless he could get the gendarmes to understand, the makings existed of a disaster. He stood before the great wooden gates of the fort with his hands to his mouth and shouted till he was hoarse. Surely the bloody men must know no adoo would do that, he thought. And at last, after what seemed an age as the sounds of shooting crept ever closer to the town, the iron-studded doors creaked open and he stepped through into the courtyard.

Using signs and the occasional word of Arabic he had learned, Kealy explained the position to the Gendarme officer. He would like to borrow the Gendarmes' Landrover, he said, to take the BATT and the Gendarmerie wounded to the helicopter pad by BATT house. The officer shrugged and smiled sympathetically but pointed without speaking to the riddled vehicle standing on shredded tyres in an ever-increasing pool of oil and water. As he looked about him Kealy began to appreciate the weight of explosive that must have landed inside the fort. Yet, despite the pounding, nowhere was the wall breached.

In despair at this latest disappointment, he was trying to force his exhausted brain to think of an alternative way to get the wounded to safety when a broad Geordie voice spoke behind him. He spun round with a surge of relief to see the grinning figure of one of the incoming squadron's soldiers framed in the doorway. A machinegun rested easily on his shoulder. For a moment they stared at each other and the soldier's grin froze as he studied Kealy's face and the normally fair hair blackened with smoke and encrusted blood. Silently he turned and walked over to the gun pit. For a full half minute he stood there while his gaze took in the dead and dying men, the wrecked gun, the empty shell and bullet cases, the grenades, and the blood everywhere, on the ripped and torn sandbag walls, on the gun, in pools on the floor. At last he broke the silence.

"Jesus wept," he said quietly.

Although to the north things were quieter, furious little bursts of fire still flared up to the south-east as the squadron mopped up. Machine-gun and rifle bullets still cracked overhead while Kealy, bone weary, stood peering with red-rimmed eyes at the helicopter flying towards him, almost touching the ground, from the direction of BATT house.

Barely realized by him, the support of the SOAF helicopters and jets had been superb. The first helicopter tried to get in to evacuate Labalaba when Kealy and Tobin were still half way across on their journey from BATT house to the fort. Chapman ran from the house to the usual landing pad on the beach two hundred yards away to receive it and since all seemed fairly quiet, threw out a green smoke grenade to signal that it was safe to land. But as the helicopter began its final approach the adoo began their second attack even more ferociously than before. Bullets began to crack about Chapman and he identified at least one 12.7 mm heavy machine gun firing towards the incoming helicopter.

His heart pounding, he fumbled in his belt for a red grenade and hurled it as far as he could. Immediately, a machine-gun began to rake the landing site. He paused a second to watch the helicopter sheering off into the mist, then turned and raced back up the beach to where a low wall provided cover. He crawled along this for fifty yards and when it was safe stood up and walked back to BATT house where he knew his medical skills would be needed.

A quarter of an hour later a shout came from the roof that another aircraft could be heard above the mist. This time Chapman selected a landing site only a hundred yards away from the house and protected by buildings. The noise of engines grew stronger as the pilot found a hole in the cloud and suddenly Chapman saw it, a brown blob streaking towards him at roof top level coming in from the sea, not a helicopter at all but a Strikemaster. He clicked on his sarbe radio.

"Hullo, Strikemaster, this is Tiger four one. Enemy are north and east of the fort. Over."

"Roger, Tiger four one. I have it visual. How far from the fort?"

"One hundred meters and closing," he replied. This was the strike which prevented Kealy and Savesaki from being overrun.

Chapman ran back up to the roof of BATT house and passed the sarbe to Bradshaw who took over control, directing the jets down the wire towards the fort and on to the enemy heavy support weapons on Jebel Ali.

Watching a brave man risk his life produces a breathless feeling almost akin to love. You feel intense admiration combined with an aching fear that his luck will run out. So the two men told me they felt as they watched the jets flying in under the mist, straight and level to give greater accuracy to their guns, while the enemy threw up a curtain of machine-gun and Kalashnikov fire until the sky seemed an impenetrable mad network of criss-crossing tracer. Then came the ripping sound of the aircrafts' 20 mm cannons before they pulled up and disappeared into the mist. Some jets were indeed hit but none fortunately badly enough to prevent their limping back to Salalah.

Bradshaw radioed back to base that it was out of the question for helicopters to attempt to reach the town at this time, so the next lift brought in the relieving squadron's soldiers to the beach. It was not until a second lift had been dropped at the same place that the first helicopter, flown by Squadron Leader Baker and already holed, was able to reach BATT house. Here he landed three prisoners from the beach and loaded up the most seriously wounded for evacuation to the Field Surgical Team at Salalah. Although quieter, bullets were still cracking about and Baker knew he had to fly his helicopter over open ground to reach the fort. Nonetheless he decided to risk it, and it was this aircraft's approach that Kealy was now watching. Harris, having done all he could for the wounded, ran out to guide it as close as he could to the gun pit. Its doors were already open and two men leapt out as it touched the ground to help lift in the wounded men. The two worst hit, Trooper Tobin and the Omani gunner were lifted aboard first. Savesaki declined to move until they were aboard and even then insisted on walking to the aircraft with wounds that would have killed any ordinary man. The enemy were now in full retreat back to the mountains and having seen the helicopter take off safely Harris and Kealy walked back to BATT house. As the centre of resistance it had attracted all manner of people throughout the battle: firqatmen, wounded or asking for ammunition or help in one form or another, townsfolk wounded by shrapnel or just frightened, and the inevitable hangers-on, mainly old men, bearded, frail and toothless who appear to offer advice and the comfort of their presence at any incident of note in Arabia. Kealy raised his eyes in surprise as he saw a figure dressed all in white bent over a wounded man.

"Doctor" Ahmed was a civilian who had received some medical training and who had been posted to Mirbat by the wali of Dhofar, qualified doctors being unobtainable. Anxious to assert his authority, Doctor Ahmed at first had been thoroughly unco-operative to the SAS men and sparks had flown on more than one occasion, but although a thorn in the side of BATT, Ahmed was symbolically important for he represented the first faltering step in the development of an Omani medical system which was eventually to cover the whole of Dhofar. Now, in emergency, he revealed his true worth.

English voices sounded outside and a group of soldiers strode into the room led by the relieving squadron's commander, Major Alistair Bowie. Bowie was a Guards officer and he had that calm, smiling authority that immediately makes things seem not quite as bad as they appeared to be. Kealy explained the situation as shortly as he could and spoke of his worry about the firqat still the other side of Jebel Ali. They would be right in the path of the retreating adoo. Even as he said it the first crackle of small arms fire sounded to the north. Kealy felt sick with helplessness. Perhaps he could take a sarbe out and see if he could direct in jets to help the trapped firqat, he suggested.

Bowie read the despair and fatigue in the man's eyes. Very

well, he agreed, but Kealy was not to go beyond Jebel Ali. The small jebel was now picketed by a platoon of the Northern Frontier Regiment that had flown in with the third helicopter at 1220.

Kealy hurried off and after several minutes scrambling and slipping on the wet shale reached the top. Mist hid everything but the first two or three hundred yards. As he had secretly known, he could see and do nothing. He settled down to wait against a sangar wall, weary beyond words, until at last the dispirited huddle of firqat appeared out of the drizzle carrying their dead and wounded and passed beneath him.

Once more he trudged back to BATT house where he found that Bowie had wasted no time in reorganizing the town's defences and establishing order again. Two Landrovers had just returned with the dead and wounded and thirty-eight enemy bodies lay in a row, their weapons and ammunition belts, all new Chinese and Russian equipment, piled in heaps nearby. A gaggle of firqat clustered about them trying to persuade some stony-faced SAS men that they needed the weapons to claim reward money to feed their families.

Within the house a medical officer and the SAS medics busily applied dressings to the minor wounded, both friendly and enemy, while in a separate room the prisoners were being interviewed by Chapman. The three sat quietly smoking cigarettes and drinking tea and Kealy was struck both by their youth and by the dignity with which they accepted their lot. These were brave men.

AFTERWORD

For his bravery and leadership at Mirbat, Captain Mike Kealy was awarded the DSO. (He later died on exercise on the Brecon Beacons in Wales). Corporal Bradshaw was awarded the Military Medal. Trooper Tobin and Trooper Labalaba, both killed in the gun pit, were posthumously awarded the DCM and a Mention in Dispatches respectively.

AIRMOBILITY
John Pimlott

Vietnam was the war of the helicopter. Although the US had used helicopters in Korea, it had been solely for light transport duties and medical evacuation. By the time of Vietnam, the gas-turbo engine had been born, and choppers could be used to lift troops over difficult terrain to landings zones (LZs) in the enemy rear, for reconnaissance – and for air-attack. To explore all the military possibilities of the helicopter, the US government set up the Army Tactical Mobility Requirements Board under Lieutenant General Howze, out of which came the concept of "airmobility" – full military capability within one heliborne unit. A test Air Assault Division was then created – the formation which would enter the Vietnam War as the legendary 1st Cavalry Division (Airmobile), or "Air Cav".

Here John Pimlott describes the 1st Air Cavalry's role in the Ia Drang Campaign of 1965, for which the Air Cav received a Presidential Unit Citation. The main chopper used at Ia Drang was the Bell UH-Id Iroquois, the armament of which was four 7.62 machine guns (two fixed, two on pintles in the side doorways) and 38 2.75 inch rockets.

ON JULY 28, 1965, President Johnson announced the commitment of the 1st Cavalry to Vietnam. The division had formally come into existence only a month before, absorbing personnel from the experimental 11th Air Assault Division (Test) and reassigned units from the 2d Infantry Division (now given cavalry designations), but the commanding officer, Major General Harry W. O. Kinnard, was eager for action. More than 400 helicopters – OH-13 Sioux for reconnaissance, UH-1 Hueys for assault and infantry lift, CH-47 Chinooks and

CH-54 Flying Cranes for heavy lift – were loaded on transports; these, together with 16,000 personnel and 1,600 vehicles, were shipped across the Pacific, approaching Vietnam in early September.

General Westmoreland's first reaction was to split the division, sending each of its three brigades to a different part of the country; but Kinnard was adamant: the whole point of airmobility, he argued, was to keep the closely integrated force together to maximize its impact.

Kinnard's view prevailed, and he was ordered to deploy his division to An Khe, 35 miles inland from Qui Nhon in the central provinces. An immense heliport (soon to be dubbed "the Golf Course") was constructed, and the 101st Airborne was drafted in to clear Route 19. On September 14, the first Regular Army helicopters flew in to An Khe.

The central provinces were not chosen at random, for, by the summer of 1965, it was becoming apparent that the area was under attack, not just from the VC but also, more significantly, it was believed, from elements of the North Vietnamese Army. Infiltration of NVA regulars down the HO Chi Minh Trail in Laos and Cambodia had been recognized for some time, but intelligence sources were now painting a much more menacing picture. They were not mistaken: a special Field Force under NVA Brigadier General Chu Huy Man was preparing to seize Kontum and Pleiku provinces, before thrusting toward the coast and splitting South Vietnam in two.

For this to succeed, the NVA had to destroy other, more westerly, Special Forces camps at Plei Me and Duc Co, opening up the main routes to Pleiku City. In the late July, 1965, the NVA 32d Regiment began the campaign by surrounding Duc Co, threatening to overwhelm its defenders, who were a mixture of South Vietnamese Special Forces and Montagnard and Nuong tribesmen, all under U.S. Special Forces control. An ARVN mechanized column was committed to relieve the base, but was caught in an ambush four miles east of Duc Co. The NVA, under heavy U.S. air attacks, eventually withdrew, having inflicted significant casualties.

The NVA 32d Regiment was joined by the 33d in early

September, linking up with the local VC main-force battalion to establish a base on the eastern slopes of Chu Pong Mountain. This was a 174-square-mile massif that straddled the border south of the Ia (River) Drang; it rose more than 500 metres above the floor of a rolling plateau of jungle that stretched the 37 miles to Pleiku City. Unknown to the Americans, General Man was about to receive a third regiment – the 66th – that would increase his command to the equivalent of a division (nine infantry battalions, each of 550 men, backed by artillery and support units). It was the first time the NVA had operated in the South at a multi-regimental level.

Camp Plei Me was attacked early on October 20, and the ARVN responded predictably: as the defenders of the base fought for survival, a mechanized column was prepared in Pleiku City. But local ARVN commanders, scared of committing their troops, stalled. It was not until Westmoreland agreed to send the 1st Brigade, 1st Cavalry, to Pleiku to guard against possible envelopment that the relief column set out, on October 22.

As the column approached Plei Me however, it was ambushed and, despite heavy U.S. air support, the commander insisted on caution. Only when Kinnard in an early display of airmobility, helicoptered artillery forward to LZs close to the ambush point did the column begin to move. Plei Me was finally relieved late on October 25, having survived only through the courage and fighting skill of its Green Beret garrison.

Westmoreland was impressed by the rapid response of 1st Cavalry, and on October 26 he agreed to "give Kinnard his head," changing the role of the division from one of reaction/reinforcement to unlimited offense within a particular area of Vietnam. Kinnard was given responsibility for most of Pleiku, Kontum, and Binh Dinh provinces in II Corp Tactical Zone and was ordered to seek out, fix, and destroy any enemy forces in the region. He gave the task to his 1st Brigade, which immediately began widespread aerial searches, hoping to find the troops responsible for the Plei Me attack. The 1st Brigade was spearheaded by the 1st Squadron,

9th Cavalry, whose task it was to fly light scout helicopters at treetop height, calling in "aero-rifle platoons" in UH-1S whenever contact was made. The brigade's main body was made up of three heliborne infantry battalions as well as artillery and aerial-rocket fire support, the latter delivered by specially adapted UH-1 "gunships."

Unaware that the Plei Me attack and ambush had been carried out by NVA regulars, the Cavalry concentrated on areas to the north and east of the camp, hoping to spot VC guerrillas returning to their home villages. Little was found, chiefly because General Man had ordered the 32d and 33d Regiments back to the Chu Pong base in the west, where they would link up with the 66th Regiment before renewing their attack on Plei Me.

It was not until 0–720 hours on November 1 that contact was made, when 9th Cavalry helicopters, ranging far and wide, spotted movement about seven miles west of Plei Me. Aero-rifle support was called up and, at 0808 hours, a group attack was made on what turned out to be an NVA field hospital. In less than 30 minutes, 15 NVA had been killed and 43 captured, along with a mound of documents and medical equipment. Isolated firefights continued throughout the day, at the end of which Kinnard could claim a "body count" of 99 NVA for 11 of his own men killed. Airmobility was beginning to bite.

It soon became obvious from the captured documents that the Cavalry were looking in the wrong place for the wrong enemy. On November 2, Kinnard shifted his search pattern to the west, where 9th Cavalry scouts had already reported jungle trails between the Chu Pong and the Ia Drang. They started sweeping the area on November 3, setting up a temporary LZ south of the river from which infantry patrols could be mounted. Late on the same day, one of these patrols ambushed elements of the NVA 66th Regiment and then helped to defend the LZ against attacks that cost the Communists a further 72 confirmed dead.

Kinnard now suspected that the Chu Pong area was a major NVA base. On November 9, he relieved the 1st Brigade of his division with the 3d ("Garry Owen") Brigade, commanded by Colonel Thomas W. Brown, and ordered it to prepare for an assault into the Communist-held area. An entire battalion of heliborne troops – the 1/7th Cavalry – was to be lifted on November 14 onto an LZ at the foot of the Chu Pong and then patrol out, searching for contacts.

The 1/7th was commanded by Lieutenant Colonel Harold G. Moore and, at first light on the 14th, he led an air reconnaissance of the eastern edge of the Chu Pong (the western side was in Cambodia and therefore "off-limits"), looking for likely LZs. He chose a clearing on the edge of the massif, later designated LZ X-Ray. After a 20-minute artillery bombardment, followed by rocket fire from support helicopters, the battalion would be transported in a series of lifts to the LZ, spearheaded by Captain John D. Herren's Company B. Once landed, they would secure the LZ and, as soon as Company A arrived, patrols would be sent out, initially to the north and northeast, where a mountain spur jutted out from the Chu Pong. Companies C and D, brought in by subsequent airlifts, would defend the LZ perimeter and move west toward the mountain itself.

Artillery fire crashed down on X-Ray at 1017 hours and, 20 minutes later, 16 lift helicopters came in at treetop height. They landed amid shattered tree stumps and waist-high grass on an LZ dominated by the immense wall of green of the Chu Pong: one sergeant looked up at the mountain and was heard to mutter in a Georgia drawl: "My Gawd, that son of a bitch is big." Moore set up his command post around a large anthill in a clump of trees near the center of the LZ and ordered Herren to start patrolling. Within minutes, his 1st Platoon had captured an NVA deserter, who willingly confirmed that the area was a major Communist base. As elements of Company A came in by the second lift, Moore directed Herren to probe toward the mountain spur in the north.

Company B went forward in textbook fashion, with 1st Platoon on the left, 2d Platoon on the right, and 3d Platoon trailing in reserve. At 1245 hours, 1st Platoon encountered an enemy force and, as a firefight developed, called for aid. Herren ordered the 2d Platoon, 27 men strong, to move across to make contact. As they did so, they bumped into a squad of NVA and started to pursue them, only to come under a hail of fire from their right flank. In seconds, the platoon was surrounded. Herren responded by ordering his 3d Platoon forward, but it soon became obvious that he was up against a large, well-disciplined enemy force.

Moore, monitoring these developments, called in airstrikes and artillery strikes before sending the newly arrived Company A to reinforce Herren. As Company A's lead platoon advanced across a dry creek bed to make contact, it, too, came under heavy fire and, as NVA mortar rounds began to hit the LZ, Moore had to suspend helicopter operations. By 1445 hours, with fewer than three companies on the ground, he was in a perilous situation. In response, Colonel Brown assigned a company of 2/7th Cavalry to fly in from An Khe as soon as possible; he then ordered 2/5th Cavalry to move to LZ Victor, five miles to the southeast of X-Ray, and to prepare to reinforce overland.

Fortunately for the Americans, enemy fire slackened under the weight of air and artillery attack, enabling the rest of 1/7th to be lifted into X-Ray at 1500 hours. This allowed Moore to reorganize his defense, leaving Companies C and D to hold the LZ while A and the remains of B regrouped for another attack to relieve the surrounded platoon. Behind a storm of artillery and rocket fire, the attack began at 1620, only to be halted after an advance of less than 150 yards. Moore had no choice but to pull his men back, leaving the trapped platoon, commanded by Sergeant Clyde E. Savage, to survive as best it could. By 1900, Company B, 2/7th, had arrived, and Moore had set up a rudimentary perimeter.

The NVA spent the night trying to wipe out Savage's platoon – in the event, three separate attacks were held off – and to move forces around to encircle the LZ. Just after dawn on November 15, they struck from the south, inflicting heavy casualties on Company C, 1/7th, before repeating the process to the east against Company D. Fire swept the LZ, and it was not until 0900 hours that more reinforcements could be helicoptered in. By then, the 2/5th Cavalry were approaching from LZ Victor and the NVA began to melt away.

Moore ordered all his companies to push out from the

perimeter, searching for American wounded and NVA stragglers. The latter were still capable of causing casualties – during a second night of battle, they tried to mount harassing attacks – but with Savage's platoon finally relieved and more reinforcements flying in, the crisis had passed. At 1030 on November 16, Moore's battalion was relieved. By then, the Cavalry had lost 79 killed and 121 wounded; the confirmed number of enemy dead was 634, but the figure may have been over 1,000.

But the Ia Drang Campaign was not yet over. On November 17, LZ X-Ray was abandoned (preparatory to B-52 bombing strikes on the Chu Pong), and the units that had replaced Moore's battalion – 2/5th and 2/7th Cavalry – were ordered to pull back to LZs Columbus and Albany to the east. The move to Columbus went without a hitch, but as 2/7th approached the clearing known as Albany, they triggered an NVA attack that caught them squarely on the flank. Company C bore the brunt, losing 41 men killed; the fighting went on through the afternoon and evening. Reinforcements were rushed in from Columbus and An Khe, but the final NVA body count of 403 was overshadowed by an American loss of 151 killed and 121 wounded.

Despite this tragedy there could be no doubt that the 1st Cavalry had fought well in the Ia Drang. Sweeps continued until November 27, when the operation was officially called off: in 33 days, Kinnard's men, in a stunning display of airmobility, had blunted a major NVA attack in the Central Highlands, killing a confirmed 1,519 NVA, wounding an estimated 1,178, and capturing 157. It had cost the 1st Air Cavalry Division 304 dead and 524 wounded, but the NVA had, for the time being, been forced back over the border into Cambodia.

THE MUSSOLINI RESCUE
Otto Skorzeny

Otto Skorzeny was a junior Waffen SS officer serving in Berlin when a chance decision resulted in his overnight appointment as Chief of Germany's Special Troops. Prompted by the success of the raid on St Nazaire (see pages 139–176) by British Commandos, Hitler ordered the setting up of a German equivalent. The Army High Command, however, regarded the order as another Hitler whim, and pushed it around departmental pending trays. Eventually, it landed up on the desk of someone who remembered a university acquaintance who might do as leader of the new unit. And so Otto Skorzeny found himself plucked from behind a desk and brevetted Chief of Special Troops. To mark the occasion he was promoted – to the rank of Captain.

As the world was soon to discover, the German army had inadvertently appointed a man who not only believed in the commando concept, but had the ability to carry it out. Born in Austria in 1908, Skorzeny was physically imposing (six-foot four, with a duelling scar from ear to chin), charismatic, and daring. Within six months of his appointment, Skorzeny had not only welded together a commando force, but had brought off the most improbable exploit of the war – the rescue of the Italian dictator, Mussolini, in September 1943 from the mountain prison where he was held by Italian forces intent on surrender to the Allies.

Other dazzling adventures quickly followed. In September 1944 Skorzeny kidnapped the son of the Hungarian Regent and occupied the Citadel of Budapest (a move which prevented Hungary concluding a separate peace with the USSR, and rescued a million encircled German troops). During the Ardennes offensive, December 1944, he organized "American Brigades" of disguised Germans to cause havoc behind Allied lines. Eisenhower was a prisoner in his own HQ for a week.

With the conclusion of the war in Europe, Skorzeny (now a Major-General) was declared by the Allied Prosecutor to be "the most dangerous man in Europe", and charged with war crimes. The most serious of these related to "fighting in enemy uniform" during the Ardennes Offensive.

At one stage it looked as though Skorzeny would hang. This fate, however, was averted when his defence lawyer called as a witness the British war hero, Wing Commander Forrest Yeo-Thomas, who revealed that the British had done the same thing in reverse as a matter of course. Skorzeny was duly acquitted.

On his release from POW camp he settled in Spain, where he returned to his pre-war occupation of engineering. One of the most influential pioneers of special forces, Skorzeny died in 1975.

The following is Skorzeny's own account of his greatest triumph, the liberation of Mussolini from Gran Sasso, a mountain range to the north of Rome.

SEPTEMBER 10TH, 1943. We had not been out of our uniforms for two nights and days, and though our general was in the same case it was essential that I should see him with a view to making the great decision.

But first I discussed all the possibilities with Radl. We both fully realized that speed was absolutely vital. Every day, every hour that we delayed increased the danger that the Duce might be removed elsewhere, nay even worse, delivered over to the Allies. This supposition subsequently turned out to be most realistic. One of the terms of the armistice agreed by General Eisenhower was that the Duce should be handed over.

A ground operation seemed hopeless from the start. An attack on the steep, rocky slopes would have cost us heavy losses, as well as giving good notice to the enemy and leaving them time to conceal their prisoner. To forestall that eventuality, the whole massif would have to be surrounded by good mountain troops. A division at least would be required. So a ground operation was ruled out.

The factor of surprise could be our only trump as it was to be feared that the prisoner's guards had orders to kill him if there was any danger of rescue. This supposition later proved well founded. Such an order could only be frustrated by lightning intervention.

There remained only two alternatives – parachute landings or gliders.

We pondered long over both and then decided in favour of the second. At such altitudes, and in the thin air, a parachute drop would involve too rapid a rate of descent for anyone equipped with the normal parachute only. We also feared that in this rocky region the parachutists would be scattered too widely, so that an immediate attack by a compact detachment would not be possible.

So a glider remained the only solution. The final decision was in the hands of the Parachute Corps experts and General Student.

What were the prospects of sucess with glider landings? When we took our air photographs to the big laboratory at Frascati on the afternoon of the 8th, we had found it completely destroyed. I asked one of my officers to look somewhere else and he eventually found an emergency laboratory at an airstrip. Unfortunately, we could not have the usual big stereos which would have shown up all the details of the mountain zone. We would have to be content with ordinary prints approximately 14 by 14 cm.

These proved good enough to enable me to recognize the triangular meadow which I had noticed as we flew over. On the suitability of this meadow as a landing-ground we based our whole plan and I accordingly drew up detailed orders for the individual parties.

General Student suggested that a parachute battalion infiltrate by night into the valley and seize the lower station of the funicular at the hour appointed for the landing. In that way we should have cover on that side and also a line of retreat if withdrawal became necessary after the operation was complete.

The talk with General Student had the desired result. Of course he realized that there were many most serious objections but he agreed that there was only one possible way short of abandoning the enterprise altogether. Then the experts in air landings – the Chief-of-Staff and the Ia Air of the Parachute Corps – were called in to give their reactions.

These two officers were at first wholly adverse to the plan. They objected that an air landing of this kind at such an altitude and without a prepared landing-ground had never been attempted before. In their view the projected operation would result in the loss of at least 80 per cent of the troops employed. The survivors would be too few to have any chance of success.

My answer was that I was fully aware of this danger, but every novel venture must have a beginning. We knew the meadow was flat and a careful landing should enable us to avoid serious casualties. "Of course, gentlemen, I am ready to carry out any alternative scheme you may suggest."

After careful consideration, General Student gave his final approval and issued his orders: "The twelve gliders required are to be flown from the south of France to Rome at once. I fix 6 a.m. on the 12th September as zero-hour. At that moment the machines must land on the plateau and the funicular station be seized by our battalion. We can assume that at that early hour the dangerous air currents so common in Italian mountain regions will be relatively weak. I will instruct the pilots personally and impress upon them the importance of the utmost care in landing. I am sure you are right, Captain Skorzeny. The operation cannot be carried out in any other way!"

After this decision had been given Radl and I worked out the details of our plan. We had to make careful calculations of the distances, make up our minds as to what arms and equipment the men should carry and, above all, prepare a large-scale plan showing the exact landing-place for each of the twelve gliders. Each glider could take ten men, i.e., a group, in addition to the pilot. Each group must know exactly what it had to do. I decided that I would go myself in the third glider so that the immediate assault by my own and the fourth group could be covered by the two groups already landed.

At the conclusion of these labours we spent a little time discussing our chances. We did not bluff ourselves that they were other than very slim. No one could really say whether

Mussolini was still on the mountain and would not be spirited away elsewhere before we arrived. There was the further question whether we could overpower the guards quickly enough to prevent anyone killing him first, and we had not forgotten the warning given by the staff officers.

We must, in any event, allow for casualties in the landings. Even without any casualties we should only be 108 men and they could not all be available at the same moment. They would have to tackle 150 Italians who knew the ground perfectly and could use the hotel as a fortress. In weapons the two opponents could be regarded as approximately equals, as our parachutists' tommy-guns gave us an advantage, compensating to some extent for the enemy's superiority in numbers, particularly if we had not suffered too badly at the outset.

While we were immersed in these calculations Radl interrupted: "May I suggest, sir, that we forget all about figures and trying to compute our chances; we both know that they are very small, but we also know that, however small, we shall stake our lives on success!"

One more thought occurred to me: how could we increase the effect of surprise, obviously our most potent weapon? We racked our brains for a long time and then Radl suddenly had a bright idea: "Why not take with us an Italian officer, someone who must be reasonably well known to the Carabinieri up there? His very presence will bluff the guards for a short time and restrain them from immediately reacting to our arrival by violence against the Duce. We must make the best possible use of the interval."

This was an excellent idea, which I promptly approved and considered how best to exploit. General Student must confer with the officer in question during the evening before the operation and somehow persuade him to come with us. To prevent leakage or betrayal, he must remain with us until the following morning.

We discussed the choice of the most suitable person with someone who knew the situation in Rome and decided upon some high-ranking officer of the former Italian headquarters in that city who had adopted a substantially neutral attitude during the recent disturbances. He must be invited to a conference at Frascati after General Student had approved the idea.

Fresh troubles now descended upon us. The reports we received during the 11th September about the movement of the gliders was very unsatisfactory. Owing to enemy air activity they had had to make various detours and bad weather had not helped. Despite these misfortunes, we hoped to the last that they would arrive in time, but we hoped in vain.

The selected Italian officer, a general, appeared punctually, but had to be politely put off till the next day and invited to a conference with General Student for 8 p.m. at the Practica di Mare airfield. Zero-hour had to be postponed, as we received news that the gliders could not arrive in Rome before the early hours of the 12th. General Student fixed it for 2 o'clock on the Sunday (12th September) as we certainly could not wait another twenty-four hours. This postponement involved awkward changes in our plans and further prejudiced our chances. Owing to the air currents and local winds to be anticipated in the middle of the day the landing would be more dangerous, and the fact that the assault was to be made at 2 p.m. (i.e., in broad daylight) set a difficult task for the detachment operating in the valley. Various changes were necessary and had to be made with the utmost speed.

In the afternoon of the Saturday I visited the garden of a monastery in Frascati where my own men and the Mors battalion had pitched their tents. For this enterprise I meant to take volunteers only, and I had no intention of keeping them in the dark as to the dangers involved. I had them paraded and made a short speech: "The long waiting-time is over. We have an important job to do to-morrow. Adolf Hitler has ordered it personally. Serious losses must be anticipated and, unfortunately, cannot be avoided. I shall of course lead you and can promise you that I will do my utmost. If we all stick together the assault will and must succeed. Anyone prepared to volunteer take one step forward!"

It gave me the greatest pleasure to see that not one of my men wanted to be left behind. To my officers and von Berlepsch commanding the one parachute company, I left the disagreeable task of refusing some of them, as the party must not exceed 108 in all. I myself selected 18 of my Waffen SS men. A small special commando was chosen for the valley detachment and another for an operation to rescue the Duce's family. I remained at the camp a little longer and was delighted with the spirit and enthusiasm everywhere displayed.

At that moment we got a terrible shock from an Allied wireless message which came through. It was to the effect that the Duce had arrived as a prisoner in Africa on board an Italian man-of-war which had come from Spezia. When I recovered from the fright I took a map and compasses. As we knew the exact moment when part of the Italian fleet left Spezia I could easily calculate that even the fastest ship could not possibly have reached Africa so soon. The wireless message must, therefore, be a hoax. Was I not justified in regarding all news from enemy sources with the greatest suspicion ever after?

Sunday, the 12th September, 1943. At 5 a.m. we marched in close order to the airfield. There we learned that the gliders were expected at 10 a.m.

I again inspected the equipment of my men, who were all wearing parachute uniform. Parachute rations for five days had been issued. I had arranged that several boxes of fruit should be sent up and we sat about, pleasantly idle, in the shade of the buildings and trees. There was an atmosphere of tension, of course, but we took care to prevent any manifestation of apprehension or nerves.

By 8 o'clock, the Italian officer had not showed up so I had to send Radl off to Rome, telling him that the man had to be produced, alive, in double quick time. The trusty Radl duly produced him, though he had the greatest difficulty in finding him in the city.

General Student had a short talk with him in my presence, Lieutenant Warger acting as interpreter. We told him of Adolf Hitler's request for his participation in the operation, with a view to minimizing the chance of bloodshed. The officer was greatly flattered by this personal request from the head of the German state and found it impossible to refuse. He agreed, thereby placing an important trump in our hands.

About eleven the first gliders came in. The towing planes were quickly refuelled and the coupled aircraft drawn up in the order in which they were to start. General Student dismissed the men of Berlepsch's company and then my men.

The pilots and the twelve group commanders were summoned to an inner room, where General Student made a short speech in which he again laid great stress on the absolute necessity for a smooth landing. He categorically forbade crash landings, in view of the danger involved.

I gave the glider commanders detailed instructions and drew a sketch on a blackboard showing the exact landing-place of each craft, after which I cleared up all outstanding points with the commanders of each group and explained the tasks allotted to them. The men had decided on their password, something guaranteed to shift all obstacles. It was "Take it easy", and the battle cry remained the watchword of the SS commandos right up to the end of the war.

Flying times, altitudes, and distances were then discussed with the Ic (Intelligence officer) of the Parachute Corps, who had been on the photographic expedition with us. He was to take his place in the first towing plane as, apart from Radl and myself, he alone knew the appearance of the ground from the air. The flying time for the 100 kilometres to be covered would be approximately one hour, so it was essential that we should start at 1 o'clock prompt.

At 12.30, there was a sudden air-raid warning. Enemy bombers were reported and before long we were hearing bomb bursts quite near. We all took cover and I cursed at the prospect of the whole enterprise being knocked on the head at the last moment. Just when I was in the depths of despair, I heard Radl's voice behind me: "Take it easy!" and confidence returned in a flash. The raid ended just before 1 o'clock. We rushed out to the tarmac and noticed several craters, though our gliders were unharmed. The men raced out to their aircraft and I gave the order to emplane, inviting the Italian General to sit in front of me on the narrow board, which was all that was available in the cramped space into which we were packed like herrings. There was in fact hardly any room for our weapons. The General looked as if he were already regretting his decision and had already shown some hesitation in following me into the glider. But I felt it was too late to bother about his feelings. There was no time for that sort of thing!

I glanced at my watch. 1 o'clock! I gave the signal to start. The engines began to roar and we were soon gliding along the tarmac and then rising into the air. We were off.

We slowly gained altitude in wide circles and the procession of gliders set course towards the north-east. The weather seemed almost ideal for our purpose. Vast banks of white cloud hung lazily at about 3,000 metres. If they did not disperse we should reach our target practically unobserved and drop out of the sky before anyone realized we were there.

The interior of the glider was most unpleasantly hot and stuffy. I suddenly noticed that the corporal sitting behind me was being sick and that the general in front had turned as green as his uniform. Flying obviously did not suit him; he certainly was not enjoying himself. The pilot reported our position as best he could and I carefully followed his indications on my map, noting when we passed over Tivoli. From the inside of the glider we could see little of the country. The cellophane side-windows were too thick and the gaps in the fabric (of which there were many) too narrow to give us any view. The German glider, type DFS 230, comprised a few steel members covered with canvas. We were somewhat backward in this field, I reflected, thinking enviously of an elegant aluminium frame.

We thrust through a thick bank of clouds to reach the altitude of 3,500 metres which had been specified. For a short time we were in a dense grey world, seeing nothing of our surroundings, and then we emerged into bright sunshine, leaving the clouds below us. At that moment the pilot of our towing machine, a Hentschel, came through on the telephone to the commander of my glider: "Flights 1 and 2 no longer ahead of us! Who's to take over the lead now?"

This was bad news. What had happened to them? At that time I did not know that I also had only seven machines instead of nine behind me. Two had fallen foul of a couple of bomb craters at the very start. I had a message put through: "We'll take over the lead ourselves!"

I got out my knife and slashed right and left in the fabric to make a hole big enough to give us something of a view. I changed my mind about our old-fashioned glider. At least it was made of something we could cut!

My peephole was enough to let us get our bearings when the cloud permitted. We had to be very smart in picking up bridges, roads, river bends and other geographical features on our maps. Even so, we had to correct our course from time to time. Our excursion should not fail through going astray. I did not dwell on the thought that we should be without covering fire when we landed.

It was just short of zero-hour when I recognized the valley of Aquila below us and also the leading vehicles of our own formation hastening along it. It would clearly be at the right place at the right time, though it must certainly have had its troubles too. We must not fail it!

"Helmets on!" I shouted as the hotel, our destination, came in sight, and then: "Slip the tow-ropes!" My words were followed by a sudden silence, broken only by the sound of the wind rushing past. The pilot turned in a wide circle, searching the ground – as I was doing – for the flat meadow appointed as our landing-ground. But a further, and ghastly, surprise was in store for us. It was triangular all right, but so far from being flat it was a steep, a very steep hillside! It could even have been a ski-jump.

We were now much nearer the rocky plateau than when we were photographing it and the conformation of the ground was more fully revealed. It was easy to see that a landing on this "meadow" was out of the question. My pilot, Lieutenant Meyer, must also have realized that the situation was critical, as I caught him looking all round. I was faced with a ticklish decision. If I obeyed the express orders of my General I should abandon the operation and try to glide down to the valley. If I was not prepared to do so, the forbidden crash-landing was the only alternative.

It did not take me long to decide. I called out: "Crash

landing! As near to the hotel as you can get!" The pilot, not hesitating for a second, tilted the starboard wing and down we came with a rush. I wondered for a moment whether the glider could take the strain in the thin air, but there was little time for speculation. With the wind shrieking in our ears we approached our target I saw Lieutenant Meyer release the parachute brake, and then followed a crash and the noise of shattering wood. I closed my eyes and stopped thinking. One last mighty heave, and we came to rest.

The bolt of the exit hatch had been wrenched away, the first man was out like a shot and I let myself fall sideways out of the glider, clutching my weapons. We were within 15 metres of the hotel! We were surrounded by jagged rocks of all sizes, which may have nearly smashed us up but had also acted as a brake so that we had taxied barely 20 metres. The parachute brake now folded up immediately behind the glider.

The first Italian sentry was standing on the edge of a slight rise at one corner of the hotel. He seemed lost in amazement. I had no time to bother about our Italian passenger, though I had noticed him falling out of the glider at my side, but rushed straight into the hotel. I was glad that I had given the order that no one must fire a shot before I did. It was essential that the surprise should be complete. I could hear my men panting behind me. I knew that they were the pick of the bunch and would stick to me like glue and ask no explanations.

We reached the hotel. All the surprised and shocked sentry required was a shout of "*mani in alto*" (hands up). Passing through an open door, we spotted an Italian soldier engaged in using a wireless set. A hasty kick sent his chair flying from under him and a few hearty blows from my machine-pistol wrecked his apparatus. On finding that the room had no exit into the interior of the hotel we hastily retraced our steps and went outside again.

We raced along the façade of the building and round the corner to find ourselves faced with a terrace 2.50 to 3 metres high. Corporal Himmel offered me his back and I was up and over in a trice. The others followed in a bunch.

My eyes swept the façade and lit on a well-known face at

one of the windows of the first storey. It was the Duce! Now I knew that our effort had not been in vain! I yelled at him: "Away from the window!" and we rushed into the entrance hall, colliding with a lot of Italian soldiers pouring out. Two machine-guns were set up on the floor of the terrace. We jumped over them and put them out of action. The Carabinieri continued to stream out and it took a few far from gentle blows from my weapon to force a way through them. My men yelled out "*mani in alto*". So far no one had fired a shot.

I was now well inside the hall. I could not look round or bother about what was happening behind me. On the right was a staircase. I leaped up it, three steps at a time, turned left along a corridor and flung open a door on the right. It was a happy choice. Mussolini and two Italian officers were standing in the middle of the room. I thrust them aside and made them stand with their backs to the door. In a moment my Untersturmführer Schwerdt appeared. He took the situation in at a glance and hustled the mightily surprised Italian officers out of the room and into the corridor. The door closed behind us.

We had succeeded in the first part of our venture. The Duce was safely in our hands. Not more than three or four minutes had passed since we arrived!

At that moment the heads of Holzer and Benz, two of my subordinates, appeared at the window. They had not been able to force their way through the crowd in the hall and so had been compelled to join me via the lightning-conductor. There was no question of my men leaving me in the lurch. I sent them to guard the corridor.

I went to the window and saw Radl and his SS men running towards the hotel. Behind them crawled Obersturmführer Merzel, the company commander of our Friedenthal special unit and in charge of glider No. 4 behind me. His glider had grounded about 100 metres from the hotel and he had broken his ankle on landing. The third group in glider No. 5 also arrived while I was watching.

I shouted out: "Everything's all right! Mount guard everywhere!"

I stayed a little while longer to watch gliders 6 and 7

crashland with Lieutenant Berlespsch and his parachute company. Then before my very eyes followed a tragedy. Glider 8 must have been caught in a gust; it wobbled and then fell like a stone landed on a rocky slope and was smashed to smithereens.

Sounds of firing could now be heard in the distance and I put my head into the corridor and shouted for the officer-in-command at the hotel. A colonel appeared from nearby and I summoned him to surrender forthwith, assuring him that any further resistance was useless. He asked me for time to consider the matter. I gave him one minute, during which Radl turned up. He had had to fight his way through and I assumed that the Italians were still holding the entrance, as no one had joined me.

The Italian colonel returned, carrying a goblet of red wine which he proffered to me with a slight bow and the words: "To the victor!"

A white bedspread, hung from the window, performed the functions of a white flag.

After giving a few orders to my men outside the hotel I was able to devote attention to Mussolini, who was standing in a corner with Untersturmführer Schwerdt in front of him. I introduced myself: "Duce, the Führer has sent me! You are free!"

Mussolini embraced me: "I knew my friend Adolf Hitler would not leave me in the lurch," he said.

The surrender was speedily carried out. The Italian other ranks had to deposit their arms in the dining-room of the hotel but I allowed the officers to keep their revolvers. I learned that we had captured a general in addition to the colonel.

I was informed by telephone that the station of the funicular had also fallen undamaged into our hands. There had been little fighting, but the troops had arrived to the second and the surprise had been complete.

Lieutenant von Berlepsch had already replaced his monocle when I called to him from the window and gave orders that reinforcements must be sent up by the funicular. I wanted to make insurance doubly sure and also show the Italian colonel that we had troops in the valley also. I then had our wireless truck in the valley called up on the telephone with instructions to send out a message to General Student that the operation had succeeded.

The first to arrive by the funicular was Major Mors, commanding the parachute formation in the valley. Of course the inevitable journalist put in an appearance. He immediately made a film to immortalize the hotel, the damaged gliders and the actors in the drama. He made a mess of it and later on I was very annoyed that the pictures in the magazine suggested that he had himself taken part in the operation. We certainly had too much to do in the first moments to find time to pose for reporters.

Major Mors then asked me to present him to the Duce, a request I was very pleased to comply with.

I was now responsible for Mussolini and my first anxiety was how we were to get him to Rome. Our plan had provided for three possibilities.

Both he and I considered that it would be too dangerous to travel 150 kilometres by road through an area which had not been occupied by German troops since the defection of Italy. I had therefore agreed with General Student that Plan A should be the sudden *coup de main* against the Italian airfield of Aquila de Abruzzi, at the entrance to the valley. We should hold it only a short time. I would give the zero-hour for this attack by wireless and a few minutes later three German He 111s would land. One of them would pick up the Duce and myself and leave at once, while the two others gave us cover and drew off any aircraft pursuing.

Plan B provided that a Fieseler-Storch should land in one of the meadows adjoining the valley station. Plan C was for Captain Gerlach to attempt a landing with the Fieseler-Storch on the plateau itself.

Our wireless truck got through to Rome with the report of our success, but when I had fixed up a new time-table with Lieutenant Berlepsch and tried to give the parachutists the zero-hour, 4 o'clock, for the attack on the airfield we found we could not make contact. That was the end of Plan A.

I had watched the landing of one of the Fieseler-Storchs in the valley through my glasses. I at once used the telephone of the funicular to have the pilot instructed to prepare to take off again at once. The answer came back that the aircraft had suffered some damage on landing and could not be ready straight away. So only the last and most dangerous alternative, Plan C, remained.

After they had been disarmed, the Italian other ranks showed themselves extremely helpful and some of them had joined with the men we had sent out to rescue the victims of the glider crash. Through our glasses we had seen some of them moving, so that we could hope that it had not been fatal to all its occupants. Other Carabinieri now helped in clearing a small strip. The biggest boulders were hastily removed, while Captain Gerlach circled overhead and waited for the agreed signal to land. He proved himself a master in the art of emergency landing, but when I told him how we proposed to make a getaway with his help he was anything but pleased with the prospect, and when I added that there would be three of us he said bluntly that the idea was impracticable.

I had to take him aside for a short but tense discussion. The strength of my arguments convinced him at last. I had indeed considered every aspect of the matter most carefully and fully realized my heavy responsibility in joining the other two. But could I possibly justify letting the Duce go alone with Gerlach? If there was a disaster, all that was left for me was a bullet from my own revolver: Adolf Hitler would never forgive such an end to our venture. As there was no other way of getting the Duce safely to Rome it was better to share the danger with him, even though my presence added to it. If we failed, the same fate would overtake us all.

In this critical hour I did not fail to consult my trusty friend, Radl. I then discussed with him and Major Mors the question of how we were to get back. The only men we wanted to take with us were the general and the colonel, and we must get them to Rome as soon as possible. The Carabinieri and their officers could be left at the hotel. The Duce had told me that he had been properly treated, so that there was no reason not to be generous. My pleasure at our success was so great that I wanted to spare my opponents.

To guard against sabotage to the cable railway I ordered

that two Italian officers should ride in each cage and that after we had got away the machinery should be damaged sufficiently to prevent its being put in working order again for some time. All other details I left to Major Mors.

Now at last, I had time to pay a little attention to the Duce. I had seen him once before, in 1943, when he was addressing the crowd from the balcony of the Palazzo Venezia. I must admit that the familiar photographs of him in full uniform bore little resemblance to the man in the ill-fitting and far from smart civilian suit who now stood before me. But there was no mistaking his striking features, though he struck me as having aged a lot. Actually he looked very ill, an impression intensified by the fact that he was unshaved and his usually smooth, powerful head was covered with short, stubbly hair. But the big, black, burning eyes were unmistakably those of the Italian dictator. They seemed to bore right into me as he talked on in his lively, southern fashion.

He gave me some intensely interesting details about his fall and imprisonment. In return I managed to give him some pleasant news: "We have also concerned ourselves with the fate of your family, Duce. Your wife and the two youngest children were interned by the new government in your country place at Bocca della Caminata. We got in touch with Donna Rachele some weeks ago. While we were landing here another of my commandos, under Hauptsturmführer Mandel, was sent to fetch your family. I'm sure they are free by now!"

The Duce shook my hand warmly. "So everything's all right. I'm very grateful to you!"

Donning a loose winter overcoat and a dark, soft hat, the Duce came out of the door. I went ahead to the waiting Storch. Mussolini took the rear seat and I stowed myself in behind. I noticed a slight hesitation before he climbed in and recollected that he was a pilot himself and could well appreciate the risks he was running.

The engine worked up to full speed and we nodded to the comrades we were leaving behind. I seized a stay in each hand and by moving my body up and down, tried to give the aircraft more thrust or lessen the weight. Gerlach signalled the men holding the wings and tail to let go and the airscrew drew us forward. I thought I heard a mixture of "Eviva's" and "Heil's" through the cellophane windows.

But, although our speed increased and we were rapidly approaching the end of the strip, we failed to rise. I swayed about madly and we had hopped over many a boulder when a yawning gully appeared right in our path. I was just thinking that this really was the end when our bird suddenly rose into the air. I breathed a silent prayer of thanksgiving!

Then the left landing-wheel hit the ground again, the machine tipped downwards and we made straight for the gully. Veering left, we shot over the edge. I closed my eyes, held my breath and again waited the inevitable end. The wind roared in our ears.

It must have been all over in a matter of seconds, for when I looked around again Gerlach had got the machine out of its dive and almost on a level keel. Now we had sufficient airspeed, even in this thin air. Flying barely 30 metres above the ground, we emerged in the Arrezzano valley.

All three of us were decidedly paler than we had been a few minutes earlier, but no words were wasted. In most unsoldierly fashion I laid my hand on the shoulder of Benito Mussolini whose rescue was now beyond doubt.

Having recovered his composure, he was soon telling me stories about the region through which we were flying at an altitude of 100 metres, carefully avoiding the hilltops. "Just here I addressed a huge crowd twenty years ago." . . . "Here's where we buried an old friend" . . . the Duce reminisced.

At length Rome lay below us, on our way to Practica di Mare. "Hold tight! Two-point landing," Gerlach shouted, reminding me of the damage to our landing-gear. Balancing on the right front and tail landing-wheels, we carefully touched down. Our trip was over.

Captain Melzer welcomed us in the name of General Student and congratulated us warmly on our success. Three He 111s were waiting for us, and after the conventions had been observed by my formally presenting their crews to the Duce, I gratefully shook Gerlach's hand on parting. There was no time to lose if we were to reach Vienna before dark.

AFTERWORD

Hitler was ecstatic with the news of Mussolini's rescue, and danced for the first time since the Fall of France. He awarded Skorzeny the Knight's Cross personally.

Acknowledgements

The editor has made all efforts to locate all persons having rights in the selections appearing in this volume, and to secure permission from the holders of such rights. Any queries regarding the use of material should be addressed to the editor c/o the publishers.

"Operation Thunderball" is an extract from *Entebbe Rescue* by Yeshayu Ben-Porat, Eitan Haber & Zeev Schiff. Copyright © 1976 Zmora, Bitan & Modar Publishers. English translation copyright © 1977 Zmora, Bitan and Modar Publishers.

"The Sea Devils" is an extract from *Sea Devils* by Count J. Valerio Borghese. Copyright © 1952 J. Valerio Borghese. English translation copyright © 1952 James Cleugh.

"The Flying Tigers" is an extract from *Way of a Fighter* by Claire L. Chennault. Copyright © 1949 Claire L. Chennault. Reprinted by permission of the Putnam Publishing Group.

"The Bull of Scapa Flow" is an extract from *Sea Wolves* by Wolfgang Frank. Copyright © 1951 Wolfgang Frank. Published by Weidenfeld & Nicholson.

"Wireless Ridge" is an extract from *2 Para Falklands* by Major-General John Frost. Copyright © 1983 Major-General John Frost. Reprinted by permission of Ashford Buchan & Enright Publishers.

"Mirbat" is an extract from *SAS: Operation Oman* by Tony Jeapes. Copyright © 1980 Tony Jeapes. Published by William Kimber.

"Saint Nazaire Commandos" is an extract from *Raiders from the Sea* by Rear-Admiral Adolphe Lepotier. Copyright © 1954 Rear-Admiral Lepotier. Published by William Kimber.

"The Last Raid on Simi" is an extract from *The Filibusters* by John Lodwick. Copyright © 1957 John Lodwick.

"Desert Scorpion" is an extract from *Private Army* by Vladimir Peniakoff ("Popski"). Copyright © 1950 Vladimir Peniakoff.
"Airmobility" is an extract from *Vietnam: The Battles* by John Pimlott. Copyright © 1990 Marshall Editions Development Ltd. Reprinted by permission of Marshall Editions Ltd.

"Twilight of the Gods" is an extract from *Dien Bien Phu* by Jules Roy. Copyright © 1963 Jules Roy. English translation copyright © 1967 Harper & Row and Faber & Faber. Reprinted by permission of Faber & Faber.

"The Mussolini Rescue" is an extract from *Otto Skorzeny's Adventures*. Copyright © 1956 Otto Skorzeny.

"Assault into Hell" is an extract from *With the Old Breed* by E. B. Sledge. Copyright © 1981 E. B. Sledge. First published by Presidio Press, California. Published in the UK by Oxford University Press.

"Project Delta" is an extract from *Green Berets at War* by Shelby L. Stanton. Copyright © 1985 Shelby L. Stanton. First published in Great Britain by Arms and Armour Press Ltd.

"Siege at Princes Gate" Copyright © 1993 Jon E. Lewis.

True Stories of the SAS and other ELITE FORCES

True Stories of the SAS AND OTHER ELITE FORCES

Edited by
Jon E. Lewis

CONTENTS

INTRODUCTION ix

THE SCUD-HUNTERS
(22 SAS, Iraq 1991)
John Amos 1

BIRTH OF A LEGEND
(SAS, North Africa 1941)
Jon E. Lewis 11

OPERATION WALLACE
(2 SAS, France 1944)
Roy Farran 18

THE KOEMBA JOB
(22 SAS, Borneo 1965)
Peter Grossman 31

RAID ON DIEPPE
(No 3 Commando, France 1942)
Peter Young 37

SON TAY
(US Special Forces, Vietnam 1970)
Leroy Thompson 51

SCALING THE HEIGHTS
(US 2nd Ranger Battalion, Normandy 1944)
O. L. Howard 58

THE ATTACK ON CORPS HQ
(2 SAS, Italy 1945)
Roy Farran 67

PATROLLING
(RM Mountain & Arctic Warfare Cadre, Falklands 1982)
Julian Thompson 96

ADVENTURE AT BRUNEVAL
(1st Parachute Battalion, France 1942)
H. St. G. Saunders 104

OPERATION BENSON
(Belgian SAS Regiment, France 1944)
G. Sadi-Kirschen 123

FIRST BLOOD
(Merrill's Marauders, Burma 1944)
Alan Baker 136

THE RESCUERS
(22 SAS, Mogadishu 1977 & London 1980)
Jon E. Lewis 146

THE SEIZURE OF WALCHEREN
(RM Commandos, Holland 1944)
H. St. G. Saunders 156

THE BATTLE OF JEBEL AKHDAR
(22 SAS, Oman 1958)
David Smiley 172

ARNHEM
(British 1st Airborne Division, Holland 1944)
G. G. Norton 188

THE BACKWATER WAR
(US NAVY SEALs, Vietnam 1967)
T. L. Bosiljevac 198

SUEZ
(40 & 42 RM Commandos, Egypt 1956)
J. C. Beadle 218

OPERATION LOYTON
(2 SAS, France 1944)
John Hislop 230

APPENDICES
SAS Chronology 260
The Philosophy of the SAS – David Stirling 263
SAS Selection – *Jon E. Lewis* 267
22 SAS Commendation, Gulf War 270
Acknowledgements 273

INTRODUCTION

". . . THESE MEN ARE highly dangerous . . . they must be ruthlessly exterminated"

So instructed Adolf Hitler in 1944. The "dangerous men" were the wartime Special Air Service of David Stirling, founded in 1941 as a small-scale raiding force in North Africa, where they had done more to demolish the Luftwaffe (courtesy of hand-placed explosives on harboured aircraft) than the RAF. The SAS had since transferred their peculiarly disruptive – and dangerous – talent to the mainland of Occupied Europe. Hence the issuing of the so-called "Fuhrer Instruction" which authorized the murder of captured SAS troops by the Gestapo. Of course, in its way, the Fuhrer Instruction was a compliment to the success of the SAS, the exemplar of special forces, then and since. This book shows why the SAS, and the other leading special force units of the world have been, and are, dangerous, but it is not a catalogue of operations, or even a history. It is a collection of accounts, some by participants and some by military writers, of the greatest deeds of the special forces, for it is by their deeds they shall be known.

There have always been elite units within armies, from the Spartan 300, the Praetorian Guard and the Persian Immortals through to such modern day equivalents as the Brigade of Guards. By dint of their greater loyalty, discipline and fighting skill, these elites were considered superior to their comrades in arms. On the battlefield, they would lead the attacking charge to certain death, or be the armed rock on which an attacking enemy would flounder. The twentieth century, however, has seen the rise of a new military elite, one which recruits from within existing – elites (forming an elite of the elite), and is dedicated to a particular form of warfare: these are the special forces, the warriors of unconventional warfare.

Perhaps the irony in the Fuhrer's detestation of the SAS is that special forces are a German invention. Although anticipations of special forces can be seen in such military formations as the Rogers' Rangers of 1763, Quantrill's Civil War Raiders, the Boer Commandos of the late 19th century, special forces were formed definitively in 1915 on the Western Front. In that year, after months of bloody slaughter, German military leaders began to look for a means of ending the deadlock. It was decided that instead of launching attacks with large bodies of men, spearhead units, known as "Sturmtruppen" (Stormtroopers) would lead a lightning assault and seek out weaknesses in the enemy's defences that conventional forces could subsequently exploit to the full. Initially, the experiments proved unsuccessful but an officer of the Garde Schutzen Battalion, Hauptmann Eric Rohr, set about perfecting the idea, and developing the weapons and equipment for a new force. The unit he created, Sturm-Battalion Ruhr, was first used successfully in December 1915. In action, the Sturm-Battalion troopers carried little kit and concentrated on fire power. New battalions were formed from volunteer frontline veterans (drafted or conscripted soldiers would not have had the necessary motivation), who were then sent on specialised training courses. These courses tended to demand absolute realism. One storm battalion officer, Ernst Junger, recorded in his wartime diary: "Sometimes I made practice attacks with the company on complicated trench systems, with live bombs, in order to turn to account the lessons of the Cambrai battle [of November 1917]". The storm units made an impressive contribution to the Michael Offensive of 1918, when the German army almost managed to rescue the war. It was for the use of such troops that the first sub-machine gun was developed, the Maschinen Pistole 1918 (also known as the Bergmann MP 18.1). Fast-moving raiders, relying on surprise, with superior weapons and training, and recruited from volunteers who were already tested soldiers – the Sturm-Battalion Ruhr was the virtual definition of a special force.

The stormtroopers, in turn, formed the model for the "kommando" of the Waffen SS during World War II. Under the leadership of Otto Skorzeny, the SS special troops pulled off one of the most daring exploits of the war, the rescue of Mussolini from the mountain fastness of Gran Sasso in 1943. In addition to these SS troops, the German army and airforce fielded a number of other special forces during the 1939–45 conflict. The use of parachute troops had been pioneered by Italy in the 1920s (curious how Italy, despite its unmilitary reputation has often been in the van of military developments; the Italians also invented the mini submarine), and picked up by the USSR in the 1930s. Duly impressed, the Germans developed their own airborne formations, which they used to stunning effect in the first years of World War II. In the invasion of the West in 1940, German parachute troops landed on top of the allegedly impregnable fortress of Eben Emael in Belgium. The 1000-strong garrison was so surprised by the drop that they promptly surrendered to their "visitors" – who numbered a mere 85. A year later, the Germans achieved their most celebrated conquest from the air, the invasion of Crete.

World War II also witnessed the raising of similar units by other countries. (Indeed, the 1939–45 conflict, with its extended supply lines, long frontiers and huge areas "behind enemy lines" was ideal special force terrain.) A small number of British military officers, prime among them Lieutenant-Colonel J. C. F Holland R. E., had begun – with the example of the First World War "stormtruppen" firmly in mind – in the late 1930s to press for the formation of irregular or guerrilla companies in the British army. These first saw expression as the "Independent Companies", created during the period of the "Phoney War", but it was only after the fall of France and the personal push of Winston Churchill that British special forces received real direction or resources. In June 1940 Colonel Dudley Clarke of the British General Staff organized the reformation of the Independent Companies as Army "Commandos", the name deriving from the freebooting Boer horse soldiers who had fought the South African War (1899–1902) during Churchill's youth. Out of these Army Commandos were, in time, spun-off other special forces. No 2 Commando, for instance, was despatched to Ringway Airport in July 1940 and ordered to become Britain's first parachute unit (see "Adventure at Bruneval", pp104–22). As the story "Birth of a Legend" shows, the SAS, along with a number of "mobs for the jobs", was formed out of a disbanded Army commando unit. Not that David Stirling, the SAS founder, recruited every commando who volunteered. Selection was rigorous, so was training, with any man not achieving or maintaining the required grade being "RTUd", returned to parent unit. (The SAS, like other special forces, still maintains a gruelling selection procedure, as can be seen from the appendix on selection for the 22nd SAS Regiment today). Meanwhile, the need for wartime commandos prompted the War Office to look for a source outside the army; their eyes alighted on the Royal Marines, who between 1942 and 1944, formed nine commando units.

The heroism and discipline of the Commandos at Dieppe in 1942 (see pp37–50) was recognized in the granting of the right to wear a distinctive green beret. Indeed, a hall-mark of a special force is that they wear an unique badge or piece of uniform. Accordingly, the Parachute Regiment has a red beret, the SAS itself a beige beret, US Special Forces a green beret (inspired by that of the British commandos), while USSR Airborne Divisions sport a striped shirt.

Although not entering World War II until 1941, the USA was quick to exploit the special force concept. At the time of the Japanese attack on Pearl Harbor in December 1941, the US had one operational parachute battalion. Within eight months, it had two parachute divisions, the 82nd ("All American") and 101st ("Screaming Eagles"). These divisions, in whole or in part, saw action in North Africa, Sicily, Italy and in France, during D-Day 1944. Later, they took part in Operation Market Garden, and when the Germans launched their counter-offensive in December 1944, both were sent as ground-troop "firebrigades" to hold the strategically important towns of Bastogne and St. Vith.

Alongside its airborne forces, the US also created three other commando-type units, the Rangers (see "Scaling the Heights"), the US Marine Corps raider battalions and the 5307th Composite Unit. Better-known as "Merrill's Marauders", the 5307th, based on the Chindits of Orde Wingate, was a deep-penetration force which would take the war into the jungles of Japanese-occupied Burma.

It is a remarkable fact that of all the special forces created during World War II only three survived 1945 and the outbreak of peace: the British Commandos, the British SAS (and then only after being disbanded and reformed) and the Belgian SAS. Special forces were viewed with mistrust by the military "top brass" (who believed them to be "private armies"), while military strategists considered that they would have no role to play in forthcoming wars, which would be either conventional meetings of armies on the field of battle or a nuclear exchange by remote control. This wisdom did not survive a decade. Warfare since 1945 has been dominated by struggles of national liberation and insurgency by Communist (or, at least self-styled Communist) forces. In other words, guerrilla warfare has been the new warfare, from the jungles of Malaya to the streets of Northern Ireland, from the deserts of Palestine to the alleyways of Algeria, by way of El Salvador, Chile and most other points of the globe. This has left Governments and Chiefs of Staff in a dilemma, since classically deployed lines of troops and tanks tend to be of little use in countering guerrillas. But who better, to catch a guerrilla than a guerrilla in uniform, a soldier from a special force? Moreover, those "general conflicts" which have been fought since 1945, like Korea, the Falklands and the Gulf War, have demonstrated all too clearly that "behind the lines" raids, disruptions, intelligence-gathering and alarm-spreading are as war-winning as ever. The last decades, consequently, have seen a resurrection of special forces, the units which put the elements of daring and surprise back into war.

If special forces tend to be viewed with a tingle of envy by other soldiers – after all special forces are invariably better trained and equipped than other units – they have won adulation from the public. It is not difficult to see why. In an age without heroes and in an age when wars can, in theory at least, be shot out across continents by push-button soldiers in the rear echelons, the trooper of the special force still fights his wars in person.

Jon E. Lewis

THE SCUD-HUNTERS
John Amos

The 22nd Special Air Service Regiment came to the attention of the world in May 1980 when troopers from its B Squadron stormed the Iranian Embassy in London and, in the full glare of the TV camera, rescued 19 hostages. It was an unusually public appearance for the unit, most of whose operations before and since have been deep behind enemy lines or in the more shadowy areas of Counter-Revolutionary Warfare (CRW).

The present day 22 SAS Regiment, the direct descendant of the wartime SAS of David Stirling (see "Birth of a Legend", pp 11–17), was formed in 1952, and began its career fighting guerrillas in Malaya (since 1957, Malaysia), Borneo, Oman and Aden. In recent decades the main SAS effort has been directed against the IRA, both in Ireland and on the mainland. The Regiment – to itself it is always "the Regiment" or "Sass", never "S.A.S." – has also used its counter-terrorist capability to help other European security forces. In May 1977 it helped Dutch marines and police to deal with the hi-jack of a passenger train by South Moluccan gunmen, and five months later worked with the German GSG9 at Mogadishu (see "The Rescuers", pp146–55). Five years on, the SAS was asked to fight a so-called "general war" in the Falklands. In 1990, the Ministry of Defence once again called on 22's special service and sent it to fight Saddam Hussein in the Gulf War. It was almost a homecoming for the Regiment, for it had been raised in the desert fifty years before. And, as the story of the 22 SAS patrol codenamed "Bravo Two Zero" shows, the intervening years had done nothing to diminish the professionalism and physical capability of the SAS trooper.

THE 22ND SAS Regiment was alerted for action within hours of Saddam Hussein sending his armour rolling into oil-rich Kuwait at 0200 (local time) on 2 August 1990. At Stirling Lines, the SAS camp situated behind a nondescript

1950s red-brick housing estate on the edge of Hereford, a small batch of troopers was issued desert kit and briefed. They were flown out to Saudi Arabia later that month, carrying hand-held designators (which "paint" targets for the laser-guided bombs of Allied aircraft), as part of the United Nations' Operation "Desert Shield", the securing of the Saudi border from further Iraqi encroachment.

More teams of SAS followed. Initially, it seemed that the SAS would be employed in their role as hostage rescuers. The commander of the 40,000-strong force which made up the British contribution to the anti-Saddam Coalition, Lt-General Sir Peter de la Billiere ("DLB"), had previously fought with 22 SAS in Oman and Malaya, and commanded the Regiment during the Falklands conflict. He had also planned the 1980 seizure of the Iranian Embassy at Prince's Gate. Now, in the Gulf, he was faced with another hostage situation, Saddam's use of "guests" as human shields at important military installations. Eventually, however, de la Billiere ruled an SAS mass rescue mission. The hostages were constantly moved and the intelligence inside Iraq was not good.

Meanwhile, the number of 22 SAS at the regimental holding area in Saudi Arabia grew steadily. By early January 1991 the force assembled totalled 300 badged SAS soldiers, plus 15 volunteers from the elite reserve team of the part-time Territorial Regiments, 21 and 23 SAS. It was the biggest gathering of the unit since the heady days of World War II.

For an agonising period, however, it looked as though the unit would be given no role in Operation "Desert Storm", the Allied offensive to remove the Iraqis from Kuwait. The SAS were gathered like so many racehorses before a race, but not sure if they would be allowed to run. The Commander-in-Chief of the Allied forces, US General H. Norman "Stormin' Norman" Schwarzkopf, intended to degrade Saddam's military capability by a huge air campaign, while finishing him off with a completely conventional – if tactically brilliant – infantry and armoured envelopment. Also, like many senior military figures, the irrascible Schwarzkopf was no admirer of special forces. Reputedly, he had met a contingent of US Special Forces in the Gulf with the greeting: "I remember you guys from Vietnam . . . you couldn't do your jobs there, and you didn't do your job in Panama. What makes you think you can do your job here?". However, de la Billiere, the only non-American on Schwarzkopf's planning staff, CENTCOM, was determined to find a job for his old Regiment. In the second week of January, de la Billiere identified a task for 22 SAS, to cut roads and cause diversions in the enemy rear, thus pulling troops away from the front. After a presentation by the SAS themselves, Schwarzkopf gave 22 SAS the go-ahead. They would cross the Iraqi border right at the beginning of the air campaign. This was scheduled to begin on 29 January. The SAS was in the war.

As the Regiment made itself ready at its holding area, the world was hypnotised by the deadline by which President Bush insisted Iraq implement United Nations' Resolution 660 (Iraqi withdrawal from Kuwait), midnight on 16 January. Saddam refused to blink or budge.

The Regiment was as surprised as most other people when hundreds of Allied aircraft and Tomahawk Cruise missiles began bombarding targets in Iraq just before dawn on 17 January. Within twenty-four hours the Iraqi airforce was all but wiped out and Saddam's command and communications system heavily mauled. Allied commanders retired to bed at the end of D-Day most satisfied.

The only nagging area of Allied doubt was Iraq's Scud surface-to-surface (SSM) missile capability. Though an outdated technology, a Soviet version of Hitler's V2, the Scud was capable of carrying nuclear and bio-chemical warheads. It could be fired from a fixed site or from a mobile launcher. Could Saddam still fire his Scuds? Would he? On the second night of the air campaign, Saddam answered all speculations by launching Scuds (all with conventional warheads) at Saudi Arabia and Israel. The six which landed in Israel injured no one, but they were political dynamite. If Israel responded militarily the fragile coalition, which included several Arab members, would be blown apart. Israel declared itself to be in a state of war, but frantic diplomacy by the Allies managed to dissuade Israel from taking immediate punitive action. Batteries of Patriot ground-to-air missiles were dispatched to Tel Aviv, Jerusalem and Haifa. The Allies diverted 30% of their air effort to Scud hunting. But in the expanses of vast Iraqi desert all too often the air strike arrived to find the Scud fired and the mobile launcher elusively camouflaged. Previously, the US military had believed that its hi-tec satellite observation system could detect Scuds before launch. Now it was finding that the Scuds could be many minutes into flight before being betrayed by the flare from their motors. Asked by the media on 19 January about the Scud menace, the normally upbeat Schwarzkopf was obliged to say that "the picture is unclear", and to grumble that looking for Scuds was like looking for the proverbial needle in the haystack.

If the C-in-C was unclear about what to do, the Scud factor gave 22 SAS an absolutely clear-cut mission. De la Billiere signalled 22 SAS that "all SAS effort should be directed against Scuds". That very same day, 19 January, the SAS was rushed 1500 km from its holding area to an FOB just inside the Saudi border with Western Iraq. The move was made in a non-stop 24 hour airlift by the RAF Special Forces flight.

The Regiment decided on two principal means of dealing with the Scud menace. It would insert into Iraq covert 8-man static patrols to watch Main Supply Routes (MSRs) and report on the movement of Scud traffic. There would be three such patrols, South, Central and North. When Scud sites and launchers were identified, US F15 and A10 airstrikes would be called down to destroy them, directed to the target by the SAS patrol using a tactical airlink. (Though the SAS patrols carried laser-designators to "paint" targets for Allied aircraft they only used them infrequently.)

Alongside the road watch patrols, there were four columns of heavily armed vehicles, "Pink Panther" Land Rovers and Unimogs, which would penetrate the "Scud Box", an area of western desert near the border with Jordan which was thought to contain around 14 mobile launchers.

As is traditional in the SAS, the decision how to deploy was left to the patrol commanders and reached after democratic discussion.

The South and Central road watch teams were inserted on 21 January, and both found that the eerily flat, featureless desert offered no possibility of concealment. The South road watch patrol aborted their mission and flew back on their insertion helicopter. The Central team also decided that the terrain was lethal, but before "bugging out" in their Land Rovers and stripped-down motorcycles called down an air strike on two Iraqi radars. After a four-night drive through 140 miles of bitingly cold desert the patrol reached Saudi Arabia. Four men needed treatment for frostbite.

Road Watch North, codenamed "Bravo Two Zero", had the most isolated insertion, landed by RAF Chinook 100 miles north-west of Baghdad. The weather was appalling, driving wind and sleet, the worst winter in this part of the Iraqi desert for thirty years. Led by Sgt Andy McNab (a pseudonym), the patrol took food and water for 14 days, explosives and ammunition for their 203s (American M16 rifles with 40mm grenade-launchers attached), Minimi machine guns, grenades, extra clothes, maps, compasses and survival equipment. Each man was carrying 209 lbs of kit. Watching a main supply route, the patrol saw a Scud launch and prepared to send their first situation report ("Sit Rep") to base. In the first of several fruitless efforts, Bravo Two Zero's signaller, Trooper Steven ("Legs") Lane prepared the radio antenna, encoded Sgt McNab's message and typed it ready for transmission. There was no answer and no amount of adjusting the set got a response.

On the second day an Iraqi military convoy rumbled across the desert towards the team and sited a battery of low-level anti-aircraft guns only yards from where they were hunkered down. The team got off a brief radio message to HQ: "Enemy triple-A gun now in position immediately to our north". The team was now in grave danger of compromise. In mid afternoon the compromise came. A young Iraqi goatherd looked down into the patrol's lying-up place (LUP), a shallow wadi, saw the troopers and ran off towards the Iraqi soldiers. Bravo Two Zero rapidly prepared to move, checking equipment and gulping down as much water as possible. They had a "fearsome tab" (march) in front of them.

There were further frantic efforts to radio base that they were now compromised and requested "exfil asap". There was again no response. The HF radio was being rendered near useless by ionospheric distortion. The men loaded their bergens and moved quickly westwards. As they cleared the bottom of the wadi they heard tracked vehicles approaching from the rear. They dropped into a depression and turned to face the enemy. An Iraqi Armoured Personnel Carrier (APC) opened fire with a 7.62 machine gun. With a scream of "Fucking let's do it!", the SAS patrol fired off a fusillade of 66 anti-armour rockets, rifle grenades and Minimis. They held off the Iraqis twice, destroying armoured personnel carriers and infantry trucks, and cut down scores of troops.

It started to get dark, and the patrol decided to get out of the contact area, moving as fast as they physically could manage with their heavy bergens. As they cleared a slope the Iraqi Triple-A battery sighted them and opened fire. A 57 mm ack-ack round hit one trooper in the back, ripping open his bergen. When extracted from it he was found to be uninjured. The rest of the patrol voted to "bin" their bergens for more speed, and eventually lost their enemy in the gloom. At a rallying point, Sgt McNab decided to use their four personal short-range TACBE (personal rescue beacons) to get in touch with an orbiting AWACS plane to bring strike aircraft down on the Iraqis. Again there was no reply. McNab did a quick appreciation of their situation. The Iraqis would expect them to make south for Saudi Arabia. Jordan was due West but was a non-combatant ally of Saddam Hussein. A hundred and twenty kilometres to the north west was Syria, a member of the anti-Saddam coalition. McNab decided to go for Syria.

Moving fast towards the Syrian border, Bravo Two Zero walked 50 miles that night, through driving sleet, pausing to rest only four times. Two troopers were in a parlous state, however. Sgt Vince Phillips had fractured a leg in the contact with the Iraqis and was finding it difficult to move. Trooper "Stan" was becoming dangerously dehydrated.

The sound of aircraft high overhead prompted another call on the TACBE. Finally, they got a response. An American pilot on a bombing mission acknowledged their call. The message was relayed to the British Special Ops HQ in Saudi

Arabia. British and American helicopters went into Iraq to search for the patrol, but a specific run to a pre-arranged rendezvous was ruled out as too dangerous.

The stop to use the TACBE proved unlucky. In the swirling, raining darkness, Sgt Phillips, Cpl "Chris" and Trooper Stan carried on walking and became separated from the rest of the patrol.

Sgt McNab and his four companions had no option but to continue on without them, hoping they would meet up later. The rain turned to snow. During rests they huddled together for warmth. In their soaked clothes the wind-chill was starting to kill them. Throughout the night they slowly made their way to the Syrian border. Resting during the next day they decided that, if they were going to make it, they would need to hi-jack a vehicle, preferably something inconspicuous. Watching by a main road they ignored military trucks. In the gathering darkness of evening they spotted the lights of a single vehicle and flagged it down. The incident has already entered Regiment folklore. Instead of the hoped for 4WD, they found before them a bright yellow New York taxi, proudly sporting chrome bumpers and whitewall tyres. The five SAS men pulled out its amazed occupants and hopped in, putting the heater on high. They made good progress towards the border, their shamags pulled up around their faces to conceal their Caucasian identity, until they became confused in the lacework of roads near the border. Along with other traffic they were stopped by Iraqi soldiers at a vehicle checkpoint. An Iraqi "jundie" (squaddie) knocked on the driver's window to ask for their papers. Trooper Legs Lane shot the Iraqi in the head with his 203. The SAS men leaped out, shot two more soldiers and ran off into the desert.

By now the lights of a town across the border were clearly visible. As they neared the border they again ran into an anti-aircraft battery. Shells and small arms fire landed all around. There were now over 1500 Iraqi troops looking for them. The SAS men had barely six miles to go, but the moon was bright. An Iraqi patrol found them hiding in a ditch. A running firefight broke out in which the SAS soldiers killed scores of Iraqis, but became separated from each other in the process. Trooper "Mark" was wounded in the elbow and ankle and captured. Another Trooper, Robert Consiglio, a Swiss-born former Royal Marine, was hit in the head as he covered the withdrawal of Trooper "Dinger" and Lance-Corporal Lane. Consiglio was the first SAS soldier of the campaign to die from enemy fire. He received a posthumous Military Medal. Lane urged "Dinger" to join him and swim the Euphrates, then in full icy flood. Lane emerged on the far bank in a state of collapse. His companion stayed with him and hid him in a nearby hut. When it became clear that Lane was going to die from hypothermia, "Dinger" attracted the attention of a civilian working nearby. By the time an Iraqi retrieval team got to Lane he was dead. He, too, was awarded a posthumous MM. "Dinger" tried to escape but was captured.

Sergeant McNab was discovered the next morning in a drainage culvert. Along with the other SAS men captured alive he suffered a month of imprisonment and torture. The latter was brutally physical and, ultimately, counter-productive. It only made the SAS men more determined not to talk. Though the Iraqi military imprisoned the men together they failed to even covertly monitor their conversations.

As for the trio missing in the desert, Sergeant Phillips was lost in driving snow on the night of 26 January. His companions, "Stan" and "Chris" turned back for him but could not find him. His body was eventually found by Iraqi soldiers and handed to the British authorities at the war's end. Later the next day, Stan went to see if he could hi-jack some transport. As he approached a parked lorry an Iraqi soldier came out of the house. The Iraqi tried to pull a weapon out. Stan shot him with his 203. Six or seven other Iraqi soldiers came running out. Stan shot three of them but then his gun jammed. The Iraqis did not kill him, only beat him unconscious with their rifle butts. When Stan failed to return to the LUP, Chris decided to set out on his own. He would be the only man from Bravo Two Zero to escape to safety.

Massively dehydrated, his feet and hands turning septic from cuts, and at one point falling unconscious and breaking his nose, Chris managed to cross the Syrian border on 30 January. He had covered 117 miles, evading hundreds of Iraqi searchers, with only two packets of biscuits for nourishment.

During the final two days he was without any water. He had filled his bottles from a small stream. When he came to drink the water his lips and mouth burned instantly. The stream was polluted with chemicals from a nearby uranium processing plant.

Inside Syria, Chris was initially treated with hostility. As he neared the capital Damascus, however, his treatment became more cordial. A civilian pin-stripe suit was run up for him as he bathed in the HQ of the Syrian secret police. That same night he was handed over to the British Embassy. It was the first anyone at SAS HQ in Saudi Arabia had heard of Bravo Two Zero since infiltration. The seven day walk of Trooper Chris across the desert is considered by the Regiment to be at least equal to that of Jack Sillitoe, an SAS "Original", who crossed the North African desert in 1942 drinking his own urine to survive. In a Regiment where the remarkable is standard, Chris's epic trek is still considered one of the most amazing escapades ever recorded.

The eight members of Road Watch North, Bravo Two Zero, killed nearly 250 Iraqis in their fight and flight across northern Iraq. After the attempt to insert the static patrols, 22 SAS effort shifted to the four mobile fighting columns. Drawn from Squadrons A and D, the columns – which contained about a dozen Land Rovers or Unimogs together with motorcycle outriders – were the biggest overland fighting force put into the field by the SAS since 1945. The columns had their own Stinger anti-aircraft and Milan anti-tank missiles, plus .5 Browning machine guns, 7.62 mm general purpose machine guns and 40 mm grenade launchers. One team found a sledge-hammer most useful. The freebooting columns, soon operating in broad daylight, scored spectacular successes as they sped into the Iraqi desert flying enormous Union flags to identify them to friendly aircraft. An Iraqi deputy commander of a gun battery taken POW proved to have on his person a map giving positions of Iraqi front lines units. On 29 January SAS columns called down F15E airstrikes on two mobile Scud launchers, plus one fixed site. On 3 February in the Wadi Amij ("Scud Alley") locality, a patrol from D Squadron called down an airstrike on a Scud convoy. Only one airstrike hit the target, so the SAS patrol hit the convoy with wire-guided Milan anti-tank missiles, an inspired last minute addition to the SAS armoury. These SAS attacks were the first military actions on the ground in the war except for the minor Iraqi cross-border attack on Khafji, Saudi Arabia, on 29 January. Group 2 from D Squadron called an airstrike on a Scud convoy on 5 February, and on the same day fought two firefights with Iraqi troops. Increasingly, the SAS destroyed Scud and launcher themselves, since some were escaping in the gap between their targetting by the SAS and the arrival of the airstrike. To service the Land Rovers and Unimogs, the SAS organised a supply column ("E Squadron") which formed a temporary workshop deep inside Iraq. Everywhere the SAS teams went they caused mayhem, and not only to the Scuds. Saddam (courtesy of the time when the West regarded him as a friend) had an advanced communications network consisting of buried fibre optic cables. The weak point in the system was that the signal needed to be boosted at above-ground relay stations. A team from 22 SAS blew up seven of these stations alongside the highway from Baghdad to Amman. When the SAS Land Rovers returned to Saudi Arabia at the end of the war, they had covered an average of 1500 miles and spent between 36 and 42 days behind the lines. The front wings of the Land Rovers were decorated with scores of silhouettes of "kills", including mobile scuds and communications towers. The SAS had also provided valuable advice to US Special Forces, operating in a "Scud Box" north of the Regiment's. It is a measure of the success of the SAS that General Norman Schwarzkopf, the "enemy" of special forces, praised the Regiment's "totally outstanding performance" in the Gulf. (See Appendix C for the full text of Schwarzkopf's letter of commendation for 22 SAS). No less than 39 awards and honours for bravery and meritorious service were given the Regiment for its part in Operation Granby, the Gulf War. There was, of course, a price to be paid for the Regiment's achievement. In addition to the three SAS soldiers from Bravo Two Zero who were killed, Trooper David Denbury from A Squadron was killed on 21 February during the ambush of a Scud convoy in North-West Iraq. A sapper attached to the Regiment was also killed in action.

BIRTH OF A LEGEND
Jon E. Lewis

Most of the North African campaign of 1940–43 was fought out in the narrow coastal strip which runs the long arc from Tunis to Cairo. South of the coastal strip lies the Sahara, an immense secret place of shifting sands and cauldron-like heat. Few paid much attention to this wilderness, but in its unguarded vastness a young British second-lieutenant saw the possibility for a new type of unit to operate. A unit which would strike swift and hard, and then disappear like a phantom into the desert from which it had emerged.

THE SPECIAL AIR Service was conceived in a hospital bed in Egypt. Injured during some unofficial parachute training David Stirling, a subaltern with No. 8 (Guards) Commando, decided to use his enforced stay in the Alexandria Scottish Military Hospital to develop a scheme for special operations in the desert.

On his release from hospital in July 1941, Stirling determined to bring his plan to the attention of the Commander-in-Chief. As C-in-Cs are not, by and large, in the habit of granting interviews to junior officers Stirling decided to ignore the usual channels. Instead, he hobbled on his crutches to British Army Middle East HQ and tricked his way past the sentry. Inside, Stirling found his way into the office of the Deputy Commander Middle East, one General Neil Ritchie. Stirling apologised to the somewhat surprised Ritchie for the unconventional call, but insisted that he had something of "great operational importance" to tell him. Ritchie offered him a seat, and Stirling pulled out the pencilled memo on a desert raiding force he had prepared in hospital.

Ritchie spent several minutes reading it. It was then

Stirling's turn to be surprised. Ritchie looked up and said brusquely, "I think this may be the sort of plan we are looking for. I will discuss it with the Commander-in-Chief and let you know our decision in the next day or so". The C-in-C was General Auckinleck, new to his command and under pressure from Churchill to mount an offensive. Stirling's plan was indeed what Auckinleck was looking for. It required few resources, and it was original. The unit Stirling proposed was to operate behind enemy lines in order to attack vulnerable targets like extended supply lines and airfields. What is more, the raids were to be carried by very small groups of men, between five and ten, rather than the standard commando force of hundreds.

Meanwhile, Ritchie looked into Stirling's background. He was pleased with what he found. David Stirling, born in 1915, was the youngest son of the aristocratic Brigadier Archibald Stirling of Keir. After three years at Cambridge, David Stirling had joined the Scots Guards, before transferring to No. 8 Commando. As part of the "Layforce" brigade, No. 8 had been dispatched to North Africa where its seaborne raids had all proved to be wash outs. The unit, along with the rest of Layforce, had been marked for disbandment. Stirling, however, had remained so keen on the commando idea that he had jumped – literally – at the chance of doing some parachuting with 'chutes that another officer in No. 8, Jock Lewes, had scrounged. The jumping trials had taken place near Mersa Matruh. The aircraft used, a lumbering Valentia bi-plane, was not equipped for parachuting and the men had secured the static lines which open the parachutes to seat legs. Stirling's parachute had caught on the door and snagged. He had descended far too rapidly and damaged his back badly on landing. Which is how he had come to be in Alexandria Hospital.

Three days after his meeting with Ritchie, Stirling was back at Middle East HQ, this time with a pass. Auckinleck saw him in person. Stirling was given permission to recruit a force of six other officers and sixty men. The unit was to be called "L Detachment, SAS Brigade". The SAS stood for Special Air Service, which did not exist. The name was dreamed up by Brigadier Dudley Clarke, a staff Intelligence Officer, as a means of convincing the enemy that the British possessed a large airborne force in North Africa. To mark his new appointment, Stirling was promoted to captain.

The recruiting took less than a week. There were two particular officers Stirling wanted. The first was Jock Lewes who was in Tobruk, where he had been carrying out small raids against enemy outposts. A scholar and Oxford rowing "blue", Lewes was also a daring soldier. He agreed to join. So did the Northern Irishman Paddy Mayne, then under close arrest for striking his commanding officer. Before the war, Mayne had been a rugby player of international rank. Most of the rest of the unit were recruited from the Guards Commando then at a camp at Genefa. Selection was based on Stirling's impression of the men at brief interviews. He also told them that if they failed to make the grade in training they would have to return to their units.

By August 1941, Stirling had established his force at Kabrit, 100 miles south of Cairo. Equipment was conspicuous by its absence. The camp consisted of two small tents for personnel, one large supply tent and a wooden sign saying "L Detachment – S.A.S.". Being, in his own words a "cheekie laddie", Stirling decided that the equipment L Detachment needed, in view of the parsimony of the Q side, would have to be "borrowed" from a New Zealand camp down the road. Thus the first – and highly unofficial – mission of L Detachment was a night raid on the New Zealand camp, filling L Detachment's one and only 3-ton truck with anything useful that could be found.

The next day, L Detachment boasted the smartest – and most luxuriously furnished – British camp in the Canal Zone. Training then began in earnest. From the start, Stirling insisted on a high standard of discipline – equal to that of the Brigade of Guards – and the pursuit of excellence. To achieve such standards demanded a combination of the right character and sheer physical fitness. One early recruit to Stirling's L Detachment, Fitzroy Maclean, recalled that: "for days and nights on end, we trudged interminably over the alternating soft sand and jagged rocks of the desert, weighed down by heavy loads of explosive, eating and drinking only what we could carry with us. In the intervals we did weapon training, physical training and training in demolitions and navigation."

Additionally, everyone joining the SAS had to be a parachutist, since Stirling envisaged airborne insertions for his force. No RAF instructors – or indeed aircraft – were available, so the SAS developed its own parachute training techniques. These involved jumping from ever higher platforms or from the backs of trucks moving at 30mph. The unit then moved on to make its first live jump, from a Bombay aircraft. Two men died when their 'chutes failed to open. "That night", recalled SAS "Original" Bob Bennett, "we went to bed with as many cigarettes as possible and smoked until morning. Next day, every man (led by Stirling himself) jumped; no-one backed out. It was then that I realised that I was with a great bunch of chaps." Thereafter parachute training progressed smoothly.

There were other problems though. Prime among them was the type of bomb which would be carried by the SAS raiding parties; it had to be small enough to be easily transportable but big enough to do the job. The requisite device was invented by Jock Lewes, a small incendiary bomb made of oil, plastic and thermite. Appropriately enough, it became known as the Lewes bomb.

Stirling sharpened his men for action with a training raid on the large RAF base at Heliopolis outside Cairo. An RAF Group-Captain had been unwise enough to tell L Detachment that their planned enterprise of attacking enemy aircraft on the ground was unrealistic. Although the airfield guards had been warned of their coming, and daily reconnaissance planes sent up, the SAS could not be kept out. After marching 90 miles across desert by night and hiding up by day, they placed stickers representing bombs on the RAF aircraft before slipping away into the desert darkness.

To celebrate their success, L Detachment were given a few days leave in Cairo. Before they had lacked an identity, but training had made them into a cohesive unit. They took pride, too, in their new unit insignia. The design of the cap badge was the result of a competition won by Sergeant Bob Tait who came up with a winged dagger emblem. David Stirling added the motto, "Who Dares Wins". The one problem was the unit's headgear: a white beret. After this drew unceremonious wolf whistles in Cairo, it was hurriedly replaced, first by a khaki forage cap, then by the famous sand-coloured beret.

After their leave, the men of L Detachment assembled to hear the details of their first real attack, scheduled for the night of 17 November 1941, when five SAS groups would parachute into the desert near Gazala and attack the five forward German fighter airfields. It was to be the opening prelude to Auckinleck's attempt to relieve Tobruk. Stirling assembled his men. "With luck", he told them, "we'll polish off Rommel's entire fighter force." There were whistles and cheers.

Alas, L Detachment's luck was out.

The weather forecast on the morning of 16 November looked ominous. The wind was strong and it looked as though it might rain – far from ideal conditions for parachuting. Even so, Stirling decided to press ahead with the mission, partly because Auckinleck expected it, mostly because many of the men who had joined the SAS had done so out of disgust for the continual cancellation of their commando operations. To call off the drop, Stirling concluded, would have been catastrophic for morale. At 19.30 the five Bombays containing L Detachment left the runway, flying first out to sea, then turning inland to cross the coast well behind German lines. The aircraft tossed around wildly in the wind, and the ground below was totally obscured by the darkness and the sandstorm.

The drop was more than a failure, it was a disaster. Of his group, Stirling was the first to jump. It was so black and murky that he could not see the ground. He waited and waited for the impact. He recorded later that it was like being suspended in space. Then there was a smashing blow. For some seconds he was unconscious but luckily nothing was broken. It took him nearly an hour to assemble the rest of his stick who had been dragged all over the desert by the wind. One man could not be found, others were injured, and vital supplies were missing. They had some Lewes bombs, but no detonators and so could not carry out their mission. Stirling resolved on the spot that never again would detonators and bombs be packed separately. There was nothing to do but call off the attack and attempt to walk the forty miles into the desert for the planned rendezvous with a motor patrol from the Long Range Desert Group (LRDG).

It took several days for the SAS parties to reach the LRDG rendezvous. Some never made it. Of the fifty one officers and men who had jumped into the storm three days before, only five officers (including Stirling himself) and eighteen men were left. Any other man would have given up the idea of a special desert force.

Stirling, however, decided to press ahead. Fortunately for him, the Eighth Army Command had more to think about than the fortunes of a small band of irregulars; the counter-offensive against Rommel had become bogged down by tough German resistance. So Stirling withdrew with the remnants of his unit to a remote oasis at Gialo, where he began preparing for another mission. He had already abandoned the idea of parachuting into the desert. At the rendezvous with the LRDG, David Lloyd-Owen of the latter unit had proposed that his patrols could get Stirling and his men to and from their targets. Although essentially a reconnaissance group, such a task was easily within the LRDG's capability. Stirling accepted with alacrity. Now, at Gialo, Stirling and his men poured over maps. A quick success was obviously necessary to wipe out the failure of the first raid, if hostile elements at GQ were not to succeed in burying the fledgling SAS.

In only a matter of days Stirling's idea was vindicated. In early December an SAS group under Paddy Mayne destroyed 24 enemy aircraft at Tamet airfield, while Bill Fraser's party destroyed 37 at Agedabia. Two weeks later, Paddy Mayne led a six-man group back to Tamet and accounted for a further 27 aircraft. A group led by Stirling himself reached the airfield at Bagush but were unable to plant their bombs. Their improvised response to this situation was to prove so successful that it was used often in future: a motorised charge down the airstrip, blazing away at the aircraft with machine guns and grenades from the back of the LRDG jeeps.

Fitzroy Maclean later wrote of the huge success of these raids:

> "Working on these lines, David achieved a series of successes which surpassed the wildest expectations of those who had originally supported his venture. No sooner had the enemy become aware of his presence in one part of the desert then he was attacking them somewhere else. Never has the element of surprise, the key to success in all irregular warfare, been more brilliantly exploited. Soon the number of aircraft destroyed was well into three figures."

It was not only aircraft which received the attention of the SAS. Stirling was quick to see the vulnerability of Rommel's Supply lines. Convoys were attacked, harbours raided. Recruits flocked to join L Detachment. Stirling himself was promoted to Major in January 1942. Seven months later, Stirling's force had grown to Regimental size (750 men) and was renamed 1 SAS.

Perhaps the real proof of the SAS concept was that it survived without the presence of its founder, it wasn't dependent on the charisma and drive of one man. David Stirling led from the front and in January 1943 he paid the price. He was captured in Tunisia by the Germans. The SAS went on without him, not only in North Africa, but into Italy, France, Holland and eventually Germany. By 1945, the idea David Stirling had conceived in his hospital bed had become more than a war-winning unit. It had become a legend.

OPERATION WALLACE
Roy Farran

Major Roy Farran joined 2 SAS Regiment in 1943, towards the close of the war in North Africa. 2 SAS was the creation of William "Bill" Stirling, elder brother of David Stirling (see pp 11-17), and run on exactly the same principles as the original Regiment. Many of 2's initial recruits came from Bill Stirling's old unit, the disbanded No. 62 Commando (also known as the Small Scale Raiding Force). Although 2 SAS did some (largely ineffectual) raiding in North Africa, its finest moments came later, during the campaign in Europe. Among them was Operation Wallace, an epic post D-Day jeep ride through occupied France led by Roy Farran.

I SUPPOSE THAT of all the operations carried out by the 2nd Special Air Service Regiment, the jeep operation "Wallace" was the one in which the greatest distance behind the enemy lines was covered. Of course, great distances were traversed in the desert operations under David Stirling and a certain amount of penetration was achieved in the first skirmishes after the landing at Taranto, but until August 1944, people still doubted that we would ever again have a fluid situation which would allow us to drive vehicles about behind the enemy front. Until D-Day there was a strong school of thought which still imagined that only the most clandestine sabotage would be possible in enemy territory in Europe. In Italy we had still been pioneering in a new form of warfare. We had been trained to operate with an unfriendly local population and all our attacks were so cautious that they could not be regarded as much more than pinprick raids. They could be compared to the behaviour of a naughty boy who knocks on perhaps two doors in a street and then runs away. There was no organised form of re-supply from the air, and after our first load of explosive was finished we had no alternative but to return somehow to the right side of the lines. In France things were different. We were supported by the whole weight of Transport Command, and although we had not yet put our theories into practice, Italy had convinced us that we had been far too conservative in our approach.

We began by building up large bases in the forested areas in Central France. These areas were chosen at random off the map without local knowledge, but proved in every instance to have been well selected by Bill Stirling. From D-Day onwards parties were dropped in to reconnoitre the areas and to receive stores with a view to active operations after our landings in Normandy. Sometimes these parties were built up to operational strength in conjunction with the Maquis, but quite often they operated completely separately. Soon after D-Day, the Special Air Service Brigade (consisting of British, French and Belgian components) had bases in Brittany, the Forest of Orleans, the Grand Massif, the Forest of Chatillon, the area around Poitieres and the Vosges.

My own squadron built up its base in the Forest of Chatillon north of Dijon. Grant Hibbert, the Advance Party Commander, therefore had one troop with sufficient stores astride a direct line from Normandy to Belfort and roughly in the centre of France.

When the Americans broke through at Avranches we were presented once more with a fluid front through which it would be possible to infiltrate small vehicles. With a base already established halfway across France and with ensured air supply for our columns, we were in a position to cause great chaos behind the Germans who were withdrawing in front of the American Third Army. The operation could not have been better timed.

On 19 August, twenty jeeps containing the remainder of my squadron were loaded into Dakotas piloted by the British 46th Group. Each aircraft carried a jeep lashed into its fuselage, plus a crew of three men – sixty men in all. We landed on the only serviceable strip on Rennes Airfield, pockmarked from many heavy bomber raids. Within twenty-four hours the column of jeeps was winding through the forest paths north of Orleans, winkling its way round pockets of Germans to the open country in the enemy rear.

We drove down muddy, deserted rides through the trees until we met the main road at Les Bordes on the banks of the Loire. The village was full of excited Maquisards, to whom we were the first Allied troops. They told us that there were large German columns in Gien, Montargis and Sully, the three villages round about. I was most impressed by the bellicose air of the French partisans, who to this day I believe to have been the best guerrillas in Europe. The local Commandant readily lent me a young guide, who was unfortunately wounded and captured a few days later. I believe he was shot by a firing squad in Semur.

Before moving further east, I sent a jeep patrol up to the village of Les Choux on the Montargis road, while we celebrated the liberation with our new-found Maquis friends in the village street. When the patrol had reported the village to be clear, we moved off again in column by minor roads. So long as we kept to the tangle of country lanes we were fairly safe, for the Germans kept mostly to the metalled highways.

There was a mishap in crossing the main Montargis road when one of the jeeps became separated from the main column. Our system was to choose a point where the road was crossed by a track and to drive across in column at top speed when it was reported clear by a forward patrol. Unfortunately, the front jeep misunderstood its role and, instead of joining on to the tail when we were all across, it stayed in its position until first light the next day. After losing contact with the rest of the squadron, Sergeant Forster led it alone across France to join us in the Forest of Chatillon. He had many exciting adventures on the way, including a collision with a German staff car when he shot four high-ranking enemy officers.

We spent the night in the Forest of Dracy behind the cabbage patch at the back of a farm. I had to use force to convince the landlord that we were British for he had barricaded his door against intruders. I knocked hard and shouted for a long time at the front door, but had no more luck than Walter de la Mare's traveller. Eventually I burst in through the back and found a tiny little Frenchman cringing in the corner with his wife. When at last he discovered that we were indeed British, he was torn between a desire to shower on us presents of bread, butter and eggs, and a fear that the Germans would discover that he had harboured us.

Most of the 22 August was spent in gathering information about enemy movements in the area, and Ramon Lee was invaluable at this stage. The local villagers soon smelled us out. Clustering around the jeeps as we sat cleaning our guns under the trees, they poured masses of misleading information into our ears. They were all terribly excited at the appearance of British troops. Amongst them was a young English girl, who had married a French farmer, and she was so thrilled by it all that she could only speak in short gasps.

We were all very satisfied that we had covered fifty miles behind the enemy front without a single serious brush with the enemy. I did not want to begin operations until we had reached Grant Hibbert's base near Chatillon, and to have covered a third of the journey in one day was a most encouraging start. I had decided to move just before dark when I reckoned that most of the German troops would be settling down for the night. Later experience proved this to be unwise since Allied aircraft had forced the Germans to move mainly under the cover of darkness, and we discovered that the best time for our own movement was around midday. For the next leg, I split the squadron into three parts – five jeeps under Ramon, eight under me and the remainder under Lieutenant David Leigh, an officer with considerable experience of jeep operations in the desert. Each party was to move at thirty-minute intervals on the same route, although they were not bound to keep to it if they ran into trouble. I was careful to instruct both Party Commanders that the present aim was to by-pass all opposition.

The Latin temperament is a most incalculable factor, especially in war, for it always does things at a rush, either forwards or backwards, and it was typical of Ramon that he should charge through the first opposition he encountered on the east side of the River Yonne. The fourth jeep in his column was destroyed by machine-gun fire, although the crew escaped with minor injuries.

When I arrived at a village called Mailly-le-Château a very excited Frenchman jumped on to the bonnet of my jeep, shouting that he was the man to lead the liberators into battle. I eventually had to quieten him by sticking a pistol in his ribs. It was a long time before I could get any sense out of the crowd, but it did appear that although there were Germans on the other side of the river, Ramon had passed through. This was difficult to understand in view of my orders, but it was clear that if his hot-headedness had led him into trouble, we would have to do what we could to get him out.

The Frenchman, now more subdued, led us down a hill to a place where the road wound under a steep cliff. He dismounted here and expressed a desire to return to the village, from which I gathered that the Germans were close. I walked round the corner alone and was immediately greeted by a burst of Spandau. From what I could see from my rather cramped position in the ditch, there were about a hundred enemy with some horse-drawn vehicles under the trees. Even if Ramon had been able to crash through in his first fine rush, I did not see how we could follow now that the element of surprise was gone. We fired a few tracers from the top of the cliff before we left and succeeded in setting a cart on fire.

The Frenchmen in the village looked rather dismayed when we retraced our steps to hook round to the south. I left a message for Lieutenant Leigh to conform to my movements and drove through the moonlight, for dusk had now fallen, to see if we could get across the bridge at Merry-sur-Yonne. Fortunately it was unguarded, although I had certain misgivings when we encountered a hay wagon, flying the white flag and containing three Germans wounded by our Bren.

We all joined up that night in the Forest of St Jean, over a hundred miles behind the front. We leagured near a Priory converted into a farm, where civilians from the village of Château Gerard found us the next morning. They brought presents of flowers, wine, butter and eggs, heaping them high on the jeeps. I was not too happy about the farmer, who was a shifty-eyed rogue and looked as though he would sell his own grandmother for two sous.

I was so angry with Ramon for his rash behaviour that I reduced his command to two jeeps, although I still allowed him to lead since his knowledge of French made him so much more useful at extracting information from the peasants. We started at five o'clock and within ten miles of the forest Ramon again ran into trouble. An unreliable civilian told him that a village called Villaines was clear of the enemy. He ran into a number of Afrika Corps troops in the streets and both his jeeps were destroyed. Ramon, as always, fought bravely and succeeded in escaping on foot to the hills, but three of our best men were left behind. Worse still, there was no way of warning me.

I was breaking all the rules by motoring along quite happily at about thirty miles an hour at the head of my column, confident that Ramon would give notice of any opposition ahead. Only the very slowest speed is wise in enemy country since it is essential that you see the enemy before he sees you. As it was, we turned a corner to come face to face with a 75-millimetre gun blocking the entire road. Even as I told Corporal Clarke, my driver, to swing into the ditch, two Germans in Afrika Corps hats fired a shell at less than ten yards' range. Perhaps it was because we were so close to the muzzle of the gun that the shell whistled over our heads to burst in the road behind.

And then we were crawling out of the wrecked jeep into the ditch with bullets spattering all round. The little Maquis guide we had picked up at Les Bordes was shot in the knee. As I huddled under the bank, I could see the spare wheel from the front of the jeep rolling down the middle of the road. There were lots of Germans practically on top of us, shouting loudly and spraying the jeep with machine-gun fire. We had crawled about five yards from the vehicle when I remembered the codes and my marked map. Carpendale, the Signals Officer, crawled back to get them. We still had the Bren, so that when we came to a convenient gully I sent the others up to the top of the bank to hold them off. I began to run the gauntlet back to organise the rest of the column.

The Germans were now running forward in line, shooting

as they came. A big blond brute with a schmeisser called upon me to surrender so I wildly fired at him with my carbine. He disappeared, but I cannot say whether he was shot or just taking cover.

I found Jim Mackie with the good old, bewildered look on his face, standing by the leading jeep. Thank God he had had the sense not to drive round the corner. In fact he at first thought that I had been blown up on a mine. I led him up a convenient lane to the right, from which his two jeeps poured enfilading fire at short range into the German flank. Corporal Clarke was still holding his own out in front with the Bren. Sergeant-Major Mitchell moved off to the left with ten men and four Brens to hold the line of the hedge, while I myself commanded the two jeeps in the centre of the road.

By now the enemy fire had become very heavy, including shells and mortar bombs. The Germans made a foolish charge along both sides of the road, giving us a magnificent shoot at less than fifty yards' range. Their casualties were very heavy and Jim Mackie's troop alone accounted for a whole platoon in a field. Instead of abandoning the attack, the idiots came on until they were so far into our rough semi-circle that we were cutting them down from three sides. I even shot a German with my own carbine – my only definite personal bag of the war.

Corporal Clarke's Bren was silent by now and I feared that he had been captured or worse. (In fact, he joined up with Ramon Lee some days later.) After we had been fighting for about an hour, a mortar and a machine-gun opened up behind us. I had been holding on in the hope that David Leigh would come along with the other jeeps, but it was now quite clearly time to break off the action. In any case his arrival had been so long delayed that I assumed that the sound of the firing had made him veer off on another tack. The trailer containing our wireless set was on fire in the middle of the road and I nearly got myself killed in a vain attempt to rescue it.

Under the cover of Jim Mackie's guns, we withdrew down a small lane which unfortunately proved to be a dead-end leading into a mill. We succeeded, however, in making our way over a stream and across country through many hedges to strike a country lane near Jeux. There we met a farm labourer who warned us that a whole Panzer Division (without its armour) was strung out in the villages between Semur and Montbard.

We drove on into the night, making a wide detour to the south of Semur. Once we lost our way in a maze of cart-tracks to the east of the main road, and the jeeps were driving about a ploughed field looking for an opening, when we noticed the headlights of a large convoy on the road below. We switched off our engines and sat in complete silence until the last lorry had passed.

Meanwhile, David Leigh had run into the same opposition at Villaines after our withdrawal. He himself was killed, and the whole party only escaped with heavy casualties. Ramon Lee found the remnants of the column and, after several more brushes with the enemy, led them back to Paris. Some of the crews were dropped in to me by parachute a few weeks later.

I was very depressed to find myself with only seven of my original twenty jeeps the next morning. We had driven all night and were very tired, but I was determined not to stop until we had reached the cover of the forest. The country was typical of the Cote d'Or in the summer: tiny green fields, white red-roofed cottages, hedges and gently undulating slopes. The roads were very dry and we had to drive very slowly to avoid putting up a tell-tale dust cloud behind.

Dawn was still touching the grass with pink when we found ourselves halted by a closed level-crossing at the foot of a sharp decline. Before there was time to withdraw the jeeps under cover, I noticed the smoke of a train coming round the shoulder of the hill. The chugging gradually became louder until we were able to see that it was a goods train of about twenty trucks. When the engine was level with the gates I gave the order to fire, and all the Vickers poured in mixed incendiaries, tracers and armour-piercing bullets at fifteen yards' range. She did not stop at once, but rolled on for about two hundred yards with her boiler enveloped in a cloud of steam. As in a *Punch* cartoon, vapour was escaping in spouts from all sorts of strange places. Two German sentries in the last truck were killed, but when at last she came to a halt, a French driver dismounted from the engine cab and looked up at the flames now licking the woodwork as much as to say, "What is the use? This must be the sixth I have lost this week. If it is not aeroplanes, something else happens."

It must have been about the middle of the morning when we were just approaching the southern limits of the Forest of Chatillon. Jim Mackie stopped in the leading jeep and I ran up to discover the cause of the delay. He was still explaining that he had noticed a radar station in a clearing beyond the trees, when a number of machine guns opened fire on our jeeps. Although we sprayed the undergrowth with our guns, I could not see from where the fire was coming and therefore thought it wiser to withdraw. We learned later that the Germans in Beaulieu Radar Station had taken us for the advance guard of the American Third Army. At one o'clock that day they blew up the control tower and withdrew along the road to Langres. By that time I had sent off Jim Mackie to try to make contact with Grant Hibbert and he was lucky enough to meet a patrol commanded by Lieutenant James Robertson (who had been dropped in by parachute a fortnight before). Together they attacked the Germans, who were evacuating Beaulieu, and caused thirty-five enemy casualties.

The reunion with Grant was a great moment. He was quite astonished at the rate at which we had crossed France. Belittling my worry at our depleted numbers, he led me with his long strides into a cunningly concealed camp under the trees. Explaining it all in a dry voice, he showed me the dumps of stores, the tents made from khaki parachutes draped between the branches, and the brushwood barriers which protected the main exits. He certainly had not wasted his month in enemy territory. The rude shelters were impossible to detect except at the shortest range, and inside they were furnished comfortably with bits of parachute equippage. Most of the men wore beards and their red berets were beginning to fade, but their morale was high.

The combined force of Farran's Operation Wallace and Grant Hibbert's Operation Hardy then commenced offensive patrolling and information gathering in the area. A visit on 29 August to a friendly farmer divulged the news that a German garrison nearby was being relieved, beginning a chain of events which led to the famous Battle of Chatillon. That same evening, Farran and Hibbert dined with the local leader of the Maquis, Colonel Claude. As Farran admitted later "it was a wonderful dinner . . . and I partly blame the actions of the next day on the quantity of red wine drunk". The SAS men suggested a wild scheme whereby they would all, SAS and Maquis, attack the German garrison in the town of Chatillon the following morning.

The combined squadron attacked Chatillon at first light. My plan was to seize the important junction of the Montbard and Dijon roads. From there we would send a foot party with Brens, carried as far as possible by jeep, to attack the north of the château. The signal for the attack to begin would be the firing of the three-inch mortar on the château from the south.

Jim Mackie crossed the aerodrome and occupied the cross-roads without incident. I then moved the remaining nine jeeps containing forty men through him into the town. We occupied all the main junctions leading into the market square, while Jaimie Robertson took the foot party round the back. I placed Sergeant-Major Mitchell with two jeeps on the Troyes-Chaumont cross-roads and Sergeant Young cut all the military telephone wires.

Dayrell began to mortar the château at about seven o'clock. He placed forty-eight bombs on the target in all. Fifteen minutes later a long column of about thirty German trucks, presumably containing the relief, arrived at the river bridge near Mackie's position on the Montbard–Dijon cross-roads. The battle was on. Sergeant Vickers, whose jeep was in the middle of the road, allowed them to approach to within twenty yards before he opened fire. The first five trucks, two of which were loaded with ammunition, were brewed up and we were treated to a glorious display of fireworks. A motorcycle combination skidded off the bridge into the river. I thought I noticed a woman in the cab of the leading vehicle, but it was too late to worry. All the sounds of war echoed in the streets – the rattle of the Brens, the rasp of the Vickers, the whine of bullets bouncing off the walls, and in the background the stonk-stonk of the mortars. I got a Bren myself and, balancing it on a wall, hosepiped the German column with red tracers. The Germans had baled out from the back of the convoy and were firing a lot of mortar bombs. Bullets were whistling everywhere and it was good to see our tracers pumping into them. Parachutist Holland was killed by a bullet in the head and a brave French civilian dragged him into a doorway.

I could hear other shooting from the centre of the town as well as firing from behind the château, so it seemed that Mitchell was also engaged, although by far the greatest weight of fire was around our position on the Montbard–Dijon cross-roads.

A pretty girl with long black hair and wearing a bright red frock put her head out of a top window to give me the "V" sign. Her smile ridiculed the bullets.

A runner came up from Mitchell to say that a number of Germans were fighting their way down the street from the château. The situation was so confused that the enemy was mortaring his own side. I sent Dayrell Morris up to reinforce the position in the centre of the town which was now hard pressed. Jaimie Robertson's Brens were firing briskly from the back of the woods to the north.

At nine o'clock, three hours after the action had begun, I felt that since Mitchell was being subjected to such strong pressure from the houses, although only one jeep had been hit, I had better give the signal for a withdrawal. The Montbard column was becoming more organised and there was still no sign of the promised Maquis reinforcements. I walked into the middle of the road, waving to the girl in the red frock, and fired two Verey lights into the air.

Grant brought out Lieutenant Robertson's troop, while I led the remainder back along the Dijon road for breakfast. On his way back with the foot party, Grant met sixty of the promised five hundred Maquis waiting on the aerodrome. He undertook to lead them into the town with a party of seven men, at the same time sending a message to ask me to co-operate in a second attack. He became involved in a street fight in which he knocked out an armoured car, but was beaten into a tight corner from which the party only narrowly escaped. A bicycle patrol of thirty Germans trapped them in a garden and, while they were fighting their way out, Corporal Brownlee was hit in the most precious part of his body. When I arrived with the main party I posted jeep ambushes on all the main roads leading out of the town, which destroyed eight German vehicles loaded high with troops. Supported by Jim Mackie in a jeep, I led a foot patrol round the east of Chatillon. It was all very quiet except for occasional firing from the direction of Grant Hibbert. With our heads bowed, we stalked round some Germans on a crest amongst some beech trees, crossed a canal by a lock and walked along the sides of the tow-path. There were several Germans around the hospital on the other side, but they did not see us.

After walking for about an hour we found ourselves in a narrow lane leading down to the Troyes road. Looking around the corner, I was astonished to see a German machine-gun post on each side, facing outwards. They were all in great-coats and had their backs to us. I could not think what to do, so we sat in a garden and waited. Lieutenant Pinci begged a bottle of wine, bread and cheese from a French cottage, so we had lunch.

I tossed up which German we should shoot in the back and it turned out to be the left-hand one. Sergeant Young took careful aim through his carbine, and when I gave the word he pulled the trigger. At the same moment, Pinci, excitable as ever, shot a German on a bicycle to the right. All hell was then let loose. I do not know from where they were coming, but our little lane was soon singing with schmeisser bullets. It was so high-banked and so open on each side as to make it a death-trap. With angry bullets buzzing round our heads, we burst into the front door of a French house. Running straight through, we scrambled down the bank to the canal.

After we had run along the tow-path to the lock, I led the party across country to the east. We had just reached the cover of a thin hedge on a skyline when two machine guns picked us out. I had not realised that we could be seen. We wriggled on our bellies along the furrows in a ploughed field with the bullets kicking up great clots of earth all round. I have never felt so tired. I knew that if we remained on that crest we would be killed and yet I could not force myself to move any faster. Sergeant Robinson, behind me, was hit in the leg and still he moved faster than I. When we had reached a little dead ground I tried to help him, but I was too exhausted. Never have I been so frightened and so incapable of helping myself.

Jim Mackie appeared and we loaded Robinson into his jeep. At the friendly farmhouse, from which we had telephoned the mayor the day before, I dressed his wounds on the kitchen table, while all the women clucked and fussed around with kettles of hot water. After we had despatched him to the Maquis hospital at Aigny-le-Duc, we motored back slowly through the forest glades to our base. The Battle of Chatillon was over. They say that we killed a hundred Germans, wounded many more and destroyed nine trucks, four cars and a motorcycle.

AFTERWORD

In theory, the action at Chatillon was something that should have been absolutely avoided by a small, lightly armed force. But Farran dared and won, and lost only one man killed.

Operation Wallace ended officially on 7 September 1944, by which time Farran's squadron was credited with 500 Germans killed or seriously wounded, 23 cars and 36 other vehicles destroyed, plus 1 train and 100,000 gallons of enemy petrol. This was achieved at a cost of 7 men killed, 7 wounded, 2 captured and 16 jeeps lost. At the end of 1944 Farran was sent to Italy as commander of 3 Squadron to launch Operation Tombola (see pp 67–95).

THE KOEMBA JOB

Peter Grossman

Between 1963 and 1966 the mountainous jungle island of Borneo became the theatre of armed warfare between the former British colony of Malaya and an expansionist Indonesia under President Sukarno. To counter the latter's infiltration of guerrilla insurgents from Indonesian Borneo (Kalimantan) into northern Malaysian Borneo, the British organized a border guard of Malaysian, British and Commonwealth troops. A main constituent of this guard was 22 SAS, which proved eventually so successful that Indonesia abandoned its confrontationist policy.

For the most part, SAS effort in Borneo took the form of the insertion of four-man patrols into the jungle, where they lived off the land, often for weeks at a time. The main responsibility of these patrols was to gather intelligence about hostile forces and to carry out a "hearts and minds" programme to secure the friendship of the natives. (Many SAS troopers, having taken part in the Malayan Emergency of 1948–1960, spoke Malay, the lingua franca of the Borneo tribes.) The standard patrol always included a signaller and a medic, while movement through the jungle followed a set procedure: the patrol would be led by a scout, with the commander, medic and signaller following behind at set intervals. The last man usually carried a Bren or 7.62 GPMG, the others SLRs and M16 rifles, although the American Armalite AR-16 assault rifle was the weapon of choice of many.

As the war in Borneo wore on, the role of the SAS began to be modified, not least because Indonesia began committing properly organized units of its army to the frontier war. By early 1964 the SAS was not only detecting incursions but guiding "killer groups" of infantry across the border into Kalimantan. And, increasingly, the Regiment's own "recces" ended in engagements with the enemy. These offensive forays, codenamed "Claret" were ultra-secret operations because any trace of British presence on Indonesian soil would have been intensely embarrassing to the British government, as well as leading to international accusations that Britain was escalating the Borneo conflict.

One such Claret operation was that led by Sergeant Don "Lofty" Large of D Squadron in May 1965 the Koemba river, a major supply route inside Kalimantan.

IN EARLY 1965 the new Commander of British Forces in Borneo, Major-General George Lea, decided that the so-called "Claret" missions should be stepped up. One objective chosen was the Koemba river, which was believed to be one of the enemy's major supply routes. There had been no less than six previous attempts by SAS patrols to reach the Koemba, but all had failed to penetrate the dense swamps which lay alongside the river like some natural, primordial security moat. A four-man patrol from D Squadron, led by Sergeant Don "Lofty" Large was ordered to investigate river traffic on the Koemba near the town of Poeri. The suspicion in the "Haunted House" (SAS squadron headquarters) was that Large's attempt would also become bogged down and fail. Large himself, however, was determined and, after studying all the maps and air photos that he could lay his hands on, found what seemed to be the only possible route. Running south from the border was a spur of high ground. With luck, the spur would run all the way to the Koemba. The main task of the patrol was information-gathering, but it was also, after a suitable interval of watching, to disrupt any military traffic found on the river.

Despite Large's optimism, the patrol's departure from Squadron HQ (SHQ) on 10 May was marred by what seemed a bad omen. Following the advice of the informal Regimental motto, "check and check again", the patrol members had spent many hours working on their weapons, before handing them over to the armoury for safe-keeping on the night before leaving. The next day, on the way to the airfield from which they were to fly to Lundu, one of the patrol, Trooper Pete Scholey, realized that he had been given the wrong SLR rifle. As his life might depend on his weapon, he was bitterly unhappy. Even a thorough strip down and check of the wrong weapon by the rest of the patrol failed to convince him that it was working perfectly.

After arriving at Lundu, the patrol was whisked to a waiting chopper and dropped that same afternoon at a "hot" landing position just on the border, from where they set off on a bearing west of their intended course to confuse any "Indos" who might discover their tracks. On the second day out the patrol ran into trouble. Large, hearing a faint sound, scouted ahead and found an Indonesian unit of around platoon strength directly in their path. The patrol was forced to take a detour through thick jungle, without making a noise or leaving a track, an exercise that tested their skills in jungle movement to the limit.

Then things got worse. On the third day, after successfully crossing tracks used by the Indonesians to intercept Claret operations, the patrol made for the spur Large hoped would lead to the bank of the river. To the team's dismay all they encountered was dense swamp, tangled with roots and screened with hanging moss and vines. A particular hazard was a carpet of huge leaves which lay on the surface of the water and crackled loudly when stepped on. Each time the patrol probed for the ridge they found themselves deeper in the jungle. Progress was exhausting, the men losing body weight by the hour. Failure began to seem certain. But there was one small encouragement: they could hear the sound of boat engines, so the river must be near. After breakfast on a piece of dry ground, the team decided to carry on, taking a route through the swamp parallel to the Koemba in the hope of finding a causeway through to the river. At first they made little headway – but then, to their amazement, they found Large's spur, rising fully 30 feet above the swamp. They negotiated the spur, which had a light covering of jungle, before coming to a rubber plantation. Cautiously skirting round this they saw before them the muddy, fast-moving water of the Koemba. They had made it.

Without wasting a moment, Large set up an observation post (OP), choosing a place on the river bank bounded by a ditch and which provided cover in the form of a tree and some bushes. He also hoped that this would be the spot the enemy would least expect an ambush to come from and that their patrols would concentrate on the jungle nearby. To celebrate their arrival, the team disregarded all normal operational procedures, cooked curries, brewed tea, and smoked cigarettes. Large wanted morale to be peak-high for the moment when action came.

The days passed, with a steady amount of boat traffic – some of it military, as SHQ had rightly suspected – passing the patrol's OP, all of it reported back to base on the radio. When Large considered that the patrol had done enough observation, he sent off a signal requesting permission to carry out their secondary task, an ambush of a boat carrying troops or war cargo. The code he used was "Request 00 Licence". Unfortunately, the officer in charge of the Operations Centre was about the only person in the world who had never seen a James Bond film and sent back a signal saying "Message not understood". Cursing the Ops Centre officer, Large sent another – and longer – coded message, with the danger that it would be intercepted by enemy signals and give a fix on the patrol's position. They received permission to execute part two of the operation and, luckily, the morse traffic was not noticed by the Indonesian army.

As for ambush tactics, Large decided that the best thing to do would be to wait until a military boat had passed the bend in the river and then rake it with fire from the rear. This would be done by his team members, Pete Scholey, Paddy Milliken and Kevin Walsh; Large himself would direct the fire and keep a watch out for any enemy, as well as dealing with any retaliation.

The team settled down and waited for a suitable target. Several launches passed but Large dismissed these as either too small or going in the wrong direction. It started to rain. Then there appeared a gleaming white launch, 45 foot long, flying military pennants. The patrol waited eagerly for the signal to fire, but it didn't come. Large had, at the last moment, spotted a woman aboard the craft, so it too escaped attack. The waiting continued, with the patrol beginning to bemoan Large's cavalier decisions to let so many craft past.

Suddenly, just as daylight was fading in an evening storm,

there appeared another big launch. As it passed Large he could see troops in uniform resting beneath its canvas canopy. He raised his thumb and the patrol leapt to their firing positions. Large took out the two sentries at the back of the boat, and Scholey, Milliken and Walsh began to pump rounds into the boat, although Scholey soon had problems with his rifle, having to cock it after each shot. The boat was quickly holed, and began to list in the water, smoke bellowing from under the canvas roof. Soldiers started jumping ship, and seconds later the craft burst into flames.

With their mission accomplished, the patrol began to effect a hasty exit, collecting their packs and making for the spur. As Large reached the top of the slope he found his way blocked by a deadly King Cobra. The snake reared up to head level, Large raised his rifle, and for several long seconds it was a "Mexican stand off", before the snake decided not to attack, and slithered off into the jungle. Pushing on, the patrol cleared the deployment tracks in the evening, breathing a small sigh of relief to find no enemy waiting for them. The patrol spent the night among some felled trees. There were some mortars fired from an enemy base in the vicinity but these landed a long way from the patrol. The Indonesians had obviously been fooled by an eastern loop the patrol had put in their route out.

The next day as the patrol made for the LZ where they had been inserted, Paddy Milliken began to suffer from a fever. The LZ was also proving too difficult to find in the featureless jungle terrain. Large made a snap decision to signal base and request a helicopter to hover over the LZ so that he could get a definite fix on it. As the patrol neared the area of the LZ a helicopter arrived, but instead of remaining above the LZ it began to circle around as though looking for the patrol. Large then switched on his SARBE (search and rescue beacon), and the helicopter soon found them. A winch cable was lowered and the patrol hoisted up and flown back to base.

Sergeant Large's patrol had been a resounding success. Although they had only destroyed one launch, they had dealt the enemy a reeling psychological blow. The Indonesians now considered that their main supply route, despite being deep inside their own territory, was vulnerable to attack. Consequently, troops had to be diverted from other tasks to guard it. It was the beginning of the end of the war in Borneo.

RAID ON DIEPPE
Peter Young

In Churchill's memorable phrase the Army Commandos were to be a seaborne "hand of steel which plucks the German sentries from their posts". Originating in a War Office concept of 1938, the Commandos first took practical shape as the Independent Companies before becoming the Commandos proper in 1940. All were volunteers who had to pass a rigorous selection course at the Commando Basic Training Centre at Achnacarry in Scotland. This lasted three months (later reduced to five weeks) and covered close combat training, offensive demolitions and amphibious assault, the last incorporating firing exercises with live ammunition. Any man not up to standard was returned to unit ("RTUd"). During WWII the principal weapons of the commandos were Bren light machine guns, Thompson sub-machine guns (model M1928A1 from 1940 to 1942, which had an automatic rate of fire of 120rpm, and from 1942 model M1), Sten guns, Mark III Lee-Enfield rifles and Garland rifles. The famous commando fighting knife was designed by two instructors at Achnacarry, Captains Fairburn and Sykes. The 178mm-long blades, made by Wilkinson Sword, were of carbon steel with a 22mm diamond shaped cross-section. The brass curled grip had an oval crossguard with its ends curved up and down. About 250,000 knives based on this design were produced between 1941 and 1946.

Peter Young joined No. 3 Commando as a second lieutenant shortly after its formation in July 1940. The unit's first commanding officer was Lt-Col J.E. Durnford-Slater, whose aim was to make 3 Commando "the greatest unit of all time". Most of the early Commando units suffered from a run of aborted missions, but 3 Commando raided Guernsey in July 1940, the Lofoten Islands in March 1941, and Vaagso in December 1941. In 1942 3 Commando was part of the force which took part in the legendary raid on Dieppe in occupied France. Two years later, 3 Commando – now led by Lt-Col Peter Young – returned to France as part of the Allied invasion of Normandy.

THE PLANNING FOR Dieppe had begun as long ago as April when I had been on the planning staff at C.O.H.Q. Dieppe was selected because it would not be one of the invasion ports whenever it was finally decided to launch the Second Front. It was within the range of fighter cover. It also had obvious disadvantages. The whole coast for some miles on either side of the town is a wall of chalk cliffs, like those between Newhaven and Brighton, and this limited the number of suitable landing beaches. The planners had to decide whether to land several miles from the town, which meant crossing small rivers on the way, or to land on the waterfront of the town in the teeth of the garrison. A landing at Dieppe itself would call for the maximum of fire support from the Navy and the Royal Air Force.

Three Commandos were allotted to the force. Nos. 3 and 4 Commandos were to silence the two coast defence batteries on either flank of the port, while No. 40, the first of the Royal Marine Commandos, was to attack shipping in the harbour and to be available as a floating reserve. The main assault was to be made by the 2nd Canadian Division.

The task of 3 Commando was to land in two groups at two beaches, near the village of Berneval, "Yellow 1", and near Belleville-sur-Mer, "Yellow 2". The Colonel was to land on Yellow 1 with the main body of the Commando, while I was to land on Yellow 2 with 3 and 4 Troops and a 3-inch mortar section. The two groups were then to move inland and together destroy Goebbels Battery of 5.9-inch guns, 450 yards inland on the outskirts of Berneval, between the village and the cliffs. The Colonel, with the general layout of the battery and its neighbourhood clearly in mind, was able to organize thorough rehearsals which were carried out on the downs behind Alfriston.

In July the raid was postponed for a month, which gave rise to the usual rumours that the whole show was off, but towards the middle of August it became obvious that it was really going to happen. First of all a detachment of U. S. Rangers arrived and later some Fusiliers-Marins – these last to act as guides.

The force embarked on the evening of August 18 and sailed from Southampton, Portsmouth, Shoreham and Newhaven about 9 p.m. No. 3 Commando sailed from Newhaven in a flotilla known as Group 5, consisting of twenty Eurekas[1]. These unarmoured landing-craft – designed not for a seventy-mile channel crossing but only for a run of five to ten miles – each carried about eighteen fully-equipped soldiers. We were escorted by a steam gunboat, a motor launch, and a larger landing-craft carrying 4 Troop. The Colonel and Commander E. B. Wyburd, RN, were leading the flotilla in the steam gunboat, so as to ensure that we did not lose our way. The Eurekas sailed in four waves five abreast, and I was in the starboard craft of the first wave, which was commanded by Lieutenant Buckee, RNVR, and the soldiers with me were the H.Q.s of my Group and of 3 Troop.

At first everyone was chiefly interested in watching the rest of the force moving out to sea, but after a time we tried to get some sleep; it was very uncomfortable and cramped in the landing-craft and I doubt if anyone dozed for more than a few minutes. About midnight we opened some tins of self-heating soup. It was tepid.

At 3.47 a.m., when we were still about an hour's run from the coast, a star shell went up on our port bow illuminating the group.

Immediately a heavy fire was opened up on us; 3- and 4-inch guns, ack-ack guns and machine-guns poured a stream of shells and tracer into the flotilla, while further star shells lit the sky. It was by far the most unpleasant moment of my life.

Five enemy craft were converging on us. It seemed impossible that our wooden landing-craft could survive for more than a few minutes. The tracer seemed to come swooping straight at us. In a few minutes we would be dead and there was absolutely nothing we could do about it. We crawled upon the face of the ocean, and always nearer to the deadly line of enemy ships. It was certainly very frightening – far more so than any land battle I ever saw before or since. I began to ram a clip into my Garand rifle. There wasn't much else to do. In the dark I found it unfamiliar. I wished I had stuck to my old Lee-Enfield. Craft and Clark were at my side. I

[1] Landing-craft Personnel (Large).

sensed that they were as unhappy as I was – which comforted me to some extent.

I was in the stern of the craft, where I had been trying to sleep; there was more room there. Now I wanted to speak to Buckee urgently. He was up forward beside the steersman. It was impossible to get to him through the soldiers crouched beneath the awning. I climbed up on to the narrow deck and ran along the side. We were still heading towards the Germans and every second brought us nearer the muzzles of their guns. I suggested to Buckee that it might be better to take some sort of avoiding action, but he replied that we were to follow the steam gunboat, which was navigating, so long as she was in action. Commander Wyburd had decided beforehand, that, should he meet the enemy at sea, he would continue on his course and fight his way through, for he felt quite rightly that any alteration in course or speed would so disorganize the group that an orderly landing would become impossible. In any case, the destroyers *Slazak* (Polish) and H.M.S. *Brocklesby* were to give support to the landing craft in the event of their being attacked by German ships. We ploughed on towards the Germans for what seemed a very long time; it has been estimated as ten minutes, but can scarcely have been as much; at the end of that time the gunboat, hit many times, reeled out of action, crossing our bows. Once more I urged Buckee to alter course and he now turned off ninety degrees to starboard.

Those of the landing-craft which escaped owed their survival to Wyburd's gallantry in keeping the gunboat on her original course, for the majority of the German gunners took his ship for their target. All his guns were put out of action, his wireless equipment was hit and about 40 per cent of those on board were wounded.

On the other hand, we in the landing-craft now found ourselves far too near to the German ships and attracting a great deal of fire. The canopy of our craft was full of holes, but the men crouching down below were not hit. We made the best speed we could for several minutes and at last found ourselves out of range; behind us tracer could still be seen but no sound reached us.

The destroyers, meanwhile, were pursuing some project of their own.

As soon as we were clear we looked about to see where the rest of the group was, only to find that we were now alone. This did not disturb us very much; Buckee had little doubt that some of the other craft would be able to find their way to the beaches even without the gunboat to navigate. We turned towards the shore and started looking for Yellow 2. It was not difficult to estimate its rough position, as a light some miles away to starboard was evidently the Dieppe lighthouse. We could now see the cliffs quite clearly and a black patch which Buckee said was the gully at Yellow 2. I thought it was Yellow 1, but Buckee insisted that he was right.

"There you are," he said, "there's your beach."

"What do we do now?" I asked, rather pointlessly.

"My orders," he replied, "are to land even if there's only one boat."

Not to be outdone, I said: "Those are my orders, too: we are to land whatever happens, even if we have to swim."

Buckee offered to land with his sailors to swell our party, but I persuaded him to remain with the craft. We arranged that if he should come under heavy fire from the cliffs he would leave us and that we would try to make our way to Dieppe and join the Canadians when the time came to withdraw. He was making directly for Yellow 2, but, fearing that there would be machine-guns in the gully, I asked him to run in about fifty yards to the right. We came in five minutes early, for it was getting light all too quickly, and touched down about 4.50 a.m.

We crossed the narrow beach, reached the foot of the cliff, turned to the left and approached the gully. The narrow cleft in the cliffs was completely choked with coils of wire with a rabbit-wire fence on the outside some ten feet high in front of it. I asked John Selwyn to tell his men to bring a Bangalore torpedo and blow a hole in the fence and was told that they had not got one in this particular boat. I said that we had better get to work with wire-cutters, but he said he had not brought any. I was vexed with Selwyn. I started to climb up the left-hand side of the gully, which looked the easier, but almost immediately lost my balance and fell back on top of Selwyn, who suggested that we were not doing much good and that it might be better to get back in the craft.

Similar thoughts were passing through my own mind at the moment, but being, I suppose, contrary by nature it needed only this to make me determined to carry on. I gave a sort of surly growl by way of reply and started climbing the other side of the cleft. When about twelve feet from the ground my Garand rifle slipped off my shoulder and into the crook of my right arm, swinging me away from the wire. I thought to myself, "If I fall off now I shall never get up," but by some miracle I managed to keep my foothold and cling on with one hand. From this point the cliff became rather less steep and I reached the top, standing on the pegs with which the Germans had secured the wire, which served as a rope. The barbs were very close together but fairly blunt and this, though it cut my hands, was not as unpleasant as it sounds. On reaching the top, I could see the back of a notice-board which turned out to have the words *"Achtung! Minen"* written on it.

The men seemed to take a very long time coming up the cliff, though Driver Cunningham collected their toggle ropes and made a rope to help them up the worst bit. As we reached the top Hopkins pointed out some landing-craft running in on Yellow 1, five of them. Later on a small ship ran in and beached between Yellow 1 and Yellow 2. This was the German armed tanker *Franz*, damaged by one of our motor launches.

By about 5.10 a.m. my whole party had reached the top and I led them into a small wood near by and organized them into three groups under Selwyn, Ruxton – a recently-joined subaltern – and myself. Some of the soldiers did not look particularly pleased at the turn of events, so I gave them a pep talk, telling them that if a party of nineteen could do any good it would be something to tell their children about. They looked a bit dubious. We had an odd assortment of arms; there was one Bren, six Thompson guns, ten rifles including my Garand, which had been given to me by the U.S. Rangers, a 3-inch mortar, which we had failed to get up the cliff, and a 2-inch mortar.

I now sent out scouts and started advancing through the

cornfields towards the road which runs along parallel with the coast about 1,000 yards inland. Looking out across the fields towards the battery we could make out absolutely nothing, though during our advance six Hurricanes came over and attacked it and were fired at by a light ack-ack gun. When we reached the road I took a careful look at the approach to the village through my field-glasses, expecting that there would be a German post at the entrance to the village. A French youth of about sixteen was passing on a bicycle when some of the men grabbed him. Though terrified, he was friendly and told me that he was trying to escape inland to avoid the fighting and that there were 200 Germans in the battery. It was obvious that he would not betray our presence, and when I told him he could go on his way he swiftly leant forward, kissed me on the cheek, leapt on his bogwheel and pedalled for the hinterland! Ruxton advanced with his group while the rest of us covered him. He soon signalled that the coast was clear and we all arrived at the edge of the village just as the battery fired its first round. We cut some telephone wires at this point and then pushed on. In an orchard to the right of the road a French peasant woman sat calmly milking a cow.

To move through the gardens at the back of the houses would have taken too long so we went up the main street. Here we met some Frenchmen wheeling a wounded woman along on a hand barrow; she had been hit during the attack by the Hurricanes soon after dawn. The guns were still firing slowly, so the sooner we reached the battery the better; I gave the order to double and we ran down the street at a pretty good pace. I questioned several inhabitants, hoping to hear that some of the men who had landed at Yellow I had also reached the village, but there was no news of them and no sign of firing from that direction. We saw quite a number of the inhabitants, some of whom were members of the local fire brigade in their brass helmets; one of the houses in the village was on fire. The people very wisely kept out of the way, though several of them waved to us, and all those we spoke to were distinctly friendly.

When we came abreast of the church we were suddenly fired on by a German machine-gun post at the corner of the road about sixty yards ahead of us. Ruxton opened fire on two Germans whom we saw cross the road and get into position in a hedge. They fired their rifles at him, but he stood his ground and returned their fire with his Thompson sub-machine gun. Selwyn joined him and opened up as well; then Abbott came up and got the Bren into action. Selwyn put Lance-Corporal Bennett behind the church and engaged this enemy post with our 2-inch mortar; the German machine-gun ceased fire.

I cannot think why we had no casualties at this point, for our party must have been an easy enough target. While this shooting was going on another group pushed on into the churchyard and engaged the enemy from there. The Germans' fire was mostly high and one burst dislodged a shower of tiles from a roof which descended on Abbott, the Bren-gunner.

The doubling had done the men good. They had now got their blood up and quite recovered their spirits. They were beginning to enjoy themselves. I re-formed them behind the church, with the intention of placing the Bren and some snipers in the tower, while the rest of us held the area. It seemed certain that the belfry would overlook the gun positions, and I had visions of picking off the German gunners one by one as they served their pieces. Unfortunately, when I went inside to look for the steps leading up the tower, I could find none. The church, a lovely medieval one, vanished in the pre-D-Day bombing, but I was told several years later by the town clerk that the steps began ten feet above ground level and were reached by a ladder which had been removed. Moreover, the view from the belfry was obscured by a row of tall trees, so perhaps it was as well that I was forced to alter my plan.

We now tried to advance on the battery through the orchard at the north-west end of the village, hoping to outflank any position which might be guarding the tracks entering the battery from the rear. We passed a slit trench and the under-carriage of an aeroplane which had been camouflaged and rigged up to look like a small gun, but then came under fire again from riflemen whom we could not see. They did not hit anybody and probably could not see us very well. Next a machine-gun opened up on us, firing three bursts, but there were so many hedges that we could not locate this either. There seemed to me to be no future in advancing blind through these orchards against a hidden enemy, and it suddenly occurred to me that we might be better off in the cornfields.

We assembled again at the edge of the village and I sent Selwyn's group to the flank of the guns, with orders to get within two hundred yards and snipe them. As he moved, my own group fired at the left-hand gun and continued to shoot while Ruxton led his men out to support Selwyn. My group then joined the other two. All three parties were fired at by small arms as we dashed to take up our new position, apparently by sentry groups posted along the edge of the orchards, but once again nobody was hit. The left-hand gun, which we imagined we could see clearly, and at which we had fired a certain amount, now turned out to be a dummy!

Once we were in among the crops I formed the men into two lines in extended order, with a good distance between each man and with the second line firing between the intervals in the first line. We now opened a hot fire at the smoke and flashes around the gun positions. Groups of riflemen were all firing at us from the battery position, but they were no marksmen.

All this time the guns went on shooting at a slow rate; possibly only one gun was in action, trying to find the range. Certainly there were no salvoes, and some of us estimated that the total number of rounds fired was no more than fifteen or twenty, though there must have been more. It seemed that the gun detachments were firing on their own account and that the observation post was not doing its job properly, possibly because we had cut their telephone wires, but more likely because of the enormous smoke-screen off Dieppe. The cloud of smoke there was very thick indeed and we ourselves could see none of the ships. To confuse the gunners the R.A.F. had dropped smoke on the battery and there was still a great deal hanging about. No doubt this air attack had upset them.

We had to fire from the kneeling position because of the height of the corn, taking snap shots and moving about, so as to offer the most difficult possible target to the enemy, but we were almost exactly at right angles to the enemy gun-line and my bullet that whistled over No. 4 gun would give a good fright to the crew of No. 1 as well – at least so we hoped. I am very far from claiming that we caused many casualties, and indeed it was very difficult to see anyone to get a shot at. It was harassing fire, more or less controlled. The guns were about twenty to thirty yards apart and surrounded by concrete walls.

After a time, at about eight o'clock, we had our reward. There was a sudden explosion about 150 yards to our front, an orange flash, and a cloud of black smoke. A shell screamed past overhead and plunged into a valley about a mile behind us. The Germans had turned their left-hand gun round and were firing it at us. Fortunately we were too close to be damaged, for the guns, not being designed to fire at point-blank range, could not be depressed sufficiently to hit us. It was nevertheless an unusual experience and for a moment I wondered what was happening. Indeed one of the soldiers came up to me and said indignantly:

"Sir! We're being mortared!" An odd deduction when a 6-inch gun was firing at us! The Germans in the Varengeville Battery used mortars against 4 Commando, but at Berneval it seems they had none, which was just as well for us. Fifteen feet of standing corn is said to stop a bullet, but I doubt if it is much protection against a mortar bomb. Selwyn told me afterwards that one of our motor launches, having taken us for the enemy, was also firing at us about this time and one of the men was hit in the ear, our first casualty. Every time the gun fired we gave it a volley of small arms, aimed at the black-and-yellow fumes which appeared. They fired four rounds at us, at the same slow rate as before, and then gave it up.

Suddenly two Messerschmitts came swooping up from our rear and flew over the battery without attacking us. Neither side seemed to know who we belonged to. We had come ashore with about 100 rounds per rifleman. Firing rapidly it would be easy to spend that much ammunition in ten minutes, so we had to be very sparing; we were continually telling the men to fire slowly so as to keep up a steady whine over the heads of the gunners. The posts in the orchard continued to fire at us without respite, but without success. We kept all our fire for the big guns.

Coast defence guns firing at a normal rate should be able to fire one or two rounds a minute, for the operation of reloading, though complicated, should not take more than about thirty seconds. We spent approximately an hour and a half in the cornfield and during that time I do not believe the battery got off more than twenty or thirty rounds, including the four aimed at us.

The shortage of ammunition was now becoming acute, and as time went by it was becoming increasingly probable that German reinforcements, including perhaps armour, would intervene. I did not care for the idea of meeting tanks in the middle of the cornfield, so I thinned out my line and sent Selwyn to form a small bridgehead round the beach, telling him that if the landing-craft was still there he was to fire three white Very lights.

So far we had paid no attention to the German observation post which clearly deserved a visit. While the remainder of the party withdrew towards the beach, Ruxton with Abbott, Craft and Clark came with me to a point on the cliff from which we had a good view of this pillbox. Ruxton saw two Germans standing on the roof and fired a burst at them with the Bren, at a range of 400 yards. They disappeared and fire was returned immediately. Ruxton continued to engage the enemy post. Clark now reported seeing three white Very lights from the beach and we wriggled back into a small valley and began to make our way back to the boat. A group of riflemen were following us, at a respectful distance, and someone else was sniping from the Dieppe side of the gully. A few of the men covered our withdrawal, firing back at the German riflemen.

Captain Selwyn now withdrew his party and embarked, while the rest of us covered their withdrawal from the top of the cliff. The landing-craft had been under fire from the observation post for some time. Riflemen had reached the cliffs about 300 yards to the east, and the solitary sniper was still plugging away from the west. Three men waiting on the beach to cover Ruxton and myself down the cliff were cursed at by the sailors for their slowness and told to get into the boat.

Once aboard they engaged the cliff-tops with the stripped

Lewis gun belonging to the craft, scoring several hits. One German dropped his rifle down the cliff.

By this time Ruxton and myself, with Abbott our Bren-gunner, had crossed the beach and were wading out to the landing-craft. It was like those dreams you have of trying desperately to walk and making no progress. Eventually we laid hold of the lifelines and were towed out to sea. About 300 yards out the craft hove to and we were dragged aboard. Quite a number of shots hit the craft at this point, and a sailor a yard away from me was severely wounded in the thigh. The battery fired a few shells at us but pretty wide of the mark. A bullet hit the smoke canister in the stern and we began to give out quite a respectable smoke-screen.

Shortly afterwards we fell in with the motor launch and transferred to her. We then returned to Newhaven, being unsuccessfully attacked on the voyage by a JU. 88 at 10.45 a.m. and entertained nobly on whisky, cocoa, and rum so that I felt distinctly warm, if somewhat tight, on arriving at Newhaven.

There was no news of the rest of the Commando when we reached Newhaven, and in the afternoon I went up to London to report at C.O.H.Q. Having been on the planning staff there at the time of the St Nazaire raid, I knew with what anxiety we had waited for any authentic information and how many days it had taken to reach us. I had an interview with Lord Louis Mountbatten and with General Haydon and was told to return for the conference which was to be held next day. I asked permission to reappear in my battledress which was rather the worse for wear, and Lord Louis replied: "What the hell, there is a war on."

I then went home to Oxshott and slept the night in my own bed.

*

The Germans were very excited at capturing some Americans. One of them, a very tall man – unfortunately his name is unknown to history – was being interrogated by a German officer.

"How many American soldiers are there in England?"

"There are 3,000,000. They are all my height and they have

to be kept behind barbed wire to stop them swimming the Channel to get at you bastards." Fortunately this German had a sense of humour.

*

What did Dieppe prove?

To the Germans it proved that their system of coast defence was sound, and in the two years that followed they continued to develop the West Wall with the intention of repelling invasion on the beaches. Infantry Regiment 571, which was in the area, had only the 2nd Battalion holding the town and yet succeeded in repulsing an attack by six battalions. The Germans were convinced that they were working on the right lines.

The expedition was extremely costly. Of the 4,961 Canadian soldiers engaged 3,363 became casualties – that is to say 68 per cent. The Germans sustained about 300 military casualties. Only thirty-seven prisoners were brought back to England, less than the number taken by our Commando at Vaagso.

Dieppe was always intended as a reconnaissance in force, and it succeeded in rubbing in certain lessons. When D-Day came in 1944 the invaders, instead of attempting to capture a port by direct assault from the sea, took their port with them and never again did they try to carry out a large-scale landing without heavy preliminary bombardment from the air and supporting fire from the sea.

At Dieppe there was no preliminary air bombardment because it was felt that this would prejudice surprise. It is not clear why a night air attack should necessarily put into the mind of the enemy commander the idea that he is going to receive a raid from the sea at dawn next morning, but this was one reason put forward. A heavy air raid shortly before a landing must cause great confusion and will give the assaulting troops a chance to strike before the defenders get really set again. St Nazaire should have proved the danger of taking on German coast defences without a proper air bombardment.

The naval force commander, Captain J. Hughes Hallet, had always insisted that a capital ship should have been employed to lend fire support to the assault. There is no doubt that the comparatively light naval losses support his view. A 6-inch cruiser such as H.M.S. *Kenya* which supported us at Vaagso might have made all the difference at Dieppe. The main German defences enfilading the beach were concentrated in the two headlands and it should not have been impossible for 6-inch guns firing at the cliffs to have brought down whole portions of them, besides destroying houses and barricades along the waterfront. The troops attacking on the main beach at Dieppe were invited to assault without proper covering fire.

Some people assumed, in view of the heavy casualties, that the enemy had warning of the raid in advance. Against this I can only say that we found the defence posts on our cliff-top near Belleville-sur-Mer unoccupied. Would the Germans have neglected these points if they had expected a raid?

We heard later that even the news of the action with the coastal convoy at night had not reached the German private soldiers, while the lighthouses at Dieppe and the Point d'Ailler (near Varengeville) remained burning until our landing-craft were close.

To sum up the results of the Dieppe raid, one can only say that if we made a mistake in attacking such a strong place without adequate fire support, at least the enemy were lulled into a sense of false security. Thereafter, they pursued a policy of coastal defence which was to be their undoing in 1944. In war the right things often happen for the wrong reasons.

SON TAY
Leroy Thompson

During the decade of direct US involvement in Vietnam, around 800 American military personnel were captured by the enemy, most of them USAAF aircrew shot down in raids over the North. The preferred tactic of the US government was to negotiate the release of the captives (with occasional success), but in 1970 it decided to sanction more direct methods. This was the daring raid by Special Forces on Son Tay, the only attempt ever made to free prisoners held in the North.

It was only natural that such a task should fall to Special Forces. Formed in 1952 – although with a lineage dating back to the wartime Office of Strategic Services (OSS) – the Special Forces had been charged from the beginning with recovery operations, especially of downed pilots, in addition to their role as Unconventional Warfare (UW) experts. Initially, Special Forces – the "Sneaky Petes" – had been viewed with suspicion by the military establishment, but had grown in both size and stature after the inauguration of President J.F. Kennedy in 1961. The new Commander-in-Chief believed that Special Forces were vital to the strategic interests of the US, especially in the Third World. Kennedy also lifted the ban on the Special Forces emblem, the green beret (based on that worn by the British Royal Marine Commandos), which had been imposed by senior army officers. The President's support for Special Forces was based on his own wartime experience as a PT boat commander running special ops. In Vietnam, Special Forces were committed heavily – and often inappropriately – to the war, and the less than satisfactory outcome of that conflict for the US led the army subsequently to downgrade its commitment to unconventional warfare. After ill-starred roles in Iran, Grenada, El Salvador and at Paitilla airfield during the Panama invasion, Special Forces demonstrated their elite status in the Gulf, where their long range reconnaissance proved invaluable at identifying Scud missiles sites.

When, on 9 May 1970, an NCO of the USAF's 1127th Field Activities Group (1127th FAG), a special intelligence unit that correlated information about American POWs in North Vietnam, spotted what appeared to be a prison full of American POWs at Son Tay, some 37 km west of Hanoi from reconnaissance photographs, he started a chain of events that would eventually lead to one of the most daring Special Forces operations of the entire war. Once the Joint Chiefs of Staff had evaluated the information from the 1127th FAG and decided that a rescue was desirable, both for the well-being of the prisoners and for the morale of American fighting men and civilians, the go-ahead was given for SACSA (the Special Assistant for Counter-insurgency and Special Activities), Brigadier-General Donald Blackburn, to begin planning a rescue mission to free the POWs held at Son Tay.

Various photo-intelligence sources, including the Big Bird reconnaissance satellite, the SR-71 Blackbird and Buffalo Hunter reconnaissance drones, were also made available to gather the information necessary for the raid. By 5 June, a full briefing had been given to the Joint Chiefs, and Blackburn had received permission to continue planning the raid. A little over a month later, on 10 July, the Joint Chiefs gave Blackburn the OK to begin implementing the plan.

Blackburn, a real fire-eater who had commanded Philippine guerrillas during World War II and the Special Operations Group in Vietnam, wanted to lead the raid himself, but because of his knowledge of sensitive intelligence matters he was precluded. Instead, the assignment went to Colonel "Bull" Simons, a highly experienced Special Forces officer who had served under Blackburn and had a reputation for getting things done. The raiding force was known as the Joint Contingency Task Group (JCTG), and the mission itself was code-named Ivory Coast. An area of Eglin Air Force Base in Florida was set aside for training the JCTG. Although Major-General Leroy Manor, the commander of USAF special operations at Eglin, was put in overall command, Simons was his deputy and in charge of leading the raiding force.

Since the optimum time for the raid appeared to be between

20/25 October, when the weather and moon would be most favourable, both men began selecting their teams: Manor, the air and planning elements, and Simons, the actual assault force. At Fort Bragg, hundreds of Special Forces troopers volunteered for the JCTG only knowing that it was hazardous and that the "Bull" would be commanding. Some 15 officers and 82 NCOs, predominantly from the 6th and 7th Special Forces Groups were chosen. As training progressed, the assault force, their backups, and the support personnel would be selected from these 97 Green Berets.

To carry out realistic training, a mock-up of the Son Tay compound was built at Eglin. So that Soviet spy satellites could not detect its presence, the mock-up was designed to be dismantled during the day and quickly set up at night for training. Since the raid itself would be at night, training at night on the mock-up was essential. As an additional training aid, a table-top model of the camp, costing some $60,000, was also built.

Detailed training of the raiding force began on 9 September. Two problems involving the elimination of guards at the prison arose during this period. Simons was dismayed to find that even his best marksmen were having trouble getting more than 25 per cent of their shots on target at night. This difficulty was solved, however, by going outside the normal Army supply channels to acquire "Singlepoint Nite Sites" for the sharpshooters' M16s. The other problem involved the need to saturate the guard towers around the Son Tay compound with fire. To solve this problem an HH-53 Super Jolly Green Giant equipped with 7.62mm miniguns was given the mission of chopping the towers down with a hail of fire.

The assault force was formed into three groups: the compound assault force of 14 men, who would actually be deposited inside the prison compound by crash landing an HH-3 helicopter; the command and security group of 20 men; and the support group of 22 men commanded by Simons himself. Five HH-53s, which could be refuelled in-flight and the HH-3 would carry the assault force.

Beginning on 28 September, the assault force practised the actual assault with the air force crews who would fly the helicopters and other aircraft, which included three C-130s (two of which were Combat Talons equipped for command and control) and A-1 strike aircraft. The landing and assault were rehearsed again and again, with many simulations being "live-fire" run-throughs. Alternative plans were also produced in case one of the three teams failed to make it to the target.

As the rehearsals progressed, Simons, a firearms enthusiast and expert, ordered his supply people to come up with additional weapons and special equipment. Eventually, the teams were equipped with 12-gauge shotguns, 30-round M16 magazines, .45 automatic pistols, CAR-15s for the compound assault force, M-79 grenade launchers, LAWs, bolt-cutters, cutting torches, chainsaws and special goggles. Some men carried cameras to record the prisoners' living conditions. Many items used in the raid had to be acquired outside of the normal Army supply channels. To ensure communications during those critical minutes on the ground, the 56 men of Simons' assault force were given 92 radios: two AN-PRC-41s to maintain contact with the Pentagon via a radio link at Monkey Mountain in South Vietnam, 10 AN-PRC-77s for calling in air strikes, 24 AN-PRC-88s for communications between the various groups on the ground, and, finally, 56 AN-PRC-90 survival radios for escape and evasion.

Although the mission had not been approved by the target date of 20/25 October, Blackburn got the go-ahead to begin moving personnel to Southeast Asia in preparation for the mission on 27 October. On 1 November, Blackburn and Simons, among others, left for Southeast Asia to lay the groundwork for the raid. By the 12th, both Blackburn and Simons were back in the States as the raiding force prepared to head for Thailand. Six days later, a few hours after the raiders had left for Takhli RTAFB (Royal Thai Air Force Base) in anticipation of receiving orders to carry out the raid, President Nixon gave the "go" order. The weather and moon had to be right for the raid to take place and conditions were deemed acceptable on the night of 20/21 November.

On the evening of 20 November, the raiders were shuttled to Udorn RTAFB from where the raid was launched at 2318 hours local time. Carrier aircraft from the *Oriskany*, *Ranger*, and *Hancock* were also launched a couple of hours later, during the early morning of the 21st, to create a diversion by staging a fake raid over Hanoi. At about 0218 on the morning of 21 November, the raid itself began. As a C-130 flare ship illuminated the area with flares, the HH-53, code-named Apple Three, opened up on the guard towers of Son Tay Prison with its miniguns, bringing them crashing down.

Shortly thereafter, the HH-3 carrying the assault party commanded by Major "Dick" Meadows, landed inside the prison compound: the whole group pressed against mattresses to cushion them against the crash. The HH-3, known as Banana One came to rest amid branches, leaves, and other debris brought down by its whirling rotors during the crash descent. On landing, "Dick" Meadows rushed out with his bullhorn shouting: "We're Americans. Keep your heads down. We're Americans. This is a rescue. We're here to get you out. Keep your heads down. Get on the floor. We'll be in your cells in a minute." The remainder of the assault party rushed into action, some men laying down suppressive fire, others streaking for the cellblocks to rescue the prisoners.

A few minutes later the command and security group landed just outside the prison's walls. The Support group led by Simons himself, however, had landed 400m off course at what was identified on the raiders' maps as a secondary school. Instead of a secondary school, they found themselves outside a barracks housing Chinese or Soviet advisors to the NVA (North Vietnamese Army). School or not, though, Simons and his men proceeded to teach its denizens a lesson. Within minutes of touching down, many of the residents of the barracks had been killed, preventing them from reinforcing the prison compound and taking the other raiders by surprise. Within 10 minutes Simons had cleared the area and his men had been lifted back to the Son Tay compound, where they assisted the assault and security elements in eliminating several guards.

Despite the smoothness of the assault, however, the raiders discovered that there were no POWs in the prison. They had been moved elsewhere some weeks before the raid. This development had not been picked up by the US intelligence, because no one had wanted to risk putting in any agents on the ground, and too much reliance had been placed on photographic intelligence.

Less than 30 minutes after the raid had started, the raiders were back on board their choppers and heading for Thailand. Casualties were light: only one raider had been wounded. The raid itself had gone almost perfectly. Even Simons' landing at the wrong complex was fortuitous as it allowed a surprise attack on an undetected enemy unit.

The raiders themselves had mixed reactions on the flight back to Thailand. They were disappointed that all of their training and effort had not resulted in the rescue of a single prisoner. However, they were also glad that they were all heading home, and justifiably proud of the precision with which the raid had been carried out.

The Son Tay raid was not a complete failure, despite the fact that no prisoners were rescued. It proved in very striking fashion that the North Vietnamese were vulnerable to attacks on installations close to home. As a result, the North Vietnamese had to tie down additional troops to guard sensitive areas, and they also lost some credibility with the Chinese and Russians, who feared that the US would continue to mount raids into North Vietnam. Indirectly, the raid also led to some improvement in the treatment of American POWs.

It should not be forgotten, either, that Simons' party had killed dozens of the enemy, many of them foreign advisors, without taking any losses themselves. The Special Forces troopers, and the air force and navy pilots had carried out their jobs with great skill. It was a classic raid – get in quick, hit hard, get out fast, inflict maximum casualties – but the intelligence had been wrong, a failure which clearly illustrated the fact that intelligence is critical to special operations, especially raids into enemy territory. It is still not known why the North Vietnamese moved their prisoners from Son Tay, but it may be speculated that a rescue attempt was foreseen as the US were steadily building up pressure for their release.

The final point proven by the Son Tay raid was one that Donald Blackburn had been making ever since being appointed SACSA. He argued that North Vietnam was vulnerable to hit-and-run raids by highly-trained special operations forces. Other such raids might have secured the release of many of the American POWs held by the Hanoi government.

SCALING THE HEIGHTS

O. L. Howard

The first rangers in US history were formed by Major Robert Roberts in 1763 as a guerrilla force to fight the native Indians and the French. The name was revived in 1942 when the US began to create commando-type units as part of its war effort in Europe, and eventually six ranger battalions were formed. The 2nd Ranger Battalion, led by Lt-Col James Rudder (hence the 2nd's informal nomenclature, "Rudder's Rangers"), was formed in April 1943 when 500 men were selected from 2000 volunteers, and completed training in the States that November – having established a US Army record of 15 miles in a 2-hour speed march. The unit was tasked with one of the most important missions in the Allied invasion of Normandy on 6 June 1944, the destruction of the German gun emplacement on the Pointe Du Hoc, a towering promontory – with seemingly unscaleable cliffs – which offered an unresricted field of fire across the Utah and Omaha invasion beaches. The exploits of the 2nd Rangers on that historic day are detailed below.

After D-Day the Rangers remained part of the US Army until their disbandment following the Korean War. They were revived in 1975 when the US Army, wishing a fresh start after the defeat in Vietnam, recruited two ranger battalions, the 1st and 2nd Battalions of the 75th Infantry Regiment. With a combined strength of 600 personnel (all airborne-qualified), the two battalions came under the 1st Special Operations Command in 1982. They played a key role in Operation Urgent Fury, the invasion of Grenada.

POINTE DU HOC was heavily fortified. The Germans, under Rommel, were no fools. They had recognized immediately the vital significance of the spot. Deep entrenchments had been dug for the troops; concrete bunkers held the spitting posts. Heavy weapons of all types, from artillery pieces to machine guns and mortars were emplaced to rake the beaches, and to annihilate any troops that might dare to land on the more inviting coastal points. But the heart of the German defenses on the great 100-foot bluff was a battery of six big coastal guns. They employed mobile French GPF 155 mm rifles among the most powerful coastal artillery in all Europe. The big, long-barreled pieces had a range of over 26,000 yards.

Pointe du Hoc *had to be knocked out* before the main landings. Otherwise those six big guns would slaughter the infantrymen in their packed landing boats or on the beaches. What was worse, they could knock out the more lightly armed troop-carrier vessels, if they ventured within five miles of the beaches. Even if the troops managed to get ashore, they would be subject to directly aimed fire from this artillery, a barrage that would pin them down, prevent them from pursuing their assigned objectives, and permit German defense forces to wipe them out easily, at their leisure.

The job of wiping out this Nazi slaughterhouse was given to the Rangers. They were the only American unit that could hope to cope with the obviously suicidal nature of the assault. Trained with and by the British Commandos, they were the toughest and most self-reliant force in the entire US Army.

Every man was a hand-picked volunteer. Just asking to join these elite troops was not nearly enough. Only the fittest and the most able fighting men were even given a chance to become part of the Ranger organization.

Back in 1942, some fifty men of the newly reactivated Rangers had taken part in the famous Canadian-British raid on Dieppe. Others had fought in the kaleidoscopic battles across the deserts of North Africa, with the 1st Infantry Division. Their smashing raider-assault attacks had broken the German defenses at Gela in the Sicily invasion. There, they had again led the way for the 1st Division.

General Omar N. Bradley, commander of the United States First Army, the invasion force, knew the Rangers well . . . from North Africa and Sicily. His choice of a Ranger unit to make the assault on Pointe du Hoc met no argument from anyone. A special (Provisional) Ranger force of two hundred men would be picked for the most crucial job. To lead the raid, Lieutenant Colonel James E. Rudder, a 34-year-old rancher from Brady, Texas, was chosen by Major General Clarence R. Huebner, C. O. of 1st Division. Once again the Rangers were to open the way for an invasion by the Big Red One division.

After it was all over, Rudder remarked wryly about this terrific assignment: "First time they told me about this mission I thought they were trying to scare me. It did give me plenty to think about, too." Most men would have been terrified at the prospect. If ever there was an assignment that carried a *Suicide* label plainly visible, this was it. But instead of fainting when told what his raiding unit was to do, Rudder gulped, grinned, and started to handpick the men who would go with him.

The men he chose from the mass volunteer list would have delighted the leathery Rangers of 1763. They were an American Ranger group in the best old colonial tradition – a motley crew of diverse personalities and bewildering ancestral backgrounds. Every man was a deadly one to have as an enemy and a prize one to have as a sidekick when the chips were down – like Saunders from Nebraska, O'Keefe from Massachusetts, Lacey from Arkansas, Cohen from New York, Lesek from Ohio, Marino from California, Desmoulins from Louisiana, Karpovich from Pennsylvania, Nilsen from Minnesota – a tough, swashbuckling, laughing crew of fighting men; the best in the history of the world, the cream of America's young men – 2nd Ranger Battalion.

Training for the great assault was carried out on the Isle of Wight, the large, offshore English island that guards the entry to the cities of Southampton and Portsmouth, and is known in peacetime as the home of the international yacht regatta of Cowes.

The Isle of Wight provided a series of cliffs, similar in many ways to the terrain the Rangers would face in Normandy. And the heavy seas, rolling in from the unprotected channel side, duplicated exactly the conditions the landing party would have to face.

The plan they practised over and over again was simplicity in design but probably certain death in execution. All they had to do was to land under fire – concentrated on them because they'd be the only target in the area – move from a presumably rough and heavy sea onto a tiny shingle beach, and openly scale a 100-foot cliff in the face of an enemy entrenched above them and commanding their route completely. Then, having mounted to the top, they were to destroy the German troops guarding the guns, and finally they were to demolish the guns themselves.

In training, they had full cooperation from both the British Commandos, and the British Alpine Club. Among the post-war achievements of that band of experienced mountaineers was the conquest of Mount Everest. They provided equipment and teachers. For example, the Rangers used special mortars, built to shoot ropes with long grappling hooks up onto the top of a cliff.

Every man in the unit had to master the art of using this equipment, to scale a hundred-foot rope up a sheer wall, carrying a full battle pack, weapons, plus extra demolition charges to be used when he succeeded in reaching the top.

Colonel Rudder tried to foresee every eventuality. But no matter how he tried, it was impossible to find a way to avoid the overwhelming probability of enormous casualties. Speed appeared to offer the only hope. It worked down to the fact that the faster they finished, the less men they would lose.

Besides scaling ropes, they practiced with lightweight steel sectional ladders, narrow and easy to carry and assemble. Fire truck extension ladders, borrowed from the London Fire Department, were mounted on platforms built into DUKW's. The DUKW's were to run ashore and throw their ladders right up against the cliff face.

Three companies of the 2nd Ranger Battalion were to spearhead the attack, two-hundred men landing in the first assault. The rest, followed by the 5th Ranger Battalion (Reinforced) would wait offshore until the toehold on the cliff top was seized. Of to the right, across Omaha Beach, C Company of the 2nd Battalion would lead the 116th Infantry Regiment in, and strike at Pointe du Hoc overland if the key battery was not captured within thirty minutes after assault began. How they were to land on the open beaches, under the fire of the unconquered strongpoint, was not made too clear. Nor was it explained what would happen to the rest of the D-day schedule, if the battery was not silenced. Certainly, the effect on the raw, unbloodied 29th Division, which was due to be landed directly under the guns of the Pointe du Hoc strongpoint was gruesomely easy to imagine. As it was, even with the battery silenced, they would have a hard enough time.

But fate had another blow to deliver. Purely by chance, the German 352nd Division had moved into the invasion area on June 5. They were running through training maneuvers, precisely at the instant the landing took place. Instead of encountering only light and isolated resistance, the invasion forces had to cope with a hard-bitten, tough fighting organization. And the Rangers had to meet a heavily reinforced garrison in their lonely cliff-side attack.

In the darkness just before dawn on June 6, the raiding force waited in landing craft off the black coast of Normandy. Night's dark shadows were rent by leaping flashes as battleships, cruisers and destroyers in the open channel fired salvo after salvo at the invisible shore. The thunderous booming of cannon and crashing roars of exploding shells echoed around the wallowing LCA's. In each assault landing boat some thirty men crouched, heavily weighted with weapons and equipment.

Aboard the 1st Division's C.P. ship, Huebner spoke one last "good luck" to Colonel Rudder, on their radio command channel. Rudder was going to lead his men in himself, over Huebner's protests. "You'll risk getting knocked off in the first minutes," objected the Division Commander, "and then where's the leadership!"

"Sorry, sir," answered the Ranger C.O. "If you order me not to go I'll have to disobey you. My men can carry on without me, but if I don't go the attack may foul up, and I'll never forgive myself." Huebner had no choice but to agree. The Ranger Commander took his place in a landing boat, right with the other men, as he meant to do.

As dawn broke the LCA's sped towards the cliffs. The assault was on.

* * *

Overhead, waves of bombers droned, spilling clusters of demolition bombs that made a welter of flaming eruptions atop the cliffs and on the plateau beyond. Careening destroyers, running like terriers behind the landing ships, raked the cliffsides with barking, crackling volleys. Screaming fighter bombers and attack planes hurtled over, skimming across the cliff tops to disappear behind them. LCT (R)'s (rocket-firing assault boats) rode behind the LCA's, sending streams of flaming rockets to burst in spectacular blasts against the cliffs. It seemed that no defense could endure the blasting barrage of fire and steel.

It seemed so – but only until the assault boats neared the shore. Then, as morning light brightened, a storm burst from the shore. Cannon and machine guns blazed out at the few oncoming LCA's. Geysers erupted in shattering roars all around the few lonely boats, pushing doggedly towards the cliff. Enemy flak guns from the Pointe and artillery from both sides raked the boats with murderous fire.

Behind the Rangers' boats wallowed a few DD tanks, supposed to support the LCA's with close gunfire. None of the amphibious tanks ever fired a shot. Swamped in the turbulent seas, they floundered and sank.

White-faced men in the assault boats heard the vicious drumming of machine-gun bullets beating against the steel sides of their boats. Plumes of water, thrown up by near-miss shell bursts, cascaded down on them. Soaked and half seasick in the rocking, pitching boats, the Rangers looked at each other grim-faced. It would be bad enough on the shore, but it was hard to sit helplessly in a boat under fire, sitting-duck targets for the guns above.

"For chrissake," bellowed one Ranger at his boat's helmsman, "can't you speed up this goddam crate! They'll make hash of us before we get near 'em, at this rate."

A shell burst with a wicked *whap-p* right alongside the boat, sending splinters of hot steel whistling into the craft. Several men grunted in surprised pain, and then slumped heavily down on the gritty floor. The man who had just shouted at the helmsman stared at a bright red, wet spot, rapidly spreading on his right shoulder. He had been hit.

Outrage and wrath roared in his voice as he yelled furiously at the helmsman again. "See what I mean! The bastards are clobbering us while you horse around out here. Get this damn boat up to that damn cliff, so I can knock off a few krauts before my arm stiffens up!"

That was the kind of man who was a United States Ranger at Pointe du Hoc. All man, unafraid, and eager for battle. A fighting man, in the hell-for-leather tradition of Roger's Rangers. In the charging assault boat the men smiled with grim amusement as they neared the shore.

At the narrow beach the leading boats grated on the rough shelf, which was pitted with dozens of shell holes, blasted out by bombs and shells. The ladder-carrying DUKW's were stalled in futile helplessness, unable to move in closer and unable to reach the cliff with their ladders.

"Fire the mortar grapples!" The C.O. shouted the command.

On the boats and the narrow shore, mortars barked again and again. The Rangers fired the grappling hooks up, but most of them fell short, held back by heavy-soaked ropes. Speed was vital. If the Germans could move to the cliff edge above, they could slaughter the men below.

"Move! Move! Move!" Colonel Rudder, bleeding from a shrapnel wound, was going from group to group. "We're forty minutes late already. *Let's get up that cliff!*"

On the cliff top, the coal-scuttle helmets of Germans were beginning to appear. Up and down the narrow beach, crackling explosions ripped at the men – potato masher grenades were being flung down by the Germans.

On his radio the C.O. spoke anxiously to his seaborne support, a destroyer racing up and back not far out from the cliff's face. U.S. Destroyer *Satterlee*, hardly half a mile offshore, brazenly rode parallel to the shore, firing at the cliff top, like a mother hen protecting its chicks. The Navy, not to be outdone by the soldiers ashore, defied every rule of safe operation, and stayed protectively near. Without the *Satterlee* the fate of the Rangers might have been annihilation. As it was, one man after another was falling under the murderous grenades from above.

Sheets of flame spouted from the *Satterlee*'s guns – volleys, fired at the cliff top. The coal scuttle helmets disappeared in a mass of flying earth, smoke and flame.

"Very nice shooting," reported the C.O. to the destroyer. "Thanks! Don't go away!"

Mortars barked again on the narrow shingle beach. This time exultant yells told of success. The grappling hooks had gone up and over – a dozen lines dangled down the cliff side.

"Up and over!" Non-coms bellowed the command. On each rope line men were clambering up, straining and sweating despite the morning chill.

Whap – Whang – Whang!

Men froze on the ropes, huddled against the cliff. More grenades!

Offshore, the *Satterlee* bellowed again. Shells screamed over the cliff edge, hardly yards above the Rangers clinging to the swaying ropes. Cracking explosions above. Then silence. The last Germans there were gone.

Sergeant Fred Morton, from Georgia, was the first man to reach the top. A desolate picture met his eyes. The tableland was scarred with shell and bomb craters. Not a gun nor a live German was in sight. Dead figures and pieces of figures in field-gray were scattered all over the grim plateau. A long line of big 240 mm shells lay spotted in a row along the edge. They had been meant to roll down onto the Rangers, and to be fired by electric wires. The bombing and shelling had cut the wires.

As the Americans gathered on the cliff top, Morton whistled softly, "Brother, what those things would have done if the wires hadn't been cut!"

Colonel Rudder took quick stock of the picture as he reached the top, a blood-soaked bandage around one arm. The Germans had quit under the fierce attack, afraid to stand before the fearless assault. The guns were gone, moved out.

Patrols of three and five men moved forward, toward the gun

emplacements. All were found to be empty of guns, though full of ammunition.

Inland, half a mile from the shore, the guns were found in an apple orchard. A few dozen German troops, desperate rear guards, were cut down by the swarming Rangers in a series of savage little skirmishes.

Pointe du Hoc was taken. Mission accomplished.

Some forty Rangers had fallen in the assault. Almost laughably small casualties for so dangerous a raid. The guns were disabled by blowing their breeches. A perimeter defense was set up, to await the arrival of the units soon to land on Omaha Beach.

For two days the little band of 2nd Battalion Rangers was to hold off repeated counterattacks by the Germans. They were to be savagely besieged. Colonel Rudder was to be wounded again, and to refuse to be evacuated. They were to lose all but ninety men of the entire attack force. They were to hold on successfully through it all, until the 116th Infantry joined up with them two days later.

THE ATTACK ON CORPS HEADQUARTERS

Roy Farran

Following the Axis surrender in North Africa in May 1943, Allied attention in World War II began to shift to Italy, and the US Seventh and British Eighth Armies landed on 10 July 1943 in southern Sicily. 1 SAS – now renamed the Special Raiding Squadron (SRS), and placed under the command of Lieutenant-Colonel Paddy Mayne – operated in advance of the main invasion forces, launching raids against enemy batteries at Capo Murro di Porco and Augusta. Meanwhile, 2 SAS operated in enemy rear areas disrupting enemy communications and troop movements. The SRS was withdrawn from Italy in October 1943, but detachments of 2 SAS continued to fight in Italy intermittently until the end of the war in Europe. These included 3 Squadron of 2 SAS, under the command of Major Roy Farran (see also "Operation Wallace", pp 18–30), which arrived in Italy in January 1945 with a general commission to disrupt enemy supply lines and co-ordinate the activities of the partisans in the North. The squadron carried out three minor operations and one major one, "Operation Tombola". This was a large-scale tactical operation involving SAS and partisans, the centrepiece of which was an attack on the German corps headquarters at Albinea in the Po Valley. Farran – now going under the nom de guerre of Major McGinty – was specifically ordered not to accompany the attack, but "accidentally" parachuted down with the advance party on 4 March. Meeting the party on the DZ was Mike Lees, British SOE liaison officer in Reggio Province, and an agreement was reached to form at "Battaglione Alleata", a mixed partisan and SAS combat group under SAS command. The new formation consisted of about 25 SAS from 3 Squadron, 30 Russian POWs and some 40 Italian partisans led by "Tito", most of whom were

"Garibaldini" or Communists. Few of the partisans had any military experience, but two weeks of intensive training by Farran welded them into an effective force, capable of using rifles, 3" mortars, Brens and heavy machine guns. Shrewdly, Farran gave the partisans a distinctive green and yellow feather hackle to wear in the berets, which they wore with pride and a sense of belonging. A notable feature of Tombola was that British junior NCOs and private soldiers were put in charge of partisan teams and, uniformly, displayed high quality leadership. "It was extraordinary", Farran later recorded, "how successful the British common soldiers were as detachment commanders. They reacted to their sudden responsibility magnificently". In this respect Tombola anticipated 22 SAS operations in Oman in the 1960s, when the Regiment fought alongside locally raised tribal levies.

MIKE LEES had long dreamed of an attack on the German corps headquarters at Albinea, a village on the flats of the Po Valley but close enough to the mountains to be tempting. In fact it was the obvious vulnerability of the Albinea headquarters that made him so keen to have British troops dropped into his valley.

The headquarters was sited around a cross-roads and was well protected by anti-aircraft guns. But the nerve centre comprised two villas, one on each side of the road to the north, which were actually unprotected by the main body of guarding troops and were on the side farthest away from us.

Lees received day by day messages concerning the headquarters. He knew the names of most of the officers and even what they ate for dinner. The girl *staffettas* [partisan couriers] maintained constant watch over their movements. At least once a week Maria or Argentina or Norice would bicycle through the camp. While the sentries wolf-whistled, our girls noted the positions of machine-guns and sentries, faithfully reporting back to us in the valley. Allied headquarters in Florence were well aware of our interest and even dropped in maps and air-photographs of Albinea. Lees's one dread was that the Germans would move before we could attack them.

This also became my fear as I became infected by Mike's enthusiasm. A damaging attack on a main headquarters would certainly be a big contribution to the Allied cause, especially if it coincided with the main offensive. And we were both excited and relieved when Fifteenth Army Group wirelessed agreement to our plans.

Those plans were simple enough. We would collect our force of one hundred men – thirty Russians, forty Italians and twenty-four British – at the extreme edge of partisan controlled territory. From there we would march by night to a farm on the northern edge of the mountains overlooking the Po Valley. We would hide in this farm for a day and then, on the following night, launch our attack on the headquarters. After causing as much damage as possible in a brief raid, we would disperse and make our separate ways back to our mountain lair where the remaining two-thirds of the battalion would protect us from pursuit.

This assault into the heart of the thickly-populated plains would be by three parallel columns from the north, the side farthest away from our protective mountains but most vulnerable to attack. The Russians were to march in the eastern column and were to swing right after entering the target area so as to form a screen that would cut off the two villas from the German troops billeted to the south. Each of the other two columns would take one of the pair of villas, thus isolated by the Russians. One of these villas was known as Villa Calvi and was, according to our information, the operational headquarters of the corps. In it we hoped to trap the German chief of staff, a certain Colonel Lemelsen, and his officers. The other, called Villa Rossi, was on the opposite side of the north-south road and was the billet of the general and other senior officers. These assault columns each consisted of an advance guard of ten British, who were to break into the houses, followed by twenty Italians. My own headquarters, which was to base itself on the road between the two villas, comprised Kirkpatrick, the piper, Morbin, my servant, Bruno the faithful and an Italian guide.

My orders were purely for destruction. No prisoners were to be taken because they would only hamper withdrawal. And the main object was to kill the German officers and to set fire to their headquarters. The raid was to last no more than twenty minutes and my signal for retreat back to the mountains would be a red Very cartridge fired into the sky.

Looking back, I cannot imagine why I neglected to tell both assault parties to seize enemy papers. Unfortunately I did not and, although it would have been easy, no one else thought of it in the heat of battle.

I knew from past experience that the German reaction would be quick and I was particularly afraid they would send help to their officers from the guardhouse at the cross-roads. German counter-action might also come from the two anti-aircraft batteries at Bottegie and Pianello, both of which were to the south and could therefore only interfere with us by sending truckloads of troops via the cross-roads. I was careful to tell Modena and his Russians to spray the cross-roads area indiscriminately with tracer bullets throughout the raid. They were not to attempt to take anything, but were to concentrate on keeping German heads under cover.

As 25th March, the day set for our attack, approached, I became afraid that the Germans suspected we were planning something. It seemed impossible that they did not know of our activities in the valley. The main body of British had dropped on 9th March and weapons poured steadily into the dropping zone at Casa Balocchi. Huge supply drops took place on 10th, 14th, 18th, 22nd and 23rd March.

My alarm was at its highest when a German patrol crossed the river at Ceredelo to the east. The Green Flame [a partisan detachment] outpost fled immediately and the Germans advanced along the road to Quara before they encountered Wooding and his Browning machine-gun. The Green Flames held firm on the hills around Wooding and there was a day-long exchange of small-arms fire. Presumably the Browning and the wild partisan fire gave the Germans an erroneous impression of our strength for they withdrew across the River Secchia before evening.

This first brush with the enemy hardened our resolve to attack on 25th March whatever the situation. Lees and I felt that our undisturbed peace in the valley could not last much longer and that if we missed our opportunity to attack Albinea then, it might never present itself again. And, although short wireless schedules with Florence precluded a long explanation,

Fifteenth Army Group proved surprisingly ready to agree to the attack before the time set for our main activities against the enemy. Up-to-date air photographs were dropped into Secchio – to our astonishment by the unorthodox method of a swooping fighter – and final orders were issued to the companies.

The sun shone brightly as I marched beside Lees at the head of twenty British parachutists chosen for the attack. It was a long and tiring approach march for a hot day, out of the safety of our valley, across the River Secchia by the footbridge at Cavola and up the heights beyond to Vallestra, where we were to meet Modena and his Russians. The men were in good spirits though heavily laden with arms and ammunition. Those left behind with Easton at Tapignola were disappointed not to be chosen, but someone had to defend our base and already I had denuded Eld at Gatta by taking three of his ten men for the raid. Among our twenty were Sergeant Guscott and Lieutenant Riccomini, two gallant members of the Special Air Service who had distinguished themselves in Walker-Brown's operation near Spezia. Though deserving rest, they both volunteered to return to the wrong side of the enemy lines for Operation Tombola. Among the best of our men, both were destined to be killed.

Behind the British straggled twenty ragged Garibaldini and Bruno with nineteen of his Goufa Nera. This selection of Garibaldini and Lee's bodyguard instead of Tito's Italians was a mixture of prudence and politics. Our own Italians were still insufficiently trained for such a raid and I thought our solidarity with the Communist partisans would be strengthened if I offered to give a place to ten Garibaldini drawn from each of the brigades of Rames and Luigi. They were commanded by Yani, a tough character, and their role was comparatively simple – to follow the British, who would kill the sentries and force the entrance into Villa Calvi. As for the Goufa Nera, Lees had insisted on taking them. Ever since he dropped into Villa Minozzo Valley, it had been his ambition to attack Albinea. And, although his job was strictly no more than liaison with the partisans from his mission at Secchio, he insisted on joining the party. I was glad to have him, especially since his Goufa Nera bodyguard were the best partisans in the valley. They were to follow Riccomini and his British into Villa Rossi.

Norice and Argentina, two of the girl *staffettas*, walked up and down the column, chatting with the men and breaking into shrill laughter at their wisecracks. Their bare legs were brown and sturdy and their short skirts ended above the knees. Norice had pinned a red beret on her long black hair. When I caught her eyes they laughed a message that had nothing to do with war.

I was worried about Lees for all my pleasure at his company. He had developed a fever, suspiciously like malaria, but refused to be left behind. He dosed himself frequently with quinine, but I did not like the unnatural drops of sweat on his forehead. Though we were all hot from marching in the sun, his face was grave and pallid beneath the sweat. And he was unusually quiet.

We left Quara behind us and began to descend gradually to river level at the Cavola footbridge. I told Kirkpatrick to play his pipes and the men trudged through the dust in time to the music. Lees strode silently beside me. Then the men broke into the song they coined up on Cisa Pass.

"We're reckless parachutists,
  At least that's what we're told,
But when action stations sounded,
  Then we don't feel quite so bold.

"We're the boys who ride the slip-stream,
  We're the heroes of the sky,
But we all know deep inside us,
  It's an awful way to die.

"Stand to the door, stand to the door,
  And my poor old knees are trembling,
Up off the floor, up off the floor,
  And I'm seeing scores of gremlins.

"Red light on! Green light on!
  Out through the door we go,
F-f-fighting for breath, b-b-battered near to death,
  Drifting down to earth below.

"We're the boys who ride the slip-stream,
We're the boys who jump for fame,
If our parachutes don't open,
Then we get there just the same.

"There's a big court of inquiry,
And the packer gets the sack,
But all the juries in creation,
Can't fetch that poor chap back."

It was sung to the tune of a famous German marching song and was in keeping with the same sense of humour that had parodied our motto, "who dares wins," to read "who cares who wins".

Once over the river, it was hard climbing up the slope of the northern bank to Vallestra and I felt sadly out of condition when we reached the top. While Sergeant Guscott sought billets and clean straw for the men in a barn, I sprawled on the grass of the village green to await the arrival of Modena and his Russians. While I lay there in the evening sun, enjoying the cool greenness of the grass, I vaguely wondered at the steady trickle of peasants who, in two's and three's with bundles over their shoulders, hurried down the track towards the river. It was some time before it occurred to me that they looked remarkably like refugees, even though I had seen the signs often enough to recognise them. Suddenly alert, I sat up and watched. Some dragged laden cattle behind them, all carried blanket-wrapped bundles and the children stayed close to their mothers' heels. The symptoms were unmistakable. Worried, I sent Riccomini off to reconnoitre.

He did not have to spy out the land for long before discovering the disturbing answer. The Germans had started a broad sweep towards our valley and had already reached Baiso, a hill-top village five miles to the north. Some of the Green Flames had moved into positions on the edge of Vallestra and peasants were evacuating the village.

Wearily, I followed him to a high point west of Vallestra to see for myself. A few partisans lay on their stomachs on the edge of the Carpineti road and, from behind the cover of rocks, pointed sten-guns towards Baiso. Occasionally they fired a burst in the general direction of the enemy and feverishly reloaded. It was comic opera war, for the Germans were at least ten times out of range, and I told Riccomini to stop this crazy firing at clouds. Through my glasses I could see a line of small black figures, silhouetted against the sky as it climbed a razor-backed ridge that led up the hill to Baiso. Twice I heard the familiar *tack-pung* of a Mauser rifle in the distance. But it seemed to me that since they were climbing up to the village and there was less than an hour before dark, the chances were that they were retiring to billets for the night.

It was a pity that we had to place pickets, for the men needed their rest, but obviously they were necessary. I told Riccomini to place them at good points for observation and walked down the hill to the village. I was just in time to see the Russians arrive – in a condition that finally destroyed any vague intentions I had of carrying on with the march to Casa Del Lupo that night. Modena had marched them from Governara at a fantastic pace and they were in the last stages of exhaustion. When he reported that they were unable to go on until the next day, I fully agreed.

But the risk was great. Clearly, if the men had been in good condition, our best chance of infiltrating through the enemy screen was to march immediately, before we became embroiled in a fight at close quarters. But if the men were so tired that they stumbled over every stone, we would probably rouse the Germans by accident anyway.

I told Guscott to disperse the rest of the men among the farm buildings. Most would get a poor rest because they were needed for pickets on the road, especially since the Germans, only expecting partisan opposition, might try a surprise attack by night.

I slept in the open on the village green. Unlike the men, who were heavily laden with arms and ammunition, I had brought my sleeping-bag. And though I was vexed that Modena should have driven his men so hard, I was glad myself of the opportunity to rest. We would certainly be more effective if we were not tired.

Fortunately dawn brought little change in the situation,

except that Lees's malaria seemed worse. The Germans were apparently in no hurry and, though many male refugees still scurried through Vallestra, the drive from Baiso was not resumed. I guessed from the terror of the peasants and the slow deliberation of the enemy advance that at least part of their motive was to press suitable Italians into forced labour. We could see through binoculars that sections of Germans were scouring the scattered farms in the valley, but they still seemed to be regarding Baiso as a base of operations, for there was no concerted drive south-ward.

Norice brought me a fried egg on a piece of bread and a mug of tea and I watched our motley throng as I ate my breakfast. Most of the British and Russians were still asleep in the straw or on duty along the Carpineti road, but a few had joined the Communist partisans on the village green. They leaned against a wall and joked with the girls.

Yani's Garibaldini were a tough-looking crew. Their clothes were in rags and their boots were cracked, but their morale seemed high. They smiled at me and I grinned back at their pinched, under-nourished faces. It was a colourful crowd – the partisans with bright scarves around their necks and red stars in their hats, the orange kerchiefs of the Goufa Nera, a sprinkling of British red berets and the summer frocks of the girls. Norice, Valda and Argentina sat among the Garibaldini, but had eyes only for the British.

A burst of machine-gun fire sounded from the high ground above the village. I knew it to be a trigger-happy Green Flame firing at the clouds, but it caused a ripple of apprehension among the partisans. Yani and one of his lieutenants, a close disciple of Commissar Eros, came over with an official request. He thought the attack on the headquarters should be abandoned. Their first duty, he said, was to join the Green Flames in defence of the valley against the German drive. I realised the time had come to explain to them all the plans for the attack.

Defection of Yani's Garibaldini would not be serious enough to cause a cancellation of our plans, for the villas would in any case be stormed by the British, but I particularly wanted them to feel a community of effort with the allied battalion. They naturally felt apprehensive about the German thrust towards Villa Minozzo, but I wanted to show that for once a partisan force had enough resolution to make a plan and to carry it out regardless of changes in the enemy's situation. In any case, I had good reason to believe that if we were dissuaded from the attack now, we would find neither determination nor opportunity to mount it again.

Riccomini called in our guards from the Carpineti road and put out the word for all companies to assemble around me on the village green. The men spilled out of the ox-sheds, pieces of straw clinging to their shabby uniforms. Modena and his Russians, squat little men with high cheek-bones and squint eyes, kept in a segregated group, but the Italians and British mixed freely. With Lees by my side, I explained the plan. After each sentence I paused and the interpreters translated first into Italian, then into German for Modena's sake and finally into Russian for his men.

The first stage was for Hans, our tame German, to ferry us in his captured truck as far as the blown bridge five miles north-west of the village on the Vallestra-Baiso road.

I told them we would start at dusk. Once assembled below the blown bridge, we would strike northward down the valley, keeping to minor tracks and skirting German posts, villages and farms. Wherever possible we would march in the three columns, but for much of the way our hundred men would be strung out in single file because the tracks would be narrow. I would lead with two British scouts and two Italian guides. To my left would be Lieutenant Ken Harvey, the Rhodesian, with nine British and the twenty Garibaldini. Behind me in the centre would be Lieutenant Riccomini, nine British, Captain Mike Lees and nineteen mixed Russians and Goufa Nera. The right-hand column would be Major Modena and his thirty Russians. Whenever the columns had to contract into Indian file, the order behind me would be Riccomini, Harvey and Modena.

There would be no smoking or talking and we would have to march fast if we were to make our lying-up point – a large farm called Casa Del Lupo – before daylight. After hiding in the farm all day, we would attack the headquarters at around eleven o'clock. Approaching in a wide sweep from the north-west, the three columns would split – the Russians to their task of isolating the target area, Harvey's column to Villa Calvi and Riccomini's column to Villa Rossi. After I fired the signal for withdrawal, each party would find its own way back to the mountains.

I showed them the air photographs with their routes marked in pencil and everybody seemed to understand. Yani, to my surprise, ceased to object and became quite enthusiastic. When all the translations were over and it seemed they understood, Kirkpatrick played an eightsome on his pipes.

Some of the SAS troopers seized the girls and danced there on the lawn to the cheers of the others. Their red berets were faded and their uniforms were unkempt but their morale was as high as ever. It was infectious and the Italians and Russians seemed light-hearted too. I knew that if I could keep them in that kind of mood for two more days the chances were good for a successful operation.

It was at that moment, while we lay on the grass watching their antics, that an Arrow runner arrived from Smith, who had remained behind with the wireless set in Secchio. He brought a curt message from Fifteenth Army Group in Florence – our attack was to be postponed for ten days because there had been a change in plans for the main offensive. I read it unbelievingly two or three times before I handed it to Mike Lees without comment. Often, during other operations behind the enemy lines, I had cursed remote control from distant staff-officers, from people who could not have the remotest idea of what was involved in a guerrilla attack. These people seemed unable to realise that assault by irregulars cannot be co-ordinated to a definite time-table. They depend so much on surprise and on prevailing conditions that they can only be carried out successfully by seizing opportunities when the time is ripe. Our girl *staffettas* had confirmed there was no unusual activity in Albinea. But in another ten days things might be different. Soon the Germans would learn that a strange partisan force with British officers had been making aggressive motions from Vallestra. And a postponement at this stage, when we were so close to the start line, would certainly not be appreciated by the Italians. They would never believe we were firm in our intention to attack the Germans. They would think we played the same game of pirates, of eternal make-believe, they played themselves. And having once worked a partisan force up into the frame of mind for an attack we could not march back, like the Duke of York, to the bottom of the hill, and repeat the manœuvre with the same enthusiasm ten days later.

I resolved to pretend the signal failed to reach us in time. Though an attack on the corps headquarters might not have as much effect now as at the time of the main offensive, it would be infinitely better than no attack at all. Lees, who was still running a high fever from malaria, agreed, but the responsibility was mine.

All day as we sheltered behind the ox-sheds of Vallestra we heard spasmodic bursts of fire and isolated rifle shots from the valley that separated us from Baiso. This was the valley over which we had to pass during the night, but I had no fears. It seemed certain from what I had seen through my field-glasses that the Germans were using Baiso as a base and were only slowly mopping-up the rugged terrain around the hill on which it sat. Sometimes we were unable to restrain the Green Flames and they fired their guns, which had a maximum effective range of eight hundred yards, at the enemy-occupied village five miles away. But I felt sure that if we only remained quiet enough in Vallestra, the Germans would again retire for the night into Baiso.

Soon after dusk Hans drove up from Ceredelo with the ten-ton truck. He had some trouble fording the river, but finally managed to arrange for the truck to be towed across by oxen. He was a typical young blond of a German, but was intellectually inclined and, I thought, was probably a communist. He showed no qualms at fighting his fellow-countrymen and Lees swore he was completely reliable.

Our ragged-looking warriors piled into the back of the truck and were driven off to the blown bridge. The peasants gaped open-mouthed as they saw these truck-loads of partisans advance towards the enemy. Incredulous, they apparently believed that we were carrying out an unprecedented counter-attack against the advancing Germans.

It was almost dark when we wound down the steep slope into the valley. I led the column, but ahead of me, constantly running back and forth, were two Italian guides and two British scouts. The noise seemed dangerously loud – weapons banging against equipment; the rattle of all the accoutrements of a heavily-armed soldier; pebbles, set loose by an unwary foot, that tumbled down the gravel slides to the streams below; the crunch of a booted foot on loose earth. Once I looked back and saw a long line of black figures silhouetted on the sky-line behind me, looming large in the half-light of evening. Often I sent a whispered message down the line for the men to be more quiet. They were trying, I knew, but the silence of the night magnified every sound.

Marching at night through enemy country is an eerie experience at the best of times. But when it is with a long line of a hundred men, all completely silent apart from involuntary noise, the strain on one's nerves is indescribable. At every farm dogs barked, causing us to pause in dread of discovery.

We crossed a stream in the valley bottom and followed a narrow track that led us close to an isolated farm. There was a light in the window and, when a dog barked, the peasant came to the door with a lamp. But he did not spot us and retired to bed after cursing the dog for awakening him.

After two hours of slow and deliberate marching we began to ascend the slope of the first valley, up towards the Carpineti road, one of the danger points. The village through which the track led was occupied by Germans and our plan was to make a detour in time. However, as we came close to the danger area, the leading British scout who, in his canvas shoes, ran constantly back and forth across the line of march, came back to warn me that we were close to some houses. I dropped flat on the ground and the whole column sank low into the darkness behind me. A whispered conference revealed that the Italian guide had lost his way. He had remained on the path too long and now, short of retracing our steps, we were compelled to cross a rockslide immediately below the occupied village. The other guide, expressing disapproval of his colleague in a stage whisper, took over.

Less than two hundred yards below the black hulks of the houses we tiptoed across the loose rocks. Voices could be heard from the village. Several dogs began to bark. And it was impossible to cross without setting free occasional pebbles with our feet.

We slowly moved over the slide, our hearts in our mouths. Once a scout thought he heard the click of a rifle bolt and we dropped flat against the loose stones for some ten minutes, the whole column motionless behind. But again we were lucky and the enemy was not aroused.

The column paused beneath the lip of the highway while the scouts reconnoitred the crossing. Then, when they came back with the message that the coast was clear, we scurried over the road and up into the rocks above like so many rabbits. We did not hesitate again until we climbed between the boulders to the safety of the cliff above and there, at last, we threw ourselves on the long grass of a saucer in the hills to take our first rest of the evening. One of the Garibaldini found a well of clear, cold water and the men drank their fill. I lay on my back, gazing up at the stars. Someone nudged my elbow and I rolled over to find Norice, the *staffetta*, sitting cross-legged beside me. She handed me a hard-boiled egg, already peeled, and a slice of bread. I smiled my thanks. With her long black hair tumbling over her face, she looked almost beautiful in the dark. Her sturdy legs, brown above white bobby-socks and Italian ski boots, were certainly better able to take this mountain marching than mine. She seemed as fresh as when we left Vallestra, but I was already exhausted.

Shaking off my lethargy, I jumped to my feet and gave the order to march again.

"*Andiamo*," I said and my whisper was echoed down the column. The tired men lumbered slowly to their feet.

It was safer now that we had passed through the immediate area of the German drive and we could walk less cautiously along the mountain paths. The long column straggled over more than a mile behind us. And now, with the benefit of a bright moon, the scouts could range farther ahead, making it less necessary to pause for signs of danger. The path wound endlessly up and down the hills, through meadows in which cattle grazed, between vineyards, ever closer to the plains. Mike Lees had hardly spoken a word since we left Vallestra. He came up to the front after crossing the highway, but only stumbled in grim silence beside me and was obviously far gone with fever. Twice I urged him to go back, but he just muttered refusal, forcing his legs to carry him forward. I still hoped to convince him to stay at Casa Del Lupo, the lying-up point, but it was only a faint hope.

When dawn came we were still a few miles short of the farm. The hills opened out into rolling meadows of green and, devoid as they were of cover, we would have been uncomfortably conspicuous if it had not been for the morning mist. This thick, wet mist, hovering three feet above the ground, effectively shrouded us from observation, which was just as well, for we were already too tired for cunning. When I could spare the energy, I glanced backward at the ragged files and noticed that the fog distorted the shapes of the men behind. We could not have wished for better conditions for an attack. During the entire march we had met no one – not even an early-rising peasant. But as the sun grew stronger, dispersing the mist, and the day advanced, we were in ever increasing danger. It was, therefore, with considerable relief that I learned from Green, one of our scouts, that he had spotted Casa Del Lupo over the next rise. I had begun to despair of ever reaching it before day broke in full force.

We climbed the path over the grassy rise and saw for ourselves. The brick buildings of a large farm perched on the peak of a hill, high above the mist.

I passed the order back for the column, most of which was still in dead ground behind the rise, to lie flat in the wet grass. Then I told Riccomini to take his British and to surround the farm. They were to approach cautiously, taking their time, for I did not want any of the occupants to escape, whether they were Italian peasants or Germans. I watched them close in slowly through the mist. Then Sergeant Guscott and two others entered the front gate. There was no sound of firing and so, assuming the coast to be clear, I led the remainder of the force into Casa Del Lupo. An old farmer and his wife were the only people in the place.

It was ideal for our purpose. The buildings lined four sides of a square court-yard and the only entrance was narrow and to the south, away from the direction of the Germans in Albinea. This farm was like a fortress and was probably so designed against raids by mountain bandits in days gone by. Our columns quietly filed into the shelter of the court-yard. As each company arrived, I allotted it both a billet and a side of the farm to protect. Every man was to keep under cover. They could sleep, although sentries were to peep cautiously from the upper windows. If anyone was observed approaching the farm, whether Italian civilian or German soldier, he was to be allowed to enter. Then, sealing the exit behind, we would hold him prisoner until the operation was over.

Lees and I made our headquarters in the farm kitchen. Both the peasant and his wife were terrified at first, but they soon recovered and became quite garrulous. In fact, while the woman cooked our breakfast, the farmer produced a dusty bottle of *grappa*. He told us German soldiers frequently visited Casa Del Lupo in search of eggs, so I passed word for our sentries to be doubly alert.

Actually, the old peasant – red of face like his traditional counterpart in Britain – was a little confused by the merry-go-round of war-time politics. He took us for Germans and only half-believed when we explained we were British. And he seemed utterly unable to comprehend that Italians were divided into two factions. He told us proudly that his son had served with the Arieti Division at Benghazi under Graziani and was now an officer in the Fascist Black Brigade at Milan. When we appeared unimpressed, he produced endless photographs showing a young man in officer's uniform, proudly standing in front of a row of light tanks. He could not understand that we were on the other side. And when, for his own sake because I feared Yani would hear him and cut his throat, I told him to put his pictures away, he was more than puzzled. But, flushed by the *grappa*, he insisted on ending the story of his son with a family joke to the effect that the boy was really the son of the village priest. Then he roared at his own humour and slapped me lovingly on the back.

Lees was very sick. He sat with his head in his hands at the kitchen table, taking alternate doses of quinine and *grappa*. But, as I had feared, my arguments were to no avail and he was adamant that he would see the operation through to the end. "I'll be all right," he repeated as I stared anxiously at the beads of sweat on his forehead. He even refused to lie down, preferring to sit hunched at the table.

At around eleven o'clock in the morning I dispatched Norice and Argentina for a last check on the defences at Albinea. I wanted to be sure that the guards had not been alerted since our move from Vallestra and that there was no change in the dispositions of their machine-guns. The girls discarded their pistols and battle-dress blouses and walked gaily out of the farm. They were more reckless than any of the Garibaldini and treated the whole adventure as a game. They were quite capable of arranging dates with the Germans for the time of the attack.

Shortly after noon Taylor pushed two Italian peasants into the kitchen at the point of his sten-gun. They were innocent neighbours, paying a friendly call on Casa Del Lupo, and had been arrested according to orders. Both denied they knew we were there, but in the same breath claimed they came to warn us of a German patrol in the neighbourhood. Having had previous experience of unreliable reports from country folk, I did not believe them, although I told Riccomini to alert our sentries. They said the Germans were on the other side of the hill, that six were searching all farms for partisans. I guessed it to be a rumour passed from shepherd to shepherd all the way from Baiso. I told Taylor to make them sit under guard in the courtyard. They would have to spend the night at Casa Del Lupo, I explained, but were free to leave in the morning. They pleaded that their families would worry and that they had livestock to feed, but I paid no heed. Three more peasants, one of whom sought our first two guests, drifted in during the day and were likewise confined to the farm. All told the same story of a German patrol. I debated sending out a section of our own men to see if the reports were true, but decided against it. And Lees agreed that we risked discovery less by keeping under cover in the farm.

Our jovial host produced bottles of wine and served a good meal of salami, spaghetti and bread. All the officers joined us in the kitchen for dinner and a last-minute briefing.

I was a little worried when the girls were late returning from their reconnaissance of Albinea and we were all relieved when they sauntered in just before dusk. All seemed normal in Albinea, they said. Norice had been right through the headquarters and even took a cigarette from a German sentry. She produced it from her blouse as evidence of her daring, her grey eyes sparkling as she poured out her report in a torrent of rapid Italian punctuated by peals of laughter. The only new information came from Argentina. She said another anti-aircraft troop of three guns had arrived at Pianello, a village to the east of Albinea.

Both girls were furious when I told them they could not accompany us on the attack and were to wait in the farm until the next morning. Norice directed most of her wrath at Lees, whose Italian was better, and screamed and wept and stamped her feet. But Lees was too sick to care. He told Bruno, the Goufa Nera leader, to take her outside, and his voice was so listless that I made a last attempt to persuade him to stay behind with the girls. But he shook his head, not bothering to argue.

I was pleased to see the mist fall again with evening. The weather could not have been more in our favour. One of the Italian peasants we confined to the farm offered to guide us down to the road and, as soon as it was properly dark, our three columns wound silently out of the arched entrance from Casa Del Lupo. I walked beside the peasant over the fields and there was no sound apart from the swishing of feet in the wet grass. The moon glowed palely through the banks of mist. I had not realised we were so close to the limit of the mountains and it was with something of a shock that, at the top of a grassy rise, I suddenly saw the Lombardy plain laid out beneath us. The hills ended so abruptly and beyond all was dark and flat except for the silver Po that shone in the moon and the pin-point dots of light that marked farms and villages below. It all seemed so close and only Albinea, presumably at our very feet, showed no lights. All around us the night was silent. It seemed so improbable that soon we were to break it with the din of battle. As I slid softly down the hill into the black abyss I looked back once. The long file was silhouetted on the sky-line against the background of mist and moon, and their figures were elongated like distant bushes in a desert heat.

My Italian guide whispered good-bye and crept off into the night. The main road, he pointed, lay only a few yards ahead. The columns stayed motionless in the wet grass while our scouts went ahead to find it. They tiptoed back, crouching despite the cover of darkness. It was twenty yards in front and there were no signs of the enemy. We moved slowly forward into the ditch and lay still again. I told the columns to fan out on either side of me, but to be careful not to get mixed in their ranks. We would reform on the other side. Then we scurried across the exposed hard-top and crawled under a thick hedge on the north side, scratching our faces and rattling our weapons alarmingly as we wriggled through.

I lay in the grass beside Kirkpatrick, the piper, Morbin and my faithful Bruno, awaiting the message that all our hundred men were safely over the road. In an amazingly short time the word came back. All were with me, even the Russians, ready in their columns to move forward again. A small Italian farm-house gleamed white in the moon and I recognised it from the air photograph. Now the responsibility for navigation was mine alone and a single mistake might lead us to disaster. I took a north bearing on my compass and began to count my steps. The columns closed up tight behind me, each man less than an arm's length from the next, and we crept stealthily forward. I tested almost every footstep before putting down my weight and paused frequently to listen for danger. A dog barked in the farm and my heart leapt. We made a detour to avoid two more buildings, neither of which I remembered from the photographs. I heard a truck pass along the road we had crossed and I threw myself flat. The others dropped to the ground behind me and we lay still for several minutes before daring to move again.

We came to a ploughed field where the going was heavy and I was terrified the sentries would hear the rattle of our equipment. Twice I stumbled into a wet ditch, stepping into it unawares in the dark. And once I heard a German shout. Then, as my count of paces told me that the time had come to swing east, I caught my parachute jacket in some barbed-wire and shook the whole fence as I broke free. Still no sound, and the men were incredibly quiet behind me. It had taken more than an hour to cover a few hundred yards.

We were on the objective before I was ready. Suddenly I found myself on the edge of the crescent-shaped wood that lay at the foot of Villa Calvi – the villa which contained the staff-officers and their operations room. I had not expected it so soon, but my navigation was accurate. Our force of a hundred men had penetrated the German headquarters undetected.

The time for action had come, but, since my excitement had been gradually mounting to a crescendo ever since we crossed the road, words seemed to stick in my throat. My mouth was dry and when I did manage to speak the words came in whispered gushes. I sent a runner back to find the Russians, to tell Modena to form his protective screen to the south. Above the half-moon wood I could see the white walls of Villa Calvi on the top of a small hill. No lights were showing and I vaguely wondered whether we had been misled, whether the villas were really occupied by Germans. The British columns stood around me in the dark, but somehow the Russians had become separated. The air was heavy and still. Not a single sound disturbed the night – no dogs barked now, no wind disturbed the trees in the woods, and the men held themselves tense, ready for my word to advance.

The runner came back. He was so quiet that he was by my side before I knew he had returned. He had failed to find Modena and the Russians. I could only assume that without waiting for orders Modena had already led his men into position. He must have branched off from the moment I changed direction to the east. We could delay no longer. At any time now the Russians might alert the sentries and surprise would be lost.

I called for Riccomini and told him to start. I would allow

him only three minutes before I let Harvey attack Villa Calvi in front of us, so it was important that he move fast. He was to remember that the main German strength lay to the south. That was the direction from which enemy machine-guns would probably fire. After twenty minutes, whether his attack was successful or not, he was to withdraw back to the mountains. If I fired a red Very light before that, he was to withdraw anyway.

I watched him go, hoping as I did so that he was not infected by my obvious fear, by the difficulty I had in speaking. Lees lumbered by his side, a big hulk of a man in the darkness. Behind him came the ten British and the Goufa Nera led by Bruno and they disappeared into the darkness towards Villa Rossi, their weapons carried at the ready.

The black silence was almost forbidding and I shivered from both cold and excitement as I cocked my carbine. I led Harvey to the edge of the wood, below the hill that led up to Villa Calvi. One of the Garibaldini pointed to the wire fence that surrounded the trees and crossed a narrow path leading up the bank to the lawns around the villa. Nailed to a tree behind it was a sign in red letters – "*Achtung – Minen.*"

There was no time to make a detour. The three minutes was up. But Ken Harvey did not falter. He swung through the fence and the British swarmed up the path behind him. Yani and his Garibaldini hesitated, but I pushed them from behind, forcing them to follow the British up the bank to the villa. The minefield was obviously non-existent, a bluff.

I began to move over to my allotted position on the road. The others had lost me somehow in the darkness, but Kirkpatrick, the Highland Light Infantry piper, was still by my side. I walked into a slit-trench and lost my carbine, but Kirkpatrick retrieved it. Then, as I was still recovering from the shock of my fall, the fighting began.

The silence was broken by a tremendous burst of fire from Villa Calvi above. It sounded like a whole Bren magazine fired without pause and, as much as if it were a signal for which both Germans and ourselves had been waiting, it triggered automatic fire from every direction – from the enemy billets to the south, from Villa Rossi and from Villa Calvi. The night was shattered by the rattle of machine-guns. I heard the harsh rasp of a spandau and knew the Germans were firing back. Bullets whistled over our heads as if the Germans could see us, which was impossible. All along the line to the south Modena's men maintained continuous fire and I saw tracers bouncing off the white walls of the guardhouse. A siren wailed from the direction of Villa Rossi. That was unfortunate because it meant the alarm had been sounded there before Riccomini entered his target. Even mortars added their thuds to the general racket and, between the rattle of small-arms fire at Villa Calvi above, I heard the thump of a bazooka.

Having loosed off the attack, I had no more control and I could only sit with Kirkpatrick and wait. I told him to play "Highland Laddie," just to let the enemy know they had more than a mere partisan attack with which to contend. The British at Calvi cheered when they heard the defiant skirl of the pipes. Our job was to cause panic and confusion and, even if we failed to clinch our attack, this had already been achieved. An enemy spandau singled us out and the bullets whizzed uncomfortably close. I pushed Kirkpatrick into a convenient slit-trench and he continued to play from a sitting position. I wondered whether I should join Harvey at Villa Calvi, but decided against it. Someone had to stay in the middle to fire the signal for withdrawal. So, while Kirkpatrick played his pipes, I sat beside him amidst the bullets, cursing myself for not having restrained Harvey a few minutes longer.

Only later, when we were on our way back to the mountains, did I piece together what had happened.

The British at Calvi crept up the bank to the edge of the lawn. Four German sentries were standing on a gravel drive in front of the villa. There was no time for finesse, so Harvey shot them down with his Bren and that initial burst of machine-gun fire which awakened the whole headquarters carried death to these sentries. Then the British charged across the lawns to the house, covered by the Garibaldini who fired into the windows. The front door was locked and several minutes elapsed before the British shot it in with a bazooka. By then Harvey and Sergeant Godwin had entered through ground-floor windows and were fighting Germans in the operations room. Bursting into one ground-floor room, Harvey was confronted by a German with a Schmeisser submachine-gun. He ducked but forgot to extinguish his flashlight. Fortunately, Sergeant Godwin, who was close on his heels, fired over his shoulder and killed the German in time. Four other Germans, including the staff-colonel, were killed on the ground floor, as were two other sentries in the outhouses. But the remainder fought back down a spiral staircase that led to the upper story. Several unsuccessful attempts were made to climb this stairway but failed in the face of intense enemy fire. The Germans were able to cover the first landing from behind balustrades and could not be seen from below. In one of these attempts Parachutist Mulvey was wounded in the knee. Then the Germans began to roll grenades down the stairs, one of them wounding Corporal Layburn. Harvey decided to raze the villa. It was impossible to take the house in the twenty minutes allowed. Working frantically against time, the British piled maps, papers, files and office furniture into a heap in the middle of the operations room. Then, with the assistance of a little explosive and some petrol found in one of the outhouses, they started the fire. Our men kept the Germans confined to the top floor, shooting up the stairs and through the windows outside, until the flames had taken good hold. After firing the rest of their bazooka bombs and most of their ammunition through the windows, they withdrew from the grounds, carrying their wounded with them.

The story at Villa Rossi was similar except that there, because firing broke out at Villa Calvi first, our raiders did not have full advantage of surprise. Riccomini's men were still in the ditch beside the road when the fighting began at Villa Calvi. They had used more caution in their approach than time allowed and were still outside the grounds when sirens sounded from the roof of their villa. Realising that surprise was lost, the British shot the three sentries in the grounds, firing through iron railings that surrounded the lawn. Then they charged the house, cheering as they heard Kirkpatrick's pipes. Several more Germans were killed in outlying buildings and most of the thirty raiders – British and Goufa Nera – crashed through the windows into the house. In the ground-floor rooms, more Germans were encountered, two of whom surrendered. These two prisoners were locked in an outhouse and presumably lived to tell the tale.

As at Villa Calvi, a furious battle took place for the upper floor. The British led attack after attack up the spiral stairway, but were always repulsed when they ran into merciless fire on the landing. Mike Lees led one attack and was severely wounded, as was Bruno, the Goufa Nera leader. Riccomini and Sergeant Guscott tried again and almost reached the top, but, there on the second landing, Riccomini met his death. He was shot through the head and died instantly. Sergeant Guscott dragged his body down. Then, angry at the loss of his leader, Sergeant Guscott led another attempt. While shouting from the landing, urging the others to follow him, he too was mortally wounded and died there on the staircase. Both had volunteered for Operation Tombola although entitled to a rest after the operations north of Spezia. Both met their end at Villa Rossi.

Then the Germans, heartened by their success, attempted to come down the stairs. A hail of fire greeted them at the bottom and three more Germans died with Riccomini and Guscott on the staircase. Kershaw, Green and Taylor decided to light a fire in the kitchen. They poured petrol on the walls, heaped up curtains and bedding from the other rooms and started the blaze. Sergeant Hughes and Ramos, one of our Spaniards, carried the wounded outside.

Meanwhile I waited nervously, wondering whether to fire the signal for withdrawal. The planned twenty minutes had long expired and I saw flames licking around the roofs of both villas, especially at Villa Calvi. German return fire was becoming more intense and mortar bombs crashed into the trees of the half-moon wood at the foot of Villa Calvi. A few Italian and Russian stragglers had already joined me. And I knew that soon trucked reinforcements would be arriving in Albinea from other German-occupied villages nearby. The time had come for retreat if we were ever to return safely to our mountain base. I pointed my Very pistol at the sky and fired three red signal flares. Immediately the alert spandau to the south sprayed bullets all around me, sending the Italians scuttling for cover.

I waited until all the British, at least, had rallied around me. They came down from Calvi in two's and three's, jubilant at their success. Corporal Layburn and Mulvey, the two wounded, hopped between them, supported by a man on each side. Those from Villa Rossi were less triumphant. They told me how Riccomini and Guscott had died and that Mike Lees was being carried on a ladder to safety by Burke and Ramos. And the Goufa Nera, they said, were also carrying Bruno, their leader.

I waited as long as I dared, but Burke, a red-headed Irishman, and Ramos never arrived with Lees. In fact, they carried him on a ladder for four days and, by some miracle, escaped capture by the hundreds of Germans who scoured the area after our raid. Considering that Lees, who was seriously wounded, weighed at least two hundred and fifty pounds, it was a tremendous feat. Both were awarded the Military Medal after they carried him to a safe hiding-place in the mountains. Bruno also evaded capture, and a few days later I arranged for a light aircraft to evacuate him and Lees to Florence. Burke and Ramos later rejoined us at Tapignola.

The sky was red from the blazing villas as we straggled west to the River Crostollo. We glanced occasionally over our shoulders at the burning headquarters and at the star shells now being fired over the area by the guns from Pianello. It was a satisfying sight. If only we could regain the safety of the mountains, the raid could be marked up as at least a partial success.

Though our withdrawal was far from organised, by astonishing good fortune most of the scattered parties managed to link together on the banks of the Crostollo. Our progress was slow, since neither Layburn nor Mulvey were capable of walking, and I was desperately anxious to cross the main road before dawn. I led them across the river and then cut south towards the hills. We were extremely tired, but there was no hope of rest for many hours. It was already getting lighter. German trucks drove helter-skelter along the road and once we hid for several minutes when we heard the rumble of tank tracks. Only Green's alertness in spotting a German unit sign saved us from walking into an anti-aircraft battery. Wearily we made yet another detour. Sounds of firing still came from Albinea and I could only guess that either some of the Russians were still in action or the Germans were shooting at themselves.

At last we crossed the road safely and began to climb into the hills. Obviously something had to be done about the wounded. Mulvey was in great pain and could go no farther, even with the help of the others. I took him into a farm-house and, after laying him on the kitchen table, did my best to bandage up his shattered knee. The peasants promised to hide him until the fuss died down and then to bring him up in an ox-cart to our mountain base. I did not like leaving him, but there was no alternative. And Mulvey himself, well aware that he risked capture, begged me to hurry away while there was still time. I gave the Italians some money and promised more after safe delivery of our comrade. Layburn could limp along with the help of two others and, with some misgivings, I allowed him to accompany us as long as he could. In the event, the Italian peasants were as good as their word and delivered Mulvey safely to the mountains. The farm was searched, but the Germans did not find him.

It was broad daylight by the time we reached Casa Del Lupo. The poor *padrone* was very frightened after the excitement of the night and at last seemed to realise that we were not Germans. He begged us to go away as soon as possible. We did not need urging. After tying Corporal Layburn's wounds with a field-dressing, I lashed him to an ancient horse we commandeered from the farmer. The horse was extremely decrepit and blind in both eyes, but it served the purpose. Layburn was much more badly hit than I had imagined. He had multiple grenade wounds in both legs and it was remarkable how he had managed to struggle along so far. I tied him tightly to the saddle with his wounded legs hanging limply by the horse's side. Though those dangling legs, dripping blood most of the way, must have been extremely painful, he never once complained.

There could be no more halts now. According to peasants

we met on the track, the countryside buzzed with Germans and we frequently skirted round danger areas. At first the mist was still thick, aiding our escape, but a light rain made the muddy path slippery underfoot. This time I did not doubt peasant rumours. We had to believe all reports of enemy patrols for it was illogical to assume they were not looking for us. We were too short of ammunition and our weapons had fallen too often in the mud for us to look for a fight.

The men were exhausted, but their morale was high. Only the loss of Ricky Riccomini and Guscott marred their good spirits. Incessantly, as we plodded through the mud, they recounted stories of their experiences during the raid. The best anecdote had it that one German officer at Villa Rossi was chased on to the lawn in his pyjamas. But as the day dragged on and I kept them marching without pause, fatigue began to tell and they trudged silently behind me, straggling raggedly down the track. I was probably more tired than most, for the old wounds in my legs ached and I doubt if I was in as good condition as the men. But I was more alive to danger than they were and knew that only a forced march across the Secchia would save us from capture.

The old horse frequently stumbled in the mud, throwing Layburn to the ground. Even on the best of going it was inclined to trip over the slightest obstacle, causing him to slip sideways in the saddle. When it finally collapsed, crushing Layburn beneath, we decided to abandon it. We made a rough stretcher from saplings and parachute blouses and four of us carried Layburn up and down the hills. I took my turn with the rest at this gruelling chore and soon we were all so tired that we could only reel blindly forward. Often, with the poles across our shoulders, we slipped to our knees in the mud. Layburn volunteered to stay behind, but the men would not hear of it. Actually I thought I made better progress when I took my turn at the stretcher, for then the weight on my shoulders made me forget the aching in my legs. We marched mechanically now, tramping wearily in step with our heads down. If we had encountered any Germans, resistance would have been impossible. Our weapons were caked with mud and we were so tired that we were incapable of anything more than this monotonous trudging along the track. We marched without scouts, for no one had enough energy to climb to higher ground. Soon I even abandoned my earlier practice of skirting around danger points and we crossed the north-south highway without any attempt at concealment. We walked openly through a village, to the amazement of the inhabitants, and were still lucky enough not to meet any Germans.

I remembered that Mark Antony made his soldierly reputation not so much from feats of arms as from his endurance while retreating from Modena through this very country. But our own endurance was close to an end. Without bothering to discover if the German drive was still in process around Baiso, I followed the route by which we had come, up the steep slope to Vallestra. Still we were lucky, although homesteads on the way were strangely silent. I gathered later that the Germans passed through this area and aimed along a Baiso-Carpineti axis, by-passing Vallestra.

We managed to conjure up enough energy to stage a little show for the villagers of Vallestra. Forming column of three's outside this village from which we had launched our raid, with Layburn leading the way on his stretcher, we marched through the streets to the music of Kirkpatrick's pipes. Women came to doorways and cheered us and little children ran beside the parade, but no men were to be seen. I hoped that the Germans in Baiso would hear the pipes and take them for defiance, for proof that we were safely beyond their reach. The men tried to pick up their sore feet and to straighten their shoulders as if they, too, realised that more by luck than good judgment we had successfully passed through the German lines without making contact.

After Vallestra, where my immediate fears were at an end, my legs refused to respond to the demands I made on them. I lagged farther and farther behind the rest, even though it was now easy going downhill to the Secchia. Some of the men took mercy on me and found a horse on which I finished the last four miles to Cavola. I was so completely exhausted that I could not appreciate the tumultous welcome given us by the Green Flames, who carried the men off to celebrate in various houses in the village. I know the mayor made some sort of speech, but I was more grateful for the bed of the local schoolmistress. She, of course, was not there, but even if she had been she would have been safe. I did not awaken for another fourteen hours. We had marched for twenty-two hours without pause and, excluding the eight-hour halt at Casa Del Lupo had been awake for more than two days.

When all was reckoned, our raid cost us three British dead and three wounded, three Italian wounded, two Russians wounded and six Russians captured. At first we thought we had killed the German general at Villa Rossi, but apparently this was not so. However, we did kill Colonel Lemelsen, the chief of staff, and many other Germans. We destroyed the two main buildings in the headquarters together with many maps and papers. Above all, we made the enemy realise that he was not safe anywhere, no matter how far behind the front.

AFTERWORD

With the termination of Tombola there was an attempt to court-martial Farran, first for parachuting himself behind enemy lines, and second for carrying on with the Albinea HQ attack after receiving the order to suspend it. Fortunately, Farran received the support of Colonel Riepe, the US officer in charge of Allied clandestine operations at 15th Army Group, who signalled SAS Brigade "FARRANS gallant actions . . . have completely sold to American part this HQ the tremendous value of SAS operations". Indeed, "Tombola" and the SAS campaign in Italy "sold" the SAS to many, and proved that it could operate in any theatre and not just the sandy wastes of North Africa.

PATROLLING
Julian Thompson

Originally formed as an instructional unit to train other Royal Marines in mountain warfare, the Mountain and Arctic Warfare Cadre was in 1981 given an operational role as a long range reconnaissance unit. All members of the Cadre are fully qualified commandos who have already been selected as junior NCOs. The qualification that sets a member of the Mountain and Arctic Warfare Cadre apart from other marines is the Mountain Leader badge. There are two levels of skill: ML1 and, below it, ML2. The ML2 course lasts for 11 months, and includes progressively harder rock climbs, combat survival skills, escape and evasion, skiing and parachuting. The course culminates in a forty-mile hike carrying full kit across Arctic terrain. Those who pass are allowed on the ML1 course, where they learn to become instructors themselves as well as taking part in a month-long exercise in Switzerland known as "Ice Flip".

Within a year of becoming operational, the M and AW Cadre was despatched to the Falklands (Malvinas) War, serving as part of 3 Commando Brigade. In the Falklands 35 men of the Cadre, led by Captain Rod Boswell, were deployed ahead of the Task Force reconnoitring enemy dispositions. They also had one engagement with Argentine Special Forces whom they routed with a textbook right-flanking assault. This was the skirmish at Top Malo House, 20 km northwest of Bluff Cove, on 31 May 1982, and is described here by the Commander of 3 Commando Brigade, Julian Thompson.

CAPTAIN BOSWELL AND nineteen of his men of the M and AW Cadre were champing at the bit at first light that morning [31 May] because a Sea King helicopter, ordered to lift them off one hour before dawn, had still not arrived. The task that these men were about to undertake had originated in a report made on 27 May by Sergeant Stone's four-man patrol, also from the Cadre, sitting on Bull Hill. They had been in position since D-Day, 21 May, one of a number of Cadre patrols, the eyes and ears of the Commando Brigade, well forward on the route to Teal and Stanley. Stone came up on the radio in clear to Boswell back at San Carlos Settlement to say that this might be the last message from his patrol because two Argentine UH-1 helicopters were hovering right over his OP. Boswell could hear the sound of the helicopters over the radio as Stone spoke. Eventually, to Stone's and everybody else's relief, the UH-1s hover-taxied away, lifted and flew off in the direction of Mount Simon. The summit of Mount Simon was in cloud, so Stone reckoned that they probably deposited their troops, patrols from a Commando Company of the Argentine Special Forces, on the lower slopes of the Onion or Mount Simon. Stone cancelled his order to his men to destroy their radios and codes and fight their way out.

However, the news that he sent back alerted the Commando Brigade Headquarters to the threat of Argentine Special Forces sitting on the high ground on the right flank of the approaches to Teal Inlet and beyond. The Argentine OPs would thus be in a position to do exactly what the M and AW Cadre were doing – report on any movement they saw on foot, in tracked vehicles or helicopters. The Commando Brigade was about to move towards Teal Inlet, so this threat to their security must be eliminated. Boswell was ordered to use the complete M and AW Cadre, less four patrols newly positioned or moving, to seek out enemy OPs on the high ground Mount Simon – Ball Mount – The Onion, fix their positions and clear them if he could, or at least find them so they could be taken out by other means. He regrouped his patrols and, by withdrawing three patrols from other tasks, adding his reserve patrol and his small headquarters, had, by 30 May, gathered nineteen men. He intended to start the insertion of his patrols on 31 May. But, on the evening of 30 May he received a message from Lieutenant Haddow's patrol. They had been marching to Mount Challenger from a position on Evelyn Hill overlooking Teal and now in the hands of 3 Para. They had been moving only at night and had been lying-up all day in an OP on the lower slopes of Mount

Simon. Haddow said that he had just seen two UH-1s deposit a patrol of sixteen men at Top Malo House 400 metres from his own position and that they had also heard several other helicopters in the vicinity. Haddow asked for fighter ground attack to destroy the enemy in the house. But with only half an hour to nightfall, the request was refused and the weather the next day might not be suitable. Boswell was told to eliminate this Argentine patrol in the morning.

He attempted to make radio contact with his patrols on the ground, including Haddow's, to order them to meet him on his chosen landing site, having secured it first. But that night, for the first and only night of the campaign, he could not get through on the radio to any of his patrols because of atmospheric conditions. He therefore planned to arrive by helicopter about one hour before first light at a landing site about 1,000 metres away and in dead ground from Top Malo House. He would then approach in darkness and assault at dawn. When, on the morning of 31 May, an hour late, the first helicopter arrived at the pick-up point at San Carlos Settlement, Boswell charged on board and angrily enquired if this was the helicopter for his task, to be told that it was for the move of Brigade Headquarters which had "higher priority". Fortunately the pilot in the aircraft Boswell had boarded was Lieutenant-Commander Thornwill, the CO of 846 Naval Air Squadron, and, when he realized the importance of Boswell's task, summoned the correct helicopter forward. When it arrived, Boswell quickly briefed the pilot, who bravely agreed to the choice of landing site close to the enemy. The nineteen men then piled into the helicopter with their rucksacks loaded with sufficient rations for a week in the field without resupply. The overloaded helicopter took off and then, in Boswell's words, "flew lower and faster than he had ever flown before" to deposit the Cadre on exactly the right spot after a forty-five kilometre flight – fine flying and typical of the splendid pilots and aircrew of 846 Naval Air Squadron.

After dumping their packs on the landing site, the Cadre set off to a fence about 1,000 metres away. Here the seven-men fire group moved off to the left to a gate, about 150 metres from Top Malo House, from where they would support the assault group. The twelve-man assault group led by Boswell skirted round to the south-east of Top Malo House, remaining below the intervening crest line. As they moved round, the fire group commander, Lieutenant Murray, spotted some peat cuttings which would give the assault group an excellent covered approach. He sent Sergeant McLean after the fire group to tell Boswell. As Boswell approached the house he called his Section Commanders, Sergeant Doyle, Sergeant Stone and Colour-Sergeant Montgomery, up to him for a final check reconnaissance. As they lay looking at the target, Boswell realised that their dark uniforms on the snow-covered ground would be a give-away to an alert sentry. So far they had apparently not been spotted, despite fears that the enemy, being Special Forces, would surely have sentries out. Boswell cancelled the close reconnaissance and the whole assault group crawled forward, only too conscious that the ground over which they were moving was overlooked by a window in the upper floor of the building, like an eye watching them.

When Boswell judged they were close enough to the house and in full view of their fire group, he gave the order "fix bayonets". Sergeant Stone said, "It's a bite, there's no one there". Boswell fired a green mini-flare, the signal for the fire group to fire six 66 mm light anti-armour rockets at the house. As the first rocket was fired, an Argentine sentry moved to the window on the upper floor. Corporal Groves, armed with a sniper rifle, shot him. As the 66 mm rockets slammed into the house it burst into flames; Boswell and the assault group charged forward, halted, fired two 66s into the house and charged again. The enemy ran out of the house into a small stream bed about 50 metres away, firing as they ran. Sergeant Doyle fell, hit through the shoulder and then Corporal Groves also fell, hit in the chest. The ammunition stacked in the house exploded as the assault group ran forward, causing them to recoil for a moment, while smoke from the burning building shielded them from the enemy lying in the stream firing at them. The fire fight went on for a few minutes as the assault group worked their way towards the enemy. Then the officer commanding the Argentine force tried to run off and was killed by two 40 mm rounds fired from M 7 grenade launchers by Corporal Barnacle and Sergeant McLean. The Argentines stood up and threw away their weapons. It was over. Five Argentines had been killed and seven wounded, the remaining five were taken prisoner. The Cadre had three wounded – Doyle, Groves and Stone. Haddow's patrol, who had watched the whole battle, came running forward waving a Union Flag as a recognition sign. They did not want to risk being shot by their own side in the excitement, with the adrenalin still flowing.

The whole operation had been a brilliant success, starting with good OP work and fieldcraft by Haddow's men, a good plan and briefing by Boswell, excellent flying by the pilot from 846 Squadron, canny use of the ground, bold and aggressive tactics and professionalism. It must be said that, despite being Special Forces, the Argentines did not have adequate sentries out, but that does not detract from the Cadre's achievement. Once again the better soldiers won. Unknown to the Cadre the assault had been watched by two other Argentine OPs who, having seen the treatment meted out to their comrades and imagining that it was their turn next, decided to call it a day. One OP stationed on the summit of Mount Simon walked into Teal Inlet where they were picked up by 45 Commando. The other walked from The Baby towards Lower Malo House and surrendered to 3 Para. Boswell, having sent out his and the enemy wounded and the enemy dead by helicopter, took his cock-a-hoop Royal Marines into Teal Inlet to be congratulated on their assault by the Brigade Commander. The Cadre from the beginning of the land campaign had been giving sterling service by its patrolling, OP work and accurate passing of information and was to continue to do so for the rest of the war. It had now, on its own, caused the elimination of the Argentine Special Forces OP line which threatened the security of the Commando Brigade's right flank.

The continued "good work" of the M and AW Cadre noted by Brigadier Thompson included a patrol on 8/9 June which gathered information about Argentine positions vital to 3 Commando Brigade as it prepared to capture Harriet, Two Sisters and Longdon mountains.

There was, however, one important gap in the information available to 3 Commando Brigade which Rowe, as Intelligence Staff Officer, had realized must be filled if at all possible before the Brigade attack. Little was known about the ground formed by the triangle from the eastern end of Two Sisters, the eastern side of Mount Harriet and Mount Tumbledown. Rowe, having been frustrated in all his requests for air photographs, knew that the only way to find out would be to get a patrol into a position to observe this ground, preferably by day. The most skilled patrollers in the Commando Brigade were the M and AW Cadre. After discussing the problem with Chester and myself, Rowe had summoned Boswell, the Cadre's Commander, on 8 June, and tasked him to get the information. Boswell briefed Lieutenant Haddow and Sergeant Wassell to take their patrols, a total of eight men, including the two leaders, to Goat Ridge that night. They were to stay in a hide on Goat Ridge during the following day and return the next night. Their tasks were to report on enemy strengths and dispositions on the north-eastern side of Mount Harriet and the south-eastern side of Two Sisters. Boswell arranged that the two patrols should go out with a troop-strength fighting patrol from K Company 42 Commando, led by Lieutenant Townsend. This patrol was tasked with checking Goat Ridge for enemy before swinging south on to the Harriet feature from the north-east. By this time the coordination of the patrolling in the Commando Brigade had been well refined, thanks to Chester's idea of instituting a "Patrol-Master", a task carried out by Major Gullan. He knew exactly what patrols were going out, their routes and tasks and, by consulting with the Brigade Intelligence Staff and other agencies, such as artillery and engineers, was able to minimize the chances of inter-unit patrol clashes and could task patrols to a Brigade plan.

The combined patrols left the eastern end of Mount Challenger after last light on 8 June. When they reached a point about 300 metres from the western end of the Goat Ridge spine-back Haddow's and Wassell's men halted and waited for the K Company patrol to move south towards the north-east slopes of Mount Harriet. They saw the K Company fighting patrol engage an enemy heavy-machine-gun position with an 84 mm round before withdrawing. The Argentine fire directed at the K Company patrol, as it conducted a fighting withdrawal, was heavy, most of it passing over Townsend's men's heads and striking around the M and AW Cadre men lying by the Goat Ridge spine-back. Haddow and Wassell noted where the fire was coming from for future reference. When all was quiet again the Cadre patrols started moving. Haddow's men worked along the north side of the narrow spine-back, while Wassell took the south side. Each patrol spent the whole night carefully creeping forward and searching the rocks and ground. They found a well-worn track that connected Mount Harriet and Two Sisters and, even though it was dark, discovered that there were strong enemy positions on the reverse, or eastern, slopes of Mount Harriet and Two Sisters. This confirmed Rowe's suspicion that Divisional Headquarters was underestimating the strength of the positions, hence his wish to get a patrol into the middle of the enemy to "eyeball" the ground.

Wassell and Haddow met at the eastern end of Goat Ridge and decided to find an OP position in which they could spend the day and observe. The spine-back was so narrow that finding a position on the eastern tip was difficult and they eventually settled for one about half-way back along the ridge. The two patrols operated as one team armed with two M79 grenade launchers and two sniper rifles, as well as their personal weapons. Haddow and Wassell sat under a rock, back to back all day, Haddow facing south and Wassell facing north. The remaining six men hid under another rock about twenty feet away, providing flank and rear protection for their two leaders. Deep in the middle of the Argentine positions, Haddow and Wassell were about forty metres away from the track connecting Two Sisters and Tumbledown which the Argentines were using as a route for administration and casevac for the positions on Two Sisters. Daylight revealed the enemy positions on the eastern slopes of Two Sisters and Mount Harriet. From their OP they could also see the enemy positions on Mount Tumbledown and Mount William. Lieutenant Haddow and Sergeant Wassell each spent the day drawing a sketch map showing the positions they had seen.

These included a large command-wire-initiated demolition consisting of barrels dug into the ground on the eastern end of Two Sisters, with wires leading back to a firing point. Assaulting troops would take heavy casualties if they were on or near these large "mines" when they exploded.

The patrol remained all day watching the Argentine soldiers moving about in what were reverse-slope positions to the Commando Brigade OPs on Wall Mountain, Challenger and Kent, but were clearly visible to the OP in the heart of the position. About three hours after dark the patrol withdrew and moved back to Mount Challenger and thence to 42 Commando's Tactical Headquarters between Challenger and Mount Kent. Here they briefed the second-in-command, Sheridan, on what they had seen, before going on to Brigade Headquarters to speak to Rowe and Gullan, the Patrol-Master. Wassell was then sent to brief 45 Commando. The information they brought back caused both Whitehead and Vaux to make alterations to the plans they were hatching in anticipation of being told to attack Two Sisters and Mount Harriet. The grid references of enemy positions that Haddow had seen on Tumbledown and Mount William were passed to 5 Infantry Brigade. This patrol was remarkable in what it achieved, bringing back a wealth of information that was to save many lives, including locating the large command-detonated mine on Two Sisters. Wassell and Haddow led their men away after the debriefing, brewed up, cleaned their weapons and crept into their "bashas" for a well-earned sleep.

ADVENTURE AT BRUNEVAL

Hilary St. George Saunders

The history of British Airborne Forces begins in June 1940 with a note from Winston Churchill to General Sir Hastings Ismay, which stated that "We should have a corps of at least five thousand parachute troops". The first force to begin paratroop training at Manchester's Ringway Airport was from No. 2 Commando, and on 13 July the men made their first jumps, from converted Armstrong-Whitworth Whitley bombers. The parachute training was supervised by Major Jock Rock, and designed to supplement the commandos' training at Achnacarry (see p 37). On 21 November the parachute force from No. 2 Commando was renamed No. 11 Special Air Service Battalion – no relation to David Stirling's SAS – and three months later 31 men from the unit parachuted deep into Italy and destroyed the Tragino aquaduct. Though they were captured, the value of British paratroopers was plain. Churchill ordered the expansion of the force and in September 1941 the 1st Parachute Brigade was formed under Colonel Richard "Windy" Gale. In February 1942 it carried out Operation Biting, the raid on Bruneval radar station.

"ONE AFTERNOON IN the middle of January 1942," records Lieutenant-Colonel J. D. Frost, D.S.O., M.C., then a major newly seconded to the Parachute Regiment from the Cameronians, "all company commanders were summoned to battalion headquarters (the 2nd Parachute Battalion) for a conference. It transpired that a company was required to move to Tilshead on Salisbury Plain for special training."

"C" Company, of which Frost was the commanding officer,

was chosen. There was, however, one difficulty. Before he could accompany his men to Tilshead he had to acquire the blue wings of the parachute soldier. That he had not already done so was due to an accident in which he had injured his knee when landing on one leg after his second jump from "the vile, loathed sausage". It was almost decided that Major Philip Teichman, a brother officer in command of "A" Company, should take over "C" until it had returned from its special training. Frost, however, "heartily disliked this idea" and prevailed upon his commanding officer to allow him to go immediately to Ringway and complete his course.

To do so in the time available before the company left meant jumping five times from an aircraft in six days. At Ringway Frost reported to Newnham, ready with every kind of argument to persuade him of the urgency of the matter. This proved unnecessary, for "I was pleasantly surprised to find that he seemed to know all about me, and one or two of the remarks he let slip gave me considerable food for thought. He referred to certain articles of equipment which they had had to procure in a hurry 'last time', and I wondered what he meant by 'last time'". Newnham was referring darkly to the first operation carried out by parachute troops against the enemy, the attack on the Tragino aqueduct in southern Italy. As will be remembered, it had taken place in February 1941, almost exactly a year before, and it is significant that twelve months had had to elapse between that operation and the descent upon the radiolocation station at Bruneval, which Frost was to lead. Some might maintain that to allow so long a time to pass between operations shewed how uninterested were the authorities on the potentialities of warfare conducted by airborne troops. To do so would be less than just. The work of Nigel Norman, Maurice Newnham, Louis Strange, John Rock and all the others at Ringway, and of Richard Gale and Eric Down and their parachute soldiers at Hardwick and elsewhere, bore not slow but rapid fruit – miraculously rapid indeed, when all the circumstances are considered.

Even in peacetime, with all the resources of a great industrial state at their disposal, eighteen months would have been a very short period in which to create from nothing all the gear required for the complicated business of arriving upon a battlefield by way of the air. And to the gear would have to be added the evolution of the training methods, and the devising of the strategy and tactics involved. But the School at Ringway and the airborne forces at Hardwick or in Scotland had neither time nor material. The country was fighting for its life, and, when in June 1940 the creation of parachute troops was decided, was facing the huge task of re-equipping an army which had left behind at Dunkirk or elsewhere in France and Belgium 7,000 tons of ammunition, 90,000 rifles, 2,300 guns, 120,000 vehicles, 8,000 Bren guns and 400 anti-tank rifles.[1] Not only had these enormous losses to be made good, but also the requirements of the Royal Navy, the Royal Air Force, the Merchant Navy, and the Home Guard and Civil Defence, and the civilian population in general had somehow to be met. But despite these commitments and the fact that "a damaged parachute and jumping-helmet captured from the Germans were the only models available, and for aircraft . . . four Whitley Mark IIs which were seldom simultaneously serviceable", those responsible for the creation of the airborne forces put them in a position to shew their mettle within seven months, and to be ready at the end of eighteen to carry out a second operation which, though very little larger, was of far greater importance. When all is said and done, and all the difficulties borne in mind, this achievement must be regarded as remarkable.

Such matters, however, were no concern of Frost, as he addressed himself to the task of becoming a trained parachutist "in five clear days". Unfortunately the days were far from clear. The weather at Ringway, he notes, "was notoriously fickle. On the slightest provocation a smoky fog would creep across the aerodrome from the direction of Manchester, which was only a few miles away, and a wind strong enough to dispel the fog very often made jumping unsafe". On the first of the five days "I was ready (at nine o'clock) just outside the hangar . . . and was still waiting there at past four in the afternoon.

[1] *History of the Second World War*, vol. ii. "Their Finest Hour", by Winston S. Churchill, p. 125.

. . . The second day was almost a replica of the first", when towards evening the fog suddenly lifted. Frost was able to make two jumps from a Whitley. The next day he was able to do his third jump, and on the day following his last two. He then returned in triumph to Hardwick, and thence brought his company down to Tilshead, "a miserable sort of place with mud everywhere", arriving towards the end of January.

Here, after an inspection by Major-General Browning, they set about training for an exercise which, Frost was informed, "would probably take place in the Isle of Wight and the whole of the War Cabinet would be there to see it". The interest and enthusiasm of "C" Company was aroused and maintained by the information conveyed by Peter Bromley-Martin, the liaison officer with divisional headquarters, that if the demonstration were convincing enough, the company would be chosen to carry out a real raid on the coast of France later on.

Alton Priors, north of Salisbury Plain, was chosen as a suitable spot to practise moving from the dropping zone to the objective, and from the objective to an imaginary coast where, after completing their task, the parachute troops would embark upon imaginary assault landing craft for the return home. Such was the plan as outlined by Bromley-Martin, but, to Frost's annoyance, he went on to explain that "as this was such a very special demonstration, the normal company organisation would have to be scrapped, and it would have to be divided into parties of different size. Each party would be given a different task, and therefore . . . would be differently organised, armed and equipped". Frost argued in vain against such a novel departure from all the then accepted principles of the tactical handling of parachute troops, but Bromley-Martin was adamant, and after much discussion the two men "parted with veiled hostility on both sides".

In the meantime Flight-Sergeant E. W. F. Cox, an expert radio engineer, was on his way to the Air Ministry in London. Arrived, he reported to an air-commodore, who at once congratulated him "on having volunteered for a special and dangerous mission". Cox had certainly volunteered for a special mission, but this was the first time that he had heard that it was likely to be dangerous. His apprehension and curiosity were still further aroused when he was told to report to Ringway to learn "all about parachute jumping". He did so and qualified as a parachutist in about the same time as it had taken Frost to acquire his wings.

While he was doing so "C" Company were busy with their rehearsal at Alton Priors. Their commanding officer and Bromley-Martin were no longer at loggerheads, for the liaison officer had been allowed to tell the truth: the demonstration before the whole of the Cabinet was a mere cover story. "Actually," said Bromley-Martin, "you will be taking the company over to the coast of France; before the end of February." The news, though "it flung a heavy cloak of responsibility" upon him, filled Frost will exultation; nor was this damped when he found that "a very detailed plan" had been made by one of the planning syndicates at Combined Operations headquarters.

This time the objective was not a snow-covered aqueduct in southern Italy, but a snow-covered hole in the ground in northern France. It held a radio location apparatus known as a giant Wurzberg. This was a device, one of a chain stretched along the coast of western Europe. These installations were designed to give warning to her German masters of the approach of hostile aircraft or ships. That they were doing so had been known for months, but the precise nature of the apparatus used in these installations was still a matter for the argument and conjecture of experts. Photographed many times, their ultimate secrets were hidden behind thick walls. The capture of one such apparatus would, it was hoped and believed, shew not only the mechanical methods of radio-detection used by the Germans, but equally, if not more important, whether these were in advance or behind those which we ourselves were using. Precisely how accurate the devices of the enemy were was a matter of no small concern to Bomber Command, which night after night went forth to battle. In this, therefore, the second operation of parachute troops, the stakes were much higher than those of the first. They were called upon, not to interfere with the problematic water supply of some Italian peasants, but to seize and bring back an instrument which was playing a very important part in the ceaseless warfare waged between the bombers of the Royal Air Force and the defences of occupied Europe.

The force given this task eventually consisted of one hundred and nineteen all ranks, divided into three parties, to which the code names of three famous sailors – Drake, Nelson and Rodney – were given. Browning chose them out of compliment to the Navy and to emphasise the fact that the projected operation was one in which all three services would play an essential part. The Air Force would take the Army to the objective, and when the Army had done its work it would be removed from France and brought back to England by the Navy. Among the one hundred end nineteen officers and men finally chosen were a small party of Sappers and a few men from "B" Company. Conspicuous among the non-commissioned officers was Company Sergeant-Major G. Strachan of the Black Watch, "a man who knew exactly how a company should be run".

The training was strenuous and everyone worked long hours, for time was short; but at weekends the admirable rule that there should be complete relaxation for twenty-four hours was strictly kept. As the winter days went by Captain J. G. Ross,[1] a Scotsman from Dundee, and Frost's second-in-command, began to receive an ever-increasing quantity of stores. These arrived at irregular moments, both by day and by night. Soon every man was equipped with the then newly invented Sten gun, something between an automatic rifle and an automatic pistol. At that time it had not been perfected – as the Canadians were to find to their cost some months later at Dieppe – and therefore contained a number of defects absent from the later model. These the parachute troops did their best to discover and remedy, being consoled by the fact that, though the new weapon might not be perfect, it was greatly superior up to a range of fifty yards to the rifle and bayonet with which they had up till then been equipped.

During the training at Alton Priors the embryo raiders made the acquaintance of No. 51 Squadron of the Royal Air Force,

[1]Later Major J. G. Ross, D. S. O.

flying Whitleys, which was to take them to their destination. It was commanded by Wing Commander P. C. Pickard, D. F. C., who before his death in action two years later in the attack on the gaol at Amiens was to be admitted three times to the Distinguished Service Order. He was an airman of the highest ability, and was well known to the general public, for he had played a leading part in the film *Target for Tonight*, at that time drawing large audiences throughout the country. After talking with the pilots, Frost and his men "were left in no doubt as to their efficiency, and we felt that if anybody was going to put us down in the right place they were the people to do it".

After some time spent on Salisbury Plain, they travelled to Inveraray on Loch Fyne, removing their parachute wings for obvious reasons of security during the journey, and there made contact with the officers and crews of the assault landing craft, whose duty it would be to take them back to England. The parent ship of these craft was the *Prince Albert*, on board which the parachute troops took up their quarters. This part of the training was found to be very enjoyable, "although it meant long hours and frequent wettings in the icy Loch". What was disconcerting, however, was the discovery that the business of embarking in the dark was not so easy as they had imagined. Moreover, the captains of the landing craft did not by any means always discover the whereabouts of the parachute troops as they waited for them on the cold lochside, and this augured ill for their successful retreat on the night of the enterprise. By then few doubted that they would reach their destination, but that they would be able to leave the shores of France after accomplishing their mission seemed less certain.

Having completed their training at Inveraray rather less than more to their satisfaction, the party returned to Tilshead, where they carried out a practice drop from the aircraft belonging to No. 51 Squadron, which had never had parachute troops on board before. "Although the ground was brick-hard there were no casualties", and it was noted that Sergeant Grieve, Seaforth Highlanders, and his men left their aircraft far more smartly than any of the other sticks.

By then Frost and his men had reached that point in their

training, well-known to all who rehearse something which they will subsequently perform in public, when nothing seems to go according to plan. The hardest part of the business would obviously be the embarkation in the dark when the operation was over, and consequently "nearly every day a small convoy of five troop-carrying vehicles" could be seen "travelling down to the Dorset coast at a steady forty miles per hour". The weather was fickle, and more than one of these journeys proved fruitless. The last rehearsal "could not have been a more dismal failure". The parachute troops were to leave their lorries at a point near the sea where the ground was flat; aircraft were to fly over and drop containers carrying their weapons and a mock attack would then be made on a fictitious radiolocation post, after which the raiders would move down to the beach and enter the landing craft. That was the plan. Very little of it was put into practice. The containers were dropped in the wrong place; the landing craft arrived at the wrong beach; the parachute troops lost themselves in a minefield ten miles from the correct spot.

The next morning Frost was faced with something of a crisis. The first available date for the operation was only forty-eight hours away, and the naval authorities, quite rightly, insisted that a further rehearsal was essential. Very fortunately the weather intervened: a postponement of the raid was inevitable, and the night of Sunday, 23rd February was spent on the shores of Southampton Water in a final exercise. This time all went well, save that a miscalculation of the time of the tide caused the landing craft to stick in the mud sixty yards from the shore. "Though," says Frost, "we walked out to heave and shove, hard and fast they remained, and we went home to bed."

Only four possible nights were now left, the Monday to the Thursday of the week beginning 24th February. A full moon, or a moon nearly so, was essential if the parachute troops were to see and recognise their objective, and the Navy required a rising tide. By then every man had been briefed in detail, new information being given to him as it arrived, which it did "in almost incredible detail". Before they set out all knew the exact position of every enemy defence, the strength, the billets, the weapons, the temper of the German garrison, and even some of their names. What the small building containing the radiolocation device looked like and its exact whereabouts were impressed on everyone by means of a scale model of remarkable fidelity. It shewed a section of high white cliff, the abrupt ending of some flat fields traversed by paths, of which one connected a circular hole in the ground holding the radar installation with a fair-sized modern villa of great vulgarity and little charm. It was quite new and approached by a rather more than semi-circular drive.

The task of Frost and "C" Company was to enable Flight-Sergeant Cox and a section of the 1st Parachute Field Squadron Royal Engineers, under Captain Denis Vernon, to dismantle the radar station, bring back parts of it, and photograph those which could not be moved. The radar experts had, therefore, to be brought to the station, protected while they dismantled it, and then removed with their booty to the boats.

The German defences were far from negligible. Their garrison consisted of three bodies of men: first the signallers and covering troops on duty at the radar post itself and the villa, who numbered about thirty; next those in immediate support, some hundred all told, stationed at La Presbytère, a cluster of farm buildings in a wooded enclosure about three hundred yards to the north of the villa. They served as billets for coast defence troops and for the signallers when off duty. Finally there was the garrison of the village of Bruneval itself, numbering forty, who might be manning the pillboxes and earthworks covering the village and the beach from which the evacuation would have to be made. These pillboxes were situated both on the top of the cliffs and at their foot where they joined the beach.

The three parties into which Frost had divided his force were of unequal strength. The largest, to which Cox, Vernon and the sappers were attached, was called "Drake", and consisted of fifty men. They were subdivided into two groups, one under Lieutenant Peter Young, whose orders were to assault the radar station itself. The other, under Frost, who would attack the villa. "Drake" was to drop first and to be followed after a short interval by the second party, known as "Nelson" and made up of Lieutenant E. C. B. Charteris, King's Own Scottish Borderers, and forty men. The third detachment, "Rodney", which was to land last after another short interval, was composed of Lieutenant John Timothy, Royal West Kent Regiment, and thirty men. They were to deal with any Germans advancing to counter-attack either the station or the beach, and to act as a general reserve.

In the later stages of planning and rehearsal Frost and his men derived much amusement from trying to imagine what the enemy in the villa in Bruneval were doing or might be doing when they arrived. The village was known to possess "a fairly well-appointed estaminet", and it was hoped that on the night chosen it would be well patronised. In order to achieve swift and overwhelming surprise every man of Frost's party was to be in his position before the assault began, and after much discussion it was decided that Frost himself should give the signal for the battle to begin by blowing his whistle just as he broke in the door of the villa. What, he wondered, should he do if the door were locked? "Ring the bell," suggested one of his men; "but in the event it proved unnecessary".

It will be observed that throughout everyone taking part in the raid, regardless of his rank, discussed the plan and was encouraged to make suggestions. This admirable practice – one with which the commando troops who wore the green beret were familiar – was followed whenever possible by those who wore the red. On more than one occasion it provoked timely suggestions which contributed to subsequent success.

One point was of paramount importance: the operation had to be timed very accurately. The force was to remain on the soil of France for just as many minutes as would be required to seize the radar apparatus, dismantle and remove it, and for not one minute longer; and those minutes had to be as few as possible, for – a fact that they did not forget – these hundred and nineteen men were thrusting themselves into the outer defences of an enemy who, with every road at his command, could bring overwhelming strength against them in a short time. Moreover, there was also the Channel tide and its vagaries to be considered. The assault craft must not be left stranded on the rocks as they had been on the mud during the final rehearsal.

The ships which were to take them back to England were under the general command of Commander E. N. Cook, Royal Australian Navy, and consisted of motor gunboats of the 14th Flotilla, assault landing craft and support landing craft. These were under Lieutenant-Commander W. G. Everett, Royal Navy. Two destroyers were detailed to act as escort. The assault landing craft were empty except for their crews; but in the support landing craft were thirty-two officers and men of the Royal Fusiliers and the South Wales Borderers, with orders to provide covering fire while the parachute troops, their task accomplished, were embarking.

By 24th February all was ready. The containers carrying demolition charges, signalling apparatus, additional weapons and other necessary gear had been packed and sent to Thruxton airfield, the last orders had been given, the last adjustments made, and the parachute troops lay down in the afternoon to take a few hours' rest. They were not unnaturally keyed up, for they had been living under a certain strain during the period of preparation. All were young, high-spirited, and possessed of their fair share of the faults and virtues of that time of life. Their behaviour had in it the "excuse of youth and heat of blood" and had therefore to be carefully watched; for, as Frost noted at the time, "if the enemy has an inkling of the project we shall be doomed". Though the many details of the attack were known to all, for all had had a share in working them out, the object and the destination of the force were kept a close secret from everyone except the officers. That the place was Bruneval and the objective the radar station close to it were only divulged at the last moment. Even so, Frost had his moments of anxiety, especially when one evening some of the wilder elements of his command arrived in camp from the public houses of Tilshead marching behind an improvised band playing "borrowed" instruments, the property of the local branch of the British Legion. "Thereafter the guardroom door yawned more widely" and the threat that such conduct would mean a swift and ignominious return to Hardwick, and thence to unit, sufficed. Though as noisy as most in their cups, no parachute soldier gave a hint of what was so soon to be in the wind.

At teatime on the 24th a message was received announcing a postponement of twenty-four hours owing to adverse weather conditions. On the next day, the 25th, and the day after, the 26th, it was repeated. "Each morning we braced ourselves for the venture, and each evening, after a further postponement, we had time to think of all the things that could go wrong." On Thursday morning, the 27th, the weather seemed no different, and Frost was expecting to be sent on leave with orders to be ready to operate in a month's time when the moon should again be favourable, when a staff officer arrived to say that the period of waiting would be extended by another twenty-four hours. "Listlessly and without much enthusiasm," the containers were once more packed and sent to the airfield.

Throughout this trying period, one with which officers and men of the Parachute Regiment became only too familiar before the end of the war, Company Sergeant-Major Strachan alone refused to be depressed. He was quite convinced that Thursday would be the day, and when at teatime, in place of the staff officer, Major-General Browning himself arrived to say that they were to take off that night, he was quietly triumphant. The weather was at last favourable. "No wind . . . and a bright moon, with a little cloud and a light haze," reported the naval commander afterwards; and his words were echoed by Wing Commander Pickard, who stated that "visibility in the area was found to be two to four miles, with excellent definition".

The men were in high spirits when they arrived at Thruxton airfield. Here they formed up and marched round the perimeter "like Guardsmen", behind pipers playing the regimental marches of Scotland. There was time for a last cigarette and a mug of tea well laced with rum before the twelve sticks entered the twelve Whitleys, silently waiting. At the last moment Frost was called to the telephone to speak to Nigel Norman in charge of the air side of the operation. France, he reported, was covered with snow, and the light anti-aircraft defences "seemed to be particularly alert".

One by one the aircraft took off, Frost flying in that piloted by Pickard. The parachutists, wrapped in sleeping-bags, gave vent to their feelings in song, the favourites being "Annie Laurie", "Lulu" and "Come sit by my side if you love me", the special song of the parachute troops of which only that line is printable. Not to be outdone by the Army, Flight-Sergeant Cox "obliged" with a solo rendering of "The Rose of Tralee". Others in other aircraft played cards – the old army game of pontoon. Among them was Corporal Stewart, an inveterate player, who was carrying a wallet well-filled with former winnings which he had steadfastly refused to leave behind. To these he was now able to add, remarking as he did so, that if he were hit whoever was near him would find himself in luck's way. . . .

From time to time Pickard sent back messages telling of their progress and whereabouts. An hour went by, and, despite the sleeping-bags, the cold inside the cramped bellies of the Whitleys was beginning to cause great discomfort. Added to this, "the huge mugs of hot tea we had drunk before taking off soon began to scream to be let out. In that restricted space, and encumbered as we were, there was, alas, no way". When they had been flying for two hours the coverings over the holes in the floors of the Whitleys, through which they were to jump, were removed, and soon afterwards they could see the coast of France near Le Havre. Their presence did not pass unnoticed by the enemy and anti-aircraft shells began to burst in the silver air about them. A number of aircraft were hit, though no serious damage was caused, but two of the Whitleys, one with Charteris on board, had to take avoiding action and in consequence arrived late and not quite at the right dropping zone.

At the moment planned the red light shone. Frost sat on the edge of the hole, and on the appearance of the green light thrust himself into space. As soon as his parachute opened he could see all the features he had expected "standing out in the bright moonlight". There was the forming-up place, a row of trees by a gully. "That they had arrived at exactly the right spot was," he was convinced, "in great part due to the excellent air photography which had been provided."

On reaching the ground Frost and his stick performed a natural function. This "was certainly not good drill, as now was the time when a stick of parachutists are most vulnerable . . . but at least it was a gesture of defiance". "The first thing that struck me," said Flight-Sergeant Cox afterwards, "was how quiet everything was and how lonely I felt, and then I heard some rustling and saw something outlined against the snow. It was a container."

It took the men composing the "Drake" contingent ten minutes to collect their weapons and form up in the belt of trees by the gully. They then set off, moving – since they had been dropped inland – towards the coast and the radar station. The only sound was the noise made by the engines of the departing Whitleys, and some distance away a few bursts of machine-gun fire aimed probably at the aircraft. From the bijou villa and the radar station beyond, "which we could see plainly, there was no sign of alarm". At a slow run Frost, Young and the men of "Drake" approached and surrounded them in silence. According to the plan, Frost made for the door of the villa. To his surprise it was open and "I nearly forgot to blow my whistle before going in. As soon as I blew it explosions, yells and the sound of automatic fire" broke the silence of the quiet night. At the head of four men, Frost, shouting "Hände hoch!" dashed into the villa, which was found to be unfurnished. Running upstairs, they killed the only German inside, who was leaning from the window of an upper room firing on Young's men now entering the buildings which housed the radar instruments.

Leaving two men in the villa, Frost with the rest made off to join Young. On reaching him he found that the Germans manning the radar post had been killed or captured. One of the prisoners had, in the confusion, leapt over the edge of the cliff, but had landed on a ledge ten feet down and been hauled back. He was immediately interrogated, was found to be a signaller and confirmed the information already known to the raiders, that the number of Germans in the immediate neighbourhood was not more than a hundred. For the moment all seemed well. Denis Vernon with the sappers had arrived, and with him was Flight-Sergeant Cox, who was beginning to inspect and dismantle those parts of the radar set which were to be taken back to England.

It was then that fire from La Presbytère opened. Fortunately it was inaccurate, but one man was killed and two bullets struck the apparatus under Sergeant Cox's hands. Frost and his men were forming a defensive perimeter round the radar set, of which most stood above ground and resembled "an old-fashioned gramophone loudspeaker", and were soon in position. Twenty minutes passed and then three enemy vehicles were observed moving behind the wood of La Presbytère. This was serious, for if they contained mortars and opened fire they would catch the parachute troops in the open and "it would be difficult to get the equipment away". The signallers reported that the small wireless sets they carried were not working, and Frost "began to feel the lack of a proper company headquarters' organisation. We had turned ourselves into an assault group for the attack on the villa, and now when I wanted some signallers, runners and my sergeant-major, they were all dispersed doing other tasks". Vernon and Cox presently reported that they had dismantled the instruments needed, the party moved towards the beach, and presently came under fire from a pillbox situated on the edge of a cliff. Several men were hit, including Company Sergeant-Major Strachan, who received three bullets in the stomach. He was dragged to cover and given morphia.

By now, however, contact had been made with the "Rodney" party further inland, though some confusion was caused by a sudden shout, "The boats are here; it's all right! Come on down!" This news – who cried it in the night whether one of the enemy, or a parachutist excited by this his first time in action is not known – was immediately contradicted by John Ross, the second-in-command. He was near the beach and shouted that the defences had not yet been taken. Obviously something was wrong, and at that moment Frost was told that the Germans had reoccupied the villa and were advancing against him. What had happened was this.

Charteris and the "Nelson" party had been dropped at the wrong place, for, as will be remembered, some of the Whitleys had had to alter course to avoid anti-aircraft fire. They had, in consequence, landed two and a half miles away from their chosen assembly point, and because of this were late in arriving at the scene of action. Without the "Nelson" party, Timothy and the "Rodney" contingent were not strong enough to attack the German pillboxes and other defences covering the beach. On landing, Charteris had at once realised that he was in the wrong valley, though "it looked very like the right one, but there was no row of trees at the bottom of it as there should have been, and it was not deep enough. I don't mind saying that this was a nasty moment". Seeing that the aircraft which he had just left had turned and was flying north, he and his men moved in that direction at that Red-Indian lope, between a fast walk and a trot, which was the gait of the trained parachutist. He soon caught sight of the lighthouse at Cap d'Antifer and this gave him his bearing. Almost at once he and his men came into contact with the enemy. Both sides were moving in single file in the moonlight, and one of the Germans attached himself to the men of "Nelson", under the impression that they belonged to his own patrol. Subsequent explanations resulted in his death. Moving in the traditional manner to the sound of the guns, in this instance the rattle of machine-gun fire, Charteris, after a running fight near the village of Bruneval, fell in with Frost close to the largest pillbox on the beach.

Their relief in meeting was mutual, and Frost immediately ordered Charteris and Timothy to attack and clear the beach. As he did so, he saw Vernon, Cox and the sappers "slipping and sliding with their heavily laden trolleys" down the frozen path from the site of the radar set towards the shore. They were accompanied by Sergeant-Major Strachan, half-walking, half-carried, calling out, under the influence of morphia, unintelligible orders.

Charteris and his men, shouting their war-cry "Caber Feigh"[1], supported by Timothy and his, rushed the beach. A house on its outskirts received "two volleys of hand grenades", while the garrison of a nearby pillbox was speedily despatched. For some moments the enemy resisted violently

[1]The antlers of the deer.

with machine-gun fire and grenades. A splinter struck Corporal Stewart on the head and laid him low. Mindful of his pontoon winnings, he called out to his nearest comrade, Lance-Corporal Freeman: "I've had it. Here's my wallet." Freeman hastened to take it and then examined Stewart, clearly visible in the bright moonlight. "You've only a scalp wound," he said, to which Stewart immediately retorted, "Gie us my bluidy wallet back, then."

The house, like the villa, was found to be empty, save for a very frightened German orderly engaged in a telephone conversation with a furious company commander some miles inland. It was broken off just as the officer was threatening the German garrison with condign punishment on the following morning for making so much noise and disturbing his rest.

The hour was now about a quarter-past two in the morning; the beach was in our hands and the instruments, dismantled by Vernon and Cox, lying upon it with the wounded. But where was the Navy? Some minutes went by and then the signallers informed Frost that they were unable to make contact with the ships which by then had been many hours at sea, for they had had to start long before the parachute troops. Signals by lamp were tried, but "still we got no reply. There was a light mist out to sea and visibility was no more than half a mile". As a last emergency Frost had arranged to fire a red Very light, first to the north and then to the south of the beach. He now did so more than once; but from the dark and heaving waters there came no sign. "With a sinking heart," he records, "I moved off the beach with my officers to rearrange our defences. It looked as though we were going to be left high and dry, and the thought was hard to bear. The prisoners were questioned as to the whereabouts of the enemy's reserves, but they were too frightened to be coherent." On each side the great cliffs loomed above the little beach and the little force, and seemed to "dominate us with ever-increasing menace".

But all was well. The men had hardly taken up their new positions, when a signaller shouted, "Sir, the boats are coming in; the boats are here. God bless the ruddy Navy, sir!" And "we saw several dark shapes glide in across the water". In obedience to their order, the covering party of Royal Fusiliers and South Wales Borderers at once directed a heavy fire upon the cliffs, of which the noise echoing to and fro was deafening. They were with difficulty persuaded to cease; but fortunately none of the parachute troops was hit. All six landing craft came in together, and for some moments a mild confusion reigned. Frost, however, was able to put the wounded and the captured radar equipment into one landing craft, and then the parachutists scrambled on board the others, each man as best he could, as the Germans began "to lob grenades and mortar bombs onto the beach". The orderly withdrawal which had been planned had gone by the board, and there was no time to make sure that everyone had been taken off. Eight men were in fact left behind; two of them were dead and six had not yet reached the beach. As he stepped on board one of the motor gunboats, her wireless operator informed Frost that he had just picked up a message from two of the six who had lost their way and only arrived at the beach after the landing craft had put out to sea again.

The raiders were taken from the open landing craft into the gunboats, which then made off for England with the landing craft in tow. Below deck, in the warmth and amid the mugs of rum, Frost and his men learned that while the flotilla had been lying offshore awaiting them a German destroyer and two E-boats had passed by less than a mile away, and "by God's good grace had failed to notice us". This was the reason why no reply had been sent to the signals of the raiders.

On board one of the gunboats was Doctor R. V. Jones, a radar expert, who informed the parachutists to their delight that Flight-Sergeant Cox and Lieutenant Vernon had been able to remove almost everything that the scientists desired to examine.

At dawn the flotilla was not more than fifteen miles from the French coast, but it was met by a squadron of Spitfires which gave it cover throughout the passage home. "We vainly tried," says Frost, "to sleep as the gunboats rolled and jerked across the Channel. I went on to the bridge as we approached Portsmouth. There were destroyers now on either side of the flotilla, and when we broke away to head for the *Victory*, they came by at speed and saluted us." A little later Pickard and his pilots were welcoming their passengers, amid a confused crowd of "staff officers, photographers and reporters".

So ended the raid on Bruneval which, at the cost of two killed, six wounded and six missing, fulfilled the exact intention of those who had planned it. Frost and Charteris were awarded the Military Cross; Young was mentioned in Dispatches; Flight-Sergeant Cox received the Military Medal, as did Sergeants Grieve and McKenzie. Company Sergeant-Major Strachan was awarded the Croix de Guerre with Palm; he recovered with great speed from his wounds, and a few weeks later was back with the 2nd Battalion.

The affair of Bruneval has been told in detail so that the hazards and opportunities of this strange and then still novel form of attack may be understood. On the day after the raid a Hurricane was sent in a reconnaissance over Bruneval and La Presbytère. Its pilot saw a number of German officers standing round the circular hole which had housed the radar apparatus and which now gaped wide and empty. He dived and opened fire with his machine-guns. The hole was quickly occupied.

OPERATION BENSON
Gilbert Sadi-Kirschen

The wartime Belgian Independent Parachute Company, despite its name, was actually part of the British SAS and fought under its direction, sharing identical training and equipment. Led by Captain E. Blondeel, the Belgium company – also known as 5 SAS and, from summer 1944, the Belgian SAS Regiment – was numerically tiny, around 300 personnel at its height, and tended to be used for small-scale intelligence-gathering operations. Below is the diary of Gilbert Sadi-Kirschen (Lt Kirschen) detailing one such operation, codenamed Benson, in France in August 1944.

The work of the Belgian SAS was not confined to spying. In one operation in the French Ardennes in August 1944, forty Belgian troopers led by Captain Blondeel killed 138 Germans in a fortnight of relentless ambushing. The Belgians also had the dubious privilege of being the first SAS troops to enter Germany – although more by accident than design. Operation Bergbang was intended to install a small Belgian force in the Liège-Maastrict area to observe Wehrmacht movements and communications. On 5 September 1944 a group of reinforcements was dropped inside the German border. They operated to some effect before being overrun and forced to retire to liberated Belgium. Towards the close of the war in Europe the Belgium SAS provided a screen, in the form of 200 troopers in jeeps and 15cwt trucks, for the Canadian II Corps as it drove through Holland, and later provided the same service inside Germany for the Polish Armoured Division. On 21 September 1945 the Belgian SAS was formerly handed over to the Belgian Government. The contemporary Belgian 1st Para-Commando Battalion is the direct descendant of the Belgian SAS and wears a beret with SAS wings in memory of its origins. The battalion's most memorable operation in recent years was the 1964 rescue of European nationals from the Congo.

London 26 August 1944.
It was the last day of my leave and I had to go back to Fairford Camp that evening. I didn't like the idea of a long journey by train and lorry. Then I thought of ringing up Special Air Service Brigade Headquarters at Moor Park. They were sure to have a jeep doing a shuttle service between London and Fairford.

Captain Blondeel answered the telephone.

"Certainly, my boy. I'm going back to Fairford this evening. Be here by four o'clock."

Blondeel had hardly set eyes on me when he said:

"Ah, there you are. How would you like to go off on an operation to-morrow evening?"

"Certainly. Where to? Belgium?"

"No, I'm sorry; north of Paris. It's another intelligence mission. SHAEF need to know every movement in that area. You'd have to send reports daily or even twice a day on the volume of traffic on the roads running from Paris to Compiègne, and Paris to Soissons. You may say they ought to be able to find that out with aerial reconnaissance, but the countryside is stiff with anti-aircraft batteries. You're also asked to pin-point these Ack-Ack batteries, so that the R.A.F. can either avoid them or beat them up, depending on how they feel.

"This time you'll be met on arrival by a reception committee provided by the local resistance, and of course that'll save you a lot of time – Oh, and I forgot to say that the name of your operation is BENSON?"

"Who's BENSON?"

"No idea. Look him up in the 'Encyclopædia Britannica.' There'll be six of you altogether – two W. T.'s of course. Who would you like?"

"Moyse and Pietquin – I was very pleased with them last time."

"Good. As second in command I thought Lieutenant Franck might be good. He's a Frenchman, and before the war he had a factory in the area where you're to operate."

"Excellent. I came across Franck during training last year and we get on well together. For the two others, let's see, what about Flips and Bouillon who were with me in Normandy. They're real toughs. They used to be in the Foreign Legion."

We were driving fast through the English countryside. It was a wonderful summer evening, and I felt far less nervous than the day before my first operation. Blondeel also was much less strung up. The Squadron hadn't had many casualties up to the present in these French operations, and the results had been satisfactory.

"We're in Belgium at last," he said. "The office was against parachuting men into Belgium, and I had to drop Paul Renkin's group into the French Ardennes, but they were attacked and crossed over into the Belgian Ardennes, where they were received with open arms by the local Maquis, and I'm hoping to send them some reinforcements very soon."

He was humming to himself at the wheel, and to my surprise, he suggested stopping and having a drink in a pub on the banks of the Thames.

"You're a lucky devil, Kirschen," he sighed suddenly, as we raised our glasses, "When I think that in a day or two you'll be overrun by the Americans and you'll be able to go and enjoy yourself in Paris."

27 August.

Fairford Camp was a foretaste of the Apocalypse: every uniform of the United Nations was to be seen, every language spoken. Scotsmen tested their weapons by firing over your head. Frenchmen checked over their W.T. sets or tried on their parachute harness. Norwegians, lying flat on their stomachs, studied their maps. There were some on their way to France and others who'd just come back, and who were telling stories of their experiences. And there were a few emaciated airmen who had just been fished out of the Channel after days in the water.

Lorries picked their way carefully between the tents looking for men who were due to leave for somewhere behind the German lines. "Who's pinched my helmet? Anyone seen my parachute?"

There was a crowd round a jeep which was armed with a machine gun, a bazooka, one or two Brens and fitted with several reserve petrol tanks. Evidently this jeep was to be dropped by parachute. We wondered what sort of state it would be in after landing.

In all this confusion I managed with great difficulty to find Freddy, who was in great spirits. He had just been told that he was to speak daily on the radio in the five o'clock broadcast to the Belgian SAS. The thought of this greatly amused him.

"The broadcast will be preceded by the first notes of 'Sur le Pont d'Avignon'" he explained. "No one could fail to recognise it, even if they were as unmusical as you are. Messages for you will begin with the words 'Hello, Loulou Two.'"

"That's charming. And what sort of stories will you tell us?"

"I'll give you the latest news of the various SAS groups, and also what schemes are being hatched in high places. As soon as your mission is over, I'll tell you if you have to come back direct or if you can stop in Paris and come back by easy stages."

Everyone talked about Paris to me as if I were already there. For this departure I felt as though I were going through an old routine. The number of people who saw me off this time was much less impressive than for my first operation. Freddy was the only one at the take-off, and he gave me a great wink as the door of the plane closed on us.

The operation was to be a short one and I was to be met on landing. I felt that things were going very well.

28 August

Things went far from well.

First, of course, the kitbag went wrong. I remembered to unhitch it as I jumped, but I didn't manage to hold on to it tightly enough as it fell. I tried to slow its fall, but all I did was to rip the skin off my fingers. That damned kitbag. I always knew it would give me trouble before I finished.

Then I saw Moyse limping up to me. He had made a good landing, but had managed to sprain his ankle walking into a rut in a cart track.

And Flips had winded himself by falling on to his kitbag and getting the barrel of his carbine stuck into the small of his back.

Franck had injured his foot pretty badly.

Otherwise everyone was all right.

There was a storm somewhere in the distance, and we found each other by the light of lightning flashes.

But what was so comforting was that there wasn't the slightest trace of the famous reception committee who were supposed to meet us. We peered vainly into the darkness. There was no movement, no shouting.

It had hardly been worth while the pilot of the Stirling who had dropped us making me spend the last twenty minutes before jumping crouched beside the hole we were to jump through . . . His idea was not to let us drop without being absolutely certain of having found the right ground, and recognising the signal letter.

"My instructions are quite clear," he had said, "if I'm not dead certain of the ground, I take you back to England."

He was a conscientious man, this Australian pilot, and his conscience was surely quite clear, having persuaded himself that he had seen the lights of the reception committee. And then he came back over the ground. He must have uttered a sigh of relief as he dropped the twenty-four containers to his imaginary reception committee. We heard the aircraft disappearing towards England, the sound of the engines getting softer and softer.

Franck came up and whispered.

"King, what are we going to do with these containers? Where are we? Has anyone found the case with the W. T. equipment in it?"

"I know no more than you do. It's so dark we'll never find the wretched containers or the cage. Besides, with four out of the six of us injured, how could we carry them? Forget the containers. Let's get out of here double quick. As soon as it gets light the Germans will realise that parachutists have been dropped. Just a minute. Do you see that red light winking over there? Maybe that's where the reception committee is waiting for us, because the pilot did say he saw lights."

In the blinding rain we walked as far as the red light. It wasn't the reception committee – it was a light on an abandoned train. Luckily there were no sentries, no Germans. Perhaps we were somewhere in liberated territory.

History repeated itself. As in Normandy, I looked for a

signpost and then I studied my map and discovered we were ten kilometres west of the ground. That meant that I was ten kilometres further away from those delights of Paris which I had been promised so consistently.

We set off walking eastwards, and after five kilometres of difficult going, we went through a village, Valescourt. An hour before dawn all we had found in the way of shelter was a miserable clump of about a dozen stunted trees. Otherwise there was nothing but bare plateau and cornfields which had already been cut. Oh, for the deep forests of Normandy.

We woke up from a short sleep, soaked to the skin. Without moving from our clump of trees we looked about us. It was a dull, grey day. We could see German cars moving along the main road about 500 yards away and in the other direction we could hear tanks and carriers clanking along cart tracks.

This place was not too healthy for us. There was no farm to be seen. It wasn't like Normandy – here all the farmers and labourers lived in the villages. Just as Franck and I were wondering how we were going to make contact with the local inhabitants we noticed a peasant on his way to work in a nearby field.

I decided to disregard all the accepted rules. I knew one should not show oneself during the day, especially when wearing uniform. I knew one should not reveal one's hide-out to local people. But our wretched little wood gave us such uncertain cover that some relaxation of the rules was justified.

I went out and accosted the peasant. We were lucky. He was the son of a Belgian farmer and he offered to give us all the help he could.

"You've come to the right place," he said. "There are Germans in every village and thousands of them pass through here, because the main roads cross at Saint-Just-en-Chaussée, a few kilometres away. Personally, I'm not in the Resistance, but I can get Monsieur Lucien to come along later. He's one of the chiefs I think. Won't you take my sandwiches? you must be hungry and cold under those trees . . ."

In our first message to London I gave our position and asked to be allowed to remain where we were, so as to observe the Paris-Beauvais and Amiens-Montdidier roads. I explained that with things as they were, it would be difficult as well as a waste of time to shift our position.

In the afternoon, Monsieur Lucien of the Resistance, came to see us. He was a local farmer, short and thick set, with bright eyes.

"The first thing to tell you," he said, "is that one of my chaps has found all the stuff that was parachuted last night. He and the others made a real good job of it and everything was unpacked and hidden away before the Jerries got up this morning."

"You didn't by any chance find my cigarettes, did you?" said Moyse.

"No, I don't think so," said Monsieur Lucien, looking slightly embarrassed. "I'll bring you some bread and smoked sausage this evening. Is this where you sleep, under the trees? It doesn't look very comfortable."

"Do you know anywhere else we could go?"

"Why not try Folly Cellar?"

"Did you say Folly?"

"The Folly's what we call the barn over there, the other side of the hill. It's a very good barn. Loving couples used to use it at one time. The entrance to the cellar is hidden by bushes. I could take you there this evening if you like."

At five that afternoon we got a message confirming that we could operate in this area. We sent them the position of an anti-aircraft battery, Lucien had told us about. I wondered what Blondeel had thought when he heard we had not been met. He'd been so proud of having that reception committee arranged for us.

At nightfall we settled ourselves in the cellar of Folly Barn. The name was ominous and so was the atmosphere of the place.

"The local couples can't have been hard to please," sighed Franck. We lay on the damp stone floor of the cellar and thought regretfully of the warm sleeping bags we had purposely left in England, to give us less weight to carry about. But at least it wasn't raining directly on us.

29 August

We lay in the cellar till Lucien came and brought us some food and a detailed summary of last night's traffic on the roads.

"I asked Dr Caillard to come and see you," he said. "He's a good doctor and a good man. He'll attend to the sprained ankle and to your hand, Captain. He should be here in a minute or two."

While waiting for the doctor to come, we went into the barn, about twenty yards away from our cellar, to try and get a message through to London.

The doctor, seeing this bunch of crocks, would hardly be impressed by us as professional parachutists, so we would try and put on a clandestine radio exhibition for his benefit.

The doctor arrived on a motor bike and introduced himself.

I've seldom seen a man so calm and methodical as he was. He dealt with Moyse's ankle and Franck's foot and while he was bandaging my hand he suddenly began to talk.

"Maybe this will interest you, Captain. Yesterday, at the crossroads at St -Just-en-Chaussée, there was a German major directing the traffic. He stopped each vehicle to examine the driver's papers and pointed out which road he should take. I was rather intrigued by all this so I stopped and watched him for a few minutes. And suddenly the major wiped his forehead and went off to the café to have a drink. I followed him and noticed he put his map on the table. While he wasn't watching I made a copy of the map." At this point he carefully unfolded a piece of paper. "There's my rough sketch. That's the Channel coast and that line there's the Somme."

"But it's incredible, Doctor. It shows every German division on the Somme. All the division numbers, the ones up in the line, and those in reserve. It even shows the position of Army Headquarters." We looked at one another astounded.

"I'm very pleased to have been of service to you," said the doctor quietly. "Good-bye, and good luck," and off he went.

We had an hour before our next sked.[1] Franck went into the cellar to shave. The five of us in the barn were sitting

[1]Radio Operator's technical term meaning "period of transmission." Derivation: Schedule.

bunched up together while the rain rattled on the roof and swept in through the door which wouldn't shut.

I began to dictate. Never had a message been composed with such fervour or coded with such care.

"Following enemy divisions on Somme. Between Abbeville-Amiens . . . Between Amiens-Peronne . . . south of Doullens . . ."

"Can you hear that noise?" whispered Pietquin.

We listened. Yes. There was a strange noise – it sounded like a carrier clanking along a muddy lane.

The noise got nearer. We grabbed our arms. The noise ceased and three yards in front of us a German self-propelled gun came to a standstill. The five or six soldiers riding on the gun carriage stared at us stupefied.

Flips and Bouillon opened fire at once. The Germans replied, firing incendiary bullets. The firing quickly became intense and then one side of the barn caught fire. Suddenly the gun carriage went into reverse and took up a position on the other side of the barn. Flips and Bouillon seized their chance, rushed outside and disappeared.

The firing started up again.

"Destroy the set, Moyse, quick." But Moyse preferred to take it to pieces. He was very expert and he only took thirty seconds to do it. Moyse was very attached to his wireless set.

I stuffed the doctor's plan into my pocket. The smoke was getting very thick and at any moment the straw would catch fire. We ran out, screened by the smoke. We threw the parts of the set into a bush and ran towards the only thing which offered any cover at all – a row of trees.

We threw ourselves down in the wet grass under the trees.

"I don't think they've seen us," said Pietquin.

For a minute or two there was silence, then the firing started up again more violently than ever. We saw two men running towards us, bullets whistling round them. Flips arrived first and threw himself down, he was followed by Franck who still had his face covered in shaving soap. He murmured: "They've got me in the arm, but it's nothing much."

"Where's Bouillon?"

"No idea."

For a moment there was a lull. The Jerries had probably

gone off to get some reinforcements, so we decided the best thing to do was to get away. But there was no cover, nothing but a field of stubble.

"We could hide under the cornstacks," Flips suggested. "They're damned small but it's better than nothing at all."

Each of us crept under one of those miserable cornstacks. The straw had gone brown with all the rain there'd been.

Franck kept a bit apart from the rest of us. I went over and gave him some sulphonamide tablets. "Don't worry about me," he said, "I can manage all right."

We waited all through that long afternoon. Between the sheaves I could see Folly Barn burning. A wave of depression swept over me. There I was, soaked to the skin, bent double, wretched, not able to move one yard and knowing that in my pocket was a document of the most vital importance which was quite valueless if I didn't succeed in getting away.

I was hungry.

And what had happened to Bouillon. I'd been so proud of coming back from Normandy with all my men.

And this was the operation which was to have gone so well, so smoothly and was to take me, after a few days, to Paris. And now it was raining torrents and I had cramp. Here and there I could see cornstacks moving a little and I guessed my men were as impatient as I was. But there was no question of leaving our hiding places before it got dark.

By nightfall we were all ravenously hungry, all of us that is except Franck who had gone off on his own with a peasant.

"We may find something to eat in a village," said Moyse. "Perhaps the Germans have left by now."

He was indulging in a little wishful thinking. We tried approaching several villages but we heard nothing but shouts and orders in German. We would have to last out until the following day.

Luckily we found a few bales of straw and made ourselves a kind of roofless hut. Compared with our cornstacks of the afternoon, it was wonderfully comfortable.

We hardly slept that night and everyone woke up about four, in a very bad temper.

"Of course it's raining," groaned Flips.

"And no smokes," added Moyse.

I had one idea only and that was to transmit the message at all costs. I had to go back to the barn.

We moved off in single file and arrived safely at the row of trees where we had hidden the previous day. I told the men to wait there, and taking my carbine, I set off towards the barn. I crawled slowly forward stopping every two or three yards to look around me in the half light of dawn. I saw no Germans near, only a column of smoke from the barn rising slowly into the air.

I went back to the trees to fetch Moyse. I wanted him to collect the parts of his set from the bush where he had hidden them.

I decided to go down to the cellar in the hope of rescuing some chocolate I had left in my haversack. As I entered, I heard a strangled voice say in French: "Who goes there?" It was Bouillon's voice. "Oh, it's you, sir. That's wonderful. I thought you were all roasted alive in the barn. I've been hiding here since yesterday. How are all the others?"

A few minutes later we were all five of us together behind the line of trees which had become our new base. But I'd learnt my lesson and I got Flips and Bouillon to keep a look-out, while Moyse and Pietquin fixed up the radio.

Making contact wasn't easy. London could hardly hear us. Pietquin put all he'd got into turning that generator handle while Moyse, swearing and groaning, adjusted the dials and knobs on the set. At last they could start sending. We held our breath.

Q.S.P. (I have an important message for you). Q.S.P. It was a long message; 125 words, each word repeated for safety and several times London stopped to ask for extra repeats.

Pietquin and fat old Flips took turns at the handle, smiling and sweating. Five hundred yards away we could see German cars going along the road. I wondered if we'd ever come to the end of the message.

We had been on the air for more than an hour when Moyse said:

"At last. They've received all of it, and I'd give a lot to see their faces when they start decoding that."

We all relaxed. Our one problem now was food. We waited for Lucien as if he had been the Messiah. Late in the afternoon he appeared. He had expected to find our remains in the smouldering ruins of Folly Barn, and he was quite surprised to find us full of life and very hungry. He went off at once in search of provisions.

While we were eating, a German battery came and took up its position between our line of trees and the barn. We felt they might have had the decency to choose somewhere else. Luckily it was very dark and yet another thunderstorm came and broke over our heads. We retired discreetly from the tactless battery and slept in our shelter of the night before. We woke to a sunny day at last. We dried our uniforms and watched the German convoys go past, thinking each one would be the last one. We went on sending reports of enemy traffic.

At midday, London had a message for us. As Moyse decoded it, he beamed all over.

"A personal message from the General, sir," he said, trying to seem unconcerned.

It was Brigadier MacLeod who sent us his personal congratulations and thanked us for the information transmitted, which was of the greatest value.

"Very good of him," said Flips, "but we were damned nearly roasted."

We listened at 5 o'clock. Freddy's voice was jubilant.

"Good work, Kiki. You should have seen the excitement here when your message arrived. Everyone rushed to telephone SHAEF. You never heard such a noise."

"You might almost think that message had given them more trouble than it gave us," said Flips, taking a large bite at a sausage.

For the last few minutes an artillery duel had been raging just over our heads. From our observation post we could see the road clearly and we followed the battle with great interest, but without understanding very much about it.

More German cars came along the road. We counted them almost mechanically. Then they got fewer and fewer. We talked in whispers, watching the road. A Jerry motor cyclist scorched past, and as the noise of his engine died away, a silence seemed to settle down on the whole countryside. The sun began to set. And then, as we were sitting there, a little surprised at this strange lack of noise, suddenly all the bells of St Just pealed out together.

1 September.

Liberation was followed by a kind of explosion of joy. We were invited everywhere, fêted, gorged, kissed. We went to St Just to fetch Franck, who had been put up by the mayor and whose wound in the arm was recovering.

Toasts, ceremonies, speeches. I managed to repeat the talk I had given at Longny a fortnight before which still suited the occasion.

In a German lorry and with American petrol, we bowled along towards Paris.

2 September.

At Paris.

3 September.

"Hello, Loulou two, Hello, Loulou two." Freddy's voice was calm and cheerful as ever. His first message was for Eddy. He promised him some food in the near future.

Eddy? So Eddy Blondeel had gone into action. I wondered where he was. Probably in the Ardennes; that was always his great ambition.

Then there were a number of short messages for Paul, Jean, John, Jean-Claude Pilou. Each name made me jump – all my friends were "in the field."

At last he got to me. "Hurry up and come home, my boy, I'm off myself this evening. So long."

We set off once more. We crossed Normandy, going via Longny to collect Regner, who had spent a pleasant convalescence at Monsieur Bignon's house.

As for good old Bignon, he'd progressed a long way since we'd last seen him. He talked about jeeps and M.P.'s and doughnuts as if he'd lived for years on the banks of the Missouri.

6 September.

Our arrival in England marked the happy ending of operation Benson. And to this day I don't know who Benson was.

FIRST BLOOD
Alan Baker

Formed in 1943, the US 5307th Composite Unit (Provisional) was a 3000-strong deep penetration force designed to fight behind Japanese lines in occupied Burma. More popularly known as "Merrill's Marauders", after its commanding officer, Frank D. Merrill, the 5307th was the only American combat unit at the disposal of Lieutenant-General Joseph "Vinegar Joe" Stilwell, then in charge of Chinese troops on the Burmese frontier. In October 1943 some of Stilwell's Chinese troops began an offensive against the Japanese in northern Burma, and in February the Marauders went out on their first mission, the establishing of a road block at Walawbum inside Burma. It was the intention of Stilwell that the Marauders' road block would be the anvil on which retreating Japanese regiments would be crushed. This account of the Marauders' first mission begins with the 5307th nearing their objective, after a ten-day march through sweltering, leech-infested jungle.

BY THE 2ND March all the Battalions were assembled at the final drop area across the River Tanai before they began the approach march to Walawbum which was about fifteen miles distant. Here Merrill issued the first combat orders to the unit. Lieutenant-Colonel Beach's 3rd battalion in the lead was to move via the villages of Sana Ga and Lagang Ga to Walawbum where it was to dig in on the high ground along the Numpyek river covering the road from the east with mortar and machine gun fire, and blocking any Japanese attempt to escape to the south. Colonel McGee and 2nd Battalion were to march via the village of Wesu Ga to the Numpyek river, which it was to cross before cutting the road about two and a half miles west of Walawbum. The 1st Battalion was to complete the envelopment by blocking the trails at Sana Ga and patrolling the Numpyek river with one combat team, while the other remained in general reserve. Thus disposed, the Marauders were to remain in position blocking the Kamaing road until the Chinese, advancing from the north, relieved them. Up to this point the Marauders had been particularly fortunate, for although two of their advanced patrols had clashed with the Japanese on 28th February the 18th Division Headquarters was still unaware that a specialised and self-contained American unit was operating on its right flank, for the radio link between the Japanese 56th Regiment's 2nd Battalion and Divisional Headquarters had broken down and it was unable to pass on the information. However, with the establishment of the main blocking position at Walawbum, well to the rear of his forward troops, the true facts of the situation were available to Tanaka [Japanese General responsible for area of northern Burma where Stilwell's offensive was taking place], and his reaction to this information was to consider that the opportunity he had been waiting for had arisen. Concluding that the Chinese were advancing so slowly that they would have little effect on the outcome of the approaching battle, he left a small screen to contain their advance and quickly deployed his troops to the rear in order to destroy the Americans.

Merrill was anxious to press on at top speed and therefore ordered the 3rd Battalion to move out before it had collected only one of three days' rations then being dropped to it. At dawn on the following day, 3rd March, all three battalions were on the move towards Walawbum. The leading platoon of the 3rd Battalion travelled so quickly that it caught up with a withdrawing Japanese patrol and inevitably ran into an ambush. Immediately standard operating procedures went into effect. The leading element established a fire base, while the two other sections moved off the trail to work round both flanks of the Japanese position. When contact was made the enemy pulled back and established another position where the same procedure was repeated. Having been considerably slowed down by these tactics the I and R [Intelligence and Reconnaissance] platoon was caught up by the 3rd Battalion's main body at Lagang Ga where a sharp fight developed in which about thirty Japanese were killed. "Khaki" Combat Team of 3rd Battalion remained at this village to establish and protect a drop zone, while "Orange" Combat Team pushed on towards the Numpyek river and dug in in the evening on the high ground on the east bank of the river where its platoons could command, with their heavy weapons, the Kamaing road and Walawbum itself. Lieutenant Weston's I and R platoon was ordered to continue due east from Lagang Ga, cross the river and then move south towards the objective, digging in a few hundred yards north of Orange Combat Team where it was in a position to protect the battalion's flank.

By night-fall on 3rd March the other two battalions were bivouac'd some two miles west of Wesu Ga where 2nd Battalion had been engaged in a fire fight that afternoon. The following day 2nd Battalion cut a trail south towards the main road, meeting no Japanese on the way, established a road block and dug themselves in by nightfall. Running through the American position was the main Japanese telephone line which linked the Japanese forward HQ at Maingkwan with the Division's rear Headquarters at Kamaing. This line was tapped by Sergeant Matsumoto, a Japanese-American, and the information he gained proved invaluable.

In the meantime, however, the Japanese from early morning on 4th March had started probing the American positions, beginning with an attack at dawn by a force of about thirty against the airstrip which Khaki Combat Team had been constructing at Lagang Ga. Aided by early morning mist and good cover from the broken ground, the Japanese managed to get very close to the Marauders' positions but they were beaten off suffering about ten killed; a further seven Japanese died when six soldiers carrying a wounded Japanese officer walked unconcernedly into the middle of 3rd Battalion's command post close to their airstrip. Orange Combat Team consolidated its position across the river from Walawbum, enfilading the river banks with its heavy machine guns, and opened the battle in its sector by mortaring Walawbum and the main road. The Japanese 56th Regiment returned the fire and attempted to find the flanks of the Americans' position, suffering heavy casualties as they tried to cross the river, and other losses from ambushes and booby traps positioned to protect the Combat Team's flanks. An estimated seventy-five Japanese were killed in actions against Orange Combat Team during the course of the day. The American losses were extraordinarily light – one killed and seven wounded.

What characterised the combat on this day was the fluidity of the situation, for units and individuals from both sides ran into each other throughout the whole area. Lieutenant-Colonel Beach on a personal reconnaissance with his orderly into Walawbum itself was discovered by some fourteen Japanese soldiers whom he fortunately managed to evade, returning to the security of the American position even though he had to cross the open river before reaching safety. Earlier, Beach had had an even more remarkable escape when walking along the trail from Lagang Ga to Orange Combat Team's position: a Japanese had stepped out on to the trail some fifteen yards ahead of him, but before he could fire the Colonel's orderly dealt with him with his tommy gun. Several Japanese machine gunners even managed to infiltrate to within a hundred yards of Merrill's command post at Wesu Ga before they were quickly flushed out and killed in a short but fierce engagement.

On 5th March the Japanese intensified their attacks on the American positions east and west of Walawbum, and 1st Battalion, blocking the trails to the north at Sana Ga and Nchet Ga, was engaged by small parties of Japanese trying to escape south to avoid the slow but powerful advance of the Chinese from the north.

Throughout the day Orange Combat Team of 3rd Battalion was subjected to continuous Japanese mortar fire and to sporadic attacks, which would have been all the heavier had the defenders not managed to mortar the Japanese themselves as they gathered at their forming up points, while to the north and south dive bombers directed by the Marauders' air liaison officers provided further harassment for the Japanese units. But the heaviest fighting of the day in this area occurred around the position of 3rd Battalion's I and R platoon across the river from Orange Combat Team. From early morning the platoon's position was hit by heavy Japanese mortar fire and from 0730 hours Lieutenant Weston's small command was subjected to continuous assaults, first from the north, then from the north-east and finally from the northwest. In all the unit was attacked by five assault groups. Fortunately Weston's Nisei [Japanese American] Intelligence Sergeant, Henry Gosho, was able, by listening to the shouted orders of the Japanese officers, to tell Weston where the next assault would be coming from so that the automatic weapons could be moved to meet it. But by 1100 hours the Japanese mortar fire was getting closer and more accurate and the platoon was being pressed hard on three sides. In addition ammunition was running very low. Weston requested mortar support from 3rd Battalion's command post at Lagang Ga, about 1,000 yards away, and directed some 235 rounds of 81mm into the Japanese assault units. However, the pressure finally became too heavy for the I and R platoon to sustain alone and Weston was ordered to withdraw by the Orange Combat Team commander, who covered the river crossing for him with machine-guns and a smoke barrage. Carrying two litters for their wounded comrades the platoon withdrew slowly, a Japanese attack on the withdrawal being repulsed by a squad from the platoon lining the west bank where Private Norman E Janis accounted for seven Japanese alone with his MI Carbine, while mortars and machine-guns knocked out two Nambu machine-guns the Japanese had set up to enfilade the river. Despite this last attack the platoon withdrew successfully, suffering no casualties, and with the satisfaction of having inflicted an estimated two-thirds casualties on the Japanese attacking force of about ninety men in the course of the morning's battle.

At 2nd Battalion's road block two and a half miles west of Walawbum the Japanese made their most sustained and severe attacks in their endeavours to force the Americans off their main communications route hoping to destroy them in the process if they could. The Marauders bore a constant barrage of shells throughout the day and beat off six determined Japanese attacks, but in spite of the heavy fighting, in which the Japanese suffered an estimated one hundred killed, only six casualties were inflicted upon the

Americans. Sergeant Matsumoto continued his message interception and later in the evening passed on to General Merrill the important news that 18th Division Headquarters had ordered a general withdrawal. However, Japanese pressure against 2nd Battalion increased and, after consultation with Lieutenant-Colonel McGee who explained that the unit was very short of ammunition and had had no food or water for thirty-six hours, Merrill ordered a withdrawal to Wesu Ga, where the battalion was to pick up supplies before moving south to join 3rd Battalion, which held the high ground on the east bank of the Numpyek river and thereby dominated the Japanese in Walawbum and effectively prevented movement on the Kamaing road. At midnight 2nd Battalion began moving out of its position with Captain Evan Darlington and the leading scouts, wary of booby traps, driving a mule ahead of the column. It was fortunate that they did for after only a short distance the mule was killed in an extensive booby-trapped area.

Tanaka's decision to withdraw was forced upon him by the slow but relentless pressure of the Chinese Provisional Tank Group, under Colonel Rothwell Brown. On 5th March after some hours of very heavy going the tanks broke out on to the track running from Wesu Ga to Maingkwan, and immediately became engaged with a body of Japanese of about company strength. In fact, the Chinese armoured unit had unwittingly bumped into and begun to attack Tanaka's Divisional Headquarters, and by so doing had put themselves in a position between him and his 56th Regiment. What further added to Tanaka's problems was that the Chinese tanks were operating along the track he had designated as the route for 55th Infantry Regiment's assault on the Marauder positions. Instead of the assault of 55th and 56th Regiments going in in echelon as he had intended they were forced to attack more or less in column, one behind the other. The 56th, at the point of assault, as has been shown, was making little progress in any case.

As a result of Brown's advance and the lack of success at Walawbum Tanaka decided to abandon his attacks on the US positions, to withdraw his troops south along a Japanese built trail some distance to the west of the Kamaing road, and to reestablish an east-west defensive line further down the Hukawng valley. On 6th March the fighting reached its peak as Tanaka manoeuvred to disengage his division from between the Chinese 22nd Division in the north and the Marauders' road block to the south.

Earlier that day Merrill had moved his command post to the airstrip at Lagang Ga and together with the 2nd Battalion and elements of 1st Battalion caught the worst artillery shelling the 5307th had so far taken from the Japanese. The Marauders dug in furiously to avoid this bombardment as the War Diary explains:

"Some didn't have foxholes and between rounds the dirt flew as they dug with helmets, bayonets and mess gear. Few men had shovels. Any available would have sold for $100.00 each at least."

In the middle of the artillery barrage a private from the first battalion, still digging his foxhole, found himself staring into the eyes of two Japanese soldiers some six feet away. Somehow he managed to avoid their grenades, the explosions of which bought in several men from the 2nd Battalion's Pioneer and Demolition platoon who quickly killed the two enemy infiltrators. This action, only some fifty yards from Merrill's Command Post, caused considerable excitement and a great deal of indiscriminate firing. At about 1600 hours Colonel Brown's Chinese tank unit met up with the Marauders at Wesu Ga where Merrill had a conference with the battalion commander of the Chinese 113th Regiment which had come to relieve the 5307th. Merrill decided that he had effectively carried out Stilwell's directive and ordered the Marauders to withdraw from their positions at midnight. His intention was to circle south once more and to cut the road again nearer Kamaing at Chanmoi, while the Chinese continued their slow but steady advance.

Meanwhile, in the area held by Orange Combat Team the bloodiest fighting of the Marauders' first operation was about to begin. Earlier in the day Khaki Combat Team of 3rd Battalion had moved down from its positions guarding the airstrip at Lagang Ga and had taken up a defensive position to the left of Major Lew's Orange Combat Team at a point where the Numpyek river makes a sharp turn, and where Khaki Combat Team could therefore act as a flank guard. Just after dawn the Japanese began sending a steady stream of mortar fire on to Orange Combat Team's positions, probably in order to cover the withdrawal of part of their main force units through Walawbum. The Marauders were well dug in, however, with their positions strongly reinforced by logs and were not particularly discomfited when the Japanese added medium artillery fire to their mortar barrage. Indeed, the Japanese themselves suffered heavy casualties when the Orange Mortar Teams hit their concentration area behind the village at the moment when several trucks were unloading, one 81 mm mortar shell scoring a direct hit on a Japanese lorry loaded with troops. Much of the success of the mortars' fire can be attributed to a Sergeant Andrew B Pung who courageously directed fire from a precarious position thirty feet up in a tree on his platoon perimeter, until a tree burst left him stunned and deafened for several days. The Marauders also managed to locate the Japanese artillery and direct aircraft dive bomb attacks against it, but in spite of this the Japanese mortars and gunners intensified their fire and the Americans braced themselves for the expected assault. At 1715 the attack came. Two companies following each other in extended formation and with heavy fire support began to cross the river, their officers waving swords and prodding stragglers along. Except for their mortar's bombardment the Marauders did not open fire until the Japanese were within forty yards. Then all weapons opened up tearing huge gaps in the Japanese lines: "The river was suddenly full of bodies and still the Japs charged on." Two heavy machine-guns, low on the river bank with clear fields of fire were especially effective sweeping back and forth across the river, each firing 5,000 rounds in the course of the attack. On the flanks the Japanese pressed forward and a desperate call for ammunition went to Khaki Combat Team, but before it could arrive the Japanese attack faltered and then fell back leaving behind 400 dead and dying. The Marauders, well-entrenched as they were, suffered not one man killed and only seven wounded.

At midnight 3rd Battalion withdrew to Wesu Ga, in accordance with Merrill's earlier decision. The next morning the leading elements of the Chinese 38th Division moving up to take over the Marauders' position bumped into a patrol of the 1st Battalion, 5307th and, not recognising the American's combat helmets nor apparently being aware of the recognition signal, started a brief engagement in which, before it could be stopped, three Chinese were severely wounded. Shortly after this the Chinese entered Walawbum against virtually no opposition. Later that day Merrill informed his officers that the first phase of the operation was over, and that the intended move to Chanmoi was cancelled as the 38th Division was already on the move in that direction. His final comment was:

"Our new mission will be made known to us soon. Please convey to your men General Stilwell's and my congratulations for a fine piece of work. Get rested and re-equipped as soon as possible and be ready to move on our next operation in three days."

With the link-up between the Chinese and the Marauders a limited success had been achieved but what Stilwell had desired was a decisive victory. From his Headquarters on 8th March it seemed as if there was a possibility that this could be achieved. He was unaware, because of communication problems, of Merrill's action in withdrawing the Marauders, and as far as he was concerned his forces (with the 22nd Chinese Division moving down from the north and west, the 38th Division with the Tank Unit in the east, and the 5307th still in position opposite Walawbum) would be able to squeeze and crush the 18th Division to death. However, the co-ordinated effort as planned by Stilwell did not come off for not only were communications between him and his field commanders very often very poor, but on most occasions the various individual units were unaware of each others' movements or positions. Co-ordination in these circumstances was simply not feasible and this factor, together with the notoriously slow advance of the Chinese Divisions, enabled Tanaka to extricate his troops from a potentially very dangerous situation. However, as a result of this operation the greater part of the Hukawng valley was in Allied hands.

As for the Marauders, in their first operation they had killed about 800 enemy soldiers, helped, with the Chinese, to force a major Japanese withdrawal and had opened the way to the Moguang river corridor leading directly to the Irrawaddy valley. In the process they had lost eight men killed, thirty-seven wounded, and 179 evacuated because of injuries and sickness. It was a start to their operations in Burma of which they could be proud.

THE RESCUERS
Jon E. Lewis

The origins of SAS counter-terrorism in urban centres date back to the "Keeni Meeni" (Swahili for moving unseen like a snake) period in Aden, during which the major commanding A Squadron SAS set up a Close Quarter Battle Course for a selected team of troopers. Thereafter, the evolution of SAS Counter-Revolutionary Warfare (CRW) proceeded almost by accident; during a period in the early 1970s when the Regiment found itself without an active campaign it offered its service to the British government as trainers of bodyguards for VIPs. The government saw this as a means of raising revenue, and hired out the Regiment to overseas heads of state. At the same time, at the Hereford HQ of 22 SAS, Bradbury Lines (later rechristened Stirling Lines in honour of the Regiment's founder), a special house was constructed to train marksmen in the skills of shooting gunmen in the close confines of a room without hitting VIPs or other hostages. Formally called the Close Quarter Battle House (CQB), it is more usually known as "the Killing House". (One exercise involves a trooper sitting amongst dummy terrorists, while other troopers burst in and riddle the dummies with live rounds). To maintain and improve the Regiment's new skill a permanent CRW Wing was set up. This remained a modest affair until the Munich massacre in September 1972, when seven Palestinians from "Black September" seized the dormitory occupied by Israeli Olympic athletes, killing two and taking nine as hostage. The West German government agreed to allow the gunmen and hostages safe passage out of the country, but as the party moved through Munich airport German security forces opened fire. In the wild gunbattle that followed all the hostages were killed. European governments became alarmed about their ability to deal with terrorism. The West Germans themselves responded by setting up Grenzschutzgruppe 9 *(GSG9), an elite counter-terrorist unit. Britain, meanwhile, turned to the SAS, who were given the resources needed to expand the CRW Wing to a cadre consisting of one officer and four instructors, who in turn would be responsible for teaching all aspects of counter-terrorist work to all troopers. In addition, a CRW team of about twenty troopers, drawn on rota from the four operational Sabre squadrons, was to be available at immediate notice to deal with any hostage or terrorist situation.*

In the aftermath of Munich, the SAS quickly established links with the CRW groups of other Western nations, including Germany's GSG9. These links would benefit both units at Mogadishu Airport in 1977 and London in 1980.

THEIR TENSE FACES blackened with camouflage paint, the commandos of the crack German anti-terrorist squad GSG9 edged slowly through the dark tropical night to the rear of the Boeing 737. Some held automatic pistols, others the Heckler & Koch MP5A2 sub-machine gun. One group of GSG9 edged to take up position under the Boeing's wings and nose, another crouched beneath its tail plane. Ladders were propped gently against the aircraft, and magnetic charges placed around the passenger doors. In readiness by the ladders waited two men from Britain's 22 SAS Regiment on temporary attachment to GSG9. The grim faced leader of GSG9, Ulrich Wegener, watched all these preparations with anticipation. Many questions racing through his mind. But one question looped and looped – could he get all the 79 hostages and crew off the hijacked airliner alive? Or would it turn into another massacre like Munich?

Wegener had commanded GSG9 from its creation in 1972, and had striven from the outset to make GSG9, recruited from the border police, an elite amongst CRW units. Rigorously selected (75 per cent of candidates fail entry) and trained, GSG9 men were also equipped with some of the most sophisticated weapons in the world, Model 19.357 Magnum handguns and Heckler & Koch MP5A2 sub-machine guns, the latter often in its MP5SD silenced version. After years of painstaking rehearsal for the real thing, GSG9 was now having the chance to prove its value – the storming of a hijacked jet on the runway of Mogadishu airport on 18 October 1977.

Five days before, at 1300 hours on 13 October, Lufthansa

Flight LH181 had lifted off the runway at Majorca's Palma airport and set course for southern France. It never reached its destination. Four Palestinian liberationists, two men and two women, had smuggled guns aboard in their baggage and had proceeded to hijack the plane in mid-flight. Their principal object was to force the West German authorities to release members of the armed revolutionary organization, Baader-Meinhof. The Palestinians also demanded a £9 million ransom.

A wild career across the skies of Europe, the Middle East and the Horn of Africa then followed as the Palestinians sought a safe haven. Meanwhile, a minister of the West German government together with a member of GSG9 had flown to London. The minister wanted Britain to use its influence in Dubai, where the hijacked aircraft was about to land, to ensure diplomatic clearance for GSG9; the representative from GSG9 considered that the SAS might have some useful equipment and knowledge. It quickly became obvious to all that an SAS team attached to GSG9 for the duration of the hijack would be a distinct advantage. The two SAS men selected were Major Alistair Morrison, MC, then second-in-command of 22 SAS, and Sergeant Barry Davies, BEM, who commanded the CT sniper group. With them went a collection of "flash-bangs", the SAS-invented magnesium-based concussion grenades which have the shock effect of stunning the enemy for valuable seconds.

Morrison and Davies flew out to Dubai, where they found Wegener and two of his men under virtual arrest. No sooner was this problem sorted out, than the hijacked aircraft flew on to the Republic of Yemen, where it for a time enjoyed sanctuary. Then the leader of the Palestinian gang, Mahmoud, killed the captain of the airliner, Jürgen Schumann, for communicating with the security forces. Now flown by the co-pilot, the Boeing proceeded to Somalia on 17 October. Wegener and the two SAS men followed. Time, however, was running out for the hostages.

At Mogadishu, Mahmoud threatened to blow up the aircraft unless all his demands were met. To emphasize his seriousness he threw the body of Schumann onto the tarmac. From that moment on there was no possibility of a peaceful outcome. As a ruse to gain a few precious hours the negotiators told Mahmoud that 11 Baader-Meinhof members were being released. Even as Mahmoud was given this misinformation the main body of GSG9 arrived from Turkey and Wegener began putting the operation to storm the airliner, codenamed "Magic Fire" and based on a plan by Morrison and Davies, into motion.

At 0100 hours on 18 October, GSG9 marksmen and troopers armed with grenade launchers moved out into the desert. Morrison and Davies began preparing their "fireworks". The operation began at 0150. While two hijackers on the flight deck were kept talking by the control tower, the assault teams and the two SAS men moved into their positions. At 0207, 23 minutes before Mahmoud's final deadline, a flaming oil drum was rolled onto the runway in front of the aircraft. Ladders were placed against the doors and magnetic charges carefully put into place. Morrison and Davies climbed silently onto the wing and along to the emergency passenger door. As the terrorists watched the fire, there was a massive explosion. The passenger doors at the rear and front of the aircraft were blown in. So was the emergency door above the port wing. Through this the SAS men threw in their flash-bangs which exploded with a deafening roar. The GSG9 assault teams waited a second or two then kicked in the passenger doors and stormed into the aircraft. A fierce gun battle followed as GSG9 troopers neutralized the Palestinians at the front and rear of the plane. Mahmoud flung two grenades that exploded harmlessly under the seats before being cut down by a burst from a Heckler & Koch. One of the women Palestinians ran into a lavatory, where she was shot in the head by Wegener. As Wegener and the SAS men had guessed, the hostages, strapped in their seats, would be safe below the line of fire. No hostages were killed in the exchange. Of the Palestinians, three were killed, one was taken prisoner. One GSG9 trooper was slightly wounded. The storming of the aircraft had taken just five minutes.

On their return to the 22 SAS camp at Hereford, Morrison and Davies extolled the virtues of the Heckler & Koch MP5A2 that they had just witnessed in action. Tests confirmed its superiority over the American Ingram sub-machine gun used by the SAS CT teams, and it became the choice of the Regiment. In addition to firing at a rate of up to 650 rpm, the 9 mm Heckler & Koch MP5A3 can, if need be, fire single shots. It is light (2 kg) and short (32.5 cm). The first time the "Hockler" was used in action by the SAS was just three years later, during the Iranian Embassy siege.

Number 16 Princes Gate, home of the Iranian embassy, overlooks the peaceful green expanse of London's Kensington Gardens. At 11.25am on the morning of Wednesday 30 April 1980, this leafy tranquillity was rudely shattered as six men wearing shamags sprayed No. 16 with bullets and stormed through the front doors. The gunmen – Faisal, Hassan, Shai, Makki, Ali and Salim – were members of Mohieddin al Nasser Martyr Group, an Arab group seeking the liberation of Khuzestan from Ayatollah Khomeini's Iran. The siege of Princes Gate had begun.

The police were on the scene almost immediately, alerted by an emergency signal by Trevor Lock, and were soon followed by Scotland Yard specialist units including C13, the anti-terrorist squad, and D11, the elite blue beret marksmen. The building was surrounded, and Scotland Yard hastily began putting in motion its siege negotiation machinery.

While no siege is ever the same as the one before or after it, most follow a definite pattern: in stage one, the authorities try to pacify the gunmen (usually with such provisions as cigarettes and food), and allow the release of ideological statements; in stage two, the hostage-takers drop their original demands, and begin negotiating their own escape; stage three is the resolution.

The Princes Gate siege moved very quickly to stage one, with Salim, the head Arab gunman announcing his demands over the telephone just after 2.35 pm: autonomy and human rights for the people of Khuzestan, and the release of 91 Arab prisoners held in Iranian jails. If his demands were not met he would blow up the Embassy, hostages and all, at noon the following day.

The SAS meanwhile had been alerted about the siege within

minutes of its start. Dusty Gray, an ex-SAS sergeant now a Metropolitan Police dog handler, telephoned the Officers' Mess at Bradbury Lines, the SAS's HQ next to the River Wye in Hereford, and said that the SAS would probably be required at the Iranian Embassy, where gunmen had taken over. That night SAS troopers from B Squadron left for London in Range Rovers, arriving at a holding area in Regent's Park Barracks in the early hours of Thursday morning. The official authority from the Ministry of Defence approving the move of the SAS teams to London arrived at Bradbury Lines some hours after they had already left.

Over the next few days the Metropolitan Police continued their "softly, softly" negotiating approach, while trying to determine exactly how many hostages were in the Embassy and where they were located. Scotland Yard's technical squad, C7, installed microphones in the chimney and walls of No. 16, covering the noise by faking Gas Board repairs at neighbouring Enismore Gardens. Gradually it became clear that there were about 25 hostages (as they discovered at the end of the siege, the exact count was 26), most of them Iranian embassy workers. Also hostage were PC Trevor Lock and two BBC sound engineers, Sim Harris and Chris Cramer. The latter, who became seriously ill with a stomach disorder, was released by the gunmen as an act of good faith. It was a bad mistake by the Arab revolutionaries: a debriefing of Cramer gave the SAS vital information about the situation inside the Embassy as they planned and trained in a new holding area only streets away from Princes Gate itself.

Inside the holding area a scale model of the Embassy had been constructed to familiarize the SAS troopers with the layout of the building they would assault if the police negotiations were to break down.

As the police negotiating team located in a forward base at No. 25 Princes Gate (of all places, the Royal School of Needlework) anticipated, the gunmen very quickly dropped their original demands. By late evening on the second day of the siege, the gunmen were requesting mediation of the siege by Arab ambassadors – and a safe passage out of the country. The British Government, under Margaret Thatcher, refused to countenance the request. To the anger of the gunmen, BBC radio news made no mention of their changed demands, the broadcast of which had been a concession agreed earlier in the day. Finally, the demands were transmitted – but the BBC got the details wrong.

For some tense moments on Saturday, the third day of the siege, it looked as though the furious Salim would start shooting. The crisis was only averted when the police promised that the BBC would put out the demands accurately that evening. The nine o'clock news duly transmitted them as its first item. The gunmen were jubilant. As they congratulated themselves, however, an SAS reconnaissance team on the roof was discovering a way into No. 16 via an improperly locked skylight. Next door, at No. 18, the Ethiopian Embassy, bricks were being removed from the dividing wall, leaving only plaster for an assault team to break through.

On Sunday 4 May, it began to look as though all the SAS preparation would be for nothing. The tension inside the Embassy had palpably slackened, and the negotiations seemed to be getting somewhere. The gunmen's demands were lessening all the time. Arab ambassadors had agreed to attend a meeting of their COBRA committee in order to decide who would mediate in the siege.

And then, on the morning of Bank Holiday Monday, 5 May, the situation worsened rapidly. Just after dawn the gunmen woke the hostages in a frustrated and nervous state. Bizarrely, Salim, who thought he had heard noises in the night, sent PC Lock to scout the building, to see whether it had been infiltrated. The hostages in Room 9 heard him report to Salim that there was nobody in the Embassy but themselves. Conversations among the gunmen indicated that they increasingly believed they had little chance of escape. At 11.00 am Salim discovered an enormous bulge in the wall separating the Iranian Embassy from the Ethiopian Embassy. Extremely agitated, he moved the male hostages into the telex room at the front of the building on the second floor. Forty minutes later, PC Lock and Sim Harris appeared on the first-floor balcony and informed the police negotiator that their captors would start killing hostages if news of the

Arab mediators was not forthcoming immediately. The police played for time, saying that there would be an update on the midday BBC news. The bulletin, however, only served to anger Salim, announcing as it did that the meeting between COBRA and the Arab ambassadors had failed to agree on the question of who would mediate. Incensed, Salim grabbed the telephone link to the police, and announced: "You have run out of time. There will be no more talking. Bring the ambassador to the phone or I will kill a hostage in forty-five minutes."

Outside, in the police forward post, the minutes ticked away with no news from the COBRA meeting, the last negotiating chip of the police. Forty-two minutes, forty-three minutes . . . The telephone rang. It was Trevor Lock to say that the gunmen had taken a hostage, the Iranian Press Attaché, and were tying him to the stairs. They were going to kill him. Salim came on to the phone shouting that the police had deceived him. At precisely 1.45 pm the distinct sound of three shots was heard from inside the embassy.

The news of the shooting was immediately forwarded to the SAS teams waiting at their holding area. They would be used after all. Operation Nimrod – the relief of the Embassy – was on. The men checked and cleaned their weapons, 9 mm Browning HP automatic pistols and Heckler & Koch ("Hockler") MP5A3 sub-machine guns. The order for the assault teams to move into place was shortly forthcoming.

At 6.50 pm, with tension mounting, the gunmen announced their demands again, with the codicil that a hostage would be shot every forty-five minutes until their demands were met. Another burst of shots was heard. The door of the Embassy opened, and a body was flung down the steps. (The body belonged to the Press Attaché shot earlier in the day. The new burst of shots was a scare tactic.) The police phoned into the Embassy's first floor, where the telephone link with the gunmen was situated. They seemed to cave in to Salim's demands, assuring him that they were not tricking him, and that a bus would be arriving in minutes to take the gunmen to Heathrow Airport, from where they would fly to the Middle East. But by talking on the phone Salim had signalled his wherabouts to the SAS teams who had taken up their start positions on the roof, and in the two buildings either side of No. 16, the Ethiopian Embassy and the Royal College of Physicians. At around this time, formal responsibility – via a handwritten note – passed from the Metropolitan Police to the SAS.

Suddenly, as the world watched Princes Gate on TV, black-clad men wearing respirators appeared on the front balconies and placed "frame-charges" against the armoured-glass window. There was an enormous explosion. The time was exactly 7.23 pm. At the back of the building and on the roof, the assault teams heard the order "Go. Go. Go." Less than 12 minutes had elapsed since the body of the Press Attaché had appeared on the Embassy steps.

The assault on the building came from three sides, with the main assault from the rear, where three pairs of troopers abseiled down from the roof. One of the first party accidentally swung his foot through an upper storey window, thereby alerting Salim to their line of assault. The pair dropped to the ground and prepared to fight their way in, while another pair landed on the balcony, broke the window and threw in stun grenades. A third pair also abseiled down, but one of them became entangled in the ropes, which meant that the rear assault could not use frame charges to blow-in the bullet proof glass. Instead a call sign from a rear troop in the garden sledge-hammered the French windows open, with the troopers swarming into the building on the ground floor. They "negotiated" a gunman in the front hall, cleared the cellars, and then raced upwards to the second floor and the telex room, where the male hostages were held by three gunmen. Meanwhile the pair who had come in through the rear first floor balcony encountered PC Lock grappling with Salim, the head gunman, who had been about to fire at an SAS trooper at the window, and shot the gunman dead.

Almost simultaneous with the rear assault, the frontal assault group stormed over the balcony on the first floor, lobbing in stun grenades through the window broken by their frame charges. Amid gushing smoke they entered and also moved towards the telex room. Another SAS team broke into the building through the plaster division left after the bricks had been removed from the wall with the Ethiopian Embassy.

Outside, at the front, the SAS shot CS gas cartridges into an upstairs room where one of the gunmen was believed to be hiding. This room caught fire, the flames spreading quickly to other rooms. (The trooper caught in the abseil rope suffered burns at this point, but was then cut free and rejoined the assault.)

The SAS converged at the telex room, as planned. The gunmen had started shooting the hostages. The Assistant Press Attaché was shot and killed, and the Chargé d'Affaires wounded before the SAS broke in. By then the gunmen were lying on the floor, trying in the smoke and noise to pass themselves off as hostages. What then happened is the subject of some dispute, but the outcome was that the SAS shot two of the gunmen dead. Afterwards, some of the hostages said that the gunmen tried to give themselves up, but were killed anyway. In the event, only one gunman escaped with his life, the one guarding the women in Room 9. The women refused to identify him as a terrorist, and he was handed over to the police. After a brief assembly at No. 14 for emotional congratulations from Home Secretary William Whitelaw, the SAS teams sped away in rented Avis vans. Behind them the Embassy was a blaze of fire and smoke.

The breaking of the siege had taken just 17 minutes. Of the 20 hostages in the building at the time of the SAS assault, 19 were brought out alive. The SAS suffered no casualties. Although mistakes were made in the assault (part of the main assault went in via a room which contained no gunmen and was blocked off from the rest of the Embassy), the speed, daring, and adaptability of the SAS assault proved the regiment an elite amongst the counter-revolutionary forces of the world.

THE SEIZURE OF WALCHEREN

Hilary St. George Saunders

Since their foundation in 1664 the Royal Marines have constituted the main body of infantry serving aboard the ships of the Royal Navy. They were largely overlooked at the beginning of World War II. A Royal Marine Division, formed in 1940 as an attempt to make amends, languished in the UK until 1942, when Mounbatten realised that it was a ready made source for the new Commando units, especially since the War Office was opposed to drawing off more Home Forces volunteers to raise additional Army Commandos. The Admiralty agreed that a Royal Marine Commando force could be formed from volunteers from the RM Division and in February 1942 it came into being at Deal in Kent, with Lt Colonel Picton Phillips as CO. The various Royal Marine Commando units (popularly known as the "Green Berets") served in, amongst other operations, the Dieppe landings of August 1942 – in which Picton Phillips was killed – Sicily 1943, Normandy 1944, Burma 1944–45, and in the November 1944 seizure of the island of Walcheren in occupied Holland.

Above a fireplace in the Library of the House of Commons there hangs a German battle map. Upon it is displayed the formidable defences of the island of Walcheren. The map is a relic of one of the fiercest actions of the war, and it was brought to its present home by Commander R. N. Prior, who was admitted to the Distinguished Service Order for his gallantry at Dieppe, and who subsequently for a time represented the Aston Division of Birmingham. The seizure of the island was carried out by No. 41 (Royal Marine) Commando under Lieutenant-Colonel E. C. E. Palmer, No. 47 (Royal Marine) Commando under Lieutenant-Colonel C. F. Phillips, D.S.O., and No. 48 (Royal Marine) Commando under Lieutenant-Colonel J. L. Moulton, D.S.O. They formed, together with No. 4 Commando under Lieutenant-Colonel R. W. P. Dawson, D.S.O. (the Loyal Regiment), the 4th Special Service Brigade under Brigadier B. W. Leicester, D.S.O.

By the end of September [1944] the brigade had been withdrawn from active operations in France to begin training for the assault on Walcheren. No. 46 (Royal Marine) Commando, whose strength in the battle of Normandy had been reduced from three hundred and fifty to two hundred, was replaced by No. 4 Commando.

The great port of Antwerp, the finest in Europe, had been seized by the 11th Armoured Division, as the climax of their swift and irresistible advance from the Seine. The British and American armies now possessed a sea base large enough to handle their supplies. Moreover, it was undamaged; the local Belgian resistance movement had seen to that. But – and here was the difficulty – Antwerp lies some forty miles from the mouth of the Scheldt, and both banks of that majestic river between Antwerp and the sea were still held in force by the enemy. The port therefore could not be used until the approaches to it could be freed; and until the port could be used, the invasion of Germany proper could not be begun. "The Allied need for Antwerp had become imperative," states Field-Marshal Viscount Montgomery. "In the 21st Army Group the administrative machine was working on a narrow enough margin, while in the American Army the maintenance situation had become extremely grave . . . It was thus necessary to devote the whole of our resources into getting Antwerp working at once, and I had to shut down on other offensive operations . . . until this object was achieved." The task entrusted to the 4th Special Service Brigade was, therefore, of the first importance.

Walcheren is shaped somewhat like a saucer, of which the rim is composed of high dunes of loose, soft sand up which infantry can scramble, but which is impassable to vehicles. There is a gap in these dunes on the western edge, and it is filled by the great dyke of Westkapelle. Behind this natural wall of sand lies the ridged Polder land of the island, a flat plain below sea level, dotted with villages and farms.

To the defences provided by nature the Germans had made formidable additions. About thirty coast defence and field batteries made up of guns of from 220 to 75 mm calibre were in position covering the north, west and south-west coasts. They were supported by concrete strong points; light anti-aircraft guns were plentiful; the beaches were heavily mined and defended on the north and south-west by three, and in places four, rows of obstacles. On the dunes above high-water mark were more mines and great fields of barbed wire. Such was the formidable fortress to be assaulted by between eight and ten thousand men of the 4th Special Service Brigade aided by two Troops of No. 10 (Inter-Allied) Commando, one Squadron of the Lothian Tank Regiment, an Assault Regiment and two Field Companies of the Royal Engineers, the 144th Pioneer Company, and the 10th Canadian Field Dressing Station. They were to be assisted by a strong naval force under the command of Captain A. F. Pugsley, D.S.O., Royal Navy, known as "T" Force. It was made up of the battleship, H.M.S. *Warspite*, the two 15-inch gun monitors H.M.S. *Erebus* and H.M.S. *Roberts*, and a support Squadron of close support landing craft.

Training for the operation was carried out on dunes near Ostend, of which the defence system, very fortunately, was almost an exact copy of that on Walcheren. Here throughout October, the combined sea and land forces rehearsed together until all knew their several parts, and many those of their comrades; for during this period a hundred Commando soldiers and marines learned to drive Weasels, tracked amphibious vehicles which, together with their kindred Buffaloes, were to take them to their objectives.

The choice of date for the attack was a problem which greatly exercised the minds of the planners. The approach by sea was a matter of great difficulty owing to the tides and the heavy swell. Local opinion considered that at that time of year – late autumn – upon only one day in three would a landing be possible even on the most sheltered part of the island, the south-west. It would be necessary to touch down before high tide, but owing to their draught the assault craft could only cross the sandbanks, placed by nature to guard the low-lying coasts, one and a half hours after low water. It was finally decided that there were two periods when conditions, which could never be favourable, would at least be possible. The first from the 1st to 4th November, the second from the 14th to 17th November.

The plan as eventually adopted comprised three phases: first, the sea dyke at Westkapelle should be breached, thus allowing the sea to enter and flood great parts of the island. The effect of this would be to hamper the movement of reserves, to drown many of the field batteries, and to enable amphibious vessels to take the seaward defences of the town in the rear. This part of the plan was put into execution almost a month before the assault. On the 3rd October, two hundred and forty-seven aircraft of Bomber Command dropped 1,262.9 tons of high explosive and 6.7 tons of incendiaries on the dyke at Westkapelle, and on the defences near at hand. The breach effected by this and subsequent attacks was three hundred and eighty yards wide; a second breach was also blown in the dyke just north of Flushing. The sea poured in, flooding all the central part of Walcheren, and for a time it was hoped that the Germans would be compelled to withdraw the greater part of their defending forces. The most formidable batteries of all, however, planted upon or in the Westkapelle dyke itself, remained well above the level of the floods. Within the circle of the dunes was a scene of waterlogged desolation. Patches of brown or black soil strewn with rusting wire and debris thrust themselves out from dun-coloured waters. Further inland, half submerged houses reared their red-tiled roofs, their occupants moving in sullen misery in small boats above their sunken fields. The island, which even on a day of sunshine wears an inhospitable air, now resembled early Dutch pictures of the Flood.

The second phase provided for heavy attacks by the Royal Air Force on coastal defences, the day before the assault; on the day itself these would be still further bombarded by the Navy and by bombers of the 2nd Tactical Air Force. Four squadrons of rocket-firing Typhoons would be in the air throughout D-day, ready to attack any target indicated. Following the preliminary air attacks, the third phase would begin. The three Royal Marine Commandos in amphibious vehicles would pass through the gap blown in the dyke and advance upon the shore, while No. 4 Commando would assault Flushing to the south. Once the Special Service Brigade were ashore and had seized their objectives, they would be immediately reinforced by a brigade of the 52nd Lowland Division.

The detailed plan for the landings was for three Troops of No. 41 (Royal Marine) Commando to go ashore on the north shoulder of the gap to cover the main landings by clearing the area between the dyke and the western edge of Westkapelle village. The remainder of the Commando, strengthened by two Troops of No. 10 (Inter-Allied) Commando, were then to land from Buffaloes and Weasels, launched from tank landing craft, clear Westkapelle and push north. No. 48 (Royal Marine) Commando, carried to battle in the same way, was to land south of the gap and move south as far as Zouteland; and No. 47 (Royal Marine) Commando, landing in the same place, was to push towards Flushing until they met with No. 4 Commando, detailed to capture that port. To support the advance of No. 41 (Royal Marine) Commando, tanks and flail tanks were to land in the first flight. Artillery support would be lavish and would be provided by the many British and Canadian batteries established in Breskens on the other side of the Scheldt opposite Walcheren. Such was the plan, and on the 1st November, 1944, it was put into execution.

On the day before, the four Commandos were depressed by the news that the weather was likely to be too thick for aircraft to fly. This, it was realized, would prove a grave handicap, for the preliminary air bombardment would not be able to take place, and that of the Navy would be hampered by a lack of spotting aircraft. Nevertheless, it was decided to sail and to leave it to the naval and Commando leaders on the spot, Pugsley and Leicester, to decide at the last moment whether or not to turn back. It was known that the batteries had been already very heavily bombed, and it was hoped – vainly as it turned out – that they had been destroyed.

Day dawned on the 1st November with a heavy mist on all the Dutch and Belgian airfields. No aircraft could take off. At Walcheren, however, conditions were better; the sky was overcast but clearing, and sea conditions were favourable. As the morning wore on the weather improved somewhat, and though the preliminary air bombardment could not take place, the Typhoons of 84 Group arrived punctually at H-hour and before nightfall had flown four hundred and twenty sorties.

Force "T" sailed from Ostend at 03.15 hours and at 07.00 hours sighted the tall lighthouse tower on Westkapelle. *Warspite*, *Erebus* and *Roberts* opened fire, while the close support craft moved into position. The German batteries north and south of the dyke immediately replied, and it was at once obvious that the preliminary bombing had failed to silence them. Their salvoes fell among the rocket-firing craft and the tank landing craft carrying the amphibians in which the Special Service Brigade was to go ashore. As H-hour, 09.45 hours approached, six of the support landing craft with Royal Marine gunnery officers on board closed the beaches and opened fire. The range was at first two thousand yards, but it fell rapidly to eight hundred, and fire was brought to bear on two batteries, W.15 immediately to the north of the gap, and W.13 to the south. Three rocket craft then moved still closer in to sear the beaches with flame. All were heavily engaged by the German defences. L. C. F. 37 received a direct hit which blew up a hundred thousand rounds of 2-pounder and Oerlikon ammunition and destroyed the vessel literally in a flash. Twenty-nine of her crew survived, though the enemy fired on the rafts and floats supporting them. The support craft maintained their fire with great resolution and suffered many casualties, but it was soon seen to be "disappointing work against the heavy concrete of the enemy pillboxes." Neither the bombs of the Royal Air Force, nor the shells of the *Warspite* and the monitors – ill-directed because of lack of observation – had hit these formidable defence works. The support craft came so close inshore that they were engaged by small arms fire, some of which entered the sighting ports, killing the gun layers behind. By the afternoon casualties among these craft were such that only six out of twenty-five remained fit for action, and two of these presently developed engine trouble. Of those on board, a hundred and seventy-two officers and men had been killed and two hundred and ten wounded. The close support fire, most gallantly maintained and nourished, had been a failure. Its place was taken soon after H-hour by attacks carried out by the rocket-firing Typhoons on selected targets.

Behind these bombarding ships the tank landing craft bearing the Commandos wallowed and rolled in the uneasy sea, spray breaking over their blunt bows. This is what the scene looked like to Lieutenant-Colonel J. B. Hillsman, waiting in an Alligator to go ashore at the head of the 8th Canadian Surgical Unit.

"The landing craft tank were tossing about in three parallel lines, and far to the north we could see the *Warspite*, *Erebus* and *Roberts* steaming along in staggered formation. The dim outline of Walcheren came slowly into view. Steadily the ships drove on until the gap could clearly be seen. I wondered what the Germans were doing and hoped they had all gone to the diversionary attacks which had now been in progress for some hours. The silence was oppressive as each lived with his own thoughts.

"Suddenly from the *Warspite* a cloud of dirty brown smoke erupted. Seconds later a dull rumble and columns of smoke arose from the island. The *Erebus* and *Roberts* followed suit, and broadside after broadside was poured into the north batteries. There still wasn't a sound from the island. Coming up from the right, parallel to shore and about a thousand yards off the island, we could now see the support craft with their rocket guns. The moan of the rockets could plainly be heard and the batteries on the south shore of the gap were soon wreathed in smoke and dust. Still not a sound from the island. Our spirits rose. It looked so easy.

"We were getting close in now and the landing craft tank in front of us turned out of line to go further back. It was our specially equipped hospital ship and we didn't want her in the muck yet. As it passed us, it struck a sea mine. There was a tremendous explosion and the entire ship was hurled into the air. It settled rapidly. Men jumped into the sea. Some were picked up by the following craft. Others floated face down in their lifebelts.

"Pin-points of light sparkled from the south batteries. The Germans were opening up at last. The whole line of support craft broke into flame and smoke. Ships blew up and were swallowed in one gulp. Others drifted aimlessly around out of control."

In these circumstances it was scarcely surprising that the touch-down of the infantry landing craft carrying the leading troops of No. 41 (Royal Marine) Commando was twenty-seven minutes late, so that those assaulting the north of the gap landed almost at the same time as No. 48 (Royal Marine) Commando south of the gap. The landing took place under heavy fire, two infantry landing craft being hit on the run-in. Once ashore, "B" Troop of No. 41 (Royal Marine) Commando took up a position on the edge of the village of Westkapelle and opened with small arms fire on strong point W.15, which it had thus been able to take in the rear. "S" Troop set up their machine guns to cover the southern fringe of the village.

The remainder of the Commando, including its headquarters, came ashore in their amphibians, and at once made for the village, meeting with fire only from the lighthouse tower on its eastern edge. This was returned and the tower was also engaged by some tanks of the 1st Lothian Regiment which had now got ashore. By 11.15 hours the village of Westkapelle itself was in its hands.

The large German battery at Domburg at once turned its attention away from the naval forces to the village. Its fire was quelled about 13.00 hours by rocket-firing Typhoons and finally silenced by the 15-inch shells of the *Warspite*. Before this happened, the Commando had begun to push steadily, if slowly, towards Domburg, the dunes upon their left, the flooded Polders upon their right. The speed of the advance was checked by numerous bodies of Germans eager to surrender, and it was not until after nightfall that the main crossroads in Domburg was reached. The Commando fought on in the glare of blazing houses still on fire from the naval bombardment.

Major Peter Wood established "P" Troop in the centre of the village with "Y" Troop covering their right flank as far as a dark mass of woodland which, now that the day was over, it was impossible to reconnoitre. Behind them "X" Troop had been held up in the dunes by a fiercely defended enemy post north-west of the village. Major P. K. Brind Sheridan led them to the assault and was badly wounded. Attempts to rescue him, which continued for twelve hours, were unsuccessful, and the strong point did not fall until 08.00 hours on the following morning, when he was found to be dead. No. 41 (Royal Marine) Commando had accomplished its task. So, too, but with even heavier losses, had No. 48 (Royal Marine) Commando south of the gap.

The first flight, consisting of "B," "X" and "Y" Troops in three tank landing craft, touched down at 10.10 hours, their Colonel being one of the first ashore. Though shelled on the way in, their casualties had not been heavy and they found their first objective, a row of concrete pillboxes, on the southern shoulder of the gap, undefended. The second, the radar station close by, was also empty. The second flight, with "A" and "X" Troops and the Machine Gun Troop on board, coming in ten minutes later, did not fare so well. One of their landing craft was hit on the way in, the shell breaking the ramp and smashing the vehicle carrying the machine guns. The best exit from the beach was soon blocked by a Buffalo, hit as it was passing through it. Shellfire was becoming heavier, and several more Buffaloes and a number of Weasels were destroyed. The advance, however, continued, and presently the leading Troops of the Commando came in contact with the defenders of strong point W.13, a battery which was causing much harm to shipping. Intense machine gun fire met Major de Stacpoole and "Y" Troop as they went in to attack. They were all killed or wounded before they could reach the enemy. Until artillery could be brought to bear upon a position embedded in concrete, further assaults would assuredly suffer a like fate; but to call for gunfire was the difficulty. The forward observing officer, Captain Blunt (Royal Artillery) was himself working his wireless set, as his two wireless operators had been hit, but the support craft with which he was in touch, was so badly damaged that it was unable to fire. Another forward observing officer, Captain A. D. Davis (Royal Artillery), was, however, able to direct two salvoes from the monitor H.M.S. *Roberts* before he and his wireless operator were killed by a mortar bomb. The third observer, Captain Skelton (Royal Canadian Artillery) had no wireless set, and had therefore only very uncertain contact with his regiment. The tanks of the 1st Lothian Regiment, of which only eight were still serviceable, were bogged in the flooded ruins of Westkapelle and could not bring their guns to bear, and to cap all, the Commando's rear link Weasel, containing a more powerful wireless set, was stuck on the beach and was out of touch with Brigade Headquarters. There was but one thing to do. Colonel Moulton himself went back to the brigade and eventually made contact with the artillery.

"Z" Troop was ordered to attack, but half the men composing it were caught by mortar fire and killed or wounded. Their places were taken by "B" Troop, and from 15.40 hours to 16.00 hours the whole fire power of the 2nd Canadian Divisional Artillery was turned upon the battery, and the garrison was further disorganized by an attack from R.A.F. Typhoons firing rockets. As they roared away, "B" Troop leapt to the assault, captured the command post, silenced the guns, and took thirty prisoners. Pushing on in the now gathering darkness, they found and captured the Battery Commander, his second-in-command, and seventy more prisoners. Subsequent examination showed that a rocket fired by one of the Typhoons had entered a casemate of the main battery and killed all the crew at their stations.

The last of the three Royal Marine Commandos to set foot on Walcheren was No. 47, which, under heavy shellfire, came through the gap soon after 11.00 hours. By some mistake three of the landing craft beached on the north instead of the south side of the gap. This was a serious matter, for several hundred yards of swiftly running bullet-lashed water separated them from the point at which they were due to begin their advance southwards towards Flushing to link up with No. 4 Commando. "B" Troop landed in the right place, but hardly had the landing craft touched the shore, when four of their vehicles were destroyed by fire. Not until 15.30 hours was the Commando assembled beneath a high sand dune some three hundred yards south of the radar station. Seventeen out of twenty of its Buffaloes were in working order, but only three of its twenty Weasels. All the Weasels carrying wireless had been sunk or knocked out, but casualties had fortunately not been heavy.

Here, in accordance with the plan, No. 47 stayed, awaiting the capture of Zouteland by No. 48. The assault began on the following morning, after a night passed struggling to bring up stores. Weasels took them as far as the radar station, after which they were carried over steep dunes through acres of loose sand. Food was short, for of the three landing craft carrying rations and ammunition, one had been sunk by a mine, and the other two had been prevented by shelling from reaching the beach.

It had been a gruelling day, and the losses on the beaches, both in men, tanks, and vehicles, had been high. The Lothian Tank Regiment, for example, which had with it ten flail tanks, eight Avres (tanks carrying bridges), four bulldozers, and two Sherman Command tanks on board four tank landing craft, were eventually put ashore with but six of the flails, six of the Avres, the two Command tanks, and two of the bulldozers. Of these, three flail tanks, four Avres and one bulldozer very shortly fell victims to the deep bomb craters surrounding the dyke and were drowned, despite the efforts of their crews who worked up to their necks in water striving to recover them. During the night three more flail tanks met the same fate, and within twenty-four hours, therefore, there were but two Command tanks and two Avres left to support the whole force. They did so with much skill and determination; before the operation was over the Shermans had fired between them fourteen hundred rounds of 75 mm and thirty boxes of Browning machine-gun ammunition.

The first night on Walcheren passed quietly, and at dawn No. 48 (Royal Marine) Commando moved forward towards Zouteland. H.M.S. *Erebus* shelled the town and soon after 11.00 hours its garrison of a hundred and fifty surrendered. Shortly before 13.00 hours No. 47 was able to advance and presently reached the outer defences of Flushing. Here support fire was called for and also attacks from aircraft, but these were not forthcoming owing to low clouds and rain. "Q" and "Z" Troops to the left lost about twelve killed and many wounded, including Major J. T. E. Vincent; but "A" and "Y" Troops on the right, moving along the dunes close to the sea, made good progress until they came under mortar fire which wounded three of their officers. The situation remained obscure and that night No. 47 successfully beat off a counter-attack. Not until the following morning, the beginning of the third day on which the brigade was on shore, did the battery in the outer defences of Flushing fall. The very large number of shells which fell upon it seem, when they did not kill, to have dazed its garrison. Many of the prisoners taken were half out of their minds, and it was noticed that the pupils of their eyes were so dilated that the whites were almost invisible.

After the capture of this battery the enemy's resistance weakened, and grew still less when a number of German officers called upon those left in the garrison to surrender.

That evening No. 47 (Royal Marine) Commando met No. 4 Commando, which had by then captured the greater part of the town of Flushing. It had landed just before first light on the 1st November. The Commando had with it part of a Dutch Troop of No. 10 (Inter-Allied) Commando and an observing officer of the Royal Artillery, a total strength of five hundred and fifty all ranks, and they embarked in twenty landing craft which put out from the harbour of Breskens at 04.15 hours. The objectives it was to capture were distributed along the southern water front of Flushing, and were given the code names of watering-places in southern England. From west to east these were: Dover, Worthing, Hove, and Brighton. Behind these was Bexhill, the shipbuilding yards, and Eastbourne, buildings in the centre of the town. Next came the Orange Mole, with behind it Seaford and Troon; and that section of the harbour running at right angles to the sea locks was called Falmouth.

The planners had the greatest difficulty in finding a suitable beach. "Uncle" beach near the Orange Mole was a dump for rubbish and therefore most suitable for vehicles, but it was protected by underwater stakes. There were many enemy strong points in that part of Flushing, but it was believed that these could be rushed and overcome, provided that the Commando landed immediately after the preliminary bombardment had lifted. The final plan was for No. 4 Commando to go ashore on "Uncle beach in three flights, the first made up of reconnoitring elements whose duty it was to find a suitable place for climbing the dyke wall, and the second carrying the all-important landing craft obstruction clearing unit and men to form a beachhead. The third flight, which was not to come in until summoned, was to pass through the beachhead, secure the barracks between Worthing and Hove, the harbour entrance at Brighton, the park, and finally the open space at Dover.

It was a formidable programme, rendered more so by the fact that it was impossible to choose the exact spot for disembarkation. No. 4 Commando, however, were extremely well trained, and the various Troops were perfectly confident that they would be able to operate at night provided that they were accurately briefed. This was done and each man went into action having studied specially prepared maps and air photographs, and with an exact knowledge of what his individual task was to be. Lieutenant-Colonel Dawson knew his men and was well aware that their pride reposed as much on the high intellectual standard they had reached as on their knowledge of their weapons and on their great physical fitness.

Any faint hopes of achieving surprise vanished on the afternoon of the 31st October, when the Germans perceived the Buffaloes swimming down the Scheldt from Terneuzen. An attempt was made to hide them by a smoke screen but it did not stretch far enough, and the enemy, well aware of the portent of these small amphibians, began to shell Breskens heavily. Fortunately he achieved negligible results and at the appointed hour, 04.00, the leading craft slipped their moorings and edged their way out of harbour. Over the heads of their occupants screamed the shells of a fierce artillery bombardment, rendered fiercer because, the weather being execrable, the Lancasters of Bomber Command were unable to play their part. Fires were soon ablaze all over the town of Flushing, which was quickly reduced to the condition in which it had been put by Lord William Stewart and his ten frigates in 1809. Suddenly the silhouette of the windmill on the Orange Mole shewed sharp and black against a background of blazing buildings and warehouses. On went the Commando, protected by patrols of landing craft watching keenly for floating mines and one-man torpedoes.

At 05.45 hours, as the plan provided, the leading assault craft reached "Uncle" beach just as the guns ceased fire. One craft struck the underwater stakes and sank, but the others, moving to the west side of the beach, landed without mishap; the men on board scrambled over the dyke wall, cut a gap in the wire and "were winkling the Germans out of their dug-outs before a shot had been fired." White tapes were laid to mark the gap, and a signal made calling on the second flight to lose no time. They came in two by two under the direction of an officer on a landing craft who shewed them where to beach. By now those first ashore had captured a strong pillbox and a 75 mm gun and were holding Orange Street.

The new arrivals made at once for the barracks and the arsenal between Hove and Worthing. No. 2 Troop divided into two. One half captured a 50 mm gun in its emplacement close to "Uncle" beach, together with twenty-five prisoners and the area commander, and then stormed along the waterfront "from pillbox to pillbox, ably supported by fire from the 50 mm gun that it had just captured." The other half cleared the ground inland from the waterfront and by 09.00 hours was firmly established between Troon and Falmouth.

The third flight was called in at 06.30 hours and landed under heavy machine gun and 20 mm cannon fire. Nevertheless it landed successfully on the Orange Mole. One of the craft carrying the mortars and wireless equipment was sunk on an obstacle twenty yards out, but its cargo was taken ashore, cleaned and brought into action under fire.

For the rest of that morning the Germans ensconced in Brighton, the merchants' harbour west of "Uncle" beach, and in the barracks at Hove, gave a certain amount of trouble, and sharp street fighting took place. There was also much fighting round Bellamy Park, and later on outside the barracks at Hove. A Piat mounted in the local cinema fired upon the embrasures of a strong point containing a Flak-vierling (a 4-barrelled 20 mm anti-aircraft gun); and a determined policy of "mouseholing" soon achieved results. Each man had been issued with a small made-up charge, and by using these the men moved from house to house through the party walls and thus avoided advancing along streets swept with machine gun fire. At one moment half a dozen Commando soldiers were to be seen on the roof of a building hanging head downwards and flinging grenades through the window of the room beneath them. Two strong points which proved obdurate were dealt with most efficiently by Typhoons swooping low over the waterfront "like falcons."

By nightfall the town was won, and for the next two days mopping-up operations were conducted against an enemy whose resistance gradually dwindled. The garrison of a building in the Boulevard Bankert were bolted like foxes until from its pillbox entrance three officers and fifty-four other ranks of the enemy, all very shaken, emerged with their hands up. No. 4 Commando had accomplished the first landing upon a waterfront since the raid on Dieppe more than two years before. The lessons learned upon that disastrous day had been well and truly applied, and the capture of Flushing by the same Commando which had destroyed the guns at Varengeville must be hailed as a classic operation of war.

The three Royal Marine Commandos of the brigade continued the work of subduing the enemy in the west of Walcheren until at dawn on the 8th November when a battery, W. 19, at the northern end of the island was overcome with the assistance of No. 4 Commando which had moved from Flushing to the reinforcement of the Marines. This period was one of steady fighting and not a few casualties. "For me the most tragical moment in the war," records Lieutenant-Colonel Pugh, "was during the final mopping-up; a Buffalo with about thirty Commando soldiers on board met a submerged mine and blew up. There were no survivors." The Marines went doggedly about their work, accepting the surrender of the enemy when it was offered, but attacking him with skill, fire, and resolution whenever he showed a tendency to resist. In this series of individual actions the Norwegian and Belgian troops attached to the Brigade from No. 10 (Inter-Allied) Commando were prominent, especially in the clearing of the woods behind Domburg.

Progress had been slow for four reasons; the weather, which blew a full gale on the third day; the mounting number of prisoners who had to be fed and guarded; the conditions of supply; and the presence everywhere of minefields. But in the early afternoon of the 8th November, all was at length over. Walcheren was in our hands with two thousand nine hundred prisoners. The way up the Scheldt to Antwerp lay open and the door to it had been unlocked by No. 4 Commando and the three Royal Marine Commandos. Their casualties had been far from light, particularly among the ranks of No. 41, who had to deplore the death of Captain P. H. Haydon who at the age of nineteen had won admission to the Distinguished Service Order in the action at Salerno, where he was badly wounded. "Quiet and hesitant," says one of his officers, "he looked like a sixth-form schoolboy, but when in action he was concise, clear-thinking and utterly fearless." He and those who fell that week most worthily upheld the traditions of the great corps to which they belonged, and which had already visited that battlefield. For the Royal Marines were no strangers to Walcheren, and in 1809 had earned the commendation of Admiral Sir Richard Strachan, the Naval commander of the ill-fated expedition of that year. He praised them for their excellent management and discipline which had enabled them alone out of an army of forty thousand men to preserve their health while all others were dying of the ague. That same excellent management and discipline enabled the officers and men serving in the same corps to achieve a signal victory a hundred and thirty-five years later, and thus to revenge the ghosts of their ancestors, who from the shadows must surely have watched their prowess and rejoiced.

THE BATTLE OF JEBEL AKHDAR

David Smiley

The ancient Sultanate of Muscat and Oman is an arid country of climactic extremes which, according to a Persian proverb, gives the visitor a foretaste of Hell. The main importance of the country, a former British colony, lies in the accident of its geography aside the Hormuz Straits, through which pass 30 per cent of the world's crude oil. In 1954 a rebellion against the autocratic (but pro-British) Sultan, led by Ghalib, the Imam of Oman and his brother Talib, threatened to destabilize the country, and the British government decided on military support for the ruling regime fearing that a new government might block the flow to the UK. An RAF bombing campaign, however, did little to break the rebellion in its heartland, the "Green Mountain" (Jebel Akhdar), an elevated, almost inaccessible plateau where Talib had assembled a formidable guerrilla army, equipped with a modern arsenal of weaponry, including .5-inch Browning machine-guns. With the failure of the air campaign, two infantry regiments were sent to scale the Jebel but failed. A plan to drop the Parachute Regiment was cancelled; the Prime Minister felt that to send such a world famous regiment over-emphasized the importance of the situation. Consequently, 22 SAS was invoked as the only other unit likely to succeed. Lt-Col Anthony Deane-Drummond, the then commanding officer of 22 SAS, was given 15 days to round up D Squadron SAS, then in the remote jungle of Malaya finishing off the campaign the Regiment had fought there since 1950, retrain and deploy it in Oman. The Regiment arrived in the Sultanate on 18 November 1958, well before time. The following account of the Regiment's Oman campaign is by Colonel David Smiley, at the time the Sultan's British Chief-of-Staff.

A WEEK LATER they came – some eighty officers and men comprising D Squadron, under Major John Watts; they were organized in four troops, or patrols, of sixteen men each, together with Squadron Headquarters. Despite their small number they wielded formidable fire-power, with their Browning machine-guns, FN rifles and Energa grenades. We had built them a camp at Beit al Falaj, but Watts, a stocky, tough, and dedicated professional, sensibly decided to lose no time in making them familiar with their new conditions; for he realized that the steep bare rocks and sharp outlines of the Jebel would require tactics quite different from those they had learnt in the swamps and jungles of Malaya. We therefore split the squadron, sending two troops on fighting patrols among the giant slabs above Tanuf and Kamah, and the other two to join Tony Hart [a British contract officer with the Muscat Regiment] at Awabi. Men from the Sultan's Armed Forces accompanied the SAS on all their patrols, an arrangement which greatly improved the morale and fighting skill of my own soldiers, who in their turn provided the SAS with valuable local knowledge.

The need for different tactics struck the SAS forcefully and tragically on one of their first patrols in the Tanuf area. In a skirmish with the rebels one of their best NCOs ["Duke" Swindells MM] incautiously showed himself on a skyline and was shot through the heart by a sniper. This sad incident at least gave them a healthy respect for the enemy, whom they had been inclined to underestimate.

The other two troops, with Hart and some of his men, climbed from Awabi by the Hijar track to the top of the Jebel, which they reached undiscovered. They then pressed on across the plateau until they came under attack from some rebels entrenched among caves in a cliff known as the Aquabat al Dhafar; although held up, they inflicted severe punishment on the enemy without loss to themselves. While a platoon of the Muscat Regiment dug themselves in at the top of the Hijar track to establish a base for further operations, the SAS tried to work their way round the Aquabat al Dhafar. But the rebels had strengthened their positions, and as we were unwilling to commit the SAS to a full scale frontal assault, a role for which they were not intended, we contented ourselves with strengthening our new base on the plateau, in the hope of demoralizing the enemy and encouraging him to divert troops there from other sections of the Jebel. At least we were firmly on the top.

Action flared again at the end of November around Tanuf, where some forty rebels suddenly launched a determined attack, supported by heavy mortars, on a company of the Northern Frontier Regiment and our troop of 5.5s. At first the defenders wavered, and almost broke, but they rallied under the spirited leadership of the Royal Marine NCOs, until the timely arrival of a troop of Life Guards racing up from Nizwa turned the scales. After a fierce battle, in which the machine-guns of the Life Guards' Ferrets took a heavy toll, the enemy withdrew; but the NFR had four men wounded, and we lost two of our gunners when one of their shells failed to clear their sangar and burst on the lip.

On 1 December the SAS troops in that area took the offensive. Eager to avenge their dead NCO and acting on the information they had gleaned on that unlucky patrol, they attacked one of the caves held by the rebels and, supported by a strike of Venoms, killed a number of the occupants; they claimed to have killed eight of them, but subsequent interrogation of prisoners revealed that only two had been killed and three wounded. All the same, it was a useful action, which raised their spirits as much as it must have depressed the enemy.

In the ensuing weeks we strengthened our positions on the other side of the Jebel. At the end of December the Trucial Oman Scouts put a squadron into the village of Hijar, out of which they maintained two troops at our new base on the top, to reinforce the existing garrison of the Muscat Regiment and SAS. A platoon from the Northern Frontier Regiment joined them, and to provide additional fire-power a dismounted party of twenty Life Guards under a Corporal of Horse carried up eight of their Browning machine-guns. We never ceased to bless the authorities for giving us these Life Guards; they really entered into the spirit of our war and, when not engaged in a protective role with their Ferrets, were happy to turn themselves into infantry and carry out arduous and dangerous duties up the mountain.

The SAS now felt they had sufficient support to mount a strong night attack on the Aquabat al Dhafar. They excelled in night operations, and under a protective barrage from the Life Guards' Brownings and the heavy mortars of the Muscat Regiment, they scaled the steep cliffs with ropes and came to close quarters with the rebels in their caves. A wild *mêlée* ensued in the darkness, with bullets, grenades and insults flying between the combatants, but the rebels fought back stubbornly and held their ground until we called off the attack. Although once again they had inflicted casualties without loss to themselves, the SAS emerged from the battle with an even greater respect for the enemy.

Although our situation was immeasurably better than in the summer, we were still a long way from victory. John Watts and I agreed that our chances of storming the Jebel with a single squadron of SAS were pretty slim, but that with a second squadron we could be reasonably certain of pulling it off. We therefore sent a signal to Deane-Drummond asking if he was prepared to let us have another squadron; he not only agreed but added that he would come himself with a small headquarters to take over command of both squadrons.

Our next problem was to secure the approval of the War Office and the F.O. We put our case to the Political Resident on one of his visits to Muscat, and obtained his promise to forward it to the Foreign Office; and in Aden the military authorities agreed to back us with the War Office. With all this support we won our clearance but, needless to say, the F.O. modified it with a proviso of their own: all British troops must be out of Muscat by the first week in April. The significance of this deadline, apparently, was that the United Nations were to discuss the Middle East situation soon afterwards, with Oman featuring large on the agenda; British diplomacy must not be embarrassed by the presence there of British troops.

Deane-Drummond arrived on New Year's Day, 1959. Our first decision was to set up a joint headquarters to co-ordinate the operations of the Sultan's Armed Forces, the SAS, and the

Royal Air Force, and we co-opted a senior RAF officer from Bahrain to serve as our Air Liaison Officer. We installed this "Tac HQ", as we called it, in the Northern Frontier Regiment's camp near Nizwa, and I moved there from Beit al Falaj on 9 January with John Goddard and a small staff.

My next problem was the chain of command. Officially all British troops serving inside the country came under my orders, and hitherto my second-in-command had been Colin Maxwell. But Deane-Drummond had to be in a position where he could give orders to his own troops, and so, to avoid complications, I appointed him my Deputy Commander. From anyone less generous hearted and unselfish than Maxwell this arrangement might have aroused strong resentment; but he accepted my decision with his usual amiability, well understanding the reasons behind it.

On 12 January A Squadron, 22 SAS Regiment flew in from Malaya, under Major John Cooper, one of the longest-serving officers in the SAS. As a corporal, Cooper had been David Stirling's driver in the Western Desert in the earliest days of the regiment, and had taken part in some of its bloodiest actions in Sicily, Italy and France. Dark and thin, with strong, expressive features and a quick though short-lived temper, he was a brilliant soldier whose thirst for adventure and danger was to bring him under my command again in the Yemen.

We sent the new arrivals to relieve D Squadron, who came back to Beit al Falaj for a few days of rest and refit; the special SAS boots had lasted only a few days on the sharp rocks of the Jebel – to the incredulous dismay of the experts in the Quartermaster General's department who had designed them – and so we replaced them with hockey boots, which were much more satisfactory. Fresh from the heat of Malaya, A Squadron needed time to adjust to conditions on the Aquabat al Dhafar, where it had turned very cold, with hail storms and even snow; water bottles froze at night and fires were a necessity, even at the risk of snipers' bullets; although, in fact, both sides took this risk and nobody ever shot at the fires.

Because of the imposition by the Foreign Office of an April deadline we had about three months in which to assault the Jebel. We had agreed that the attack must be launched at night and during a period of full moon – it would be impracticable in total darkness; the full moon period came at the end of each of the next three months, which meant that the last weeks in January, February and March were the vital ones. We would make our first attempt at the end of January, which would give us two more chances if we failed. We must therefore plan on a very tight schedule, for we had a bare three weeks before our first attempt in which to move all troops to their take-off positions, organize their reinforcement and supply, re-deploy our garrisons, find reliable guides and co-ordinate the support of loyal tribal irregulars – in close consultation, of course, with Sayid Tarik.

At the same time I was faced with a difficult problem in diplomacy. The O.C. Northern Frontier Regiment, a British Seconded Officer, had an unfortunate habit of quarrelling with everyone with whom he came in contact. Already his Contract Officers had formed up to me, one after the other, to tell me they would "soldier no more" under him; I had to transfer them and replace them with seconded officers, which meant there were no Arabic-speaking officers in the regiment. Next he alienated the Life Guards at Nizwa, giving them orders which he was not empowered to give them but which, presented with even a minimum of tact, they would almost certainly have accepted; it is only fair to add that, in return, the Life Guards officers baited him unmercifully. The consequence for me was that I had to spend precious time smoothing ruffled feelings as well as preparing for war.

The primary object in all our planning was to gain a foothold as quickly as possible on the top of the Jebel, near the rebel headquarters, and hold it for the reception of air supply drops and as a firm base for further operations. Surprise was obviously essential in order to avoid the heavy casualties that we must expect if the assault were opposed. The Aquabat al Dhafar was too far away from the main rebel strongholds of Habib, Saiq and Sharaijah, and in any case the enemy was already well entrenched on the Aquabat, where he was expecting us to attack; we must encourage him in that expectation and hope he would concentrate the main body of his forces on the northern side of the plateau. On the other hand the shortest approaches to the rebel villages, the tracks leading from Tanuf and Kamah, were known to be guarded.

Deane-Drummond and I made several flights over the Jebel, cruising slowly just above the ground and scanning the smooth faces of rock to find a route that men and donkeys could climb. At length Deane-Drummond made his choice, a sloping buttress thrusting out above the Wadi Kamah on its eastern side. We sketched it, mapped it, studied photographs of it, and imprinted every detail of it on our minds; there appeared to be no track, but the slope looked feasible for the pack animals except in one place – a sharp ridge connecting the two main features – where we hoped the Sappers would be able to improve the going.

This approach had two main advantages: first, it was unguarded, so far as we could see, and it was most unlikely the enemy would except an attack by such a route; secondly, our men could climb it in one night – in about 9½ hours by our reckoning – and so by dawn the leading troops could be in position on the top, where they could receive supplies by air.

Following standard Army practice, we gave a code-name to each of the tactical features on the way up. Our principal objective, the top of the Jebel, we christened "Beercan"; the first prominent peak on the approach to it became "Pyramid", while the sharp ridge connecting the two, which we had already noticed from the air, received the name of "Causeway". There was a lesser crest about a third of the way up to Pyramid, which we called "Vincent", and our final objective, a peak beyond Beercan overlooking the village of Habib, went down in our operations plan as "Colin".

The two SAS squadrons would lead the assault, for I had received strict instructions from Aden that all other troops – Life Guards, Trucial Oman Scouts, and Sultan's Armed Forces – were to be used only in support of the SAS. These orders caused some natural disappointment to the Sultan's forces, who had tried for so long to reach the top, and who had in fact been the first to get there – when Tony Hart had taken his platoon of the Muscat Regiment up the Hijar track. However, they accepted the situation philosophically, especially as they themselves had important roles to play: first, they would make diversionary attacks before the main assault; secondly, they would follow closely upon the heels of the SAS and take over successive features as they were captured; and thirdly, they would consolidate the top of the Jebel and hold it against attack while the SAS pressed forward.

"Once we're on the top," I told Deane-Drummond, "and the aircraft have made their supply drops, we'll have to play things off the cuff. It'll depend on a lot of factors we can't foresee at this stage, such as the rebels' reaction and the whereabouts of their leaders. Remember, from our point of view – that is, from the Sultan's – the capture of Talib, Ghalib, and Suleiman is very nearly as important as the capture of Beercan."

We agreed that if there was no serious opposition Deane-Drummond would push his patrols on to Habib, Saiq and Sharaijah, while our supporting troops cleared the enemy from the Kamah track and opened it up for the donkey columns.

We planned to launch our attack on the night of 25 January, at the beginning of the full moon period, which would allow us to postpone the operation if the weather forecasts were unfavourable. It was vital for us to have at least twenty-four hours of good weather following the assault, to allow the RAF to drop their containers accurately; otherwise the leading troops would arrive on the plateau short of food, water and ammunition, for we couldn't expect the donkeys to get there in time.

Talib must by now have realized that an attack was imminent, but he had no idea from which direction it would come. In order to confuse him we mounted a series of diversions during the weeks before 25 January in different parts of the Jebel. Between 8 and 22 January D Squadron of the SAS and A Company of the Northern Frontier Regiment carried out offensive patrols from Tanuf, and drove the rebels from some high ground they were using as an observation post. From 18–22 January A Squadron of the SAS, supported by the squadron of Trucial Oman Scouts, made probing attacks against the Aquabat al Dhafar; but on the night of 23 January A Squadron disengaged all but one of its troops and, after a forced march across the mountain, came down to join D Squadron near Tanuf. The following night A Company of the Northern Frontier Regiment engaged the enemy again near Tanuf, while C Company put in an attack from Izki. On every occasion we met strong opposition – C Company had a particularly hard time, losing one soldier killed and several wounded – which showed us the enemy was reacting as we hoped.

But the most brilliant, and one of the most successful of our deceptions involved no fighting at all. "I'm prepared to bet," said Malcolm Dennison, my Intelligence Officer, "that if we call leaders of the donkey men together on the night before the assault, and tell them in strictest confidence and under the most ferocious penalties that the following night they'll be leading their donkeys up the Tanuf track, Talib will have the news within twenty-four hours." In fact, we learned afterwards, Talib received the news in twelve hours.

Our plan of attack was necessarily simple, even primitive. The operation was essentially a straight slog up the mountain face, and everything would depend on whether we achieved surprise; even when we postponed it for twenty-four hours because of a poor weather forecast – a wise decision, as it turned out – there was no need to alter the details. There were to be three phases: in the first A Squadron of the SAS would capture Vincent, and D Squadron would occupy Pyramid, Beercan, and Colin before first light. In the second C Company of the Northern Frontier Regiment would relieve A Squadron on Vincent, while the dismounted troop of Life Guards took over Pyramid; and lastly, A Squadron would consolidate their position on Beercan and D Squadron on Colin.

Two groups of irregulars would be taking part: on the southern side fifty Beni Ruawha tribesmen under Major John Clarke, a Sultan's Contract Officer, would accompany the SAS squadrons, while a force of two hundred Abryeen and a platoon of the Muscat Regiment, under the command of Jasper Coates, would create a diversion in the north and, if unopposed, would climb the Jebel by two tracks leading from Awabi. These two tribes were hereditary enemies of Suleiman and his Beni Riyam, and welcomed a chance to pay off old scores; the Abryeen, in particular, needed to restore their honour after their failure the previous summer to protect the lines of communication of the Muscat and Oman Field Force.

There would be air support the following morning: Venoms from Sharjah would strafe any pockets of resistance, while three Valettas from Bahrein would make a total of nine container drops on Beercan. We also had two helicopters ready at Nizwa to evacuate casualties to our Field Hospital there. If the weather was still bad we should be absolutely dependent for supplies on the donkey columns; the prospect worried me and my only consolation was that we had a few Omani jebel donkeys to supplement the poor little Somalis.

Just before the assault began, on the evening of 26 January, I drove in my Land Rover to the assembly points where our men were waiting. Unlike Deane-Drummond, who was going with his men up the mountain, I should have to spend the night in "Tac HQ" glued to the wireless; as overall commander I had to be in a position where I could exercise control at every stage of the operation, and I could only do so from headquarters, where I should be receiving regular progress reports from all units throughout the assault. I found the SAS cheerful and relaxed, with the easy self-confidence of experienced professionals who knew their job and had no doubt that they could do it; my own SAF were more subdued but there was no mistaking their determination to do what was required of them. The tribesmen of the Beni Ruawah formed a picturesque if ragged group in their flowing robes, their only uniform a red armband to distinguish them from the enemy on the plateau. John Clarke was standing by himself surveying them with his habitual air of profound gloom; behind his melancholy manner, I knew, were efficiency and courage as well as a wry sense of humour.

"Do your boys know what they're supposed to do?" I asked him.

"Yes, they know what they're supposed to do." He paused. "God only knows if they'll feel like doing it."

The assault was to begin at 8.30 pm. I returned to the camp in a mood of intense excitement, tinged with impatience as I awaited the first reports in our improvised operations room.

I felt no apprehension about the result. We had done our planning with care and thoroughness, allowing for every possible contingency, providing for every conceivable mishap; the progress reports would give me an up-to-date picture of the battle and I could deal with any emergency over the wireless. I had the best possible men for the job, in first class condition and equipped with the most modern weapons, I never doubted the outcome.

Outside, the night was cool and clear and mostly very silent. Once I heard faint shots from the mountain as our leading troops brushed with an outpost, but it soon became evident that we had indeed taken the enemy by surprise. Our deception plans, as we discovered next day, had been completely successful. The rebels had reinforced their pickets on the Aquabat al Dhafar – eight hours' march away, on the other side of the plateau – to more than a hundred strong, and both Talib and Suleiman had gone there to supervise the defence in person; their remaining strength was concentrated on the Tanuf track. There was only one outpost guarding our route – two men with a .5 Browning that was too heavy to move. They were half asleep in their cave, secure in the belief that no attack would come their way, when a soldier of the SAS stalked them and killed them both with a grenade.

In the half light before dawn enemy mortars and machine-guns opened fire on C Company of the Northern Frontier Regiment from the Kamah slab, but our 5.5″ guns, thirsting for targets, quickly put them out of action. The SAS suffered the only casualties of the entire operation when a chance bullet hit and exploded an Energa grenade in a soldier's pack; he and the two men following him were badly wounded and two of them died within twenty-four hours. The only serious obstacle on the route was the ridge known as Causeway; here the donkeys were utterly defeated, but one of the SAS squadrons shed their packs and heavy equipment and scaled it with ropes in a couple of hours. Beercan, our objective on top of the plateau, was in our hands by dawn; the entire climb had taken 9½ hours.

While some of our troops consolidated on Beercan and others pushed forward to occupy Colin and the village of Habib, the three Valettas from Bahrein made their supply drops –

nearly 30,000 lbs in all, including equipment, ammunition, food, and – most important – water. But the Venoms making their low level runs over the plateau found no targets for their guns and rockets; the opposition seemed to have melted away and the only signs of rebel activity to greet our men as they dug in on the heights they had captured were some twenty shame-faced Beni Riyam who came up to them in disconsolate little groups to surrender.

The total collapse of enemy resistance came as a surprise to us, and it was not until later in the morning that the mystery was solved. Prisoners told us that when they had seen the containers coming down on parachutes, the rebels had thought they were parachutists; without waiting to verify their first impression they had panicked and dispersed to their caves and villages. And so the little Somali donkeys had helped us after all, by their very uselessness; it was because of our total lack of confidence in them that we had originally asked for the supply drops. If only we could have told them of it, perhaps the irony would have consoled them in their long and lonely exile.

One of the "Casevac" helicopters took off from the camp at dawn to fetch the two most seriously wounded of the SAS casualties. When it returned I watched while the orderlies gently offloaded the unconscious men, and went to the hospital with them myself before returning to greet Sayid Tarik, who had come to offer his congratulations on our victory. Although I was sad about the loss of two good soldiers from such an evil stroke of fortune, I had to admit that in every other respect we had been fantastically lucky.

Immediately afterwards Tarik and I climbed aboard the helicopter to be lifted to the top of the Jebel. As we flew up the mountain I could make out in the growing light the Life Guards pickets holding the heights which the SAS had captured; they had taken the Biza machine-guns off their Ferrets and carried them for nine hours up the mountain – a remarkable effort on the part of men who weren't even trained as infantry. Around the crest of Vincent groups of Somali donkeys huddled miserably on the rock face, unable to climb any higher; they had been more of a hindrance than a help, the troops told me afterwards, although the big Omani jebel donkeys had carried on as far as Pyramid.

We landed at Pyramid, on a small pad the troops had marked out for the helicopters. As we hovered above it I saw in the distance a long column of SAS winding across the plateau towards Saiq; they might have been on an exercise, so peaceful was the scene. All the same, I came nearer to death a few minutes later than I had done in all the campaign – and a very stupid and messy death at that. I was anxious to photograph Tarik as he emerged from the helicopter, for I thought he would make a fine picture in his turban, robes, bandolier and assorted weaponry; and so I leaped out as soon as we touched down, clutching my cine-camera and ducking low to keep well clear of the main rotor blade. As I ran round the back of the aircraft to catch Tarik climbing out on the other side, I forgot there was another rotor on the tail. I saw people in the crowd gesticulating frantically, and sensed they were shouting at me, but the noise of the engines drowned their voices and I paid no attention. It was only when I skirted the tail and felt the breath of the blade an inch or two from my ear that I realized how near I had come to extinction.

The Beni Riyam prisoners were standing in a silent little knot nearby, their eyes flickering nervously towards Sayid Tarik as he strode over to them. He shook each one warmly by the hand and they gathered round him, sitting on their haunches in a circle while he questioned them gently about our most immediate problem, the whereabouts of Talib, Ghalib and Suleiman. Although I doubt if they gave away anything, or even if they knew anything, they quickly shed their reserve and launched into animated and friendly conversation, obviously greatly relieved to find him so genial. After a few minutes he bade them farewell, telling them to return to their villages and persuade their fellow-tribesmen to come in and hand over their arms, with assurances that we would treat them well. They evidently obeyed him, for during the next two days parties of rebels began to drift in and surrender; no more than a trickle at first, the numbers increased over the next few days as it became known that we were taking no reprisals.

We flew on to Beercan to join Tony Deane-Drummond,

who was in high spirits despite his exhausting climb. He had been talking on the wireless with his leading troops.

"They've just occupied Saiq," he announced. "Why don't we fly over there and take a look?"

During the short ten minute flight I looked down on the green, scrub-covered plateau bathed in the clear morning sunlight, a welcome contrast with the baking rock and sand among which I had been living for the last nine months; orchards and terraced vineyards covered the slopes below Saiq, and fields of millet and sorghum, interspersed with almond trees and apricots, spread their blend of colours over the fringes of the plain. In the village the SAS had just disarmed a small group of tribesmen, some of whom squatted on the ground in sullen and dejected silence while others protested loudly that they had been on our side all the time and cursed Suleiman for the trouble he had brought upon his people.

One of them went so far as to offer to show us Suleiman's cave. We accepted eagerly and followed him for about half an hour into the hills, walking warily with our rifles at the ready and accompanied by a small escort of soldiers. The entrance to Suleiman's cave was a large hole in the rock. We found nobody there, but a fire still burned inside, indicating that the occupants had left pretty recently. Leading off from this cavern was a veritable rabbit warren of smaller caves, into which we had to crawl on hands and knees by the light of electric torches which we had luckily remembered to bring. They were too numerous for us to explore in any detail, but we entered a few, where we found a rich treasury of loot: there were stores of arms, ammunition, and food as well as Suleiman's personal possessions, which included a new Singer sewing machine; also, to our astonishment and delight, there were boxes of documents and bundles of letters giving confidential details about the organization of the rebels and their secret sympathizers in the Sultanate. Under Tarik's direction we collected a few of the most important papers and posted SAS guards to keep watch on the caves until we could send for the rest. Before leaving we each took something of Suleiman's as a souvenir – mine was a fine round brass coffee tray, on which I still serve coffee to my guests at home in Spain.

Suleiman's documents, which included nearly a thousand letters, provided our intelligence officers with a complete picture of the enemy network throughout the country. They gave us the names of prominent citizens of Muscat who were deeply compromised; of Sheikhs and village headmen who, under a cloak of loyalty to the Sultan, were actively helping the Imam; of mine-layers and arms smugglers, and of askers who assisted them or let them pass. Some, no doubt, were merely re-insuring against the possibility of a rebel victory; but one asker leader, supposedly in charge of an important and troublesome stretch of road, was revealed as the principal mine-layer.

I could not understand why Suleiman, however hasty his flight, had been so criminally careless as to leave behind such damaging evidence; although not conspicuous for his loyalty to friends in time of trouble, he could hardly have meant to betray them in this manner. The most charitable explanation is that when he had left his headquarters for the Aquabat al Dhafar to meet what he had believed to be our main attack, he had expected to return at leisure as a victor; but after the collapse of the rebels he had been forced to escape as best he could, and had no chance to revisit the cave. In that case the parachute scare had indeed served us well.

That same afternoon our troops entered Sharaijah unopposed. In the village they found only women and children, the elderly and the crippled; the young men were still hiding in the surrounding rocks and caves. With the capture of this village, the last on the plateau, the battle of the Jebel Akhdar was over; it only remained for us to establish our authority throughout the area we had just occupied. I detailed some of the troops to consolidate positions at strategic points against any possible counter-attack – although it was difficult to see where it could come from; others I sent out in strong patrols to track down the rebel leaders and search for arms. The task of making contact with the villagers still in hiding, and persuading them to surrender their weapons and return to their homes, I entrusted to our tribal irregulars.

AFTERWORD

The SAS would fight another successful campaign in Oman, this time a six-year war, 1970–76, against communist insurgents in the southern province of Dhofar. The Dhofar war saw 22 SAS in one of its most desperate actions, the battle of Mirbat, where an eight-man SAS detachment led by Captain Mike Kealy was attacked by 250 guerrillas. The SAS won the battle, suffering two troopers KIA.

ARNHEM
G. G. Norton

The example of the German airborne invasion of Crete in May 1941 and the success of Britain's own 1st Parachute Brigade at Bruneval (see "Adventure at Bruneval"), prompted an urgent request for the expansion of Britain's airborne capability. In April 1942 the Airborne Forces Depot at Hardwicke Hall was duly founded. From that point on the British Airborne formations (the "Red Berets") continued to grow both in numbers and in the reputation they held amongst enemy and Allied forces alike. Of their many distinguished actions in World War II, none is better known than Operation Market Garden – the drop on Arnhem. Afterwards, Dwight Eisenhower, the Allied Commander Europe, would say of the British 1st Airborne Division at Arnhem: "There has been no single performance by any unit that has more greatly inspired me or excited my admiration . . ."

IN AUGUST 1944, General Montgomery proposed an Allied offensive based on one powerful thrust through Holland and across the Rhine, to isolate and occupy the Ruhr, thus depriving Germany of more than half her industrial potential. The plan required many divisions and virtually all the logistic support available to the Allies in Europe. Partly because he did not wish to halt all the other Armies, which were going well, particularly in the south, partly because he regarded such an advance as risky, Eisenhower rejected the proposal. But he did agree to a modified scheme, whereby the 21st Army Group would attempt the narrow thrust to and beyond the Rhine, largely supported from its own resources.

The plan was to lay an "airborne carpet" along the Eindhoven-Arnhem road, across which the British 2nd Army could advance quickly to and beyond the Rhine, the last great natural barrier to the Reich, and turn the Siegfried Line. The essential task of the airborne operation was to seize intact the bridges over the canals and rivers en route, notably those at Grave, over the River Maas, the crossing of the Maas-Waal Canal, the great steel bridge over the Waal at Nijmegen and the road bridge over the Rhine at Arnhem.

Three airborne divisions – the US 82nd and 101st and the British 1st, together forming the 1st Airborne Corps of the newly formed 1st Allied Airborne Army under Lieutenant-General Lewis H. Brereton, USAAF – were assigned to the operation. Dropping simultaneously, the Americans were to open the corridor from Eindhoven to Nijmegen and the British to seize the bridge at Arnhem. The Airborne Corps was to operate for 48 hours unsupported, though the 2nd Army was expected to link up by the end of that time. Such was the plan. An airborne action relies for success on the element of surprise, enabling the lightly-armed soldiers to seize their objectives before the defenders can bring superior forces and fire-power to bear. This limitation puts them at an overwhelming disadvantage if the enemy can quickly bring against them self-propelled guns and tanks. Three factors combined to deprive the 1st Airborne Division of this advantage in the battle of Arnhem.

First, and, as it proved, most critical, there were insufficient aircraft available to lift the whole division on the first day. Only the 1st Parachute Brigade, 1st Air-landing Brigade, plus Divisional HQ and some supporting arms, could be carried in the initial lift. The 4th Parachute Brigade and 1st Polish Parachute Brigade, the latter under the command of the 1st Division for the operation, would drop on D + 1 and D + 2 respectively. Thus only half the division could benefit from surprise at all, and of this, most of the Air-landing Brigade was detailed to protect the dropping zones for the subsequent lifts. So far as the battle for the bridge was concerned, only the 1st Parachute Brigade was available on the first day.

Secondly, the open areas south and south-east of the bridge were waterlogged and crossed by eight-foot-wide irrigation ditches. These made them unsuitable for massed glider landings and less than ideal for parachuting. Furthermore, anti-aircraft defences in the area of Arnhem were believed to be strong. Major-General Urquhart, GOC 1st Airborne Division, finally selected dropping and landing zones to the west, the furthest eight miles away.

Thirdly, Allied intelligence was misleading. Although the division was warned that counter-attacks by Germans at Brigade strength, supported by tanks and self-propelled guns, were possible, it was not known that the 9th and 10th Divisions of the 2nd SS Panzer Corps were refitting east and north-east of Arnhem: or, more accurately, information to this effect reached the 2nd Army HQ from the Dutch Resistance, but was discounted. As a result, instead of being faced with a brigade group, the 1st Airborne Division was to be met by a Panzer Corps.

The plan assumed that the Airborne Reconnaissance Squadron, followed by the 1st Parachute Brigade, would reach the bridge quickly. The remainder of the division were to take up blocking positions on the approaches the next day, and the Poles to relieve the 1st Brigade on D + 2, to create a reserve. In view of the scale of the opposition which actually materialized, this plan could work only if everything went smoothly – which, after a deceptively propitious start, it did not.

The first lift arrived on time on September 17, there was little flak, and a very high percentage of the parachute and glider troops reached their RVs as planned.[1] But amongst the 38 gliders (out of 320) that failed to arrive were some of the armoured jeeps of the Reconnaissance Squadron. The weather, too, important for the timely arrival of later lifts for re-supply, and for fighter-bomber support, clamped down. In the light of what has been said above regarding the extended lift, the irony of this needs no emphasis. Nevertheless, provided that the 2nd Army could keep to their planned timetable, success was still possible.

[1]With them went no fewer than 15 Army Chaplains, of whom two were killed, ten taken prisoner, and three crossed the river during the final withdrawal.

The 1st Brigade set off on foot for the objective. The 2nd Battalion, under the command of Lieutenant-Colonel J. D. Frost, the veteran of Bruneval, the retreat from Oudna, and Sicily, advanced to Heelsum and then on by the southern road running close to the north bank of the river. At the same time, the 3rd Battalion advanced on the main Heelsum-Arnhem road to approach the bridge from the north. The 1st Battalion initially remained with Brigade HQ, in reserve.

In Heelsum, the 2nd Battalion ambushed some German vehicles and took 20 prisoners. Members of the Dutch Resistance passed information that there were few Germans in Arnhem itself, and the battalion pressed on towards the bridge, which was still six miles away. They arrived at the railway bridge too late to prevent its destruction, met and overcame opposition in Doorwerthsche Wood, but were held up by enemy occupying the high wooded ground called Den Brink. "B" Company was sent to capture it while Frost with "A" Company hurried on into the town in the fading dusk, killing or capturing small scattered parties of enemy on the way.

Between 2030 and 2100 hours, they reached the road bridge: it was still intact. Swiftly and silently they secured the northern end; and Frost ordered Lieutenant J. H. Grayburn to lead his platoon across. The Germans were solidly established, with an armoured car's machine guns and two 20 mms firing straight along the bridge. There was no cover, and Grayburn was hit almost at once; yet he pressed on until ordered to retire, and thus initiated 48 hours of resourceful leadership and unassailable courage that led, eventually, to his death and the award of the VC – one of five won during the next nine days at Arnhem. In an attempt to cross lower down and so outflank the Germans, Frost sent a platoon to the pontoon bridge, but it too had gone, and there were no barges.

That night, therefore, the road bridge was still in one piece but far from secure. All Frost could do was commandeer and fortify the nearby houses at the northern end, and try and gather in the missing members of his battalion. By morning his force had grown to between 300 and 400 men.

Meanwhile, the 3rd Battalion had run into infantry, supported by armoured cars, at a road junction west of Oosterbeek. The armoured cars were eventually destroyed by PIAT[1] fire; but the infantry continued to hold them up. "C" Company, ordered to find an alternative route to the bridge, became split up, the platoons fighting individual actions until, much reduced in numbers, they met at the railway station in Arnhem. After another skirmish in the town, what was left of the company finally reached the bridge and joined the 2nd Battalion. The rest of the 3rd Battalion advanced from the crossroads before dawn on the 18th, and fought their way to the railway station. Here they were halted by concentrated fire from 88 mm guns. Throughout the day they continued to battle against increasing enemy pressure from infantry, supported by self-propelled guns and intense mortar fire, and suffered heavy casualties. A final attempt to continue at 1600 hours made no progress; and the battalion, now split into two groups, found itself surrounded. At dawn on the 19th all that were left reached the river bank and seized a large house called the Pavilion; but could advance no further. Here they were joined eventually by the remnants of the 1st Battalion.

The 1st Battalion had enjoyed no better fortune. Advancing along the railway, they were soon engaged in confused and desperate fighting with an enemy, reinforced with tanks and armoured half-tracks, who had moved in behind the other two battalions. Fierce and sporadic clashes continued throughout the night of September 17–18, and the battalion's casualties were heavy. It was impossible to make headway. At dawn on the 18th, the battalion attempted to disengage and bypass the enemy to the south, moving through back gardens and houses and continuously sniped at. The battalion history notes that the enemy defences had been thoroughly prepared, and there were few gaps in the fire plan.

Attacks and counter-attacks continued throughout the day; and that evening, after 24 hours fighting, while Frost and the

[1]Projector Infantry Anti-tank. The rifleman's anti-tank weapon firing an HE Bomb effective against armoured vehicles up to a range of about 120 yards.

2nd Battalion were desperately clinging on to the northern end of the bridge and praying for the arrival either of reinforcements from the 1st and 3rd, or of XXX Corps from the south, the 1st Battalion had been brought to a standstill in the north-western suburbs, and the 3rd was similarly held up near the St Elizabeth Hospital. From here they established radio contact with the 2nd Battalion at the bridge who were calling urgently for reinforcement. But the 1st Battalion, reduced by this time to barely 100 men, could do no more.

General Urquhart himself became embroiled in the confused and bitter fighting. When visiting his units after landing on the 17th, he found Brigadier Lathbury with the 3rd Battalion. Together they were forced to remain with the battalion; and when they were eventually able to proceed, they were immediately involved in fighting the enemy at close quarters. Lathbury was wounded, and General Urquhart personally despatched one enemy soldier with his pistol. "It is seldom in modern war that the commander of a division has an opportunity to fight the enemy at such close quarters", Urquhart wrote; and the author of *Red Beret* comments: "But this division was airborne, and every man in it, from its commander to the most junior private, was trained to arms and expected to use them at any moment". One remembers the exploits of the glider full of staff officers at large in Sicily.

At the bridge at dawn on the 18th, Colonel Frost found himself in command of a mixed force that had grown to some 600–700 men, with a few six-pounder anti-tank guns. At 1130 hours the bridge was rushed from the south by five armoured cars and six half-tracks. The armoured cars were knocked out by the six-pounders; the half-tracks by the Sappers from a building overlooking the bridge, and their crews killed. "When we dealt with them", Frost wrote, "they smoked and burned in front of us almost to the end of the battle"; and they effectively blocked the bridge to further traffic.

That morning the second lift was due. Owing to fog in England, it did not take off until after midday; and although this drop was as near-perfect as the first, these battalions, too, were soon in trouble, pinned down here and there in their attempts to reach the bridge, for the Germans had effectively sealed off the centre of Arnhem. The 10th Battalion ran into guns and tanks on the Utrecht road and had to dig in; and it was here that Captain L. E. Queripel of the 10th Battalion distinguished himself repeatedly through a long and fire-swept day. Wounded in the face and both arms, he was last seen covering the withdrawal of his men with the handful of grenades they had left. He also won a posthumous VC.

By the second day, therefore, all the forces that had dropped to reinforce Frost and his men at the bridge were themselves on the defensive; and the day's ill fortune was still incomplete. The resupply drop that afternoon went astray and fell, complete, into enemy hands; and the arrival of the Polish Parachute Brigade by glider provoked a furious German retaliation, which fell most severely on the 4th Parachute Brigade, who found themselves marooned in the suburbs of Oosterbeek. It was at this point that General Urquhart was forced to admit that nothing they could do would enable his forces to reach the bridge, and he formed a defensive perimeter where he was, in the hope that the 2nd Army would arrive before it was too late. During this contraction, the three battalions, the 10th, 11th and 156th, were all virtually wiped out. In this sector on the following day, the 20th, the third VC of the battle was won, by Lance/Sergeant J. D. Baskeyfield who, first with his section and later single-handed, accounted for two tanks and two self-propelled guns. He, too, was killed. Arnhem was like that. By sheer guts and fighting ability, the men of the 1st Airborne Division maintained a moral superiority over the enemy to the last, exemplified by Grayburn, Queripel, Baskeyfield, and, not least, by Major R. H. Cain of the 2nd Battalion, South Staffordshire Regiment, who stopped tanks, self-propelled guns, flame-throwers and infantry alike with PIAT-fire and finally with a 2-inch mortar. Unlike the others, however, he lived to tell the tale.

Meanwhile, at the bridge, mortar and shell fire continued all through the 18th, and steadily demolished the buildings in which the force was holding out. On the evening of the 18th, although a further attack was beaten off, and the enemy lost two tanks and many troops, four of the defenders' houses were set alight and had to be evacuated. At sunset, a spirited bayonet charge, accompanied by the battle cry of "Whoa Mohammed!"[1] dispersed more German infantry who were forming up for yet another attack.

Sporadic fighting continued during that night, though, in a lull some time after midnight, Frost was able to sleep briefly for the first time in two days. All next day heavy shelling and mortar fire continued, interspersed with attacks by tanks firing into the houses, and infantry assaults. But in spite of mounting casualties, and a growing shortage of ammunition, the defenders held on, sustained a little by rumours that relief was on the way. By midnight on the 19th, the key house commanding the northern end of the bridge had been burned down and the force, now dangerously weakened, were under constant small-arms fire.

September 20 brought no relief; yet, hounded from house to house, they were still able to deny the Germans the bridge – or even the satisfaction of blowing it up. Grayburn saw to that. Colonel Frost was badly wounded, though he continued to take major decisions, water was short, and all the radios were out of action. By an ironic domestic touch, however, Frost was still able to talk to Divisional HQ by telephone, thanks to the operators of the Dutch Resistance, whom, for their temerity, the Germans subsequently murdered. News that the 2nd Army would attack the southern end of the bridge that afternoon sent hopes high. But no help came, or could come; and during the day they were forced out of the shells of their battered, burning houses until they were fighting in the ruins close to, or beneath, the bridge. Enemy aircraft strafed the positions. The six-pounders were out of action and PIAT ammunition was exhausted. Tanks could advance almost with impunity. Finally, only a school in which the wounded had been gathered remained; and that evening it was set on fire. Under a flag of truce, they, with Frost among them, were taken away by the Germans.

[1]This improbable exhortation derived from the 2nd Battalion's time in Tunisia in early 1943. One of the native donkey-drivers thus addressed his charges, and it became the battle-cry of the 1st Brigade.

Now only a handful remained, 120 officers and men, commanded by Major C. H. F. Gough of the Reconnaissance Squadron; and at dawn on September 21 they made a final attempt to regain the houses from which they had been prised. The attack failed, and with that failure, the operation. The bridge was back in German hands; and the surviving remnant, a mere 50 or so, melted away, to try and reach the perimeter, or cross the Rhine. A few, a very few, succeeded in doing this.

It is worth recapping. According to the plan, the bridge was to have been taken, and held for not more than 48 hours, by the entire 1st Airborne Division. By then, XXX Corps, storming up from the south, should have relieved them. As things turned out, the bridge was held for three days and four nights – from the evening of the 17th to dawn on the 21st – by less than one complete battalion.

The bridge – the central purpose of the operation – had gone. The fragmented battalions within the perimeter, shrunk now into the western edge of Oosterbeek with a foothold on the river bank, held on for four days more. Hungry, thirsty, tired to the bone, and with the casualties steadily mounting, they drove off attack after attack. Attempts to reinforce them from across the river were as doomed as those to supply them from the air. And the latter were haunted by a tragic irony. Time and time again the RAF pilots flew straight into the wall of flak; many of them continued their run with their aircraft on fire; but, as one officer on the ground described it, "We thought that some would not face it and would jettison their cargoes, in which case we should get them, for they would fall short and therefore in our lines; but they all stuck to their course and went on . . ."[1] Herein lay the tragedy. The planned dropping zones had not been captured, but the message informing the RAF of the necessary changes had never got through. The troops on the ground did everything they knew to mark the new zones; but among the trees, their signals were virtually invisible from

[1]One of them was Flight Lieutenant D. S. A. Lord, DFC, of 271 Squadron, Transport Command, who circled for eight minutes and made two runs with his starboard wing blazing, and crashed with his aircraft. He was awarded a posthumous VC.

the air; and less than 8 per cent of the stores dropped were recovered. On the worst day, September 21, the RAF lost a fifth of their aircraft in these brave, forlorn sorties.

Meanwhile, the two US Divisions had dropped on September 17, and the 2nd Army operations to advance up the "carpet" to Arnhem began successfully enough. Men of the 101st Division seized their objectives, though one bridge was found destroyed. The Guards Armoured Division built a replacement and pressed on towards the 82nd, holding Grave and the high ground south-east of Nijmegen. The 82nd Division, however, had been driven back from their final objective – the bridge over the River Waal north of Nijmegen. It was recaptured, intact, by the Guards Armoured Division and 504 US Parachute Regiment.

All this time, though, south of Grave, enemy counter-attacks delayed operations, and, combined with fierce resistance north of the Waal, blunted the point of the 2nd Army's advance. Far from being a rapid thrust against light opposition, it became a savage slogging match: far from relieving the 1st Airborne inside 48 hours, the 2nd Army was never able to reach them at all.

The 43rd Infantry Division finally took over the lead and succeeded in reaching the Polish Brigade. But enemy pressure on the 2nd Army's flanks prevented a full-scale link-up with the perimeter across the river. Some hardy members of the 4th Dorsets crossed the Rhine, but it was too little, and too late. During the night of 25th/26th the survivors of the 1st Airborne Division were ordered to withdraw south of the Rhine. Of the 10,095 all ranks, including glider pilots, who landed, fewer than 3,000 returned across the river.

The bid to end the war in 1944 had failed: the battle of Arnhem was over.

THE BACKWATER WAR
T. L. Bosiljevac

Taking their name from the elements they are trained to fight in, under and on – Sea, Air, Land – the US Navy's SEALs have their origins in the wartime Underwater Demolition Teams (UDTs) which cleared safe lanes through German beach defences for the 1944 Allied invasion of Normandy. During the Korean War UDTs prepared the way for the amphibious landing at Inchon. In 1960 a US Navy study suggested the need for units even more specialized than the UDTs, and in 1962 President John F. Kennedy authorized the establishment of two new teams bearing the appropriate acronym of SEAL. Recruited principally from the UDTs, the SEALs were soon deployed in Vietnam. Although they would later see action throughout the warzone, their initial area of operations was the Mekong Delta in the southernmost corner of Vietnam. With its immense patchwork of swamps, river and rice paddies, the delta was a natural stronghold for the VC (Viet Cong). The tasks assigned the SEALs, as can be seen from the following account of their operations in 1967, ranged from setting up listening posts to monitor VC movements to the demolition of VC bunkers. More often than not, the SEALs were sent out in three-man detachments with the simple order, "Sat Cong" (kill communists). In the first operations insertion was by Mike boat (heavily armed riverine craft), but later by Boston Whaler (16ft glass-fibre craft with a very shallow draft), IBS (inflatable boat, small), even submarine. The SEALs' Vietnam arsenal included the 5.56 mm M63A1 Stoner light machine gun – which was highly valued by SEAL teams since it could be easily converted for a number of different roles, including sub-machine gun and assault rifle – the M60 GPMG, the M79 grenade launcher, and the 9 mm M45 "Carl Gustav" sub-machine gun, which was popular due to its reliability. For clandestine ops, the SEALs carried the 9 mm Smith and

Wesson Mark 22 Model 0 silenced pistol, nicknamed the "hush puppy" since it was developed originally for silencing enemy guard dogs. Combat knives such as the Randall, Ka-bar and Gerber were standard. "Tiger stripe" camouflage fatigues were often worn in preference to the usual combat-issue green leaf-pattern uniform, and many SEALs wore blue jeans, finding that these best withstood the Mekong mosquitoes. A special combat coat was developed for the use of SEALs, made of camouflaged material, with a built-in flotation chamber, and designed to carry everything that a SEAL would need on a mission. During the Vietnam War the SEALs were credited with 580 VC killed. Since Vietnam SEAL teams have also seen service in the invasion of Panama, Grenada and in the 1991 Gulf War.

By the beginning of 1967, nearly 400,000 US servicemen were involved in Vietnam. The war continued to build on all fronts, and the United States continued to pressure the North Vietnamese and Vietcong to find an end to the conflict. Navy Special Warfare involvement also expanded during the year. To date, only one frogman had been killed in UDT/SEAL operations in-country. The success of SEAL Team One platoons led to a wider role in the conflict for both SEAL teams. The West-Coast-based SEAL Team One expanded in manpower, putting additional operational platoons into the Mekong Delta. Meanwhile, for the first time, SEAL Team Two began to deploy platoons into the war zone at the beginning of 1967. This year would mark a great increase in the Delta fighting. The war in the backwaters of the canals and rivers would no longer be limited to the Rung Sat Special Zone (RSSZ).

The Vietcong increased their attacks on Saigon shipping in the RSSZ during January 1967. Out of a dozen incidents, three involved minings, while the majority of the others involved ambushes. Two SEAL squads were inserted by Mike boat to patrol the RSSZ on 6 January. While conducting their reconnaissance mission along the Rach Muoi Creek, the SEALs discovered a small base camp and subsequently destroyed it. Another patrol on the 9th was detected by enemy forces as it searched a small complex fourteen miles south of Nha Be. While at least four VC attempted to surround the SEALs, the frogmen slipped into the Rach Cat Lai Be Creek and swam quietly downriver. They silently passed a large enemy base camp, but escaped to their helicopter extraction point. Once out of the area, air strikes were called in on the communist forces with unknown results.

Documents captured in December 1966 during Operation Charleston revealed that the VC were using several fresh-water wells in the RSSZ for resupply. Subsequent aerial photography confirmed that the VC were using numerous trails leading to the wells. SEALs were immediately ordered to destroy them. On 12 January 1967, two six-man teams were inserted by helo; using explosives, the teams demolished eight wells near Thanh Thoi Hamlet in the lower RSSZ. Intelligence reports from a US Army advisor in Can Gio two months later indicated that this action caused great hardship among the communist units in the vicinity, forcing them to carry water from a much greater distance. Four days later, the SEALs destroyed a large rice cache they discovered in a camp twelve miles south of Nha Be.

While the SEALs were moving to insert for one of the demolition operations, another VC ambush of an LCM riverboat occurred on 20 January. Many of the SEALs and navy crewmen onboard were wounded and one Vietnamese officer was killed, but the US forces fought back aggressively and ended their mission by killing four enemy soldiers and capturing nearly 360 VC suspects, along with numerous documents and a large quantity of supplies. Most of the detainees turned out to be active Vietcong. The SEALs had been operating in conjunction with a US Army unit that was sweeping the area. The SEALs mission had been to patrol the river and prevent enemy forces from evading the army sweep.

Other patrols reconned the mangroves for VC activity, many times finding their movement hampered by thick vegetation. On 9 January, one patrol was forced to extract by McQuire Rig via a helicopter winch after it was unable to make its way to a riverine extraction site. A small and deserted VC camp and rice cache were found and destroyed by men from SEAL Team One on the 16th. The cache, which held an estimated 17.5 tons of rice, was scattered by 160 pounds of explosives that the frogmen had requested via helicopter.

Although missions were run almost daily, only a handful of enemy contacts resulted. On countless patrols, the SEALs heard the Vietcong use small-arms fire in patterns, as signaling and warning from one enemy unit to another. It was easy for the communists to hear the approach of the river vessels used for insertion and extraction by the SEALs. The VC sensed the presence of the new, deadly navy units and gave them a wide berth.

Also during January, Operation Deckhouse V utilized men from UDT [Underwater Demolition Team] 12 to find and mark safe channels in the Co Chien and Ham Luong rivers. The success of the operation in the Than Phu Secret Zone was due in large part to the fact that the UDT missions included channel searches, surf observations (SUROBS), mine searches, and salvage work.

On 2 and 3 February, four SEAL Team One squads conducted a series of patrolling sweeps in the RSSZ. Several VC bunkers and a concrete cistern were demolished, and four enemy sampans were fired upon. Additionally, a small quantity of ordnance and equipment was captured. Patrols all throughout the spring consisted of intelligence recons, listening posts, and ambushes, and there was a marked improvement in the objectives of the missions compared to the earlier, freestyle ambushes of the year before. A few of the operations were designed to abduct Vietcong for the purpose of gaining intelligence through interrogation. Many team members saw fresh evidence of enemy forces in certain areas, but few actually made any contact.

Almost immediately after arriving in-country on 31 January, SEAL Team Two patrols commenced operations. Prior to leaving the continental United States (Conus), two SEAL Team Two platoons, consisting of two officers and ten enlisted each, stopped over for two weeks in San Diego to train and confer with SEAL Team One elements. During their stop on the West Coast, the men trained in weapons and tactics in the desert located east of the city, received intelligence updates and briefs, and prepared their equipment for deployment.

The group, which was to include a specially trained scout dog named Prince, arrived at Binh Thuy airfield outside Can Tho at the end of the month. From there, they moved to Nha Be, where some initial orientation missions were run with elements from Team One before the East Coast units struck out into their own designated areas of operation in the Mekong Delta along the Bassac River and its tributaries.

On 7 February, one platoon advised the 32nd Vietnamese Ranger Battalion and called in air and artillery support for the unit. Yet, this type of initial mission was of little consequence. It took a few weeks to iron out problems concerning exactly how the SEALs were to be employed in the Delta. Many of the same questions that had faced SEAL Team One elements in the RSSZ a year before were now echoed in the Delta regions where other platoons were hoping to work. By the second week in March, these issues had been resolved. The Team Two SEALs were to perform the majority of their missions within five kilometers of the major rivers in the Delta, but they could penetrate further inland with special approval.

At times, the elements became the gravest enemy of all. Well before dawn on 13 February, men from UDT 12's Det Charlie launched from the deck of the *Tunny* in motorized IBSs off Sa Huynh in II Corps. Large swells met the men as they anchored the command boat just outside the surf zone and sent two swimmer scouts ashore. In the darkness of the squall, the command boat capsized as it was hit by an estimated twenty-foot breaker. The three men onboard were unceremoniously dumped into the water. They struggled to the beach as the other boat was rocked by the high surf and fought to remain upright. UDT men in the second boat activated an emergency flare to notify the sub of the situation. The *Tunny* began to respond to the call for assistance and launched a third IBS.

The frogmen from the command boat were barely able to make their way ashore and link up with the scout swimmers stranded on the beach. After burying their radio and the remains of their boat, they began several attempts to swim through the surf. Three of the men made it to the second boat just before 0600. Meanwhile, the *Tunny* had moved to within 1,300 yards of the beach and anchored. She called on a nearby LST (Landing Ship, Tank), the USS *Westchester County*, for additional help. The LST launched an amphibious landing craft to join in the search. Just after it had launched, another swimmer was reported recovered by the second IBS. The last swimmer was recovered by the landing craft about an hour later, and the vessel linked up with the sub to transfer all hands. Luckily, the frogmen were uninjured, although they were exhausted by the ordeal. The necessary hydrographic data was finally obtained, and Operation Deckhouse VI, designed as another marine assault to throw the communists in I Corps off balance, was launched on 16 February.

New methods and tactics were developed by the frogmen, mostly as a result of trial and error. The SEALs were beginning to discover that wearing boots into enemy territory was a dead giveaway. Enemy forces went barefoot in most areas, and they would easily pick up the tracks of their enemy's footwear. Many SEAL platoons began to go barefoot themselves and carried a pair of lightweight coral booties or tennis shoes to be used only in certain terrain. In the mud and on the hard-packed trails, bare feet additionally proved more sensitive and made careful movement along booby-trapped trails more positive. A low-strung booby-trap tripwire was more easily sensed on bare skin. Stalking without boots also proved to be an absolutely silent method to penetrate an enemy camp. Squad radios were used in the spring without impressive results. They seemed too noisy for the small units attempting to remain as ghosts in the brush.

U.S. ground troop involvement in Vietnam continued to expand steadily. In the third week of February, Operation Junction City was conducted in III Corps near the Cambodian border. The largest military operation to date, it involved 22 U.S. battalions in a sweep-and-destroy operation that targeted guerrilla base camps in the South. On 3 March, UDT 11 relieved UDT 12 as the forward-deployed Underwater Demolition Team in WESTPAC. UDT 12 later received the Navy Unit Commendation for its 1966–1967 WESTPAC cruise. The citation noted that the frogmen reconned over 120 miles of beaches, rivers and harbors in the combat zone and provided other valuable services to the Seventh Fleet's amphibious forces. Also in March, UDT 11 received the same award for operations between January 1964 and September 1966. Its effort included the reconnaissance of over 110 miles of beaches and rivers and countless missions in support of the Pacific Fleet's operations.

Six LDNN were assigned to conduct training operations with U.S. Navy SEALs out of Nha Be beginning on 9 March. In the initial after action reports, the Americans felt that the LDNN accompanying the units would be of greater value given a little more time and experience. On the 11th, a 2nd Platoon ambush (its first real contact of the tour) interdicted an enemy resupply attempt fifteen miles southeast of Can Tho. Four VC were killed, while the SEALs were extracted by riverine craft under fire. On 12 March, twenty sensors were emplanted by a SEAL Team One platoon in Vam Sat. On 15 March, Admirals Sharp and Ward and General Westmoreland visited Seal Team One's Detachment Golf to express their personal admiration for the job the SEALs were tackling all over the Delta. That same day, a small SEAL Team One ambush netted three VC killed and several weapons and a small amount of operational equipment from an enemy sampan.

The mud, tidal flows, and nipa palms were not always the only environmental hazard. On a riverine abduction/ambush mission on 17 March, a SEAL Team One frogman encountered an obnoxious crocodile. The amphibian finally forced the frogman to flee his position and shoot in self-defense. "At the bank, in about three feet of water, I saw what looked like a stump. The stump started moving closer to me. I stopped. It came closer and closer, and when it was about six feet away, I saw that the stump had two eyes and was pointing its snout at me . . . I moved back about three or four feet, pointed my M-16 at him and fired," he later related. The noise compromised the ambush location and caused the men to extract.

Always with a markedly unique sense of humor, frogmen throughout Vietnam faced their physical adversities with directness. A sign composed and posted by the SEALs at Nha Be read:

Welcome to the Nha Be summer resort. For your pleasure we provide *Swimming Facilities*: Delightful frolics under the ships in the harbor. *Boating Excursions*: Try one of our famous moonlight cruises down the river. *Camping Trips*: Enjoy a night out in the open air as you sit comfortably and companionably beside a trail or a stream.

On 19 March, a SEAL Team One patrol carried a sniper rifle on an ambush/abduction mission with poor results. It seemed to be more trouble than benefit to lug the precision weapon through the mud and thick vegetation, only to find fields of fire that could be covered easily by a weapon with regular iron sights. The biggest problem was that the sniper weapon was not an effective tool at night for SEAL operations at that stage in the war, as the SEALs reported.

The SEALs also attempted to pioneer other new techniques in order to gain the upper hand against the sly and elusive enemy. While most squads inserted by riverine craft into their patrol areas, some swam from their boats to shore. A SEAL Team One group on 19 March jumped from the stern of its PBR as it continued to move up a river. In this way, the engine noise continued at the same pitch and would not indicate to VC close at hand that men had been placed ashore. The team inserted with minimal equipment. No radios were carried. Each man had his weapon, two magazines of ammunition, a flare, and a red lens flashlight. Many platoons and squads used this method during the war to insert. It was found in the early years that the engine noise at about 1,500 to 1,800 RPM from a PBR created enough ambient noise to cover the technique. Another method was to coordinate an overflight of helicopters. Their noise and distraction would often cover the noise of a team inserting or closing on a target.

Other patrols utilized false insertions and extractions to try to catch the enemy. The riverine craft would feint putting men ashore at various points to make the VC nervous and force them to move, a process similar to hunters flushing a rabbit or quail from the bush. The SEALs would then try to catch the VC in ambush. During "false extractions," half of the team would depart the patrol area as others remained in place to lure the enemy into a sense of security as they saw and heard the partial patrol depart. A variation of the false extraction, the double-back ambush had the entire patrol fake a withdrawal to the water as if they were extracting. They would then hook around onto their own trail and lay an ambush for anyone tailing or tracking them. The men of SEAL Team Two were shifted slightly once again to take advantage of these unorthodox tactics that they and other SEALs were mastering. On 31 March, 2nd platoon was moved to the PBR base at My Tho to begin operations in that part of the Delta.

In April, more emphasis was placed on intelligence collection to determine VC patterns, locations, and lines of communication and supply. SEALs were sent out to occupy observation and listening posts concealed in dense undergrowth for up to seven days at a time. On one such operation, a SEAL officer who had won an Olympic Gold Medal in swimming in 1960 lay silently along a river with three of his men. The enemy force spotted them and surrounded the entire area. For the next nineteen hours, the numerically superior VC searched for the squad, which hid in dense vegetation and chest-deep mud. At one point, one particular Vietnamese nearly stepped on the SEAL officer. The frogmen remained undetected and slipped away.

On 4 April, SEAL Team One's Kilo platoon arrived in-country, followed three days later by Lima platoon. On 7 April, the newly arrived Kilo platoon from Team One was transiting to an operational area near the mouth of the Vam Sat River within the RSSZ when its riverine craft entered a Vietcong ambush. This time, the SEALs' luck ran out. The vessel took heavy fire, and was only able to limp out of the area to escape the hail of enemy ordnance. In addition to small-arms fire, the boat was also struck by several enemy rockets. It was one of these B-40 rockets that killed three SEALs onboard: Lt. Daniel Mann, Interior Communications Electrician Third Class Donald Boston, and Radioman Third Class Robert Neal. After removing itself from the area to the Soirap River, the riverine craft evacuated the dead and wounded by helo.

In the after-action report, the SEALs indicated that the LCM had been used for a recon by fire on this operation. As the craft traveled upriver, its organic weapons were fired ashore into the brush to try to get an equal response from the enemy. By doing so, the enemy would reveal his location, and the SEALs, along with close air support, could overwhelm them. On the 7 April operation, the recon by fire had created an aggressive response from the Vietcong. The SEALs, who did not agree with being a part of this technique, felt that the craft should be used to quietly insert and extract them and for communications relay and support. Another hard lesson had been learned.

On the 18th, a three-man SEAL listening post killed three Vietcong communications-liaison personnel as they attempted a route crossing near Giai Island. At the end of the month, two SEAL squads conducted a daylight raid twelve miles southeast of Can Tho. Six VC were killed and one captured in the action.

On the evening of the first day of May, the USS *Tunny* bottomed out off the coast of Phouc Tien Province in the southern part of I Corps. A team from UDT 11's Det Charlie locked out of the sub with their equipment and boats. After ascending to the surface, the boat was inflated and the men climbed aboard with their gear. Using an underwater acoustic pinger, the submarine vectored the frogmen toward the target beach. A large number of small indigenous craft were sighted, but the group slipped ashore undetected. Using a new communications device, the men remained in contact with the sub via a length of wire taken from an MK 37–1 wireguided torpedo. Following the reconnaissance, the team paddled back to the *Tunny*, which snagged their towing line with its periscope. The *Tunny* then towed the boats into deeper waters and surfaced for recovery. Another beach recon had been successfully completed.

Later in May, Det Bravo from UDT 11 came under heavy mortar attack while supporting Operation Hickory in the Demilitarized Zone (DMZ). Teamwork and organization in the face of enemy fire helped expedite the evacuation and recovery of the wounded.

On several operations later in the spring, teams laid sensors deep in enemy-controlled territory. The McQuire Rig was used further for extraction when patrols were unable to find a landing zone large enough for a helo to touch down. Other teams found that U.S. Army artillery spotting rounds could be fired within hearing range of the patrols as an aid to navigation when their operational areas lacked noteworthy navigational terrain features in the swamps.

When laying in ambush, the SEALs at times would use hand grenades rather than weapons fire for small contacts so as not to give away their exact position in case the small contact turned out to be part of a much larger enemy element. On 17 May, one SEAL Team One platoon even tried to use a PBR as bait. As the craft lay beached along a riverbank, the team set ambush positions to its front in the hopes that a few VC would attempt to get close enough to take a shot at the naval craft. One enemy soldier was seen creeping through the bush and was engaged, but he slipped away cleanly. The cat-and-mouse game continued.

The first two SEAL Team Two platoons were now nearing the end of their tours. They prepared to return to the States, where they could instruct other East Coast frogmen on the methods of this new backwater war. On May 30, 4th platoon from Team Two relieved 2nd platoon in-country. The debriefings of 2nd platoon members helped prepare other SEALs for their first encounter with the Vietnam Delta war. The West Coasters continued to rotate men into the war and became ever more experienced. Echo platoon from Team One arrived at Nha Be on 16 June and immediately began running operations.

In May, SEAL Detachment Bravo was established to advise Vietnamese Provincial Reconnaissance Units (PRUs) in the Delta. Half of SEAL Team Two's 4th platoon was assigned advisory roles as well as men from SEAL Team One. The mission of the detachment was to lead and advise the PRUs in their operations against the cadre of the communist guerrillas within the various provinces. Field units would react to intelligence reports and attempt to capture or kill known guerrilla leaders.

The indigenous PRUs were a hardened lot of warriors. Many were criminals who chose to fight for the South rather than waste away in a Vietnamese jail. Some were former Vietcong. In all, it took the strong leadership of the army's Green Berets and the navy's SEALs to control these fighters in combat. Contrary to the popular impression, the PRUs did not specialize in covert assassination, though they did target specific VC leaders for abduction and capture. By detaining and questioning the captives, the Allies were able to ferret out more of the enemy infrastructure. If the PRUs could not net their targets, they often killed them in open combat.

On 7 June, a five-man SEAL Team Two patrol was conducting a demolition strike against a Vietcong rest area near the northern tip of Tan Dinh Island. Several enemy soldiers were seen manoeuvring to set an ambush against the Americans, and the patrol leader immediately engaged them, killing one VC. An estimated twelve to fifteen other VC then opened fire on the frogmen, and the SEALs pulled back under fire. Two other Vietcong were subsequently killed in the engagement, while the Americans escaped unharmed.

Two squads attacked an enemy hamlet in a daylight raid two miles southwest of My Tho on the 18th. Three VC were killed, three wounded, and four others captured.

Naval planners met at the end of June under Admiral Veth in a SEAL symposium to decide the future employment of SEALs in order to increase their already substantial effectiveness. At the same time, frogmen continued to rotate into the combat zone. On 26 June, 5th platoon from SEAL Team Two relieved 3rd platoon in-country. UDT 11's Det Bravo conducted river surveys and assisted in reconnaissance operations in the Mekong Delta during June and July.

Other operations continued. Three Vietcong leaders, two men and a woman, were kidnapped from their base in II Corps, twenty miles northeast of Phan Thiet in the Le Hong Phong Secret Zone, by Team One SEALs from Juliett and Kilo platoons. They launched their commando raid on 4 July 1967 from an offshore destroyer, the USS *Brush*. One other VC was killed as she attempted to flee the raiding party. Important documents concerning enemy political actions were also captured. The SEALs launched their mission in small rubber boats and used swimmer scouts to recon their beach landing site prior to coming ashore. The dark moon and clear weather allowed them to move quietly in the sand dunes and steep hills of the region. Naval gunfire support played only a small supporting role to ground units throughout the war, but 164 rounds of naval gunfire were expended by *Brush* in strong support of this SEAL raid. *Brush* and other naval vessels proved to be much more than passive insertion craft for SEALs on many operations.

Several other contacts, involving numerous VC killed in action, were made by SEALs while patrolling throughout July, mostly as a result of a refinement of tactics and techniques. On 9 July, one of the operations by a squad from Team Two's 4th platoon captured important documents concerning the VC infrastructure in the Binh Dai Special Zone. The ambush patrol fired on several VC along the Bong Ca Creek on the final day of their mission, twenty-eight miles southeast of Ben Tre. Four enemy soldiers were killed in the raid. Included in the seized information were two map overlays and a list of VC personnel from six districts. The captured data resulted in a larger operation conducted by the ARVN Seventh Division on 17 July.

Two SEAL squads were landed in Bien Hoa Province near the suspected headquarters of the Vietcong commander of the RSSZ on 20 July. Four VC were killed by the teams as they attempted to slip out of the area using two different sampans. Numerous supplies and weapons were captured, but the VC commander was not located. A SEAL Team One group was compromised on a mission on 21 July after having to shoot an aggressive wild pig; the team was extracted shortly thereafter. At the end of the month, a SEAL patrol contacted an enemy force of unknown size while conducting a daylight raid on a base camp on Ilo Ilo Island. After a brief fight, the enemy broke and ran. The SEALs destroyed fourteen structures in the camp.

UDT 11's Det Delta was based at Danang, with smaller teams "farmed out" to locations at Chu Lai and Cua Viet. On 15 July, Det Delta was forced to move unexpectedly from

Camp Tien Sha to the Tien Sha Annex. The men of the unit did all they could to improve their physical circumstance, building a center for all the UDT detachments to enjoy as they rotated off the ARG and other vessels for rest and recuperation. Other detachments from UDT 12 and 13 worked out of the Danang base in their rotations through Vietnam later in the war. The facility was affectionately dubbed "Frogsville" by men in the teams.

Besides their explosives employment in the I Corps area, the men also took advantage of other opportunities that presented themselves. From 16 to 22 August, one officer and two enlisted men from the detachment attended U.S. Army Airborne School at Phan Rang in South Vietnam. The condensed course lasted eight days. By this time in the late 1960s, it was becoming more common for all frogmen to be qualified parachutists. Dets Echo and Foxtrot from UDT 11 were located aboard two different amphibious ready groups. The teams participated in nine different amphibious operations in Vietnam during the cruise. During one operation, Beau Charger, the beach party came under heavy mortar attack near Cam Pao. The officer in charge received the Vietnamese Cross of Gallantry for his actions, which organized the force and evacuated wounded and nonessential personnel from the beach.

Two SEAL squads landed in an area near the mouth of the My Tho River on the night of 1 August and conducted a three-hour patrol. Three VC were killed and one captured in the fighting, while numerous documents and weaponry were also discovered. A number of intelligence documents, along with forty 82 mm mortar rounds, were recovered from two sampans, which were ambushed by a SEAL Team Two squad on 2 August. In early August, the Army's 199th Infantry Brigade requested recon assistance from Det Golf in the Delta. A combined SEAL/LDNN ambush team from Nha Be killed five Vietcong nineteen miles south of Saigon on 7 August. Two sampans had entered their kill zone, but only one was successful in escaping. Also in August, one SEAL ambush by Echo platoon led to the capture of ten pounds of valuable enemy documents carried by a VC courier in the

RSSZ. Five VC were killed by Team One ambushers on the 6th.

It seemed that the combined efforts of all the SEAL squads was beginning to gel for naval planners. The navy could never hope to stop the flow of men and arms into the Delta using riverine craft, but their defensive patrols had a great impact. With the addition of several SEAL platoons, the navy had a significant offensive reaction force. The enemy forces seemed unable to predict where the SEALs would strike next. One thing they could predict, however, was that when they met the SEALs, the VC almost always took casualties. Most were lucky to escape with a wound. Although the SEALs continued to run a variety of patrols, the riverine ambush remained the simplest and most effective operation for the frogmen. On the 11th, an ambush patrol from Team One was forced to extract when one member was bitten by a spider and had a severe reaction. Only a quick medevac saved his life. The man had been clearing a field of fire in preparation for occupying an ambush site. The Delta environment alone was sometimes the worst enemy of all.

In a large operation on 16 August, twenty frogmen and six Vietnamese swept the island of Culaodung. Located in the mouth of the Bassac River, the island had long been a VC stronghold. A defector provided reports, placing the number of enemy troops on the island at about two hundred men. The assault run began after dawn, and at 0900, the river craft were turned toward the bank. Overhead, three Seawolf helos provided fire support. For five hours, the SEALs fought brief skirmishes and destroyed bunkers and hootches (native shacks or quonset huts used as barracks) used by the Vietcong. Fourteen tons of rice were destroyed, along with fifty-three huts, fourteen bunkers, and six sampans. Only three VC stood to face the frogmen. All three were killed in the fighting. "The Vietcong are really shook when we go into their backyard and hit them," one SEAL officer said. "Well, we hit them today and they'll know they're no longer safe in the areas they control."

A Vietcong defector led another group of SEALs from 5th platoon into a VC camp on 18 August. Three enemy leaders were killed, and an armory and printing facility were destroyed. Alfa platoon from SEAL Team One arrived in-country in August and began operations. It was during August that a third direct-action platoon from SEAL Team One was committed to operations in Vietnam, joining the four others already conducting missions (two from each coast). The expansion was further evidence that naval planners were now much more comfortable with the SEALs' operations and welcomed their proliferation throughout the IV Corps region.

One particular SEAL ambush in 1967 in Kien Giang Province provided a surprise to a frogman force. The SEALs had been watching a reported supply route used by enemy forces on a remote canal. Late in the afternoon of the second day of their surveillance, a VC sampan floated into the kill zone. Besides the two indigenous guerrillas onboard, a tall, heavy Caucasian with a beard rode in the bow. He was dressed in what looked like a khaki uniform and was holding a communist assault rifle. Just as the craft pulled into the area, the communists became leery, as if sensing the danger nearby. Although initially startled at seeing the white man, the SEALs immediately let the law of the barroom prevail – when a fight is unavoidable, strike first, and strike hard. The frogmen unleashed a hail of fire into the enemy force. The Caucasian was hit in the chest in the initial burst of fire and went overboard. The VC attempted to jump in and assist him. Just then, a superior Vietcong force appeared and counterattacked. Outnumbered and outgunned, the SEALs fought a running gun battle to an area where they could extract. Later, they were debriefed about the incident by an intelligence officer. They were told to remain silent about the action. South Vietnamese intelligence had reported that the white man had been a Russian. It would remain a little-known fact that the guerrillas and North Vietnamese were assisted in their Third World brushfire war by a host of foreign advisors and technicians, including Soviets, Chinese, Eastern Bloc, Cuban, Korean, and other communist nationals.

Rotations for all the teams continued. On 25 August, Det Charlie from UDT 11 moved to Okinawa to conduct readiness training while the USS *Tunny* underwent maintenance in

Yokosuka, Japan. On 28 August, 6th platoon from the East Coast's SEAL Team Two relieved a West Coast platoon from SEAL Team One in-country. While the war was of primary concern to the men in the field, the political front proved just as unstable. On 3 September, Nguyen Van Thieu was elected president of South Vietnam, ending a series of power struggles between top leaders of the South which had occurred since the assassination of Diem in 1963. Besides the communist insurgency, the South Vietnamese fought many internal struggles for control.

During September and October, small high-speed fiberglass boats, called "Boston Whalers," were first tested by riverine forces. One application used by the SEALs was to recover ambushed sampans before they had a chance to sink or slip further downriver. These craft accounted for a higher confirmation of enemy KIA and the capture of even more documents and equipment as a result of higher recovery rates.

On 16 September, three SEAL platoons inserted and swept Tan Dinh Island as part of Operation Crimson Tide. Three VC were killed, a number captured, and a large VC staging area was destroyed. On 21 September, a SEAL Team One Alfa platoon ambush decimated a VC sapper squad, which was enroute to mine the Long Tau River. Seven VC were killed in the action, and their equipment was captured. Another ambush on the 28th along the Thi Vai River, seventeen miles east of Nha Be, killed four VC and wounded one. One sampan and numerous documents were recovered. Combined SEAL/LDNN missions on 13 and 28 September resulted in eleven Vietcong killed.

On 6 October, Signalman Third Class Leslie Funk, a member of SEAL Team One, drowned while training for operations in the RSSZ. He was initially pronounced as missing, but his status was changed when his body was found. With the heavier operational commitment, the teams were beginning to sustain additional casualties. On occasion, the VC now chose to stand against the frogmen. During an operation on 13 October, one particular SEAL stopped a VC attempt to overrun his unit with a heavy and accurate volume of 40 mm grenade fire. Six enemy soldiers were killed by his defense.

At times, the SEALs scored heavily by capturing documents or a key VC leader. Additional Crimson Tide sweeps of Tan Dinh Island on 19, 21, and 23 October saw light action for the SEALs; seven enemy soldiers were killed and several captured. One of the captives was identified as the man who had murdered the national police chief in 1962. South Vietnamese soldiers working with the SEALs had to be restrained from killing the prisoner on the spot following the identification. SEAL riverine ambushes on the 21st and 23rd killed four Vietcong.

As the weather cleared toward the end of the year, more emphasis was placed on ambushes since this tactic yielded the largest volume of captured enemy documents. Enemy documents continued to be a tremendous intelligence resource. The East Coast SEAL platoons were now becoming manned by combat-experienced men, much the same as SEAL Team One platoons. On 24 October, 7th platoon from Virginia relieved 4th platoon.

On 31 October, a SEAL ambush twenty-six miles southeast of My Tho killed two enemy soldiers. As the frogmen swept the area, they received weapons fire from a bunker complex and immediately went into the attack. Two more VC were killed, and the SEALs demolished fourteen bunkers and twenty structures, capturing several hundred rounds of ammunition.

Eight ambushes during November and December were successful in making contact. An ambush team on 12 November along the Ba Gioi River, twelve miles east southeast of Nha Be, listened to a Vietcong unit training with weapons and grenades throughout the day. Before withdrawing by riverine craft, the SEALs finally killed three enemy soldiers in a sampan as the VC transited the area. On 15 November, a SEAL Team Two squad killed a VC district security chief in a riverine ambush. The man had long eluded South Vietnamese forces and was notorious for atrocities he had participated in and supervised.

The Vietcong continued to employ innovative munitions against the Allies. One SEAL received severe injuries to his left hand when he attempted to disarm a simple grenade booby-trap. It was then determined that the device was specially rigged to detonate when the grenade spoon was depressed toward the grenade body. The surprise caused a serious injury, but it resulted in the dissemination of the intelligence to other units which then began to watch out for similar devices around VC base camps.

On 25 November, another SEAL Team Two platoon patrolled to several hootches and placed them under observation in the predawn hours. After light, two Vietnamese attempted to escape the area and were fired upon by the Americans. The shouting of fifteen to twenty men was then heard from three sides, and the SEALs called for a riverine craft to extract. During exfiltration, heavy fire was received from the three sides, and the SEALs fought their way to the river, at one time overrunning a bunker directly in the path of their escape route and occupied by four Vietcong. Six VC in all were killed in the action.

Late in the year, one SEAL Team One squad found that using low-flying helos over its area covered the noise of a riverine craft used to insert the team. On three consecutive patrols, they were able to make contact by using this ruse.

From 16 to 24 November, 7th platoon elements operated in Giao Duc District during Operation Cuu Long. They killed fifteen VC and captured eleven, along with one B-40 rocket, an AK-47, and sixteen Chicom rifles. The platoon also destroyed eighty bunkers and seven sampans. The same platoon killed three enemy soldiers and captured one other in a sweep operation ten miles southwest of My Tho. UDT 12 officially relieved UDT 11 of its WESTPAC duties as of 4 December. On 9 December, SEAL Team One's Bravo Platoon relieved Echo platoon in-country; 8th platoon from the East Coast relieved 5th platoon.

The 7th platoon killed six VC and captured one other while attempting to insert and move to a planned ambush site on 20 December. On 23 December, the newly arrived Bravo platoon inserted six miles east of Nha Be for a thirty-six-hour recon/ambush patrol. The team began to patrol toward the southeast and east and had moved only a short distance before being contacted by heavy weapons fire. While acting as point man for the operation in the RSSZ, Seaman Frank Antone was hit by small-arms fire from the initial Vietcong burst and killed. The team had been patrolling deep inside enemy territory and had penetrated a VC regimental headquarters. The men fought their way to an extraction point and called for helo support. Antone, a Vietnamese LDNN also killed in the fight, and several other wounded men were extracted by McQuire Rig. The rest of the team was pulled out by army helos.

At the end of 1967, nearly 500,000 U.S. servicemen were serving in Vietnam. The U.S. ground role continued to grow and had yet to peak. For the men of Naval Special Warfare, the war was now becoming an everyday reality, and 1967 became the first year that almost all the teams were deeply committed to the conflict. The beaches of every corps area were becoming quite familiar to UDT surveyors. By the end of the year, a majority of UDT and SEAL Team members were combat veterans, unlike the year before. As 1967 began, the SEALs were just gaining strong recognition for their abilities in the RSSZ. As the year ended, the frogmen were developing into an effective offensive naval instrument throughout the Mekong Delta. Their independent squad-size operations were netting significant results when appraised as a whole. Like the overall conventional capability, however, the men of Naval Special Warfare had yet to peak in number and effectiveness.

SUEZ
J. C. Beadle

The accession of the strongly nationalistic President Abdel Nasser to power in Egypt was quickly followed by demands for the withdrawal of British forces stationed there. On 31 March 1956 the last British military units left the country, although Britain retained a large share in the company which ran the Suez canal. On 26 July, President Nasser nationalized the canal company in order to finance the Aswan High Dam project. He also forbade Israel use of the canal, a contravention of the 1888 treaty which allowed its free use by all nations. Israel determined to invade the Sinai peninsula as a reprisal. An agreement was also reached by Israel with Britain and France that they would intervene soon after the Israelis moved, ostensibly to protect the canal from the warring parties. Among the British units committed to the Suez invasion were the Royal Marines 40 and 42 Commandos. Both Commandos had their origin in World War II RM Commandos (see "The Seizure of Walcheren") which were disbanded in 1946, but reformed afterwards.

THE PLAN INVOLVED a sea-borne assault on Port Said to land 40 Commando (left) and 42 Commando (right), either side of the Casino Pier. The assault troops were to be carried in LVTs and LCAs, to land at 0445 hours with H Hour 35 minutes after sunrise. The landing would be preceded by air strikes and Naval gun support to destroy gun and beach defences. The French sea-borne assault was to commence on Port Fouad at 0705 hours followed by a British parachute battalion descent 10 minutes later onto Gamil airfield. The French parachutists were to drop on Port Fouad and 45 Commando was to land by helicopter in the area of the interior basin.

The task of 40 and 42 Commandos was to establish a

beach-head and, at H plus 20 minutes, a squadron of tanks would land to support them in the break out from the beach-head. 40 Commando would then advance along the Bund and capture the four shipping basins. On their right, 42 Commando would advance along the Shari Mohammed Ali to capture the bridge over the interior basin and water works. 45 Commando, after landing in the area to the north of the interior basin, was to relieve 42 Commando at the bridges and provide a stop at the north end of the causeway. When this phase was completed the three Commandos would each dominate an area of the city.

On 26 September, 40 Commando embarked in ships of the A W Squadron and carried out close support live firings with HMS *Duchess* at Filfla Island, off the west coast of Malta. Lt Gen Sir Hugh Stockwell, Commander Land Forces, visited the unit the following day and gave a rousing talk to the men. The intensive training of all elements of the Commando units and A W Squadron continued throughout September and into October. There was considerable emphasis on house to house fighting (firing blank ammunition) but this could only be practised in two derelict barrack blocks near Brigade HQ. There were no facilities for a tactical grenade throwing range and live grenade training was confined to one bay on the rifle range. Exercising with tanks of "C" Squadron was hampered by a Maltese Government restriction on the movement of armoured vehicles. Nevertheless the tank crews and commandos established a good working relationship.

Brig Madoc returned from London on 13 October with details of a new Winter Plan and Lt Gen Stockwell arrived in Malta on 17 October to attend the planning conferences. Before any changes could be implemented the plan was shelved. The men were by this time fully trained, very fit and wondering whether they would ever get to Egypt. A sense of excitement swept through St Andrews Barracks on 23 October when the Brigade was brought to 24 hours notice but the order was rescinded and the situation continued as before.

In the diplomatic arena the complex discussions, postures and promises between governments of countries immediately involved with the Suez crisis, as well as recriminations between political parties, were coming to a head. France, committed to the support of Israel, had increased the delivery of fighter aircraft to 60 a month. Israel, responding to border incidents made a raid in strength across the Egyptian border. The Jordan Nationalist Socialist Party, campaigning against the Anglo-Jordan treaty was elected to power. Israel commenced to mobilise on 25 October, accusing Egypt of making incursions into Israel. At 1700 hours, 29 October, Israeli armoured units attacked Egypt.

The British and French Prime Ministers, having already decided a course of action in the event of Israel invading Egypt, delivered an ultimatum to Cairo and Tel Aviv on 30 October stating, that unless they withdrew their forces ten miles from the Suez Canal, Great Britain and France would take their own measures to enforce the decision and occupy Port Said, Ismalia and Suez. When the announcement was made in the House of Commons at 1600 hours, Labour protested that such action independent of the USA and UNO would be a risky gamble. (At the time of the ultimatum Israel's ground forces had not reached the 10 mile limit and could therefore continue to advance to this demarcation. But Egyptian ground forces would have to abandon positions still held on the east side of the canal). The ultimatum was rejected by Col Nasser.

Commando Brigade operation and administrative orders were issued to HQ staffs at 2330 hours 28 October and the following morning the Commando units received orders to prepare for a major amphibious exercise, including the waterproofing of vehicles and the issue of ammunition. This procedure took 24 hours but the embarkation of the Brigade (less 45 Commando) comprising 178 officers and 2,300 other ranks, with over 550 vehicles including 51 Centurion tanks, was completed by 2230 hours 30 October. 40 Commando was allocated to LST *Reggio*, commanded by Lt Cdr I. Stoop and LCT *Bastion* under command of Lt Cdr R. Davidson. At 2359 hours the A W Squadron, consisting of the HQ ship HMS *Meon*, 3 LST(A)s, 5 LSTs and 8 LCTs, sailed from Grand Harbour.

The landing-craft usually turned to port on leaving harbour

for exercise landings in one of the bays. However, Sgt Gratrix remembers "On this occasion we turned to starboard and kept going out to sea. After half an hour a voice on the tannoy said we were heading for Suez. The convoy sailed in two lines at an average speed of six knots, the speed of the slowest vessel. At this point in proceedings Port Said seemed a long way distant". 45 Commando, who would cover the distance more quickly in the aircraft carriers HMS *Ocean* and *Theseus* sailed on 2 November. Cdr E. Bruce, in LCT *Sallyport* recorded "To get into the habit of things we had 'Action stations' from the time of sailing. Life belts were always worn and the ship was in a war cruising state."

Late evening on 31 October, Brig Madoc received a signal from the Allied Task Force Commander, ordering the cancellation of the helicopter assault by 45 Commando as the task of capturing the bridges had been allocated to a French parachute force. In consequence 45 Commando would be available to Brig Madoc as a floating reserve. This late alteration had to be notified to personnel dispersed in 20 ships in the convoy and with the landing only a few days ahead the Brigadier decided that 40 Commando's task would remain more or less unchanged. After the break-out from the beach-head 42 Commando was to advance to the southern end of the city, to prevent infiltration from the Arab quarter and link up with 40 Commando south of the built up area. 45 Commando would remain in reserve, and when ordered by the Brigade Commander, would be carried by helicopters to the beach-head to support 40 and 42 Commandos as required. Finally, 45 Commando would proceed on foot to join up with the French parachutists at the bridges.

On 4 November new orders were received which required the Allied parachute troops to drop on 5 November, a day earlier than planned. The sea-borne landing would be made on 6 November as arranged but naval gun support, to exclude all guns of 6-in calibre and above, would only be fired in reply to Egyptian gun-fire. Only if events indicated an opposed landing would drenching fire from support ships be ordered. The change in orders relating to gun-fire support was decided at a very senior level in UK to minimise Egyptian casualties, but it left the question of whether the Commandos would have gun-support to cover the landing uncertain. Confirmation that it would be available was not made known to Brig Madoc until 60 minutes before H-hour.

Daily broadcasts received from the BBC London were not conducive to bolstering morale. The daily exchanges by MPs in the House of Commons could not be construed as supportive and statements by the Leader of the Opposition were so demoralising that on one occasion the ships broadcast system on LCT *Bastion* was turned off. The slow progress of the convoy was monitored by the USA Sixth Fleet. Boldly, in daylight on 4 November, a submarine of the US Navy surfaced and passed through the lines of British ships. No recognition colours were hoisted and no crew were to be seen. During the night of Landing Day minus two (L-2), the convoy increased speed in the direction of Port Said. On L-1 all was ready. According to Cdr Bruce in LCT *Sallyport* "The French assault element had just joined us and the place bristled with escorts. The paratroops had gone in 20 hours early, and then came news of a local armistice. Perhaps rather an anti-climax. However at 2300 hours came the news that the armistice was off and an opposed landing could be expected. The night was not so dark and I could make out the shapes of the battleship astern of us, then the carriers with the choppers. I heard their bugle call at 0200 hours. That was action stations for us also." At first light Brig Madoc could see Port Said in the distance with a dense pall of black smoke drifting over the city from a burning oil tank to the south. Lecturing to the staff of the Royal Naval Staff College in May 1957 he said "There were no lights showing and no signs of life."

40 and 42 Commandos transferred to their LVTs and LCAs and set off towards the beach. 40 Commando landed at 0447 hours, two minutes after H-hour. Their first task was to establish a small beach-head, with 42 Commando carrying out a similar assignment on their right. During the run-in there was very little shooting and the actual landing was carried out without much incident. There were no mines on the beach and it is interesting to note that there were only two beaches at Port Said where an amphibious assault could land.

The other at Gamil airfield was heavily mined with anti-tank and anti-personnel mines.

The commandos in the landing craft were pleased to see that the fire support was right on time. The RAF dealt with coastal defences from H-55 to H-45 and then HMS *Diamond* and HMS *Duchess* opened up, firing nearly 1,400 rounds of 4.5-inch, in direct support of the landing force. At H-5 the Fleet Air Arm delivered a strike on the Beach area 400 yards ahead of the LVTs. The first wave of LVTs carrying A and X Troops towards the beach was fired on during the last stage of the run-in and while crossing the beach but there were no casualties. Machine-guns were found in the beach huts where they had been abandoned by their crews. Had they been more determined they could have created untold mayhem.

The first wave ashore was involved in limited fighting to capture the buildings at the back of the beach. A Troop, led by Capt R. Grant, had the task of clearing a large block of flats, about 200 yards from the beach-head. According to Sgt Gratrix "Our 2-inch mortar-man laid smoke as near as possible to the building and we advanced a section at a time. In the process of clearing the flats two Egyptian soldiers were killed and one wounded". The 3.5-inch rocket launcher was used with great success to winkle out enemy positions in buildings. X Troop led by Maj A. P. Willasey-Wilsey, met stiffer opposition in the buildings on the right, killing 15 Egyptian soldiers and capturing three more before the area was finally cleared.

The second wave of seven LCAs carrying B, P and Y Troops, and the Commando Tac HQ, landed at 0450 hours. Y Troop, led by Capt D. Morgan, captured Liberation Barracks, to the south of De Lesseps statue while B Troop, led by Capt M. Marston, cleared the Fishing Harbour area and the breakwater before becoming reserve Troop. The HQ Troop element led by Capt C. J. Verdon, took over and established B Echelon in Liberation Barracks. The third wave, consisting of the remainder of HQ and S Troop landed at 0500 hours and the 3-inch Mortar Group set up base plates, but no calls were made by the rifle Troops for fire support.

The Fishing Harbour had been secured by 0700 hours and

it was possible to call in LCT *Bastion*, carrying the Anti-Tank Platoon and first-line vehicles. A few shells passed over the ship in both directions during the run-in and on the approach along the Western Wall the commandos found themselves looking directly into the muzzles of six, 3-pounder guns. From Lt Whitehead's viewpoint on *Bastion* "It was not a pretty sight and for one moment we thought we would be lucky to go much further." Fortunately for the commandos the undamaged guns had been abandoned by the Egyptian gunners. Once ashore the 17-pounders, towed by Stuarts and crewed by gunners from 1st Battalion Royal Berkshire Regiment, deployed to cover the Rue al Gamhuriyah and Rue Vingt Trois Juillet.

The Royal Navy soon discovered that the Egyptians had sunk a number of ships in the Canal entrance thereby blocking access to the Commercial Basin and quays. The superstructures of five ships were clearly visible and it was suspected that more vessels were completely submerged. Minesweepers, attempting to clear a path for the LSTs, lost their sweeps on the submerged obstructions and had to give up the task. Alternative berths for the LSTs were found alongside the Casino Hotel and in the Fishing Harbour.

The supporting armour, consisting of 11 Troop C Sqn 6 RTR, landed in the beach-head at 0535 hours to join up with the Commandos. P Troop, led by Lt J. P. Gardner, with the Centurion tanks in support, advanced along the Quai Sultan Hussein as far as the Port Police Station, completing the first leg of 40 Commando's Phase II in 15 minutes despite coming under fire at each road junction from buildings in the town. A marine was wounded while crossing these obstacles and a JNCO and marine were hit by shell splinters from a round fired by one of the tanks which exploded against the dockyard railings ahead of them. Another unfortunate casualty was caused by the back-blast of a 106 mm anti-tank missile, fired from the roof of Liberation Barracks. The blast dislodged a coping stone which fell on a signaller below.

Capt Grant received orders to proceed with A Troop and one Centurion tank in support, to release the British Consul from house arrest. The approach along the Suez Canal met with some opposition and took about an hour. As Sgt Gratrix remembers it "The Consulate stood on the corner of some lovely ornamental gardens which were about 300 yds square. The buildings on this corner had to be cleared floor by floor and when cleared coloured markers – in the shape of a cross – were placed on the flat roofs to warn the Fleet Air Arm pilots that the commandos were in occupation. My section came under fire from a building on the other side of the gardens but the tank commander had spotted this and silenced the position with two HE shells". The 3.5-inch rocket launchers were also used to good effect by A Troop on enemy positions in buildings.

The Consulate square was strongly held by Egyptian infantry and A Troop had to fight hard to clear the way to the British Embassy. At the height of the engagement S Troop commander Capt Cooper, armed with his sniper rifle, went forward to see how the situation was progressing. In typical officers school playlet style his greeting to Capt Grant was "Hello Dicky, what's the form?" As he spoke a bullet flattened itself on the wall between them. "That!" replied Dicky Grant, stating the most precise assessment of the situation!

By the time the area had been cleared 23 Egyptian soldiers had been killed and a further 14 had been taken prisoner. Information provided by the prisoners indicated that eight of their number had been sent to kill the British Consul. In the clearance operation over 200 Soviet manufactured weapons and a large quantity of ammunition was found in the buildings overlooking the square.

Elsewhere the battle was progressing well. The French paratroops were in possession of Port Fouad and the British 3rd Parachute Battalion, having captured Gamil Airfield, was fighting its way via the Coastguard Barracks and hospital towards shanty town. The British paratroops met stiff opposition and a call was made for Naval gun support to neutralise the area. At the beach-head, 42 Commando had silenced opposition on their right flank and proceeded along the Shard Mohammed with amphibians and 10 Centurion tanks in support. Their progress was harassed by small arms fire and grenades thrown from buildings. The power station and cold storage depot – their objectives to the south of the built up area – were well defended by the Egyptians and there was some stiff fighting before they eventually captured these buildings.

One and a half hours after H Hour, the leading elements of 45 Commando, accompanied by the CGRM, were brought in by helicopter to land near the De Lesseps statue. The shuttle service proceeded as programmed and, according to Cdr Bruce watching the landings "It looked good, and I laughed to see the commandos so crowded that one man had to sit with his legs dangling out". While they were preparing to move along the Shard Mohammed to back up 42 Commando, a Royal Navy plane made a strike on the area, wounding 45 Commando's CO, Lt Col N. H. Tailyour, and causing 17 other casualties. Maj R. Crombie assumed command and the Commando continued the follow up to make contact with 42 Commando. Lt D. Edwards, leading a 40 Commando house-clearing team, later said "I could hardly believe my eyes when I glanced at a passing figure and recognised Gen Hardy, whose obvious intention was to have a ring-side view of the action."

By using the Fishing Harbour more extensively than planned the Navy overcame the problems of the blockaded Canal, and instead of being two hours behind schedule in bringing in the first LST, were soon ahead of programme. The beach party worked desperately hard to clear berths for the landing-craft ferrying troops and equipment from the ships. The ships blocking the Canal prevented access to the berths near Navy House, but in any event this continued to be an unhealthy area in which to remain for long.

In the meantime Y Troop, under the command of Capt Morgan, led the advance of 40 Commando with gun support from two of the four Centurion tanks allocated to the unit. Enemy resistance from the area of the huts at the north-west corner of the Commercial Basin was eliminated after one Egyptian had been taken prisoner and two had been killed. Movement along the western side was held up for a time by accurate fire from the direction of the town, resulting in the death of Mne L. Dudhill. The Centurions neutralised the enemy fire enabling the advance to continue to the Suez Canal building. Here, the opposition was quickly overrun leaving two enemy dead. During this time the tank armament and troop LMGs were used effectively against the Egyptian infantry who could be seen withdrawing southward from the town centre.

B Troop, commanded by Capt M. A. Marston, assumed the lead along the northern side of the Arsenal Basin. Almost immediately the forward sections came under intense and accurate fire from the Customs Houses on their left, killing Mne R. J. Fudge and wounding another marine. One section of the troop occupied the Police Station, where they disarmed and took custody of 12 policemen who were in the building. Wireless contact with the tanks was lost at this point and a runner was sent to X Troop with a request to secure the northern flank and neutralise enemy fire from the direction of the town and railway station.

Lt E. A. Ufton, led a section of B Troop in an attack on the Customs House. Two marines fell wounded as they raced forward but having gained an entry they cleared the area immediately in front of them and then moved to the next floor from which emanated much of the enemy fire. Two more sections led by Lt P. W. McCarthy entered the building to complete the clearance of the ground floor. The Egyptians, who had taken cover behind the customs inspection tables and in the rabbit-warren of cubicles and offices in the large hall, put up a fierce resistance and, in the process of forcing an entry into this area Lt McCarthy was killed and two marines were wounded. Lt Ufton assumed command and continued with the difficult task of clearing a determined enemy from the customs hall. His task was almost completed when he was killed by one of the enemy who had taken cover in the last office to be searched. The Egyptians had lost 17 killed. Two were wounded and another was found hiding in a cupboard.

X Troop continued with the clearance of Navy House Quay, using fire support provided by the tanks. Each of the postal and customs buildings were occupied by enemy troops and nearly all of them continued to fight until they were killed. Navy House, former HQ of the Royal Navy, was strongly defended and in order to overcome this resistance Lt Col Tweed called for an air-strike. This was delivered with great effect by Fleet Air Arm Sea Hawks just before the light faded. It did not completely silence the enemy and to minimise casualties the quay was cordoned off for the night. Two officers and six marines of X Troop were wounded in this final encounter. The Egyptians had lost a further 17 killed and four officers and six ratings of the Egyptian Navy surrendered at noon the following day.

While this local battle had been in progress P Troop, commanded by Capt P. Gardner, had been clearing small groups of enemy from the buildings along the waterfront. There were several consulates in the locality including that of the United States Embassy. Arriving at this particular building the troop commander was confronted by an irate official who said "Young man, if one of your marines steps across this threshold it will be an act of war against the United States of America". Employing considerable Royal Marine diplomacy, Capt Gardner tactfully placated the agitated embassy official while the lead section concentrated on silencing a particularly bothersome sniper hidden in an adjacent block of flats. A helpful tank gunner pierced the wall of the building with a round of armour piercing shot and followed up with a round of high explosive through the same hole for good measure.

Earlier in the day the Egyptian Garrison Commander had been taken to Brig Madoc's HQ where he asked if a cease-fire could be arranged. The Brigadier told him that he was not empowered to do so and in any case, if a cease-fire was ordered it would have to be on the same conditions as had been refused the night before when Brig Butler of the Parachute Brigade had tried to arrange a cease-fire with the Egyptian authorities. The Garrison Commander informed Brig Madoc that he was prepared to accept these conditions and the Brigadier signalled the HQ ship HMS *Tyne* accordingly. The Egyptian Commander was then taken to the house of the Italian Consul who was trying to negotiate a cease-fire.

By mid-afternoon Brig Madoc had established his HQ in a block of flats on the seafront and it was here that he first heard of the cease-fire on the BBC news broadcast at 2000 hours. By this time the 2nd Parachute Battalion and Guards Independent Parachute Company had disembarked and assembled at Raswa in readiness for the push to Ismailia.

An hour later the BBC announced that the Prime Minister had informed the House of Commons that a cease-fire would take place at Port Said at midnight. The British Force was not aware at the time that the USA had threatened economic sanctions against Britain unless the action was brought to an end. The cease-fire, confirmed from HMS *Tyne* at 2315 hours, was implemented by the British and French. However, information of the cease-fire did not appear to have reached all the Egyptians. Spasmodic shooting continued from their positions during the night and an ammunition dump close to X Troop's locality exploded as fires spread in that direction.

The next morning the Commando Brigade re-organised and took control of the city with 45 Commando on the west side, 42 Commando in the centre and 40 Commando on the east side. Over 2,000 weapons were collected by 40 Commando personnel in house to house searches and guards were mounted to prevent Egyptians looting valuable stores from the dockyard.

On 9 November, Gen Stockwell informed Brig Madoc and Brig Butler that 3 Commando Brigade and the 16th Parachute Brigade were to leave Port Said. The Parachute Brigade, less 42 Commando and transport, sailed in HMT *Empire Fowey* on 14 November. 42 Commando remained in Port Said for a further 10 days and then joined the Brigade in Malta for a brief period before returning to England on 1 December.

OPERATION LOYTON
John Hislop

Lasting two months and involving 91 men, "Loyton" was one of the most ambitious operations mounted by 2 SAS (see also pp 18–30 and pp 67–95) in the liberation of France. Tasked by Operation Instruction No. 38 to gather intelligence on enemy movements, and attack enemy installations in cooperation with the Resistance, in the Vosges area of eastern France, an advance SAS party, accompanied by a Phantom patrol and a Jedburgh team, parachuted in on 13 August 1944. John Hislop dropped with the advance. More drops took place in the following days, including that of the commanding officer of 2 SAS, Brian Franks.

WE WERE KEPT hanging about for several days, ready to go, and even got as far as forming up beside the aeroplane, only to have the flight cancelled at the last moment because of an adverse weather report.

It was wearing to the nerves, and though the putting off of our departure at the last minute brought a certain easing of the tension, the knowledge that it was only a temporary respite from the inevitable soon built it up again.

At last, on the somewhat ominous date of August 13th, we left from Fairford aerodrome.

We had been briefed already; so we knew our dropping zone, which was close to a small village called La Petite Raon, a few miles north of St Dié, also our rendezvous, in case there was any hitch in the arrangements for the local Maquis to meet us and guide us there. As the password between the Maquis and ourselves, we were to say, "Nous sommes les guerriers de Malicoco", the Maquis replying, "Bamboula vous attend."

The less erudite members of the party found these verbal exchanges rather beyond them, and it was fortunate that when the time came our arrival was accepted without question.

Meticulously we checked and packed our equipment, revised our briefing and mentally went through the procedure to be followed for jumping and after landing – making sure we were properly hooked up, releasing the kit-bag on the descent, rolling up and disposing of our parachutes as soon as we had touched down, and so on. It all served to while the time away and calm the nerves.

The heat of the day waned as evening approached. At dusk we assembled by the aeroplane and a warm, still, fine night, ideal for flying, gradually descended.

The final preliminaries seemed to take ages, but at last they were completed, we climbed on board, cheerful but a trifle subdued, and at about 10 p.m. took off. In that pre-jet era air travel was a comparatively slow business, and our plane droned tediously through the night towards its destination. The flight was uneventful; we ran into no anti-aircraft fire, nor were we attacked by enemy planes: there was no reason for the Germans to suspect that allied parachutists were being flown into the area towards which we were heading, nor did our route pass over or lead to any important bombing targets. We sat, lay or reclined as comfortably as the comfortless interior of the plane allowed, dozing, eating sweets and talking little, beyond exchanging remarks on our progress, or some banality. Occasionally the dispatcher would bring news of our whereabouts from the pilot, and as the miles slipped by without incident I could not help feeling a sense of relief, regardless of what might await us at the end of our journey. It became hot and stuffy and I began to wish that I had not put on so many clothes; but everything we took had to be carried and my rucksack was so full of equipment that there was no room in it for my battledress blouse or sweater. Dozing, I seemed to be in a confused version of the Hammam Turkish baths in Jermyn Street, where occasionally I had spent the night in pre-war days.

About two o'clock in the morning the dispatcher aroused us with the warning that soon we would be over the D. Z. He passed round a bottle of rum for anyone who cared to take a swig, but on the principle that most jockeys ride best sober, I did not have one. We got to our feet and began preparing for the drop; each man strapping his kitbag to one leg – the right, I think it was – getting into his correct position in his respective stick and hooking up the end of the static line of the man in front to the fuselage of the plane. Nervous excitement drove away the last tentacles of sleep and fatigue, and I could not help my hands trembling slightly as they used to do when I was dressing to ride in a steeplechase.

The dispatcher walked down the line checking each man, which was a wise precaution, since, somehow, Henry Druce's static line had been passed through his parachute harness. Had this not been discovered he would have been suspended indefinitely and irrecoverably beneath the aeroplane after he had jumped.

Finally, we were all ready and the doors of the aperture through which we were to jump were opened, letting in a refreshing stream of air. Our plane was one in which the parachutists' exit was through a large coffin-shape hole in the floor; so that the jumper had only to put forward the leg to which his kit-bag was attached to be whipped down and through it by the weight, with no danger of "ringing the bell" and without option of any last-second change of mind about jumping.

The first stick was made up of the SAS personnel, less David Dill, who led our stick.

The plane had been coming down gradually as we approached the D. Z., till it was at a height of about 800 to 1,000 feet, when the pilot began his run-in. The men stood poised, taut, yet cool, like swimmers awaiting the start of a race.

As we neared the D. Z., a clearing in a valley bounded by wooded hills, the blaze of the guiding fires on the ground came into view. I remember wondering whether the local Maquis hadn't overdone the illuminations a bit – they looked like bonfires in celebration of Guy Fawkes' night – and speculating on the possibility of the Germans seeing and investigating it, though they were supposed to be only a few troops in the area, and those of indifferent calibre.

The plane sank lower, the noise of its engine changed in

tone and lessened, and the pilot began his final approach. The red light went on, changed to green, the dispatcher shouted "Go", and like pins in a bowling alley the first stick vanished through the floor. To the crescendo of its engine, the plane at once started to climb again before swinging round for the second run-in.

We took up our positions and waited. By this time I was trembling with excitement and tension, my heart pounding like a mechanical hammer, as I stood jammed between the man in front and behind – the tighter a stick is packed, the quicker it gets out, thus lessening the chance of dropping outside the area of the D.Z. I felt a sense of claustrophobia blended with suspense and discomfort which, though it cannot have lasted more than two or three minutes, seemed interminable.

Just as it became almost unbearable, the green light went on and in an instant I was out.

The plunge into the night air and the brief, soothing caress of the slipstream as it twirled me about before my parachute opened, was as refreshing as diving into a cool stream on a stiflingly hot day.

This sybaritic illusion was dispelled immediately by the opening of my parachute and the start of my descent, hastened beyond normal speed by the weight of the kit-bag. As soon as the opening of my parachute put me on an even keel I pulled the cord to release the kit-bag from my leg, but only one strap became undone and the kit-bag remained attached by the other, swinging about like a dog who has taken hold of a trouser-leg and will not let go. This was not a particularly happy situation. With some 50 lbs heaving to and fro on my leg there was a sporting chance that if I landed awkwardly it would be broken, which rather disturbing thought at once occurred to me. Meanwhile the illuminations were getting nearer and, added to the bonfires, so it seemed to me, was enough noise to wake the entire German force in the Vosges. As one of the Maquis let off a firearm, either out of exuberance or by mistake – a far from infrequent occurrence, as we were to find later – it crossed my mind that the enemy might even be among the reception committee.

Only the bottom leg-strap of my kit-bag being secure, I

began to haul in the cord attached to the top of the kit-bag in order to check its movement, the fulcrum of which was my ankle, before we hit the ground. Progress in this manoeuvre was barely keeping pace with my descent and I was not feeling too happy about the outcome. But just as the ground started to come up to meet me – that odd impression during the final stage of a parachute jump – I got the kit-bag more or less under control. Another couple of seconds and I crashed through the branches of a sapling and landed gently and comfortably on my back in the undergrowth. Before I could rise, a member of the Maquis appeared on the scene and began to help me out of my harness. Out of breath and in my best Wellington French I spluttered out the pass-word, but for the interest he took I might have been quoting the starting prices at the last Plumpton meeting. All he wanted was a cigarette, the parachute material and any items of equipment for which I had no further use.

Greatly relieved to have reached the ground unimpaired and not in hostile society, I extracted my rucksack from the kitbag, of which, together with my helmet, my companion took charge, saving me from burying them. Then I followed him to the clearing where the party were re-assembling.

We were the first parachutists to have dropped into this part of France and from the curiosity we aroused we might have come from another planet. Enthusiastic and curious Maquisards shook us by the hand, fingered our equipment, asked for cigarettes and exchanged greetings. There were no serious casualties: Henry Druce was concussed, Robert de Lesseps seared his hand paying out the cord attached to his kit-bag, and one of the S.O.E. team dropped from another plane sprained his ankle.

Gradually some sort of order developed out of the chaos: fires were stamped out and we formed into a semblance of a column, the Maquis taking up part of our baggage. The sky was beginning to pale and with the approach of dawn a sense of urgency to get as far away from the D.Z. as soon as possible was conveyed finally to the rank and file of the Maquis by their leaders and ourselves.

At last we set off for our rendezvous, some ten hours walking distance across the mountains. As we left the open, grassed area of the D.Z. for the concealment of the woods, I felt a certain relief. We had been hanging around too long on the scene of the conflagration and tumult which, I felt, would soon be discovered by the Germans.

In the cool of the early morning, after the long, cramped, stuffy flight, it was pleasant to stretch one's legs and march. Soon we had put one ridge between us and the D.Z., so that even if the Germans had learned of our arrival and discovered where we had landed it would not have been easy for them to know where to seek us. As the morning climbed from behind the mountains to mark the new day, it began to get hot, despite the cooling shade of the trees under which most of our path lay. Our guides, used to the mountains, walked swiftly and easily up the steep inclines, but as the hours went by I began to feel the pressure. Apart from the effects of fatigue from loss of nervous energy, which excitement and anticipation had produced, and the weight of my rucksack, the weakness left by the attacks of jaundice and tonsillitis earlier in the year made itself evident. The sweat poured off me in rivulets, I gasped for breath and my limbs felt like lead. After each halt I lay exhausted till it was time to move on, and found it more and more difficult to hoist my rucksack on to my back when I got up. I stripped off my battledress blouse, sweater and shirt from beneath my camouflaged parachutist's jacket, and whenever I got the chance laved my face and neck with the beautifully cool, clear water from the mountain springs which, happily, seemed to be everywhere. At no time has the difference between fitness and lack of it been more deeply impressed upon me. My lamentable condition awakened a foreboding as to how I was going to cope with the exigencies which lay ahead, but the march itself seemed to put me right, because from the next day on I felt a new man. The impurities were sweated out of my system and climbing the mountains cleared my mind and attuned my muscles to a pitch which soon enabled me to return to a physical state which ordinary training had failed to achieve.

By evening we reached our destination. It was an encampment made of logs, on top of a wooded mountain, neatly built and well equipped with tables, benches, sleeping cabins and so on, the whole seeming as if it had been lifted straight out of one of Fenimore Cooper's books. The Tricolor flew from a flag-staff, and at sunset it was hauled down with military ceremony.

The Maquis were quite well supplied with food of a primitive nature: coffee made of acorns, coarse, brown bread, meat and various vegetables. We had brought rations of our own, which we pooled, the Maquis cooking for us.

I slept deeply and well, waking to a beautiful, sunny day, the clear mountain air and the stillness of the forest making it difficult to believe that we were at war.

Our first wireless schedule was due that morning, and guided by one of the Maquis, Davis and I took the set some seven miles away, preparatory to getting through to base. The Maquis stressed the danger of operating near camp, or in the same place two days running, in case the Germans succeeded in fixing our position through a direction finder.

The place chosen for us was a part of the forest where the trees were tall and deciduous and fairly widely spread, giving a noble, cathedral-like impression. Nearby some woodmen were working with a pair of oxen, and their musical cries, interspersed with the crack of an ox-whip, were the only sounds to break the stillness of the morning.

At the appointed time, we opened up. To the wireless operator this moment, the making of the first call, is a tense and thrilling experience. Hundreds of miles away he can visualise the base operator – probably someone to whom he has often worked in training – tapping out the call sign. And with all senses concentrated he waits for the thin, staccato note, tuned at will between alto and treble, to carry the code to his ears. Straightaway, the first letters of the call-sign spelt themselves out, pure and distinct. Davis held up his thumb to signify the good news, though he had no need, since I caught the welcome sound myself. But the instant we started to answer the set went dead, as a thin, faint needle of smoke emerged from the transmitter, betokening that it had burnt out. Mortifying though this set-back was, it was not a disaster, since Jakie had taken the precaution to equip each patrol with two sets. And our Maquis friend nobly volunteered to go back to fetch the second one, so that we could come up on the next schedule.

Davis and I lay beneath the trees awaiting his return, talking, or silently enjoying the peace and beauty of our surroundings. It was an unbelievable contrast to the happenings of the previous twenty-four hours, and feeling that the most should be made of it I clung to the passing minutes with that luxury of enjoyment felt when waking before it is time to get up. Our friend returned in time for the next schedule, when all went well. Indeed, the wireless communication throughout the operation worked perfectly.

Meanwhile, Henry Druce had recovered from his concussion and he, David and Robert began a series of conferences with the Maquis leaders, all of whom were known by pseudonyms, such as Maximum and Felix. The talks were not productive: Maximum, of whom my recollection is of a figure in appearance something between a game-keeper and an actor, and his colleagues were obscure of purpose, jealous of their position and unco-operative.

It was a difficult and delicate situation. Until we were re-supplied we had to rely on the Maquis feeding us, while they knew and controlled the few D.Z.s in the area.

Four or five days passed in this way. Once, a thunderstorm broke in the night, but the next days continued fine, warm and sunny. Each morning at the same time a German reconnaissance plane used to fly over the area. At first there was no sign of its having noticed our camp, but on about the fifth day after our arrival the Maquis reported that the Germans had searched the D.Z., thrown a widely dispersed ring of troops round the base of the camp, and were moving more troops into the area. Henry then decided that it was time that we moved out, a point of policy with which, for once, the Maquis leaders were in full agreement. The plan was to split up into two parties and move by separate routes to a rendezvous in a different area. Henry, David and my patrol were to go with one party, Robert, Lodge, Crossfield and Hall with the other, the Maquis being divided equally between the two.

We set off after breakfast, getting out of the immediate area of the camp without seeing any Germans. The route lay along a path through the woods, easy to pick out, David Dill and Dusty Crossfield walking about a hundred yards ahead of the main body, as an advance guard. It was pleasant going: the ground smooth and springy beneath our feet, the branches shielding us from the heat of the sun and the gradations of light, shade and colour in the scenery an ease and joy to the eye.

Henry and the rest of the English marched together, the Maquis following in a group behind us, chattering quietly like starlings roosting for the night.

We had been going for about two hours when David and Dusty, who had disappeared round a bend in front of us, came running back. They had caught sight of a German detachment fallen out at the side of the path ahead of them, but had not been seen. At once Henry ordered everyone to get into hiding and stay quiet until the Germans, who evidently were on a route-march, had fallen in again and passed by. His briefing before we left England was to keep our arrival in the area secret from the Germans if possible, and to avoid contact with them until a base had been established and more SAS troops had been dropped into the area.

A hundred yards or so to the side of the track was a small hollow, in which the English party lay down. The Maquis deployed and hid among the trees and bushes on the same side of the track. Behind us the ground fell steeply down to a valley, the hillside thickly covered with trees and scrub. Our hollow could not have been bettered as a hiding place, though badly sited for fighting, since the lie of the land was such that it was impossible to see an approaching enemy until he was right on top of us. But since concealment and not battle was the immediate aim, it appeared to serve the purpose.

After a few minutes, we heard the Germans moving along the track. They were marching at ease, and their voices drifted over to us, interspersed with the clink of equipment.

We listened, still and tense, as the sounds came nearer, drew level, and moved on. Just as it seemed that all was well we heard a shout of "*Achtung*!", so high in note as to give the impression that it was uttered by a eunuch – a peculiarity of the Germans which we found not uncommon. Then came a shot, and the cry ended in a gurgle. At once followed orders shouted in German, firing, and cries from the French. From our position it was impossible to see, though not difficult to surmise, what was going on. It transpired that a curious member of the Maquis had been unable to resist the temptation to look up before the Germans had passed out of sight, was spotted and had shot the soldier giving the warning. Our first visual evidence of the situation was the Maquis dashing by in flight. "We'll have to leave our kit and run for it", Henry Druce said. By this time the Germans had set up a machine gun overlooking the hill down which the Maquis were fleeing, this being the only way of escape. Our wireless was packed in the rucksacks, but was useless to the enemy without the crystals and code-book, which I had on me; this was one consolation, as it was impossible to carry the rucksacks or get out and redistribute the wireless. Henry Druce had the presence of mind to leave a stick of explosive timed to go off in half an hour in his rucksack, for the benefit of any German who might carry it off.

Henry directed that we should make a dash in two groups, my patrol in one, he and the rest in the other. Our hollow lay just short of the top of the slope, with a path running across the hillside a little below it. We crept out of our hollow and moved down through the scrub to the edge of the path, which the Germans were covering with intermittent machine-gun fire. I collected my patrol and waited until immediately after a burst of fire had ended, then gave the order to take off. When they saw us crossing the path the Germans opened fire again, but by then we were out of sight in the undergrowth and tearing down the hillside.

I caught a glimpse of Davis just in front of me and to my left as we disappeared into the undergrowth, and the others were close by me. About three parts of the way down the hill, which was some four hundred yards from the path near the top, I stopped to review the situation. The rest of the patrol were beside me, except for Davis, whom I never saw again. So dense was the undergrowth that it was not surprising that he lost touch with us; and there was also the possibility that he had been hit. As it turned out, he was unharmed but lost contact with us. Eventually, he made his way to a village, but was betrayed to the Germans and put to death, which was the fate of all SAS on the operation who fell into their hands.

Besides the other members of our patrol who joined me were three of the French: a young man called Marcel, a boy of about sixteen, and an elderly simpleton, whose presence in the Maquis is difficult to explain; probably he had attached himself to them in the hope of getting better rations than he would have received otherwise.

We lay hidden beneath the bushes, regaining our lost breath; and I pondered the next move. We could hear Germans shouting orders and calling to each other, and every now and then a burst of machine-gun fire.

Gradually, the voices became fainter, the bursts of firing less frequent, and it seemed that the hunt was being called off. Finally there was silence.

It was late afternoon when the Germans appeared to have moved away, but I suspected that they might have left some troops behind to watch the area, so I made up my mind to lie low until just before dawn, when it was light enough to see where we were going, and then slip right out of the area.

For comfort while marching in the heat of the day I had taken off my shirt and battledress blouse, leaving my body stripped to the waist beneath my parachute smock. As night fell and it became colder I began to regret this. Still, it was a minor discomfort, offset by the relief of being safe, at least for the present. At the first glint of light we moved off quietly, Marcel knew the country and volunteered to guide us to another valley, within reach of a village from which we could obtain food and, perhaps, information about the rest of our two parties.

A few hundred yards ahead we came to a path, which was being patrolled by a sentry, who looked cold, sleepy and bored. We slipped across unnoticed when he moved to the far end of his beat, and as we began to climb up the far side of the valley, hidden once more by the welcome undergrowth, I felt the thankfulness of a rider who has crossed the last fence safely in a steeplechase on a bad jumper. We pressed on, resting every now and then for the sake of the elderly man and the boy, till we had put some ten miles behind us. We halted high up on a hill thickly wooded with fir trees and clumps of undergrowth, in which we were able to find a hiding place invisible from a few yards away. There was no sign of any Germans and the stillness of the morning was broken only by the sounds of rural life drifting up faintly from a village in the valley below.

I had a consultation with Marcel, whom I was lucky to have with me. Energetic, resourceful and intelligent, he had refined good looks and an air of sophistication, which suggested the townsman rather than the countryman. We concluded that it would be best if he reconnoitred the village, to see whether he could learn any news of our companions, and find some food. As a Frenchman of the district he would attract little attention, whereas an Englishman in uniform might be received with mixed feelings, and possibly be betrayed to the Germans.

As Marcel began the descent down the hillside, I lay back in the warmth of the morning, letting my thoughts revolve at their will. It seemed that whatever military operation in which I became involved went wrong: first there was Dunkirk, then this. And I pondered the prospects of the immediate future. If Henry and the others had got away safely and we succeeded in finding them, well and good; a plan of operation could be worked out between us. Otherwise, the alternatives seemed to be to join up with the Maquis or try to make our way back through the German lines. For the moment, there was nothing to do except await Marcel's return.

A couple of hours later he came back, accompanied by another Frenchman. The latter was a cheerful, burly, loquacious type, with a full, ruddy, clean-shaven face and an alert, vigorous air. As they approached, I remember wondering about the advisability of his being brought right up to our hiding place, as not all those in occupied France welcomed the appearance of British troops or agents, and it was always possible that he might be in league with the Germans or the Milice. Perhaps the stranger sensed my doubts, for at once, in rusty but comprehensible English, he explained himself. "Me was merchant seaman. Have been in England; I know

Cardiff, Newcastle, Liverpool – I seen the Grand National!" This last observation established him in my estimation: in these circumstances the odds against coming across someone who had seen the Grand National were so remote that the portent could only be favourable. I informed him that I had ridden in the race, which impressed him; and the doubts which had filled my mind changed to a feeling of warmth and trust. He and Marcel had brought some food with them, and the seaman undertook to supply us while we remained in the area, for which I agreed to pay him out of the operational money with which we had been provided, and which, fortunately, I had in a trouser pocket.

I made up my mind to wait a day or two in the area, in the hope of hearing something about my companions: there seemed no point in starting to wander about the Vosges in search of them at once. As it happened, the choice of plan was a happy one. A few days later Marcel, who visited the village daily, returned with the news that Henry and others of the party had been located and that a rendezvous had been fixed for that night.

The respite of those few days was a halcyon calm after the stormy passage of our encounter and escape, which I welcomed. It emphasised, once again, the extraordinary contrasts found in the complex pattern of war. Here was beauty and tranquillity, the hours revolving round us softly and smoothly. From the pearl-grey of first light to the saffron splendour of evening there was nothing to disturb the solitude and peace. The faint sounds of village life rose and fell like the strains of distant music. At the height of the day I would lie full-length in a patch of sunlight, absorbing its warmth and dozing with animal enjoyment. My thoughts strayed down corridors of the past and pondered what lay beyond the door of the future. I repeated in my mind favourite pieces of poetry and memorised others copied into a pocket book which, happily, was in one of my pockets. It contained excerpts from Siegfried Sassoon, Walter de la Mare, W. B. Yeats, one or two of Shakespeare's sonnets, passages out of *The Crock of Gold*, and various other pieces of verse or prose which had caught my fancy. It was to prove a solace both to me and to some of my companions throughout the operation, becoming known as The Anthology.

A further mental stand-by were the many lines of Milton learnt at Wellington for the School Certificate and later in life, through having developed a delight in the beauty of his language. In times of stress it is the resources of the mind rather than those of the body which enable the individual to face the issue.

When we arrived at the rendezvous we found Henry, David, Dusty and the S.O.E. officer, Gough, together with a number of the Maquis. We were also joined by Robert, whose party had fared no better than ours. They had run into some Germans and Hall had been killed, Lodge captured and, as we learnt later, murdered. Henry then resolved to attach ourselves to the Maquis, which was the only way of getting any food, and to send a message back to England through the French underground, explaining our position and asking for re-supplies.

By now the Germans were very much alive to our presence, and began to move more troops into the area. We had to keep on the move continually. Every now and then the Germans would find our camp and move on it to attack, but always we got away. The forests of the area were a great boon, since they made it difficult for the Germans to find us and, having done so, to pin us down. They did not seem anxious to stray far from the tracks and never ventured into the woods after dark.

We had enough to eat, our diet consisting chiefly of brown bread, soup, ersatz coffee, potatoes and an apparently inexhaustible supply of Camembert cheese of a brand called Le Petit Recollet. We built lean-to's beneath which to sleep, laying branches on the ground on which to lie, this being appreciably warmer than lying on the bare ground. When it rained, fires could be lit with safety, as the mist made the smoke invisible. Except for the cold at nights, the chronic diarrhoea produced by the unaccustomed diet, to which the French were immune, and the sudden, periodical appearance of the Germans, life was tolerable, if uncomfortable and somewhat nerve-racking.

When we moved camp, unless surprised by the Germans,

we always travelled by night. A Maquis guide would lead the way, sometimes in impenetrable darkness and through thick woods, when we would follow holding on to each other's belts, so as not to lose contact.

Eventually we got in touch with England through the French underground. News came that we would be re-supplied and the map reference of the D.Z., code-sign for signals between aeroplane and ground by torch, and the date and time of the drop were given us.

For five or six nights running we sat out on the D.Z. waiting for the plane. But either there was no sign of it or there was no reply to our signals, and we began to wonder whether the drop would ever materialise. At length, just as we were preparing to leave the D.Z. after manning it for most of the night, we heard the drone of an approaching aircraft. Our party had been joined by a Canadian pilot who had been shot down over France and looked after by the French Resistance, and he used to accompany us to the D.Z., as he was able to tell from the sound of the engine whether an aircraft belonged to the enemy or the Allies. This was a help, as several of the planes to pass over the D.Z. had been German ones. He identified this as British, and when it was directly overhead we gave the signal. It was answered correctly from the plane, which then wheeled round for the run-in. We waited anxiously and excitedly. Then it was back again, and within seconds dark shapes were floating down towards us. To our surprise, for we had not been warned of this, men as well as containers arrived. Altogether about twenty SAS, including Brian Franks, who had taken over command from Bill Stirling, and Christopher Sykes, the writer and brother of Sir Richard Sykes of Sledmere, also Peter Johnsen and his patrol from Phantom. This changed the whole outlook. Peter had brought two wireless sets and three first-rate men, his patrol corporal, Joe Owens, and two signallers, Bannermann and Bell, so that we could set up direct communication once more. We merged our two patrols, this time so distributing the wireless that no vital part was carried in a rucksack, and if we had to abandon the latter we would still have the wireless.

As quickly as possible we collected the containers and got

rid of them and the parachutes. Some confusion resulted from one of the Maquis letting off a Sten gun accidentally, which caused the new-comers to think that the Germans had arrived on the scene – we had become accustomed to this sort of occurrence by now – and to add to the diversion one of the French threw a fit.

It was well after midnight when the plane arrived, and by the time we had cleared the D. Z. morning was breaking. We moved into the woods and lay in hiding for the rest of the day. The Germans must have heard the plane and suspected that there had been a drop, for a few hours after we left the scene they arrived. After looking round they began to shell an area which, I presume, they thought we might be occupying, but it was nowhere near our position. When evening fell we moved away and set up camp some miles distant, towards the top of a hill above a village called Moussey. So far as anything in our nomadic existence could be so termed, this was to be our permanent base. From time to time we left it, either as a precaution or to operate in different areas. After a few days, and influenced by the unimaginative quality of the German mind, which would lead them to believe that we would not return to the area so soon after the drop, we moved into a farmhouse close to the D. Z.

Brian Franks took command and, provided with ample rations, arms and explosives, we were able at last to operate with some effect, instead of being chased about the countryside in the role of what was little more than escaped prisoners of war.

The arrival of supplies made a marked difference to our life. It meant the luxury of a sleeping bag, the warmth of more clothing and the benefit of better rations. While the experiences of the past weeks were not severe, they were beginning to prove wearing. Added to this the uncertainty and lack of purpose surrounding us did not improve matters. The unexpected appearance of Brian and his companions, and the weapons and wireless they brought dispelled this aspect of gloom.

I found Brian, whom I had known slightly before the war, an excellent commander. In build tall, lean and athletic, he was by nature cheerful, understanding, full of initiative and brave, appreciated the exigencies of the circumstances in which we were operating, had a clear and decisive mind and left us to get on with working the wireless without interference. His messages were brief and to the point, as opposed to those from the Brigadier, which tended to be verbose and not always pertinent. As we took down and decoded the tedious contents of his less inspired efforts, we often cursed his lack of imagination regarding the conditions in which we were operating and wished he could be given a course in message writing. Once we had to close down half way through a call because of the Germans moving in on us. It gave Joe Owens and me the amusement of sending one of the more colourful code-messages on the handkerchief provided by the gentleman in Baker Street. In clear it read: "Closing down owing to enemy attack."

Brian had several conferences with the Maquis leaders, but found them no easier than did Henry; so he determined that we would operate on our own, with a small team of Maquis, who would act as cooks, guides and general helpers.

With periodical changes and interruptions, life took on a new set pattern. Twice a day we had a wireless schedule, coding and sending messages, receiving and decoding others. We also listened in to a special channel of the BBC allotted to us and run by the actor John Chandos, who was in Phantom. The messages were always preceded by a few bars of "Sur le Pont d'Avignon", followed by "Hello Romo, Hello Romo", and then the message, sometimes in clear, at others half in clear and half in code. If opportunity allowed, lighter features were broadcast, one (chiefly for my benefit) being a repeat of Frankie More O'Ferrall's commentary on the St Leger won by Tehran, a result which gave me a measure of satisfaction, since before leaving I had given a short talk on current racing over the same wave-length and tipped Tehran to win the race.

Parties of the SAS would go out on operations, such as mining roads, reconnoitring concentrations of enemy armour and noting the map-reference, which we would send back on the wireless, enabling the RAF to come over to bomb them, and ambushing unsuspecting German troops. Every now and then we would be supplied, when all of us assembled at the D.Z. to receive the drops. It was hard work, since the place had to be cleared by first light and everything had to be carried to whichever camp we were occupying, these always being high up a mountain.

I learned to adapt myself to circumstances. When it rained, I found that it was better to wrap my sleeping bag round me instead of getting into it wet, which made it difficult if not impossible to dry. In this way, lying on a bed of branches and covered from head to foot with a waterproof gas-cape, I have slept soundly and comfortably through nights of pouring rain.

We had not been in the farmhouse by the last D.Z. many days when, one evening, a large detachment of German troops appeared down the drive. They had no idea that we were in the area, and approached casually, probably in search of food or billets. They were no more than a hundred yards away when they came into view, but by the time they reached the front door the farmer, his wife and the rest of us were out at the back door and into the woods. Marching through the night, we went back to our base above Moussey unpursued.

Virtually all our movements about the country took place at night, the darkness being one of our best friends. The pitch-black nights, when we had to hold on to each other's belts to avoid losing touch completely, were varied by those of brilliant moonlight. In the forest this gave strange and weird effects of silver and ebony, casting grotesque shapes and shadows, which to the imaginative mind could represent anything from a spectre to a German. For me the scene used to conjure up thoughts of James Stephens's vivid and terrifying story *Etched in Moonlight*.

More SAS were dropped into the area later on, though through losses and departures back through the lines we were never all together at the same time. Several men, including a pre-war racing acquaintance, Denny Reynolds, were captured – all later being murdered – near a lake called Lac de la Mer; "Lac des Cygnes", Christopher Sykes renamed it. And after being separated from the main body following a skirmish, two of the Phantom men, Bell and Sullivan, went back through the lines, as did some SAS men involved in the same action.

Scope was added to our operations by several Jeeps being dropped in, landing intact, a parachute at each corner. They were used with great success until finally captured, the star operator in them being Johnny Manners, younger brother of the Duke of Rutland.

The French in the area were extremely loyal to us, though many suffered on our account, an aspect of which Christopher Sykes has written in his excellent book *Four Studies in Loyalty*. One of the sufferers was poor Père Georges, a veteran of the 1914–18 war, in whose farm we sheltered for a while during a spell of wet weather. In the end he paid for his hospitality to us by being shot by the Germans. He lived in a house which might have come out of Grimms' Fairy Tales. It backed on to the forest, the front giving a clear view down the hillside; so that anyone approaching from the only path leading to the house could be seen a long way off. Père Georges was a small, cheery, friendly man, who loved to talk of his experiences in the Kaiser's war and was, I think, glad of our company and conversation.

We used to take it in turn to keep watch from his apple store, the window of which overlooked the path up the hill; and when the memory of those vigils returns the smell of apples and the beating of the rain on the roof provides its accompaniment, giving a feeling of sadness which, perhaps, was the portent of that good man's cruel end.

In the strange and extreme variations of those times were some of the happiest and most tranquil moments of my life. A few hours rest in safety, a meal, a warm and dry place to sleep; these became every luxury that could be wished for. The worries of ordinary civilian life did not exist, and in my case there was no wife, child or parent dependent upon my existence.

It was pointless to be anxious about the future, because its nature was unpredictable. We lived from day to day, as it were, playing each ball according to the way fate bowled it.

Unreality and incongruity hovered as a Puck-like influence over all our doings. One morning I was alone in the camp above Moussey, when a message arrived from the village that an agent had appeared from St Dié, bringing an important document, which he would hand only to a British officer. The agent was hiding in a cottage a few miles away, and the Maquis agreed to provide me with a guide to it. I was fitted out with a black cloak, which I put on over my uniform and set off with the guide, a demure little country girl of about sixteen. We must have presented an odd couple as we walked along. We skirted the village, which was still occupied by Germans; but by that time we had become contemptuous of their presence, since they had made it clearly evident that they were considerably more frightened of us than we were of them. "The grey lice", Brian nicknamed them, for so they looked when we watched them from up the mountains, as they moved about in the valleys far beneath. A couple of Frenchmen stared at us suspiciously, and for a moment I wondered whether they were Milice, but they made no further move and we walked on through the mellow autumn morning. Eventually we came to the cottage, which lay by itself just off a track through the valley. All was still and peaceful, but from the precautions which the agent took to hide himself it might have been surrounded by Germans. In the company of a dubious-looking blonde girl – subsequently she proved to have been acting at one time for the Germans – he cowered in the corner of an upper room. He was a thin, pale, nervous man, with hawk-life features and a hunted look. Our hosts, a smallholder and his wife, seemed amused at his apprehension and caution. The document which he had brought was a map of the German defences of St Dié, which Henry Druce, who made trips through the German lines as casually as if he had been crossing Bond Street, eventually delivered to the Americans. The farmer and his wife insisted that my guide and I stay for a meal with them. They gave us an excellent one, asking us to guess what we had been eating. It tasted like venison, which I named it, but in fact was goat.

"If you and Peter would like a bit of variety you can go out this evening and mine a road," Brian said to me one day. I was delighted at the offer and so was Peter, both from the aspect of the novelty it represented to us and the excitement of a venture tempered with a minimum of risk.

Our Sapper officer, Dusty Miller, explained exactly how to lay the explosives, fuses and wires, which was a simple and straightforward operation; and Brian showed us the position where they were to be placed, on the map. We loaded the equipment into our rucksacks and waited for night to fall before setting off.

Another and purely selfish reason for our welcoming the expedition was that by this time we were very short of food, and there was the possibility of getting something to eat from the inhabitants of the village through which we had to pass.

It was a fine evening, not cold, and we had plenty of time in which to accomplish the task. So we set off at an easy pace, relaxed in mind, but with the unconscious alertness which the circumstances of our sojourn in the Vosges had developed.

We took the usual, rough track down the hill into Moussey, which at this hour was as dark and silent as a catacomb. In the hope of finding some food we knocked at one or two doors quietly, but either the occupants did not open up or they had nothing to spare. So we went on our way, which led past the house of a friendly, buxom woman and her daughter, whom we knew as loyal supporters and good friends. They lived on the outskirts of the village and when we reached the house we made our way round to the back and tapped on the door.

The women opened it cautiously, but recognising who we were welcomed us in. "It's good to see you. At first we thought it might be the Germans; they were here a few hours ago, asking a lot of questions and looking round the place, but they won't come back now. Come in and we'll find you something to eat."

Gratefully we entered and sat down in the kitchen. The room was dimly lit, for security, the windows covered so that no chink of light was visible from without.

The scene had a dramatic quality: the faint, flickering light, which made the objects in its immediate vicinity stand out in unnatural clarity against the blackness of the remoter corners of the room; the unkempt, brigand-like appearance of Peter and me; the neat, clean, simple attire of the two women; the glow of the kitchen stove; and the air of secrecy which our hushed voices emphasised.

At the same time there was about it all a feeling of extraordinary warmth, comfort, friendliness and security. It reawakened an atmosphere of childhood: sitting at home on a winter's evening deep in a story of mystery or danger, which quickened the pulse with excitement and suspense. And if a tremor of fear crept down the spine a glance at the familiar and comforting surroundings soon allayed it.

So we sat talking, of the war, news of the district, our doings, home and other topics, as the mother prepared us a dish of potatoes. By the standards of peace-time it might have passed for frugal fare, but to us it was a Lucullan repast; nothing could have tasted better.

When we had finished we thanked our hostess, gathered up our equipment and slipped quietly out of the house. "Bon courage!" the women whispered before they shut the door after us. Outside there was no sign of anyone. The night was silent and fresh, and we walked comfortably and quickly towards our objective. A couple of miles or so out of the village, two or three hundred yards away to our left, we heard sounds of activity coming from a grove of trees. There was a clanging as if of hammering on metal, sounds of voices and a glare of arc lamps shining through the trees. We moved close enough to recognise the language as German and came to the conclusion that it must be an armoured repair unit working.

We made our way back to the road and pressed on, till once more only the sounds of nature broke the night. Eventually we came to the spot where the charges were to be laid. It was a short and simple job, though with the passage of time I am unable to describe the procedure.

When we had finished we set off back to camp, along the route we had taken. When we reached the place where we had heard the sounds of hammering there was no light or anything to be heard. We hurried by and reached our camp before dawn. I never discovered the outcome of our efforts; perhaps the charges did not go off.

Not long after this, we were in our base camp late one afternoon, when several bursts of firing sounded further down the hill. "John, you might go and see what it's all about, if you can. You'd better take a man with you," Brian said to me. Accompanied by one of the SAS – so far as I remember his name was Jack Spencer and he came from Spilsby – I started off. I went ahead, placing Spencer to my left and about fifty yards behind me.

It was a damp misty day and the afternoon light was beginning to fade. The firing had ceased and except for the drip of moisture from the trees – the scene brought back passages of *Bleak House* – there was no sound. I walked on quietly and slowly, peering into the Cimmerian gloom. The only sign of life was a figure meandering through the wood, head bent and gaze to the ground, dressed in what looked like a grey dressing-gown. "An old woman looking for sticks for her fire," was the first thought that struck me. Unaware of my presence, the figure moved nearer, until I could see that it was, indeed, a German. I sank into a kneeling position and raised my American carbine, ready to fire. As the German approached, heedless of his peril, I had time to think of what I was about to do. I had no particular wish to take anyone's life, especially in this leisurely and rather cold-blooded fashion, but this, after all, was what I had hired myself to the Army to do, and if I did not kill the German there was every probability that he would kill me. So I aimed at that part of the grey dressing gown behind which I supposed his heart lay, and waited for him to come close enough to ensure his demise. Suddenly he looked up and saw me. An expression of surprise and terror crossed his yellowish face, and the cigarette which he had been smoking fell from his lips as I pressed the trigger – and nothing happened. Desperately I worked the bolt and tried again, while he unslung his rifle shouting "*Hände hoch*! *Hände hoch*!" But still nothing happened.

All acquainted with the American carbine will know that this estimable weapon has one peculiarity: the safety-catch and the button releasing the magazine are placed rather close together. In the heat of the moment I had pressed the latter instead of the former, resulting in the magazine falling out.

Then he started to shoot at me. His marksmanship must have been deplorable, as he cannot have been more than thirty or forty yards away and got off two or three shots without hitting me, before Jack Spencer opened up on him and he ran away. The encounter produced no immediate repercussion, but we left the area before daybreak, to be on the safe side.

As September gave way to October, our position began to deteriorate. The weather broke, making flying impossible, so that we could not be resupplied. Hoping to starve us out, the Germans had stripped the countryside, leaving the French with hardly enough to live on, let alone feed us; we were beginning to run short of arms and explosives; one wireless set was out of action and the remaining one was on its last legs. Also, the Germans were becoming increasingly irritated at our presence and stepped up their efforts to hunt us down, so that we dared not stay more than a day or two in the same place.

About the third week in October we returned to the Moussey base. Late in the afternoon of our arrival we heard an ominous sound – a large number of troops moving round us. We could not see them, but from all sides came faint, though unmistakable noises – steel against stone, the crack of a broken twig and, what was more disquieting, the whine of dogs. We could do nothing but keep absolutely quiet and hope for the best, but the outlook was not pleasant. It seemed impossible that they could not find us; and when they did we would be outnumbered beyond reasonable hope of survival.

I was sitting with Peter Johnsen and an SAS officer, Peter Power, who had joined us after being dropped into another area. At our feet were the embers of a dying fire. Peter Johnsen had been drying a pair of socks at it, and as he turned them over I noticed that his hand trembled slightly with tension. His face, in which the candour and comeliness of youth lay untouched by the erosion of worldly experiences, was pale and taut; and in his eyes was a look not exactly of fear but more of sorrow, as if for the years ahead which he must have realised could soon be snatched from him for ever. He had taken part in a SAS operation before joining Loyton, and had come through the past weeks with a courage, coolness and sense of responsibility beyond his years, standing up to the physical and mental strain, where others of his sensitivity and youth might easily have broken down. To have undergone all this and then be deprived of the fullness of life seemed a bitter injustice. He looked at that moment the personification of Raleigh in *Journey's End*, a symbol of all the anguish, sacrifice and futility embodied in war. And my heart grieved for him.

My case was different. I had to some extent lived my life, done much of what I wished to do and achieved at least some position in my chosen calling. The past years had smiled on me, and if the end of the road lay just ahead I was entitled to feel no remorse. Peter Power was sitting back, half reclining, against the trunk of a tree, relaxed, motionless and as inscrutable as a sphinx. As ever he was smoking – he could smoke more unobtrusively than anyone I have known, the cigarette barely burning and as still as if it were glued to his lips. His strong, ruddy face with the scar on the cheek left by a bullet received in the North African campaign was expressionless. He might have been engaged in a game of poker, waiting for his opponent to declare his hand.

The Midian-like sounds continued, seeming, if anything, to be closing in on us; but because of the thickness of the forest there was nothing to be seen. I thought, "this looks like the finish", and considered how best I could meet it. I had no illusions as to my probable fate if captured, finding contemplation of that eventuality most distasteful. While not unduly fearful of dying, I had grave doubts as to my ability to withhold information against the Gestapo's methods of extracting it; and I determined that a certain end fighting would be preferable to becoming the subject of their ingenuity in making me talk. To my state after death I gave no thought. While believing vaguely in an after life I was sceptical of religion in general. My spiritual problem of the moment was to depart this world in a manner approximating as closely as possible to that expected of a good SAS soldier.

This gloomy reverie was dispelled sharply by a noise, which I felt beyond doubt would bring the whole surrounding force upon us in a matter of seconds: someone dislodged an empty tin, which clattered down the hillside from stone to stone, making as much din as if it had been tied to the tail of a cat loosed in an empty cathedral. Yet, astonishingly, it produced no reaction: the sounds went on as before, then gradually became fainter till finally they ceased. For minutes we dared neither move nor speak, but as the dusk deepened and nothing broke the silence we relaxed, and in hushed voices began to discuss the extraordinary affair. The whole occurrence seemed a version of Kipling's Lost Legion.

That night we left the area. It was an opportune move, for shortly afterwards the Germans put in a strong attack on the camp, supported by tanks and guns. This suggested that their previous visit had been a reconnaissance, the result of which defeated their objective, since it gave us sufficient warning to get out before they attacked. The one tragic result of the incident was the capture and subsequent death of David Dill, when he went back to the camp to see if there was any sign of Henry Druce, who was due there on his return from an expedition through the German lines. David was a sad loss and it was ironical that, having survived from the original drop, he should meet this fate on what was to prove the last stage of the operation.

Brian now decided to send a message suggesting that the operation should be brought to an end. Bad weather had made re-supply by air impossible, we had almost run out of food, ammunition and explosives, had lost all the jeeps, and in consequence could serve no useful purpose by staying. Besides, the Germans were making renewed efforts against us and it must be only a matter of time before they succeeded.

This news gladdened me. My enthusiasm for the operation was wearing thin, and the prospect of a continued game of hide-and-seek with the Germans, in steadily worsening conditions, made no appeal to me. When I learned of Brian's proposal we were halted on the side of a hill with a magnificent vista right away towards the American lines. The latening afternoon was Turneresque in colouring. David Dill had not yet set off on his fatal journey and, side-by-side, we reclined against the slope, basking in the warmth of the sun as we gazed into the gold and vermilion haze of the far distance, where lay safety: a Pisgah-like sight, which poor David was never to realise.

We received a message from England ordering us to end

the operation and make our way back through the German lines. Brian resolved that we should do so in small parties, and that in case any final action should be required, one party consisting of himself, Peter Power, Christopher Sykes, an SAS sergeant called Chalky White and a Phantom wireless team, should remain behind for as long as was necessary. I sent Peter off with the two operators, Johnston and Bannerman to make their way back through the lines, Joe Owens and I comprising the Phantom wireless team staying behind.

Joe Owens was the senior non-commissioned member of the Phantom detachment and volunteered for the task. He was as good a soldier and companion in time of stress as anyone could wish for. Short in height, he was squarely built, tough, intelligent, and sensible. Unselfish, cheerful and patient, he was a true gentleman by nature and earned the confidence and devotion as much of his officers as his men. His home was, and still is, in Newcastle-on-Tyne, and he had once served in the Merchant Navy – he walked like a man who had been at sea. Peter and I had found Joe a great stand-by during the whole operation, and it was largely due to his skill and care that communication never failed.

Before setting out, Brian arranged that we should meet at a sawmill some miles away and on our route towards the American lines. We made our way there in separate parties, the Phantom detachment forming one of them. It was a day's march and we reached the area at nightfall. We sheltered in a deserted sawmill, not far from the one at which we were due to rendezvous, completing the journey in the morning.

At our meeting place we found the others. Some of them, including Christopher Sykes, went off to try to obtain food for the journey from one of our contacts in the forest. The rest deployed in the woods overlooking the sawmill and the house beside it.

The scene which followed is described by Christopher in the chapter, "In Times of Stress", in his book, *Four Studies in Loyalty*.

The family in the house had helped us in the past and the Gestapo, having discovered this, arrived to take away the husband. Not finding him, they departed after saying that they would return and, if he was not at home when they came back, they would burn the place down.

That afternoon the Gestapo appeared, five of them. From our hiding place we watched the scene, as from the dress circle of a theatre. The Germans called out the family, an old woman, a younger one and a child, and started to cross-examine them. The rain was teeming down and they stood in the open while the inquisition dragged on, the victims in a state of terror and distress.

It was as much as we could do to resist killing the five Germans, which would have been only too easy, but we dared not do so for fear of the appalling reprisals on the district, which would have resulted in due course. Besides, we could not have taken the old woman and the child with us, and had they been left behind the probability was that they would have been caught and shot. In helpless mortification we were compelled to see out the tragedy.

When they had finished making their enquiries, the Germans turned the woman and child into the road, set fire to the buildings and, having collected all the chickens and put them into one of their cars, drove away.

We went down to offer what comfort we could and to express our gratitude for their loyalty in not betraying us. They had been questioned persistently about our whereabouts and by giving us away could have saved their home and their belongings, but they remained staunch in face of the destruction of all they possessed.

Sadly we watched the closing scene. In Christopher's words: "They were last seen walking down the road towards the Northern valley, in the pouring rain, weeping bitterly. They were the last French people any of us saw before reaching the American Army."

Each party was to make their way back through the lines by a different route, in order to lessen the danger of capture. There was no sign of David Dill or Henry Druce and it transpired that the latter and Robert, having reached the camp and found it deserted, returned through the lines, knowing that this was the intention.

All the parties except Brian's departed. This left me as the last of the original group to drop into the area more than two months before. Had I been a true fighting soldier such as Roy Farran, whose SAS operation in Italy was one of the finest military feats of the war, doubtless I would have been in a different frame of mind. As it was, my only aim now was to reach the American lines safely. My nerves were becoming edgy, increasing cold and shortage of rations had not improved my physical state, and the shaky condition of the wireless was a constant source of worry. On the morning after the others had gone, we sent a message asking if there was any further task required of us before we, too, began our journey back. It was a brilliant, sunny day, and wireless communication was perfect. In a few minutes we had sent the message and received the answer. Decoding it I could not help a thrill of joy: it read that we were to return forthwith. Joe Owens and I broke up and buried the wireless, and burnt the code-book. There was an air of finality about this, for the destruction of the wireless meant the severing of our only link with home; for by now the Maquis in the area had been scattered by the Germans, and getting a message to England through them would have been a doubtful, if not impossible procedure.

The first major obstacle facing us on our journey towards the American lines was the river Meurthe. We reached the banks at nightfall and were examining the possibility of crossing by a railway bridge, when we caught sight of two sentries guarding it, so moved away down the bank. They must have heard or seen us, because they lobbed a couple of hand-grenades over the parapet, but by then we were well out of range. Our attempt at finding an unguarded bridge over the Meurthe was due to White being unable to swim; but after this experience we gave up the idea, hoping instead to get him across, supported between two of us. Further down the bank we came to a part of the river which looked reasonably easy to swim. We got rid of our sleeping-bags and packs and climbed down into the stream. After the first shock of entering the water it was not so cold as I had expected, and I got well into the middle before having to strike out. The river was about thirty yards wide, so we were not out of our depth for long, and Brian and Peter Power got White across between them without difficulty.

We climbed the far bank, relieved at having put the Meurthe behind us, and forgot the cold and discomfort of our soaking clothes.

I felt a sense of joy and elation such as I cannot remember experiencing before or since. The river had been the first serious problem of our way back, and with it behind us there was the knowledge that at least one less hazard lay ahead.

John Hislop eventually made it to American lines. Loyton cost the SAS two dead, and 31 captured, all of whom were executed by the Gestapo as per Hitler's instruction. Of the 210 villagers from Moussey who were rounded up by the Gestapo for cooperating with the SAS and Maquis, only 70 returned home. At the time, Hislop believed that Loyton had been an "expensive failure". But as he says:

It was not until later that the discovery was made of the disruption and alarm to which our presence gave rise among the Germans. The troops in the area were kept in a state of permanent tension, never knowing when they were likely to be ambushed, or blown up by a mine laid on a road, or the strength of our force and how to pin it down.

Instead of being able to contain the district with a few sparsely scattered units of mediocre calibre, they had to divert an increasing number of first-class fighting troops from the American front until, finally, an entire SS Division was withdrawn for the sole purpose of destroying us. This threw a very different light on the operation, for it showed that the comparatively little material damage we inflicted was more than counterbalanced by the number and quality of the German troops which our presence tied down.

SAS CHRONOLOGY

July 1941:
The SAS, then designated "L" Detachment, raised in North Africa by Lt David Stirling. Total strength 6 officers, 60 NCOS and men.

Nov 1941 – Jan 1943:
SAS patrols raid German and Italian airfields and installations in the Western Desert, destroying over 250 aircraft on the ground. Stirling, now Lieut.-Col., captured January 1943. A second SAS Regiment is created by the founder's brother, William "Bill" Stirling, and a large waterborne element developed, known as the Special Boat Section.

Feb 1943 – Dec 1943:
1 SAS renamed SRS (Special Raiding Squadron) and put under the command of Lieut.-Col. Paddy Mayne. The Special Boat Section becomes the SBS (Special Boat Service). SRS raids in Sicily and Italy, 2 SAS fought in Italy.

Jan 1944:
SAS units, less SBS, formed into SAS Brigade under command of Brigadier R. W. McLeod.

June 1944:
SAS parachute into France before D-Day. SAS order of battle for D-Day:

HQ SAS Brigade
1st SAS Regt — 2nd SAS Regt
3rd (French) SAS Regt — 4th (French) SAS Regt
5th (Belgian) SAS Regiment

1944–45:
1, 2, 3, 4 and 5 SAS serve in, variously, France, Belgium, Holland, Italy and Germany.

Oct 1945:
SAS Regiments disbanded. 3 and 4 SAS go to French Army; 5 SAS go to Belgian Army.

1949:
21 SAS Regiment (TA) (Artists), a territorial unit, raised and based in London.

1950:
Maj J. M. Calvert raises the Malaya Scouts to fight Chinese Communists in Malaya.

1951:
The Malaya Scouts and M Squadron 21 SAS combine to form 22 SAS.

1952–57:
22 SAS in Malaya.

1958–76:
22 SAS serve in the Gulf, in Oman, Dhofar, Aden.

1963–65:
22 SAS in Borneo during "Confrontation" war with Indonesia.

1970:
SAS deployed in counter-terrorist role in Northern Ireland, in Britain and elsewhere.

1980:
Princes Gate.

1982:
The SAS in the Falklands.

1991:
SAS serve in the Gulf War.

THE PHILOSOPHY OF THE SAS
David Stirling

To understand the SAS role it is important first to grasp the essential difference between the function of Airborne Forces and Commandos on the one hand and that of the wartime Special Operations Executive on the other. Airborne Forces and Commandos provided advance elements in achieving tactical objectives and undertook tactically scaled raids, while the SOE was a *para*-military formation operating mainly out of uniform.

In contrast, the SAS has always been a strictly military unit, has always operated in uniform (except occasionally when seeking special information) and has functioned exclusively in the *strategic* field of operations. Such operations consisted mainly of: firstly, raids in depth behind the enemy lines, attacking HQ nerve centres, landing grounds, supply lines and so on; and, secondly, the mounting of sustained strategic offensive activity from secret bases within hostile territory and, if the opportunity existed, recruiting, training, arming and co-ordinating local guerrilla elements.

The SAS had to be capable of arriving in the target area by air and, therefore, by parachute; by sea, often by submarine and folboat; or by land, by foot or jeep-borne penetration through or around the enemy lines. To ensure surprise the SAS usually arrived in the target area at night and this required a high degree of proficiency in all the arrival methods adopted for any particular operation.

Strategic operations demand, for the achievement of success, a total exploitation of surprise and of guile – accordingly, a bedrock principle of the Regiment was its organization into modules or sub-units of four men. Each of the four men was trained to a high level of proficiency in the whole range of the SAS capability and, additionally, each man was trained to have at least one special expertise according to his particular aptitude. In carrying out an operation – often in the pitch-dark – each SAS man in each module was exercising his own individual perception and judgment at full strength. The SAS four-man module could be viable as an operational entity on its own, or be combined with as many other modules as an operation might require.

In the early days of the SAS Middle East HQ sometimes tended to regard us as a baby Commando capable of "teasing" the enemy deep behind the lines during the quieter periods but available, in the circumstances of a major defensive or offensive confrontation, to undertake essentially tactical tasks immediately behind or on the flank of an aroused enemy. It took some further successful raids to persuade HQ to acknowledge that our role should remain an exclusively strategic one.

In today's SAS the importance of good security is thoroughly instilled into every man. Certain delicate operational roles require the Secret Service to invest in the SAS Command highly classified intelligence necessary for the effective planning of these operations and, just as importantly, for special training. For such intelligence to be entrusted to the SAS, its security disciplines have to be beyond reproach.

As the SAS was operating at a distance of up to 1,000 miles from Army HQ, an exceptionally efficient wireless communication was essential. Frequently we would require interpretation of air photographs of target areas, taken while an SAS unit was already deep in the desert on its way to attack them. An effective communication system became even more important to the SAS in Europe. [Their own dedicated and special communications are still an essential feature of SAS operations].

Recruitment was a problem, as we had to depend on volunteer recruitment from existing Army units. Not unnaturally, Commanding Officers were reluctant to see their most enterprising individuals transfer to the SAS, but eventually

Middle East HQ gave us firm backing and we were usually able to recruit a few volunteers from each of the formations which had undergone general military and desert training. We always aimed to give each new recruit a very testing preliminary course before he was finally accepted for the SAS. Today the SAS is even more ruthless in its recruitment procedures.

Once selected, our training programme for a man was an exhaustive one and was designed to give him thorough self-confidence and, just as importantly, equal confidence in his fellow soldiers' capacity to outclass and outwit the enemy by use of SAS operational techniques.

We kept a careful track record of each man and capitalized whenever possible on the special aptitude he might display in various skills such as advanced sabotage technique, mechanics, enemy weaponry, night-time navigation and medical knowledge, etc. This register of each man's special skills was vital to make sure that each of our modules of four men was a well-balanced entity. Historical precedents, demonstrating how vital this concept could be to the winning of wars, were ignored and we, therefore, had to start again nearly from scratch. Luckily, the British, for one, now acknowledge the validity of the strategic raid, hence the continuing existence of the SAS Regiment. The SAS today fully recognizes its obligation to exploit new ideas and new development in equipment and, generally, to keep a wide open mind to innovation and invention.

From the start the SAS Regiment has had some firmly held tenets from which we must never depart. They are:

1. the unrelenting pursuit of excellence;
2. maintaining the highest standards of discipline in all aspects of the daily life of the SAS soldier, from the occasional precision drilling on the parade ground even to his personal turnout on leave. We always reckoned that a high standard of self-discipline in each soldier was the only effective foundation for Regimental discipline. Commitment to the SAS pursuit of excellence becomes a sham if any *single one* of the disciplinary standards is allowed to slip;

3. the SAS brooks no sense of class and, particularly, not among the wives. This might sound a bit portentous but it epitomizes the SAS philosophy. The traditional idea of a crack regiment was one officered by the aristocracy and, indeed, these regiments deservedly won great renown for their dependability and their gallantry in wartime and for their parade-ground panache in peacetime. In the SAS we share with the Brigade of Guards a deep respect for quality, but we have an entirely different outlook. We believe, as did the ancient Greeks who originated the word "aristocracy", that every man with the right attitude and talents, regardless of birth and riches, has a capacity in his own lifetime of reaching that status in its true sense; in fact in our SAS context an individual soldier might prefer to go on serving as an N.C.O. rather than have to leave the Regiment in order to obtain an officer's commission. All ranks in the SAS are of "one company" in which a sense of class is both alien and ludicrous. A visit to the Sergeants' Mess at SAS HQ in Hereford vividly conveys what I mean;
4. humility and humour: both these virtues are indispensable in the everyday life of officers and men – particularly so in the case of the SAS which is often regarded as an élite Regiment. Without frequent recourse to humour and humility, our special status could cause resentment in other units of the British Army and an unbecoming conceit and big-headedness in our own soldiers.

SAS SELECTION
Jon E. Lewis

A SPECIAL FORCE is ultimately only as special as the men (and, just occasionally, the women) who make up its ranks. To find and maintain the highest calibre of soldier, virtually all special forces have a military course which would-be members must pass. No course is more demanding than that required to join 22 Special Air Service Regiment.

Since the Regiment's reformation in Malaya after the Second World War, Selection Training has been based on a course devised in 1953 by Major John Woodhouse. It is designed to enlist only those who have the right qualities: mental and physical toughness, self-reliance and the intelligence to think through problems in any circumstance. The egalitarian anti-military culture of 22 SAS, together with the smallness of its basic component, the four-man patrol, and the isolated nature of commando work, also requires a soldier with a particular character. "Selection", as ex-SAS Regimental Adjutant Major Dare Newell has put it, "is designed rather to find the individualist with a sense of self-discipline than the man who is primarily a good member of a team. For the diciplined individualist will always fit well into a team when teamwork is required, but a man selected for team work is by no means always suitable for work outside the team."

The selection course for the full-time, regular 22 Regiment, based at Stirling Lines, Hereford, lasts for one month. As it is impossible to enter the SAS directly, each volunteer must have had previous service with a regular unit. The only civilians allowed to try for selection are members of the SAS's two part-time, Territorial Regiments, 21 and 23 SAS. The course is run twice a year, once in the summer and once in the winter.

It begins with a three-week build up period for soldiers (two for officers), which allows each volunteer a chance to get up to the physical standard required. The emphasis is on cross-country marches over the Black Mountains and Brecon Beacons in nearby South Wales in which the distance covered, carrying rifle and pack (bergen), increases every day. So does the weight of the pack, from 11 kg to 25 kg. As SAS troopers must all be proficient at navigation, basic tuition in map and compass work is given to those who need it. At the beginning of Selection the marches are done in groups, but as the course progresses the candidate works alone. Each man is given a bergen, a compass and map and a rendezvous (RV) he has to make for. There is a time limit for the march, but the candidate is not told what it is. For much of the march he will have to jog. It is usually raining and his bergen will get heavier and heavier. When he reaches the RV he is given another one and so on. To increase his anxiety and to test his ability to deal with the unexpected he might be asked to perform a task at the RV, such a stripping down an unfamiliar weapon.

By the fourth week, Test Week, the culmination of Selection, the numbers on the course will have dropped significantly. Many have left of their own accord, while others have been rejected ("binned" in SAS parlance). Those who remain are exhausted, their stamina and judgment eroded by 21 days of exercises which begin at 4 a.m. and end at 10.30 p.m. It is now that the selectors subject the candidate to the endurance march, the "Long Drag" or "Fan Dance", a 40-mile land-navigation exercise which has to be completed in 20 hours or less. Most candidates, because of map reading errors in the difficult mountainous terrain, end up marching/jogging considerably more than 40 miles. Only the most determined and fit candidates have made it to the "Long Drag"; even so, a handful of them will fail here. Some have even died doing the "Long Drag" including, tragically, the SAS hero of the 1972 Battle of Mirbat, Major Mike Kealy, who retook the march to test his own fitness after a spell doing administrative work.

Those who pass the endurance march are then gathered in the SAS barracks at Stirling Lines, where they are told the bad news: they are not yet in the SAS. They must now endure, after a mere week's leave, Continuation Training.

Continuation Training lasts for around four months and tutors the potential recruit in all the SAS patrol skills: standard operating procedures (SOPs), weapons-training, demolitions and reconnaissance. Each student receives instruction in signalling, a vitally important skill for long-range patrolling. All SAS troopers must achieve British Army Regimental Signaller standard which includes being able to transmit and receive Morse Code at a minimum of eight words a minute. In addition, tuition is given in SAS field medicine techniques.

After these fundamentals, the candidates then go on Combat and Survival training, which lasts three weeks and takes place on Exmoor. Here the prospective troopers learn all aspects of living in hostile environments: laying traps, building shelters, finding food and water. The Combat and Survival phase ends in an Escape and Evasion exercise, where candidates must not only live off the land but do so for three days while being hunted by the "enemy", usually soldiers from local infantry battalions. At the conclusion of the exercise, candidates are subjected to 24-hour realistic interrogation (the Resistance-to-Interrogation exercise) of the sort they might face if captured by the enemy. The interrogation includes elements of physical hardship, sensory deprivation, and psychological torture. Any candidate who "breaks" is rejected.

Those that get through have then finished Continuation. However, they are then tested, along with three other hopefuls, by a four-man Jungle Training patrol in the Far East. If any man in the patrol fails, the others are also "binned". Only at the end of all this testing, and on completion of a basic parachute course, will the volunteer be accepted into the Regiment and given the beige SAS beret and cloth badge bearing the famous winged dagger. Out of every hundred hopefuls who go to Stirling Lines for Selection only some 5–10 will end up being "badged" SAS.

22 SAS COMMENDATION, GULF WAR

On 9 March 1991, the Commander-in-Chief, General H. Norman Schwarzkopf, sent the following Letter of Commendation to Sir Patrick Hine, British Commander of Gulf Operations.

SUBJECT
Letter of Commendation for the
22d Special Air Service (SAS) Regiment.

1. I wish to officially commend the 22d Special Air Service (SAS) Regiment for their totally outstanding performance of military operations during Operation Desert Storm.
2. Shortly after the initiation of the strategic air campaign, it became apparent that the Coalition forces would be unable to eliminate Iraq's firing of Scud missiles from western Iraq into Israel. The continued firing of Scuds on Israel carried with it enormous unfavorable political ramifications and could, in fact, have resulted in the dismantling of the carefully crafted Coalition. Such a dismantling would have adversely affected in ways difficult to measure the ultimate outcome of the military campaign. It became apparent that the only way that the Coalition could succeed in reducing these Scud launches was by physically placing military forces on the ground in the vicinity of the western launch sites. At that time, the majority of available Coalition forces were committed to the forthcoming military campaign in the eastern portion of the theater of operations.

Further, none of these forces possessed the requisite skills and abilities required to conduct such a dangerous operation. The only force deemed qualified for this critical mission was the 22d Special Air Service (SAS) Regiment.

3. From the first day they were assigned their mission until the last day of the conflict, the performance of the 22d Special Air Service (SAS) Regiment was courageous and highly professional. The area in which they were committed proved to contain far more numerous enemy forces than had been predicted by every intelligence estimate, the terrain was much more difficult than expected and the weather conditions were unseasonably brutal. Despite these hazards, in a very short period of time the 22d Special Air Service (SAS) Regiment was successful in totally denying the central corridor of western Iraq to Iraqi Scud units. The result was that the principal areas used by the Iraqis to fire Scuds on Tel Aviv were no longer available to them. They were required to move their Scud missile firing forces to the northwest portion of Iraq and from that location the firing of Scud missiles was essentially militarily ineffective.

4. When it became necessary to introduce United States Special Operations Forces into the area to attempt to close down the northwest Scud areas, the 22d Special Air Service (SAS) Regiment provided invaluable assistance to the US forces. They took every possible measure to ensure that US forces were thoroughly briefed and were able to profit from the valuable lessons that had been learned by earlier SAS deployments into Western Iraq.

I am completely convinced that had US forces not received these thorough indoctrinations by SAS personnel US forces would have suffered a much higher rate of casualties than was ultimately the case. Further, the SAS and US joint forces the immediately merged into a combined fighting force where the synergetic effect of these fine units ultimately caused the enemy to be convinced that they were facing forces in western Iraq that were more than tenfold the size of those they were actually facing. As a result, large numbers of enemy forces that might otherwise have been deployed in the eastern theater were tied down in western Iraq.

5. The performance of the 22d Special Air Service (SAS)

Regiment during Operation Desert Storm was in the highest traditions of the professional military service and in keeping with the proud history and tradition that has been established by that regiment. Please ensure that this commendation receives appropriate attention and is passed on to the unit and its members.

H. NORMAN SCHWARZKOPF
General, US Army Commander in Chief.

ACKNOWLEDGEMENTS

THE EDITOR HAS made every effort to locate all persons having any rights in the selections which appear in this anthology and to secure permission from the holders of such rights. Any queries regarding the use of material should be addressed to the editor c/o the publisher.

"The Scud-hunters" is copyright © 1995 John Amos (pseud. Jon E. Lewis); "Birth of a Legend" is copyright © 1995 Jon E. Lewis; "Operation Wallace" is an extract from *Winged Dagger* by Roy Farran. Copyright © 1948 Roy Farran. First published in the UK by Collins. New edition 1986 Arms and Armour Press; "The Raid on Dieppe" is copyright © 1964 Peter Young. Reprinted by permission of London Management and Mrs Mary Delion; "Son Tay" by Leroy Thompson first appeared in *Elite*. Copyright © 1987 Marshall Cavendish Partworks Ltd; "Scaling the Heights" is an extract from *Eye-Witness World War II Battles*, ed. Howard Oleck. Copyright © 1963 Belmont Ltd; "The Attack on Corps HQ" is an extract from *Operation Tombola* by Roy Farran. Copyright © 1960 Roy Farran. First published in the UK by Collins; "Patrolling" is an extract from *No Picnic* by Julian Thompson. Copyright © 1984 Julian Thompson. Reprinted by permission of Leo Cooper Ltd; "Adventure at Bruneval" is an extract from *Red Beret* by Hilary St George Saunders, published by Michael Joseph. Copyright © 1950 Hilary St George Saunders; "Operation Benson" is an extract from *Six Friends Arrive Tonight* by Gilbert Sadi-Kirschen, published by Nicholson & Watson 1949; "First Blood" is an extract from *Merrill's Marauders*. Copyright © 1972 Pan/Ballantine; "The Rescuers" is copyright © 1995 Jon E. Lewis; "The Battle of Jebel Akhdar" is an extract from *Arabian Assignment* by David Smiley. Copyright © 1965

David Smiley. Reprinted by permission of Leo Cooper Ltd; "Arnhem" is an extract from The *Red Devils* by G.G. Norton. Copyright © 1987 G.G. Norton. Reprinted by permission of Leo Cooper; "The Backwater War" is an extract from *Seals* by T.L. Bosiljevac. Copyright © 1990 T.L. Bosiljevac. First published in the USA by Presidio Press. Published in the UK by Greenhill Books; "Suez" is an extract from *The Light Blue Lanyard* by J.C. Beadle. Copyright © 1993 Square 1 Publications; "Operation Loyton" is an extract from *Anything but a Soldier* by John Hislop. Copyright © 1965 John Hislop; "SAS Selection" and editorial matter is copyright © 1995 Jon E. Lewis.